PUBLIC FINANCE

PUBLIC FINANCE

Revenues and Expenditures in a Democratic Society

Richard E. Wagner

Florida State University

LITTLE, BROWN AND COMPANY

Boston   Toronto

Library of Congress Cataloging in Publication Data

Wagner, Richard E.
  Public finance.

  Includes bibliographies and index.
  1. Finance, Public. 2. Revenue.
3. Expenditures, Public. I. Title.
HF141.W343   1983   350.72   82–13009
ISBN 0–316–91684–6

Library of Congress Catalog Card No. 82–13009

ISBN 0-316-91684-6

9 8 7 6 5 4 3 2 1

MV

Published simultaneously in Canada
by Little, Brown & Company (Canada) Limited

Printed in the United States of America

To Barbara, Stephanie, and Valerie

Preface

This book is intended to serve as a text for upper division courses in public finance (or public economics, as it is sometimes alternatively called). As an upper division text, this book is written under the assumption that its readers have digested an introductory course in microeconomic theory.

Much of the course of intellectual advancement is a result of scholars trying to explain what they formerly thought was outside the purview of their efforts: They came to ask themselves "Why?" about material they had formerly accepted as given data. It is no different in public finance. Until the past half-generation or so, scholarship in public finance generally accepted budgetary choices as given data and sought to explain the consequences of various taxes and, to a lesser extent, expenditures that resulted as people reacted to those (unexplained) choices. Lately, perhaps prodded by an increasing curiosity about the reasons for the long-continuing growth of government, fiscal scholars have come to incorporate the observed patterns of budgetary choices into the domain of their analysis. Public finance still includes earlier types of topics such as the effect of progressive income taxation or social security on real income and its distribution. But in addition it now includes efforts to explain why the personal income tax or social security program has acquired its present dimensions and characteristics.

This book gives roughly equal attention to the coordinate facets of public finance: the causes and consequences of public choices regarding revenues and expenditures. As might be expected in any field that has been undergoing a substantial expansion in its research agenda, public finance contains a mixture of older topics about which there is often, though not always, considerable agreement and newer topics about which there is sometimes much disagreement. I have not avoided areas of disagreement and controversy in this book. The exploration of unsettled areas often provides a good opportunity both to reinforce what has been learned and to probe the limits of that knowledge. I have, however, tried to be judicious in my treatment of such areas. Because this is a text and not a treatise, I have made sparse use of citations to the massive literature written by those scholars whose work informs this book. Brief annotated bibliographies have been appended to each chapter, however, and these should serve to introduce the interested reader to the underlying professional literature.

My debts in writing this book are numerous. There are, of course, the numerous scholars just alluded to from whom I have learned by studying their works. More immediately in writing this book, I have received valuable advice on parts or all of a preliminary draft from a number of colleagues: Judith B. Cox (University of Washington), John H. Goddeeris (Michigan State University), Timothy J. Gronberg (Texas A & M University), Barry P. Keating (University of Notre Dame), Robert J. Mackay (University of Maryland), Morgan O. Reynolds (Texas A & M University), and Roy Van Til (Bentley College). I have not always taken their advice in revising the manuscript, but I have nearly always found that I learned something by reflecting upon their thoughts and reactions. Mary Parsons and Mary Schneider typed and retyped the manuscript with accuracy, speed, and general good cheer, and I am exceedingly grateful to them, as I am to Al Hockwalt, Kate Campbell, and Elizabeth Schaaf from Little, Brown, who were so very helpful in guiding me through the many activities required to convert an initial manuscript into a finished book.

Brief Contents

Contents

PUBLIC
FINANCE

1

Introduction to Public Economics

Economics seeks to understand how societies deal with scarcity, the condition of life in which the resources available to the members of a society are insufficient to fulfill all their wants. In the presence of scarcity, a society must make choices about what to produce, how to produce, and for whom to produce. Since a society cannot produce all the books, shoes, bread, vacations, and so on that its members would like to have, it must somehow choose what it will and will not produce.[1] It must decide how to allocate its resources for production —how many resources to devote to producing consumer goods, to capital goods, to the development of knowledge and new technologies, and so on. The more a society uses resources to produce capital goods and to develop new technologies, the more it is emphasizing future consumption over present consumption. To implement the choices about what to produce, a society must also make related choices about *how* to produce. A society that chooses efficient processes for production will be better able to satisfy the wants of its members.

The choice of whom to produce for is likewise related to the other economic choices a society must make. If some people like beef and others prefer fish, a society that emphasizes the production of beef is making a choice that favors those who like beef. One important

[1] To say a "society" makes choices about what to produce is simply a shorthand way of saying that the interaction of the individuals who constitute a society brings about a pattern of resource usage that produces some things but not others. There may not be any conscious, collective choice about what to produce, but only a large number of individual choices — the aggregate of which might be described as a "social choice." Nonetheless, to speak of a society as choosing is linguistically convenient, and it creates no confusion so long as "society" is not mistakenly reified.

facet of a society's choice of for whom to produce is its choice of how to deal with unanticipated shortages. When crop failures, foreign embargoes, labor strikes, and the like cause the quantity of goods available to fall below anticipated levels, choices must be made about which wants to satisfy and which to leave unfulfilled.

THE MARKET ECONOMY

There are many ways a society might make its economic choices, but make them it must. The two most common economic systems in which a society can organize itself to make its economic choices are a command economy and a market economy. In a command economy, choices about production are made in principle by a central planning agency. In actual practice, however, there is rarely a pure command economy. Many of the plans and targets announced by a central planning agency are constructed from information provided by individuals within the society. To the extent that this happens, it is doubtful that the planning agency is truly imposing its own distinct will on the economy. Some degree of individual autonomy necessarily characterizes all complex economies simply because the information required to operate a complex economy overwhelms the information-processing capacity of any planning agency.

A market economy is one in which choices about production result from the individual choices of the members of the society. The particular features of market economies can vary a great deal. The United States is considered a market economy, yet the government controls many prices and many conditions of work. It was also considered a market economy when the government did not exercise such controls. This book explores the public economy within the context of a society in which economic activity is organized through markets rather than through central planning, while keeping in mind that the two categories are not free of ambiguity.

It is easy to take for granted such a routine thing as eating breakfast, yet the ability to eat breakfast is the result of coordination among millions of people throughout the world. In a market economy, this coordination emerges through the interplay of people pursuing their own interests within an institutional order characterized by property and contract. People have the right to own chickens, fields of grain, and the like, and to contract with others over the disposition of their property. People make choices to raise chickens or to grow grain in anticipation that others will buy their output, in this case that people will want eggs or dry cereal for breakfast. Within the system of profit and loss inherent in the institutions of property and contract, people become wealthier as they are more successful in producing what others want. If consumers begin to prefer dry cereal to eggs, the price of cereal initially will rise as shortages occur and the price of eggs will fall as producers are left with surpluses. This shift in prices is a signal to producers that consumers have changed their preferences in favor of cereal, and it simultaneously provides producers with an incentive to reduce production of eggs and to increase production of cereal. To a substantial extent, economic theory studies how a market economy generates a coordinated pattern of choices regarding *what, how,* and *for whom.*[2]

GOVERNMENT IN THE ECONOMIC ORDER

The operation of a market economy has some structural resemblance to playing a game. A game requires a set of rules, and different rules define different games. Even if the players agree to the rules of the game, an umpire or a referee is usually required to enforce the rules and to resolve disputes that inevitably arise. Government's two distinct roles in a market economy can be seen in these terms. In one capacity, government acts as a referee to enforce the rules by which the market economy operates. In the other capacity, government acts as one of the players.

The rules of a market economy are based in the institutions of property and contract. For economic coordination to take place within a market economy, the rights and duties of ownership must be secure and the terms of contract must be enforceable. In the course of economic activity, disputes may arise over the precise nature of ownership claims, contractual obligations, and so on. Two parties may disagree, for instance, about the applicability of the law to a particular business situation. Advances in technology may create new situations, as when photocopying a book is cheaper than buying it. Individuals such as burglars may see violence as more effective in gaining desired resources than is conformity to the rules of property and contract.

Regardless of the reasons disputes arise, a market economy requires a policing and refereeing agency. When government performs this protective function, people are able to increase their wealth only through peaceful means consistent with the rules of property and contract. The government's role applies both to internal sources of violence, as when one member of society violates the rights of another

---

[2] It also studies how discoordination can arise, how different patterns might be chosen, and the consequences of those choices.

member, and to external sources of violence, as when members of a
society seek to acquire wealth through conquest. Police and military
are aspects of the protective state that operates to maintain the social
peace essential for the coordination of economic activities.

Government acts as a participant in a market economy when it
makes choices about what, how, and for whom to produce in addition to maintaining the framework of order in which those choices are
made. There are numerous ways in which government makes such
choices: it offers educational opportunities to the members of society;
it provides insurance coverage against unemployment, illness, and
flooding; it maintains a system of parks for outdoor recreation, and
so on.

PUBLIC ECONOMICS

The study of public economics has two main branches, *public choice*
and *applied microeconomics*. The first examines public choices that
emerge, as market choices do, as a result of people pursuing their
interests within a particular institutional order. Of the numerous
institutional regimes within which fiscal choices can be made, our
focus in this book is on democracy.

The conduct of government in a democracy resembles in many respects that of a cooperative or club. True, people voluntarily join a
cooperative or club and are able to leave it at will, but they acquire
membership in a government by virtue of residence and can escape
its jurisdiction only by emigration. Nevertheless, the difference between the voluntary nature of a cooperative or club and the compulsory nature of a government may be more apparent than real, at least
in certain circumstances. Cooperatives, clubs, and governments all
supply services to their members on the one hand and derive revenues
on the other. The analysis of the supply of services seeks to explain
such things as the total size of the government's budget and its ap-
portionment among the various categories of expenditure. In studying
the derivation of revenues, we seek to understand why governments
raise the revenues they do and in the particular forms they do.

The second branch of public economics, applied microeconomics, examines the reactions of individual citizens to public choices.
Whereas public choice might try to explain the size of the Social
Security program, applied microeconomics would deal with the impact of the program on personal saving. Applied microeconomics treats
public choices relating to taxes and expenditures as facts of nature,
"givens," and analyzes their consequences as individuals react to
those choices.

ORGANIZATION OF THIS BOOK

This book is concerned with the fiscal choices of governments and the consequences of those choices. Although overall we are less concerned with normative statements about desirable fiscal choices, we discuss the normative foundations of public economics in Part I: Chapter 2 deals with the meaning of efficiency in public economics and Chapter 3 examines various efforts to develop standards of equity and justice.

Part II covers the central features of the theory of public choice as it applies to democratic forms of government. Chapter 4 surveys voting as a means of making collective choices about the use of resources. Most fiscal choices take place in representative assemblies, and Chapter 5 examines those features of representational government that have substantial interest for the theory of public choice. The choices of the legislature are usually implemented by governmental agencies, and Chapter 6 explores the present theory of bureaucracy. The literature on public choice contains two divergent approaches to democracy. One emphasizes democracy as essentially a cooperative enterprise that advances the common interests of the members of the society. The other emphasizes democracy as a factional or monopolistic enterprise that produces gains for some at the expense of others. Chapter 7 examines these two approaches, paying particular attention to the circumstances under which one or the other type of democracy is likely to predominate.

Parts III and IV explore the economic consequences of the budgetary choices of government. Part III focuses on the various methods of financing government. Chapter 8 discusses the direct pricing of services as a method of financing government. Taxation, the dominant method of financing government today, is explored in Chapters 9 through 12. Although there are many forms of taxation, they fall into a few broad categories. Taxation may be based on the value of the flow of goods during some period of time or on the value of the stock of goods at some point in time. Those values may reflect transactions on either the product or the factor side of the market. Taxes on personal income and corporation income — the subject of Chapters 9 and 10, respectively — are levied on the flow of services on the factor side of the market. Chapter 11 considers the taxation of consumer expenditures, which represent flows on the product side of the market. Chapter 12 looks at the taxation of asset value; that is, the value of stocks at some point in time. Besides pricing and taxing, governments finance their activities by borrowing or by creating money; Chapter 13 examines these two methods of government finance.

Part IV investigates various aspects of the expenditure side of the government's budget. Chapter 14 addresses briefly the conceptual framework for presenting public budgets and the procedures through which such budgets are made. Chapter 15 discusses the substantial interest that has arisen in developing techniques to analyze the efficiency of alternative public programs. Chapter 16 considers spending on national defense, which is the largest item of federal expenditure as measured by the actual use of resources by government. Chapter 17 examines spending on what has come to be called the welfare state, the largest overall item of federal expenditure, although it involves government mainly in the transfer rather than the use of resources. Chapter 18 explores the particular features of a federal form of organization for the public economy.

SUGGESTIONS FOR FURTHER READING

The fundamental functions of any economic system are set forth in Frank H. Knight, *The Economic Organization* (New York: Augustus M. Kelley, 1951). For a historical survey of economic thought approached from the perspective of economic coordination, see Joseph J. Spengler, "The Problem of Order in Economic Affairs," in *Essays in Economic Thought,* edited by Joseph J. Spengler and William R. Allen (Chicago: Rand McNally, 1960), pp. 6–34 (originally published in *Southern Economic Journal* 15 [July 1948], pp. 1–29). The distinction between the protective and the productive activities of government is explained in James M. Buchanan, *The Limits of Liberty* (Chicago: University of Chicago Press, 1975), particularly pp. 68–70. For an interesting description of the integrated political-economic approach to public economics developed by Italian scholars, see James M. Buchanan, "La scienza delle finance: The Italian Tradition in Fiscal Theory," *Fiscal Theory and Political Economy,* edited by Buchanan (Chapel Hill: University of North Carolina Press, 1960), pp. 24–74.

For a compilation of many types of data on the revenues and expenditures of American governments, see *Facts and Figures on Government Finance* (Washington, D.C.: Tax Foundation, Inc.), published biannually. For a presentation of much pertinent data on the growth of government in the countries listed in Tables 1.1 and 1.2 in the appendix, see G. Warren Nutter, *Growth of Government in the West* (Washington, D.C.: American Enterprise Institute, 1978).

This text assumes the reader has principles-level experience with microeconomics. The modern classic treatment of public economics at an advanced level is Richard A. Musgrave's treatise, *The Theory of Public Finance* (New York: McGraw-Hill, 1959). The first two-thirds of this book is still a highly valuable statement of numerous topics in public economics, although it will probably be inaccessible to students with no experience in intermediate microeconomics; the final third of the book is devoted mainly to topics in fiscal policy, which has since become the province of courses in macroeconomics and monetary theory. For an advanced treatment of topics that have developed since the publication of Musgrave's book, see Anthony B. Atkinson and Joseph E. Stiglitz, *Lectures on Public Economics* (New York: McGraw-Hill, 1980).

APPENDIX:
SOME QUANTITATIVE INFORMATION

Various data regarding taxes and expenditures will be introduced where appropriate throughout the text. A preliminary look at some pertinent data may be helpful in forming an initial impression of the place of government in contemporary economic life. One of the dominant themes of recent history has been the steady growth of government's participation in the economy. This participation can be measured in many ways, with either government expenditures or government revenues as a percentage of gross national product (GNP) being common measures. These two measures are not identical because governments can finance their expenditures by borrowing, by creating money, and by charging prices for services. Nonetheless, the measures show roughly similar patterns over time.

Table 1.1 shows tax revenues as a percentage of gross national product for twenty-three nations between 1955 and 1978. A pattern of continual expansion in the relative importance of government in the economy emerges strongly from an inspection of this table. Only nine of the nations listed had tax revenues exceeding 25 percent of GNP in 1955, and none had tax revenues exceeding 40 percent of GNP. By 1968, sixteen nations had tax revenues in excess of 25 percent, although none had yet surpassed 40 percent. But by 1978, twenty of the nations had surpassed the 25 percent share, and seven had tax revenues greater than 40 percent of GNP.

There are many particular bases against which governments can assess tax liability. Table 1.2 shows the distribution of tax revenues by type of tax for twenty-three nations in 1978. Three of the four categories of tax described in Table 1.2 relate closely to the types of taxes examined in Part III of this book. Taxes on income and profits refer to the taxation of both personal income and corporation income, the subject matter of Chapters 9 and 10, respectively. Taxes on goods and services refer to the taxation of consumption, which is examined in Chapter 11. Other taxes refer mainly to various taxes on wealth, which form the subject matter of Chapter 12. Social Security contributions are related to taxes on income, representing a proportional tax on wage income up to a maximum amount; this form of taxation is examined in Chapter 17.

A quick inspection of Table 1.2 shows that the twenty-three nations

TABLE 1.1 Tax Revenues as a Percentage
of Gross National Product

Country	1955	1968	1978
Australia	21.9	24.6	28.8
Austria	29.3	35.3	41.4
Belgium	22.6	34.3	44.2
Canada	23.7	29.6	31.1
Denmark	24.0	36.1	43.6
Finland	26.6	33.7	36.5
France	32.1	35.4	39.7
Germany, West	31.9	32.1	37.8
Greece	18.8	24.3	28.1
Ireland	21.5	29.1	33.4
Italy	24.3	28.8	32.6
Japan	18.2	17.9	24.1
Luxembourg	n.a.	29.8	49.9
Netherlands	26.2	38.8	46.8
New Zealand	26.4	25.9	30.4
Norway	29.2	37.7	46.9
Portugal	15.9	19.9	26.2
Spain	n.a.	16.4	22.8
Sweden	27.9	39.8	53.5
Switzerland	18.4	22.6	31.5
Turkey	n.a.	17.1	22.5
United Kingdom	28.5	34.8	34.5
United States	24.9	27.5	30.2

Source: Facts and Figures on Government Finance, 15th ed. and 21st ed. (Washington, D.C.: Tax Foundation, Inc., 1969 and 1981), p. 32 and p. 38, respectively.

of Table 1.1 vary substantially in their patterns of taxation. In six nations income taxes are about twice or more as important as consumption taxes: Japan, Luxembourg, New Zealand, Sweden, Switzerland, and the United States. In three nations consumption taxes are about twice as important as a source of revenue as income taxes: France, Greece, and Portugal. Table 1.2 also illustrates the considerable variation in the relative importance of social security taxes and various forms of taxation of wealth.

Table 1.3 shows the various sources of revenue at each level of government in the United States for 1979. These data point to a fairly strong tendency toward a separation of tax sources by level of government. The taxation of individual and corporation income provides nearly 60 percent of federal revenues and nearly 90 percent of federal tax revenues. Insurance trust revenue, which comes primarily from the Social Security program, is not treated as tax revenue, yet the in-

TABLE 1.2 Distribution of Tax Revenues
by Type of Tax, 1978

Country	Percentage of Total Tax Revenue[a]			
	Taxes on Income and Profits	Taxes on Goods and Services	Social Security Contri- butions	Other Taxes[b]
Australia	54.4	31.4	—	14.3
Austria	26.9	31.6	30.6	10.9
Belgium	41.1	26.1	30.0	2.8
Canada	44.8	32.2	11.8	11.2
Denmark	54.2	38.3	1.3	6.2
Finland	48.5	39.0	10.3	2.3
France	17.9	31.3	42.0	8.8
Germany, West	35.7	26.1	33.9	4.4
Greece	15.5	43.9	28.0	12.6
Ireland	33.6	46.6	13.7	6.0
Italy	29.3	26.3	40.7	3.7
Japan	40.4	17.2	29.5	12.9
Luxembourg	48.0	17.6	28.5	5.9
Netherlands	32.7	25.6	37.3	4.4
New Zealand	67.9	23.4	—	8.7
Norway	41.4	37.9	18.0	2.7
Portugal	21.7	38.0	29.8	10.5
Spain	23.7	21.4	49.5	5.4
Sweden	45.2	23.8	26.7	4.3
Switzerland	42.7	20.4	29.8	7.2
Turkey	47.9	31.2	15.0	5.9
United Kingdom	41.1	26.5	18.3	14.0
United States	45.9	17.0	25.0	12.1

[a] Percents may not sum to 100 because of rounding.
[b] Includes taxes on net worth, property, gifts, and inheritances, among others.
Source: Facts and Figures on Government Finance, 21st ed. (Washington, D.C.: Tax Foundation, Inc., 1981), p. 38.

surance trust is mainly a proportional tax on wage and salary income (as explained in Chapter 17). If such revenues are treated as tax revenues, the dominant position of income taxation becomes even stronger. The dominant form of revenue for state governments is the taxation of consumption, which accounts for over one-half of state tax revenues. At the local level of government, nearly 80 percent of tax revenues comes from the taxation of property, mainly of real estate. Local governments also derive nearly as much revenue from fees and charges as they collect in property taxes. One notable feature of the revenues for state and local governments is the relative

TABLE 1.3 U.S. Government Revenues by Source and Level of Government, 1979 (billions of dollars)

Source of Revenue	All Governments		Federal Government		State Governments		Local Governments	
	Amount	Percentage of Total	Amount	Percentage of Total	Amount	Percentage of Total	Amount	Percentage of Total
Total Revenues, own sources	$829.4	100.0	$499.6	100.0	$189.9	100.0	$139.9	100.0
Tax Revenues	524.4	63.2	318.9	63.8	124.9	65.8	80.6	57.6
Individual income	254.8	30.7	217.8	43.6	32.6	17.2	4.3	3.1
Corporation income	77.8	9.4	65.7	13.2	12.1	6.4	—	0.0
Property	64.9	7.8	—	0.0	2.5	1.3	62.5	44.7
Sales and excises	101.0	12.2	26.7	5.3	63.7	33.5	10.6	7.6
Other taxes	26.0	3.1	8.7	1.7	14.0	7.4	3.3	2.4
User Charges and Prices	138.7	16.7	53.5	10.7	29.6	15.6	55.6	39.7
Insurance Trust	166.2	20.0	127.2	25.5	35.4	18.6	3.7	2.6
Intergovernmental Revenue	a		1.3	0.3	57.1	30.1	94.8	67.8

[a] Intergovernmental revenues are payments received from the other levels of government. Because they do not add up to the total amount of revenues available to all levels of government, they are eliminated in the combined total.

Source: Facts and Figures on Government Finance, 21st ed. (Washington, D.C.: Tax Foundation, Inc., 1981), p. 20.

importance of intergovernmental revenue, consisting mainly of transfers of revenue from state governments to local governments and from the federal government to state and local governments. This source of revenue is nearly one-half of the tax revenue of state governments, and it exceeds the tax revenue of local governments.

The tax revenue that government extracts from its citizens is spent on a wide variety of services. Governments typically provide education for their citizens, protect them from fire and from other humans, dam rivers, construct highways, insure against unemployment, and subsidize retirement, among numerous other services. Table 1.4 shows how each level of government in the United States distributed its spending among thirteen categories in 1979. The federal government apportioned nearly 30 percent of its spending in 1979 to military-related activities (including foreign aid). Payments from its insurance trust programs accounted for nearly one-third of total federal spending. State governments directed about 20 percent of their total spending to each of two categories, education and public welfare. The expenditures of local governments were dominated by education, which totaled nearly 40 percent of local expenditures.

Table 1.5 presents some data on the growth of government spending in the United States for all levels of government. These data show a generally rising share of government expenditure as a percentage of GNP throughout the period since 1929, except for the reduction in expenditure upon the conclusion of World War II. By 1949 the government's share in GNP had fallen back to within 4 percentage points of its 1939 share, although the federal government occupied a larger share in comparison to the state and local governments than it did in 1939. The wartime mobilization of the economy by the federal government occurred at the expense of both private citizens and state and local governments. Between 1939 and 1944, the federal government's share of GNP increased by over 35 percentage points. The share of GNP left for private citizens fell by nearly 30 percentage points, and the share left for state and local governments fell by nearly 6 percentage points. The federal government's share in GNP fell sharply when the war ended, but it has been rising more or less steadily since then. From a 16 percent share of GNP in 1949, federal expenditures increased to 23 percent by 1980. The share of the federal government in the economy has more than doubled since the beginning of World War II. In contrast, the share of GNP occupied by state and local governments did not regain its prewar position until the late 1960s. In 1980, this share stood at 10.2 percent of GNP, about half a percentage point higher than the prewar share.

Table 1.6 presents data on the changing composition of federal spending since 1960. In 1960, defense-related expenditures made up

TABLE 1.4 U.S. Government Expenditures by Function and Level of Government, 1979 (billions of dollars)

Function	All Governments		Federal Governments		State Governments		Local Governments	
	Amount	Percentage of Total	Amount	Percentage of Total	Amount	Percentage of Total	Amount	Percentage of Total
Total Direct Expenditures	$832.4	100.0	$452.0	100.0	$148.7	100.0	$231.7	100.0
Defense-Related	128.5	15.4	128.5	28.4	—	0.0	—	0.0
Education	129.4	15.5	10.0	2.2	31.5	21.2	87.9	37.9
Highways	29.0	3.5	0.6	0.1	17.1	11.5	11.4	4.9
Public Welfare	59.1	7.1	18.7	4.1	28.7	19.3	11.7	5.0
Hospitals	25.7	3.1	4.7	1.0	10.2	6.9	10.8	4.7
Health	11.4	1.4	4.2	0.9	3.6	2.4	3.6	1.6
Police	13.9	1.7	1.7	0.4	1.8	1.2	10.4	4.5
Natural Resources	30.3	3.6	25.6	5.7	3.6	2.4	1.1	0.5
Housing and Urban Renewal	8.0	1.0	3.2	0.7	0.2	0.1	4.5	1.9
Transportation, Air, and Water	7.0	0.8	4.1	0.9	0.6	0.4	2.4	1.0
Interest on Debt	61.8	7.4	48.8	10.8	5.8	3.9	7.2	3.1
Insurance Trust	170.9	20.5	147.4	32.6	20.1	13.5	3.4	1.5
Other	157.2	18.9	54.5	12.1	25.5	17.1	77.3	33.4

Source: Facts and Figures on Government Finance, 21st ed. (Washington, D.C.: Tax Foundation, Inc., 1981), p. 17.

TABLE 1.5 U.S. Government Expenditures in Relation to Selected Years, Gross National Product by Level of Government

| | | Government Expenditures | | | | | |
| | | Amount (in billions)[a,b] | | | As Percentage of GNP[b] | | |
Year	GNP	Total	Federal	State and Local	Total	Federal	State and Local
1929	$ 103.4	$ 10.3	$ 2.6	$ 7.6	10.0	2.5	7.4
1934	65.3	12.9	6.4	6.5	19.7	9.8	9.9
1939	90.9	17.6	8.9	8.6	19.3	9.8	9.5
1944	210.6	103.0	95.5	7.5	48.9	45.3	3.6
1949	258.3	59.3	41.3	18.0	23.0	16.0	7.0
1954	366.8	97.0	69.8	27.2	26.4	19.0	7.4
1959	487.9	131.0	91.0	40.0	26.9	18.6	8.2
1964	637.7	176.3	118.2	58.1	27.6	18.5	9.1
1969	944.0	286.8	188.4	98.4	30.4	20.0	10.4
1974	1,434.2	460.0	299.3	160.6	32.1	20.9	11.2
1976	1,718.0	574.9	384.8	190.1	33.5	22.4	11.1
1978	2,156.1	681.8	460.7	221.2	31.6	21.4	10.3
1980	2,626.5	868.5	601.6	266.9	33.1	22.9	10.2

[a] Federal grants-in-aid to state and local governments are included in federal data and excluded from state and local data to avoid duplication.

[b] Parts may not sum to total because of rounding.

Source: Facts and Figures on Government Finance, 21st ed. (Washington, D.C.: Tax Foundation, Inc., 1981), p. 36.

53 percent of total federal budget outlays. By 1970 this share had declined to 42 percent, and by 1980 it had fallen to 25 percent. Moreover, in real terms after allowing for the decline in the value of the dollar through inflation, defense-related outlays were, if anything, slightly lower in 1980 than they were in 1960. While the absolute dollar amount of defense-related spending increased by nearly 174 percent between 1960 and 1980, the value of the dollar declined by about 178 percent. The declining share for defense-related expenditures contrasts sharply with the rising share for income security and social services, a category that includes Social Security, education, training, and employment assistance programs. In 1960 this category of expenditure occupied 21 percent of the federal budget. By 1970 its share had risen to 26 percent, and by 1980 it had captured 39 percent of the federal budget. Income security expenditures expanded to fill about two-thirds of the portion left by the declining relative importance of defense-related expenditures. Between 1960 and 1980,

TABLE 1.6   Federal Budget Outlays by Function,
Selected Years, 1960–1982 (in billions)

Function	1960	1970	1980	1982[a]
Total Budget Outlays	$92.2	$196.6	$579.6	$695.3
Defense-Related	49.0	82.9	146.6	200.0
Income Security and Social Services	19.3	51.7	223.9	267.2
Commerce and Transportation	4.8	9.1	28.9	23.0
Health	.8	13.1	58.2	73.4
Natural Resources and Energy	1.0	4.1	20.1	20.6
Agriculture	3.3	5.2	4.8	4.4
Science, Space, and Technology	.4	4.5	5.7	6.9
Community Development	1.0	2.4	10.1	8.1
Interest	8.3	18.3	64.5	82.5
Other	4.5	5.5	16.9	9.2

[a] Estimated.
Source: Facts and Figures on Government Finance, 20th ed. and 21st ed.
(Washington, D.C.: Tax Foundation, Inc., 1979 and 1981), pp. 81 and 89,
respectively.

defense-related spending fell by 28 percentage points as a share of
the federal budget, while income security expenditures increased by
18 percentage points. The comparative levels of defense-related and
income security expenditures, which together account for about two-
thirds of the federal budget, constitute one of the more controversial
aspects of federal expenditure policy, and it is largely for this reason
that these topics are explored in Chapters 16 and 17.

I

NORMATIVE FOUNDATIONS FOR PUBLIC ECONOMICS

2

Efficiency and the Public Economy

Efforts to formulate criteria for assessing the economic conduct of government have generally addressed two concerns: that government's use of resources should reflect the valuations of the people who constitute the society and that government should act equitably or justly. These two concerns are reflected in the principles of efficiency and of equity or justice. Although both principles may be widely held, their application to concrete situations may sometimes create controversy. Moreover, efficiency and justice may conflict, in which case questions of supremacy or trade-off arise. This chapter and Chapter 3 explore the criteria of efficiency and justice for fiscal conduct.

INDIVIDUAL VALUES AND THE MEANING
OF EFFICIENCY IN GOVERNMENT

The outcomes of the market economy tend to reflect individual valuations, commonly described as *consumer sovereignty*. People in their capacities as consumers are free to accept or reject the offerings of sellers, and a seller can acquire business only to the extent that customers think one offering serves their wants better than does another offering. What is produced is determined by the pattern of effective consumer demands; that is, consumers' willingness and ability to pay for products. Efficiency as a norm for fiscal conduct holds that budgetary choices should reflect individual valuations in essentially the same manner that a market economy reflects those valuations. In public economics this is commonly described as the *benefit principle*, and it represents an effort to extend consumer sovereignty to the conduct of government.

The benefit principle developed out of the various versions of the contract theory of the state, all of which characterized the relation between citizens and government as essentially contractual. Citizens make contributions to the state through the taxes they pay, and they receive services of value in return in the same way that consumers pay for goods received in market transactions. The norms of the market economy follow from a general acceptance of liberal values, which emphasize individual autonomy within a framework of law, exercised to the extent that it does not infringe on the recognized rights of others. The benefit principle of public economics assesses the use of resources by government against the same liberal values of individual autonomy. Citizen sovereignty in the public economy is complementary to consumer sovereignty in the market economy.

EXTERNALITY AND INCOMPLETENESS IN THE LEGAL ORDER

A market economy promotes reallocations of resources from less valued to more valued uses. The ability of a market economy to direct resources to the most highly valued uses requires a legal order that permits the exclusive ownership of all valued resources and that allows the owners of resources to alienate or transfer their ownership to others. Without the *exclusivity* and *alienability of ownership*, a market economy cannot promote the most highly valued uses of resources. If resources are not allocated to their most highly valued uses, a *misallocation* of resources results.

Exclusivity of Ownership

If ownership is exclusive, the owner can prevent use by others. With nonexclusive or common ownership, no such ability exists. Both forms of ownership can be found, for example, in oyster farming. Connecticut, Delaware, Georgia, New Jersey, and New York organize oyster farming predominately through exclusive ownership, with oyster beds being leased to particular farmers. In contrast, Alabama, Florida, Mississippi, and Texas organize oyster farming predominately through nonexclusive ownership. In these states, farmers can harvest oysters in any oyster bed they choose. Some states have a mix of ownership forms.[1]

---

[1] Different ownership arrangements in the farming of oysters are described and analyzed in Richard J. Angello and Lawrence P. Donnelley, "Property Rights and Efficiency in the Oyster Industry," *Journal of Law and Economics* 18 (October 1975), pp. 521–533.

The choice between these forms of ownership has important economic implications. When oyster beds are exclusively or privately owned, owners have a strong incentive to act to maximize the value of their beds. To do this, farmers must avoid harvesting immature oysters. If immature oysters harvested today are worth $100, and if these same oysters would be worth $140 in one year, the delay in harvesting yields a return of 40 percent. As long as the rate of interest is less than 40 percent, the owner of the oyster bed will become wealthier by letting the oysters mature than by harvesting the immature ones. Furthermore, the farmer will replenish the cultch—deposits of rock or shell vital for the growth of oysters—that is scooped up along with the oysters if the expense of replacing it is less than the increase in the value of the oyster bed that results from its replacement.

When oyster beds are subject to nonexclusive or common ownership, individual farmers have less incentive to refrain from activities that diminish the value of the oyster bed. Suppose one hundred people farm oysters under common ownership. If one farmer returns immature oysters and replenishes cultch, the value of the oysters yielded by the bed will increase, but 99 percent of this increased value will accrue to the ninety-nine other farmers. Conversely, a farmer who reduces the value of the bed by harvesting immature oysters and by failing to replenish cultch will bear only 1 percent of the reduction in value. Common ownership is unlikely to promote a value-maximizing use of resources. Indeed, government regulations specifing such things as the minimum-size oyster that can be harvested and the replenishment of cultch are testimony to the different incentives created by alternative forms of ownership. Such regulations, however, are rarely if ever fully effective in duplicating the incentives that private ownership creates naturally. Richard Angello and Lawrence Donnelley estimate that a conversion of commonly owned oyster beds to private ownership would increase by about 50 percent the value of the output from farming oysters.[2]

Alienability of Ownership

Besides being exclusive, ownership must be alienable, or transferable, from one person to another if a market economy is to direct resources to their most highly valued uses. Suppose land used for growing corn is worth $2,000 per acre, and one person owns 500 acres and another person owns 100 adjoining acres. Suppose the second person thinks an amusement park would be a more valuable use of the land;

[2] Ibid., pp. 532–533.

that is, that the value of the land will be more than $200,000 if it is used as an amusement park. As long as the value people place on amusement exceeds the value they place on corn, a conversion of land from cornfield to park will increase the value of the services yielded by the land. This increased value will be reflected in a rise in the price of the land. The owner is likely to increase the size of the park so long as the anticipated increase in land value from doing so exceeds $2,000 per acre and until the value added by the last or marginal acre falls to $2,000.

Once the entire 100-acre parcel is converted to park, it is possible that additional land will also be worth more than $2,000 per acre as park. If so, and if land is transferable, the developer could buy or lease additional acreage from the farmer. Suppose the marginal value of park land falls to $2,000 with the addition of the fiftieth acre and the farmer and the developer agree to transfer title of that land for $125,000. The simple fact of agreement implies that the developer thinks the land is worth at least as much as, and probably more than, $125,000 as an amusement park and that the farmer thinks the land is worth no more than, and probably less than, $125,000 for growing corn. The contract reflects a consensus of both parties that the land is at least as valuable, and probably more valuable, as a park than as a cornfield. However, should ownership be nonalienable, perhaps because a zoning ordinance prohibits nonagricultural uses, such a reallocation of land to a more valuable use could not take place.

Incomplete Ownership and Externality

The developer and the farmer may agree to a sale or lease of land, and any such agreement implies that, from their perspectives or judgments, the land is shifted to a more highly valued use. But what if there are other people who are not party to the contract but who are damaged by or who benefit from the contract? The water supply for the park may come from wells that the developer drills on the property. If the water table in the adjoining area consequently drops, the costs of pumping water and drilling wells will increase for other people in the area. These people are damaged by the contract between the farmer and the developer just as surely as if the farmer and the developer had conspired to siphon off some of these people's water. As another result of the sale, traffic to and from the park might create congestion on the roads in the area, thereby increasing the time it takes residents to leave or return to their homes, or the increased noise level in the evenings might cause some of them difficulty in getting to sleep.

Such third-party consequences of transactions are referred to as *externalities.* If they affect third parties positively, they are called *external benefits;* if their effect is negative, they are called *external costs.* Suppose food-processing plants emit both an odor that is highly offensive and soot that soils clothing, vehicles, and buildings, thereby increasing the expenses of laundering, cleaning, and painting. If the plants are able to avoid responsibility for the damage done by their smell and soot, their cost of production will be lower and their output higher than if they had to compensate local residents for the damages. As Figure 2.1 illustrates, the supply curve of the food-processing industry, which is the horizontal summation of the marginal cost curves of the individual firms, is lower than it would be if the firms were responsible for the damages. If the food processors were required to pay compensation for the damages, individual firms

---

FIGURE 2.1   External Diseconomy

Consumer demands for the industry's output are described by d, and industry supply, which is the summation of the marginal cost curves of individual firms, is described by S. The price of the industry's output is P_1 per unit and the rate of output is Q_1. Suppose the amount of uncompensated damage imposed on residents from odor and soot is ab per unit of output. The curve S^* shows what the industry supply curve would be if the firms had to buy the agreement of the residents to emit odor and soot; ab indicates the value residents place on the damage done by the odor and soot. With a higher marginal cost of production, industry output would fall to Q_2 and price would rise to P_2. Of this price, $P_2 - P_2^*$ would be paid as compensation for damages, and P_2^* would be paid to suppliers of other inputs.

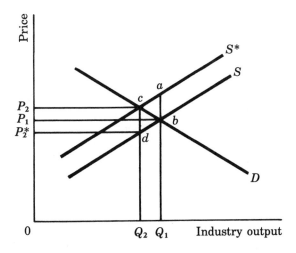

would face higher marginal costs of production and the industry's supply curve would shift upward. A tax on output might seem to be a way of offsetting this *external diseconomy*. In Figure 2.1, the value of the external diseconomy is *ab* per unit of output. As a result of this divergence, the value of the industry output to consumers, P_1, is less, by *ab*, than the cost of that output, with this cost being the value to consumers of the best alternative output that could have been produced with the same resources. Should the government impose a tax of *ab* per unit of output, the marginal cost curves of individual firms would rise by this amount, and this rise would in turn be reflected in the upward shift in the industry supply curve. If the tax is calculated properly, it will induce the firms to act in the same manner they would have acted had they been required to buy the consent of residents to emit odor and soot; in the case of the tax, however, the payments will accrue to government rather than to the people actually damaged by the odor and soot.

Reciprocal Nature of Externality

Externality relationships are reciprocal. From one perspective the food processors impose damages on residents, but from another perspective the residents damage the food processors. After all, should the residents move away, the externality would not exist. The relation between bees and various fruits and herbs illustrates this reciprocal character. Suppose a beekeeper's bees fly into an adjoining cherry orchard and pollinate the cherry blossoms. These bees increase the yield from the orchard, but the pollination of cherry blossoms yields no honey in return. The beekeeper will expand the number of colonies as long as the revenue from the added production of honey exceeds the cost of the additional colonies. As described in Figure 2.2, the beekeeper will keep Q_1 colonies and the price per colony will be P_1. This solution is based on the presumption that bees are kept only because of the honey they yield to the beekeeper. But bees are also valued by the owners of cherry orchards for their pollination services. If beekeepers could somehow be paid for the services the bees yield to the cherry orchards, they would keep more bees, and an increased yield of cherries would result. If the government gives a subsidy for keeping bees, the number of colonies kept will expand. The subsidy has the effect of paying the beekeepers for the pollination services their bees provide for the owners of cherry orchards.[3]

---

[3] Many complexities surround the use of taxes or subsidies as a way of dealing with external economies or diseconomies. Among other things, a tax could be assessed against the product a factory produces, or it could be assessed against some measure of the soot it emits. The choice of approach to taxation could

FIGURE 2.2 External Economy

Suppose the demand for bees by beekeepers is based only on the value of the honey the bees produce, represented by the demand curve D_H. In this situation the number of colonies is Q_1 and the price per colony is P_1. Suppose the value of the pollination services to cherry orchards is ab per colony of bees. If the beekeeper takes the value of these pollination services into account, the demand for bees would rise to $D_H + D_P$, which would lead to an output of Q_2 colonies and a price of P_2 per colony. Should government impose a subsidy of cd ($= ab$) per colony, the supply curve of bees to beekeepers would shift downward to S^*. In this situation, beekeepers would select Q_2 colonies. Even though the bees are valued at only P_2^* per colony for their honey at this larger rate of output, the subsidy for pollination services leads beekeepers to act as if they had taken into account the interests of the owners of cherry orchards in making their decisions as to how many bees to keep.

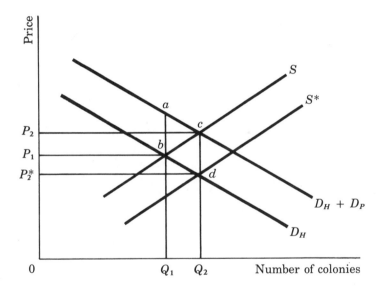

The reciprocal nature of externality relationships means that the affected parties all have an incentive to reach some agreement con-

have important implications for the way in which a firm decides to produce. Similarly, a subsidy could be based on the amount of honey grown by a beekeeper, or it could be based on the number of colonies the beekeeper has. The choice of one base for subsidization over another may affect the production choices of the beekeeper. A subsidy based simply on the number of colonies would create some incentive to substitute less expensive for more expensive colonies. A subsidy based on the volume of honey produced would create some incentive for the beekeeper to substitute the production of high-volume honey for that of low-volume honey.

cerning the use of resources. As long as ownership is exclusive and transferable, such agreements are likely to be reached. If orchard owners would gain by the presence of more bees, they can pay the beekeepers to keep more bees. (Alternatively, the orchard owners could raise their own bees.) As long as the value of the increased yield of cherries together with the value of the increased volume of honey exceeds the cost of the additional bees, both parties will be able to agree about an expansion in the number of colonies. The beekeepers will be willing to keep more colonies because the orchard owners' payment makes it profitable to do so. If the bees become sufficiently numerous that no agreement is possible over a further infusion of bees into the orchard, all relevant demands for the services of bees—both as producers of honey and as pollinators—will have been reflected in the outcome of the market economy.

The agreement between the orchard owner and the beekeeper increases the wealth of each. In terms of Figure 2.2, the beekeeper values expansions in output beyond Q_1 at the price indicated by D_H. The cost of that expansion is indicated by S. To expand output from Q_1 to Q_2, the beekeeper must receive at least bdc. If the beekeeper receives exactly this amount for the expansion, he will be as wealthy as he would have been without the expansion; if he receives more than this amount, he will be wealthier. As for the orchard owner, the value of the additional bees is indicated by $abdc$, the difference between $(D_H + D_P)$ and D_H. If the orchard owner pays this amount for the added output, he will be no wealthier than before, but for any lesser payment he will be wealthier. The amount shown by abc in Figure 2.2 represents the potential gain to both parties from an agreement that will increase the number of bees, and this agreement will erase any resource misallocations that might otherwise have resulted.

Considerable evidence shows that market processes take into account the demands for honey and for pollination services.[4] In cases where no honey is yielded but where pollination services are necessary for the setting of fruit, as with cherry trees, orchard owners pay pollination fees to beekeepers. In cases where pollination services are not required but where the yield of honey is high, as with mint, beekeepers pay apiary rents to landowners for the right to place their hives amid the mint.

It is essentially the same situation with smoke and soot, as well as for any other case of externality. As long as the damage done by the smoke and soot exceeds the cost to the food processors of re-

[4] See Steven N. S. Cheung, "The Fable of the Bees: An Economic Investigation," *Journal of Law and Economics* 16 (April 1973), pp. 11–33; and David B. Johnson, "Meade, Bees, and Externalities," *Journal of Law and Economics* 16 (April 1973), pp. 35–52.

ducing their emission of smoke and soot, it will be possible for the affected parties to reach some agreement to reduce the emission of smoke and soot. If the food processors have the right to use the air as they choose, those who are harmed by the smoke and soot will be able to pay the food processors to emit less smoke and soot. On the other hand, if surrounding residents have a right to clean air, the food processors will be unable to buy the consent of those residents to emit as much smoke and soot as they emitted under common ownership. Regardless of who has the right to determine the use of the air, the same outcome results, as long as the right of ownership in air is exclusive and transferable — the use of the air in its most highly valued manner.

The ability of such transfers of ownership to erase the misallocations of resources that might otherwise result is referred to as the *Coase theorem*.[5] There are difficult cases in which the rearrangement of ownership may not operate as simply as it does in other cases. A comparison of the bees and the food-processing plants is instructive. Formally, both situations are identical, but it may be less difficult for a market economy to reallocate resources from less valued to more valued uses in relationships such as those between beekeepers and orchard owners than in relationships between polluting factories and residents of the affected area. Ownership rights are clearly established and easily transferable between the beekeeper and the orchard owner, so the common interest of both parties in having resources reallocated from less valued to more valued uses will be acted upon relatively easily by both parties. With respect to the factories and the residents, however, ownership rights are generally nonexclusive and nontransferable. When people are unable to buy and sell rights to the use of air, there is no incentive for market transactions to bring about the allocation of resources to their most highly valued uses.

There are several reasons why ownership might be nonexclusive and nontransferable. Technologically, it may be difficult, if not impossible, to measure the use of resources, in this case the emission of polluting substances. It is particularly difficult with mobile sources of pollution. Residents of a city may be able to measure the degradation in air quality caused by a particular factory, but measuring the degradation caused by automobiles that travel on the streets is another matter. An area plagued by acid rain faces essentially the same problem in attempting to measure the pollution attributable to different sources. Technological limitations aside, some agreements may

5 Ronald H. Coase, "The Problem of Social Cost," *Journal of Law and Economics* 3 (October 1960), pp. 1–44.

be costly to organize. Widely dispersed victims of industrial pollution, for example, might have trouble agreeing among themselves about how best to deal with the polluting plants.

In such situations, the cost of defining and enforcing a system of ownership might be so high that administrative control is more effective than contractual arrangements in bringing about the most highly valued use of resources. The fact that some activities can be organized hierarchically at a lower cost than they could be organized through explicit contracts is one reason for the development of business firms.[6] When the cost of defining and enforcing ownership rights is taken into account, situations can arise in which governmental direction of resource use might lead to higher-valued use of resources than would otherwise result. Moreover, new situations continually arise in which formerly existing patterns of ownership may no longer be effective. Water may initially be owned in common, and people may freely satisfy their demands for water by drilling wells. As the area develops and more wells are drilled, the water table may fall, in which case it can be said that one person's drilling a well imposes external costs on others. Because water is common property, conflict will erupt among various claimants of right to the water. There are many ways this conflict may be settled or kept in check. Regardless of the particular form it takes, settlement of the conflict will involve the participation of government, because the protective function of government includes the maintenance of internal order.

EXTERNALITY, SHARED CONSUMPTION, AND COLLECTIVE GOODS

Under exclusive ownership, an owner can prevent use by others unless the parties reach an agreement about payment in exchange for use. In cases where it is prohibitively expensive to prevent use by others, ownership is nonexclusive, and the market system does not necessarily operate to bring about the movement of resources toward more highly valued uses. If someone provides flood control for an area by constructing a dam and a drainage network, all residents of the flood plain will benefit, regardless of whether they pay for the protection. It is difficult to see how flood control could be provided through ordinary market transactions.

To the extent that it is costly to prevent the use of such goods or

[6] See Ronald H. Coase, "The Nature of the Firm," *Economica* 4 (November 1937), pp. 386–405; and Armen A. Alchian and Harold Demsetz, "Production, Information Costs, and Economic Organization," *American Economic Review* 62 (September 1972), pp. 777–795.

services by those who do not pay for them, there will be some tendency for people to avoid making payments for such services. If people can consume with or without making a payment, some *free riding* is likely. In the presence of free riding, a market system will provide such goods and services either in lesser quantity than people might desire or not at all. A market system is a means of achieving social cooperation, but such cooperation breaks down in the presence of nonexclusive ownership. The resulting situation, in which people's pursuit of their own interests undermines rather than supports social cooperation, is referred to as a *prisoners' dilemma.*

Figure 2.3 illustrates this dilemma, for two persons rather than for a society of many. Each person faces the choice of making or not making a payment for the flood control project. The four cells in Figure 2.3 describe the values of the resulting outcomes to each of the two participants. The values of the different outcomes for person A appear in the upper left of each cell, and the values for person B appear in the lower right of each cell. If A contributes to the project and B does not, A bears the full cost and B receives the benefit of the project without cost. The value of this outcome is −$75 for A and $125 for B, as shown in quadrant II. This situation is called a dilemma because each person is better off if they both contribute to the project than if neither does, yet the outcome is that neither contributes. Consider the situation from the perspective of person A. If A assumes B will contribute to the project, A's own best choice is to not contribute. By not contributing when B does, A realizes a return of $125(III). But if A also contributes, the return is only $50(I). If A assumes B will not contribute to the project, A's best choice is still to not contribute. In this case A's return is $0(IV), but if A contributes and B does not, A's return is −$75(II). Regardless of what A assumes B will do, therefore, A's best choice is to not contribute. The same reasoning obviously applies to B. Consequently, with neither person making a contribution, they each gain nothing, whereas if they both contribute, they would each gain $50.

Although the prisoners' dilemma was developed here for a two-person situation, it is commonly used to illustrate the difficulties that arise in a market economy when ownership is nonexclusive as well as to illustrate the potential gain from cooperative action. Cooperative action often arises voluntarily, because, as the dilemma illustrates, cooperative action offers gains to all participants. As the number of people involved increases, however, it generally becomes increasingly costly to achieve cooperation. The situation becomes less like the relationship between the beekeeper and the orchard owner and more like the relationship between the food processor and surrounding residents.

FIGURE 2.3 Prisoners' Dilemma

Each entry in this figure represents the difference between benefits and contributions. It is assumed that each person can contribute either zero or $200. The benefit from the contributions accrues as a reduction in the anticipated damage from flooding. If neither person contributes, the anticipated reduction in damage is, of course, zero. If one $200 contribution is made, the anticipated reduction in damage is assumed to be $125, regardless of who makes the contribution. If both people make $200 contributions, the anticipated reduction in damage is assumed to be $250 for each person. Hence, if A and B each contribute $200, each receives a net benefit of $50, as shown in quadrant I. If B contributes $200 while A contributes nothing, B receives a net benefit of −$75 while A receives a net benefit of $125, as shown in quadrant III.

Outcome for person B

	Contribute	Not contribute
Contribute	$50 / $50 (I)	−$75 / $125 (II)
Not contribute	$125 / −$75 (III)	$0 / $0 (IV)

Outcome for person A

Although the market system might fail to reallocate resources to their most valued uses when ownership is nonexclusive, government intervention might be a means of doing so. If taxes are imposed on those who lie in the flood plain, free riding will be curtailed. People no longer would have a choice of contributing or not contributing to the flood control program, unless they tried to avoid paying taxes. It would be more costly to avoid taxes than to refrain from contributing to the flood control program, however, because the state uses its police power to collect taxes but not to secure agreement among many individuals acting privately. An effective or efficient government, according to the benefit principle, is one that acts to bring about those outcomes that would result under exclusive and transferable ownership, if such a system of ownership had been workable in the first place.

An important part of government expenditures for public or collective goods relates to the maintenance of order, either externally as in military spending or internally as in spending on police and courts. Other services often provided by government represent efforts to enhance the productivity of the market economy. Such government efforts as highways, fire protection, flood control, and the support of scientific research are services for which exclusive and transferable ownership can be expensive to implement. The provision of such services by government is a means of supporting the operation of the market economy in shifting resources from less valued to more valued uses.

THE BENEFIT PRINCIPLE

The benefit principle of public economics describes government as undertaking those activities that could not be undertaken efficiently through ordinary market transactions. In the absence of exclusive and transferable ownership, collective provision of goods or services may be superior to market provision. Such collective provision is assessed by how closely it reflects the valuations of the individual members of society. In other words, the benefit principle represents what can be called a consensual approach to the public economy.

Nonrivalry in Consumption

Nonexclusive ownership generally arises in situations where a single unit of production simultaneously provides units of consumption for many people. The transmission of a radio or television program over the air makes that program available to all people living within the broadcast area unless the program is scrambled and the receiver possesses a descrambling device. The provision of a dam makes flood protection available to all who live within the flood plain unless the flood waters somehow can be kept away from the properties of only those who pay for protection. Such services are *nonrival* in consumption: one person's consumption does not prevent the others from consuming the service at the same time. Goods that are nonrival in consumption are called *collective goods*.

In contrast, numerous goods are characterized by rivalry in

consumption. An ear of corn eaten by one person is not available to anyone else. A shirt worn by one person is not available for wear by anyone else. Goods for which one person's consumption rivals the consumption of others are called *private goods*. In other words, a private good can be apportioned among individual consumers so that the sum of the amounts consumed by all people equals the total production of the good, whereas a collective good is one for which the total amount produced is equally available for each person's consumption.

To some extent, exclusivity of ownership characterizes goods that are rival in consumption (private goods), and nonexclusivity characterizes goods that are nonrival (collective goods). It is generally easier to exclude those who don't pay from consuming an ear of corn or a shirt than it is to exclude them from taking advantage of flood protection or a broadcast. These correspondences between rivalry in consumption and exclusivity in ownership are by no means perfect. A lighthouse is characterized by nonrivalry in consumption. It simultaneously protects all ships in its vicinity and each ship is able to consume the entire output of the lighthouse, the protective beam. The lighthouse may not be wholly free from rivalry in consumption, however. It provides more protection for ships that pass relatively close to dangerous areas than for ships that pass farther away from such areas. As the number of ships in an area increases, access to the beam is perhaps reduced because of congestion. Nonetheless, a lighthouse possesses substantial nonrivalry in consumption, yet there is a history of lighthouse services being provided through market transactions.[7] A police force that protects one person in a city is simultaneously available to protect all the other residents, although there is some rivalry in that some neighborhoods can be patrolled more intensively than others and time spent on one case is time not available to be spent on other cases.

The case of entirely nonrival consumption may be a small one. It might seem as though the polar categories of collective and private goods can be usefully replaced by a spectrum of degrees of rivalry in consumption. Flood control and broadcasting would be close to the collective end, police services not as close, and shoes, corn, and beer would be located at the private end. Such a classification would not make any distinction between services provided by government and those provided through markets. Government provides many services that fall at or close to the private end of the spectrum: camping spaces, mortgage loans, food stamps.

---

[7] See Ronald H. Coase, "The Lighthouse in Economics," *Journal of Law and Economics* 17 (October 1974), pp. 357–376.

At the same time, many services lying closer to the collective end of the spectrum are provided through market transactions: viewings of motion pictures, spectator sports, hotel lobbies. A motion picture theater provides one production unit, a showing, which in turn provides as many consumption units as there are seats in the theater. If a theater seats 1,000 people, rivalry in consumption will not arise until the theater is full. As long as there are fewer than 1,000 people in attendance, the addition of one more viewer will not prevent someone else from watching the same showing. One unit of production is consumed by each of up to 1,000 consumers. There is, of course, some rivalry in consumption because not all seats are equally desirable. As the number of viewers increases, people must sit farther back, closer up, or more to the sides, locations that most people regard as less desirable. Nonetheless, a motion picture theater illustrates the market provision of a collective good, an item of shared consumption, that is made possible by exclusive ownership.

Collective goods give rise to difficulties in economic coordination and calculation only when exclusivity of ownership is exceedingly costly to implement. Suppose, for instance, the technology of showing films was such that films could be shown only on cloudy evenings because the picture had to be reflected against a cloud. A showing could then be viewed by anyone within sight of the cloud, and exclusion, while imaginable, would hardly be practical. The market provision of motion pictures would be unlikely to prosper in this technological setting. The exhibitor would be unable to charge viewers because they could not be prevented from watching the showing. If people enjoyed watching motion pictures, some means of charging viewers would have to be found in order for the exhibitor to maintain a business. Alternatively, some collective or governmental support would be required, the effect of which would be, according to the benefit principle, to bring about what would have happened had the exhibitor been able to exclude noncontributors from watching the showing.

Optimality in the Provision of Collective Goods

The benefit principle attempts to describe the salient characteristics of budgetary choices that reflect individual valuations. Figure 2.4 illustrates this use of the benefit principle. For simplicity, the community that makes the choice is assumed to consist of three people or, for a more realistic situation, three equal-sized groups of people with identical preferences. As with market provision of services, the benefit principle has demand and supply elements: people have demands for services to be supplied by government, and there is a cost of providing those services. The horizontal marginal cost curve (*mc*)

FIGURE 2.4 Benefit Principle and Lindahl Prices

The curves D_1, D_2, and D_3 show the demands for three people or three
equal-sized groups of people. The curve D–the vertical summation of those
individual demands–represents the valuation that people place on
successive rates of output of the service, while the curve MC represents the
marginal cost of that service; that is, the value placed on what must be
sacrificed to secure additional amounts of the service in question. At any
rate of output less that Q_2, say Q_1, people value the collectively provided
service more highly than they value what they must sacrifice in exchange,
and this divergence is indicated by ab. At any output in excess of Q_2, say
Q_3, people value the collectively provided service less highly than they
value what they must give up in return, and this deficiency is illustrated
by cd. Q_2 is the rate of output that corresponds to the requirement of the
benefit principle: It is the rate of output that would have been generated
through market transactions had such transactions been possible. In other
words, all three persons or groups could agree to the provision of Q_2, with
each person paying a share in the total cost equal to or less than their own
valuations; that is, the sum of the individual valuations, $P_1 + P_2 + P_3$,
equals the marginal cost of the service.

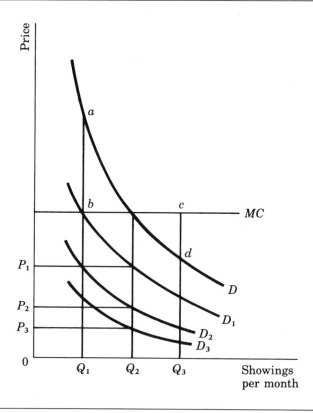

in the figure indicates that the rental price of films is a constant amount per showing. The community must decide how many films to show per month and how to apportion the expense of those showings among its members.

The benefit principle describes outcomes characterized by consensus among the members of the community. In a market economy people increase their purchases of goods as long as they think the value of the goods exceeds the cost they pay or the value of what they must relinquish in exchange. Suppose showings cost $10 each and that for five showings per month, Persons 1, 2, and 3 place valuations of $8, $6, and $5 on a showing. Person 1 would prefer one more showing as long as it costs less than $8, and persons 2 and 3 would prefer one more showing if it costs them less than $6 and $5, respectively. Since a showing costs the three together only $10 and since the three together would be willing to pay up to $19 for this showing, some consensus would be possible about financing a sixth showing. There are numerous distributions of the $10 payment among the three that would leave all three better off. One is an equal distribution, in which each pays $3.33; other distributions of the $10 cost —(6, 3, 1), (2, 4, 4), (3, 5, 2), to name just a few—are also possible. There are potential gains to all three from an agreement to increase the number of showings, and there are many particular ways in which they can share those gains.

As long as the sum of the valuations placed on an additional showing by the members of the community exceeds the cost of an additional showing, consensus is possible regarding an increase in the number of showings. Suppose that for the twelfth showing, the respective valuations were $5, $3, and $2. This corresponds to the situation described by Q_2 in Figure 2.4. An increase in showings beyond this number is valued at something less than $10, so it will be impossible to attain consensus for the increase. When the sum of the individual valuations is less than $10, there is no way that the $10 cost can be distributed among the three in such a way that all three are better off with the additional showing than they would have been had they retained their share of the cost. Moreover, the only distribution of the cost of the twelfth showing that will both cover the $10 cost and will command consensus is one where the three people pay $5, $3, and $2, respectively. These figures correspond to the individual prices P_1, P_2, and P_3 in Figure 2.4 and are commonly called *Lindahl prices*, after Erik Lindahl, the Swedish economist who developed the central idea behind the analytical construction represented in Figure 2.4.

Lindahl's formulation of the benefit principle conveys a simple message. When the conditions for Lindahl equilibrium are fulfilled, as indicated by Q_2 in Figure 2.4, all of the gains from trade involved in budgetary expansion have been fully exploited. It is no longer possible for the members of the community to agree on mutually profitable expansions in the size of the budget (or contractions, if the starting point is to the right of Q_2). Conversely, as long as the conditions for Lindahl equilibrium are unsatisfied, gains from trade involved in budgetary changes are possible such that at least some members of the community benefit and no member is harmed. As long as an activity undertaken by government represents a more productive use of resources than the best alternative use of those resources, as evaluated by the members of the community, it is possible in principle to attain some consensus among the members of the comunity over an expansion in the activity. The benefit principle of public economics, then, assesses collective outcomes in terms of their ability to reflect the consent of the governed.

Some Complexities in Lindahl Pricing

In the formulation of the benefit principle described by Figure 2.4, people pay tax prices equal to the valuations they place on the marginal or final unit of the collective service. The price paid for the marginal unit was assumed in Figure 2.4 to equal the average price paid for all units. A more general assumption would distinguish between conditions that apply to the marginal unit of the collective service and conditions that apply to the entire cost. Strictly speaking, the benefit principle refers only to the prices that individuals pay for the marginal unit of the collective service. It does not lead automatically to a model of the overall distribution of the cost of all collective output among all the citizens. There are two conceptual difficulties that prevent a simple movement from marginal conditions to distribution of the total tax burden among citizens: (1) there is no necessity that the average price each person pays for collective output equals the marginal price and (2) such an equality of average and marginal prices will be impossible unless the collective output is produced with constant cost. The fact that marginal magnitudes may diverge from average magnitudes does not disturb the central perspective of the benefit principle, but it does complicate it.

The complexities that arise when average and marginal magnitudes diverge, and the reasons they arise, are illustrated in Figure 2.5. Suppose the marginal cost of collective output is $10 per unit and that at some rate of output, say Q_2, the marginal valuations for Persons 1 and 2 are $10 and $6, respectively. Further suppose that in

FIGURE 2.5 Benefit Principle with Nonuniform Tax Prices

The demands for some collective good for two people or groups of people are shown by D_1 and D_2, and the summation of those demands is shown by D. Regardless of whether marginal cost is constant, MC_1, or decreasing, MC_2, the Lindahl equilibrium rate of output is Q_1 and the Lindahl marginal prices are P_1 and P_2. Person 1 would be willing to provide the entire expense of the first Q_2 units of output. Moreover, as long as Person 1 pays any amount less than Q_2bdQ_1 for the expansion of output from Q_2 to Q_1, he or she will be better off with the expansion. Although the two people pay marginal prices of P_1 and P_2, Lindahl equilibrium is also consistent with a distribution of total cost such that Person 1 pays $0cbdQ_1$ and Person 2 pays only bda. In this event nearly all of the joint gain from the provision of the collective service accrues to Person 2.

With decreasing marginal cost, a system of constant marginal tax prices will encounter budget deficits. The total cost of the Q_1 units of output is c^*aQ_10, but pricing at the constant marginal tax prices of P_1 and P_2 will raise only $0caQ_1$ in revenue. There will be a budget deficit of cc^*a that can be covered only through some system of prices where the average price charged to at least one person is in excess of the Lindahl price that reflects that person's valuation of the marginal unit of the collective service.

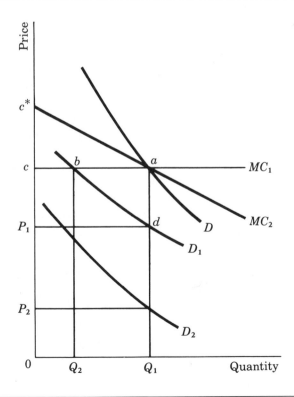

Lindahl equilibrium the Lindahl prices are $7 and $3 for 1 and 2. Moreover, let the quanitities described by Q_2 and Q_1 be 5 and 10 units, respectively. To provide 10 units of output requires a budget of $100. Although the Lindahl prices are $7 and $3 when output is 10 units, the taxes borne by 1 and 2 are not necessarily $70 and $30, respectively. Lindahl prices simply mean that the $10 expense of the final unit of output must be apportioned such that 1 pays $7 and 2 pays $3. To move from the Lindahl prices of $7 and $3 on the marginal unit to an assignment of the total expense of the budget—$70 to 1 and $30 to 2—is to dictate a particular distribution of the joint gains from the provision of the collective service. This is not required by any principle of conformity to individual valuations.

Consider the positions of 1 and 2 in trying to agree to the provision of five units of the collective service, as opposed to none. Person 1 values the fifth unit at $10 and the earlier units at more than $10. Against an option of no provision, 1 would be willing to cover the full expense of providing five units. This is implied by the location of 1's demand curve, D_1, above the marginal cost curve for output less than Q_2. Person 1 would not be willing to cover the full expense of increased output beyond 5 units. However, as long as the sum of the valuations of 1 and 2 exceeds the marginal cost of the service, two inferences can be drawn: (1) it will be possible for 1 and 2 to agree to finance an expansion in output, and (2) there is more than one way to distribute the cost of that additional output such that each person is better off than before.

Suppose 1's and 2's marginal valuations of the sixth unit of output are $9 and $5, respectively. By acting cooperatively, 1 and 2 can secure for $10 something they value jointly at $14; there is clearly room for them to agree to provide the sixth unit. At the same time, there are many distributions of the cost of the sixth unit that will leave both parties better off than they would be otherwise. Person 1 could pay $8 and person 2 could pay $2, or they could pay $7 and $3 or $6 and $4, respectively. These three distributions of cost require each participant to pay less than the value placed upon the service.

There can be many distributions of the $100 required to finance the 10 units of output, all of which are consistent with the requirement that Lindahl prices be $7 and $3 for the tenth unit. Although it is analytically convenient to work with constant marginal tax-prices, innumerable other distributions of the gains from collective provision of the service are also consistent with the benefit principle.

If the unit cost of the collective service is constant, it is possible for marginal prices to equal average prices. Although this equality is not required by the benefit principle, it would not contradict that principle either. If the unit cost of collective output is not constant, however, it will be impossible for average prices to equal marginal prices for all people. Suppose the unit cost of the collective service declines as output increases. If marginal cost is still $10 for the tenth unit of output, it will be higher for smaller rates of output. Average cost will exceed $10 per unit, so the total cost of providing 10 units will exceed $100. If marginal tax-price is constant, total revenue will be insufficient to finance the collective service. A budget deficit will result, as illustrated by cc^*a in Figure 2.5.[8]

FROM NORMS TO REALITY?

The benefit principle strives to assess actual outcomes on the basis of the liberal premise that government should reflect the consent of the governed. There are numerous ways actual outcomes may reflect the consent of the governed. Different initial distributions of wealth will result in different patterns of demands and costs and different concrete expressions of the consent of the governed. To speak of governmental outcomes as reflecting a consensus among citizens implies first of all a consensus about the legitimacy of the existing institutional order. In this chapter we have assumed that the existing order is regarded as legitimate. (Chapter 3 deals with some aspects of this assumption.)   .

Even given this basic consensus, one might wonder how the benefit principle can be put into operation. The benefit principle is a purely formal effort to describe the character of collective outcomes that reflect the consent of the governed, but those outcomes depend on the personal valuations of the individual members of society. There is no way that an outsider can read those individual valuations and compute functions that correspond to those in Figure 2.4. Nonetheless, it is possible to assess the success with which different institutional regimes make collective choices that reflect the consent of the governed, as described by Figure 2.4. A requirement that budgetary choices be made by unanimous consent would be one such institutional regime. People will approve of expansions in collective output only as long as the gain they anticipate exceeds the cost they think they will bear. Therefore, it is possible to achieve unanimous support for an expansion in output as long as the sum of gains exceeds the sum of the costs. If the sum of the gains is less than the sum of the

---

[8] Should the unit cost of the collective service increase with output, the use of constant marginal tax prices will produce a budget surplus. Although the Lindahl prices add up to $10 for the tenth unit, the total expense of 10 units of output will be less than $100.

costs, unanimity will be impossible to attain. A community that actually operated under a rule of unanimous consent and that agreed to provide twelve showings of films per month when the marginal cost was $10 per showing could be described according to a construction such as Figure 2.4.

A requirement of unanimous consent may be feasible with relatively small numbers of people, but as the numbers of people rise so will the cost of reaching agreement. Four people may sit around a table in a bar discussing how to finance a campaign to attack the rats that plague them. These people may disagree about such matters as the severity of the problem, the extensiveness of the campaign that should be waged, and the share of the burden each should bear, but it is nonetheless reasonable to imagine that they can reach some agreement so long as there truly are mutual gains from waging a joint campaign against the rats. But what if there are 4,000 people in the rat-infested area? An effort to achieve a consensus in terms of the benefit principle is less likely to be successful under a requirement of unanimous consent. People are less likely to be truthful in revealing their valuations when unanimity is required among 4,000 people than when it is required among only 4 people. With only 4 participants, each person's statement or misstatement of what the service is worth is likely to affect significantly the amount of the service to be provided. If each of the 4 people has the same valuation but if one of them claims to place no value on the service, the amount of the service will be reduced by one-fourth. On the other hand, if all 4,000 people have the same valuation, one person's claim to place no value on the service will reduce the amount provided by only 0.025 percent. As the size of the group increases, a person's misstatement of valuation and, hence, contribution to the cost of the service exerts a smaller impact on the amount of the service actually provided. Furthermore, as the size of the group rises, claims of friendship and other types of personal relationships will operate less strongly to encourage truthful statements of valuations. For such reasons as these, free-rider problems are thought to arise among large numbers of people. Unanimous consent or voluntary support of collective endeavors may work relatively well when the number of participants is small, but as the number of participants increases, people will be increasingly tempted to take a free ride.

The problem of the free rider in large groups has been used to rationalize taxation as a way to finance collective output. The unanimity associated with the purest form of the benefit principle allows people to choose how much to contribute to the support of some collective service. If free-rider problems become more severe as the number of people in the group increases, individual choices to not contribute to the service may lead to an underprovision of the service compared with the situation that would exist if this prisoners' dilemma could be avoided. Consequently, taxation has been used as a means of financing government to overcome the free-rider problem and achieve the most equitable distribution of costs of services for large groups of people.

While taxes are compulsory extractions, they could conceivably be consistent with the benefit principle. This is illustrated by Figure 2.6, in which it is assumed that individual demands for some collective service have unitary income and price elasticities. If the income elasticity of demand is unitary, a person who has twice the income of

FIGURE 2.6 Benefit Principle, Consensus, and Proportional Taxation

The curves D_1 and D_2 indicate the demand curves for two people, with D_2 lying above D_1 because Person 2 has a higher income than Person 1. Assume the demand functions have unitary price and income elasticities. At price P_1, Person 1 demands Q_1 units. If Person 2 faces the same price but has twice the income, he or she will demand twice as many units as Person 1. This larger quantity is indicated by Q_2. A proportional income tax increases the price a person must pay in proportion to the amount of that person's income. With a doubling of income, the price doubles as well. This higher price paid by Person 2 is shown by P_2. With a unitary price elasticity of demand, the doubling of price reduces by half the quantity demanded. Consequently, Person 2 also demands Q_1 units of output, and consensus emerges over the provision of collective output.

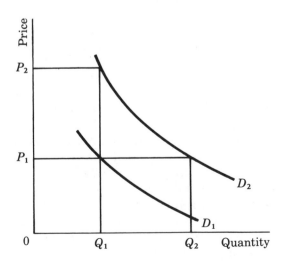

another will want twice the amount of the collective good at the same price. If the collective service is financed by a proportional tax on income, however, the price paid per unit of collective output will double as income doubles. With a unitary price elasticity, the doubling of the price will reduce by half the quantity demanded, thereby offsetting the increased demand that would otherwise have resulted because of the doubling of income. In other words, if individual demands for some collective service are accurately characterized by unitary price and income elasticities of demand, the financing of that service through a proportional tax on income would duplicate the outcome described by the benefit principle (leaving aside complexities that might arise because of nonconstant cost). In this case, it appears that people are forced to make mandatory payments rather than voluntary contributions, but actually the extractions of taxes would command consensus. The use of proportional taxation is simply a means of overcoming the prisoners' dilemma that would result if voluntary contributions were the only method for financing collective services. The use of the tax to finance collective output would be supported consensually.

To say that taxation can be rationalized as a means of overcoming the free-rider problem is not to imply that tax finance actually or necessarily overcomes that problem. The reality of taxation may be quite different from the rationalization given for it. The free-rider rationalization, as filtered through the benefit principle, provides that people pay taxes equivalent to the prices they would have paid if contract and exchange could have been relied on in the first place. Figure 2.6, based on the assumption of unitary price and income elasticities of demand, illustrates a situation in which proportional income taxation would achieve this result. If government is financed by nonproportional taxation, however, or if the relevant elasticities are nonunitary, or if people desire different amounts of some public service for reasons other than differences in income or tax prices, tax finance need not correspond to the requirements of the benefit principle. In the absence of taxation, the problem of the free rider is said to arise when people make contributions that are less than the value they truly place on the collective service. With taxation, people can be forced to suffer tax extractions that exceed the value they place on the collective service. These people can be called *forced riders*. While the presence of free riders under a regime of voluntary contribution may lead to underprovision of some collective services, the presence of forced riders under a regime of tax finance can likewise lead to overprovision, with under- and overprovision defined with reference to the benefit principle.

The presence of free riding gives government an opportunity to act as a positive-sum participant in the economic order. By providing those services that would not be provided through ordinary market transactions, government can participate in the process of shifting resources from less valued to more valued uses. The presence of forced riding opens the possibility that government can also act as a negative-sum participant. By providing more services through taxation than might be agreed to voluntarily, government shifts resources from more valued to less valued uses. In other words, government can act both as a positive-sum, value-enhancing and as a negative-sum, value-diminishing participant in the economic order. Actually, there are two ways government can act as a negative-sum participant in the economic order: It can expand spending beyond the point where the value of the service to members of society equals the cost of the service, and it can refrain from undertaking programs for which the sum of the individual valuations exceeds the cost. Both types of situations are possible, and the extent to which they might occur and the type of institutional arrangements under which they might occur constitute a substantial portion of the subject matter of Part II.

SUGGESTIONS FOR FURTHER READING

For seminal explorations of the relation between individual values and the manifestation of those values through government, see Kenneth J. Arrow, *Social Choice and Individual Values,* 2nd ed. (New York: John Wiley, 1963); and William J. Baumol, *Welfare Economics and the Theory of the State,* 2nd ed. (London: G. Bell and Sons, 1965). Charles K. Rowley and Alan T. Peacock, *Welfare Economics: A Liberal Restatement* (New York: John Wiley, 1975), examine the implications of liberalism for welfare economics.

Externalities and collective goods are explored in numerous works. For a sample of material, see James M. Buchanan, *Demand and Supply of Public Goods* (Chicago: Rand McNally, 1968); and John G. Head, *Public Goods and Public Welfare* (Durham, N.C.: Duke University Press, 1974). Some of the classic references in the theory of collective goods are Paul A. Samuelson, "The Pure Theory of Public Expenditure," *Review of Economics and Statistics* 36 (November 1954), pp. 387–389; Howard R. Bowen, "The Interpretation of Voting in the Allocation of Economic Resources," *Quarterly Journal of Economics* 58 (November 1943), pp. 27–48; Erik Lindahl, "Just Taxation — A Positive Solution" (1919) in *Classics in the Theory of Public Finance,* edited by Richard A. Musgrave and Alan T. Peacock (London: Macmillan, 1958), pp. 168–176; and Knut Wicksell, "A New Principle of Just Taxation," in *Classics in the Theory of Public Finance,* edited by Musgrave and Peacock, pp. 72–118. Randall G. Holcombe, "Concepts of Public Sector Equilibrium,"

National Tax Journal 33 (March 1980), pp. 77–88, surveys a variety of seminal works.

The benefit principle of public economics is explained fully in Richard A. Musgrave, *The Theory of Public Finance* (New York: McGraw-Hill, 1959), pp. 61–89. Considerable controversy has arisen over whether the fundamental distinction is between collective and private goods or between services to which all people have equal access and services to which access is limited, regardless of whether people are excluded because they don't contribute to the cost of the service, don't contribute to the campaign fund of the governing party, or for some other reason. For an examination of this point, which argues that there is little if anything that is necessarily of equal access, see Kenneth D. Goldin, "Equal Access vs. Selective Access: A Critique of Public Goods Theory," *Public Choice* 29 (Spring 1977), pp. 53–71. With reference to television, see Jora R. Minasian, "Television Pricing and the Theory of Public Goods," *Journal of Law and Economics* 7 (October 1964), pp. 71–80.

The free-rider problem is developed in Mancur Olson, Jr., *The Logic of Collective Action* (Cambridge, Mass.: Harvard University Press, 1965). On forced riders in relation to free riders, see Earl R. Brubaker, "Free Rider, Free Revelation, or Golden Rule?" *Journal of Law and Economics* 18 (April 1975), pp. 147–161. Also see Harold Demsetz, "The Private Production of Public Goods," *Journal of Law and Economics* 13 (October 1970), pp. 293–306; and Thomas E. Borcherding, "Competition, Exclusion, and the Optimal Supply of Public Goods," *Journal of Law and Economics* 21 (April 1978), pp. 111–132.

3

Equity, Justice, and the Public Economy

The benefit principle of public economics is typically stated as a norm of *efficiency*, which automatically brings to mind a contrasting norm of *equity* or *justice*. The benefit principle assesses collective outcomes by the degree to which they reflect individual valuations, but the particular pattern of those valuations depends on the distribution of wealth. A society's choices about production are determined by the dollar votes of its members, and changes in the distribution of wealth may bring about changes in the patterns of resource utilization. Application of the benefit principle must therefore be based on a presumption that the distribution of wealth is proper because this quality of properness renders legitimate the particular patterns of outcomes called for by the benefit principle.

PRODUCTIVE AND DISTRIBUTIVE ASPECTS OF OWNERSHIP

As Chapter 2 explained, exclusive and transferable ownership generally operates to increase the wealth of a society. While this point was illustrated with reference to oyster beds, its validity is general. The development of ownership rights in oyster beds strengthens the incentive to use those beds in ways that enhance their value. In consequence, the availability of oysters to the members of society increases. There are numerous ways in which the increased wealth that results from the development of exclusive and transferable ownership can be shared. However, while the granting of ownership where none existed before will increase the yield, and hence the value, of the oyster beds, those who acquire title to the oyster beds will become wealthier than those who do not.

Creation of Wealth Through Ownership

Figure 3.1 illustrates both how the development of exclusive and transferable ownership leads to the creation of wealth and how the particular way in which ownership is created can affect the distribution of wealth among the members of society. Suppose all people who farm oysters under common ownership are equally adept and hard working, so that each farmer can expect to garner the same harvest as the other farmers. People will be attracted to the farming of oysters as long as they can earn at least as much doing it as they could earn in other employment. Under common ownership, the number of farmers who work an oyster bed will increase so long as the average return to oyster farmers exceeds what they can earn in other employments. The increase in the total oyster harvest that results from the effort of an additional farmer, however, is less than the average return, and this lesser amount is the marginal product of the additional oyster farmer.

Under common ownership, each oyster farmer earns the average yield of all oyster farmers. The yield generated by any particular oyster farmer has two components: (1) his own harvest and (2) the reduction in the number of oysters harvested by the other farmers. The first component is the average product of an oyster farmer, w, when there are L_1 farmers. The L_1th farmer, however, actually increases the value of the oysters harvested by only w', which is his marginal product. The divergence between average and marginal products is the second component alone: the reduction in the value of oysters harvested by the other farmers. Any particular farmer, then, imposes external costs on the other farmers, but under common ownership these costs are not borne by any particular farmer.

Under exclusive ownership of oyster beds, an owner will increase the application of labor to harvesting oysters only to the point where the yield from that labor equals the wage rate that must be paid for that labor, with that wage rate being equal to the wage rate in alternative, competitive employment. Consequently, exclusive and transferable ownership will lead to a decrease in the number of farmers working the oyster bed to L_2, and at this point the yield generated by one more oyster farmer equals the yield from the employment of that person in some other activity. The right to the ownership of oyster beds is now valuable, as indicated by the excess of the average yield per oyster farmer, w^*, over the marginal yield, w, which is the wage rate paid to oyster farmers under exclusive ownership. This social gain

FIGURE 3.1 Ownership Arrangements and the
Creation of Wealth

People who earn w per day in other activities will be attracted to oyster
farming if they can receive more than w per day (assuming they regard the
occupations equivalently in other relevant respects). Equilibrium will result
when the return to each oyster farmer is w per day. There will be L_1
people working as oyster farmers under common ownership because each
farmer will earn approximately the average of all oyster farmers. Each
farmer earns the average product AP, but the marginal product, MP,
indicates the increase in total output that results from the effort of one
more farmer. When the quantity of labor supplied to oyster farming is L_1,
the marginal return is only w', which is less than the marginal return of
labor elsewhere in the economy, w. But with exclusive ownership, labor
will be applied to farming oysters only until the marginal return to oyster
farming equals the marginal return elsewhere. Only L_2 units of labor will
be supplied to oyster farming. At this outcome, there will now be profits to
oyster farming of ww^*ab per day, and these profits will show up as an
increase in the value of the oyster bed.

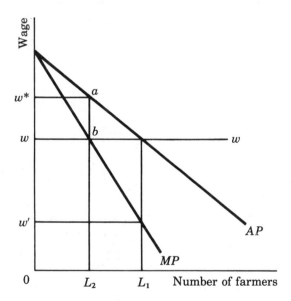

is represented in Figure 3.1 as ww^*ab. This magnitude is the rental
value of the oyster bed, and it indicates the increase in income attributable to the creation of ownership rights in oyster beds.[1]

[1] This rental value could be expressed alternatively as an increase in the capital
value of the oyster beds. The relationship between measures of income and
capital is described in Chapter 10, but we can note here that an increase in
annual income of $100 will, with a 10 percent rate of interest, increase the
capital value of the oyster bed by $1,000.

Distributive Consequences of Ownership

The creation of exclusive ownership in oyster beds is wealth enhancing, and this increased wealth can be distributed in many different ways. If all who farmed the oyster bed under common property were given a proportionate share of ownership, the increased wealth would be distributed equally among the farmers. Ownership could also be limited to only a subset of the farmers, possibly even to just one farmer. In that case, those farmers who did not share in the ownership would not share in the increased wealth. Instead, those farmers would receive the same return they received under common ownership, indicated by w in Figure 3.1, which they would receive as wages, working either as oyster farmers or in some other occupation. Those farmers would not be made poorer by the development of exclusive ownership, but neither would they share in the added wealth that resulted from the creation of ownership.

More generally, the replacement in any society of inefficient institutions (such as represented by common ownership) with efficient institutions (such as represented by exclusive and transferable ownership) will increase the wealth of that society. This is not to say, however, that each member of society will become wealthier; in some cases, some might even become poorer. Exclusive and transferable ownership strengthens incentives for the creation of wealth, but the distribution of that wealth will depend on the distribution of ownership titles among the members of society. In Figure 3.2, all points along the efficiency frontier, YX, describe the outcome of economic activity under efficient institutions. Some points describe person A as being substantially wealthier than person B, and vice versa. The efficiency locus itself might describe an economy operating under exclusive ownership, and the different points on this locus could correspond to different distributions of shares of ownership between the two persons.

The interior points on Figure 3.2 correspond to the outcomes of economic activity that takes place under inefficient institutions, as in the case of common ownership of oyster beds. For any distribution of wealth under common ownership, there will be some distribution of ownership rights that will increase the wealth of all parties. However, the wealth of all parties will not necessarily increase if common ownership is replaced by exclusive ownership. Some who would fare relatively well under common ownership might end up poorer under exclusive ownership. In the discussion above, the oyster farmers who received no right of ownership would fare just as well as they did under common ownership. Those farmers who subsequently worked

FIGURE 3.2 Allocative and Distributive Consequences of Ownership Arrangements

Under common ownership, two people might attain the distribution of wealth represented by *c*. The development of exclusive and transferable ownership permits an increase in wealth. Point *a* represents the case in which all of the increase in wealth accrues to Person A, and point *b* represents the case in which it all accrues to Person B. At any point between *a* and *b*, both persons are wealthier than they would have been under common ownership. The frontier *YX* represents the locus of distributions of wealth under exclusive ownership, with movements toward the Y-intercept and X-intercept indicating increasing concentrations of wealth with ownership by A and B, respectively. All interior points such as *c*, *f*, and *g* represent distributions of wealth under common ownership. For any such distribution, there are various outcomes under exclusive ownership that will leave both parties wealthier. If *g* characterizes the starting position under common ownership, any creation of exclusive ownership that results in some distribution along *da* will leave both parties wealthier than under common ownership. Some people could be worse off under exclusive ownership than they were under common ownership. If *g* is the outcome under common ownership and if *b* or *e* is the outcome under exclusive ownership, Person A will be poorer under exclusive ownership.

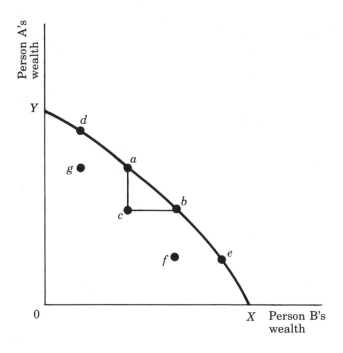

for the farmers that received a right of ownership would receive a wage rate equal to the return they received under common ownership.

The same relationship would hold for those farmers who had to seek other employment after the reduction in the amount of oyster farming. In this case, the creation of ownership would give something of value to some people but take nothing of value away from anyone. The movement from c would thus be constrained to the region ab. But in some cases the creation of ownership might foreclose opportunities to some people, a movement, say, from c to a region such as be. Several parcels of property might adjoin a lake that is common property and that is used as a dump. If the lake is converted to exclusive ownership, those people who do not acquire ownership might be poorer, even though total wealth has been increased. In this instance, the creation of private ownership forecloses some people's ability to use the lake as a depository for sewage without having to buy someone else's agreement.

The interplay between questions of allocative efficiency and distributive equity or justice has played a large part in normative writings on public economics. The concern with equity or justice is part of the study of social order, which public economics treats by considering governmental conduct that is congruent with and supportive of an economic order in a peaceful society. Justice can be advanced as a norm simply because it is thought to be an end in itself. Alternatively, and perhaps more probably, justice is thought to be an instrument of order. Order, stability, and social peace may be what people desire, but these probably require that the members of a society generally sense that they are better off in their particular social order than in some alternative order. A few thugs can be handled by police, but widespread disrespect jeopardizes the social order. Concerns about distributive justice perhaps reflect an assumption that the legitimacy or stability of a regime depends in some manner on the distribution of wealth in society or perhaps on the fairness of the process by which wealth is produced or acquired.

SACRIFICE THEORIES OF TAXATION

A major strand of public economics that deals with equity and justice assumes that individual tax burdens should reflect not individual valuations of collective outcomes but an equality of sacrifice on the part of all citizens. This norm is generally called the *ability-to-pay principle*, and it is based on equity rather than efficiency, as in the case of the benefit principle.

Equality Among Equals

Sacrifice theories typically describe fairness or equity in taxation as requiring people to sacrifice equally for the provision of collective services. Equal sacrifice has two aspects: the relation among equally situated people, commonly assumed to be people with the same income or wealth, and the relation among people who are not equally situated.

Horizontal equity requires that equals should sacrifice equally for the support of collective services. Income is the most commonly used indicator of equality, although such other indicators as consumption or wealth could be used instead.

Even if income is accepted as the appropriate indicator of equality, complex issues arise in any effort to apply the principle of horizontal equity. Various people may have equal monetary incomes, but this does not mean they would be equal by some other definition of income. Monetary measures of income neglect nonmonetary forms of income. The value of home-grown food consumed by farmers is commonly given as an example of nonmonetary income. Compared with someone else with the same monetary income, the farmer is able to have the same diet with less expenditure, thereby making it possible to spend more on other objects of consumption. The imputed rental value of owner-occupied housing is another, much larger illustration of nonmonetary income. Of two people who have equal monetary incomes, the one who lives in his own house will have a higher total income than the person who lives in a rented house.[2] Numerous other nonmonetary forms of income could be described. When nonmonetary forms of income are present, an application of the horizontal equity principle based only on monetary income will classify as equal people who are really unequal.

The use to which income is put might also in some cases constitute a legitimate basis for modifying the application of horizontal equity. Tax laws reflect an assumption that two families with equal incomes but with unequal medical expenses should not be regarded as equally situated. To some extent, items such as medical expenses and occupational expenses are regarded as expenses of living rather than as objects of consumption. Likewise, two families with equal incomes but with unequal numbers of dependents appear not to be regarded as equally situated.

Perhaps one of the strongest limitations on the principle of horizontal equity is that it is restricted to the taxing side of the budget. Horizontal equity requires all people with the same income to pay the

---

[2] The reason for this is examined in Chapter 9.

same tax. But what if some of those people receive greater benefits from public expenditures than others? Some might be frequent users of a public park, while others avoid the park entirely because they are allergic to insect bites. All are taxed equally, but not all are treated equally by the government's fiscal operations. Alternatively, someone with children generally makes more use of public services than someone without children. Schools are the primary example, but people with children are also likely to receive greater benefit from other public services such as parks, libraries, and public health.

Since fiscal affairs are two-sided, a principle of equity that is limited to one side of the budget is necessarily of limited applicability. The principle that citizens who are equally situated should make equal sacrifices for the support of government is one that encounters numerous difficulties in application because the basis of equality is ambiguous. The selection of a base on which to judge equality is necessarily arbitrary, and the principle can be applied only after this arbitrary selection is made.

Inequality Among Unequals?

Vertical equity is the proposition that unequals should sacrifice unequally for the support of collective services, and it is subject to the same ambiguities about an indicator of equality as is horizontal equity. For purposes of discussion, however, we will set aside such ambiguities to concentrate on the central features of vertical equity.

The sacrifice approach ignores the uses to which taxes are put and simply assumes that all citizens sacrifice equally for the support of government. What, however, is being sacrificed? If it is money, the principle of equal sacrifice would require that all citizens pay the same tax. But the sacrifice approach construes the sacrifice as the use (or utility) of the part of a person's income that is lost through taxation and thus holds that each citizen should make the same sacrifice of utility for the support of government. Utility is not directly observable, however, and taxes are assessed in money. Therefore, the sacrifice approach to taxation can be applied only after some relationship between utility and money has been determined. The tax will be based on a person's income and paid in money, but the significance of this payment will be assessed in terms of the sacrifice in utility that results.

Equal sacrifice would thus require that each person lose the same total utility through taxation, and this requirement is called *equal absolute* or *equal total sacrifice*. Equal sacrifice can also be defined in terms of the percentage of total utility that is sacrificed through taxation. *Equal proportional sacrifice* requires that each person sacrifice the same percentage of his or her total utility. Finally, equality of sacrifice can be defined by the requirement that each person sacrifice the same marginal utility, this approach is called *equal marginal sacrifice.*

Sacrifice theories have been concerned with the development of norms about the proper distribution of the tax burden among citizens. Such theories assume that the size of the budget has already been determined, or at least is irrelevant, and that the question at issue is simply how to distribute taxes so that all citizens make equal sacrifices. Sacrifice approaches focus predominantly on the justification for different distributions of tax burdens. In particular, these theories have sought to determine appropriate applications for *progressive taxation*, in which the average rate of tax rises with income; *proportional taxation*, in which the average rate of tax is constant; and *regressive taxation*, in which the average rate of tax declines as income rises. The requirement of equal sacrifice can yield a variety of conclusions, in part because there are three different conceptions of equal sacrifice and in part because the conclusions depend on the precise assumption made about the utility people receive from their income. It is assumed that utility increases with income, but ambiguity arises in the assumption about how rapidly it does so.[3] If it rises at a constant rate, the marginal utility of income is constant, but if it rises at a decreasing rate, the marginal utility of income declines. The assumption made about the marginal utility of income affects the application of the principle of equal sacrifice.

Equal absolute sacrifice requires that the same loss in utility be imposed on each citizen. If the marginal utility of income is constant, a dollar taken away in tax represents the same loss in utility regardless of the taxpayer's income, and therefore each person will be required to pay the same amount of tax. Suppose, however, that marginal utility is constant but equality of sacrifice is defined as the equal proportional requirement that each person sacrifice the same percentage of his or her pretax utility. With a constant marginal utility of income, a tax that takes away the same percentage of each person's pretax utility is one that takes away the same percentage of each person's pretax income. Proportional income taxation is required in this case.

The ambiguity about the required form of taxation is not reduced by assuming a diminishing marginal utility of income. Suppose equality of sacrifice is defined as equal absolute sacrifice. If the marginal

---

[3] One can avoid much ambiguity by assuming, conveniently even if not realistically, that utility can be measured and compared among people, which is the same in effect as assuming that all people have the same utility schedule.

utility of income declines as income rises, a dollar sacrificed at a higher income entails less loss of utility than a dollar sacrificed at a lower income. To make the sacrifices of utility equal, the sacrifice of a dollar at a lower income must be accompanied by the sacrifice of more than a dollar at a higher income. This requirement is consistent with regressive taxation as well as with proportional and progressive taxation. The form of tax that is actually called for depends not simply on the assumption about a diminishing marginal utility of income but on an assumption about how rapidly the marginal utility income declines.

If equality of sacrifice is defined as equal proportional sacrifice, the specific form of tax that is required still depends on an assumption about the rate at which the marginal utility of income declines. In that case, each person is required to sacrifice the same percentage of his or her pretax utility. This means that total tax payments will rise with income, but whether it requires regressive, proportional, or progressive taxation depends again on the rate at which the marginal utility of income declines.

An unambiguous application of the sacrifice approach to taxation results when the requirement of equal marginal sacrifice is combined with the assumption of a declining marginal utility of income. Under the assumptions commonly adopted by those who use a sacrifice approach to taxation, a wealthier person will always have a lower marginal utility than a poorer person, so a tax will always involve less sacrifice of utility when it is assessed against a wealthier person than when it is assessed against a poorer person. Consequently, a poorer person will pay no tax until the wealthier person has paid so much tax that his or her posttax income equals the pretax income of the poorer person. If marginal utility is assumed to decline with income and if the relation between income and utility is assumed to be the same for all people, the principle of equal marginal sacrifice calls for a government budget financed by paring posttax incomes from the top down. The extent of leveling down will vary directly with the size of the government's budget.

DISTRIBUTIVE JUSTICE AND
THE EQUALIZATION OF INCOMES

Within the framework of the sacrifice approach to taxation, the extent to which government is an instrument for the promotion of equality is limited by the size of its budget. Equality is not promoted directly as an end but indirectly as a by-product of a particular way of equalizing the sacrifices required by taxation. Many people have argued that equality should be viewed as an end to be promoted directly by government. If this argument is accepted, the desirable degree of equality is invariant to the size of the government's budget, even though government uses its taxing and spending powers to achieve the desired degree of equality.

The various efforts to specify a desired degree of equality generally start from the same utilitarian framework adopted by the sacrifice approaches. Figure 3.3 illustrates that if marginal utility declines as income increases and if people have the same income-utility schedule, a government that maximizes the sum of the utilities of each citizen promotes equality in the distribution of income. It taxes the income of those who have above-average incomes and transfers incomes to those who have below-average incomes. If the marginal utility of income declines and if people have identical income-utility schedules, aggregate social utility — the sum of the utilities of each member of society — is always higher when income is distributed equally than when it is distributed unequally.

If people differ in their income-utility schedules, which is most probably the case, full equality is no longer required by the sacrifice approach. The maximization of aggregate utility could even require the imposition of taxes on those with lower incomes and the awarding of transfers to those with higher incomes. Suppose that in Figure 3.3 B's marginal utility schedule is described by the dashed line U_B^*. At I_1, B's marginal utility exceeds A's by b^*a, and this excess is the increase in aggregate utility that would result from a transfer of one dollar from A to B. In this case, aggregate utility would be maximized at point I_1^*.[4] Moreover, to some extent those who have high incomes have them because they have chosen to forgo the leisure they could otherwise have had.[5] Presumably, this is because they had a high utility for income, whereas those who chose leisure had a lower utility for income. To the extent that income reflects a choice about how much effort to devote to earning income, there will be some positive association between higher incomes and higher income-utility sched-

[4] If people differ in their income-utility schedules, but if it is impossible to know which people belong to which schedules, expected utility will be maximized when income is equalized. This treatment of lack of information about people and their utility schedules assumes that, with respect to Figure 3.3, A and B are equally likely to possess either of the possible utility functions; expected utility is maximized when each person is assumed to possess an average of those utility functions. Hence, this case, which appears to allow for differences in income-utility schedules among people, is formally just a special case of an assumption that all people possess identical income-utility functions.

[5] Alan S. Blinder, *Toward an Economic Theory of Income Distribution* (Cambridge, Mass.: MIT Press, 1974), pp. 119–141, estimates that about 30 percent of the variation in annual income is due to differences in choices between work and leisure.

FIGURE 3.3 Declining Marginal Utility and
Equalization of Income

Assume Persons A and B have identical income-utility schedules. A's
marginal utility schedule runs from left to right and B's runs from right to
left. Income is distributed equally at I_0, where each person has the same
marginal utility. Should B's income be higher than A's, as at I_1, the
marginal utility of income (U) is higher to A than it is to B. The transfer of
one dollar from B to A will increase aggregate utility by ab because a is
the gain in utility to A and b is the loss in utility to B. Aggregate utility
will always be increased by a transfer of income from the person with
higher income to the person with lower income. (The marginal utility
function U_B^* represents an assumption that A and B have different income-
utility schedules, and the point of this assumption is developed in the text.)

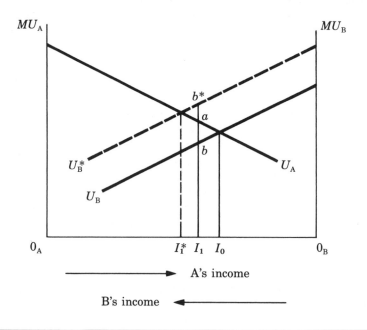

ules. Such an association contradicts the assumption that each person
is equally likely to possess each of the possible utility functions and,
hence, the rationale for full equalization.

Trade-off Between Equality and Income

The preceding discussion assumed there was a fixed amount of income
available for distribution. If the income available for distribution depends on its distribution, however, the earlier analysis of equalization

TABLE 3.1 Income Equalization in the Presence of
Disincentive Effects

Tax Rate	Pretax Income		Tax and Transfer	Posttax Income		Utility[a]	
	A	B		A	B	A	B
0%	$100	$20	$ 0	$100	$20	10,000	3,600
20%	80	20	16	64	36	8,704	5,904
40%	60	20	24	36	44	5,904	6,864
60%	40	20	24	16	44	2,944	6,864
80%	20	20	16	4	36	784	5,904
100%	0	20	0	0	20	0	3,600

[a] Utility is calculated as $U = 200I - I^2$, where I denotes posttax income.

must be modified. Even if all people have the same income-utility schedule, maximization of aggregate utility no longer requires the complete equalization of income. As equalization takes place, those with high income, from whom taxes are extracted, reduce their effort to earn income. As a result of this disincentive effect of the tax, the extent of equalization called for by the distributive criteria of maximizing aggregate utility will be lessened.

These considerations are illustrated numerically in Table 3.1, which shows the application of different rates of tax on the person with the higher income, and transfers of income made to the person with the lower income. It also shows that the total income in the society falls as the rate of tax rises, indicating that the person who is taxed earns less income as the rate of tax increases. At a zero rate of tax, A is assumed to earn $100 and B to earn $20. Suppose a tax of 20 percent is imposed on A, with the proceeds transferred to B. If A now earns only $80, $16 is paid in tax and posttax income is $64. B earns $20 and receives a transfer of $16, giving a posttransfer income of $36. If the tax rate is 40 percent, A will earn only $60. After paying $24 in tax, A's posttax income is $36. B earns $20 and receives $24 in transfer, giving a posttransfer income of $44.

The outcome in Table 3.1 that maximizes aggregate utility depends on the income-utility schedule. Suppose the total utility derived from income is

$$U = 200I - I^2.$$

This function has declining marginal utility

$$MU = 200 - 2I, \quad (I \leq 100).$$

If there is no disincentive effect from taxation, aggregate utility is maximized when the tax rate is 40 percent. This rate leaves each person with a posttax income of $60, and aggregate utility is 16,800. If disincentive effects are present, however, less equalization is required. Table 3.1 is constructed under the assumption that person A reduces his or her pretax income, either by working less or by working in the underground economy, by $1 for each percentage point increase in the rate of tax. Among the five options shown in Table 3.1, the tax rate of 20 percent has the highest aggregate utility. Moving from a 20 percent to a 40 percent rate of tax increases the posttax income and utility of B and decreases those of A by an even greater amount. The presence of disincentive effects reduces the extent of equalization required to maximize aggregate utility. As such disincentive effects operate more strongly, less equalization is required. Furthermore, if B, the transferee, reduces income-earning activities in response to the receipt of transfers, the required degree of equalization could be lowered even more. If B reduces earnings by $1 for each $2 of transfer received, Table 3.1 shows that aggregate utility is higher with a zero rate of tax than with a 20 percent rate.

One interesting variant of the utilitarian approach to distributive justice arises when the marginal utility of income is assumed to be constant. When utility is proportional to income, the maximization of aggregate utility is equivalent to the maximization of aggregate income. In this case, equalization is supported only to the extent that the taxes required for equalization actually increase the income earned by those being taxed. As we will see in Chapter 9, it is conceivable that taxation might have this effect over some range of rates, with the extent of equalization limited to an incentive-enhancing range of taxation. Application of the utilitarian criteria produces less of an egalitarian orientation when the marginal utility of income is assumed to be constant than when it is assumed to decline with income.

Economists commonly assume that the marginal utility of income declines, although it is rarely clear whether this assumption is based on introspection, on evidence, or on a preference for the conclusions that seem to follow. Assumptions of diminishing marginal utility of income are often based on observations that people will reject an opportunity to play certain types of mathematically fair games. A two-person game in which one person pays $100 to the other if a coin comes up heads and the other person pays $100 if it comes up tails is mathematically fair: For each player the expected value of playing the game is equal to zero or, more generally, is equal to the expense of playing the game. Refusal to play such a game has been rationalized on the grounds that winning $100 increases utility by less than losing \$100 reduces it. While the expected value may be zero dollars, it is negative in terms of utility.

Observation of a refusal to play a fair game can be reconciled with an assumption of diminishing marginal utility of income, which is commonly described as *risk aversion*. The purchase of insurance is likewise consistent with an assumption of a diminishing marginal utility of income. By buying insurance, the purchaser is essentially accepting some assured average return in preference to the risk or gamble that he or she would face without the insurance. Refusal to play a fair game can, of course, also be reconciled with a dislike of gambling. People may choose to establish their own businesses despite the large chance of failure and yet refuse to accept a gamble that offers the same expected value.

Rather than approaching distributive justice from the perspective of maximizing aggregate utility, John Rawls, in a widely heralded work, argues that distributive justice should focus on maximizing the utility of the least advantaged person in society.[6] The central feature of an economy in this *minimax* perspective, as it is in the utilitarian perspective, is its distribution of utility. An economy may be characterized by many different potential outcomes in terms of total income and its distribution, and each such outcome is referred to as a *state* of that economy. Among all possible states, the utilitarian perspective selects the one that maximizes the sum of utilities. The minimax perspective selects the one that maximizes the utility of the person with the least utility in the society. In the minimax perspective, a state of an economy that offered greater total utility than an alternative state would be selected only if the least advantaged person received higher utility.

Comparison of Distributional Outcomes

Figure 3.4 compares the various approaches to distributive justice. The utility possibility locus, *ab*, illustrates for a two-person economy the possible distributions of utility that correspond to the possible distributions of income in the economy. Essentially, the utility possibility frontier in Figure 3.4 corresponds to the data given in Table 3.1. For the most part, person A achieves a higher utility level than person B, which indicates that A possesses an advantage in the production of income. In the range where B's utility is higher than A's, *aE*, total utility (and income) is relatively low. That range comes about because A has been taxed relatively heavily, with the proceeds of the tax

[6] John Rawls, *A Theory of Justice* (Cambridge, Mass.: Harvard University Press, 1971).

FIGURE 3.4 Three Approaches to Distributive Justice

The utility possibility locus, *ab*, shows the distribution of utility between
Persons A and B that would result from different states of the economy. An
egalitarian criterion would select *E*, which represents the farthest attainable
point on the 45° line of equality. The minimax criteria advocated by Rawls
accept departures from equality to the extent that they increase the utility
of the least advantaged person. The minimax criteria yields *M* as the
preferred state, because this maximizes the utility of Person B. The
utilitarian criterion maximizes the sum of the utilities, and the preferred
state is *U*, where the line with the slope of −1 (indicating an equal
weighting of each person's units of utility) is tangent to the utility-
possibility frontier.

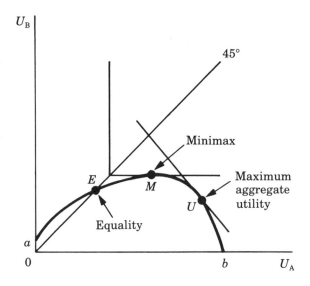

transferred to B. The low total utility in that range reflects the low
income that is earned because of the disincentive effect of the tax-and-
transfer.

There are three main approaches to the evaluation of distributional
outcomes, all illustrated in Figure 3.4. One approach adopts perfect
equality as an ideal. As implied by *E* in the figure, this approach
results in a substantial disincentive effect, which is responsible for a
low level of aggregate income and utility. The minimax perspective
allows deviations from perfect equality to the extent that the deviations increase the utility of the least advantaged person. In Figure 3.4,
M corresponds to the minimax criterion; the movement from *E* to *M*
increases the utility of both persons, even though it increases A's

utility by more than it increases B's. The utilitarian criterion is shown by U; it maximizes the aggregate utility, which occurs when a line with a slope of -1 is tangent to the utility possibility frontier. In going from M to U, the utility of person A increases by more than the utility of person B decreases.

The utilitarian and the minimax approaches to distributive justice both assess an economic order in terms of its ability to generate income and utility; both are based on a utilitarian ethic for evaluating economic outcomes. They differ only in their assumptions about the preferences people would exhibit in a state of extreme uncertainty. As we have seen, the movement from M to U in Figure 3.4 entails a decrease in one person's utility and a proportionally greater increase in the utility of the other. Both the utilitarian and the minimax approaches are based on an assumption about the choice a person would make if faced with an equally likely chance of occupying either position in the distribution. The minimax position, M, might correspond to a distribution of, say, 60–40, and the utilitarian position, U, might correspond to 90–30.

How are these possible alternative states of an economy to be assessed? In attempting to answer this question, expositors make an effort to assume the posture of some impartial spectator or observer. John Rawls uses the construct of the "veil of ignorance," in which both participants know they must choose between 60–40 and 90–30, but neither knows anything about which position he or she is likely to occupy. Each position appears equally likely. John Harsanyi, one of the main articulators of the utilitarian position, uses the construct of "moral preferences," which describes the hypothetical preferences a person would have if placed in the position of acting in an impartial and impersonal manner; that is, if each person assumed he or she had an equally likely chance of occupying each possible place in the distribution of income.[7]

The utilitarian formulation, which selects 90–30 over 60–40, reflects an assumption of *risk neutrality*. A choice between the two outcomes is made on the basis of which offers the higher expected value. If each outcome is equally likely, the higher expected value results when the state of the economy that maximizes aggregate utility is chosen. The 90–30 state has an expected value of 60, whereas the 60–40 state has an expected value of 50. If people are risk averse, they will be willing to accept some reduction in expected return in exchange for having some floor placed under the lowest possible re-

[7] John C. Harsanyi, "Cardinal Welfare, Individualistic Ethics, and Interpersonal Comparisons of Utility," *Journal of Political Economy* 63 (August 1955), pp. 309–321.

turn. This is, after all, the rationale for buying insurance: It lowers one's expected wealth, but it also puts a floor under the minimum outcome, and such a floor would not exist in the absence of insurance. Although the 90–30 state has a higher expected return than the 60–40 state, it also has the lower of the low returns. It is conceivable that a person would choose to participate in a lottery where the prizes were 60 and 40 over one where they were 90 and 30. Such a person would be choosing to give up the higher expected return of 10 in exchange for being able to avoid the prospect of actually receiving only 30 rather than 40.

The minimax criterion, however, entails infinite risk aversion: There is no possible increase in expected return that will be sufficient to offset even the smallest reduction in the size of the smallest return. A person who is risk averse might prefer 60–40 to 90–30, but there is some increase in the higher return that will be sufficient to offset the choice. Although 60–40 might be preferred to 90–30, 120–30, say, might be preferred to 60–40. Under the minimax criterion, however, it does not matter how high the higher return is in the option with the higher expected value. The option with the lower expected value will always be selected, and what is sufficient for its selection is that its lower return is higher than the lower return of the option with the higher expected value. To put the point somewhat differently, the minimax criterion will select a certain return of $100 over a 90 percent chance of $1,000 and a 10 percent chance of $99. This property of infinite risk aversion has perhaps been the main source of objections raised against the minimax criterion for the evaluation of economic outcomes, although such a basis for rejecting minimax need not imply acceptance of the utilitarian criterion based on risk neutrality. In principle, some intermediate position between M and U could be advocated.

Equality: Of Outcome or of Opportunity?

The various utilitarian approaches to distributive justice attempt to develop criteria for evaluating the distributive outcomes of economic activity. One important difficulty with the approach is that some differences in the distribution of income are actually necessary for achieving equality in the underlying distribution of utility. An observed distribution of 60–40, for instance, may reflect an underlying equality of utility, in the sense that each person may be willing, at those particular incomes, to trade places with the other. Stated alternatively, each person may be indifferent between the two positions *and* the various requirements (effort, postponed consumption, and so on) associated with those positions. If some degree of inequality in measured incomes is necessary for achieving an underlying equality of utility, the significance of an ex post assessment of outcomes becomes problematical. For this reason, an ex ante consideration of the degree of equality in the opportunities available to people may be a more appropriate approach to appraising the distributive properties of an economic system.

If occupations differ in their nonmonetary advantages and in the monetary expenses involved in entering and pursuing them, they must differ in their monetary returns as well if their returns are to be truly equal. Occupations that require long and expensive training before one can earn a livelihood will require higher monetary returns than unskilled occupations, just to compensate for the greater cost of preparation. When occupations vary in features other than their measured income, some offsetting inequality in measured income will be necessary to produce a true equality in the real incomes or utilities made possible by those occupations. Some inequality in the distribution of monetary income is necessary precisely because occupations differ in such elements as their nonmonetary advantages and monetary expenses.

Not all inequality among incomes reflects the differences in such things as the costs of preparing for and practicing an occupation and the nonmonetary returns to that occupation. People differ in their abilities and in the opportunities they confront, and these differences will reduce the extent to which differences in income simply offset differences in other aspects of different occupations. One frequently cited source of inequality of opportunity among children is the variation in parents' income. Wealthier parents can provide their children with more opportunities for acquiring material goods than can less wealthy parents. These opportunities can range from intangibles such as a more expensive education to material things such as providing shares in a business. It is easy to see why inheritance is often criticized because it is a source of inequality of opportunity. With inheritance, some people are able to start out in life with higher material standards of living than others, not because of their own effort or good fortune but because they were born into wealthier families. Inheritance would destroy what might otherwise be a fair race by giving some people head starts. If so, some form of taxation of inheritance might be reasonable as a means of promoting greater equality of starting positions.

The arguments about how inheritance acts as a source of inequality of opportunity are based on a game or sporting analogy: Life is viewed essentially as a footrace in which the earlier finishers get larger prizes superior educational opportunities, or of anything else is viewed as (incomes) than the later finishers. The inheritance of wealth, or of analogous to giving some people head starts. Equality of opportunity might require that all people start the race at the same point. What seems to be of concern in this analogy is that the race start fairly, not that everyone finish at the same time; the latter result would characterize equality of outcome rather than of opportunity. To this end, a reduction in the ability of people to inherit material wealth or educational opportunities might seem necessary if people are to start on an equal basis in the race for life's rewards.

On closer inspection, however, the distinction between equality of opportunity and equality of outcome seems difficult to maintain. What if some people are simply born faster afoot than others? Is it truly fair, or consonant with equality of opportunity, to require the naturally slow to start from the same place as the naturally fast? It could easily be argued that equality of opportunity requires a set of handicaps such that all people have the same likelihood of winning. If the handicaps are designed properly, all should expect to arrive at the finish line at the same time. Speedier people would be handicapped, perhaps by carrying additional weight or possibly by starting farther back in the race. Equality of opportunity, interpreted as a requirement that each person have the same expected outcome in the race for riches, would require more than the abolition of inheritance. It would require that people have equal expected values of lifetime income, with the measure of income adjusted to account for differences in the expenses of preparing for and practicing different occupations. A set of taxes and subsidies based on some idea of economic potential would seem to be necessary to promote equality of opportunity, and equality of opportunity would become identical with equality of outcome, when the proper adjustments to measures of income were incorporated.

Moreover, the positive correlation between the economic position of parents and that of children may be both inescapable and of questionable normative significance. One aspect of successful parenthood is the passing on of values and interests. It is to be expected that there will be some tendency for families with plumbers to beget plumbers, for families with physicians to beget physicians, and so on. Some inheritance of economic position would surely characterize a free, well-ordered society, even though no one felt stifled in his or her personal development. It would even be possible to construct a model of an economy that perfectly reproduced itself, in that carpenters begat carpenters and only carpenters, and so on. In practice, of course, there would always be some divergence between the experiences of parents and the choices of children, even assuming that parents were pleased with their choices and transmitted that sentiment to their children. Moreover, the ever-changing nature of societies ensures that they will not duplicate themselves.

The importance of the family in personal development and value formation works to create some positive correlation between the economic positions of parents and children. So does the differentiation among people in their interests and capacities. What may be of concern is not so much the correlation between the economic positions of parents and children as the extent to which people feel stifled by their backgrounds and locked into modes of life they do not truly choose to pursue. The widespread growth of such a sense may very well undermine the basis for social order. If so, the legitimacy or stability of a social order would seem to require conditions that prevent the growth of such sentiments. Objective measures of the results of economic activity do not seem to be able to describe the extent to which this stifling of personal development occurs, so some alternative approach to defining equality of opportunity seems necessary. There may be an analogy with the analysis of equalizing differences in the distribution of income. Once it is recognized that occupations differ in such things as their agreeableness, the costs of preparing and practicing, hazardousness, and so on, there is no way to determine that one distribution of income is more in accordance with egalitarian criteria than another. That people differ in their preferences and capabilities reinforces this impossibility. As restraints on freedom of contract in the employment of labor are removed, however, it becomes more nearly true that differences in earnings among occupations will at the margin reflect offsetting differences in people's evaluations of those other attributes.

Freedom of Contract

Although equality of opportunity cannot be defined in terms of objective relations among people, it can perhaps be approached in terms of restrictions placed on the ability of people to conduct their lives peaceably. One of the significant features of economic life in recent times has been the erosion of freedom of contract in the use of one's talents. As a result, sheltered positions are created and the involuntary inheritance of economic status increases. Professional licensure, minimum wages, and union monopoly are a few of many instances in which freedom of contract has been abridged and sheltered statuses have been created. If a union is able to restrict the supply of labor to an industry, the members of the union will receive higher wages. That restriction in the supply of labor, however, will bring an offsetting expansion in the supply of labor in nonunionized occupations.

This expansion implies, in turn, a lowering of wages in the nonunionized occupations. The conferral of sheltered status to labor unions increases the wages of union members while reducing the wages of nonunion workers. This holds for all efforts to restrict freedom of contract in the employment of talents: Those who secure the restriction gain at the expense of the remainder of society.

Several studies of the impact of labor unions on the earnings of union and nonunion labor serve as illustrations of the fact that restrictions on freedom of contract benefit some people at the expense of others. The seminal study in this area is that of H. G. Lewis, who estimated that unions have in recent years produced a 10 to 15 percent income transfer from nonunionized workers to themselves.[8] As already noted, this transfer has two elements: the rise in the wages of unionized workers because of the reduction in the supply of unionized labor and the decline in the wages of nonunionized workers because of the offsetting increase in the supply of nonunionized labor. Numerous other types of restrictions on freedom of contract, including minimum wage requirements and a variety of licensing provisions, work in essentially the same manner. To some extent, therefore, the problems involved in people's being locked into undesired positions in life can be attacked by policies that move toward freedom in the conduct of economic activity. Indeed, in an economic order based on freedom of contract, inheritance may have relatively little permanent impact on economic positions. In a competitive economic order, people are free to employ their talents as they choose, and substantial fluidity seems to characterize individual economic positions.[9] For reasons we will explore in Part II, however, there are strong tendencies for legislation to impose further restrictions on freedom of contract rather than to remove those that exist.

POLITICS AND DISTRIBUTION:
RATIONALIZATION VERSUS EXPLANATION

The various efforts to formulate notions of distributive justice generally reflect an assumption that what Robert Nozick has called the *minimal state* — in which government is limited to protection against

---

[8] H. G. Lewis, *Unionism and Relative Wages in the United States* (Chicago: University of Chicago Press, 1963).

[9] On the fluidity of wealth positions across generations, see Alan S. Blinder, "Inequality and Mobility in the Distribution of Wealth," *Kyklos* 29 (No. 4, 1976), pp. 607–638. For a similar consideration of fluidity in year-to-year economic positions, see Bradley R. Schiller, "Relative Earnings Mobility in the United States," *American Economic Review* 67 (December 1977), pp. 926–941.

force, theft, and fraud, along with the protection of contracts — would contradict canons of distributive justice.[10] One of the important tasks of government is thus to prevent a concentration of income and wealth, which will both satisfy some conditions of equity or justice and promote the stability of the existing social order.

This standard rationalization for the conduct of government may, however, diverge significantly from the actual conduct of government. As we have seen, in many instances government actually seems to promote inequality of outcomes and of opportunities through a variety of restrictions on freedom of contract. The distribution of wealth, income, or utility that emerges in existing democratic societies such as the United States may well violate reasonable canons of justice or equity. But this situation may also have resulted because of, or at least been supported by, government programs and policies rather than being a natural outcome of the minimal state that government is seeking to offset. In other words, in some instances government may act to equalize opportunities while in others it may act in contrary fashion, and the net impact may well be to inject important sources of inequality of opportunity into the economic order. Regardless, the impact of government programs and policies on distributional outcomes is ultimately a positive rather than a normative question, and positive questions dominate the remainder of this book.

SUGGESTIONS FOR FURTHER READING

Sacrifice theories of taxation are surveyed carefully in Richard A Musgrave, *The Theory of Public Finance* (New York: McGraw-Hill, 1959), pp. 90–115. The minimax approach to distributive justice is presented in John Rawls, *A Theory of Justice* (Cambridge, Mass.: Harvard University Press, 1971). The utilitarian alternative to the minimax principle is contained in several of the essays in John C. Harsanyi, *Essays on Ethics, Social Behavior, and Scientific Explanation* (Dordrecht, Netherlands: Reidel, 1976).

An extensive literature has developed on the notion of an optimal income tax, in which transfers from the rich to the poor produce a gain in utility of income and a loss resulting from various disincentive effects. Much of this literature is summarized in Anthony B. Atkinson and Joseph E. Stiglitz, *Lectures on Public Economics* (New York: McGraw-Hill, 1980), especially pp. 394–423. For somewhat different approaches to this same topic, see Arthur M. Okun, *Equality and Efficiency: The Big Trade-off* (Washington, D.C.: Brookings Institution, 1975); and Lester C. Thurow, *The Zero-Sum Society: Distribution and the Possibilities for Eco-*

[10] Robert Nozick, *Anarchy, State, and Utopia* (New York: Basic Books, 1974).

nomic Change (New York: Basic Books, 1980). Harold M. Hochman and James D. Rodgers, in "Pareto Optimal Redistribution," *American Economic Review* 59 (September 1969), pp. 542–557, seek to merge notions of efficiency and equity by exploring the extent to which transfers of income might be advantageous for all parties.

Equality of opportunity and equality of outcomes are contrasted in Milton and Rose Friedman, *Free to Choose* (New York: Harcourt, Brace, Jovanovich, 1980), pp. 128–149. On eudaemonism, the approach to equality of opportunity that underlies the closing pages of this chapter, see David L. Norton, *Personal Destinies: A Philosophy of Ethical Individualism* (Princeton, N.J.: Princeton University Press, 1976). For an interesting effort to explain how the legitimacy of a regime is based on the judgments of individuals about the value to them of a particular constitutional order, see Ronald Rogowski, *Rational Legitimacy: A Theory of Political Support* (Princeton, N.J.: Princeton University Press, 1974). On government as a net producer of inequality, see Walter E. Williams, "Government Sanctioned Restraints That Reduce Economic Opportunities for Minorities," *Policy Review*, No. 2 (Fall 1977), pp. 7–30. The discrepancy between common rationalizations for government programs to transfer income and the apparent actual consequences of those programs is explored in E. C. Pasour, Jr., "Pareto Optimality as a Guide to Income Redistribution," *Public Choice* 36 (No. 1, 1981), pp. 75–87.

II

PUBLIC CHOICE IN DEMOCRATIC REGIMES

4

Voting and Resource Utilization

Although the conceptual distinction between public goods and private goods is central to the theory of public goods, it seems to be of limited relevance in actually distinguishing between activities that are undertaken collectively and those that are undertaken privately. Government undertakes many activities that are predominantly public, but it also undertakes many that are predominantly private. At the same time, numerous activities that are predominantly public, as defined in Chapter 2, are provided privately. Movie theaters, for instance, are largely provided privately and libraries are mainly provided collectively, yet there is little essential difference between the two. Once a book or a movie has been produced, one person's use does not preclude use by others. Libraries and theaters both provide multiple units of consumption from a single unit of production. Although a library book can be read by only one person at a time and a theater seat can hold only one person at a time, a library book can be passed from reader to reader just as a theater seat can be passed from viewer to viewer. It is also relatively inexpensive to exclude those who do not pay from using either facility.

Until recently, the theory of public goods has been more concerned with describing norms for governmental conduct than with developing explanations of governmental behavior. Any effort to do the latter must recognize that many goods and services are provided both collectively and privately. It is not a matter, for instance, of recreation, food, education, or police being provided *either* collectively *or* privately. Education is supplied by both government and private firms. Most police services are provided by government, but many private police organizations serve businesses and individual citizens. Similarly, recreation is supplied by both government and private firms: Campgrounds, for instance, are supplied by the national government, by state and local governments, and by private companies. Food is distributed almost entirely privately, but the production of food takes place in many situations that involve collective financing, such as irrigation projects, agricultural research, and school lunches.

Industries often contain a mix of private and public producers. The national government provides numerous outdoor recreation facilities within its national parks, forests, and seashores, many of which are operated by private concessionaires. State and local governments supply a wide variety of recreational facilities, ranging from small-scale community parks and playgrounds to large-scale state parks that are similar to some of the national parks and seashore preserves. Recreational facilities such as fishing, water skiing, and camping also are supplied by private enterprise, and there is much variation in the provision of modern accoutrements. A description of the outdoor recreation industry shows a substantial intermingling of collective and private agencies, as is the case for almost any industry.

A person's demand for freshwater fishing does not usually depend on whether the opportunity to fish is supplied collectively or privately. If there are opportunities for profit from satisfying the demands for freshwater fishing, entrepreneurs will compete among themselves to satisfy that demand. There is no inherent reason why this entrepreneurial exploitation of profit opportunities must manifest itself only privately and not collectively. A private entrepreneur may supply the opportunity to fish by creating a reservoir, stocking it with fish, and charging a price for the right to fish. Private entrepreneurs compete among themselves to provide goods and services desired by the populace, and the more successful they are, the more they will profit. A political entrepreneur may also provide the opportunity to fish. Political entrepreneurs, like private entrepreneurs, compete among themselves to provide goods and services desired by citizens, and the more successful they are, the more they will profit. Customarily, however, political enterpreneurs reap their profit in the form of future electoral support rather than directly in the form of money.[1]

The various efforts to describe norms for optimality in the supply of public goods and for equity in the distribution of income and wealth may have little to do with the actual conduct of government. The derivation of norms for efficiency or equity in budgetary outcomes does not by itself ensure that those norms will be satisfied

---

[1] If they earn it in the form of money, they do so indirectly, such as through an increase in the expected value of postpolitical employment in the private sector.

through ordinary processes of budgetary choice. Actual budgetary outcomes are constrained and guided by the incentives politicians encounter, just as outcomes in the marketplace depend on the incentives faced by various participants. If outcomes that violate norms of efficiency or equity are rewarded more heavily than are outcomes that conform to those norms, inefficiency and inequity are the likely results. An understanding of actual budgetary outcomes, as distinct from a formulation of budgetary norms, requires an examination of the institutional framework within which budgetary choices are made. Part II of this book examines this institutional framework, and Chapters 4 and 5 form a subunit on fiscal legislation. Chapter 4 describes the properties of voting as a vehicle for making budgetary choices; as such, this chapter essentially describes a theory of budgetary choice under direct democracy. The properties of different voting rules are also applicable to voting within legislative assemblies, and Chapter 5 provides a foundation for an examination of representative government.

FISCAL CHOICE WITH MAJORITY RULE

In a democracy, fiscal choices typically require the approval of a majority of participants. In a wide variety of circumstances, the use of majority rule for making fiscal choices amounts to a delegation of that choice to a particular member of the collectivity, namely the person whose preference on the issue is the median preference within the collectivity. This property of majority voting makes it possible in many cases to explain the salient characteristics of fiscal choices by explaining the choice of the *median voter.*

The ability of the median voter to dominate the outcome is easy to understand. Suppose three people are to decide the route for a day-long hike. These people differ somewhat in the amount of energy they wish to expend on the hike, but they also prefer to hike together rather than to hike separately. The three adopt a procedure for reaching a collective choice, and this rule of procedure is part of the constitutional or institutional framework within which particular choices will be made. The procedure follows a particular format for determining the option preferred by the majority. Two motions are put forward and a vote is taken. A subsequent motion may in turn be put forward against the winner of the initial vote, and this process of comparing a new motion with the winner in the previous vote continues until a motion is found that cannot be defeated by other motions. Presentation of motions and the taking of votes represents a discussion about which route to take, and the discussion continues until there is nothing more to discuss; that is, until a motion that secures the permanent approval of a majority is obtained.

Suppose distance is the only dimension on which the participants differ, and suppose one person prefers a five-mile hike, another a ten-mile hike, and the third a fifteen-mile hike. Further suppose that each person's evaluation of distances other than the preferred distance declines uniformly both for increases and decreases in distances. Figure 4.1 describes the preferences of the three hikers. If a motion to hike five miles is put forth against one to hike ten miles, the ten-mile hike will secure majority support, because the person who wants to hike fifteen miles will support a motion to hike ten miles over a motion to hike five miles. If a motion to hike fifteen miles is put forward against the motion for a ten-mile hike, the ten-mile hike would again secure majority support. In this case, the second vote will come from the person who prefers to hike five miles but who rather would go ten miles than fifteen miles. In any event, majority voting effectively delegates the collective choice to the person whose preference is the median for the collectivity.

Budgetary choices can be viewed within this same framework. Suppose three people face the task of choosing how much of some service, say of parkland, to provide collectively. Although parks can differ in many dimensions, just as hiking routes can, let us suppose for simplicity that the only relevant dimension is number of acres of some standardized quality. Forms of taxation involve, among other things, methods of assigning prices to different people, and the number of acres a person prefers depends on the price that must be paid. A proportional income tax, for instance, assigns a price to each person equal to the product of that person's share of taxable income and the unit cost of collective output. If the cost of public output is $100 per unit, a person whose income is 1 percent of taxable income will pay a tax-price of $1 per unit produced under a proportional income tax. The number of units such a person will choose depends on demand, just as it does for consumer choices in the marketplace.

Figure 4.2 illustrates budgetary choice under the assumption that each person pays the same tax-price. This form of taxation is called a *poll* or *head tax*. Other forms of taxation could be assumed instead, in which case different people would pay different tax-prices. Such an alternative assumption about the form of taxation would complicate the presentation but would not modify the central point. With a different pattern of prices, the quantities different people prefer will change, but there will still be a person whose preferred quantity is the median for the collectivity. A person's order of preference will still generally decline the more the actual choice differs from his or her preferred choice. Changes in the form of taxation may even change the

---

FIGURE 4.1 Preference Orderings for Three Voters

The order of preference of three people for hikes between five and fifteen miles is shown in this figure. Person A prefers a hike of five miles and evaluates successively longer distances with decreasing favor, as shown by the line AA. Person C prefers a fifteen-mile hike and evaluates successively shorter distances with decreasing favor, as shown by the line CC. Person B prefers a ten-mile hike and evaluates both shorter and longer distances with decreasing favor, as line BB shows. Any motion to increase the distance from five miles toward ten miles will be preferred by a B and C, and so all such motions would gain majority support. Majority support also exists for all motions to decrease the distance from fifteen toward ten miles; in this case A and B provide the majority support. Only against a motion to hike ten miles is it impossible to find a majority to support some motion to change the distance hiked, and so a motion to hike ten miles is the majority motion.

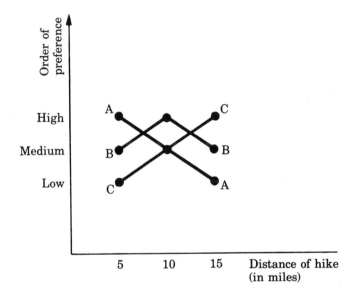

identity of the median voter, as well as the amount preferred by the median voter. Nonetheless, majority rule is still a method of collective choice that is equivalent to delegating choice for the collectivity to a single person, namely the person whose preference is the median for the choice being made.

Circumstances can arise in which a majority motion does not exist. This possibility becomes more likely when the object of choice has more than a single dimension because notions of more and less take on

FIGURE 4.2 Budgetary Choice Under Majority Voting

D_1, D_2, and D_3 are individual demand functions, and each person is assumed to share equally in the cost of the service, meaning that the total cost per unit is $3P_0$. The preferred rates of supply for the three persons are X_1, X_2, and X_3, respectively. Any motion to expand output from X_1 toward X_2 will be supported by Persons 2 and 3 because the value they place on added output, as indicated by the height of their demand curves, exceeds the cost they bear for the expansion, P_0. Likewise, any motion to contract output from X_3 toward X_2 will secure majority approval, in this case the approval of Persons 1 and 2. Only at X_2 will there no longer exist a motion for change that can secure majority approval. The rate of output X_2 is the majority motion.

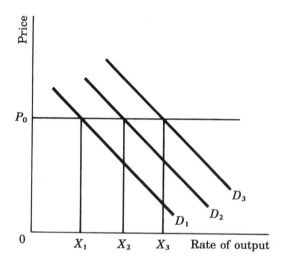

some ambiguity. Parkland may vary not only in its acreage but also in whether it is designed mainly for athletics (A), camping (C), or picnicking (P). Instead of choosing among different sizes of some standard-quality park, suppose a collectivity is to choose which type of park to establish, possibly through a choice of locations, each of which is best suited for one type of park. Suppose the personal preference orderings are as shown in Table 4.1. V_1 prefers an athletic emphasis over an emphasis on camping, but he prefers an emphasis on camping to one on picnicking, and so on for the other voters. In this situation a majority motion does not exist. Any motion that is proposed can be defeated by some other motion. In a vote between the athletic facility and the camping facility, the athletic facility will win, but in a vote between the athletic facility and the picnic facility,

TABLE 4.1 Preference Orderings: Three Voters and
Three Motions

V_1	V_2	V_3
A	C	P
C	P	A
P	A	C

the picnic facility will win. In a vote between the picnic facility and
the camping facility, the camping facility will win. Instead of a majority motion, there is a *cyclical majority*, and the outcome depends
on the order of voting. Suppose the rules of voting specify that initially two of the three motions must be paired, with the motion that
wins being paired against the remaining motion, and with the motion
that then prevails being declared the winner. If the first vote is between A and C, P will be the winning motion; if the first vote is
between A and P, C will win; and if the first vote is between C and P,
A will win. Thus, the ability to set the order of voting, or, more generally, to set the agenda for considering the options for choice can be
a means of influencing actual outcomes.[2]

Cyclical majorities have received much attention because they are
often thought to indicate a defect in voting processes. In the case
where there are three equally likely options, the probability that a
majority motion does not exist has been estimated to be about 5.5
percent for three voters and to approach 9 percent as the number of
voters becomes indefinitely large.[3] If majority voting is regarded as
having unique, normative significance, the absence of a majority motion seems understandably troublesome. Yet the normative significance of majority voting may be less than commonly thought, at least
in light of the benefit principle described in Chapter 2 and the economic analysis of majority voting throughout Part II.

Furthermore, even if a majority motion exists, not all voting procedures will produce that motion as the collective choice. Only in a
round-robin vote, a procedure that continually pairs one motion
against another until only one motion remains, will the majority motion necessarily be the choice, assuming that such a motion exists in

[2] This possibility is discussed in Chapter 5.
[3] Frank De Meyer and Charles R. Plott, "The Probability of a Cyclical Majority," *Econometrica* 38 (March 1970), pp. 345–354; and Thomas J. Hansen
and Barry L. Prince, "The Paradox of Voting: An Elementary Solution for
the Case of Three Alternatives," *Public Choice* 15 (Summer 1973), pp. 103–117.

TABLE 4.2 Preference Orderings: Five Voters and Five Motions

V_1	V_2	V_3	V_4	V_5
A	B	C	D	A
E	E	E	E	E
B	C	D	A	B
C	D	A	B	C
D	A	B	C	D

the first place. As an alternative system, plurality voting, in which one election is held and in which the option with the largest number of votes wins, will not necessarily select the majority motion, as Table 4.2 illustrates. With the preference schedules shown there for five voters and five motions, motion A would capture a plurality, for it would receive two votes and no other motion would receive more than one vote. Motion E would receive no votes, and yet it is actually the majority motion; it would defeat all of the other motions in a series of paired choices: It would defeat B, C, and D by 4 to 1 and it would defeat A by 3 to 2.

MAJORITY RULE, WEALTH TRANSFERS, AND BUDGETARY OUTCOMES

To the extent that majority voting delegates choice to the person whose preference is the median for the collectivity, budgetary outcomes can be explained by examining the median voter's choice. Moreover, the median voter's choice can be compared with the standard of the benefit principle. A simple numerical example may help to illustrate the point, in a way that conforms generally with Figure 2.4. Assume a collectivity consists of three people (or of three equal-sized groups), with the demand functions for some collectively supplied service, X, being $P_{A,B} = 20/X$ for two people (two-thirds of the group) and $P_C = 10/X$ for one person (the remaining one-third of the group). If X is provided under constant cost with $MC = \$10$, the rate of output required by the benefit principle is found, as we saw in Chapter 2, by adding the individual demand functions vertically and setting the aggregate demand equal to marginal cost. In the illustration at hand, this operation gives

$$2(20/X) + 10/X = 10,$$

which yields $X = 5$.

The distribution of marginal tax-prices is found by inserting the collective output into the individual demand functions, which in this illustration yields $P_A = P_B = \$4$ and $P_C = \$2$. At these marginal tax-prices, each person prefers five units of output, so there is consensus about this budgetary outcome.[4]

Suppose instead that public output is financed through a head tax, so that each person pays a tax-price of \$3.33 per unit. Those with majority preferences (persons or groups A and B) will prefer a rate of output of six units, which can be found by substituting \$3.33 for $P_{A,B}$ above and solving for X. Those with minority preferences (person or group C) will prefer an output of three units, which can be found by substituting \$3.33 for P_C above and solving for X. The collective choice will thus be six units, as this is the amount preferred by the median voter, who is a member of the winning majority coalition. This actual outcome now exceeds the outcome required by the benefit principle. The marginal cost of the sixth unit of output is \$10, but its value to the members of the collectivity is only \$8.33 — \$3.33 each to A and B and \$1.67 to C. Although the cost of the additional unit exceeds its value, it is supplied nonetheless because the members of the majority coalition receive net benefits from this budgetary expansion.

This simple example illustrates how majority rule can encourage coalition politics of taxing and transferring, in which the members of the winning coalition secure wealth transfers at the expense of the members of the losing coalition. Suppose a society consists of five people (or five equal-sized groups), with each person assigned a tax liability of \$100. The problem of budgetary choice in this instance is to choose how to spend the \$500. Suppose one possible project, or class of projects, distributes its benefits uniformly over the population, while another project, or class of projects, concentrates its benefits on a subset of the population. Any majority of three will gain more from the selection of the concentrated program than from the uniform program. With a uniform distribution, an average of \$100 can be spent on each person, but if spending is limited to a project desired by only three people, average spending per beneficiary will be \$167. Indeed, the

---

[4] The benefit principle is stated in terms of marginal prices. Average prices may diverge from marginal prices, and to the extent that they do the distribution of income will be modified, with those whose average price is less than their marginal price becoming wealthier and those whose average price exceeds marginal price becoming poorer. If individual demand functions are of zero income elasticity, there will be no impact on budgetary choice. Otherwise, the median voter may choose a smaller or larger quantity, depending on whether the divergence makes him or her poorer or wealthier. We have overlooked such possibilities here because they would have made the exposition more complex without affecting the central point. For a discussion of this point, see James M. Buchanan, *The Demand and Supply of Public Goods* (Chicago: Rand McNally, 1968), pp. 37–46.

smaller the size of the winning coalition; that is, the closer its size approaches a bare majority, the larger the average gain to the members of that coalition. Not all political activity involves zero-sum transfers from losers to winners, of course; some also involves the positive-sum provision of jointly beneficial activities. Nonetheless, to the extent that majority rule encourages such zero-sum activities, wealth will be transferred from the members of the minority coalition to the members of the majority.

As explained in Chapter 3, a transfer of wealth may violate precepts of justice, or it may not. In either event, it does not violate the benefit principle because a transfer does not, by itself, disturb the relation between the value yielded by resources devoted to the collective satisfaction of wants and the value yielded by resources devoted to the private satisfaction of wants. Typically, however, wealth transfers will modify the marginal tax-price the median voter pays, and this in turn will change that voter's desired rate of output. If the median voter's tax-price falls below that required by the benefit principle, an inefficiently large rate of public output will result, as we just saw.

It is also possible for the median voter to choose a rate of output that is inefficiently small compared with that required by the benefit principle. With reference to the illustration developed above, suppose only Person A has the demand function $P_A = 20/X$, while Persons B and C have the demand function $P_{B,C} = 10/X$. Assuming marginal cost is still \$10 per unit, the rate of output required by the benefit principle can now be found by solving

$$20/X + 2(10/X) = 10,$$

which yields $X = 4$ and which requires marginal prices of $P_A = \$5$ and $P_B = P_C = \$2.50$. Under a requirement of equal cost sharing, however, the median voter pays a tax price of \$3.33 per unit and will choose to provide only three units of output. In this case the budget is smaller than required by the benefit principle. An expansion in output from three to four units will shift resources from the service of wants that are valued at \$10 (marginal cost) to the service of wants that are valued at approximately \$11.67.[5] To achieve this expansion to four units of output would also impose an excess of cost over benefit on Persons B and C, and so it would fail to command majority support.

[5] The sum of the marginal valuations when $X = 3$ is \$13.33, which is found by substituting 3 for X in the demand functions and adding. When $X = 4$, the sum of the marginal valuations is \$10. If marginal value declines uniformly over this range of output, the aggregate value of increasing output from three to four units is $(\frac{1}{2})(\$13.33 + \$10) = \$11.67$.

Whether majority voting will lead to a budget that is too large or too small compared with the benefit principle cannot be answered a priori. It is an empirical matter that depends, among other things, on the types of controlling coalitions that form and on the types of constraining rules that characterize the fiscal constitution of a society. Indeed, it is even possible for majority rule to yield the budgetary outcome required by the benefit principle. This will happen if the marginal value of collective output to the median voter, at the median voter's preferred rate of output, is equal to the average of the marginal values of all voters. Suppose marginal cost is still $10 per unit but that the individual demand functions are $P_A = 10/X$, $P_B = 20/X$, and $P_C = 30/X$. In this case the benefit principle requires six units of output, as can be found by solving $10/X + 20/X + 30/X = 10$. With equal cost sharing, Person B is the median voter, who desires $20/3.33 = 6$ units of output. If preferences are distributed symmetrically and people pay equal tax-prices, majority voting will generate the budgetary outcome required by the benefit principle.

The requirement of a symmetrical distribution of marginal valuations is a strict one, as is the requirement of equal tax-prices. Even if people have symmetrical valuations of collective output, they may not pay equal tax-prices. Majority voting may produce tax discrimination by a shift of some of the burden of taxation from the members of the majority coalition to those outside it. Alternatively, although tax-prices might be equal throughout the population, the services provided by government may be valued especially heavily by a subset of the population. A successful majority coalition can practice fiscal discrimination on either the taxing or the spending side of the budget.

The properties of fiscal discrimination in producing budgetary inefficiency seem to be generally equivalent to those of A. C. Pigou's classic smoke-spouting factory.[6] Because the factory does not include the damage caused by its smoke as part of its cost of production, the price of the factory's output is excessively low. People who buy the factory's output are in effect subsidized by those who are damaged by the pollution. A majority coalition is similar to the smoke-producing factory. Its members make budgetary choices on the basis of the marginal costs they bear. If they are able to place part of the cost of those choices on others, for whom marginal cost exceeds marginal valuation, the majority coalition will choose to supply an inefficiently large amount of the service.

Majority voting can be a means for the generation of externalities.

[6] A. C. Pigou, *The Economics of Welfare,* 4th ed. (London: Macmillan, 1932), pp. 183–184.

But to look at it this way raises again some of the issues about property rights that were examined in Chapter 2. The right of the factory to spout smoke into the air is itself a factor of production. If the value of the additional output produced by using the more smoke-intensive means of production exceeds the loss in value owing to dirtier clothes, it will be socially inefficient to reduce smoke emissions from the factory. The amount of smoke will be excessive only if the value of the additional output is less than the other values that are destroyed by the creation of a dirtier environment. If the factory smoke is excessive and the factory has the legal right to pollute the air, the residents of the affected area would be able to pay the factory to reduce its emissions. If the property rights were reversed, however, the factory would not be able to buy the consent of the community to dump its smoke. As we saw in Chapter 2, the factory smoke will be reduced to efficient levels under either assignment of property rights. So long as transaction costs are relatively low, the particular rules of liability may have little effect on the allocation of resources.[7]

Similarly, majority voting will not generate budgetary inefficiency if votes can be bought and sold for money.[8] The members of the losing minority will be able to pay the members of the majority coalition to refrain from increasing collective output. This can be seen with reference to the earlier illustration in which marginal cost was $10, A and B had the demand functions $P_{A,B} = 20/X$, and C's demand function was $P_C = 10/X$. The rate of output required by the benefit principle is $X = 5$, but majority voting with equal tax-prices generates $X = 6$. If votes could be bought and sold for money, however, the inefficient expansion in output would not take place. Assuming marginal valuations decline uniformly between $X = 5$ and $X = 6$, the gain to A and B is 33.5 cents each (marginal value exceeds cost by 67 cents at $X = 4$ and is equal to cost at $X = 5$). The loss to C is $1.50 (cost exceeds marginal value by $1.33 at $X = 4$ and by $1.66 at $X = 5$). For any payment between 67 cents and $1.50, all parties would be better off than they would be through budgetary expansion. So long as they receive more than 33.5 cents each, A and B are better off with the money than with the increased collective output, and as long as C is able to buy their support for less than $1.50, C is better off buying the votes than paying for the additional collective output.

[7] This is the central theme of Ronald H. Coase, "The Problem of Social Cost," *Journal of Law and Economics* 3 (October 1960), pp. 1–44.

[8] This point is developed in James M. Buchanan and Gordon Tullock, *The Calculus of Consent* (Ann Arbor: University of Michigan Press, 1962), pp. 147–169.

Logrolling, Political Exchange, and Fiscal Outcomes

When multiple issues are subject to collective choice, the outcome preferred by the median voter has less explanatory power because various types of exchanges of support among issues are possible, and these exchanges can produce outcomes that diverge from those preferred by the median voter. *Logrolling* is a form of exchange in which support on one issue is traded for support on another issue, and it may occur either explicitly or implicitly. Explicit logrolling is a direct exchange of support among issues. Implicit logrolling involves the creation of a package of issues to be supported by the members of a coalition; the construction of political platforms is implicit logrolling. In that case, exchanges are implicitly contained in the package offered for electoral decision.

Regardless of the type of logrolling, we presently have relatively little knowledge of its properties. Although there is no such thing as a median voter model in the presence of logrolling over multiple issues, some of the salient characteristics are the same: no necessary dominance of the outcome called for by the benefit principle, and the possibility that the resulting expenditure will be either excessive or insufficient compared with the benefit principle.

The main properties of logrolling can be described with a comparatively simple illustration. Suppose a community contains three people (or three equal-sized groups) who must choose collectively the rates of output of three public services. Let P_{XA} denote Person A's demand for X, P_{YB} denote Person B's demand for Y, and so on. The postulated demand functions are shown in Table 4.3. Under the assumption that marginal cost (as well as average cost) is \$30 per unit, the rate of output of X required by the benefit principle can be found by solving

$$(20 - X) + (10 - X) + (6 - X) = 30,$$

TABLE 4.3 Demand Functions: Three Voters and Three Services

Person	Demand for X	Demand for Y	Demand for Z
A	$P_{XA} = 20 - X$	$P_{YA} = 10 - Y$	$P_{ZA} = 6 - Z$
B	$P_{XB} = 10 - X$	$P_{YB} = 6 - Y$	$P_{ZB} = 20 - Z$
C	$P_{XC} = 6 - X$	$P_{YC} = 20 - Y$	$P_{ZC} = 10 - Z$

which gives $X = 2$. By extension of this argument, the benefit principle also requires that $Y = 2$ and $Z = 2$. However, should each issue be decided independently under a regime of equal tax-prices, the median preference will be zero for each of the three services. This can be determined by substituting $10 for the relevant P variable and solving for desired output. In all three cases, the median of the desired quantities is zero.

When issues of collective choice are resolved jointly rather than independently, exchanges of support may be beneficial to the participants. A priori, the three majority coalitions (A, B), (B, C), and (A, C) are equally likely to emerge. To illustrate the point, consider a coalition between A and C over the provision of X and Y. The outcome under independent voting, (0, 0, 0), is clearly not stable when support can be traded over issues. Consider the gains to A and C from supporting (1, 1, 0) in place of (0, 0, 0). The marginal cost of doing this is $20 to each member of the coalition because a total of two units of output are provided and Person B bears the same cost. The marginal benefit can be approximated by evaluating the demand functions at the midpoint of the 0–1 range; this is $29 for A ($19.50 from X and $9.50 from Y) and $25 for C ($5.50 from X and $19.50 from Y). This same line of reasoning shows that A and C will continue to gain from budgetary expansion until (3, 3, 0) is chosen. At that point, the marginal benefit for A is $24, and for C it is $20. Person C will value expansions in output beyond (3, 3, 0) less highly than the cost of such expansions.

In this illustration, logrolling leads to an overexpansion of X and Y because three units of each are provided, whereas two are required by the benefit principle. At the same time, however, the benefit principle requires the provision of two units of Z, but none are provided. The reason for this is that the provision of even the first unit of Z has a marginal cost in excess of marginal benefit for A and C. Furthermore, although there is too much provision of X and Y and too little provision of Z, compared with the requirement of the benefit principle, the overall budget of $180 is exactly the size required by the benefit principle.

These results are, of course, built into the initial illustration, and different initial data will generate different results. What is of general value in this illustration is that the trading of support through logrolling does not necessarily bring about outcomes compatible with the benefit principle and that particular services may be either over- or underprovided. In addition, even though the overall size of the budget may be considered correct, the composition of the budget may diverge from that required by the benefit principle. The particular outcomes that transpire depend on the particular coalitions that form. Regardless of outcomes, however, there seems to be no general tendency for logrolling under majority voting to promote efficiency in the use of resources.

MAJORITARIAN AND CONSENSUAL DEMOCRACY

Knut Wicksell recognized in the late nineteenth century that majority rule as a procedure or rule for making collective choices cannot claim any particular ability to reflect the consent of the governed, as the idea of consent is expressed by the benefit principle. He was well aware of the negative-sum properties of majoritarian democracy, its tendency to spend excessively on some activities and insufficiently on others.[9] Wicksell took seriously the normative proposition that collective outcomes should reflect the valuations of the citizenry and went on to explore what this implied for the actual conduct of collective choice in Sweden in his time. Within a parliament that was broadly representative of the citizenry, unanimity among the members of parliament would surely reflect a substantial consensus of the citizenry. Besides adopting unanimity as a point of reference, Wicksell also described a set of procedures to be followed in making fiscal choices. A legislative sponsor of a proposal for public expenditure would simultaneously have to present a proposal to cover the cost of the program. The expenditure and the method of payment would be voted on as a unit. Under the unanimity requirement, the resulting outcome would be compatible with the benefit principle because a proposal that was agreed to unanimously could not require some people to pay marginal tax-prices in excess of their marginal valuations. Of course, should the valuations some people place on the marginal unit exceed the price they pay for the unit, the budget would be inefficiently small, and consensus could be attained for an increase in collective output. The budgetary outcome required by the benefit principle is, as a first approximation, the largest budget that can receive unanimous support.

The condition that unanimity is only a first approximation to a concrete method of implementing the benefit principle is important. Unanimity ensures against the enactment of programs that, while being worthwhile to the members of a controlling coalition, are not

---

[9] Knut Wicksell, "A New Principle of Just Taxation," in *Classics in the Theory of Public Finance*, edited by Richard A. Musgrave and Alan T. Peacock (London: Macmillan, 1958), pp. 72–118, is a translation of the core of Wicksell's work on the constitutional framework for collective choice.

worthwhile overall. The more inclusive the voting rule, however, the more costly it will be to secure unanimity. Even though a program may be regarded as worthwhile by 999 people, it will be more costly to secure the agreement of all those people than to secure the agreement of only 800 of them. Similarly, it will be more costly to obtain the agreement of 800 people than to obtain the agreement of only 500. A program may be regarded as worthwhile, but, as we saw in Chapter 2, there are many ways of distributing the cost of the inframarginal units, and people will have some incentive to withhold their consent in an effort to secure a pattern of payment that is more favorable to them. Although there are gains from exchanging support in reaching collective agreements, there are also individual interests in securing larger rather than smaller shares of those gains. Hence, it should generally be more costly to secure the consent of a larger share of a group of a given size than to secure the consent of a smaller share, and probably the rise in cost will become particularly pronounced as the degree of consent approaches unanimity.

In light of this increasing costliness of securing higher degrees of consent, Wicksell suggested that *approximate unanimity*, which he estimated to be somewhere between 75 to 90 percent consent, could reasonably be regarded as a practical indication of consensual democracy. With such a degree of consensus required to enact collective choices, budgetary outcomes that resulted from a legislature that was broadly representative of the citizenry could be described reasonably closely by a construction such as that represented by Figure 2.4. The choice of a voting rule for making budgetary decisions can be approached as a problem of cost minimization, illustrated in Figure 4.3. As the voting rule becomes more inclusive, the anticipated cost to any person of inefficient outcomes, as reflected in negative-sum expansions in output, declines. Under unanimity this cost must be zero. At the other extreme, the cost of inefficient outcomes will be maximal if any single person in the polity is able to choose for the collectivity. On the other hand, there will be no cost of securing group agreement if any single person is able to choose for the collectivity, and the cost of reaching agreement will be highest when unanimity is required. Within this framework, an optimal voting rule is one that minimizes these two costs. As a practical matter, Wicksell thought that the point of minimal cost would occur in the vicinity of 75 to 90 percent agreement, reflecting the assumption that the cost of reaching group agreement will rise relatively slowly until a substantial degree of consent is required.

Perhaps the most significant feature of the cost-minimization analysis of different rules for making collective choices is that unanimity, not majority rule, is the benchmark set by the benefit principle. This

FIGURE 4.3 Optimal Inclusiveness of a Voting Rule

The function *EC* describes the external cost from collective action as the degree of consent varies. If any single person can initiate action for the collectivity, external cost will be at its maximum. If unanimity is required, external cost will be zero. The function *DC*, decision cost, illustrates the cost of agreeing to undertake collective action. With a rule that any one person can choose for the collectivity, such cost is zero. It is maximal when everyone in the collectivity must agree. The function *TC* represents the sum of the external and decision costs for all degrees of consent. The degree of consent represented by *N** is that which minimizes the total cost of collective choice and therefore maximizes the benefits from collective choice.

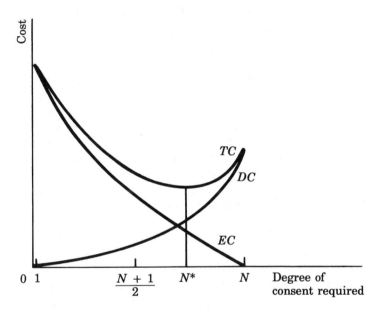

line of analysis goes on to suggest that departures from unanimity may themselves be agreed to consensually, once the costs of decision making are taken into account. It is also worth noting that, as a complement to approximate unanimity in voting on proposed expenditures, a previously approved expenditure would be eliminated from the budget if a motion for elimination received between 10 and 25 percent support. This is fully consistent with the requirements of consensual democracy because such a vote would indicate that the program no longer commands the 75 to 90 percent degree of support that is required by consensual democracy.

DEMAND REVELATION   *Clake*
AND CONSENSUAL DEMOCRACY

The Wicksellian approach to consensual democracy looks for an institutional order within which budgetary choices will tend to reflect the consent of the governed, with consent described by an analytical construction such as that in Figure 2.4 An alternative approach to consensual democracy looks to the development of different techniques of voting that will overcome incentives to free riding. The emphasis here is on techniques that will induce people to honestly reveal their preferences for collective output. To the extent that such a voting technique can be developed, it might be possible to compute outcomes that accord with a construction such as Figure 2.4.

The *demand-revealing process* is one method of voting that seeks to induce such revelation of preference. To see how the demand-revealing process works, consider first its application to a simple choice between two options, X and Y, which can represent any case where discrete options exist as alternative candidates or choices. There are three voters, A, B, and C, each of whom is asked to state the amount that they value one option over the other. Table 4.4 shows hypothetical values stated by three voters. Voter A, for instance, prefers X over Y by $30. After all voters have stated their preferences, the efficient choice can be computed easily; it is simply the option that in the aggregate is valued more highly. In the illustration in Table 4.4, the efficient choice is X, which is valued $10 more highly than Y.

But how can people be relied on to reveal their preferences honestly? After all, if such statements could be relied on, it would seem to be a simple matter to have people submit such statements and then compute an efficient choice. As noted earlier, people have an incentive to understate their preferences if their tax payments are to be based on those statements. The demand-revealing process con-

TABLE 4.4   Demand Revelation: Three Voters and Two Options

Voter	Differential Value of Option	
	X	Y
A	$30	0
B	0	$60
C	$40	0

tains an incentive to overcome this free-rider problem, through the imposition of a peculiar tax. This tax is charged to each voter whose vote, as reflected in his or her statement of preference, changes the outcome from what it would have been had no preference been expressed. The amount of this tax is equal to the cost that such decisive voters impose on the other parties to the choice because of their ability to change the outcome from what it would otherwise have been. Nicolaus Tideman and Gordon Tullock refer to this tax as a *Clarke tax*, after Edward H. Clarke, the initiator of the recent interest in the demand-revealing process.[10]

The operation of the Clarke tax and the demand-revealing process can be shown in Table 4.4. If voter A abstains, his or her differential value would be zero for each option, which in turn would yield total values for X and Y of $40 and $60 respectively. A's abstention changes the outcome from X to Y. A's Clarke tax is the amount that it takes to bring X into equality with Y; this amount is $20. If voter C abstains, the resulting values of X and Y would be $30 and $60 respectively, and the outcome would be changed from X to Y. Since it would take $30 to bring X into equality with Y, $30 is the Clarke tax that would be charged to C. If B's vote is dropped from consideration, however, the outcome is not changed, so B would not pay a Clarke tax.

How is it that the Clarke tax induces a revelation of preferences? If voter A, who states his or her differential preference for X as $30, ends up paying a Clarke tax of $20, might not he or she be better off by stating some lower value of preference? Suppose A states a lower value of $10. In this case option Y wins. Although A avoids the $20 Clarke tax, he or she loses an option worth $30 in the process. If a person understates preferences sufficiently to change the outcome, the Clarke tax will be avoided but the value of the option foregone will be even larger. Moreover, there is no incentive even for small misstatements of preference. Suppose A states a preference of $25, perhaps thinking that some small dishonesty will save a little tax but will not significantly endanger chances for the enactment of X. If A's vote is taken away, the vote now changes from $65 and $60 for X and Y, respectively, to $40 and $60. The removal of A's vote changes the outcome, so A will be assessed a Clarke tax. The amount of the tax will be $20, just as it would be with a truthful statement of preferences. The reason the size of the tax does not change is that its amount depends on the statements made by all

---

[10] T. Nicolaus Tideman and Gordon Tullock, "A New and Superior Process for Making Social Choices," *Journal of Political Economy* 84 (December 1976), pp. 1145–1159.

the *other* participants in the choice. If a Clarke tax is to be assessed against a voter, the amount of that tax will be invariant to that voter's statement of preference. There is no gain from either large or small misstatements of preference. The Clarke tax creates incentives for the truthful revelation of preferences, in contrast to the incentive for understatement that would result if those statements were to be used directly in assigning tax liability.

By extension of the principle of the Clarke tax, the demand-revealing process can be applied to such continuous-choice situations as the choice of output of some public good, although this application is somewhat more complex than the application to a binary choice. With continuous choice, each voter must state the values of successive units of collective output. Essentially, this is a statement of a demand function, although rather than specifying an equation it might generally suffice if the voter evaluates several discrete options. In this case, as Figure 4.4 illustrates, the demand-revealing process has two parts and resembles a two-part tariff: One part is a fixed charge that is assigned to each person; the other part is a variable charge that corresponds to the Clarke tax. This variable charge is computed by having each person submit a statement of demand for the collective service. The individual demands are then summed to derive an aggregate demand for the service, in the same manner as is done for a binary choice.

The individual expressions of demand correspond to votes on motions to provide various quantities of the collective service. Each person's own expression of demand is then subtracted from the aggregate demand, which amounts to taking away one person's vote and examining the resulting change in outcome. The fixed-charge component is designed to cover the total cost of collective output, and there are many ways of applying it. A proportional tax on income is a relatively simple way; each person's share of the cost equals his or her share in taxable income.

It is the variable charge — the Clarke tax — that induces the honest revelation of preference. Similar to the discrete case, the vote of any particular person is eliminated and the resulting outcome is ascertained. In this case, the resulting outcome occurs at the point where the sum of the expressed demands of all other people intersects the aggregate marginal cost for all other people. With continuous choice, the Clarke tax constructs a synthetic supply schedule for each person. This schedule is the difference between the marginal cost of the collective service and the aggregate of the demands expressed by all other members of the collectivity. As with the choice between discrete options, the Clarke tax creates an incentive for a

FIGURE 4.4 Demand-Revealing Process and Public Goods

The curve d_i shows the demand for some service as stated by Person i, and D shows the sum of those stated demands. The individual's own statement of demand is subtracted from the aggregate demand, to give the curve $D - d_i$. The object in making this subtraction is to judge the resulting impact on the collective outcome. In this illustration, the collective outcome is reduced from Q to Q^*, which is what the collective choice would be if Person i's preference were to lie along P_i rather than being represented by d_i. But what gives this person, or any person, an incentive to make an honest statement of preference? A synthetic supply schedule, S_i, is constructed and defined as equal to the marginal cost (MC) of the collective output less the difference between the aggregate expressed demand and the particular individual's expressed demand. When $D - d_i$ is $1, the presumed marginal cost of the service, S_i, equals zero. $S_i = P_i$ when $D - d_i = \$1 - P_i$, with the remainder of S_i constructed in similar fashion. The Clarke tax, which tends to encourage a truthful revelation of preference, is the divergence between $D - d_i$ and $\$1 - P_i$. By misstating preference, as in placing no value on the service, P_i is substituted as a statement of preference. As a result, the person who renders such a misstatement will actually be worse off by the amount indicated by the shaded triangle than he or she would have been with a truthful statement.

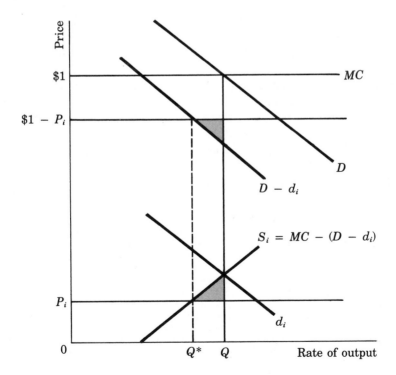

truthful statement of preference. Should a decisive voter understate his preference, the saving in Clarke tax will be less than the reduction in the value that person places on the lost collective output. For this reason, the demand-revealing process has a tendency to encourage a truthful revelation of preferences, and it is a method of voting that is basically consistent with a consensual evaluation of public output.

The statement about consensual evaluation may, however, require some qualification in light of the arbitrariness with which the fixed portion of the tax may be assigned. The tax share or price assigned to any particular person could be lowered or raised, with offsetting changes made in the shares assigned to the others, without affecting the tendency for the efficient quantity to emerge, so long as any resulting change in the distribution of income does not affect the aggregate demand for the collective good. But the benefit principle, at least as formulated by Wicksell and Lindahl, operates in terms of people paying marginal tax-prices equal to their marginal evaluations of collective output. Such prices as P_i are determined within the benefit principle model as part of the process of consensus formation, and they become equal to marginal evaluations as a necessary condition of consensual choice. The arbitrariness with which P_i could be set might seem to do some damage to the interpretation of the demand-revealing process as being consistent with consensual democracy, although the demand-revealing process is certainly intended to operate within the framework of consensual democracy.[11]

It must be noted that the demand-revealing process does not overcome the weak incentive people have to become informed about the options for choice; that weak incentive is common to all instances of collective choice. The demand-revealing process provides some consensual outcome, although the basis for that consensus may be relatively poorly informed. More significant, there is still a question

[11] Under some circumstances, however, the conflict with the benefit principle may be relatively weak. If the income elasticity of demand for collective output is unity, the use of a proportional income tax to assign the fixed tax-prices will generally reflect differences in individual demands for collective output. Although unitary elasticity is unlikely to be a faithful description of individual demands, so long as income differences loom large as sources of difference in individual demands, a proportional tax on income will be less than wholly arbitrary in relation to the tax-prices that would be required by the benefit principle. In this regard, it is interesting to note that Antonio de Viti de Marco, in his model of the cooperative state, in which the activities of government actually reflect an exchange or consensual relationship rather than a relationship of sovereignty or compulsion, assumed that the demand for public services varied in proportion to income. See Antonio de Viti de Marco, *First Principles of Public Finance*, translated from the Italian by Edith Pavlo Marget (London: Jonathan Cape, 1936), p. 116.

of the supply of entrepreneurship in politics. A voting rule is applied
to options for choice, with different rules possessing different characteristics. How do these options arise in the first place? In a market
they arise through the actions of entrepreneurs searching for profits.
In politics they must similarly arise through some form of entrepreneurial activity. This question of entrepreneurship raises questions
concerning the conduct of legislative assemblies, the functioning of
political parties, and related topics, all the subject of the next chapter.

SUGGESTIONS FOR FURTHER READING

A seminal work stressing the similarities between market competition and
political competition is Anthony Downs, *An Economic Theory of Democracy* (New York: Harper & Row, 1957). A similarly influential work on
the theory of voting is Duncan Black, *Theory of Committees and Elections* (Cambridge: Cambridge University Press, 1958). For an exploration of the circumstances in which choice by the median voter will lead
to a collective choice that is consistent with the benefit principle, see
Howard R. Bowen, "The Interpretation of Voting in the Allocation of
Economic Resources," *Quarterly Journal of Economics* 58 (November
1943), pp. 27–48. For an interesting study of how, until 1968, school districts in Florida enacted their budgetary choices in a manner that followed the choice preferred by the median voter, see Randall G. Holcombe, "The Florida System: A Bowen Equilibrium Referendum Process,"
National Tax Journal 30 (March 1977), pp. 77–84.

On the possible absence of a majority motion as evidence of a difficulty
for democratic government, see Kenneth J. Arrow, *Social Choice and
Individual Values* (New York: Wiley, 1951). For a contrary argument
that the absence of a majority motion may be valuable within a system
of majoritarian democracy, see James M. Buchanan, "Social Choice, Democracy, and Free Markets," in *Fiscal Theory and Political Economy*,
edited by Buchanan (Chapel Hill: University of North Carolina Press,
1960), pp. 75–89. See also Martin J. Bailey, "The Possibility of Rational
Social Choice in an Economy," *Journal of Political Economy* 87 (February 1979), pp. 37–56. On the tendency of majority voting to promote
the formation of coalitions of the smallest size consistent with winning,
see William H. Riker, *The Theory of Political Coalitions* (New Haven:
Yale University Press, 1962). The wasteful properties of majority voting
are explored in Gordon Tullock, "Some Problems of Majority Voting,"
Journal of Political Economy 67 (December 1959), pp. 571–579. For a
spirited defense of majority voting in the context of Tullock's critique,
see Anthony Downs, "In Defense of Majority Voting," *Journal of Political
Economy* 69 (April 1961), pp. 192–199. Dennis C. Mueller, *Public Choice*
(London: Cambridge University Press, 1979), presents a thorough survey
of the contemporary literature on the effort to understand the conduct of
government.

The original contribution to demand revelation is Edward H. Clarke, "Multipart Pricing of Public Goods," *Public Choice* 11 (Fall 1971), pp. 17–33. For a symposium on the demand-revealing process, see *Public Choice* 29 (Spring 1977, Supplement). Edward H. Clarke, *Demand Revelation and the Provision of Public Goods* (Cambridge, Mass.: Ballinger, 1980), is a valuable statement by the originator of the interest in demand revelation. For an experimental study with a similar orientation, see Vernon L. Smith, "The Principle of Unanimity and Voluntary Consent in Social Choice," *Journal of Political Economy* 85 (December 1977), pp. 1125–1139.

5

Representative Government and the Political Marketplace

To some extent, people vote directly on options for resource utilization: Local elections on proposals to issue bonds are common, there are town meetings in New England, and the western states permit comparatively heavy use of referenda. For the most part, however, voting on options for resource utilization is the province of elected representatives, with individual citizens voting only on the choice of who represents them. The analysis of voting in Chapter 4 applies to voting within legislatures and committees as well as to voting by citizens. Yet some properties of collective choice are unique to representative government, and we explore some of these properties in this chapter.

THE DEMAND FOR LEGISLATION

The production of legislation clearly has economic aspects. Some people desire various types of legislation, and other people supply legislation. The combination creates a market for legislation. As a point of departure, the demand for legislation would seem to be essentially the same as the demand for any product or service. Legislation is desired because it is useful to the recipient, and the less it costs, the more people will demand. The way in which legislation may advance the interests of the consumer depends, of course, on the particular interests of the consumer as well as on the type of legislation. Nonetheless, legislation is a source of utility to consumers, and we can apply the general framework of the theory of consumer choice to the demand for legislation.

Some legislation may be demanded by all or most citizens, while other legislation may be demanded by only a few. Instances of general or universal demand correspond to the common descriptions of the theory of collective goods. A desire to be free from attack by a foreign nation is surely one instance of such a demand, and a desire to be free from attack by a member of one's own nation is another. Much legislation deals with the provision of such common or general demands. Much legislation also deals with the provision of the specific wants of a subset of citizens, often at the expense of the remainder of the citizenry. In this case, legislation is not so much a means of increasing the general level of well-being as of transferring income or wealth from some people to others. Sometimes those who benefit in this process of transferring (as contrasted with creating) wealth may constitute a majority of the citizenry. At other times they may constitute only a minority. In either case, the legislation provides utility only to a subset of citizens, not to all citizens, although the cost of that legislation may be borne by everyone. If owners of property in coastal areas threatened by hurricanes secure legislation that provides subsidies for insurance and reconstruction, they gain at the expense of the remainder of the citizenry who pay the subsidies. The class of such examples is large, and an important feature of such legislation is its ability to transfer wealth from the general citizenry to those whose demands are satisfied by the legislation.

Some central features of the demand for legislation can be explored by considering the gains to a set of producers from forming a cartel. The cartel converts a competitive industry into a monopoly. In creating a cartel, the various competitive suppliers in an industry agree to reduce their output, which in turn brings about an increase in the price of the product. Figure 5.1 illustrates how such an agreement can increase profits for the firms in the industry. Cartels are, of course, illegal in the United States. Even if they were legal, they would face a strong pull to break down because each member has an incentive to chisel on the agreement. The reason for this incentive is simple and is illustrated in Figure 5.1. The cartel agreement requires that the individual firms reduce their output to below what it was in a competitive market. The cartel price exceeds the firm's marginal cost, however, and the extent of this excess shows the gain a member of the cartel can realize by expanding its own output beyond that called for by the cartel agreement. Any individual firm will therefore be tempted to produce more than it produced prior to the agreement. The members of a cartel are caught in a prisoners'

FIGURE 5.1 Gains to an Individual Firm from Creating a Cartel

Each firm in a competitive industry produces an output Q_c and the industry price is P_c. The cartel acts as if it were a monopoly and as if the individual firms were production plants; it restricts output and increases price. Let the output of a single firm be Q_m, with industry output being nQ_m, assuming either that the firm depicted is an average member of the cartel or that the cartel is composed of identical members. The resulting monopoly price is P_m. The cartel members will make a monopoly price of $P_m - C_m$ per unit of output, or a total profit per period indicated by the rectangle $P_m abC_m$. The industry profit will, of course, be n times as large.

Individual members of the cartel can increase their profits if they can violate the cartel agreement without detection. At a price of P_m, a member of the cartel will maximize profits at an output rate Q_m^*. To the extent that members attempt to profit by this opportunity for chiseling, total output will expand, the price will fall, and the cartel's effectiveness will erode.

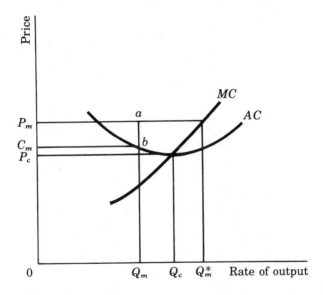

dilemma. Each member would most prefer to undercut the cartel price while the other members maintain that price. As a result the cartel tends to break down, leaving the members worse off than they would have been had they refrained from undercutting the agreement — yet undercutting is rational from the perspective of individual members.

Successful, sustained collusions seem to require legislation. At least legislation seems to be a means of enhancing the durability of cartels. Such legislation not only renders antitrust laws inapplicable but also allows the regulatory agency to act as an enforcing agency against the price-cutting temptations of member firms. The formation and maintenance of a cartel is, of course, valuable to the members of the industry. In terms of Figure 5.1, each firm receives cartel or monopoly profits equal to the excess of price over average cost multiplied by the number of units it sells.

Suppose that eggs are supplied competitively and that the formation of a cartel to market eggs within a state would yield profits to an average producer of $1,000 per year.[1] For a cartel of 1,000 producers, the annual gain from a successful cartel agreement would be $1 million. The present value of that agreement would, of course, depend on the rate of discount and on the anticipated durability of the agreement. If the agreement were anticipated to be of indefinite durability and the rate of discount were 10 percent, a successful agreement would have a present value of $10 million to the members of the cartel. Higher discount rates and a decrease in anticipated durability would reduce the present value of the agreement. If the agreement were anticipated to last only four years, for example, and if the rate of discount were 20 percent, the present value, with interest compounded annually, would be just under $2.6 million.[2]

Clearly, the greater the durability of legislation that grants monopoly profits to favored interests, the greater the value of that legislation to those interests. It may be impossible, even with the backing of legislation, for the members of a cartel to prevent erosion of their monopoly profits, however. Even though the Civil Aeronautics Board (CAB) regulated the prices airlines charged and prevented entry into the industry, it was unable to prevent the erosion of the airline cartel's profits. The CAB was effective in preventing price cutting, precluding entry by new airlines, and protecting routes, but it was not able to offset the incentive of members to compete for business through what is sometimes called quality competition.

Suppose a member of the cartel serves a route for which the regulated price of an airline seat is $200 and the marginal cost of a seat is $100. By offering such "extras" as roomier planes, more frequent flights, a three-night stay in a resort hotel for $25, and so on, airlines can attract additional business. As long as the cost of the extra services being offered is less than $100, a member of the cartel has an incentive to compete for additional business by providing

[1] For an interesting examination of cartels in the supply of eggs, see Thomas Borcherding and Gary W. Dorosh, *The Egg Marketing Board* (Vancouver, B. C.: Fraser Institute, 1981). This study found that the marketing board was responsible for an increase of about 20 percent in the price of eggs.

[2] Computed as follows: $(\$1,000,000/1.2) + (\$1,000,000/1.2^2) + (\$1,000,000/1.2^3) + (\$1,000,000/1.2^4) = \$2,588,735.$

more valued or higher-quality services because any patronage that results will still contribute more in revenue than it adds in cost.

We should not make too much of the temporary nature of the monopoly profits that favorable legislation may create even if it is incapable of preventing eventual erosion. For a firm that discounts the future at 10 percent, annual profits of $1 million have a present value of $10 million if they are anticipated to last indefinitely. But even if those profits are anticipated to last only seven years, their present value of $4.9 million is still nearly half their value at indefinite durability. Seven years is practically half as good as forever in this instance.[3]

THE SUPPLY OF LEGISLATION

Legislation is utility enhancing or wealth enhancing, sometimes for citizens generally and sometimes for a subset of the citizenry. In the latter case, the gains to one subset may come at the expense of the rest of society, as when consumers pay higher prices for eggs because legislation creates a monopoly over what would otherwise be the competitive provision of eggs. The supply of legislation, like the supply of any product or service, can be understood largely in terms of its ability to yield a return to the suppliers. Both political parties and individual legislators are suppliers of legislation, and both realize returns from their roles as suppliers. Political parties supply their members to legislatures, and those members (legislators) supply legislation to the citizenry.

The individual politicians who belong to a party and to a legislature are analogous to the partners in a business partnership. As in partnerships, some of the legislators are senior to others and therefore more influential within the party and the legislature. The electoral system provides the rules by which someone becomes a partner —that is, joins the legislature as a member of a particular party. In the United States, legislators are distributed according to geography, and the legislator for some designated geographical territory is elected by citizens (clients in the business analogy) who live in that territory.

The constitutional framework of a society influences the number of parties that participate in supplying legislators, and it also constrains the process by which legislators enact legislation. If voters have only one vote and if the candidate who receives the largest

---

[3] With a 20 percent rate of discount, the present value of $1 million for four years is $2.6 million, which is more than half the $5 million it would be if that amount were to continue indefinitely.

number of votes is elected to join the legislature, a two-party system tends to emerge. It is easy to understand why this is so. Suppose that three parties are competing for election and that voter support is equally distributed among the parties. Over a sequence of elections, each party can expect to win one-third of the elections and, accordingly, hold office one-third of the time. But this outcome is not stable. If two of the parties were to merge, the new party would win every election, and the individual supporters of the original parties could expect to be in office half of the time rather than one-third of the time. Suppose one party were to attract supporters away from one or both of the others parties, boosting its electoral share to, say, 40 percent and reducing the shares of the other two parties to 30 percent each. In this case, the more popular party can expect to hold office indefinitely, unless something else happens, such as a merger of the two smaller parties. Thus there are strong reasons why an electoral system that elects a single candidate by plurality will tend to produce two parties.[4]

The returns to legislators from being elected can have many dimensions: basic salary and expense allowances, business for a law firm in which a legislator is a partner, bribes, the prospect of postlegislative employment in a business that has extensive dealings with government, a fascination with politics and the use of power, a sense of vocation in helping the nation or community deal effectively with the problems before it, and so on. We do not need to be concerned with the reasons legislators run for office any more than with the reasons accountants become accountants or lawyers become lawyers. The relative importance of material and nonmaterial considerations varies among legislators as well as among other people in other occupations. However, all are engaged to a large extent in satisfying or supplying the demands of their clients.

Regardless of legislators' ultimate source of motivation, they are engaged in producing legislation that their clients wish to have; otherwise they will find it difficult to remain elected. The relationship between legislators and clients is not, of course, formalized as in the case of accountants or lawyers and their clients, but legislators are, like accountants or lawyers, in the business of promoting the interests of their clients. Legislators get elected because a sufficient number of people in their geographical territories think they will best serve their interests. They must maintain this support to get reelected, which requires that they follow through in promoting the interests of an electorate.

---

[4] Other electoral systems may produce a different pattern of parties. A system in which several candidates are elected from a single district, with each voter casting only one vote, tends to produce multiple parties.

Several features of the organization of legislatures increase the value of the legislation produced, both to the legislators and to the party. A party can engage in producing and selling legislation. When it does so, it must develop and market its product, legislation, just as any business would engage in product development and marketing. Among other things, the party must acquire knowledge about probable market (that is, citizen) reactions to possible legislative offerings. By placing its own members on committees and subcommittees that are tailored to particular interests, a party can effectively gauge the demand for various types of legislation. If it chooses to support legislation responsive to the demands of the largest or most valued group of citizens, the party can increase its profit from the provision of the legislation.[5]

As long as the legislative assembly by and large enacts what the various committees approve, the use of committees can enable the governing party to increase the value to itself of the legislative agenda. For instance, if the legislative session is 200 days long and if it takes the legislature an average of one day of deliberation to gauge demand, the legislature will be able to enact a maximum of 200 bills. If the legislature is separated into 20 committees, however, and if each committee can produce one bill a day, assuming the legislature enacts the bills the committees sponsor, the total legislature will be able to produce 4,000 bills. The practice of assigning legislators to committees according to their interest in different types of legislation can help the political party achieve maximum value from the legislation that is enacted.

For the most part, the market for legislation works tacitly rather than explicitly. Those who gain from the legislation, certain subsets of the citizenry, will to some extent pay for it, which allows sellers, the legislators and political parties, to capture some of the gains as well. There is no open market for votes on various bills, although such instances do surface from time to time. The tacit nature of the market for legislation does not deny that those who gain from individual pieces of legislation dissipate part of their gains by making payments to the suppliers. Rather it suggests that the payments take such tacit forms as campaign contributions, support of favored causes, the use of particular law firms, and the like. To speak of a market for legislation is not to deny that legislation may reflect a concern with promoting the common good; it does suggest, though, that a substantial component of legislation can be understood as serving

[5] Arleen Leibowitz and Robert Tollison, "A Theory of Legislative Organization: Making the Most of Your Majority," *Quarterly Journal of Economics* 94 (March 1980), pp. 261–277, examines how a committee system allows a governing party to increase the value of the agenda it is able to enact.

special interests, even if this is to the detriment of the common interest.

The survival value of such legislation, as we saw previously, can be understood in terms of the pattern of costs and gains produced by a system of majoritarian democracy. An economic approach to the production of legislation suggests that legislation is supplied because it advances the interests of those on the demand and the supply sides of the market. The nature of those interests and the concrete character of the legislation that results depend on the constitutional order that constrains political activity. Legislation will take on different patterns, for instance, when legislative action is taken by majority rule and when it is taken under some system of qualified majority or some procedure for demand revelation. This proposition is, of course, no different from the proposition that a chemical manufacturer will act differently if it has to buy the consent of a downstream user to dump wastes into a river than if it does not.

POLITICAL ENTREPRENEURSHIP
AND MAJORITARIAN DEMOCRACY

Economists who study the economic consequences of political institutions are increasingly recognizing that majoritarian democracy is to some extent a vehicle for the creation of externalities. In a majoritarian democracy, those who possess the ability to commit resources to specific uses can impose part of the cost of their choices on others. Suppose an entrepreneur thinks that the assembly of land, utilities, boats, and water slides that are necessary to develop a park at a nearby lake will be a profitable activity. If this judgment is correct, resources will have been reallocated from less valuable to more valuable uses, and consumers as well as the entrepreneur will gain from this reallocation. If the entrepreneur's choice proves mistaken and leads to a loss, resources will have been shifted to less valued uses, leaving both the entrepreneur and the members of society generally worse off.

It is, of course, in no one's power to guarantee that a particular employment of resources will prove to be profitable — that is, will shift resources from less valued to more valued uses. The failures of entrepreneurial undertakings are negative verdicts on presumptions of the entrepreneurs that they were undertaking positive-sum transformations of resources. Negative-sum tranformations of resources are unavoidable, even without the difficulties that might arise because ownership may be ill defined, nonexclusive, and nontransferable. A regime of property and contract cannot prevent negative-sum transformations of resources, but its residual-claimant property, in which the entrepreneur reaps the profits from positive-sum transformations and bears the losses from negative-sum transformations, induces more careful and judicious judgment than if the profits and losses of entrepreneurial choices were borne by the entire population. It also offers a stronger incentive to curb negative-sum transformations once they are recognized.

Majoritarian democracy operates under a somewhat different pattern of incentive. Among other things, it offers an incentive to undertake negative-sum transformations of resource so long as the gains can be concentrated among a controlling subset of the population. A 200-acre park may have been the profit-maximizing choice under a regime of property and contract. Suppose, however, that use of the park is concentrated among a bare majority of population but that taxes are apportioned uniformly throughout the population. In this case, users receive nearly a 50 percent subsidy, financed by the taxes extracted from the nonusers. Just as chemical manufacturers will use rivers more intensively as sewers when they can impose part of the cost of doing so on others, so the users of the park will support a larger and more costly facility when they can impose part of its cost on others. Indeed, this property of majoritarian democracy was what James Madison recognized as the "violence of faction" (*Federalist*, No. 10) and that he sought to control by designing a constitution that restrained the latent interest of parliamentary majorities in passing the costs of their choices on to the remainder of society.

An important aspect of majoritarian democracy is the incentive it offers participants for using legislation as a means of transferring wealth, with those transfers taking place through expansions in various programs of public expenditure and regulation. On initial inspection, we might see such wealth transfers as only zero sum and not negative sum because the winners' gain comes at the losers' expense. However, to the extent that those transfers reduce the net return people can anticipate from working and saving, people may do less of each. When this happens, wealth is destroyed and not simply transferred. Moreover, the availability of such transfers as a potential source of wealth will induce people to shift resources away from creating wealth and toward pursuing transfers. Less effort will be devoted to the production and marketing of, say, eggs and more will be devoted to seeking wealth transfers through favorable action from an egg marketing board. These activities that focus on transfers of wealth are essentially nonproductive, yet they may yield greater personal returns than would result from the expenditure of additional effort in the production of eggs. Any shift of resources from pursuing the creation of wealth to seeking the transfer of wealth

— as well as activities involved in guarding against such transfers — is actually a destruction of wealth.

Although negative-sum transformations of resources are unavoidable when entrepreneurs lack omniscience about such things as consumer preferences, there seem to be asymmetries in prevailing political institutions that increase such transformations compared with what would happen under a regime of property and contract. There are asymmetries both between the locus of the costs and the benefits of government programs and between the knowledge held by the gainers and that held by the losers of public programs. The benefits are generally more concentrated than the costs. This gives gainers a stronger interest in supporting programs than it gives losers an interest in opposing those programs; it seems generally less costly to inform those who benefit than to inform those who bear the cost. It is surely less costly for potential users of a proposed campground and park to learn what they will gain than it is for the others to learn what they will lose, perhaps an otherwise lower tax bill. It is less costly for domestic automobile producers and the United Auto Workers to learn of the benefits they will receive from a program limiting Japanese imports than it is for citizens to learn of the costs to them of the program, such as higher prices of cars and higher taxes.

Indeed, protectionist legislation has long served to illustrate how asymmetries in the degree of interest among people can promote the survival of negative-sum activities and programs. Even though the loss to consumers may exceed the gain to producers, the concentrated interest of producers dominates the diffused interest of consumers. Consider the government's imposition of restrictions on the import of beef. Such a restriction in the supply of beef increases its price. For producers of beef, this price increase translates directly into an increase in income. Consumers of beef, however, spend money on many products, so a rise in the price of beef will cause only a relatively small drop in their real incomes. If consumers spend 5 percent of their income on beef, a 10 percent rise in the price of beef will, as a first approximation, reduce their real income by just 0.5 percent. But for the producers of beef, that 10 percent increase in price will, as a first approximation, increase their real income by 10 percent. Through such asymmetries, negative-sum programs that transfer wealth to the winners acquire in the process an ability to survive in a system of majoritarian democracy.[6]

The asymmetries that we have noted, as well as others that have

[6] This thesis was sketched by Anthony Downs in *An Economic Theory of Democracy* (New York: Harper & Row, 1957), and extended by Mancur Olson, Jr., in *The Logic of Collective Action* (Cambridge, Mass.: Harvard University Press, 1965).

been discussed in various writings, are all reflections of the one fundamental asymmetry we noted earlier: the absence of a quid pro quo relationship between the claims government places on citizens and the services it renders in return. The negative-sum expansion of government becomes possible and actually results because there is no contractual relationship between government and individual citizens. Those who have no use for the campground and park must pay for it anyway; those who would like to use it can — to the extent they are able to place the cost on others — do so without paying for it. One important incentive that seems to characterize majoritarian democracy is the incentive to design policies that take from some citizens to give to others, with wealth being dissipated in the process.

REPRESENTATION, MAJORITY RULE, AND MINORITY DOMINANCE

It is easy to understand how a system of majoritarian democracy can enact negative-sum legislation that benefits a majority of citizens at the expense of a minority. But, as we noted above, it is also possible for legislation to benefit a minority at the expense of a majority. This can come about if losses imposed on individuals are sufficiently small that it becomes impossible for anyone to marshal the losers in opposition to the legislation. The creation of an egg marketing board, for instance, may transfer $50,000 to each of 1,000 growers. But the $50 million loss suffered by the general public will impose a per capita loss of only $5 in a state with 10 million people.[7]

People must invest some effort in finding out enough about the issue to reach this determination. It may not be worthwhile for many people to make that effort when the stakes are relatively small. Even if a person were to invest enough effort to acquire knowledge about the loss to consumers from the creation of an egg marketing board, he could not act effectively on that information. He could not prevent the loss without convincing a sufficient number of other people about it. Accordingly, it is rational for people to be more innocent about the cost of proposed legislation — except where they have a concentrated interest — than about the cost of options available to them privately because only in the latter case is it possible to gain directly from knowledge they acquire. Consequently, legislators will gain

---

[7] Strictly speaking, the per capita loss will be a little more than $5. Besides the transfer, a further loss arises because resources are shifted out of the production of eggs into other avenues of production where they are valued less highly. This excess burden or deadweight loss is also part of the cost inflicted on the general public.

little in trying to oppose such programs as the creation of egg marketing boards because they will be unable to convince their constituents of their opposition.

Representative democracy can also delegate choice to a minority in other ways. At base, a requirement of majority approval within a legislature may imply the approval of only one-quarter of the underlying population, even setting aside possible asymmetries such as those resulting from lack of information among some constituents. Suppose a government has eighty-one citizens, grouped into nine legislative districts of nine members each. Assuming there are no asymmetries, a bill can pass in the legislature even if it benefits only twenty-five citizens at the expense of the remaining fifty-six. This would result if the bill had the support of five residents in each of five districts and no support elsewhere. Indeed, as the number of districts expands, the minimum degree of support consistent with a majority in the legislature approaches 25 percent.

This point is intuitively simple. Suppose a bill has a bare majority of support in a bare majority of districts. As the number of districts expands, this becomes the support of just over one-half of the voters in just over one-half of the districts, or just over one-quarter of the voters, assuming equally populous districts. Suppose the government is on an island in which five of the districts incorporate coastal areas and four are exclusively interior. In each of the coastal districts, five residents own coastal property and four reside in the interior of the district. A proposal is advanced for some coastal development project that will provide benefits to the owners of coastal property, paid for by taxes on all. This means a net loss for the owners of interior property. While the legislators of the four interior districts would oppose the bill, the legislators of the five coastal districts would support it. Majority rule would approve a bill that had nearly 70 percent opposition, and the degree of opposition could approach 75 percent and still be supported by a majority within the legislature.

Even if a bill benefits only a minority of legislative districts at the expense of a majority, it can still be enacted through logrolling. The coastal development bill may benefit only one legislative district and so by itself would not pass the legislature. But if support on that bill can be tied in with support on bills favored by legislators in other districts, it is possible to find a set of bills that receives majority support. In this case, each bill benefits a minority at the expense of a majority, and the entire set of bills enacted is negative sum.

Table 5.1 presents hypothetical data that illustrate this point.[8]

[8] For an experimental study that supports this point, see Richard D. McKelvey and Peter C. Ordeshook, "Vote Trading: An Experimental Study," *Public Choice* 35, No. 2 (1980), pp. 151–184.

TABLE 5.1 Hypothetical Value of Bills A–E, by
Legislative District

District	Value of Bill if Enacted (in dollars)				
	A	B	C	D	E
1	10	−2	−4	−4	−2
2	−2	10	−2	−4	−4
3	−4	−2	10	−2	−4
4	−4	−4	−2	10	−2
5	−2	−4	−4	−2	10

There are five legislative districts, each of which support a bill of interest to the residents of that district only, which means four-fifths of the cost of each bill will be imposed on the residents of the other districts. Each of the five bills is worth $10 to the members of the sponsoring district and imposes a total loss of $12 on the other four districts. The value-maximizing outcome is the one in which all five bills fail. With majority voting, however, there are five equally likely coalitions, with each coalition able to enact three bills.

A coalition between districts 1, 2, and 3 will enact bills A, B, and C and reject bills D and E. District 1 gains $10 by the passage of A, while it loses $2 from the passage of B and $4 from the passage of C, giving it a net gain of $4. District 2 gains $10 from the passage of B, and it loses $2 each from the passage of A and C, giving it a net gain of $6. District 3 gains $10 from the passage of C, while it loses $4 from the passage of A and $2 from the passage of B, giving it a net gain of $4. District 4 loses $4 each from the passage of A and B and loses $2 from the passage of C, giving it a net loss of $10. District 5 loses $2 from the passage of A and $4 each from the passage of B and C, giving it a net loss of $10. Regardless of the particular coalition that forms, there will be a net social loss of $6. This loss, however, will be concentrated among those who are excluded from the winning coalition. The members of the winning coalition will gain, although the size of their gains will be less than the size of the losses to the others. In many cases, then, a system of majority voting within a legislative assembly is actually equivalent to a system of minority rule within the population represented.

Majoritarian democracy understandably is open to the enactment of programs that benefit a majority at the expense of a minority, and such programs tend to be expanded beyond efficient size because such expansions are a vehicle for achieving the transfers of wealth that majoritarian democracy encourages. As we have seen, though, majoritarian, representative democracy can also lead to the enactment of programs that benefit a minority at the expense of a majority, which results in even more social waste.

To illustrate this point, Peter Aranson and Peter Ordeshook have asked rhetorically what would happen to a bill to provide special benefits for blacksmiths, financed by general taxes, if there were only 218 blacksmiths left in the United States, with each living in a different congressional district and distributed among at least twenty-six states.[9] The imposition of a loss of 1 cent per person would provide a transfer of about $1,000 per blacksmith. So long as it is costly to become informed on an issue, legislation that imposes comparatively small costs on many for the substantial benefit of a few seems to have survival value in a system of majoritarian democracy.

SUGGESTIONS FOR FURTHER READING

Robert E. McCormick and Robert D. Tollison, *Politicians, Legislation, and the Economy* (Boston: Martinus Nijhoff, 1981), explores the extent to which legislation can be understood as a process of transferring wealth from losers to winners, with different constitutional orders serving as different types of constraint upon this process. Richard D. Auster and Morris Silver, *The State as a Firm* (Boston: Martinus Nijhoff, 1979), treats government as a monopolistic firm, with democracy being one particular form of ownership in which its diffused and nontransferable character is of pivotal importance. Albert Breton, *The Economic Theory of Representative Government* (Chicago: Aldine, 1974), also emphasizes what can be called the monopolistic over the competitive aspects of democratic government.

The use of regulation as a means of transferring wealth to favored interests — that is, those who purchase the legislation, rather than promoting some notion of the public interest — has been the subject of an increasing volume of literature. A survey of these alternative approaches to regulation is presented in Richard A. Posner, "Theories of Economic Regulation," *Bell Journal of Economics and Management Science* 5 (Autumn 1974), pp. 335–358. The seminal treatment of what has come to be called rent seeking as a negative-sum activity in which resources are diverted from productive into appropriative activity is Gordon Tullock, "The Welfare Costs of Tariffs, Monopolies, and Theft," *Western Economic Journal* 5 (June 1967), pp. 224–232. Tullock's essential point is explored in an international context in Anne O. Krueger, "The Political Economy

[9] Peter H. Aranson and Peter C. Ordeshook, "A Prolegomenon to a Theory of the Failure of Representative Democracy," in *American Re-evolution: Papers and Proceedings,* edited by R. Auster and B. Sears (Tucson: University of Arizona Press, 1977), pp. 23–46.

of the Rent-Seeking Society," *American Economic Review* 64 (June 1974), pp. 291–303. For a collection of essays on rent seeking, see James M. Buchanan, Robert D. Tollison, and Gordon Tullock, editors, *Toward a Theory of the Rent-Seeking Society* (College Station: Texas A&M University Press, 1980).

Dwight R. Lee and Daniel Orr, "Two Laws of Survival for Ascriptive Government Policies," pp. 113–124 in *Toward a Theory of the Rent-Seeking Society,* examines the transitory nature of monopoly profits created through regulation. Paul H. Rubin, "On the Form of Special Interest Legislation," *Public Choice* 21 (Spring 1975), pp. 79–90, examines how the use of relatively inefficient forms of legislation may increase the durability of the transfers created by that legislation. William M. Landes and Richard A. Posner, "The Independent Judiciary in an Interest-Group Perspective," *Journal of Law and Economics* 18 (December 1975), pp. 875–901, describes how an independent judiciary also increases the durability of the wealth transfers created by legislation. For an effort to distinguish between elements of self-interest and general interest in legislative outcomes, see James B. Kau and Paul H. Rubin, "Self-Interest, Ideology, and Logrolling in Congressional Voting," *Journal of Law and Economics* 22 (October 1979), pp. 365–384.

6

Bureaucracy
and the Supply
of Public Output

Legislatures enact programs of expenditure and regulation, and the implementation of these programs rests with a variety of executive departments and independent agencies. The Department of Transportation implements many transportation programs, but so do independent agencies such as the Civil Aeronautics Board and the Federal Aviation Administration. In this book we refer to both executive departments and independent agencies by the generic term *bureaus*, which are nonprofit organizations whose activities are financed through appropriations from the legislature. Sometimes the legislature's appropriations are supplemented by fees collected from users. In a few instances, such as municipally owned utilities, such fees may be the exclusive source of revenue, at least for annual operating expenses if not for capital expenses.

Public bureaus differ from profit-seeking firms both in the form of ownership and in the method of financing. Unlike firms, bureaus possess no residual-claimant status; any profits or losses are diffused among taxpayers rather than concentrated on those who make the choices concerning the use of resources. Shares of ownership in bureaus are nontransferable. A resident of a particular jurisdiction acquires, as it were, one share of ownership upon taking residence, maintains this share as long as residence is maintained, and can — and indeed must — relinquish this share upon moving out of the jurisdiction. Firms derive their revenues from the payments of their customers. Bureaus, however, rarely price their services, and some of those that do also receive additional revenues through legislative appropriations. The differences in forms of ownership and sources of revenue generate systematic differences in the conduct of firms and bureaus. This chapter explores two main topics regarding the supply of services by public bureaus: the differences between bureaus and firms in their patterns of resource utilization and the reasons for the use of bureaus in place of some alternative arrangement such as governmental contracting with firms.

OWNERSHIP, INCENTIVE, AND ORGANIZATIONAL CONDUCT

The impact of institutional framework on organizational performance has been an important part of economics at least since Adam Smith enunciated the general principle that "public services are never better performed than when their [public officials'] reward comes only in consequence of their being performed, and is proportioned to the diligence employed in performing them." [1] A corollary of this principle is, of course, that the manner in which public services are performed depends on the way in which performance is rewarded. The stronger the connection between payment and performance, the more intensely public officials will exert themselves to perform effectively. Prison officials will surely make more strenuous efforts to develop successful programs of prisoner rehabilitation if their own compensation varies directly with the earnings of released prisoners, or even inversely with the rate of recidivism of prisoners in their charge, than if their compensation is based simply on the number of years they have been on the job. Similarly, parole officials will surely make more strenuous efforts to predict the future conduct of potential parolees if their own compensation varies inversely with the number of parole violations, or directly with the subsequent earnings of parolees, than if their compensation is invariant to such factors.

Despite this link between the diligence of effort and the form of compensation, it may not be a simple matter to choose an appropriate form of compensation. Smith noted that in his time it was common to pay lawyers according to the number of words they wrote.[2] The result was, predictably, voluminous legal documents. Alternatively, in the early days of Soviet planning some manufacturers of nails were paid by the ton, which was thought to provide an incentive to

---

[1] Adam Smith, *Wealth of Nations* (New York: Modern Library, 1937 [1776]), p. 678. On this general characteristic of Smith's approach to economics, see Nathan Rosenberg, "Some Institutional Aspects of the *Wealth of Nations*," *Journal of Political Economy* 68 (December 1960), pp. 557–570.

[2] Smith, *Wealth of Nations*, p. 680.

produce. However, much of the resulting output was useful only to fasten railroad tracks to their ties. When the Soviets attempted to correct this malincentive by basing payment on the number of nails produced, many of the nails that subsequently were produced were useful for little other than light carpentry. Similarly, if police officers are paid by the number of arrests they make or the number of traffic citations they issue, they certainly will make more arrests or issue more citations than if they are paid simply by the week or month. But recognition that diligence in endeavors such as issuing citations varies directly with the extent to which that diligence is rewarded does not imply that such a means of payment would be desirable because desirable performance may involve more than a single-minded devotion to making arrests or issuing citations. To some extent, then, the development of forms of compensation that implement Adam Smith's dictum becomes problematic, despite the apparently reasonable-sounding character of that dictum.

In a market setting, the existence of a residual-claimant status resolves these matters of incentive. The manufacturer of nails is not simply induced to be diligent in producing nails. He is above all else induced to produce nails of the type that are most valuable to his customers, for otherwise customers will not buy and the producer will earn nothing for his efforts. The lawyer is not induced simply to maximize the pages written, but to maximize the value of his services to his clients. Without a residual-claimant status, and in the presence of an alternative form of incentive payment as described above, there would seem to be no basis on which to argue that legal services, nails, police protection, or anything else will be produced so as to maximize its value to consumers.

The residual-claimant status of business firms tends to induce them to produce their output with the least cost, as well as to produce the type or quality of product that consumers want. To fail to do this would diminish the wealth of the residual claimant. If a private police or detective service could conduct its present scale of operation for $1 million, but spends $1.2 million instead, the owners of the firm will bear the $200,000 loss.[3] In contrast, the nontransferability of ownership rights in public bureaus diminishes this incentive to produce output with the least cost. For one thing, any losses (or profits) are diffused throughout the entire population, instead of being concentrated on those responsible for the bureau's conduct. Moreover, an excess of actual cost of production over potential minimum cost

---

[3] With a tax on corporate profits, this loss would be shared with the government through a reduction in tax liability.

can be, in the absence of residual claimancy, a means by which the bureau's "profits" are captured.

Appropriation of Profits in Bureaus

The first reason for higher cost of output — the diffusion of the costs and gains from excessive expenses — would seem to require little further comment. The second reason, however, raises more interesting questions. Bureaus may be nonprofit institutions in name, but this does not mean they are nonprofit in fact. Although bureau profits may not be directly appropriable by bureau officials, there may be indirect methods of appropriation. The higher cost of bureau services may be a sign not of bureau inefficiency, but of the appropriation of profits, with an excess of actual expenditures over the amount required to provide a particular quality of output being a technique for appropriating those profits.

Different bureaus face different opportunities for appropriating profits and, looking ahead, different bureaus reflect different types of legislative interests. A public hospital, for instance, may appropriate profits by overinvesting in expensive equipment that is underutilized, perhaps to subsidize the research of the physicians whose interests dominate the bureau. A highway department may appropriate profits by awarding contracts at higher than necessary prices, perhaps to a construction firm owned by a relative of a high-level official. A public school may appropriate profits by paying a higher than necessary fee to its law firm, which may have as a partner the chairman of the legislature's education committee. The ways in which profits can be appropriated through expenditures that are higher than necessary are practically limitless. Moreover, the pattern of appropriation that results is unlikely to be random or haphazard but is likely to be systematically related to the interests of high-level officials in the bureau and of those legislators who have oversight responsibility for the bureau.

Whenever any excess of revenues over expenses cannot be directly appropriated, it is unlikely that any such excess will arise in the first place. Public bureaus certainly do not compete among themselves to return unspent revenues to the treasury. There is no incentive to do so. Bureau officials cannot capture a share of what they return. There can be an incentive, however, to appropriate the profits indirectly through a rise in expenditures to meet the revenues that have been provided through appropriations. To the extent that this happens, the actual expenditures of a bureau will exceed the amount for which the output could have been provided; this excess represents both the bureau's profit and the form by which that profit is indirectly appropriated. Empirically, this appropriation of profit will show up as a higher cost for a service provided by a bureau than for the same service provided by a private firm. A bureau's cost function will be higher than a firm's because the additional spending is the vehicle by which profits are appropriated. If bureaus were converted to firms, the appropriation of profits would take place directly, with the cost function then being equal to that of profit-seeking firms.

Empirical Studies

A variety of examples exist where firms and bureaus provide similar services, and the presence of such duplication makes possible some empirical examination of the appropriation of profits in bureaus, or at least of the higher cost of output. A number of such studies have been undertaken recently, and while they do not all reach the same conclusion, the weight of evidence seems to suggest that bureaus provide services in more costly fashion than do firms. David Davies examined the comparative efficiency of two Australian airlines, one a private firm with transferable ownership rights and the other a public bureau with nontransferable ownership.[4] The Australian government specified routes, schedules, prices, and type of aircraft so as to achieve approximately identical conditions for each carrier. In spite of this strenuous effort to equalize competition, the productivity of the private firm seems to have been considerably higher than the productivity of the public bureau over the 1958–1969 period initially examined by Davies, as well as over the 1969–1974 period he subsequently examined. The private firm carried an average of 10.73 tons of freight and mail per employee while the public bureau carried only 4.86 tons per employee. Similarly, the private firm carried an average of 337 passengers per employee and the public bureau carried an average of only 279 passengers. Finally, the private firm earned an average of $9,627 per employee, while the public bureau earned only $8,428 per employee.

Roger Ahlbrandt compared the costliness of public bureaus and private firms in providing fire protection.[5] Scottsdale, Arizona, contracts with a private company for the provision of fire services, al-

---

[4] David G. Davies, "The Efficiency of Public Versus Private Firms: The Case of Australia's Two Airlines," *Journal of Law and Economics* 14 (April 1971), pp. 149–165. For further information, see Davies, "Property Rights and Economic Efficiency: The Australian Case Revisited," *Journal of Law and Economics* 20 (April 1977), pp. 223–226.

[5] Roger Ahlbrandt, "Efficiency in the Provision of Fire Services," *Public Choice* 16 (Fall 1973), pp. 1–16.

though public provision of fire protection is far more common nation-wide. Ahlbrandt estimated a cost function for forty-four public fire departments in the Seattle, Washington, metropolitan area and then used this estimate to predict fire protection expenses for cities in Arizona in which fire protection was provided by public bureaus. The relationship that Ahlbrandt estimated for the cities in the Seattle area predicted accurately the expenses of publicly provided fire protection in Arizona, but it did not predict accurately the expenses of fire protection in Scottsdale. Ahlbrandt's prediction was that the annual per capita expense of fire protection in Scottsdale would be $7.10, but the actual expense was only $3.78. There could, of course, be something unique about Scottsdale that sets it apart from other Arizona cities. If so, it could not be inferred that Scottsdale's lower cost was attributable to its private provision of fire protection. Ahlbrandt could find no other sources of difference, however, which suggests that the difference in cost seems reasonably attributable to the difference in method of providing fire protection.

In a similar vein, Robert Spann examined refuse collection in Monmouth County, New Jersey.[6] He compared annual per capita expenses of refuse collection by public sanitation bureaus and collection by private contractors. While the annual expense was $8.33 for collection by public bureaus, it was only $5.84 for collection by private firms. In this instance, public bureaus were 43 percent more costly than private firms. James Bennett and Manuel Johnson examined refuse collection in Fairfax County, Virginia.[7] About one-third of the homes in the area used a once-weekly public service, costing an average of $126.80 per year. The remainder used various private collection services, usually with twice-weekly collections. The average annual cost of private collection was $85.76. In this instance, public refuse collection was nearly 50 percent more expensive than private collection and also involved less frequent service.

Other studies could also be reported, most of which would generally reinforce the proposition that provision by public bureaus is more costly than provision by private firms. We should note that the higher cost of bureau supply does not mean that bureaus are lax, inefficient

[6] Robert M. Spann, "Public Versus Private Provision of Governmental Services," in *Budgets and Bureaucrats,* edited by Thomas E. Borcherding (Durham, N.C.: Duke University Press, 1977), pp. 71–89.

[7] James T. Bennett and Manuel H. Johnson, "Public Versus Private Provision of Collective Goods and Services: Garbage Collection Revisited," *Public Choice* 34, No. 1 (1979), pp. 55–63. For a survey of a variety of studies on this topic, covering such services as refuse collection, fire protection, debt collection, hospitals and health care, ship repair, utilities, and airline service, see Bennett and Johnson, "Tax Reduction Without Sacrifice: Private-Sector Production of Public Services," *Public Finance Quarterly* 8 (October 1980), pp. 363–396.

organizations where people come to work late, leave early, take long lunch breaks, and play cards in between. Rather, such observations are consistent with the proposition that bureaus are tightly run organizations in which people work as hard as their counterparts in private firms. It is not that private firms encourage diligence and public bureaus encourage sloth; both encourage diligence, but the different institutional environments channel that diligence in different directions.

Likewise, the finding that public bureaus produce in a more costly manner than private firms is not universal. Douglas Caves and Laurits Christensen found essentially no difference between public and private railroads in Canada in the rates of productivity growth over the 1956–1975 period.[8] Some studies have even found public bureaus to produce in a less costly manner than private firms. Donn Pescatrice and John Trapani studied electric utilities in the United States between 1965 and 1970, thirty-three of which were private, twenty-three public.[9] They estimated that the public firms were about 24 to 33 percent cheaper than the private firms, possibly because the method by which the rates of private utilities are commonly regulated — so as to achieve a target rate of return on the firm's capital base — can in some cases give regulated private utilities an incentive to produce in a more costly, capital-intensive manner than they would produce in the absence of regulation.

It can be instructive to explore cases where public provision of a service seems to be less expensive than private provision. For one thing, the actual services provided may differ systematically in quality. A number of states give a monopoly to state liquor stores over the sale of alcoholic beverages. A study of the cost of providing alcoholic beverages in public bureaus and in private firms may well show that state stores have a lower cost per case of product sold. In this instance the interests advanced by the legislation creating the state monopoly may be those of the relatively few producers whose products are sold in the state and of the prohibitionists who, unable to attain prohibition, are able to make access to alcoholic beverages more difficult. The cost of private provision might be higher because the competitive process leads private firms to stock a wide variety of merchandise, keep long hours, and cash checks and accept credit cards, whereas the public stores would not do such things. Moreover, a number of private stores may serve the same area covered by a

[8] Douglas W. Caves and Laurits R. Christensen, "The Relative Efficiency of Public and Private Firms in a Competitive Environment: The Case of Canadian Railroads," *Journal of Political Economy* 88 (October 1980), pp. 958–976.

[9] Donn R. Pescatrice and John M. Trapani III, "The Performance and Objectives of Public and Private Utilities Operating in the United States," *Journal of Public Economics* 13 (April 1980), pp. 259–276.

single public store, so the system of private stores would save customers' time.

Instances in which the public provision of a service seems to be less expensive than private provision may not disturb the central point about the dissipation of profits resulting from legislation, but it can create an awareness that the way in which the profits resulting from legislation are dissipated can take on many specific forms. In some cases the profits from legislation may be appropriated in a cost-reducing manner, at least with respect to the way cost is typically assessed in such studies.

BUREAUS AND THE LEGISLATURE

Besides the absence of transferable ownership, bureaus differ from firms in the identity of their customers. The people who use a private campground or attend a private school are the customers whom the firm must continue to please in order to succeed. Bureaus, however, are not financed by fees paid by individual customers. People pay no fees for public schools, except for universities, and they pay only nominal fees for public parks and campgrounds. The bureau's customers are not the people who queue for space at a campground or try to get satisfaction from their child's teacher or principal. Rather, the bureau's customers must properly be considered the legislature and the interests the legislature represents in particular legislation. Although the user pays for a private school or campground, the legislature, not the parent or the camper, pays for public schools and campgrounds. Accordingly, the bureau does not have to please the parent or the camper directly to prosper. It has to please the legislature, which may amount to something quite different from pleasing customers or citizens generally. This difference in the identity of the customer should lead to differences in the nature of the services provided by public bureaus, because services become adapted to the particular interests reflected in the relevant legislation. In some cases this may imply higher-quality services, such as more equipment in hospitals. In other cases it may mean lower-quality services, such as longer waits and shorter hours of operation of numerous retail-like activities of government bureaus. The difference in the identity of their customers creates differences in the incentives private firms and public bureaus have to emphasize certain characteristics of services over others.

To some extent, of course, the legislature will reflect the interests of citizens. But the interests that are reflected will in many cases be the interests of particular citizens rather than the interests of citizens generally. Those special interests that will be pleased by the bureau's performance may represent a quite different set of people than those who use the bureau's services. E. G. West has found evidence that public schooling reflects to a large degree the interests of educators rather than the interests of parents and children, and that it may also reflect the interests of a particular subset of parents and children.[10] West's evidence suggests that public schooling has made a minimal contribution, at best, to literacy, good citizenship, and the like, but it has made a substantial contribution to the incomes of educators, especially school administrators. If public education results from legislation that promotes the interests of educators, and perhaps of particular subsets of citizens, there must be other people whose interests suffer. As we have seen, when legislation rewards some interests, it must penalize others.

The "poor" performance of public bureaus when viewed from a general-interest perspective may not be quite so poor when viewed from the perspective of the bureau's true customers, the legislature and the particular interest groups that secured the pertinent legislation. This result is implicit in — indeed, would seem to be required by — the special-interest approach to the production of legislation in a majoritarian democracy.

There has been much interest in recent years in developing models of public bureaus. One of the most influential contributions to this literature was made by William Niskanen.[11] The central feature of Niskanen's model is that bureaus receive their financing through annual appropriations from the legislature rather than through prices paid directly by customers. The bureau is a monopoly supplier of output to the legislature. Moreover, bureaus do not charge per-unit prices, but rather offer their entire output in exchange for an entire budget. A public school, for instance, does not price its various outputs to each child, with each child in turn being able to pick and choose to develop some desired mix of offerings. Instead, the community is charged a lump sum for the entire package of services the school system provides. Niskanen argues that this type of arrangement allows bureaus to extract an all-or-nothing offer from the legislature, as illustrated by Figure 6.1.[12] Consequently, the bureau's

[10] On this attribute of public school legislation, see E. G. West, "The Political Economy of American Public School Legislation," *Journal of Law and Economics* 10 (October 1967), pp. 101–128.

[11] William A. Niskanen, *Bureaucracy and Representative Government* (Chicago: Aldine, 1971). For further elaboration, see Niskanen, "Bureaucrats and Politicians," *Journal of Law and Economics* 18 (December 1975), pp. 617–643.

[12] An all-or-nothing offer leaves the buyer indifferent between the amount purchased and having none of the product. The seller captures the full amount of consumers' surplus, so the buyer is no better off with the product than without it.

FIGURE 6.1 Niskanen's Model of Bureaucracy

Consider a service, the demand for which is described by D and which is supplied under conditions of long-run constant cost, $LMC = LAC$. A private monopoly supplies the rate of output X_1, where marginal revenue MR equals marginal cost, and makes a profit of bc per unit of output. The competitive rate of output is X_2. At this rate, the consumers' surplus is adP. The monopoly bureau would be able to extract approximately this consumers' surplus by offering the legislature the rate of output X_3 in exchange for the total budget, $0X_3ep$, where $def = adP$. (The demand curve D_{AN} is the all-or-nothing demand curve.) With the total surplus extracted, consumers are indifferent between X_3 as the rate of output and a zero rate of output. The excessive size of the budget is indicated by edf, which is equal to the consumers' surplus under competitive supply. At the bureau's chosen rate of output, X_3, the value to customers of the marginal unit of X falls short of the marginal cost of X by ef. Although the implicit price of the bureau's output is P per unit, the bureau's output is not offered at a per-unit price. Rather the bureau exchanges the total output, X_3, for a lump-sum appropriation of $0X_3ep$.

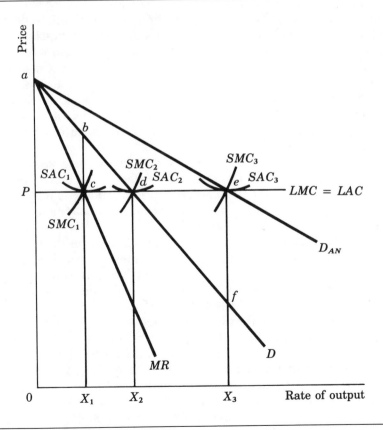

budget and output expand beyond what might be called a competitive or optimum level — that is, the level corresponding to the benefit principle of public economics. The reason for this is twofold: Legislatures are assumed to be passive in dealing with bureaus, and bureau officials are assumed to gain directly as the bureau's budget is enlarged.

The assumption of budget maximization has been the subject of some controversy, mainly because a budget-maximizing strategy may not always correspond to a utility-maximizing strategy. Seeking a larger budget, as well as managing that budget, for example, reduces the leisure time available to bureau officials. Nonetheless, the assumption of budget maximization probably does not lead one too far astray in conducting an analysis, at least as a first-order approximation. Such things as salary, the perquisites of office, reputation and power, and the ability to award patronage all increase with the size of a bureau's budget.

What seems to be more problematic is the assumption that the lump-sum appropriation means the bureau gives the legislature an all-or-nothing offer. This characterization of the relation between the bureau and the legislature sees the legislature as a passive appropriator of funds and collector of revenues. But such a characterization puts the legislature in the position of not pursuing its own interest. After all, the legislature creates the bureau, and it can always choose to purchase its output from private firms. Why should it choose to buy more output than it wants from bureaus when it makes the choice of whether to deal with bureaus or with private firms in the first place?

The relationship between bureaus and legislatures seems more mutually supportive than adversarial. If the legislature creates bureaus and finances them through lump-sum appropriations, it must be because it judges this method of public provision to be a more effective vehicle for pursuing its interests. One of those interests deals with "selling" legislation to special interests. This interest of the legislature seems better served through dealing with bureaus than through dealing with firms. If the legislature contracts with private firms, the effort of firms to compete for business by offering low bids (equal to marginal cost with competitive bidding) will provide information about the profits or rents that legislation creates. Competition will erode those rents, thereby reducing the value of holding a seat in the legislature. A state legislature may appropriate $500 million for schooling when it could provide the same schooling for $400 million by using private contractors. It would be difficult for the legislature to spend $500 million in the presence of bids offering the same services for $400 million. Yet the added $100 million represents the indirect appropriation of the profit or rent from the legislation — that is, the income to those who participate in the market for legislation.

THE BUREAU-LEGISLATURE RELATIONSHIP

The legislature generally can implement legislation either by awarding appropriations to public bureaus or by giving contracts to private firms. Given that the legislature chooses to enact laws to control immigration, for instance, it can implement those laws either by awarding appropriations to a bureau to enforce those laws or by giving a contract to a private firm or firms to handle such tasks as selecting immigrants and rounding up illegal aliens. The legislature has the same choice concerning the method of implementation for practically all legislation: The legislature chooses to control the smuggling of drugs, the violation of antitrust laws, the use of nationally owned forests, and so on, and it can implement those laws either by awarding appropriations to bureaus or by giving contracts to firms.[13]

There seem to be two main reasons why the legislature might choose to deal with a bureau. Consistent with the use of legislation to advance common interests, the legislature might deal with a bureau in situations where it is exceedingly difficult, if not impossible, to stipulate clearly a workable contract. It might be relatively simple to award a bounty for the rounding up of illegal aliens, but it might be more difficult to develop a contract that would give proper guidelines and incentives for selecting among potential immigrants. If the legislature decided it wanted to allow 350,000 immigrants per year, without regard to other considerations, it would be simple to stipulate a contract between the legislature and some firm to select the requisite number of immigrants. If other factors were also judged relevant, but difficult to stipulate concretely, as in cases where possible political persecution or considerations of foreign policy are considered pertinent, it might be more difficult to develop a clear contractual relationship between the legislature and private firms. In such cases, the creation of public bureaus might be a way of avoiding the disputes and litigation that might arise because of that difficulty.

The other main reason why the legislature might choose to deal with bureaus rather than with firms is, as we have seen, that the use of bureaus makes it easier to create rents for people who purchase

---

[13] On the implementation of legislation through private firms, see William M. Landes and Richard A. Posner, "The Private Enforcement of Law," *Journal of Legal Studies* 4 (January 1975), pp. 1–46; and Gary S. Becker and George J. Stigler, "Law Enforcement, Malfeasance, and Compensation of Enforcers," *Journal of Legal Studies* 3 (January 1974), pp. 1–18.

the relevant legislation. If legislation is implemented by private firms and if contracts for implementation are awarded through competitive bidding, the ability of the legislature to sell legislation to highest bidders will be curtailed. The use of public bureaus to implement legislation can increase the value of the legislation that the legislature is able to sell. The nonprofit status of bureaus in conjunction with the tenure created by civil service ensures that bureaus will change their interpretation of legislative intent more slowly than the composition of the legislature will change. Thus use of bureaus strengthens the ability of the legislature to make long-term commitments, which in turn strengthens the demand for the product the legislature sells — legislation.[14] Moreover, assignments to oversight committees within the legislature are generally made in such a way that there is a congruence of interest between the legislature and the bureau; the legislators on the oversight committee will generally have particularly strong interests in the enactment of legislation that will be implemented by the bureau. Members of the legislative committees that oversee highway bureaus generally have the same interest in budgetary expansion that the bureaus have. Members of the legislative committees responsible for regulating financial institutions will generally have the same interests as the regulatory bureaus. Because bureaus and the legislative committees with which they deal generally have similar interests, the two can be expected to share in the rents that are created through the supply of legislation.[15]

To say that there is a general congruence of interest between bureaus and the legislature is not to deny that conflict can arise over the division of the rents created by legislation. The legislature may create a bureau rather than contract with a profit-seeking firm because doing this allows the legislature to capture rents that could not be captured with competitive bidding. At the same time, however, the absence of residual claimancy means that such a simple indicator as a rate of profit cannot be used by the legislature to gauge the success with which the bureau conducts its activities. The task of monitoring is more complex in the absence of residual claimancy, and this complexity probably operates to increase the bureau's share in the profits from legislation. The nonprofit status of bureaus

[14] On the independent judiciary, see William M. Landes and Richard A. Posner, "The Independent Judiciary in an Interest-Group Perspective," *Journal of Law and Economics* 18 (December 1975), pp. 875–901.

[15] For one interesting study of the congruence of interest between the bureau and the responsible legislative committee, see Charles R. Plott, "Some Organizational Influences on Urban Renewal Decisions," *American Economic Review,* Proceedings, 58 (May 1968), pp. 306–321.

means that monitoring of the bureau by the legislature often involves some confounding of inputs and outputs. It is relatively easy to measure many of the inputs into the provision of police or fire services, but the outputs are not nearly as easy to measure. This difficulty is not inherent in the nature of the service but is created by the nonprofit status of bureaus. The services provided by public police and fire departments are essentially no different from those provided by private detective and security services. The only difference is that the profit-seeking status of the private firms provides an unambiguous indicator of the success with which they have used the resources at their disposal. With public bureaus there is a general inability to specify output, or at least many of its dimensions, essentially because of the absence of a contractual relationship between the bureau and the users of its output. Resource cost therefore becomes by default a primary indicator of a bureau's output.

The output of a bureau has many components, only some of which are relatively visible. Legislative monitoring accordingly tends to focus on the relatively visible components of output, and in response the bureau can be expected to emphasize the production of those components. In Veterans Administration hospitals, for example, the number of patient days seems to be a relatively visible indicator of output, while the quality of care is difficult to monitor and, hence, relatively invisible. If this is true, and if bureaus act as described, VA hospitals will tend to treat relatively simple illnesses and hospitalize patients for relatively long periods. Evidence compiled by Cotton Lindsay conforms generally to this expectation.[16] Compared with private hospitals, VA hospitals tend to have longer stays for the same treatment, as shown in Table 6.1. Furthermore, VA hospitals tend to have lower staff-patient ratios, averaging about 1.5, whereas the ratio in proprietary hospitals is about 2.5. This result is consistent with, although not required by, the assumption that the quality of care is relatively invisible and hence underprovided in VA hospitals, if it is also assumed that a lower staff-patient ratio corresponds to lower-quality treatment.

AGENDA FORMATION
AND REVERSION BUDGETING

The process of forming an agenda for making collective choices can support and exploit the complementary relationship between bureaus

[16] Cotton M. Lindsay, "A Theory of Government Enterprise," *Journal of Political Economy* 84 (October 1976), pp. 1061–1077.

TABLE 6.1 Average Length of Stay, in Days, by Surgical Procedure

Procedure	VA Hospital	Proprietary Hospital
Pilonidal cyst	15.7	5.8
Diabetes mellitus	19.0	9.0
Acute coronary occlusion	31.5	21.7
Hemorrhoidectomy	15.3	2.1
Tonsils and adenoids	6.4	2.4
Duodenum ulcer	15.2	6.7
Appendicitis	12.1	6.9
Inguinal hernia	17.1	7.2
Gastroenteritis and colitis	11.1	7.7
Gallstones	26.5	11.9
Pyelitis, cystitis, nephritis	14.6	6.0
Kidney stones	18.6	8.2
Prostate	22.1	9.7

Source: Cotton M. Lindsay, "A Theory of Government Enterprise," *Journal of Political Economy* 84 (October 1976), p. 1073. Reprinted by permission of the University of Chicago Press. © 1976 by the University of Chicago Press.

and the legislature. In many cases, the ability to specify the agenda for considering and choosing among options for collective choice is, in effect, the ability to make the actual choice. Whoever controls such things as the options to be voted on and the sequence of motions can channel, and perhaps even control, the outcome.

Suppose a club that is oriented toward outdoor activities is considering how to spend a month during the summer and that there are three sets of options that command support among the membership. One option is between traveling by canoe (C) and hiking (H). A second option is between undertaking activity in a flat (F) or in a mountainous (M) terrain. The third option is between spending the month in a northern (N), relatively cool location or spending it in a southern (S), relatively warm location. Table 6.2 shows hypothetical preference orderings for three people (or for three groups of people) who constitute the membership of the club. Person A most strongly prefers to go camping in flat terrain in the south, with camping on flat terrain in the north ranking second, and so on. Person B most strongly prefers to go hiking in mountainous terrain in the north, with hiking in flat terrain in the north ranking second. Person C most strongly prefers to go hiking in mountainous terrain in the south, with hiking in flat terrain in the south ranking second.

Suppose the membership agrees to be bound by the choice of the

TABLE 6.2 Preference Orderings for Three People[a]

Person A	Person B	Person C
CFS	HMN	HMS
CFN	HFN	HFS
CMS	CFN	HMN
CMN	CMN	HFN
HMN	CFS	CFS
HFN	CMS	CMS
HFS	HFS	CFN
HMS	HMS	CMN

[a] There are three sets of options: between canoeing (C) and hiking (H), between flat (F) and mountainous (M) terrain, and between a northern (N), cool location and a southern (S), warm location.

majority and further agrees to delegate to a person or a committee the task of selecting a procedure for arriving at a majority choice. To the extent that the person who chooses the agenda by which choices are to be made knows or has a good idea of the preferences of the membership, he can control, or at least channel, the choices actually made. Suppose that the person (or rules committee) is able to specify the order in which business is to be considered and that he would like the club to choose to take a hiking trip in mountainous terrain in the north. By specifying an agenda in which pairwise choices are to be made in turn between camping and hiking, then between flat and mountainous terrain, and finally between a northern and a southern location, the outcome he desires will result. Persons B and C will prefer hiking to camping. Given that hiking has been chosen, all three persons will prefer mountainous to flat terrain, and given that hiking in mountainous terrain has been chosen, persons A and B will prefer doing it in the north.

Suppose the person who sets the agenda wants to go camping in flat terrain in the south. This outcome is equally possible to engineer by making the first vote between north and south. Then the order of the following two votes does not matter. In a vote between north and south, Persons A and C will choose the south. Given that the south has been chosen, a choice between camping and hiking will find Persons A and B choosing camping. Given that camping in the south has been chosen, all participants will prefer doing it in flat to mountainous terrain. Likewise, any number of preferences can be engineered.

Reversion budgeting, an illustration of agenda formation, is a process in which people are faced with a choice between two budget proposals, with the rejection of one proposal entailing the acceptance of the other. Oregon has reversion budgeting on education expenditure. If a referendum on education spending is rejected for any particular year, the budget reverts automatically to one defined by

$$E = (\text{BASE})\ (1.06)^{\,t-1916}$$

where BASE is total school taxes levied in 1916 and t is the current year. If the budget proposal for a particular year is rejected, the budget reverts to an amount that is equal to spending in 1916, increased by 6 percent per year. This reversion budget can be levied without voter approval.[17]

Reversion budgeting is a particular form of agenda formation. A vote is taken on a particular motion, and this motion can either be accepted or rejected. If it is rejected, the budget reverts automatically to some alternative that is not subject to choice. If that reversion budget is lower than the budget size most preferred by the pivotal voter or group of voters, a range of budget motions in excess of that voter's preference will be considered and one motion chosen nonetheless. Figure 6.2 illustrates how reversion budgeting can increase the size of the budget that the median voter (or controlling coalition or other choice-making entity) will choose. The new budget motion given to the median voter may entail a greater than desired expenditure, but as long as that greater amount leaves the median voter better off than he would be under the lower reversion budget, the median voter will support the larger budget. In their study of reversion budgeting in Oregon, Thomas Romer and Howard Rosenthal found that between 1970 and 1977, voter rejections of the budget proposals of the school board led to increased budget proposals in 25 cases and to decreased budget proposals 569 cases.[18] If the proposed budget failed because the school board was not fully cognizant of the preference of voters, the school board would have been equally likely to err in the direction of underestimating the desires of voters for educational expenditure as in overestimating those desires. But if this were the case, school boards should subsequently have proposed budgetary increases with equal frequency as they proposed budgetary decreases, particularly since school boards are able to propose referenda on still larger budgets if a particular budget proposal passes. That school

[17] Reversion budgeting on education spending in Oregon is discussed in Thomas Romer and Howard Rosenthal, "Bureaucrats Versus Voters: On the Political Economy of Resource Allocation by Direct Democracy," *Quarterly Journal of Economics* 93 (November 1979), pp. 563–587.
[18] Ibid., p. 584.

FIGURE 6.2 Reversion Budgeting and the Median Voter

A median voter whose utility function is described by such indifference curves as P_1^M and P_2^M and who faces the budget constraint between private and collective output denoted by PC, will choose C_M as the rate of collective output. Suppose the median voter is faced instead with the choice of accepting or rejecting the budget C_M^*. If the budget reverts to C_R if C_M^* is rejected, the median voter will be indifferent between the two options. But if the reversion budget is slightly less than C_R, or if the proposed budget is slightly less than C_M^*, the median voter will choose a larger budget than he or she truly desires because that larger budget is preferable to the reversion budget that will result if the proposed budget is rejected.

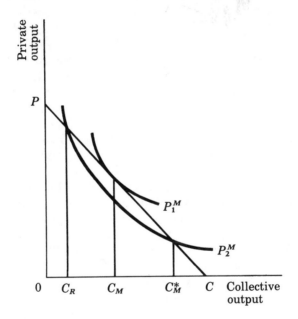

boards in Oregon chose budgetary decreases twenty times more frequently in response to the initial referenda than they chose budgetary increases is strong indication that school boards are biased systematically toward increasing expenditures beyond the level desired by the median voter.

Other types of reversion budgeting could be illustrated that would reinforce the point that the person or committee that controls the agenda can have considerable ability to enact desired programs despite voter preferences to the contrary.

COMPETING BUREAUS AND
A COMPETITIVE BUREAUCRACY?

One bureau does not operate in isolation from other bureaus. Bureaus compete for appropriations, just as the various legislative committees do. Increased appropriations for tanks for the army means reduced appropriations for, say, food stamps, although an increased appropriation for one bureau may not take place fully through reduced appropriations for other bureaus. Instead, some of the increased appropriations for some bureaus may take place through a growth in government revenue; that is, through reduced disposable income for citizens. In response to the development of a variety of models in which bureaus practice such monopoly schemes as agenda setting and all-or-none offers, a variety of suggestions has arisen in support of some notion of competing bureaus. Such increased competition is seen as a means of rendering bureaus less bureaucratic. It is perhaps easy to see why competition among bureaus might be thought to operate similarly to competition among firms. If bureaus compete among themselves for the right to supply a legislative sponsor, the demand curve faced by any one bureau becomes more elastic. This reduces the ability of any particular bureau to act as if it were a monopolist, which in turn retards the tendency toward excessive supply. Such competition might also strengthen the adversary system within the bureaucracy. Bureaus that supply services that are weak substitutes for one another are less likely to stimulate effective adversary proceedings than are bureaus that provide close substitutes because the technical knowledge possessed within the latter set of bureaus will enhance the effectiveness of such proceedings.

The calls for competition among bureaus, however, seem to run afoul of the central institutional features of majoritarian democracy. After all, the provision of services through nonprofit bureaus financed by taxation arises not through accident but by legislative choice. Supply by public bureaus would seem to be an integral feature of majoritarian democracy because bureaus are essential to the process of creating and capturing rents through legislation. If there were no such rents, bureaus would serve no function that could not be provided by private firms. Competition among bureaus would seem to be no more a matter of legislative general interest than is competition among committees. For the most part, the division of territory among legislative committees operates to enhance the value of the legislation that the governing party enacts. Competition among committees for the production of legislation would seem generally to run contrary to those profit-maximizing interests, and the organization of the legislature reflects the recognition that such competition generally subverts those interests. Since bureaus are created to implement legislation, even though the activities of the bureaus could in many cases be contracted out to private firms, the bureaucratic method seems to be chosen because it supports legislative interests. The promotion of competition among bureaus would run contrary to the interests of political parties engaged in the sale of legislation to highest bidders. In other words, the practice of organizing bureaus in such a way that each possesses exclusive territory is consistent with the perspective that the party in control of the legislature is trying to maximize the value of the agenda it enacts. Bureaus will become profit oriented or efficiency oriented when the legislature does; the organization of the bureaucracy is derived from the legislature's pursuit of its own interest, and the incentives provided to bureaus accordingly can be expected to be modified only as the incentives of the legislature change.

SUGGESTIONS FOR FURTHER READING

An important early treatment that contrasts management within bureaus with management within profit-seeking firms is Ludwig von Mises, *Bureaucracy* (New Haven: Yale University Press, 1944). For a development and elaboration of how the conduct of bureaus is guided by the incentive features of their nonowned, tax-financed status, see Gordon Tullock, *The Politics of Bureaucracy* (Washington, D.C.: Public Affairs Press, 1965); and Anthony Downs, *Inside Bureaucracy* (Boston: Little, Brown, 1967). Further aspects and implications of the divergence in incentives between firms and bureaus are explored in Roland N. McKean, "Divergence Between Individual and Total Costs Within Government," *American Economic Review,* Proceedings, 54 (May 1964), pp. 43–249; McKean, "The Unseen Hand in Government," *American Economic Review* 55 (June 1965), pp. 496–505; and McKean, "Property Rights Within Government and Devices to Increase Governmental Efficiency," *Southern Economic Journal* 39 (October 1972), pp. 177–186. *Budgets and Bureaucrats,* edited by Thomas E. Borcherding (Durham, N.C.: Duke University Press, 1977), contains a series of essays on the budgetary impact of bureaucracy, building largely on Niskanen's treatment of bureaucracy.

Important critiques of Niskanen's approach to bureaucracy are developed in Jean-Luc Migué and Gérard Bélanger, "Toward a General Theory of Managerial Discretion," *Public Choice* 17 (Spring 1974), pp. 27–43; Albert Breton and Ronald Wintrobe, "The Equilibrium Size of a Budget-Maximizing Bureau: A Note on Niskanen's Theory of Bureaucracy," *Journal of Political Economy* 83 (February 1975), pp. 195–207; and Gary J. Miller "Bureaucratic Compliance as a Game on the Unit Square," *Public Choice* 29 (Spring 1977), pp. 37–51. For a general survey of non-profit organizations from a perspective similar to that developed in this chapter, see Barry P. Keating and Maryann O. Keating, *Not-for-Profit* (Glen Ridge, N.J.: Thomas Horton and Daughters, 1980).

For further examination of agenda formation, see Thomas Romer and Howard Rosenthal, "Political Resource Allocation, Controlled Agenda, and the Status Quo," *Public Choice* 33 (No. 4, 1978), pp. 27–43; Robert J. Mackay and Carolyn L. Weaver, "Monopoly Bureaus and Fiscal Outcomes: Deductive Models and Implications for Reform," in *Policy Analysis and Deductive Reasoning,* edited by Gordon Tullock and Richard E. Wagner (Lexington, Mass.: D. C. Health, 1978), pp. 141–165; and Arthur Denzau, Robert Mackay, and Carolyn Weaver, "Spending Limitations, Agenda Control, and Voters' Expectations," *National Tax Journal* 32 (June 1979, Supplement), pp. 189–200. For an interesting experimental study, see Charles R. Plott and Michael E. Levine, "A Model of Agenda Influence on Committee Decisions," *American Economic Review* 68 (March 1978), pp. 146–160.

The influence of different patterns of organization of education bureaus on education spending in the United States is examined in Eugenia Froedge Toma, "Bureaucratic Structures and Educational Spending," *Southern Economic Journal* 47 (January 1981), pp. 640–654. The employment history of officials in three bureaus — the Civil Aeronautics Board, Interstate Commerce Commission, and Federal Communications Commission — is explored, describing clearly the complementarity of interest between the regulatory bureaus and the regulated industries, in Ross D. Eckert, "The Life Cycle of Regulatory Commissioners," *Journal of Law and Economics* 24 (April 1981), pp. 113–120. For an exploration of the possibility that bureaus become more inefficient over time because of their nonownership, see R. D. Auster, "The GPITPC and Institutional Entropy," *Public Choice* 19 (Fall 1974), pp. 77–83.

7

Contrasting Models
of Collective Choice

Warren Nutter examined the growth of government in sixteen Western democracies over the 1950–1974 period and found that government spending was universally rising as a share of national income.[1] This share ranged from 22 to 39 percent among the sixteen countries in 1950 and from 29 to 64 percent in 1974. When these countries were ranked by their shares of government in national income, the median percentage went from 31 in 1950 to 52 in 1974. There is relatively little dispute about the facts of the growth of government. There is, however, much dispute about the proper interpretation to give to or conclusion to draw from those facts. Two main classes of explanation have been advanced for the growth of government. One class sees this growth as a positive-sum response by government to such things as changes in technologies and in people's desires. The other sees this growth as representing to an important extent the operation of negative-sum elements in existing political institutions. Proponents of this second theory see problems in the growth of government and have tended to favor limiting the size of government to restrict those negative-sum elements. Some of the methods that have been suggested include limiting government taxing or spending to some percentage of an aggregate measure such as personal income and restricting the tax base or the tax rate applicable to a particular base. This occurred in California, where Proposition 13 limited the

[1] G. Warren Nutter, *Growth of Government in the West* (Washington, D.C.: American Enterprise Institute, 1978). The countries Nutter studied were Australia, Austria, Belgium, Canada, Denmark, France, Italy, Japan, Luxembourg, Netherlands, Norway, Sweden, Switzerland, United Kingdom, United States, and West Germany.

property tax to 1 percent of market value. Two categories of models of collective choice have been developed: One emphasizes the cooperative, positive-sum aspects of social life and the other notes that democratic institutions can give substantial scope to various discordant, wealth-eroding aspects of social life. One set of models raises concerns about the growth of government, and the other does not.

TWO CATEGORIES OF DEMOCRACY

It is common to think of democracy as constituting a single category of government, with distinguishing features of particular instances being of relatively minor importance. Some democracies may be parliamentary, while others have separately elected legislatures and executives. Some democracies may encourage direct citizen participation through a wide use of referenda, while others leave decision making exclusively to elected representatives. Some democracies have relatively homogeneous populations, and others have comparatively heterogeneous populations. The main distinction of interest for the theory of public economics is between democracies that tend to unleash the cooperative aspects of social life while restraining the factional aspects and democracies in which the "violence of faction" is given freer rein to pursue its negative-sum tendencies.

Italian writers on public economics, starting in the late nineteenth century, developed two alternative models of government.[2] One model emphasized the cooperative aspect of collective action and described government as a means of providing services of common value that could not be supplied efficiently through market transactions. This approach to government coincides with the benefit principle of public economics. The other model looked upon government as a means by which those who gain control of government exploit their position at the expense of the rest of society. The Italian writers described such a model in terms of a ruling class or oligarchy, but the simple model of majoritarian democracy we used in earlier chapters would fit as well, for it too describes outcomes in terms of the ability of a dominant set of citizens to exploit a subordinate set.

The first category of democratic government has been referred to as cooperative, concordant, or consensual democracy. Regardless of nomenclature, it describes a system of government in which decisions concerning the use of resources tend to reflect the consent of the

[2] The contribution of Italian scholars is surveyed in James M. Buchanan, "The Italian Tradition in Fiscal Theory," in *Fiscal Theory and Political Economy,* edited by Buchanan (Chapel Hill: University of North Carolina Press, 1960), pp. 24–74.

governed. In the second category of democratic government, such decisions can at most be said to reflect the consent of a dominant subset of society, which can only be a minority subset. This category of democracy has been referred to as monopolistic, discordant, or majoritarian democracy. This distinction between models of collective choice in democratic systems is not one so much between separate alternatives as one of the degree of applicability of those models. Concordant or consensual democracies emphasize the positive-sum aspects of collective choice. Discordant or majoritarian democracies may well undertake various programs of a positive-sum nature, but in addition they place considerable emphasis on imposing burdens on some people so as to award benefits to others.

Although it may be difficult if not impossible to classify democracies into the cooperative and monopolistic categories simply by inspecting their constitutions and related features of their political systems, it seems possible nonetheless to make a reasonable inference as to which type is dominant in a particular case. The benefit principle of public economics, which describes a model of concordant or consensual democracy, provides a framework for developing such an inference. Figure 7.1 illustrates several of the issues that arise in the model of consensual democracy.

Suppose each person pays a marginal tax-price equal to his marginal valuation of the collective service, and the sum of the marginal valuations equals the marginal cost of the service. In this case, all members of society agree to the same rate of collective output, X_0, given the tax-prices P_0^A and P_0^B. What makes this unanimity possible, of course, is the dependence of tax-prices on individual demands. Those with higher demands pay sufficiently higher prices so that their desired quantity is the same as those with lower demands, who pay lower prices.

The rule of unanimity is a particular way of implementing a principle of consensus in collective choice, but there are other institutional processes that also reflect a principle of consensus. The principle of consensus is more inclusive than a rule of unanimity. As we saw in Chapter 2, a market economy reflects a principle of consensus in the use of resources. Within the framework provided by property and contract, decisions concerning resource utilization reflect a consensus that resources are being used in what people anticipate will be their most valued employments. Disagreement about the value of particular uses of resources is resolved as a person who thinks an alternative use is more valuable than the present use buys control of those resources from the present owner. Although a market economy is a system of consensual decision making, it is not one that requires unanimity in decisions concerning the use of resources.

FIGURE 7.1 Consensus on Collective Output

The demand functions for some collective good for two persons (or equal-sized groups) are described by D_A and D_B, with D being the aggregate demand function. If marginal cost is MC, X_O is the rate of output required by the benefit principle. Person B pays a marginal tax-price of P_O^B, and A pays a marginal tax-price of P_O^A. The rate of output X_O will command unanimous support.

Suppose instead the marginal tax-price is the same for all, as indicated by P. A now prefers $\overline{X}_A$ and B prefers $\overline{X}_B$. Suppose $\overline{X}_A + \overline{X}_B = 2X_O$. If so, and if the conflict over desired output is resolved by averaging the competing motions, X_O will be the outcome. At this outcome, B enjoys a marginal value in excess of price, as indicated by $P_O^B - \overline{P}$, while A finds that price exceeds marginal value, as indicated by $\overline{P} - P_O^A$. In this case, B will want an expansion in output, and A will seek a reduction. Other methods of resolving the conflict might settle it in favor of A or B. Regardless, there will be discord over the existing rate of collective output when the benefit principle is not satisfied.

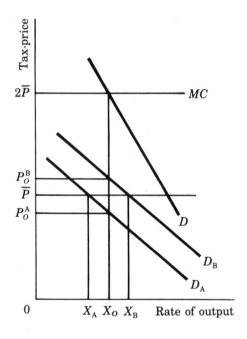

It is possible for majority rule to be consistent with consensus in the use of resources, as a further consideration of Figure 7.1 can illustrate. Suppose the population falls into two categories, low demanders and high demanders, on any particular issue. Further suppose that people are randomly distributed between these two categories over the various issues that arise for collective choice but that all people pay the same tax-price. Half the population wants the smaller quantity, X_A, and half wants the larger quantity X_B. When only a single issue is subject to choice, discord is inescapable. But suppose high demanders on one issue are low demanders on another issue. Although such people find themselves paying more for the service than they value it in one case and less in the other, there may well be a consensus that the system is producing desirable outcomes. These people may prefer majority rule to unanimity because they think it is a costly rule for making collective choices and, moreover, because they recognize that majority rule works in such a way that, on average, people pay marginal tax-prices equal to their marginal valuations, even if they do not do so for each item of collective expenditure.

This characterization of majority rule as being, on average, essentially equivalent to unanimity may not be accurate, however, as Figure 7.2 illustrates. Suppose the high demanders are the dominant group and that the prevailing tax system assigns the same tax-price to all. The high demanders will establish their preferred rate of output. The low demanders will pay more for that output than they value it. In this case, a subset of the population will systematically support an across-the-board reduction in collective output. The presence of such systematic support for a reduction in collective output, as contrasted with support for reductions in some outputs and increases in others, indicates that substantial elements of majoritarian or discordant democracy are present.[3]

Majoritarian Democracy and the Size of Government

Majoritarian or discordant democracy tends to generate an expansion in the size of government. This expansion is the means by which the transfers of income and wealth take place between those who secure the desired legislation and those who pay for it. On initial inspection, we might think such transfers are only zero sum and not negative sum. A shifting of tax burdens from one set of citizens to another, for instance, would seem to involve only a transfer of wealth. Although it is unpleasant to be a loser in this process, transfers do not by themselves move resources from more valued to less valued uses.

---

[3] More generally, some people can support general reductions in the scope of government while others support a general increase. In any event, the presence of such conflict implies that government cannot be regarded as consensual because the ability of some people to gain or lose by proportionate expansions or contractions in the size of government indicates a pattern of systematic bias that is inconsistent with a principle of consensus.

FIGURE 7.2 Conflict Between High Demanders and Low
Demanders

The demand function for some collectively supplied output is described by
D_B for one set of citizens and D_A for another set. Suppose the prevailing
system of taxation imposes an equal sharing of tax burdens on all, making
P the tax-price for members of each group. High demanders want X_B and
low demanders want X_A. If the high demanders are dominant, X_B is the
outcome and low demanders will favor a reduction in the size of the budget
because $P - V_A$ indicates the excess of marginal cost over marginal values
for the low demanders.

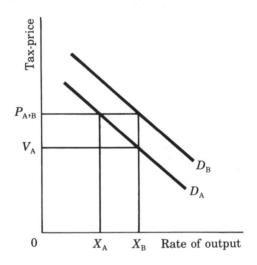

But to the extent that the transfers are accomplished by reducing
marginal tax-prices paid by members of the winning coalition, resources will be shifted into less valued uses, as Figure 7.3 illustrates.
Starting from a situation in which all people face the same tax-price,
suppose the tax-price is lowered to the members of the winning coalition and increased to the members of the losing coalition. At this
lower tax-price, the members of the winning coalition will support
an expansion in collective output, and this expansion will involve a
shift of resources from more valued to less valued uses. At the new
equilibrium, marginal cost equals marginal value to members of the
winning coalition, but marginal cost exceeds marginal value for the
rest of society.

Besides tax discrimination, a winning coalition can also practice
expenditure discrimination. As Figure 7.4 illustrates, expenditure discrimination results when people pay the same tax despite differing

FIGURE 7.3 Tax Discrimination

Suppose all members of a collectivity can be described by the demand function D_i, and let P_i be the marginal tax-price that corresponds to the benefit principle. Accordingly, the efficient rate of output is X_i. However, suppose a winning coalition enacts a program of tax revision that lowers its tax-prices and increases the tax-prices paid by the rest of society. These new prices are described by P_W and P_L respectively. If output remains at X_i, wealth will have been transferred, but the marginal value of resources applied to the provision of collective wants will equal the marginal value of resources applied to the provision of private wants. However, at the price P_W the members of the winning coalition will want X_W as the rate of output. As this expansion takes place, resources are shifted from the satisfaction of more valued into the satisfaction of less valued wants. If the two groups are of equal size, the marginal value of collective output at the rate of output X_W is $2P_W$, whereas the marginal cost is $P_W + P_L$.

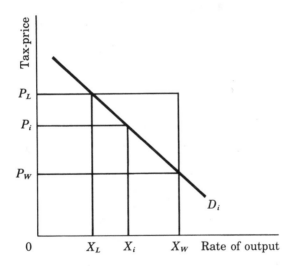

demands for collective output. Residents of interior areas may pay the same tax-price for a program of subsidized insurance as do residents along the coastal areas threatened by flooding. If people can be classified into low demanders and high demanders, and if they face a common tax-price, they will differ in their desired rates of output. The benefit principle will call for an intermediate rate of output and for marginal tax-prices that vary directly with people's demands for collective output. However, if the high demanders make up the winning coalition, the actual rate of output will exceed the efficient rate. If the low demanders are the winning coalition, the

FIGURE 7.4 Expenditure Discrimination

Of two equal-sized groups of people, high demanders are represented by D_H and low demanders by D_L. Suppose prevailing tax requirements assign equal tax-prices to the two groups. This would happen, at least on average, if each group had the same average income and if government was financed by a proportional income tax. It would also happen under progressive taxation, if the distribution of income was also the same within each group. The marginal cost of the service, according to the standard construction of the benefit principle, is $2P$, and the sum of the individual demands is D. The efficient rate of output is X_B. However, if the high demanders dominate the outcome, the choice of output will be X_H. At this outcome, resources devoted to the supply of collective output are valued less highly than resources devoted to the supply of private output, as indicated by the divergence cd. In contrast, if the low demanders dominate the outcome, output will be X_L. In this case, resources devoted to public output will be more valuable than resources devoted to private output, as shown by the divergence ab.

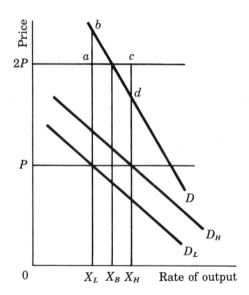

rate of output will fall short of the efficient rate. The latter outcome is also negative sum, because resources are still being employed to satisfy wants that are valued less highly than other wants those resources could satisfy. In either case, there will be discord over the outcome, although there is some reason to think that high demanders will tend to dominate low demanders in the market for legislation, mainly because, as we saw in Chapter 6, legislation will generally be of greater value to high demanders, who in turn will be willing to pay more for its enactment.

A winning coalition on a particular issue may well comprise only a minority of the citizenry. As long as legislators tend not to oppose bills for which there is no organized opposition, and as long as interest groups generally allocate their resources more effectively to secure passage of their desired bills than to defeat the bills of others, such special or minority interests will tend to dominate legislative outcomes. William Niskanen argues that existing political processes do not reflect the general interest of the citizenry because representatives and citizens face a difference in incentives; representatives bear most of the decision-making costs, but citizens bear most of the external costs of the resulting decisions.[4] Consequently, Congress will adopt voting rules and parliamentary procedures that promote minority rule as a by-product of their efforts to economize on the costs of decision making that they bear. Related to this bias within legislatures, there have been several examinations of how the costliness of political participation adds to the control of the bureaucracy over budgetary outcomes.[5] Both the bureaucracy and the legislature will generally be biased toward an expansion in the size of government because this expansion is the vehicle by which wealth is transferred from losers to winners, the wealth that is dissipated in the process notwithstanding.

LIMITING THE SIZE OF GOVERNMENT

The development of various models of democratic fiscal processes that show a tendency for a negative-sum growth of government has been accompanied by a growing interest in limiting the growth of government. If budgets tend to be too large, compared with the criteria of the benefit principle, it might seem as though the excesses of majoritarian democracy can be controlled by imposing some suitable upper bound on the size of government budgets. This seemingly straightforward presumption is not, however, so easy to implement as it may appear. For one thing, the budget power and the police power are interchangeable means by which government can direct the use of resources. Governments could eliminate their spending on education simply by requiring parents to send their children to

---

[4] William A. Niskanen, "The Pathology of Politics," in *Capitalism and Freedom: Problems and Prospects,* edited by Richard T. Selden (Charlottesville: University Press of Virginia, 1974), pp. 20–35.

[5] See, for instance, Robert J. Mackay and Carolyn L. Weaver, "Monopoly Bureaus and Fiscal Outcomes," in *Policy Analysis and Deductive Reasoning,* edited by Gordon Tullock and Richard E. Wagner (Lexington, Mass.: D. C. Heath, 1978), pp. 141–165.

school at their expense for a stipulated number of years, for instance. Such a requirement would involve substantial transfers of wealth from people who have school-age children to people who do not. Governmental spending on education could be reduced to zero, but it could hardly be claimed that government's influence over the use of resources in society has been lessened.

It has long been common for communities to protect themselves against the transmission of rabies by requiring the owners of pets to have their pets inoculated. Alternatively, government could provide such inoculations as a public health service and finance them through its budget. In either case, the impact of government on the use of resources is essentially the same. The place of government in the economy is affected relatively little by whether government hires labor and capital or compels their employment in particular activities. The more closely the police power and the budget power are able to serve interchangeably to influence the use of resources in society, the less reliable is the budget as an indicator of the extent of government control over economic activity.[6] If government growth is a vehicle for transferring wealth, then government grows because such transfers have positive survival value under majoritarian democracy. The imposition of limits on the size of government budgets would seem to do little to alter those incentives. If this is so, one major impact of a budget limit would be to induce a greater use of the police power to achieve the transfers of resources that accompany the production of legislation and that otherwise would be accomplished through the budget.

Even if a budget limit is not offset by an expanded use of the police power, or even if it is only partially offset, it is possible for a budget limit actually to intensify the negative-sum impact of government, for the same reason that the negative-sum impact occurs in the first place. Whether the imposition of a limit on government budgets will be positive sum or negative sum depends on the type of budget reduction that takes place in response to the limit. This possibility can be illustrated with a simple model. Suppose there are five people (or sets of people) in the collectivity and that two programs, A and B, are undertaken by government. Each program is financed by the imposition of a tax of $10 on each person:

$$T_{A,B} = (10, 10, 10, 10, 10).$$

One expenditure program is universally beneficial, and that program

---

[6] For an examination of a variety of uses of legal regulations that substitute for budgetary outlays, see Murray L. Weidenbaum, *Government-Mandated Price Increases* (Washington, D.C.: American Enterprise Institute, 1975).

is valued by each person as representing a 20 percent return on tax payments:

$$E_A = (12, 12, 12, 12, 12).$$

The other program provides particular benefits to a majority, and no benefits to the minority:

$$E_B = (14, 14, 14, 0, 0).$$

This second program provides a 40 percent return to the members of the majority, although the aggregate return is -16 percent. Under majority rule, both programs will be enacted, and the size of the government's budget will be $100.

Now if a budget limit of $50 is introduced, one of the two programs must be eliminated. Within the framework of majoritarian democracy, program A would seem to be the leading candidate for elimination because program B is more valuable to the dominant majority than is program A. If so, the budget limit will bring about the elimination of the positive-sum program while maintaining the negative-sum program, thereby rendering government more of a negative-sum participant in the division of labor than it was before the limit was imposed. The reason why such cuts might be concentrated on positive-sum programs is intuitively simple and is based on the same asymmetries that are used to explain the enactment of negative-sum programs in the first place. The tendencies for intense minorities to triumph over passive majorities also has a counterpart here. Compare two candidates for cutting: a program that provides moderate net benefits for all and a program that provides high net benefits for a minority of the population, low net costs for much of the population, and overall costs that exceed the benefits. Because of the tendency for the interests of intense minorities to prevail, the generally beneficial program is more likely to be cut than the negative-sum program with concentrated beneficiaries. Once again, the same line of reasoning that explains the tendency for majoritarian democracy to enact negative-sum, wealth-eroding programs also explains why budget limits may actually intensify the negative-sum components of the government's budget.

WICKSELL, CONSENSUS, AND THE ENTERPRISE PRINCIPLE IN GOVERNMENT

The explanations that have been developed about how government promotes certain types of negative-sum outcomes all rely in various ways on the absence of a quid pro quo or contractual relationship between the taxes government takes from people and the services it provides. Remedy for negative-sum outcomes might seem more effectively pursued through the formation of a quid pro quo relationship between citizens and government than through such ad hoc devices as budget limits. As a quid pro quo relationship develops, a system of majoritarian democracy gives way to one of consensual democracy. With the creation of some form of quid pro quo relationship, government will expand in size as long as people agree that the value of the services they receive in return for their contribution exceeds the value of whatever else they might have bought with those contributions. If people do not think this is so, government will shrink in size. Under consensual democracy, government becomes subject to the same rules of and incentives for economical conduct as do private citizens, instead of remaining outside those rules, as it does under majoritarian democracy.

A disjunction is commonly thought to exist between activities in which consensus can operate and activities in which it cannot. It is often suggested that property and contract — the consensual framework of the market economy — will not work in some areas because of free riding. This common assumption may not be fully correct. Experimental work by Peter Bohm, for instance, has found that people generally reveal their preferences rather than trying to free ride, in cases where an effort is made to organize the provision of shared-consumption activities through contract.[7] As Earl Brubaker has argued in trying to explain the discrepancy between Bohm's experimental study and the intuitive hunches of most of the literature on public goods, what may be dominant in people's minds is not a desire to free ride per se, but only a desire to be assured that they will not be fleeced by those who do free ride.[8] In the typical formulations of the free-rider problem, those who are truthful about their evaluation of objects of shared consumption must pay on the basis of their stated evaluations at the same time as those who understate their evaluations are able to reduce their payments.

If people are not interested so much in free riding as in ensuring against getting fleeced by those who understate their evaluations, free riding may not be as significant as commonly thought. As long as motions to provide items of shared consumption take the general form that no facility will be provided and no taxes actually levied unless the sum of expressed individual desires to contribute exceeds a specified amount, people who are truthful in expressing their pref-

[7] Peter Bohm, "Estimating Demand for Public Goods: An Experiment," *European Economic Review* 3, No. 2 (1972), pp. 111–130.
[8] Earl R. Brubaker, "Free Ride, Free Revelation, or Golden Rule?" *Journal of Law and Economics* 18 (April 1975), pp. 147–161.

erences will not be harmed significantly by those who are not. Through the use of some form of "precontract excludability," to use Brubaker's terminology, the free-rider problem could perhaps be largely overcome within government, in which case the entrepreneurial principle based on contract could come to guide the use of resources by government. Suppose a group of people were considering the draining of a swamp. Under the common formulations of the free-rider problem, each person would declare an evaluation for different drainage proposals, and those declarations would be collected. Someone who made an honest declaration would be taxed that amount, while someone who understated the evaluation would be taxed on that lesser declaration. Each of ten people might truthfully think the project is worth a $100 contribution, but the actual contributions will be less than $1,000 because some people will understate their evaluations. The size of the project will be less than efficient, and those who are truthful will bear a disproportionately heavy share of the burden. But with precontract excludability, a person's announced evaluation is actually collected by the government only if the sum of the evaluations exceeds some stipulated amount. A person might announce an evaluation of $100, but that announcement would not constitute a liability for payment unless the total announced evaluations exceeded, say, $900.

Indeed, the generally ignored problem of the forced rider, from whom taxes are extracted but who receives no value in return, may be more severe than the problem of the free rider. Both free riders and forced riders can be offset through the development of some contractual basis for organizing the provision of shared consumption. As Brubaker notes:

> The opportunities for eliciting more nearly voluntary economic expression of individual priorities for collective goods may be far greater than most of the contemporary orthodox literature suggests. If so, it may be eminently worthwhile to explore more carefully means to expand the scope of voluntary arrangements for provision of collective needs while perhaps in some measure of correspondence reducing reliance on coercive institutions with their own potentially detrimental effects.[9]

In a related line of analysis, Harold Demsetz has noted that there is no obstacle to market provision of shared-consumption goods as long as the entrepreneurs who organize the supply of such goods are able to exclude nonpurchasers from consumption. Moreover, the market process through which such goods are produced will result in the

---

[9] Ibid., p. 158.

same pattern of differential prices among people specified by the theory of public goods, as represented by Figure 2.3.[10]

The only difficulty with the organization of shared consumption through contract, Demsetz suggests, arises when nonpurchasers cannot be excluded from consumption. Even in that case, however, there are opportunities for tie-in arrangements in which the consumption of such an item is tied to the consumption of something else that is purchased privately. Both advertisers and those who produce television sets have an incentive to see that programs are broadcast, for instance, and, even in the absence of a technology to charge people for their use of television signals, those signals will be provided. Admittedly, tie-ins for the provision of such collective goods may not be efficient when compared with some idealized, nonattainable model of perfectly working government. But actual government provision takes place within a system of majoritarian democracy, which necessarily gives survival value to various inefficient, wealth-destroying collective choices that transfer wealth to winning coalitions. Clearly this arrangement does not mesh perfectly with some utopian idealization of a public goods theory. In any comparison of realizable alternatives, however, it is necessary to recognize that the method of price and profit finance has the advantage of being more consistent with the essential requirements for positive-sum conduct — that is, consensual decision making — than does tax finance.

Existing thinking about government has perhaps been oriented too much toward two distinct principles for economic organization: contract, which is appropriate for the provision of items of private consumption, and compulsion, which is appropriate for the provision of items of shared consumption. But there is only one principle for effective economical conduct in the use of resources, as Wicksell recognized, and implementation of this principle requires, in some fashion, a system of consensual decision making concerning the use of resources. It is interesting and instructive to note that hotels, amusement parks, apartment complexes, and shopping centers all illustrate the organization of shared consumption through contract.[11] The corridors and elevators of a hotel are equivalent to the streets and sidewalks of a city; both are means by which people can get from place to place. Just as numerous questions can be raised concerning the allocation of resources to streets and sidewalks, so can the same list of questions be raised with respect to corridors and ele-

---

[10] Harold Demsetz, "The Private Production of Public Goods," *Journal of Law and Economics* 13 (October 1970), pp. 293–306.

[11] See the interesting treatment of this point in Spencer H. MacCallum, *The Art of Community* (Menlo Park, Calif.: Institute for Humane Studies, 1970).

vators. Both can be kept more or less clean, more or less brightly lit, and constructed of a lesser or higher quality, all of which are decisions about the use of resources. Likewise, cities and hotels both provide for open spaces of varying types; again, a choice is made in both instances as to how many resources to devote to such objects of shared consumption. Moreover, hotels, like cities, typically contain a variety of stores and shops that provide services for private consumption. Indeed, a hotel offers a package of private consumption and shared consumption. Such communal services as police, fire, sanitation, recreation, and transportation are in effect provided by the profits earned from the provision of such private services as rooms, meals, and shops.

GOVERNMENT AND THE AGENT-PRINCIPAL RELATIONSHIP

The agent-principal relationship is pervasive in economic affairs. The relations between physician and patient, attorney and client, and manager and stockholder are common illustrations. In all such relationships, a principal who lacks either the time or the talent to perform a task engages an agent to do so. Ideally from the principal's perspective, the agent will act in the same manner as would the principal if only the principal possessed the appropriate talent and chose to devote the required time to the task. However, the agent-principal relationship includes the potential for the agent to act contrary to the principal's interests. It is often suggested, for instance, that managers will to some extent run corporations for their own benefit rather than for the benefit of stockholders. Profits received by stockholders decline as managers transfer wealth to themselves through such means as higher than necessary salaries and expense-account living.

There are two reasons why managers of a corporation might restrain themselves in this exploitation of stockholders. They might do so because they do not want to exploit stockholders "excessively," in which case benevolence would be the source of restraint. Managers might do so because they do not want to lose their jobs. While benevolence exists in most people to varying degrees, it has long been recognized that self-interest is generally a far more powerful force. Accordingly, the tightness of the relationship between agents and principals will depend primarily on the extent to which it is in the self-interest of agents to subsume their interests to those of their principals, or, stated differently, on the extent to which the self-interest of agents lies in advancing the self-interest of principals.

This extent depends in turn on the institutional order within which the agent-principal relationship takes place.

Suppose corporate managers pursue their interests at the expense of owners. The net return received by stockholders will fall below the potential return. If ownership shares are marketable, this decline in return will depress the market value of those shares. Suppose a corporation earns a net income of $1 million annually when managers fully pursue the interests of stockholders. With a 10 percent rate of discount, the value of the firm will be $10 million; if ownership is divided into one million shares, each will be worth $10. But suppose managers preempt for themselves $100,000 of what otherwise would accrue to stockholders. Net income falls to $900,000, the value of the firm falls to $9 million, and the price of an ownership share falls to $9. This decline in the value of ownership is a signal that the corporation is not being managed as efficiently as it might be, as judged by the interests of the owners. At the same time, the deviation between the actual price of ownership and the potential price indicates the capital gain that can be attained by tightening the agent-principal relationship; someone who is able to buy the corporation for $9 million and provide it with managers who did not transfer wealth to themselves will reap a capital gain of $1 million as the value of the corporation returns to $10 million.

The relationship between politicians and citizens is another form of an agent-principal relationship. A government is a nonprofit cooperative in which management is entrusted to politicians, who act as agents for the citizenry. There are some important institutional differences between governments and corporations, and these differences influence the character of the specific agent-principal relationship. Ownership shares in government are nontransferable. Since they cannot be bought and sold, they can acquire no capital value. There is no divergence between actual and potential capital value to provide knowledge about profit opportunities and to generate incentive to act on that knowledge. Moreover, it is impossible to specialize in ownership. People cannot acquire multiple shares of ownership; ownership is acquired by virtue of residency and must be relinquished on changing residency. It seems as though public managers have at least as much, and probably more, ability to transfer wealth from citizens to themselves as corporate managers have vis-à-vis stockholders.

A CONSTITUTIONAL DENOUEMENT

It is common to think that escape from the negative-sum predicament of contemporary democracy resides in electing the right politicians, who will set matters right. The analysis of majoritarian democracy that has been developing in recent literature suggests, however, that the predicament results not so much from self-serving people holding office as from the incentives that ordinary people confront. Tax-transfer politics seems likely to dominate the agenda of majoritarian democracy, and as long as it does government seems destined to act to a significant extent as a negative-sum participant in the division of labor in society. At base, there are really two categories of democracy, which represent different modes of decision making concerning the use of resources. In one, decisions concerning resource utilization are essentially consensual, while in the other they represent the outcome of some clash between warring factions. This recognition, of course, was central to the argument of the *Federalist Papers*, it undergirds the initial effort of the American Constitution to avoid majoritarian democracy, it informs Knut Wicksell's monumental contribution to public economics, was similarly recognized by a variety of Italian scholars who saw public economics as the intersection of economics and politics, and informs a growing contemporary literature on the economic properties of contemporary political institutions.[12]

Within classical liberalism, government is viewed as the umpire for the market economy, but not as a participant, except to the extent that it provides those public goods that people cannot provide effectively for themselves — begging all questions of how it is possible to limit government under these conditions. Politics and economics are treated as distinct spheres of activity, in which each sphere possesses its own rules and institutions. But if government is organized according to majoritarian principles, it will inevitably become a participant in economic life because people will seek the rents that such participation will create. If economics and politics are recognized as non-separable spheres of human conduct, the idea of separate rules and institutions for each sphere cannot be maintained. An integrated, unified treatment of politics and economics — political economy — becomes necessary.

Models of budget-maximizing bureaucrats have played a sizable part in much of the recent literature on collective choice. For the most part, these models of bureau conduct have a pejorative connotation. But what is wrong with budget-maximizing bureaus? Profit-maximizing firms do not occupy a pejorative place in economics. Yet

---

[12] The relation between the *Federalist Papers* and the American Constitution is examined from a similar perspective in Vincent Ostrom, *The Political Theory of a Compound Republic* (Blacksburg, Va.: Center for Study of Public Choice, Virginia Polytechnic Institute, 1971); and Gottfried Dietze, *The Federalist* (Baltimore: Johns Hopkins University Press, 1960).

the two motivations would seem to be essentially identical. Both profit maximization and budget maximization are shorthand statements of the assumption that people try to act effectively rather than ineffectively in what they set out to do, and with respect to organizations effectiveness is generally pursued through efforts at expansion. There are, of course, limits on the size of any particular organization, imposed by competition from other organizations, among other factors. Nonetheless, the efforts of an organization to expand to the limits created by similar efforts of other organizations are acknowledged to be an important, beneficial feature of a market economy. But why isn't it the same with governmental organizations, the various bureaus that provide services? At base, the answer must lie in the nonconsensual framework within which government operates. If so, remedy would seem to lie in the creation of some consensual order, rather than in an attempt to impose direct limits on the expansionary interests of public officials. Budget maximization within a system of majoritarian democracy can be negative sum as it proceeds by rewarding some at the expense of others in society. But budget maximization within a system of consensual democracy might reflect the creative participation of government in the social division of labor.

At base, the advocacy of budget limits, the imposition of restraints on bureau expansion, and the like would seem to reflect an assumption that negative-sum activities of government (beyond those negative-sum activities that are inherent in a market economy) are inherent in democratic government. If so, the only hope for reducing the negative-sum outcomes would seem to lie in restricting the range of political outcomes. But as the simple model we have just considered illustrates, it is by no means obvious that quantitative limits will reduce inefficient programs relative to efficient programs. If the negative-sum outcomes are seen as a by-product of a particular and modifiable institutional order, modification of this order offers the possibility that the pursuit of interests through government will become harmonized with the pursuit of interests in market conduct, with both collective and private economic organizations tending to promote the common wealth. Regardless, it is increasingly recognized that the workings of governmental institutions should command a central place in the study of public economics, for the study of public economics must properly be an exercise in political economy.

SUGGESTIONS FOR FURTHER READING

The growth of government has received much attention in recent years. Regarding the United States, see Roger A. Freeman, *The Growth of*

American Government (Stanford, Calif.: Hoover Institution Press, 1975); and James T. Bennett and Manuel H. Johnson, *The Political Economy of Federal Government Growth: 1959–1978* (College Station: Texas A&M University Press, 1980). For a historical survey of the growth of government in the United States, see Jonathan R. T. Hughes, *The Governmental Habit: Economic Controls from Colonial Times to the Present* (New York: Basic Books, 1977). The transformation of consensual to majoritarian democracy in the United States is chronicled in Terry L. Anderson and Peter J. Hill, *The Birth of a Transfer Society* (Stanford, Calif.: Hoover Institution Press, 1980). A conceptual model of this type of transformation is described in Randall G. Holcombe, "Contractarian Model of the Decline in Classical Liberalism," *Public Choice* 35, No. 3 (1980), pp. 277–286. Relatedly, though from a somewhat different perspective, see the analysis of conflict and constitutional interpretation in Jürgen Backhaus, "Constitutional Guarantees and the Distribution of Power and Wealth," *Public Choice* 33, No. 3 (1978), pp. 45–63.

For more general conceptual treatments of the growth of government, see Allan H. Meltzer and Scott F. Richard, "A Rational Theory of the Size of Government," *Journal of Political Economy* 89 (October 1981), pp. 914–927; Sam Peltzman, "The Growth of Government," *Journal of Law and Economics* 23 (October 1980), pp. 209–287; and Karl Brunner, "Reflections on the Political Economy of Government: The Persistent Growth of Government," *Schweizerische Zeitschrift für Volkswirtschaft und Statistik* 114 (September 1978), pp. 649–680. On limiting government spending, see Alvin Rabushka, "Tax and Spending Limits," in *The United States in the 1980s*, edited by Peter Duignan and Alvin Rabushka (Stanford, Calif.: Hoover Institution Press, 1980), pp. 85–108. On limiting tax bases, see Geoffrey Brennan and James M. Buchanan, *The Power to Tax: Analytical Foundations of a Fiscal Constitution* (Cambridge: Cambridge University Press, 1980). A symposium on tax and expenditure limitation is contained in a special issue of the *National Tax Journal* (32, June 1979, Supplement).

A seminal treatise that contrasts majoritarian and consensual democracy is James M. Buchanan and Gordon Tullock, *The Calculus of Consent* (Ann Arbor: University of Michigan Press, 1962). Heinrich W. Ursprung distinguishes between concordant democracy and democracy by opposition in his essay "Voting Behaviour in a System of Concordant Democracy," *Public Choice* 35, No. 3 (1980), pp. 349–362. On the referendum as a vehicle for concordant democracy, see Eli M. Noam, "The Efficiency of Direct Democracy," *Journal of Political Economy* 88 (August 1980), pp. 803–810. For a related and interesting comparison of representative and direct democracy, see Werner W. Pommerehene and Friedrich Schneider, "Fiscal Illusion, Political Institutions, and Local Public Spending," *Kyklos* 31, No. 3 (1978), pp. 381–408. For an important recognition that consensual democracy does not require approximate unanimity as much as non-discrimination, which may be implemented under a variety of voting rules, see W. H. Hutt, "Unanimity Versus Non-Discrimination (As Criteria for Constitutional Validity)," in *Individual Freedom: Selected Works of*

William H. Hutt, edited by Svetozar Pejovich and David Klingaman (Westport, Conn.: Greenwood Press, 1975), pp. 14–33. For a further exploration of the provision of shared consumption through a regime grounded in property and contract, see Thomas E. Borcherding, "Competition, Exclusion, and the Optimal Supply of Public Goods," *Journal of Law and Economics* 21 (April 1978), pp. 111–132.

Richard D. Auster and Morris Silver, *The State as a Firm* (Boston: Martinus Nijhoff, 1979), argue that government can be usefully looked upon as a monopolistic firm, with democracy being a particular form of ownership. The agent-principal relationship as it concerns corporations is explored in Henry G. Manne, "Mergers and the Market for Corporate Control," *Journal of Political Economy* 73 (April 1965), pp. 110–120; Michael C. Jensen and William H. Meckling, "Theory of the Firm: Managerial Behavior, Agency Costs and Ownership Structure," *Journal of Financial Economics* 3 (October 1976), pp. 305–360; and Eugene F. Fama, "Agency Problems and the Theory of the Firm," *Journal of Political Economy* 88 (April 1980), pp. 288–307. A similar perspective is applied to government in Robert J. Barro, "The Control of Politicians: An Economic Model," *Public Choice* 14 (Spring 1973), pp. 19–42. Hans van den Doel, *Democracy and Welfare Economics* (Cambridge: Cambridge University Press, 1979), surveys different forms of democracy from the perspective of welfare economics.

III

METHODS OF FINANCING GOVERNMENT

8

User Charges and the Enterprise Principle

For the most part, governments garner their revenues by imposing taxes on their citizens. Under a system of tax finance, there is no immediate relation between the revenues government extracts from people and the value people place on the services government provides. In contrast, user charges entail a direct relation between extractions made and services rendered. In its pure form a government's supply of a service, with the use of charges and prices, operates identically to the supply of a service by a business firm through market transactions. In both cases, people can consume the service only by paying the required price, and the supply of the service is financed by the revenue derived from the sale of the service. In a less than pure form, the revenues derived from user charges make up a substantial part of the total revenues available to finance the activity, and the remaining revenues are raised through taxation.

Many local governments engage directly in the supply of such utility services as electricity, gas, and water, which are often provided in other localities by private corporations. These services are financed by charges imposed on users for the services rendered. Local governments also commonly provide such services as refuse collection, bus service, and hospital care, and in such instances it is common for charges to cover a significant portion of total expenditures on such services. Tax revenues are used only to cover the excess of expenses over revenues from user changes. Cities also charge people for parking in metered spaces, they "charge" by issuing citations for parking in restricted spaces, they charge the promoters of events such as concerts and carnivals for special police services, and they impose a variety of licensing fees on businesses. The U.S. Postal Service charges users for carrying mail, although total revenues fall short of the expenses incurred by the postal service. This deficit is financed by tax revenues. In many cases in which user pricing is not feasible for one reason or another, tax earmarking may serve as a substitute means of financing services. Even though it may not be feasible to price highway services directly, a tax on gasoline to finance highways may be a substitute means of charging highway users for the supply of highway services.

The direct sale of services is practiced at all levels of government, but it is especially important at the local level in the United States. As Table 1.3 showed for 1979, user charges provided more than 10 percent of all the revenues raised by the federal government, over 15 percent of the revenues raised by state governments, and nearly 35 percent of the revenues raised by local governments.

WELFARE NORMS FOR PUBLIC PRICES

User pricing is feasible only when the service to be financed is divisible among users; otherwise it is impossible to charge people according to their use of the service. The user pricing of divisible services thus contrasts with the tax financing of indivisible services. Because the output from a program of, say, mosquito control is not divisible among the residents of the affected area, individuals cannot choose to purchase their preferred output of the service. User pricing therefore is not a feasible means of financing the provision of mosquito control. By contrast, the supply of water is divisible among consumers, so it is feasible to charge people according to their consumption of water. Besides the requirement of divisibility, the expense of excluding those who do not pay the charge must be comparatively low in order for user charges to be feasible. It is relatively inexpensive to monitor a person's consumption of water and to charge accordingly, but it is relatively expensive at this time to monitor a person's use of city streets. Although the use of city streets is divisible among users, it is also relatively expensive to charge people according to their use.

In those cases where user charges are considered an appropriate means of financing an activity, what is the appropriate price to charge? This normative question about setting prices has been the dominant concern in the literature on user pricing. One substantial body of thought suggests that public prices should be set equal to the marginal costs of the services provided. This line of thought construes the central problem of public administration as one of instructing enterprise managers to follow a rule setting price equal to marginal cost. This rule is generally thought to produce efficiency in resource utilization so long as marginal cost does not decrease as output increases.

Marginal-Cost Pricing and Constant Cost

Figure 8.1 illustrates the central idea of a rule that sets price equal to marginal cost in a case where marginal cost is constant over output. The demand curve reflects the value people place on the service in question, and the marginal cost curve reflects the value people place on the output they must forgo to receive the service in question. When price equals marginal cost, the value people place on what they get equals the value they place on what they must sacrifice in exchange. Accordingly, any movement away from marginal-cost pricing will, under constant cost, entail a reduction in value of the resulting output. When a public enterprise that is subject to constant marginal cost sets price equal to marginal cost, it acts in the same way as a competitive firm would act.

The equivalence between such a public enterprise and a competitive firm can also be seen by examining the effect of an increase in demand in Figure 8.1. With the increase in demand, people want to buy more than can be produced, if short-run cost is rising. By setting price equal to short-run marginal cost, the enterprise will receive profits because short-run marginal cost exceeds short-run average cost. In a competitive industry, those profits attract entry, which increases capacity in the industry. The public enterprise will essentially act in the same fashion if it uses those profits to expand its scale of operation. Once this scale has increased to the point where short-run marginal cost equals long-run marginal cost, profits will have vanished and the enterprise will have no further incentive to change its scale of operation.

Marginal-Cost Pricing and Increasing Cost

When a public enterprise produces under conditions of increasing cost, a rule that sets price equal to marginal cost might seem to have essentially the same properties as it had under constant cost. But this is not so, as Figure 8.2 illustrates. At the rate of output at which marginal cost equals price, X_0 in Figure 8.2, profits are being received because marginal cost exceeds average cost. But the cost of expanding output beyond X_0 (which is described by MC) exceeds the value of that output (described by D). This situation is identical to that discussed in Chapter 2 where application of the benefit principle led to budget surpluses under increasing cost as long as average tax-price and marginal tax-price were equal. In such circumstances,

---

FIGURE 8.1 Marginal-Cost Pricing with Constant Cost

The demand for some service is described by D_0, and marginal cost is equal to average cost. A public enterprise that follows a rule for setting price equal to marginal cost will set a price of P_0 per unit and provide X_0 units of output. That this rate of output is welfare maximizing is easily seen: When output is less than X_0, the value people place on added output (shown by D_0) exceeds the cost of that output, and when output exceeds X_0, the value they place on added output is less than the cost of that output.

If the demand for the service rises to D_1, people will want X_1 at the price of P_0. If short-run cost is rising, as shown by SMC_0 and SAC_0, a rule of marginal-cost pricing will, in the short run, provide X_S output at a price of P_S. The average cost of that output is C_S per unit, so profits of $P_S - C_S$ per unit are being earned in the short run. Those profits will make it possible to finance an expansion in output until X_1 results, at which time profits are no longer being received.

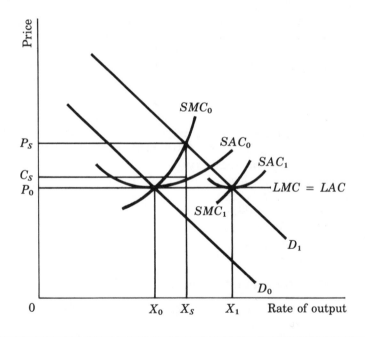

the prices people pay for inframarginal units of output will exceed the cost of that output.

The presence of such profits raises conceptual difficulties. The profits could be returned to users of the service, but there are many different ways this could be done and the choice among the options can affect the distribution of wealth. Alternatively, the profits could be used to finance other collective activities not financed by user

FIGURE 8.2 Marginal-Cost Pricing with Increasing Average Cost

A rule of setting price equal to marginal cost produces a price of P_0 and an output of X_0. At this rate of output, average cost is C_0, so profits of $P_0 - C_0$ per unit are received. If those profits are dissipated through an expansion in output to X_1, the marginal cost of that output will exceed its marginal value by ab.

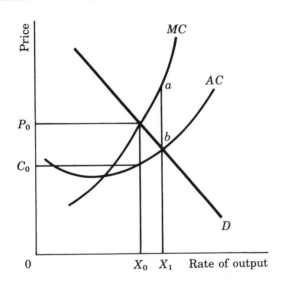

charges. In this case, the distribution of wealth will still be affected, at least as long as people differ in their demand for services that might be financed from those profits. In any event, a rule of setting price equal to marginal cost is not as easily applicable when average cost is increasing as it is when average cost is constant because the method selected for the dissipation of the profits will influence the distribution of wealth in society.

Marginal-Cost Pricing and Decreasing Cost

When average cost is decreasing, a rule that sets price equal to marginal cost will incur losses because price will be less than average cost. Those losses raise essentially the same welfare issues as those raised by profits under increasing cost. Figure 8.3 illustrates the central point. Although a loss results when price is set equal to marginal cost, the value that people place on additional output equals the cost of that output. But if the loss is avoided by setting price equal to average

FIGURE 8.3 Marginal-Cost Pricing with Decreasing Average Cost

Marginal-cost pricing yields a price of P_0 and a rate of output X_0. At this rate of output, however, average cost is C_0. A loss of $C_0 - P_0$ per unit of output results. Losses can be avoided under average-cost pricing, in which case a price of P_1 is established. At this price, however, the value people place on one additional unit of output exceeds the cost of that output by ab, which is the difference between the demand price and the marginal cost of the service.

Suppose a price of P_1 is established for the first X_1 units of output. It is easy to see that the consumers of X will potentially be able to agree on some method of financing expansions in output beyond X_1, as long as the demand price exceeds the marginal cost. This means that price will no longer be uniform over output. Rather, price will be P_1 for the first X_1 units, and it will be lower for outputs between X_1 and X_0. The price of the X_0th unit will be P_0.

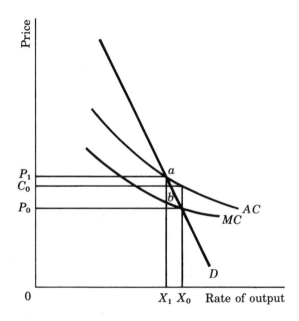

cost, output is reduced, and at this lower rate of output the value people place on additional output exceeds the cost of that output. The avoidance of losses by using average-cost pricing means that resources are diverted from the more valued to less valued uses. Much controversy has centered on different ways of covering the loss that would result from marginal-cost pricing. So long as people differ in the way they are required to pay to cover the loss, the choice among those methods of payment will entail a choice among different distributions of wealth. This difficulty is, of course, the same one that arises with the dissipation of profits under increasing cost.

Various forms of multipart pricing have captured much interest as methods of financing services that are subject to decreasing cost. Such forms of pricing can, among other things, be shown to be agreeable in principle to the users of the service. Suppose initially that price is set at average cost. At this rate of output, the value people place on additional output exceeds the cost they must bear for that output, as Figure 8.3 illustrates. It will be conceptually possible for all users of the service to agree to a system of lower marginal prices for blocks or units of output beyond those provided under average-cost pricing. Indeed, multipart pricing is widely used. Numerous services are financed by levying both a charge that varies directly with the amount consumed and a charge that is independent of consumption. Golf courses often levy both a flat annual fee and a per-unit fee for each round of golf. Telephone services are financed by applying a fixed installation charge, a recurring but fixed equipment fee, and a price that varies directly with the amount of service consumed. Although the specific form of multipart pricing may differ from case to case, all forms create a divergence between the average price of a service and the marginal price. By doing this, a multipart tariff makes it possible to reconcile the conflict between average-cost and marginal-cost pricing, and to do so in a way that is conceivably agreeable to all consumers of the service.[1]

Zero Marginal Cost

An extreme form of declining average cost occurs when marginal cost is zero. The examples that have been used to illustrate this case typically involve a long-lived asset that, once produced, will yield services with little if any additional expense. A bridge is a common illustration: The expenses of annual maintenance are quite small in comparison to the expense of construction, and the bridge's durability is quite high. Figure 8.4 illustrates this case. Suppose the bridge is financed at average cost, which will amortize the expense of the

---

[1] The feasibility of user pricing will, of course, vary inversely with the cost of operating the pricing system. In some cases the cost of operating a multipart tariff may be so high as to make it infeasible. If so, the conflict between average-cost and marginal-cost pricing will remain. Moreover, to say that a normative rationalization for a program of multipart pricing can be developed is not to imply that existing systems of multipart pricing actually conform to the requirements of that rationalization, as opposed to serving other interests and purposes.

FIGURE 8.4 Marginal-Cost Pricing with Zero Marginal Cost

The daily demand for bridge crossings is described by D, but its marginal cost is zero. If price is set at P, people will make X crossings per day, and the government's daily revenue will be $OPaX$. At that rate of output, the value to users of one more crossing is P, while the cost of that crossing is zero. An expansion in output beyond X will result in a more valued pattern of resource utilization. Only when output is X' will resources be used in their most valuable manner. At this output, the value of additional output will equal the cost of that output, with both being zero. By being charged a price of zero, consumers gain in disposable income what the government loses in revenue, but in addition consumers gain by the excess of value over cost that they capture, aXX', which is called consumers' surplus.

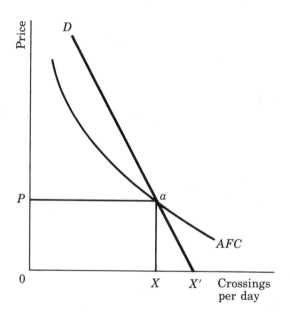

bridge over its expected lifetime, and that there is no traffic conges-tion. The imposition of a user price will induce some travelers to avoid the bridge who would otherwise have used it. Some crossings will be prevented by the charge even though the cost of those cross-ings is zero. The value of the existing stock of resources in society will be increased by allowing those crossings.

If price is set at zero, however, a question arises as to how to finance the bridge. This is the same question that comes up in the more general case of decreasing average cost. Indeed, the case of zero (or practically zero) marginal cost is but a special, extreme case of decreasing average cost. As we saw in the case of decreasing average cost in general, there is no necessity to impose a requirement that all units of output carry the same price. With zero marginal cost, as with decreasing average cost in general, there will be gains from exchange because the beneficiaries of the facility will agree to some form of multipart pricing, in which the *marginal* unit is priced at marginal cost and in which the beneficiaries pay an average price equal to average cost. This might be done in numerous ways. A simple illustration that corresponds to a variety of pricing practices would be the payment of an annual lump-sum charge for the right to use the bridge in conjunction with a set of declining prices for additional crossings beyond a stipulated level of usage.

The assumption of zero marginal cost also raises questions about the time dimension of marginal cost. Is a bridge an illustration of zero marginal cost? It might be argued that it is really only a case of low marginal cost, because there are some annual expenses of maintenance. For purposes of discussion and clarity of thought, however, assume there are no such annual expenses. That is, the bridge, once built, requires no additional care, and when the period of its useful life runs out, it suddenly collapses. If the marginal cost of a bridge that lasts fifty years is zero, what is the marginal cost of a bridge that lasts ten years? Or of one that lasts five years? What about the marginal cost of a bridge that lasts only one year? One point implied by questions such as these is that the marginal cost of anything is zero once it has been produced.[2] Cost is an anticipation of the value sacrificed by choosing one course of activity over another.[3] The cost of building a bridge is the anticipated, but never realized, value of some alternative use of resources that is displaced by the construction of the bridge. There is clearly a long-run marginal cost to building a bridge, and furthermore, this cost can have such dimensions as the durability and the capacity of the bridge.

A bridge that is already built has no marginal cost. But this is also true for the marginal cost of, say, beer already brewed. Indeed, the marginal cost of anything that has already been produced is zero, because marginal cost is the anticipated value of an option that is rejected when an alternative course of production is chosen. Cost is borne when the choice is made. A rule of marginal-cost pricing would

---

[2] This point is developed in Roland N. McKean and Jora R. Minasian, "On Achieving Pareto Optimality — Regardless of Cost," *Western Economic Journal* 4 (December 1966), pp. 14–23.

[3] For an explanation of this, see James M. Buchanan, *Cost and Choice* (Chicago: Markham, 1969).

seem to require the zero pricing, not just of bridges but of everything that has already been produced. To follow such a pricing rule would, however, destroy the incentive to engage in production in the first place. Pricing, in other words, serves the function of validating — or dashing — anticipations about the value of decisions concerning production because it is such information that guides future choices about the use of resources. The present stock of goods is costless because it has arrived as a result of decisions made previously. What is not costless is the future stock of goods, decisions about which are yet to be made.

There seems to be little point in evaluating pricing rules according to their ability to cover the cost of what has already been produced. What matters most about pricing rules is the way they guide future choices about the use of resources. The present is a product of past choices, and it is therefore beyond control. Only the future can be influenced by present choices. In this light, a truly universal application of marginal-cost pricing would set zero prices for everything in stock, not just for bridges. The consequence of doing this, of course, would be to destroy incentives for future production.

Stated alternatively, if incentives to produce are to be maintained, cost must refer to a period of time sufficient to allow for reproduction of the activity. Moreover, a pricing rule must allow for the generation of knowledge pertinent to a decision to reproduce. Beer already produced has no cost, but to disallow the pricing of beer would be to prevent its future production. The cost of beer pertains to a period of production long enough to allow for reproduction of beer. At the same time, the pricing of beer generates information about the aptness of earlier decisions about production, and that information aids present decision making about future production. It is the same with bridges or other long-lived assets. Bridges last longer than trucks, which in turn last longer than pencils. Each has marginal cost, though, and each differs in the time before reproduction will be required. In all instances, prices are one means of conveying knowledge about the aptness of past choices about production, and they provide useful information about future choices. This is not to argue normatively that a bridge with a fifty-year life should be priced, but only to note that it is misleading to speak of it as having no marginal cost. Marginal cost is forward looking, not backward looking, and a consideration of this simple point, besides raising questions about a number of long-standing rules of public pricing, focuses attention on the properties of different institutional regimes in providing incentives for future production activities, which are the only activities a society can do anything about.

TAX EARMARKING, TRUST FUNDING, AND QUASI-PRICING

As an alternative to charging consumers directly for their consumption, a service can be taxed, with the proceeds of that tax serving as a substitute for direct pricing. Highways are financed to a large extent from the proceeds of taxes on gasoline and related products. Tax liability depends on the consumption of gasoline, but as long as the consumption of gasoline corresponds closely to the consumption of highway services, the earmarking of revenues from a tax on gasoline for expenditure on highways is a close substitute for the direct pricing of highway services. Likewise, people's use of a sewer system is related to their consumption of water, although certainly not perfectly. The imposition of a tax based on water consumption, with those revenues used to finance the provision of sewerage, will similarly work to some degree as a substitute for the direct pricing of sewer services.

It is possible to conceptualize circumstances in which an earmarked tax will be a perfect substitute for user pricing. Consider the financing of highway services from a trust fund created by revenues from a tax on gasoline. Suppose that traffic density is uniform throughout the day, making it possible to ignore difficulties caused by traffic congestion, and also suppose that all cars get 20 miles per gallon of gasoline. In this setting, a gasoline tax of 20 cents per gallon is equivalent to a highway charge of 1 cent per mile. If 1 cent per mile is the marginal cost of highway services, a 20-cent-per-gallon tax on gasoline becomes a form of marginal-cost pricing. In this case, tax earmarking is a perfect substitute for the financing of highway services directly through user pricing.[4]

There are several reasons why actual gasoline taxes might serve only as an imperfect substitute for direct user pricing. For one thing, traffic density is not uniform throughout the day. Highways are subject to peak-load congestion during the morning and evening rush hours. Usage of highways during the peak-load hours is more costly than at other times because peak-load users impose congestion costs on other users at that time. A system of marginal-cost pricing would impose a higher price during the peak rush hours, one effect of which would be to transfer some usage from peak to off-peak hours. Tax earmarking can do nothing to alleviate peak-load congestion.

---

[4] This assumes that the gasoline tax is paid by consumers of gasoline, rather than by producers. Such issues of incidence, which exist for any earmarked tax, are examined in Chapter 11.

Furthermore, cars are not identical in their consumption of gasoline per mile traveled. The more miles per gallon a car gets, the lower its implicit charge for highway services will be when those services are financed through a tax on gasoline. A car that gets 40 miles per gallon will pay only half as much per mile as a car that gets 20 miles per gallon. What holds for financing highway services through a tax on gasoline holds generally for attempts to charge for one service by taxing some complementary activity instead. Moreover, changing circumstances over time may subsequently render inappropriate a quasi-price that was once appropriate. Suppose again that all cars get 20 miles per gallon and that traffic density is uniform throughout the day. If the income elasticity of demand for highway services is unity, a 10 percent rise in income will generate a 10 percent increase in the demand for highway services, as indicated, say, by miles driven. The revenue to finance the supply of highway services, however, is determined in the market for gasoline, as there is no market for highway services. If the amount of highway services consumed per gallon of gasoline remains unchanged when income rises, a 10 percent rise in income will also generate a 10 percent rise in revenue from the gasoline tax.

If the rise in income changes the demand for gasoline, most likely by changing the types of cars bought but possibly also by changing such characteristics of driving as speed, tax revenues will not rise at the same rate as the consumption of highway services. If the demand for gasoline grows more slowly than the demand for highway services, tax revenues will be insufficient to finance the supply of highway services, unless the rate of tax is increased. If demand for gasoline grows more rapidly than the demand for highway services, tax revenues will exceed the amount required to finance the supply of highway services, unless the tax rate is reduced.[5]

User pricing, or even quasi-pricing, is a more sensitive means of transmitting knowledge about consumer preferences than is general-fund financing. Under general-fund financing, several services are provided jointly through a budget. A change in the willingness of people to approve of taxation conveys less information about their evaluations of particular services than can be learned when services are financed by user charges. There is clearly scope for the development of user pricing in such areas as highways, education, libraries,

[5] See, for instance, Walter W. McMahon and Case M. Sprenkle, "A Theory of Earmarking," *National Tax Journal* 23 (September 1970), pp. 255–261. More generally on earmarking, see James M. Buchanan, "The Economics of Earmarked Taxes," *Journal of Political Economy* 71 (October 1963), pp. 457–469; and Charles J. Goetz, "Earmarked Taxes and Majority Rule Budgetary Processes," *American Economic Review* 58 (March 1968), pp. 128–136.

recreation, museums, health, and refuse collection, to name some frequently cited areas.

General support for a principle of user pricing still leaves unanswered the selection of a particular price. A particular pricing scheme must be selected, and the choice of a scheme is by no means inconsequential. James Johnson examined ten formulas for setting user charges for sewers and found substantial variation in the percentage of the total charge placed on various users.[6] The percentage of the burden placed on residential users ranged from 33.1 percent to 94.2 percent. The burden on commercial users ranged from 5.3 percent to 25.7 precent, while the burden on industrial users ranged from 0.4 percent to 51.2 percent. Johnson estimated that residential users would pay 94.2 percent of all charges if charges were uniform per user, whereas commercial and industrial users would pay only 5.3 and 0.4 percent respectively. By contrast, residential users would pay only 33.1 percent and industrial users would pay 51.2 percent if charges were a constant rate per pound of sewage discharged. The highest relative payment for commercial users, 25.7 percent, would result when charges were levied proportionate to assessed property value.

The potential arbitrariness that appears to exist in the choice of method of charging users can be expected to vary with the competition the public enterprise faces. The more intense competition is, the less scope for arbitrariness the enterprise will have in choosing pricing schemes because it will be constrained by the need to compete for customers. When competition is absent, it may possess some freedom to choose among possible pricing schemes, with the choice among schemes perhaps favoring some classes of buyers at the expense of others. To introduce such considerations as these, however, is to get into positive issues about the actual conduct of public enterprises.

INHERENT AMBIGUITY IN PRICING RULES

The normative approach to public pricing aims to describe a pricing rule for public enterprises to follow. Once such a rule has been articulated, it might seem to be a relatively simple matter to evaluate the conduct of a public enterprise by observing how closely it follows the rule. Doing this is not as simple as it might seem. The cost of making one choice concerning production is the value of some alter-

---

[6] James A. Johnson, "The Distribution of the Burden of Sewer User Charges Under Various Charge Formulas," *National Tax Journal* 22 (December 1969), pp. 472–485.

native choice that could have been made at that time but was rejected
in favor of the choice actually made. The cost of a comparatively
simple activity such as choosing how many cattle to add to a herd
depends on judgments about such things as the future prices of beef
and feed, among many other relevant variables. A number of people
all instructed by and sincerely interested in following such a rule as
choosing a size of herd that maximizes profit can reasonably be expected to make different choices, with those choices reflecting different evaluations of such things as anticipated future prices of beef,
feed, transportation, and the like. Hence, it is impossible to determine from the actual choices people make the degree to which they
are faithful to a rule of maximizing profits. Although some people
may make greater profits than others after the fact, they could all be
described as attempting to maximize profits or as following a rule
to equate marginal revenue and marginal cost.

People who act within the same institutional setting, say one of
residual claimancy or profit-and-loss, can choose different options in
light of the same data because, among other things, they vary in their
assessment of the likelihood of possibilities. Consequently, it is certainly reasonable to expect people to make different choices under
different institutional settings, even though the data on which those
choices are based do not differ. If a person in one setting shares in the
profits and covers part of the loss, while in a second setting a person is
paid through a fixed salary and has options for higher wealth in securing future employment with a present client, the cost of choosing one
course of action over another is likely to differ between those settings.
In the former setting, profit maximization is likely to be the dominant
motivation, but in the latter setting some willingness to sacrifice
profits to give business to a potential future employer has relatively
stronger survival value.

Any effort to understand the actual conduct of public enterprises,
rather than simply describing norms for their desired conduct, takes
on added interest once it is recognized that cost, and the degree to
which pricing rules are adhered to, is not an objective fact but rather
depends on the evaluation by some person of the options for choice.
One question that arises in discussions of user pricing is, Why have
such pricing in the first place? If user pricing is to finance water,
electricity, refuse collection, sewerage, postal services, hospitals, and
the like, why have those services been provided by public enterprises?
If a utility is to set prices equal to marginal cost, with the intention
of this rule being to simulate results in a competitive market, why
provide the service through a public enterprise? Why not rely on a
real competitive market? It is one thing to give a rationalization for
the services a public enterprise can provide, but it can be quite a

different matter to develop an understanding of the interests a public enterprise might actually serve.

Many services for which user pricing is either practiced or advocated are services for which competitive provision is easy to imagine, with education and recreation serving as significant examples. Other services seem to correspond to some extent to the common illustration of natural monopoly, such as various utility services in which the efficient-sized production unit will be so large as to control most of the market. Both categories of service raise the same question of ascertaining the interests served by public enterprises because such an understanding makes it possible in turn to understand the functioning of user charges. In the presence of a natural monopoly, one option is to let it exist and to charge a monopoly price. Another is to sell the right to operate the monopoly, in which event competitive bidding will essentially transfer the monopoly profits from the owners of the monopoly to taxpayers generally. A third option is to impose competitive pricing through regulation, as one application of a rule of marginal-cost pricing. Figure 8.5 illustrates these various possibilities.

Where does public operation fit in? It might be argued that public regulators cannot acquire the knowledge necessary to set prices equal to marginal cost, or to follow some other pricing rule, without actually operating the enterprise. If this is so, public operation is necessary to implement marginal-cost pricing, or whatever other pricing rule is thought to be appropriate, in light of the difficulty of monitoring the organization from the outside.

On what grounds can it reasonably be thought that making the enterprise public will cause it to follow such a pricing rule, even setting aside the impossibility of determining objectively whether such a rule is being followed? A private enterprise can be described as tending to conform to an output rule of setting marginal revenue equal to marginal cost because the market system rewards people more highly the more accurate their anticipations are about such things as future conditions of demand and production. A competitive system of private enterprises can be described as following a rule of setting price equal to marginal cost because otherwise profit opportunities would be unexploited. Simply converting an enterprise from private to public ownership would hardly seem sufficient to cause it to conform to some desired pricing rule. Likewise, the prices that are actually established by public enterprises would seem to depend on the costs and gains of different pricing policies to enterprise managers.

It has often been observed that public enterprises have more uniform prices than private enterprises in situations with periods of peak

FIGURE 8.5 Public Enterprise and Natural Monopoly

If unregulated, the monopoly will produce the output X_m, where marginal
revenue equals marginal cost. The price of its product will be P_m, and its
average cost will be C_m per unit, giving the monopoly a profit of $P_m - C_m$
per unit of output. If the government institutes competive bidding for the
right to operate the monopoly, the bid will, as a first approximation, equal
the amount of the monopoly profit. Consumers will still pay the monopoly
price for the monopoly rate of output, but now what were formerly
monopoly profits become revenues for the government instead.
Alternatively, the government could impose a maximum price of P_c, which
would correspond to the competitive outcome if the industry is capable of
competitive organization, in which case the rate of output will be X_c.

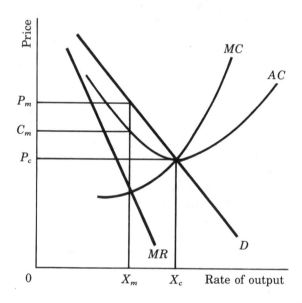

demands and of slack demands.[7] Such differences in pricing seem consistent with the different incentives typically contained in the different organizations, as Figure 8.6 illustrates. Suppose uniform pricing
is initially practiced within an enterprise, and consider the imposition
of a system of variable prices designed to ration capacity throughout
the day. That system of prices will reduce the claims on the system
during the peak period and will transfer some of those claims to the
slack period, where the excess capacity will likewise be reduced. If

[7] See, for instance, Sam Peltzman, "Pricing in Public and Private Enterprises:
Electric Utilities in the United States," *Journal of Law and Economics* 14
(April 1971), pp. 109–147.

FIGURE 8.6 Pricing Options with Variable Demands

The demand for some service, say ridership on a transit system, is higher during some periods of the day, as indicated by D_p, than it is at others, as indicated by D_s. Suppose the system can transport X_c riders before congestion costs set in. By charging a price of P_p during the peak period and a price of P_s during the slack period, the congestion-free capacity will be fully utilized throughout the day. On the other hand, should some uniform, intermediate price be used, say P_u, usage will be less than capacity during the slack period, as shown by X_s^u, and in excess of capacity during the peak period, as shown by X_p^u.

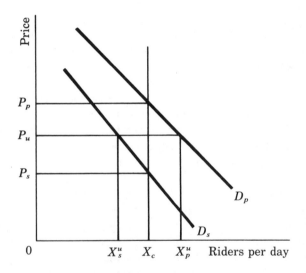

the peak demand is less elastic than the slack demand at the uniform price, which seems likely because peak usage is surely less volitional than slack usage, the imposition of variable pricing will increase total revenue.

This can be seen most clearly if it is assumed that peak demand is inelastic and that slack demand is elastic at the uniform price. In this case, the rise in peak price will result in a less than proportionate reduction in consumption, thereby increasing revenues received from the peak demanders. At the same time, the reduction in slack price will result in a more than proportionate increase in consumption, which similarly increases the revenues received from the slack demanders. An enterprise that resorts to such a program of differential prices can increase the revenues generated by the facility for no change in output, simply by shifting some usage from the congested peak period to the uncongested slack period. A profit-seeking enterprise would have a clear incentive to engage in such differential pricing.

What might account for the lesser use made of such differential pricing by public enterprises? Are there systematic differences in the incentives faced by managers of public enterprises that weaken the gains they secure from differential pricing? As we saw in Chapter 6, profits within public enterprises are not appropriable, at least under present arrangements. Yet making profits nonappropriable does not erase the desire for profits; it only changes the form in which profits can be sought. Public enterprises have no particular reason to impose variable pricing because they cannot capture the profits. There are, however, several reasons why public enterprises are interested in "profits." One reason has to do with the income and prestige that typically vary directly with the size of the enterprise. Another has to do with expanded opportunities for awarding contracts, for new buses, for construction, and the like, to favored firms. Still another reason has to do with opportunities for subsequently attaining lucrative positions in the private sector that perhaps are enhanced by the experience of managing a larger rather than a smaller enterprise.

Uniform pricing creates an excess demand during the peak period, and the resulting congestion may be an effective way of creating a coalition in support of an expansion in the capacity of the enterprise. As long as the demand price of peak demanders exceeds the uniform price they actually pay by more than the price of the taxes they must bear to expand capacity, they will generally support expansions in capacity. As we explored in several earlier chapters, there are circumstances in which such an expansion in capacity will be forthcoming under a system of majoritarian democracy — and such expansions will commonly advance the interests of enterprise managers more effectively than will the imposition of some form of variable pricing, at least as long as profits remain unappropriable.

The creation of public enterprises where private enterprises, including publicly regulated ones, could provide an alternative source of supply is a legislative choice. An understanding of public enterprises requires an understanding of the interests served by the legislation that creates and maintains the enterprise. It has been estimated, for instance, that the price of first-class mail covers 100 percent of the estimated expenses associated with carrying it, while the price of second-class mail covers only 23 percent of its estimated expenses.[8] Although postal services are provided largely through user

[8] Leonard Waverman, "Pricing Principles: How Should Postal Rates Be Set?," in *Perspectives on Postal Service Issues,* edited by Roger Sherman (Washington, D.C.: American Enterprise Institute, 1980), p. 12.

pricing, the structure of prices that results is certainly not one that would reasonably be expected to result if the postal service were profit seeking and if competitors were free to carry first-class mail. The conjunction of prohibitions on the private carrying of first-class mail and the structure of rates set by the postal service create, among other things, a subsidization of the commercial interests served by second-class mail by those who mainly or exclusively use first-class mail. The creation of public enterprises and the establishment of a particular pattern of enterprise prices is perhaps best understood, at least within a system of majoritarian democracy, as a means of subsidizing particular, dominant interests, with the prices being part of the process of subsidization (and of taxation), rather than as an efficiency-enhancing device. Public enterprises seem to possess some of the attributes of the organization of economic activity through contract, for people are charged for services rendered. But public enterprises operate under conditions of the nonappropriability of profits and, moreover, commonly receive supporting budgetary appropriations as well. Public enterprises often receive additional, legal protections from competition, as if the protection provided by budgetary appropriations and the exemption from taxation were insufficient to ensure survival. Consequently, public enterprises seem to be part of the system of majoritarian democracy in which particular interests are advanced at the expense of the interests of others in society.[9]

SUGGESTIONS FOR FURTHER READING

For a number of essays, theoretical and practical, on user charges, see *Public Prices for Public Products,* edited by Selma J. Mushkin (Washington, D.C.: Urban Institute, 1972). Careful discussions of the possible scope for user pricing in state and local government are contained in Alice J. Vandermeulen, "Reform of a State Fee Structure: Principles, Pitfalls, and Proposals for Increasing Revenue," *National Tax Journal* 17 (December 1964), pp. 394–402; and Jacob Stockfish, "Fees and Service Charges as Source of City Revenue: A Case Study of Los Angeles," *National Tax Journal* 13 (June 1960), pp. 97–121.

For discussions of user pricing in terms of its potential applicability, see Werner Z. Hirsch, *The Economics of State and Local Government* (New York: McGraw-Hill, 1970), pp. 43–47; William S. Vickrey, "Gen-

---

[9] To some extent the services provided by public enterprises may have some attributes of public goods, in that indirect benefits to others are provided simultaneously with the direct benefits to the buyer. Education is often considered an example. To the extent that this is so, a combination of pricing and tax financing can be viewed as a means of charging buyers directly for their benefits while charging indirect beneficiaries through taxation.

eral and Specific Financing of Urban Services," in *Public Expenditure Decisions in the Urban Community,* edited by Howard G. Schaller (Washington, D.C.: Resources for the Future, 1963), pp. 62–90; Milton Z. Kafoglis, "Local Service Charges," in *State and Local Tax Problems,* edited by Harry L. Johnson (Knoxville: University of Tennessee Press, 1969), pp. 164–186; and Thomas J. DiLorenzo and Paul B. Downing, "User Charges and Special Districts," in *Management Policies in Local Government Finance,* edited by J. Richard Aronson and Eli Schwartz (Washington, D.C.: International City Management Association, 1981), pp. 184–210.

The literature on marginal cost pricing is voluminous. An extensive, valuable survey of marginal-cost pricing is the two-article series by Nancy D. Ruggles, "The Welfare Basis of the Marginal Cost Pricing Principle," *Review of Economic Studies* 17, No. 1 (1949), pp. 29–46; and "Recent Developments in the Theory of Marginal Cost Pricing," *Review of Economic Studies* 17, No. 2 (1950), pp. 107–126. A classic treatment of multipart pricing is Ronald H. Coase, "The Marginal Cost Controversy," *Economica* 13 (August 1946), pp. 169–182.

For an examination of the need to distinguish between the average price paid for an entire bundle and the price paid for the marginal addition to that bundle, see James M. Buchanan, "A Public Choice Approach to Public Utility Pricing," *Public Choice* 5 (Fall 1968), pp. 1–17. Any illusions about the possibility of assessing objectively whether an enterprise is following such a rule as setting price equal to marginal cost is dashed in G. F. Thirlby, "The Ruler," *South African Journal of Economics* 14 (December 1946), pp. 253–276; and Jack Wiseman, "Uncertainty, Costs, and Collectivist Economic Planning," *Economica* 20 (May 1953), pp. 118–128. These essays by Thirlby and Wiseman, along with several other pertinent essays, are reprinted in *L.S.E. Essays on Cost,* edited by James M. Buchanan and G. F. Thirlby (London: Weidenfeld and Nicolson, 1973).

9

Taxation of Personal Income

Taxation is a mandatory transfer of control over some resources that takes place between individual members of society and government. This transfer can occur in numerous ways. It was once common for taxes to be assessed and paid in kind, as when the state would claim a portion of a farmer's crop or draft people to build roads or fight wars. In contemporary times, taxes are usually assessed and paid in money, with the assessment based on some type of economic transaction. There are numerous types of transactions against which taxes can be assessed, and they can be put into a few main categories. People act simultaneously as producers and as consumers. When they act as producers, they supply their services and receive payments in return. When people act as consumers, they use the payments they have received as producers to buy the various goods and services that have been produced in the society. Taxes can be assessed against people as producers and as consumers, against the sources or the uses of income. The former is income taxation and the latter is taxation on expenditure or consumption. This chapter and Chapter 10 explore different forms of taxing the sources of income — the taxation of personal income in this chapter and the taxation of corporation income in the next. Chapter 11 examines the taxation of the uses of income. Taxation can also be based on the value of productive assets, rather than on the value of the services yielded by those assets, and Chapter 12 considers this form of taxation.

STRUCTURE OF THE PERSONAL INCOME TAX

In its central structure, even if not in its actual operation, the personal income tax in the United States is relatively simple. The calculation of a person's tax liability can be divided into four stages: Total income is determined; various adjustments are made and the result is adjusted gross income; deductions and exemptions are subtracted, which yields taxable income; and a schedule of tax rates is then applied to find tax liability. *Total income* is defined to fit the purposes of tax administration, and it is not the same as personal income, which is constructed to measure the aggregate amount of economic activity. Total income includes most but not all of the income that people receive. It includes such obvious things as wages and salaries, interest, dividends, and rents. It also includes 40 percent of any increase in the value of capital assets between the time they were bought and the time they were sold, provided that those assets were held at least one year. Receipts of alimony also are part of total income, as are winnings from gambling or lotteries. Unemployment compensation is perhaps best described as part of total income in principle, but it is often excluded from total income in practice. It is part of total income only to the extent that the sum of unemployment compensation and all other elements of total income exceed $20,000 for a single person and $25,000 for a married couple filing a joint return. A single person with unemployment compensation of $5,000 and other income of $15,000 will be able to exclude the full $5,000 from total income. But if unemployment compensation totals, say, $6,000, $1,000 of that amount will be eligible for inclusion in total income, although only 50 percent of that amount will actually have to be included.

Several types of income are not viewed as part of total income. Payments through all of the programs administered by the Veterans Administration are excluded from total income. The interest people receive from holding tax-exempt bonds issued by state and local governments is also excluded from total income. Social Security payments and welfare benefits are income to the recipients but are not part of total income under the personal income tax. Besides these exclusions by definition, the personal tax allows several *adjustments to income*, which are subtracted from total income to arrive at *adjusted gross income*. The expenses of moving and finding new housing that are incurred as a result of changing jobs, provided that the new job is located at least thirty-five miles farther from the former residence than was the old job, is an adjustment to income. So are such business-related expenses as travel and entertainment on the part of employees. Savings that are placed in various retirement accounts are, with certain restrictions, also an adjustment to income. So are payments of alimony, which complements the treatment of the receipt of alimony as income.

Once adjusted gross income has been determined, a variety of deductions and exemptions are allowed to calculate *taxable income*. Medical and dental expenses can be deducted from adjusted gross income, basically when they exceed 3 percent of adjusted gross income. The main forms of state and local taxes are also deductible from adjusted gross income: income taxes, real estate taxes, personal property taxes, and general sales taxes. Most interest payments are also deductible, including interest on mortgages, personal loans, and installment purchases. Contributions to organizations the Internal Revenue Service rules qualified are also deductible. These organizations include all governmental units and most charitable and educational organizations, including foundations. Contributions made directly to people, unlike contributions funneled through organizations, are not deductible. Losses suffered through theft and such natural events as fires and floods are also deductible.

Many of these deductions from adjusted gross income raise complex issues of tax practice and administration, and a whole subculture of accountants, lawyers, and other tax advisers has arisen to deal with the complex mechanics that lie beneath the simple principle of allowing certain expenditures to be deducted from adjusted gross income to determine taxable income. Aside from these deductions, personal exemptions of $1,000 are also allowed from adjusted gross income. A person with two dependents can accordingly claim an exemption of $3,000. People who are over sixty-five years of age or who are blind can declare an additional exemption. A blind person over the age of sixty-five can claim a personal exemption of $3,000.

Once taxable income has been determined by subtracting deductions and personal exemptions from adjusted gross income, a person's tax liability can be readily computed. Table 9.1 shows the tax rate schedules for single people in 1980, and the 1982 portion of the table shows the initial impact of the tax-reduction program of the Reagan administration. Actually, the initial step in that program took place in 1981, although it was a short one: the 1980 rate schedule remained applicable, but tax liability was reduced by 1.25 percent from what it would have been in 1980. The 1982 tax reduction represents an across-the-board reduction of 10 percent from 1981, and further reductions of 10 percent for 1983 and 5 percent for 1984 are scheduled.

Furthermore, starting in 1985, such features of the income tax as the tax brackets, personal exemption, and amount of income at which tax liability begins are scheduled to be indexed for inflation. In the absence of indexing, people are placed in higher-rate brackets by

TABLE 9.1 Tax Rate Schedules for Single Taxpayers, 1980 and 1982

1980

Taxable Income over	Taxable Income but not over	Tax	of amount over
$0	$2,300	$0	
2,300	3,400	14%	$2,300
3,400	4,400	154+16%	3,400
4,400	6,500	314+18%	4,400
6,500	8,500	692+19%	6,500
8,500	10,800	1,072+21%	8,500
10,800	12,900	1,555+24%	10,800
12,900	15,000	2,059+26%	12,900
15,000	18,200	2,605+30%	15,000
18,200	23,500	3,565+34%	18,200
23,500	28,800	5,367+39%	23,500
28,800	34,100	7,434+44%	28,800
34,100	41,500	9,766+49%	34,100
41,500	55,300	13,392+55%	41,500
55,300	81,800	20,982+63%	55,300
81,800	108,300	37,677+68%	81,800
108,300	—	55,697+70%	108,300

1982

Taxable Income over	Taxable Income but not over	Tax	of amount over
$0	$2,300	$0	
2,300	3,400	12%	$2,300
3,400	4,400	132+14%	3,400
4,400	6,500	272+16%	4,400
6,500	8,500	608+17%	6,500
8,500	10,800	948+19%	8,500
10,800	12,900	1,385+22%	10,800
12,900	15,000	1,847+23%	12,900
15,000	18,200	2,330+27%	15,000
18,200	23,500	3,194+31%	18,200
23,500	28,800	4,837+35%	23,500
28,800	34,100	6,692+40%	28,800
34,100	41,500	8,812+44%	34,100
41,500	—	12,068+50%	41,500

inflation, even though their real income does not rise. A single person with taxable income of $10,000 in 1980 would have paid a tax of $1,387. With a 10 percent rate of inflation for two years, that income would rise to $12,100, which would have been taxed at $1,867 under the 1980 schedule. Without any change in real income and without any effort to legislate an increase in taxes, such a person's tax burden would have increased from 13.9 percent of taxable income in 1980 to 15.4 percent in 1982. With indexing, however, the various tax brackets increase with the rate of inflation. The tax bracket between $10,800 and $12,900 of taxable income, in which people were taxed at 24 percent on income over $10,800, would range between $12,600 and $14,190 after one year of 10 percent inflation. In similar fashion, the income level at which tax liability starts would be increased from $2,300 to $2,530 after one year of 10 percent inflation. Moreover, the personal exemption would rise to $1,100.

Indexing the central features of a tax structure prevents inflation from automatically increasing the rates of tax people pay. In this regard, it is interesting to note that the so-called tax reductions sponsored by the Reagan administration may not be so much tax reductions as allowances for inflation. In the presence of a 10 percent rate of inflation, those reductions accomplish essentially the same thing that indexing would have accomplished — that is, leaving real rates of tax unchanged if real income is unchanged. Look again at the person with income of $10,000 in 1980 and $12,100 in 1982 after two years of 10 percent inflation. Under the tax schedule enacted for 1982, that person would have paid a tax of $1,671, which is 13.8 percent of taxable income, practically the same percentage as would have been paid on $10,000 in 1980 and substantially lower than the 15.4 percent that would otherwise have been paid in 1982. The higher the rate of inflation, the less the so-called tax reduction reduces the real burden of taxes and the more it prevents an increase in the real burden that would otherwise have resulted.

The personal income tax is called a *progressive tax* because the average rate of tax people pay rises with their income. Someone whose 1980 taxable income was $10,000 would pay a total tax of $1,387, or nearly 14 percent of taxable income. This is the *average rate of tax:* tax liability divided by taxable income. The last dollar of income earned, however, is taxed at 21 percent, and this is the *marginal rate of tax:* the rate of tax applicable to the last dollar of income. For a single person with taxable income of $20,000, total tax liability in 1980 would have been $4,177, an average tax rate of nearly 21 percent. The marginal rate of tax in this case would have been 34 percent. In subsequent sections of this chapter, the distinction between average and marginal rates of tax will be important when we examine the effects of income taxation on such things as the incentives people have to work and to save.

Unlike a progressive income tax, a *proportional income tax* imposes the same rate of tax regardless of income. If income is taxed at a proportional rate of 20 percent, someone with an income of $10,000 will pay $2,000 in tax and someone with an income of $20,000 will pay $4,000. A *degressive tax* combines elements of proportional and progressive taxation; it allows a basic exemption of income, and income above that exemption level is taxed at a single rate. If the exemption level is $10,000 and if the rate of tax is 20 percent, people with $20,000 and $30,000 incomes will pay $2,000 and $4,000 of tax, respectively. The former person will pay 10 percent of income as tax, whereas the latter will pay 13.3 percent. As income rises, the average rate of tax rises, as it does with progressive taxation. However, the share of additional income that is taken in tax remains constant at 20 percent, as under proportional income taxation. Degressive taxation has recently attracted increasing attention under the heading of *flat-rate taxation,* and this topic will be examined later in this chapter.

THE DEFINITION OF INCOME

When it is approached from the perspective of public law and for purposes of taxation, income is defined to be simply what the government says it is, period. Appropriate conceptualizations about the essential nature of income may well affect the legal definition of income, but considerations of the ease with which particular definitions of income can be administered through reporting and auditing different types of transactions are also important to the legal definition. Likewise, the political strength of various interests affected by different definitions of what does or does not constitute income for tax purposes is relevant. Although the legal definition of income does not correspond to any of the main conceptualizations of income in economics, such efforts at conceptualization provide bases for criticism of various definitions that have emerged through administrative and political processes. It is certainly understandable that the definition of income is a primary point of controversy as it relates to the operation of a system of income taxation, for once income has been defined in a manner subject to successful administration, the calculation of tax liability is a simple matter of arithmetic.

Henry Simons's treatise on the taxation of personal income, still influential after half a century, was subtitled "The Definition of

Income as a Problem of Fiscal Policy." [1] Scholars generally agree
that income should be treated as the maximum amount of consumption possible without eroding the capital stock that makes such consumption possible in the first place. Amid this general agreement,
however, controversial areas of application exist, mainly concerning
what it means to avoid eroding the stock of capital. Specifically, this
controversy relates directly to the continuing controversy over the
treatment of capital appreciation within the personal income tax. At
present, 40 cents of each dollar of capital gain is included in total
income. It is sometimes argued that the 60 percent that is excluded
from total income is a special tax benefit for those who receive income through capital gains. But it is also argued that capital gains
are not part of income in the first place. If this is so, the present
tax treatment of capital gains does not represent favored tax treatment for those who receive capital gains, but rather it represents
the imposition of a penalty on them, although less of a penalty than
would be imposed if capital gains were taxed fully as income.

Capital Gains

The controversy over the treatment of capital gains within the income tax centers on what is really entailed by a requirement to avoid
the consumption of capital. The Haig-Simons approach to the definition of income, named after Robert Haig and Henry Simons, defines
income as the maximum amount that a person can consume during
a year without reducing net worth below its initial value.[2] Income,
in other words, is equal to consumption plus any change in net worth
during the year in question. Suppose the person starts the year with
a net worth of $100,000 and earns $15,000 during the year. If net
worth at the end of the year is $150,000, that person's income dur-
ing the year would be $65,000 according to the Haig-Simons approach.
He could have consumed as much as $65,000 during the year without
reducing his net worth below its initial level of $100,000. Alterna-
tively, should that person's net worth at the end of the year have
been only $90,000, income during the year would have been only
$5,000. In this case, the maximum he could have consumed during

---

[1] Henry C. Simons, *Personal Income Taxation* (Chicago: University of Chicago
Press, 1938). For evidence that Simons's work is still timely, see Kenneth LeM.
Carter, "Canadian Tax Reform and Henry Simons," *Journal of Law and Eco-
nomics* 11 (October 1968), pp. 231–242; and John Bossons, "The Value of a
Comprehensive Tax Base as a Tax Reform Goal," *Journal of Law and Eco-
nomics* 13 (October 1970), pp. 327–363.

[2] See Simons, *Personal Income Taxation,* pp. 41–102; and Robert M. Haig,
The Federal Income Tax (New York: Columbia University Press, 1921).

the year while maintaining net worth at its initial level of $100,000 is $5,000.

The Haig-Simons approach derives income by adding changes in net worth or capital value to consumption. In contrast, the Fisherian approach, named after Irving Fisher, is based on a sharp distinction between income and capital.[3] An economy contains a stock of productive assets, and those assets yield a flow of output. *Net income* is the annual value of the output that can be sustained indefinitely, after allowance has been made for such things as depreciation necessary to maintain the stock of assets. *Net worth*, or capital value, is the value of those assets and is the present value-equivalent of the anticipated stream of future output. You should not think, however, that income and capital are distinct, independent magnitudes. On the contrary, they are two different measures of the same phenomenon — the ability to yield services of value to people.

A winery, for instance, possesses such assets as land, vines, and casks. It earns income each year from the sale of wine it has produced. The value of the assets bears a definite relationship to the annual income. Defined correctly, income has the property of being potentially perpetual if proper care is given to capital maintenance, if consumer tastes do not change, and if unforeseen catastrophes do not occur. Suppose the winery's net income is $10,000. If people value one year's yield from the winery at $10,000, how much will they value the winery? The value of the winery will be the present value-equivalent of the future yields of wine that can reasonably be anticipated. An annual income of $10,000 in perpetuity is equivalent to a capital value of $100,000, if the rate of interest is 10 percent. In other words, $100,000 invested at 10 percent will yield annual incomes of $10,000 in perpetuity.

Suppose the annual net income yielded by the winery increases from $10,000 to $15,000 and that this higher income is anticipated to continue indefinitely. If people's time preferences (the rates at which they are willing to sacrifice present consumption for future consumption) have not changed, the value of the winery will increase from $100,000 to $150,000. If people value the services yielded during a single year at $15,000, they will value the right to those services in perpetuity at $150,000, assuming a 10 percent rate of interest. The increased value of the winery and the increased annual flow of income generated by the winery are, as noted above, simply two alternative measures of the same thing: Income is a measure of the sustainable value of output during a single year, and capital is a measure of the present value-equivalent of the value of that output

---

[3] Irving Fisher, *The Theory of Interest* (New York: Macmillan, 1930).

that is anticipated to result in future years. The $50,000 increase in capital value is not distinct from the $5,000 increase in annual income; each is simply a different way of describing the increased ability of the winery to yield services that people value.

The Haig-Simons and the Fisherian approaches both seek to define income as the maximum amount that can be consumed without eroding the stock of capital. Since the former treats capital gains as income and the latter does not, they cannot both correctly avoid the consumption of capital. At base, the Fisherian approach seems to be the correct one, at least in principle, although there are cases in practice where this may not be so (we discuss some such cases in the next section). Since income and capital are not distinct magnitudes, it is impossible to consume capital gains without consuming capital. In the year when the winery's net income increases from $10,000 to $15,000 and its capital value increases from $100,000 to $150,000, the most that can be consumed without consuming capital is $15,000, not $65,000.

To understand why capital appreciation cannot be converted into consumption without consuming capital, it is helpful to strip away the nominal, monetary magnitudes of the illustration to expose the underlying real magnitudes. What does it mean, in real terms, to consume $15,000, or $65,000, in the illustration at hand? Suppose the initial situation represents a vineyard that contains 100 vines, with each vine yielding an average of 20 bottles of wine that sell for a net price of $5 per bottle. The net income of the winery in this case is $10,000, and its capital value is $100,000 in the presence of a 10 percent interest rate. There are several reasons why the value of the vineyard might subsequently increase: The demand for wine might increase, the productivity of the vineyard might increase, and people's time preferences might fall, which in turn would lower the rate of interest. Regardless of the reason for the increase in the value of the winery, the central point remains the same; namely, that increases in capital value cannot be converted to consumption without eroding the real stock of capital.

Suppose the demand for wine increases sufficiently to allow an increase in the net price of wine to $7.50 per bottle. Consequently, annual net income rises to $15,000 and, with a 10 percent rate of interest, the value of the vineyard rises to $150,000. The Haig-Simons approach holds that $65,000 can be consumed without consuming any of the capital stock, whereas the Fisherian approach holds that only $15,000 can be consumed. Which is correct? The consumption of $15,000 represents, in real terms, the consumption of 2,000 bottles of wine, which is the entire annual yield of the vineyard. The wine need not be consumed by the owner, of course, for the owner can exchange the wine for other items of consumption. Nonetheless, the consumption of $15,000 worth of other items is equivalent to the consumption of 2,000 bottles of wine.

Therefore, the consumption of $65,000 must represent the consumption of 8,667 bottles of wine, or their equivalent. With the annual yield from the vineyard being only 2,000 bottles, an additional 6,667 bottles, or their equivalent, must be consumed if consumption is to equal $65,000 worth of output. But what does the consumption of these additional 6,667 bottles of wine *really* represent? With a 10 percent rate of interest, one vine that produces 20 bottles of wine annually is itself equivalent to 200 bottles of wine; this is, in real terms, the meaning of a statement that a vine that produces a net income of $150 will itself be valued at $1,500 at a 10 percent rate of interest. Hence, if the value of one vine is equivalent to the value of 200 bottles of wine, the consumption of 6,667 bottles of wine represents, in real terms, the consumption of 33 vines, or one-third of the vineyard. Rather than actually consuming this share of the vineyard, of course, it could be sold and the proceeds used to finance a different type of consumption. This added complexity would change nothing essential, because such additional consumption would still be possible only by virtue of capital consumption somewhere else in the economy. The vineyard may still be standing whole despite the consumption of $65,000, but only because the capital consumption took other specific forms. The Fisherian approach, and not the Haig-Simons approach, is consistent with maintaining the real stock of capital.

Owner-Occupied Housing

The treatment of owner-occupied housing within the income tax ranks second, perhaps, to the treatment of capital gains as a subject of controversy in the definition of income. An owner-occupant really functions in two capacities simultaneously: as an owner of housing that is to be rented to earn income and as a tenant who rents housing from the owner. Although these two distinct capacities are merged for the owner-occupant, they can be distinguished nonetheless. If an owner rents a house to someone else, the rental payments the owner receives are treated as income. But if the owner lives in the house, the implicit rental income he receives from himself in his capacity as tenant is not treated as income. Administratively, it would perhaps be difficult to assess income figures in such cases, although such imputations are made in the national income accounts and appear as a component of gross national product and national income.

Regardless of possible administrative difficulties, housing is an asset that yields a flow of services over a period of time. With either the Haig-Simons or the Fisherian approach to the definition of income, the value of such services constitutes income, even though the two approaches differ in their treatment of changes in the value of the house. In principle, an increase in the value of a house would reflect an increase in the value of the services that the house provides. To treat the increase in capital value as income when the house is sold, as is the case at present, represents in principle a double taxation of income.

Gulfs often separate practice from principle, however. With respect to housing, the income flow is never taxed in the first place because owner-occupants are not required to report their implicit rental income as part of their total income. The taxation of the increase in the value of a house upon its sale need not, in this case, represent double taxation because the income was not taxed in the first place. Alternatively, the taxation of capital gains upon the sale of housing, although not the taxation of capital gains generally, may perhaps be seen as an indirect means of taxing the income that owner-occupants implicitly receive from their houses.

Nonmonetary Forms of Income

Additional problems arise when it is recognized that not all income accrues in monetary form; nonmonetary forms of income are usually exceedingly difficult to detect and measure. The case of a farmer who feeds a family from food grown on his farm has become a paradigm of income accruing in nonmonetary form. The net income received from the sale of crops is an element of total income, but the value of the crops that are consumed within the farmer's family are not part of total income. A mechanic who repairs a farmer's truck in exchange for chickens and eggs also earns income but in a form that, in practice, is rarely taxed. In this case, unlike the case of the home-grown food, the value of the chicken and eggs received through such a barter transaction is legally considered part of total income and is supposed to be reported as income.

Nonmonetary income can also extend to various intangible sources of well-being. A person may prefer sunshine and dislike cold midwestern winters sufficiently to require $10,000 more per year to choose to live in Michigan rather than Texas, other things being equal. If the person rejects an offer of $50,000 to work in Michigan in favor of one for $40,000 in Texas, it can be said that $10,000 is a nonmonetary form of income that accrues from living in Texas. Living in Texas is itself a source of gain, as evidenced by the $10,000 premium it would take to make Michigan preferred to Texas, but it is not part of total income. The higher the rate of tax, the more valuable such nontaxable sources of well-being become. If people generally prefer sun to frost, a rise in the national rate of income taxation will bring about a shift in preferred location in favor of sunny places, because a lesser share of total income is being taxed in the sunny places.

This point is a simple one to illustrate. Suppose $10,000 is the differential value placed on location in Texas over location in Michigan. If the national tax rate is 20 percent, a gross income of $62,500 in Michigan will be equivalent to a gross income of $50,000 in Texas because after tax the differential is $10,000 — $50,000 in Michigan and $40,000 in Texas. Now suppose the national tax rate is increased to 30 percent. Net income in Michigan falls to $43,750, while in Texas it falls to $35,000. The differential is less than $10,000, so people will migrate from Michigan to Texas, and this migration will continue until the $10,000 differential is restored.

TAX PREFERENCES AND THE TAX EXPENDITURE BUDGET [4]

Tax expenditures are defined by the Congressional Budget and Impoundment Act of 1974 as "revenue losses attributable to provisions of federal tax laws which allow a special exclusion, exemption, or deduction from gross income or which provide a special credit, a preferential rate of tax, or a deferral of tax liability." [5] The Congressional Budget Office has estimated that tax expenditures will run about $200 billion for 1981, with about three-quarters of that amount being assigned to provisions of the personal income tax and the remainder being assigned to provisions of the corporation income tax. Within the personal income tax, there are two main categories of tax expenditure: exemptions from total income and deductions from adjusted gross income.

Various types of employer contributions to fringe benefits for employees constitute most of the exemptions from total income. Employers often contribute to the pension plans of their employees. These contributions are not treated as part of the total income of the employees, yet they do increase the future consumption opportunities of the employees they cover. It has been estimated that if

[4] For further detail on this topic, see Richard E. Wagner, *The Tax Expenditure Budget: An Exercise in Fiscal Impressionism* (Washington, D.C.: Tax Foundation, 1979).

[5] Public Law 93-344, 3(a)(3).

those contributions were treated as part of total income, federal tax collections would rise by more than $10 billion — and it is the aggregation of all the various forms of tax expenditure that yields the $200 billion estimated for 1981. Employer contributions to medical insurance and medical care for employees are similarly excluded from the total income of the employees, and yet those contributions also increase the consumption opportunities of the employees. Some of the other examples of exclusions from total income that are included in the tax expenditure budget are Social Security benefits received by retired persons, workers' compensation benefits, and the interest people receive from tax-exempt bonds issued by state and local governments.

Among the deductions from adjusted gross income, the largest are those allowed for the payment of state and local taxes. These deductions reduce a person's taxable income, and it is estimated that their elimination would raise taxable income sufficiently to increase federal tax collections by more than $10 billion. The deductibility of interest on mortgages and other forms of borrowing is another major category in the tax expenditure budget. This deduction has received increasing attention in recent years because it gives people an incentive to spend on housing and consumer goods, which competes with investment in plant and equipment. A person in the 40 percent rate bracket who borrows so as to incur $10,000 annually in interest payments really pays only $6,000, because federal tax liability is reduced by $4,000. Among the other primary deductions from adjusted gross income that are elements of the tax expenditure budget are those allowed for charitable contributions and for medical expenses.

To call something a tax preference does not mean that the beneficiary of the preference is the nominal taxpayer whose taxes appear to be reduced. The exclusion of interest income on state and local bonds provides an illustration of this point. Suppose taxable bonds carry an interest rate of 14 percent. To simplify the numerical aspects of the illustration, further suppose the marginal-rate bracket of people who buy bonds is 50 percent. Consequently, their net return after tax is 7 percent. This implies, in turn, that the equilibrium rate of interest on nontaxable state and local bonds will be 7 percent. This is easy to see: If state and local bonds are offered at a rate higher than 7 percent, there will be an excess demand for them because buyers can get a higher net return on those bonds than they can get from taxable bonds or other investments. This excess demand will result in the price of the bonds being bid up, and this rise in price will continue until the net yield falls to 7 percent.

Although the bondholder-cum-taxpayer pays no tax on the interest income, he is no better off than had he purchased taxable bonds at

14 percent. In one case he receives a nontaxable return of 7 percent, while in the other case he receives a taxable return of 14 percent, which in turn is taxed at 50 percent. It is taxpayers in the governments that issue the bonds, not the buyers of those bonds, who are better off, for they must tax themselves only sufficiently to pay a 7 percent rate of interest rather than 14 percent. The tax-exempt status of state and local bond interest represents a preference not so much to the holders of those bonds as to the taxpayers in the state and local governments that issue the bonds. The exemption of interest does, of course, reduce federal tax collections from what they would otherwise have been. Ultimately, then, the tax-exempt status of interest income on state and local bonds is a means by which the federal government transfers tax revenues to state and local governments, with these transfers being essentially in proportion to the amount of debt issued by the various governments.[6]

The deductibility of mortgage interest and local property taxes and the exclusion of the imputed rental value of owner-occupied housing are often thought to constitute a set of tax preferences for homeowners. As we saw above, the exclusion of imputed rental value understates the income of homeowners relative to renters. The deductibility of mortgage interest and property taxes, however, is not so clearly a preference for owners relative to renters. Certainly, the deductibility of mortgage interest reduces the price of borrowing to buy housing and hence encourages such borrowing. Likewise, the deductibility of local property taxes, as well as of nonproperty taxes, lowers the price to residents of state and local governments of financing activities through taxation, compared with financing them through user charges, which are not deductible.

These deductions do not seem to constitute a preference for homeowners relative to renters, as long as payments for mortgage interest and for property taxes are deductible by the owner of rental property. Suppose mortgage interest and property taxes are not deductible in determining taxable income. In equilibrium, the market for rental housing will operate to yield a return on housing equal to the return that can be obtained on other forms of investment. If we

[6] Actually, some of the reduction in federal tax revenues can accrue to bondholders in the highest marginal-rate brackets, but this complexity does not change the essential point being made. If the rate of interest on tax-exempt bonds is 7 percent while it is 14 percent on taxable bonds, people whose marginal tax rate exceeds 50 percent can gain by buying such bonds. Someone whose marginal rate is 70 percent will receive a net return of only 4.2 percent by buying taxable bonds. Although the tax-exempt bond provides a higher return for such a taxpayer, the differential rate of return is only 2.8 percent (7% − 4.2%), not the 7 percent it is commonly thought to be and that it is held to be within the context of the tax expenditure budget.

introduce deductibility of mortgage interest and property taxes, clearly the owner-occupant pays lower taxes. But what about the renter? Initially, the owner's net income from investment in rental housing rises. This encourages investment in rental housing, and the expansion in supply will continue until rents fall sufficiently to equate the net return on investment in rental housing with the net return on other forms of investment. The deductibility of mortgage interest and property taxes will have benefited the renters of housing as much as it benefited owner-occupants. If mortgage interest and property taxes are not deductible for owners of rental property, there will, of course, be no benefits to tenants either. In this case, however, it is just as correct to say that the nondeductibility for the owners of rental property imposes a penalty on renters as to say that the deductibility status of owner-occupants gives them a tax preference.

The choice between these two statements may well reflect fundamentally different normative perspectives about the relation between citizens and the state, similar to differing perspectives about whether a glass of water is half full or half empty. To say whether the recipient of the glass of water was penalized or shown favoritism depends on some normative assumption regarding rightful expectation. To say that renters are penalized relative to owner-occupants, and to look to removal of that penalty as the means of rectification, is to take the treatment of owner-occupants as a norm. Individual claims to income are the norm, taxation is an infringement, albeit one that people may agree to, and the government infringes more heavily on renters. But to say that owner-occupants are given a tax preference because renters are not also able to benefit from deductibility, and to look to removal of that preference as the means of rectification, is to take the treatment of renters as a norm. Taxation, or government's claim to income, is the norm; a failure to tax is a preference; and government confers a preference on owner-occupants relative to renters. The former position regards the renter as overburdened relative to the owner-occupant; the latter position regards the owner-occupant as differentially favored relative to the renter.

Consider a comparison of a single person in the 22 percent marginal-rate bracket with a taxable income of $12,000 for 1982, with a single person in the 40 percent rate bracket with a taxable income of $30,000. Suppose each person makes a charitable contribution of $1,000. The $1,000 deduction reduces the first person's tax bill by $220, which means that the contribution reduces disposable income by $780. The $1,000 contribution reduces the second person's tax bill by $400, so disposable income declines by only $600. Within the framework of the tax expenditure budget, the charitable contribution of the first person is subsidized 22 cents on the dollar, while for the second person it is subsidized 40 cents on the dollar. The higher the tax rate, the larger the reduction in the tax bill per dollar of contribution — that is, the higher the rate of subsidy. If government's claim to income is taken as the point of reference, the person in the 40 percent rate bracket is being given a preference of $180 over the person in the 22 percent bracket.

If the individual's title to income is taken as the point of reference, however, the deductibility of charitable bequests may be necessary for achieving equity in tax treatment.[7] The deduction reflects the presumption that a person who otherwise has a taxable income of $12,000 and who makes a charitable contribution of $1,000 is in the same position as a person whose taxable income is $11,000 and who makes no charitable contribution. It likewise reflects the judgment that a person whose taxable income would otherwise be $30,000 but who makes a $1,000 charitable contribution is in the same position as a person whose taxable income is $29,000 and who makes no charitable contribution. Indeed, a person who otherwise has a taxable income of $30,000 but who makes a charitable contribution of $19,000 is in the same position as a person who would otherwise have taxable income of $12,000 but who makes a $1,000 charitable contribution. From this perspective, the charitable deduction is not a means of subsidizing especially heavily the charitable activities of those who have higher adjusted gross incomes, as it is described by the tax expenditure budget.

Income belongs to citizens, and they relinquish command over some of that income to government in exchange for various services. To say that a tax on personal income is one means by which that command over resources is transferred, with total income defined to include some transactions and to exclude others and with deductions for various transactions allowed before determining taxable income, is simply to describe the basis on which individual shares in that transfer of command over resources are determined. There can be numerous reasons for exclusions and deductions, ranging from consensual beliefs about equity and the value of various transactions to the cruder tax-and-subsidy aspects of majoritarian democracy. Regardless of the reasons for deductions, within the income-as-belonging-

[7] See, for instance, William D. Andrews, "Personal Deductions in an Ideal Income Tax," *Harvard Law Review* 86 (December 1972), pp. 309–385; Boris I. Bittker, "The Propriety and Vitality of a Federal Income Tax Deduction for Private Philanthropy," in *Tax Impacts on Philanthropy* (Princeton, N.J.: Tax Institute of America, 1972), pp. 145–170; and Roger A. Freeman, *Tax Loopholes: The Legend and the Reality* (Washington, D.C.: American Enterprise Institute, 1973).

to-citizens perspective there is no presumption that a difference in tax liability owing to differences in exemptions or deductions is necessarily open to a claim of inequity, as it is in the tax-expenditure perspective. Furthermore, if such a claim of inequity were advanced, there is no presumption that correction of that inequity requires increasing the tax burden on the one person as against lowering it on the other.

INCOME TAXATION AND THE LABOR-LEISURE CHOICE

There are several ways in which income taxation might influence the way people use their time. It may cause them to substitute leisure for work. It may cause them to substitute work that is nontaxable or that can easily escape tax for work that is taxable. It may also cause them to substitute nonmonetary for monetary sources of income. The influence of income taxation on a person's choice between leisure and work provides a useful point of departure for analysis. People are endowed with time, and they must choose how to allocate it, usually considered in terms of a twenty-four-hour day. Leisure is command over one's own time. Monetary income, which is used to buy desired products and services, is acquired by supplying one's time to others in exchange for the payment of a sum of money.

How people apportion their time between leisure and labor depends on their preferences for leisure and for income as well as on the rate at which they can exchange leisure for income.[8] These considerations are illustrated in Figure 9.1. Assuming an absence of tax, suppose a proportional income tax of 40 percent is imposed. The posttax budget constraint rotates inward, indicating that each hour of leisure sacrificed now yields only 60 percent as high a return in income as it did before the tax was imposed. Depending on the nature of a person's preference function, the tax can increase, decrease, or leave unchanged the amount of leisure taken and, hence, the amount of labor supplied. On the one hand, the tax reduces the net return per hour of labor. Since the net wage rate is the opportunity cost or price of an hour of leisure, the tax makes taking leisure more attractive than supplying labor. On the other hand, the tax reduces

[8] It is often objected that working habits are largely institutionalized, so a person is typically unable to select a preferable combination of work and leisure. Employers must compete for labor, however, and one result of such competition is a tendency for the workday (or for the standard form of labor contract) to reflect that which is generally preferred by the labor force.

FIGURE 9.1   Proportional Taxation and Demand for Leisure

The slope of the budget line *il* is the negative of the wage rate. At *l*, no income is earned and twenty-four hours of leisure are taken. If the wage rate is $5 per hour, at *i* no leisure is taken and $120 of income is earned. The combination I_1, L_1 indicates the amount of income earned and of leisure taken by a person whose preference function is described by P_1. The imposition of a 40 percent rate of tax pivots the budget constraint inward to *li'*, for now each hour of leisure sacrificed returns only $3. The effect of the tax on the amounts of leisure taken and labor supplied depends on the person's preference function between income and leisure. If it is as described by P_2, less leisure will be taken and more labor will be supplied after the tax is imposed. If it is as described by P_4, the reverse will hold. If it is as described by P_3, there will be no change in the hours of leisure taken and labor supplied.

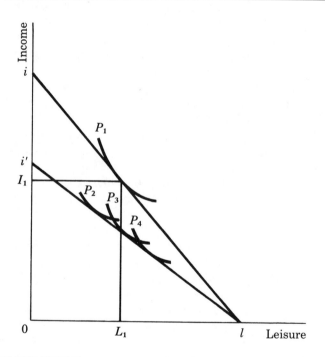

a person's net income, which can lead the person to take less leisure, assuming leisure is a normal good.

The impact of the tax on the supply of labor may become less ambiguous when we see that it is impossible to impose a general tax without allowing for some offsetting effect elsewhere in the economy. If everyone is taxed 40 percent of their income, what will be done with the resulting revenue? One option is to reduce other forms of tax. If this is done, an analysis of the effect of the tax on the supply of labor will have to take this tax reduction into account. What really happens in this case is not the imposition of a tax but the replacement of one tax with another. Another option is to use the revenue to finance the supply of some collective service, in which case the tax does not represent so much a reduction in real income as a use of income collectively to provide something of value. Indeed, if this service is valued equally at the margin with alternative private services that could have been purchased, the tax will impose no reduction in real income. The tax, taken by itself, will reduce real income, but so will the expenditure on a collective service, taken by itself, increase real income. Figure 9.2 illustrates this case. Although real income is unchanged by the combined tax-and-expenditure, the price of leisure has fallen relative to the price of earning income.[9] With a lower price and no change in real income, more leisure will be demanded.[10] Since the amount of labor supplied per day is simply twenty-four hours minus the amount of leisure taken, the increase in tax-cum-expenditure reduces the amount of labor supplied. The higher the rate of tax, the more reduction there will be in the supply of labor.

Although a general increase in tax-cum-expenditure would seem clearly to reduce the amount of labor supplied, an increase (or decrease) in the progressivity of an income tax will have an ambiguous impact on the amount of labor supplied. The replacement of a proportional income tax with a progressive tax of equal yield will, when applied to a particular person, reduce the amount of labor that person supplies.[11] The more progressive the tax, the greater the reduction in the amount of labor supplied. But this result for one person

[9] The impact on the amount of leisure demanded will vary depending on whether the public service is complementary primarily to the consumption of leisure or to the consumption of private goods and services. The construction of Figure 9.2 assumes neutrality, which seems the appropriate assumption in the absence of evidence to the contrary. On this issue, see Gordon Winston, "Taxes, Leisure, and Public Goods," *Economica* 32 (February 1965), pp. 65–69.

[10] It is common practice to describe unchanged real income as an unchanged level of indifference. The construction in Figure 9.2 defines constant real income as the ability to consume some combination along the original opportunity set. This definition, unlike the common one, is open to empirical observation. This point is explored in Martin J. Bailey, "The Marshallian Demand Curve," *Journal of Political Economy* 62 (June 1954), pp. 255–261.

[11] One illustration of a progressive tax would be a budget constraint like *lai** in Figure 9.2, in which *la* of income is exempt from tax and additional income is taxed at the rate indicated by one minus the slope of *ai**. More realistically, progressive taxes have several brackets, not just one. This means that as income rises, points are reached at which the budget constraint kinks to a flatter slope and remains linear at this flatter slope until a new bracket is reached, at which point the slope becomes flatter still.

FIGURE 9.2 Taxation-cum-Expenditure and Demand for Leisure

The budget constraint li and the choice of L_1 as the quantity of leisure are repeated from Figure 9.1, as is the posttax budget constraint, li'. The expenditure of the tax revenues is represented by an upward shift in the budget constraint to l^*i^*, where la represents the value of the collectively supplied service, which can be thought of as a lump-sum transfer of income. Since the original budget constraint, li, indicates the real opportunity set available to the economy and to the individual depicted here, the resulting equilibrium with the tax-cum-expenditure must lie on the original budget constraint and, of course, be tangent to the new budget constraint lai^*. Accordingly, more leisure is demanded, as shown by L_2.

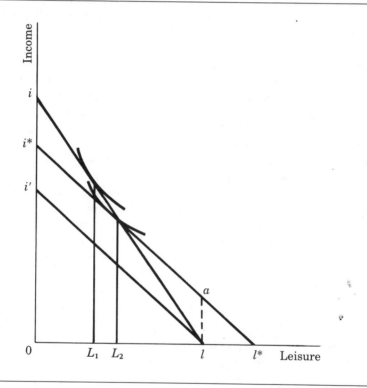

---

cannot be extended to a society. When the analysis is applied to an individual, income effects are absent. All that remains is the substitution effect, which promotes leisure and discourages labor. But the choice between proportional and progressive income taxation cannot be conducted and examined in a context in which each person pays the same tax bill. The very *raison d'être* of a progressive income tax is that some people will pay more tax and others will pay less. Income effects are an integral part of any comparison of proportional and progressive income taxes, but ambiguity arises when income effects are introduced because income effects and substitution effects will operate in opposing directions for some taxpayers.

The substitution effect is determined by the marginal rate of tax; the income effect is determined by the average rate of tax. An increase in the average rate of tax reduces net income, which decreases the demand for leisure. An increase in the marginal rate of tax reduces the price of leisure, so more leisure will be demanded. Changes in the same direction in marginal and average rates of tax thus have opposing effects on the amount of leisure people will take and, hence, on the amount of labor they will supply. The effect on average and marginal rates of tax of replacing a proportional income tax with a progressive tax of equal yield is illustrated in Figure 9.3. Under proportional income taxation, the average rate of tax equals the marginal rate of tax. With progressive income taxation, the marginal rate of tax exceeds the average rate of tax. The replacement of proportional taxation with progressive taxation of equal yield creates three distinct sets of people ordered by their income. Only for the middle income set is the effect of a progressive tax unambiguous. For that set, the marginal rate of tax is increased and the average rate of tax is reduced. Both the substitution effect and income effect operate to increase the amount of leisure demanded. For the lower income set, marginal and average tax rates are lowered, and the substitution effect reduces the amount of leisure demanded but the income effect increases that demand. For the upper set, marginal and average rates of tax are both increased. Although the increase in the marginal rate of tax increases the amount of leisure demanded, the increase in the average rate of tax reduces the demand for leisure.

Because of the conceptual impasse that results from the impact of progressive income taxation on the amount of labor supplied, empirical analysis might seem appropriate, and in fact a number of studies have been done. George Break asked British accountants and lawyers about the effect of taxation on their choices regarding the supply of labor.[12] Ten percent of Break's sample stated that high tax rates created an incentive to supply additional labor, while 13 percent stated that high tax rates created a disincentive. In a follow-up survey, Donald Fields and W. Stanbury found that high tax rates induced 11 percent of the respondents to supply more labor, an increase of one percentage point from that reported by Break. Nineteen percent of the Fields and Stanbury sample stated that high tax rates induced them to supply less labor, an increase

[12] George F. Break, "Income Taxes and Incentives to Work: An Empirical Study," *American Economic Review* 47 (September 1957), pp. 529–549.

FIGURE 9.3 Income and Substitution Effects with Progressive and
Proportional Taxation

With a proportional income tax, the average rate of tax (AT) equals the
marginal rate (MT), as illustrated by the rate t. With a progressive rate of
tax, the average rate of tax rises with income, which means that the
marginal rate of tax must lie above the average rate. In the comparison
between a progressive tax and a proportional tax, people fall into one of
three categories. People in category A have relatively low incomes, and
both their marginal and their average rates of tax are lower under a
progressive tax than they would be under a proportional tax. People in
category C have relatively high incomes, and both their marginal and
average rates of tax are higher under a progressive tax than they would be
under a proportional tax. For people in category B, the middle income
range, the marginal rate is higher under progressive taxation but the
average rate is lower.

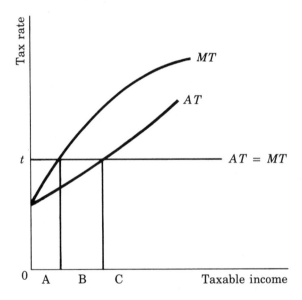

of six percent from that reported by Break.[13] Daniel Holland, in a
similar study, found that 15 percent of those sampled felt that high
tax rates induced them to supply less labor.[14]

[13] Donald B. Fields and W. T. Stanbury, "Incentives, Disincentives, and the
Income Tax," *Public Finance* 25, No. 3 (1970), pp. 381–415.

[14] Daniel M. Holland, "The Effect of Taxation on Effort: Some Results for
Business Executives," *Proceedings of the National Tax Association, 1969* (Columbus, Ohio: National Tax Association, 1970), pp. 428–516.

Such findings as these are, of course, hardly overwhelming about the disincentive effects of high, if not progressive, taxation. At the same time, it must be noted that conceptual analysis also provides ambiguous results for relatively high income groups, which are the groups represented in the studies. Moreover, such studies confound the income effect and the substitution effect of tax rates. In a more general study, which separated income and substitution effects, Jerry Hausman estimated that the income tax reduced the hours worked by husbands by an average of 8 percent compared with what would have occurred under a lump-sum tax of equal yield.[15] (He also estimated that the reduction in the amount of labor supplied would have been only 1 percent with a proportional income tax.) For the most part the reduction in labor supplied would be stronger for wives in Hausman's study because they typically face higher marginal tax rates than do husbands. If the husband is the primary wage earner, the marginal tax rate applicable to the first dollar of the wife's earnings is the rate applicable to the last dollar of the husband's earnings. Indeed, Hausman estimated that the tax reduced the amount of labor supplied by wives by about 30 percent because of the generally higher marginal rates of tax applicable to the income earned by wives.

TAX AVOIDANCE AND ALTERNATIVE FORMS OF INCOME

The analysis of the effect of income taxation on the supply of labor involves more than just a consideration of the choice between leisure and labor. By taxing only monetary forms of income, the personal income tax encourages the substitution of various nonmonetary and nontaxable forms of income for monetary payments. In the presence of an income tax, there often can be gains from trade between employers and employees for nonmonetary and nontaxable forms of income. Suppose an employer must increase an employee's net income by $10,000 per year to retain him. If the marginal rate of tax is 20 percent, the employer must increase the employee's gross income by $12,500, but if the marginal rate of tax is 40 percent, the employer must increase the employee's gross income by $16,667. An increase in the rate of tax increases the cost to the firm of achieving any increase in net monetary compensation.

[15] Jerry A. Hausman, "Labor Supply," in *How Taxes Affect Economic Behavior*, edited by Henry J. Aaron and Joseph A. Pechman (Washington, D.C.: Brookings Institution, 1981), pp. 27–72.

Alternatively, the employer could provide the employee with some fringe benefit valued by the employee at $10,000, say some combination of insurance and investment counseling. The employee will receive an increase in income but not in the form of a direct, taxable payment (although possible ways of taxing fringe benefits are continually being advocated by the U.S. Treasury Department). A fringe benefit that costs the firm $10,000 will be valued by the employee as equivalent to $10,000 in money only if the employee was spending at least $10,000 on the activity in question before the benefit was provided. Otherwise, the fringe benefit may be less valuable than a cash payment, as Figure 9.4 shows. If that is the case, the fringe benefit will have to be valued at something more than $10,000 by the employee to be regarded as equivalent to a cash payment of $10,000. With a 40 percent marginal tax rate, as long as the benefit costs the employer less than $16,667 and is valued by the employee at more than $10,000, it is potentially profitable for both the employer and employee to substitute the fringe benefit for the monetary payment.

The higher the rate of tax on income, the greater will be the scope for mutual gains from trade of nontaxable forms of income. It is cheaper for an enterprise to give a given, posttax monetary raise to a person in the 20 percent rate bracket than to give one to a person in the 50 percent bracket. Progressive rates of income taxation would seem especially to encourage the use of nonmonetary forms of payment in the higher income brackets.

People can also reduce their tax liability through tax evasion or tax avoidance, and such activities become increasingly profitable as marginal tax rates increase. People can evade tax by failing to report all of their income, which is facilitated if at least part of income is received in cash payments, is attained through barter, or results from overstatement of personal exemptions. Besides tax evasion, people may try to legally avoid tax liability by rearranging various types of transactions. By carefully timing sales of assets or donations to charity, for instance, taxpayers can reduce their liability. A large part of the demand for accounting and legal services comes from the demand by taxpayers for tax avoidance, and increases in tax rates increase that demand.

As rates of tax rise, it also becomes relatively more profitable to pursue added income through seeking political favors than through engaging in genuine production. If the marginal rate of tax is 20 percent, a person must earn an additional $12,500 of taxable income to increase net income by $10,000. But if the marginal rate of tax is 50 percent, a person must increase pretax income by $20,000 to secure the $10,000 increase in posttax income. This 30 percent in-

FIGURE 9.4 Fringe Benefits and Monetary Income

An employee initially faces the budget constraint C_1F_1 and chooses B_1 of insurance and investment counseling. If the employer subsequently provides B_3 of such services as a fringe benefit, the employee's budget constraint becomes C_1AF_2. The highest level of indifference the employee can attain is i_2. This is less than the level that could have been attained if that same amount had been given as a cash payment. In the latter case, the budget constraint would have been C_2F_2, and the higher level of indifference, i_3, would have been attained.

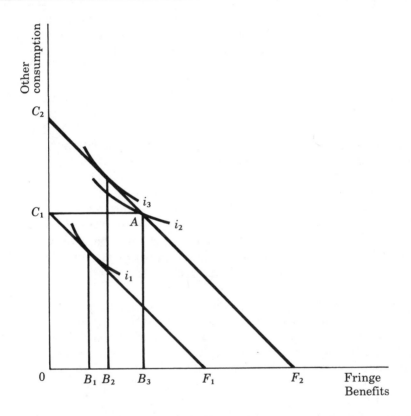

crease in marginal tax rate increases by $7,500 the cost of earning an additional $10,000. To approach the matter from a different direction, a person subject to a marginal tax rate of 20 percent can reduce tax liability by $1,000 only if taxable income is reduced by $5,000. But if the marginal tax rate is 50 percent, a $1,000 reduction in tax liability can be attained by securing a reduction in taxable income of only $2,000. With increases in the marginal rate of tax, it becomes increasingly profitable to lobby for or otherwise seek favorable tax legislation and administrative rulings as a source of disposable income rather than resorting to forthrightly productive effort.

RELATIVE LABOR SUPPLIES AND FACTOR INCOMES

Although most analyses of the disincentive effect of income taxation have focused on the aggregate supply of labor, the ability of income taxation to alter the occupational composition of the labor force may well be a more significant consequence of income taxation. In a competitive labor market, there will be a tendency for the net advantages of different occupations to be equalized at the margin. This proposition is simply a corollary of the proposition that a competitive market will not result in profit opportunities continually remaining unexploited. With respect to the supply of labor, if people require an average of $5,000 more to practice occupation A than to practice occupation B, an income differential of $10,000 in favor of A will be eroded through competition, as the supply of labor increases in A relative to B. Some of this change in labor supply may take place through shifts from B to A, but for labor markets much of the adjustment will occur through changes in the rate of entry into the different occupations. Nonetheless, there will be a tendency for competition to bring about a differential in earnings that reflects and offsets the advantages and disadvantages associated with different occupations.

To some extent, differences in earnings among occupations are necessary to offset differences in their relative agreeableness, the regularity and certainty of their returns, and the cost of acquiring and maintaining requisite skills. If one occupation requires $3,000 more per year to practice than another, it will tend to generate an offsettingly higher annual income. If this differential did not exist, say if the two occupations yielded the same income, people would alter their choices of labor supply. As people switch their choice from the occupation that is more costly to practice to the one that is less costly, either through outright shifts by existing practitioners or through changes in the rate of entry by new workers, relative wages will rise in the more costly occupation because of the shift in relative labor supplies. This shift in supply will continue until the necessary differential is established.[16]

---

[16] While the differences discussed here are required by and compatible with a competitive labor market, there are other differences that are due to monopo-

Income taxation can alter the relative returns among occupations, and, to the extent it does so, the composition of the labor force will change in response. *This effect will occur even if the aggregate supply of labor, say as measured in terms of annual hours worked, remains unchanged.* This impact can occur under both proportional and progressive income taxation, but the impact will be stronger under progressive taxation. Suppose two occupations, A and B, are equivalent in all relevant respects, except that A is relatively hazardous and B is quite safe. A might involve painting bridges while riding in wind-buffeted scaffolding 300 feet above the ground, while B involves painting single-family houses. In the absence of income taxation, assume that the average annual returns to people working at A and B are $20,000 and $15,000, respectively. Assuming that no other possible sources of equalizing differences exist, this difference of $5,000 reflects the negative evaluation people place on the hazards involved in occupation A.

What would be the impact on the division of the labor force between A and B of a proportional income tax of 20 percent? After enactment of the tax, the posttax return falls to $16,000 in A and $12,000 in B. The tax favors occupation B because nonmonetary aspects of the occupation (its greater safety in this instance, or its location in Texas in an earlier example) are not included in the tax base. When the posttax differential in net income falls to $4,000, the labor market is no longer in equilibrium. There will now be an excess supply of labor in A. Labor will shift from A to B, and as this happens pretax income rises in A and falls in B. This shift in the composition of the labor force will continue until the net differential of $5,000 is attained once again. In the new equilibrium, pretax income in A might be, say, $20,625, while pretax income in B is $14,375. In this event, posttax returns in A and B will be $16,500 and $11,500, respectively, which maintains the $5,000 differential.[17]

---

listic influences. These sources, which would dissipate in a competitive regime, include occupational licensing, minimum wages, and union control over entry into employments, particularly those for which the associated products are in relatively inelastic demand. The main interest in this chapter, however, is not the theory of wage differences, but the impact of taxation on such differences.

[17] People may differ in their assessment of the hazards encountered in occupation A, and, as labor supplies shift, the marginal person may come to evaluate the necessary compensation for the hazards as somewhat less than $5,000. Bringing in such complicating considerations, however, does not modify the essential point being made. Also, the compensating differentials people attach to various occupations may be in the form of a percentage difference in wages rather than an absolute amount. Instead of taking an additional $5,000 to get people to paint bridges, it may require, say, a 20 percent premium over what they can get for painting houses. In either case, the central point is the same. For a study of the extent to which occupational hazards are reflected in wage

In general, a proportional income tax increases the supply of labor in occupations in which nonmonetary advantages are more significant because those advantages are free of tax.

Whatever impact a proportional income tax has on the labor supply, a progressive income tax has an even stronger impact because a progressive income tax discriminates among occupations on the basis of their monetary returns. In terms of the preceding illustration, the replacement of a proportional income tax by a progressive income tax increases the tax paid by people in occupation A and lowers the tax paid by people in occupation B. As a result, the differential between the two occupations will be narrowed to something less than $5,000, which means there will be an excess supply of labor in A. Restoration of equilibrium in the labor market requires a shift in the composition of the labor force away from A toward B. As people change their occupational choices, pretax income in A will increase relative to that in B. Through this adjustment in pretax income in response to the progressive tax, part of the tax burden that appears to be paid by those with higher incomes is actually paid by those with lower incomes. The pretax income received by practitioners of the lower-paying but less hazardous occupation, B, will decline relative to the posttax income received by practitioners of occupation A. Accordingly, the impact of the tax on the redistribution of income is lessened from what it would have been before adjustments were made in the composition of the labor force.

Indeed, conditions are conceivable under which a progressive income tax will have no impact on the distribution of posttax income compared with what would result under a proportional income tax. This is possible even if the aggregate supply of labor, say as measured by total hours worked, is unaffected by the tax. Even though the supply of labor may be of zero elasticity in the aggregate, it is possible for it to be quite, even perfectly, elastic to any particular occupation.

Consider two occupations, H and L, with H possessing a higher income than L because of such features as higher costs of preparation and practice. In comparing a progressive tax with a proportional tax, it is useful to think of the progressive tax as constituting two conceptually separable components: a proportional tax and a set of tax surcharges on high-earning activities that are used to finance a

differentials, see Richard Thaler and Sherwin Rosen, "The Value of Saving a Life: Evidence from the Labor Market," in *Household Production and Consumption,* edited by Nestor E. Terleckyj (New York: Columbia University Press, 1975), pp. 265–298.

set of tax rebates on low-earning activities. The system of surcharges and rebates will modify the composition of the labor force,
inducing transfers of labor from H, where the surcharge is levied,
to L, where the rebates are offered. The progressive income tax alters
the net returns to the different types of labor, which in turn alter
the composition of the labor force in favor of the occupation that
becomes more attractive, L.

Figure 9.5 illustrates the analysis. The extent to which labor will
shift from H to L depends on the elasticity of the supply of labor
to the two occupations. If the labor supply functions of each occupation are horizontal (perfectly elastic) at the wage differential that
reflects the higher costs of preparing for and practicing in H, the
only effect of the progressive tax will be to induce a transfer of labor
from H to L of sufficient magnitude to restore the necessary differential. After the tax is imposed, pretax incomes will be higher in
H and lower in L by an amount that leaves the posttax differential
unchanged from what it would be under proportional taxation. In
this case, the replacement of a proportional income tax with a progressive income tax has no effect upon the distribution of posttax
income. The change in the form of the tax leads to an increase in
the inequality in the distribution of pretax income that is sufficient
to negate the change in the distribution of tax payments required
by the change in the form of the tax.

Although the progressive income tax does not alter the distribution of income in this case, it does alter the composition of the labor
force, and this change has economic interest. When labor shifts
from H to L, people are shifting from activities in which the other
members of society value their output more highly into activities
where their output is valued less highly. An excess burden, or welfare loss, results from this impact of progressive taxation. In equilibrium, the willingness of people to pay, say, $20 per hour for one
service and $10 per hour for another service indicates that people
value the former service twice as much as they value the latter.
What prevents more of the more highly valued service from being
supplied in a competitive market are the various costs associated
with supplying that service, and these costs are expressed by the
equalizing differential. However, if people who are willing to provide the more highly valued service are compelled or induced to provide the less valued service instead, perhaps because the more highly
valued service is taxed and the less highly valued service is subsidized, a welfare loss equivalent to $10 per hour of service supplied
will result.

The case where labor supplies are perfectly elastic among occupa-

FIGURE 9.5 Impact of Progressive Taxation
on Relative Labor Supplies

Part a of the figure describes the market for type-H labor and part b
describes the market for the type-L labor. Assume initially that the labor
market has adjusted to a proportional income tax. The relative supplies of
the labor are H_0 and L_0 in H and L respectively. Initial wages are W_0^H in H
and W_0^L in L, and this differential can be thought of as representing the
higher cost of preparing for the practicing H.
   The imposition of a progressive tax modifies the proportional tax by
imposing a surtax on earnings in H and providing a rebate on earnings in
L. The effect of the surtax is shown by the demand function D_t, which
shows that for any given wage those who provide their labor receive less
than they received before the change in tax, indicated by D. Similarly, the
rebate is shown by D_s in part b, which means that for any given wage,
recipients keep more than they did before, shown by D. In other words, the
vertical distances between D and D_t and between D and D_s are the tax and
subsidy, respectively, per hour worked. In response to the change in the
pattern of net returns in favor of L, relative labor supplies change to L_1 in
L and H_1 in H. The increased supply of labor in L reduces pretax earnings
to W_1^L. The reduced amount of labor supplied in H increases pretax
earnings to W_1^H. As a result, the posttax differential is the same as it was
under proportional taxation, although the composition of the labor force
has changed.

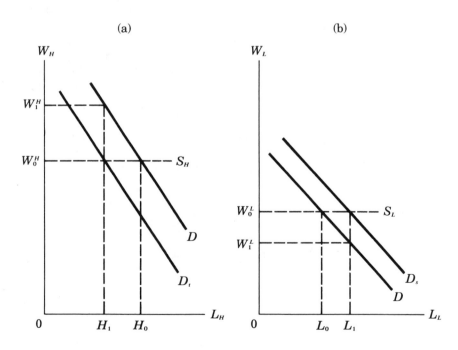

tions is, of course, a polar one. If labor supplies are less than perfectly elastic, the transfer of labor will cease before pretax income has risen in H and fallen in L sufficiently to restore the original posttax differential. Nonetheless, the tax will still increase the pretax differential in the distribution of income, thereby shifting part of the tax from those with high incomes onto those with low incomes. It is common to assess the redistributive impact of progressive taxation by comparing posttax incomes with what they would be under a proportional tax of equal yield, assuming that pretax incomes would be unaffected by the change in tax. This procedure is legitimate only if it can be assumed that relative labor supplies are invariant to taxation — that is, that they are invariant to net returns. This, of course, cannot be assumed because it is contradictory to basic economic knowledge. Even if the supply of labor is inelastic in the aggregate, it can be elastic to any particular employment.

The impact of progressive taxation can at best be assessed only partially by exploring its impact on the aggregate supply of labor. The ability of progressive taxation to alter relative labor supplies is a simple implication of the assumption that relative supplies of labor respond to changes in net returns. It seems clear that the redistributive impact of progressive taxation has been overestimated as a result of analytical attention being focused on the labor-leisure choice rather than on the composition of the labor force. Correspondingly, the excess-burden effects of progressive taxation, in terms of the composition of the labor force, have been underemphasized. The relation between income taxation and labor markets has, however, been receiving increasing attention, and it can be expected that our knowledge of probable empirical magnitudes will increase accordingly.[18]

---

[18] In this regard Morgan Reynolds and Eugene Smolensky, *Public Expenditures, Taxes, and the Distribution of Income* (New York: Academic Press, 1977), examined the effect of taxes and public expenditures on the distribution of income for 1950, 1961, and 1970. When any particular year is examined, the combined effect of taxes and expenditures entails a substantial equalization of income. Moreover, the relative size of government in the economy nearly doubled during the period studied. But the degree of equality seems to have been roughly the same in 1970 as it was in 1950. The ability of progressive taxation to alter relative labor supplies, and to do so in a manner that offsets the nominal redistributive impact of the tax, is consistent with their concluding statement: "It appears to be a common view that, even in a predominantly market economy, the distribution of income, however defined, is subject to governmental modification. We are not convinced that the conventional wisdom is correct" (p. 96). Relatedly, the effect of the income tax in encouraging self-employment is examined in James E. Long, "The Income Tax and Self-Employment," *National Tax Journal* 35 (March 1982), pp. 31–42.

FLAT-RATE TAXATION

Flat-rate taxation, which has become a topic of general interest, would replace the schedule of rising marginal rates shown in Table 9.1 with a single rate. Federal tax collections under the personal income tax presently run about 19 percent of taxable income. As a first approximation, therefore, the levy of a 19 percent rate of tax on taxable income as it is currently defined would collect the same amount of revenue as is now collected under the progressive rate structure. The condition "first approximation" deserves emphasis. Taxable income, as well as such other aggregate magnitudes as adjusted gross income and personal income, represents the value of transactions that take place under existing tax arrangements. To some extent tax arrangements influence the types of transactions people make. The replacement of the progressive rate structure with a flat-rat tax would alter taxable income and, therefore, the rate of tax required to raise the same amount of revenue currently raised. One significant impact of high marginal rates of tax is to drive transactions into the "underground economy" to escape taxation. The higher the marginal rate of tax, the greater the payoff people realize from moving their transactions underground. Because it lowers the benefits of underground transactions relative to the costs, a reduction in marginal rates of tax should reduce the size of the underground economy. To the extent that this happens, a flat-rate tax would increase taxable income as it is currently defined, which means that the current amount of revenue could be raised by a flat rate of something less than 19 percent.

Moreover, much of the discussion about flat-rate taxation has taken place under the assumption that the base of taxable income would be broadened. If the various deductions and exemptions that are used in deriving taxable income are disallowed, the tax base would be equal to adjusted gross income. Tax collections are presently about 14 percent of adjusted gross income, so, again as a first approximation, a flat-rate tax of 14 percent on adjusted gross income would raise the same amount of revenue as is now raised under the progressive rate structure. In addition, to the extent that the flat-rate tax encouraged some shift from underground to open activity, the tax base would rise and the required rate of tax would fall below 14 percent. Similarly, if the tax base is defined as broadly as personal income, a tax rate of about 11 percent would raise as much revenue as is now raised, not accounting for the probable increase in the tax base that would result from the reduction in the marginal rate of tax.

Opposing and Supporting Arguments

The main argument that has been advanced by critics of a flat-rate tax is that it would reduce the tax burdens of people with high incomes by increasing the tax burdens of low-income people. This possible shift in the burden of taxation can be seen most easily if we assume that taxable income is unchanged by the introduction of a flat-rate tax. Each dollar of income would then be taxed at 19 percent instead of at the existing schedule of progressive rates. As a perusal of Table 9.1 shows, tax liability would increase for all single taxpayers with taxable incomes of less than $20,400. A single person with a taxable income of $10,800 in 1982 would pay a tax of $1,385 under the progressive tax but would pay $2,052 under a flat-rate tax of 19 percent. When taxable income is $20,400, single taxpayers would pay $3,876 under both types of tax. As income rises above $20,400, single taxpayers would pay less under the flat-rate tax than under the progressive tax. A single person with taxable income of $28,800 in 1982 would pay a tax of $6,692 under the progressive tax and $5,472 under the flat-rate tax.

It is easy to overestimate the significance of this redistributive impact, however. As we noted in the preceding section, the replacement of a proportional income tax with a progressive tax of equal yield is not as redistributive as it might appear, once shifts in relative factor supplies are taken into account. It is invalid to compare the distribution of tax payments under progressive taxation with the distribution that would result if the same revenue were raised under proportional taxation because to do so we must assume that the pretax distribution of income remains the same. A change from progressive to proportional taxation, however, will induce a change in relative labor supplies, and the distribution of pretax income will change in response. People with high incomes earn more before tax under progressive taxation than they would earn under proportional taxation, and vice versa for people with low incomes. Consequently, a shift from a progressive to a flat-rate tax of equal yield would cause adjustments in the labor market that would reduce pretax income in the upper ranges and increase pretax income in the lower ranges. A flat-rate tax therefore would not increase posttax inequality as much as it might seem at first, just as a progressive tax does not reduce posttax inequality as much as it might appear.

Additionally, a flat-rate tax has incentive effects that will bring about some shift of economic activity from the underground economy into the open. Because the incentive to go underground rises with the marginal rate of tax, reported taxable income should increase in the upper income ranges when a flat-rate tax is instituted. People in the upper income ranges would possess a larger share of *reported* taxable income, and some shifting of the tax burden from lower-income taxpayers to higher-income taxpayers would occur.

Any expansion in the definition of the tax base would further confound simple comparison of the redistributive consequences of a shift to a flat-rate tax. People in higher-rate brackets who might gain by having a lower tax liability under a flat-rate tax might lose if the tax base is broadened; the lower tax rate applied to a broader base might entail an increase in tax liability. A single person with taxable income of $28,800 in 1982 who is on the boundary of the 35 and 40 percent rate brackets and who takes large deductions for interest and taxes may pay more tax under a flat-rate tax if those deductions are no longer allowed than under the present progressive tax. It is, of course, unlikely that the implementation of a flat-rate tax that collects the same total revenue as the present progressive tax would collect the same amount of revenue from each taxpayer. Some people are likely to pay more tax and others less, but accurate generalization about the redistributive impact of such a change in tax is not possible.

Supporters of flat-rate taxation have emphasized the efficiency- or wealth-enhancing properties of such a tax. With a flat-rate tax, many complex issues of tax administration would vanish. Inflation would no longer be able to push people into higher-rate brackets, so the various complexities introduced by tax indexing would not arise. People who have fluctuating incomes would pay the same amount of tax as people who have stable incomes, so there would be no complexities introduced by income averaging. Such savings in tax administration would be attained even if the tax base were not changed. To the extent that the base is broadened, other savings in tax administration would occur, and as deductions are eliminated, tax administration would be simplified further. If payments of interest were no longer deductible from gross income, records pertaining to interest payments would no longer be necessary; fewer resources would be devoted to tax administration, and those released resources could be devoted to other activities.[19]

This saving in tax administration is only part of the advantages that supporters attribute to flat-rate taxation. The main advantage is the change in the pattern of economic activity that they claim

---

[19] Some people will, of course, lose from tax simplification, especially in the short run. Accountants, lawyers, and other tax-related professionals would experience a decreased demand for their services under tax simplification. The short-run effect would be a reduction in their earnings; the long-run effect would be a reduction in the size of those professions.

would result when tax considerations become less important in people's choices concerning the use of resources. We have already seen that progressive taxation might influence the pattern of economic activity by reducing the labor supply, by increasing underground activity, and by shifting the composition of the labor force. These activities occur because the progressive rate structure induces people to search for ways of rearranging transactions to reduce their tax liability. Flat-rate taxation would eliminate much of this need and would modify the pattern of economic activity in the process.

The ways in which progressive taxation induces people to rearrange transactions range from the simple to the very complex. The simplest adjustments involve shifting income from the present year when income is high to a future year when income is likely to be low. A shift of $1,000 in the 50 percent bracket one year to the 22 percent bracket in a future year reduces anticipated taxes by $380. In many cases, such deferred compensation involves a loss of interest that must be set against the tax saving. But in many cases it is possible to earn interest and defer the tax on that interest as well. This is particularly true of such retirement programs as Keogh plans and Individual Retirement Accounts (IRAs). Income is excluded from the tax base when it is earned, and it becomes part of the tax base only when the funds are withdrawn after retirement, when income and the rate of tax are lower. Other efforts to time and arrange transactions to reduce tax liability are more complex, but they all represent responses to the incentives created by high and rising marginal rates of tax. Because flat-rate taxation reduces the importance of tax considerations in choices concerning the use of resources, supporters of flat-rate taxation argue that a more efficient pattern of resource usage will result.[20]

Impact on Earnings of Men and Women

Although most discussion of flat-rate taxation has centered on its probable impact on the distribution of the tax burden among income classes and the efficiency-enhancing properties of tax simplification, one of the interesting aspects of a flat-rate tax is its probable impact on the relative earnings of men and women. On average in the United States, women earn about 60 percent as much as men. In a market economy, people tend to be paid according to the value of their contribution in production; equal pay for equal work is an

[20] The pattern of resource misallocation that presently results is similar to the misallocation of resources between corporate and noncorporate enterprises because of the taxation of corporation income, which we examine in Chapter 10.

attribute of a market economy.[21] This difference in earnings means that, on average, the value of the marginal product of women is about 60 percent that of men.

This observation is fully consistent with the proposition that women have the same productive potential as men, provided only that women on average make choices that develop their potential less fully than men. The progressive income tax has much to do with making such choices rational. Consequently, the replacement of the progressive tax with a flat-rate tax would tend to equalize the incentives men and women have to develop their potential, thereby equalizing average earnings. The effect of progressive taxation on the incentives of men and women can be seen by considering the tax schedule for married taxpayers shown in Table 9.2. Suppose the husband and the wife have identical potential for developing talents and acquiring skills, which if fully developed would yield a taxable income of $20,000 each.

But what incentives to invest in human capital do these people face? It is useful to think of one person as choosing an investment in human capital and the second choosing an investment in human capital in light of the first person's choice. The first person is called a *primary earner;* the second person, a *secondary earner.* For the most part in American families, husbands are primary earners and wives are secondary earners, although the reverse clearly holds in some cases. Suppose the husband's investment in human capital yields a taxable income of $20,000. The marginal rate of tax on the yield from this investment is 22 percent.

How does the progressive income tax influence the incentive to invest in human capital by the secondary earner? If the wife makes the same investment as her husband, the family's taxable income would rise to $40,000, and the marginal rate of tax applicable to the wife's earnings would be 39 percent. The family would receive little additional Social Security coverage, so the Social Security tax that the wife would have to pay would drive her marginal rate of

---

[21] It is sometimes argued that women are on average equally productive as men, with the differential in earnings being attributed to sex discrimination. This is a difficult argument to make because it rests on an assumption that people will systematically refuse to accept money that is theirs for the taking. Suppose a newspaper publisher can get the same output from women as from men, with women being available for only 60 percent of the wage of men. A publisher who hired women in place of men could produce the same output at less cost, thereby increasing the value of the newspaper. Publishers who do not hire women over men in this situation are throwing money away. A coherent explanation of economic life has yet to be built on the assumption that people consistently and generally refuse to accept gifts. Moreover, the process of competition for equally productive but lower-priced women will raise the earnings of women relative to men until equality is attained.

TABLE 9.2   Tax Rate Schedule for Married Taxpayers Filing Joint Returns, 1982

Taxable Income		Tax	
over	but not over		of amount over
$ 0	$ 3,400	$ —	—
3,400	5,500	12%	$ 3,400
5,500	7,600	252+14%	5,500
7,600	11,900	546+16%	7,600
11,900	16,000	1,234+19%	11,900
16,000	20,200	2,013+22%	16,000
20,200	24,600	2,937+25%	20,200
24,600	29,900	4,037+29%	24,600
29,900	35,200	5,574+33%	29,900
35,200	45,800	7,323+39%	35,200
45,800	60,000	11,457+44%	45,800
60,000	85,600	17,705+49%	60,000
85,600	—	30,249+50%	85,600

tax above 52 percent. This difference in tax treatment between husbands and wives (more generally, between primary and secondary earners) under the progressive income tax creates an incentive for wives to de-emphasize the formation of marketable human capital relative to human capital that yields nonmarket, nontaxed returns, such as shopping, cooking, sewing, maintenance, and the like. A flat-rate income tax is one way of removing this penalty against secondary earners, and its enactment would provide roughly equal incentives for men and women to invest in human capital. To the extent that men and women have equal capacities and preferences for market and nonmarket uses of human capital, a flat-rate tax should erode the differential in earnings between men and women.[22]

Rather than seeking to offset such tax-induced biases in the incentives to invest in human capital, an effort could be made to promote equality of earnings by sex but without modifying incentives to invest in human capital. Suppose an equal-pay provision requires each employer to pay the same average wage to men and women employees. Figure 9.6 illustrates several noteworthy features of such an effort. For one thing, the legislation would benefit some women at the expense of others. Some women would find employ-

[22] For an examination of this point, see Paul McGouldrick, "Why Women Earn Less," *Policy Review,* no. 18 (Fall 1981), pp. 63–76.

FIGURE 9.6 Equal-Pay Legislation and the Labor Market

The demand functions of employers for primary and secondary earners are represented by D_p and D_s respectively. To simplify the geometry, we assume that the supply function is identical for both types of earners. Employment of primary earners is L_p, and their wage is W_p. L_s secondary earners are employed, and they receive a wage of W_s. If an equal-pay provision is implemented at W_p, only L_s' secondary earners will find employment. The equal-pay requirement will cause unemployment of $L_s - L_s'$ secondary earners. (It will also increase the number of secondary earners seeking employment to L_p.) Moreover, when only L_s' secondary earners can find employment, they will be willing to work for only W_s'. The wage difference $W_p - W_s'$ indicates the strength of the incentive employers and unemployed secondary earners have to find some way of contracting around the equal-pay provision.

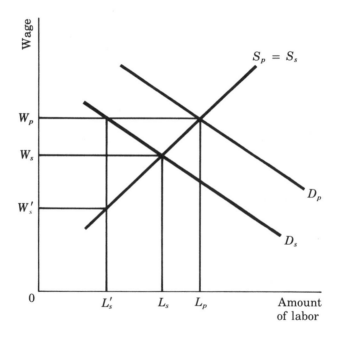

ment at the higher wage, but others would become unemployed. The legislation would transfer income from women whose market-oriented human capital is of relatively low value to women whose market-oriented human capital is of relatively high value. Among other things, single and professional women would gain at the expense of other women.

The equal-pay requirement would also result in a contradiction by creating incentives for people to contract around the legislation. At the higher wage, more women would be willing to supply their labor than employers are willing to hire. At the new and lower level of employment of women, some unemployed women would be willing to work for less than the required wage. How this contradiction is resolved depends on a number of circumstances, and no universal answer can be formulated. One possible approach is a reduction in the use of standard labor contracts. Employers, rather than hiring employees under a contract subject to the equal-pay requirement, could deal with women as independent contractors. The opportunities for the development of such alternatives depend at least to some extent on the constraints provided by legislation. Prevailing legislation makes it illegal for people to contract with a manufacturer of clothing to do sewing in their own homes, for instance. The development of a flat-rate tax, however, would not create contradictory incentives and would tend naturally to diminish the difference in earnings between men and women, to the extent that men and women have the same capacities and preferences for market and nonmarket activities.

RISK TAKING AND ENTREPRENEURSHIP

Choices made today to commit resources to production will not be evaluated by consumers until some time has elapsed. In some cases, as in the production of eggs, the period of production will be relatively short. In other cases, as in making hickory furniture, this period of production will be relatively long. In all instances, however, time must elapse between the decision to produce and the evaluation by consumers of that decision. Hence, the value of specific factors of production will not be known with certainty until after production has been completed and the product sold. The value of a furniture maker's choice to produce a particular chair will not be known with certainty until the reactions of potential customers have been revealed through their purchasing decisions. Yet many of the resource owners who cooperate in producing the chair (the suppliers of wood, saws, glue, warehouse space, and so on) are paid for their services before a market evaluation of their services has been rendered.

The furniture maker contracts with such input suppliers for their services even though the value of those services has not been established with certainty and cannot be established until sometime in the future. The terms of contract are based on the participants' anticipation of the value of those services, which is based on an expectation about how well the chair will sell. If some resource owners are guaranteed a payment for their services even though it is impossible to determine the value of those services at the time of payment, someone must provide that guarantee. This person is called an *entrepreneur*. Some people must be entrepreneurs if others are to receive guaranteed fees or prices for the productive inputs they supply. If the value of their services as revealed in the choices of consumers is less than the value on which factor payments are based, the entrepreneur or residual claimant bears the loss. Conversely, if the resulting value exceeds the value on which the guaranteed payments were based, the entrepreneur reaps the profit. Regardless, entrepreneurship is an essential feature of the process of production because it is the means by which someone accepts ultimate responsibility for choices concerning production.

The return to entrepreneurship is a return to the bearing of uncertainty through the role of residual claimant. Uncertainty can be distinguished from risk in that risk, but not uncertainty, can be insured against.[23] Although entrepreneurship and risk taking are different activities, for our purposes they can be treated together because the impact of income taxation on the bearing of uncertainty will generally be similar to its impact on the bearing of risk. A substantial body of literature has arisen in the effort to explore the impact of income taxation on risk taking and entrepreneurship. Most of this literature has actually been concerned with financial investments such as stocks and bonds rather than with entrepreneurial choices regarding the use of resources. Nonetheless, we can use the central analytical framework to explore the impact of income taxation on entrepreneurial choices regarding the investment of resources in particular uses.

Figure 9.7 illustrates the central features of what can become a relatively complex analytical framework that explores the impact of income taxation on the supply of risk taking and entrepreneurship. Not surprisingly, the results are dependent on assumptions about individual utility functions and the underlying motivation concerning choices about investment. The central analytical features are similar to those in the labor-leisure choice. Investments, or entrepreneurial choices generally, can be characterized by an expected return and a standard deviation. A furniture manufacturer may expect to earn 20 percent on a particular chair, based on, say, a 50–50 chance of earning either a 40 percent or a zero percent return. This expected return is variable and not certain, and the standard deviation is one

[23] The distinction between risk and uncertainty was the central theme of Frank H. Knight, *Risk, Uncertainty, and Profit* (Boston: Houghton Mifflin, 1921).

FIGURE 9.7 Enterpreneurial Choice Without Taxation

The indifference map illustrated by indifference curves i_0, i_1, and i_2 shows the utility is presumed to increase as the mean return rises and to decrease as the standard deviation of that return rises. The opportunity locus, OR, shows the boundary of attainable combinations of mean return and standard deviation, with all combinations to the right of the boundary being unattainable. In light of the budget constraint and preference map depicted here, a pattern of investment choices will be made that can be characterized as having an expected return of M_1 and a standard deviation of S_1.

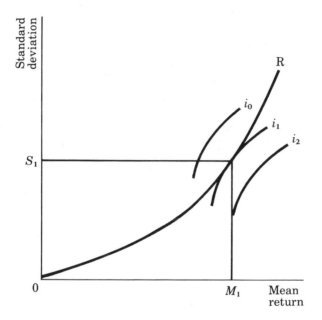

possible measure of this variability. In the literature, the expected return and its standard deviation are generally assumed to be positively correlated; an increase in the standard deviation is taken to denote an increase in the risk associated with the choice. Utility is assumed to vary positively with the mean return and negatively with the standard deviation. An individual's choice is characterized as one of maximizing utility subject to a budget constraint, as is the choice between earning income and taking leisure.

The impact of income taxation on risk taking and entrepreneurship can be explored in several ways. The tax can be proportional to income or it can be progressive. Income can be taxed without offsets for losses, or offsets can be allowed for losses. In all such cases, an

increase in the rate of tax on income will reduce the return from a
given pattern of investment, and the matter to explore is whether
the individual adjustments in response to the tax will result in an
increase or decrease in the supply of risk taking and entrepreneurship. Consider first the case of proportional income tax, with full
offsets from the tax base being allowed for losses, as illustrated in
Figure 9.8. What is relevant from the perspective of the individual is

---

FIGURE 9.8 Entrepreneurial Choice with Taxation

The opportunity locus, OR, and the indifference curve, i_1, which describe a
pattern of choice in which the expected return is M_1 and the standard
deviation is S_1, are repeated from Figure 9.7. The imposition of a
proportional income tax with full offsets for losses shrinks the opportunity
locus to OR_t, with the extent of shrinkage varying with the rate of
taxation. That is, any combination of M and S on OR is reduced by the tax
to a corresponding point on R_t. For instance, $(M_3, S_3) = (1 - t)(M_1, S_1)$
along γ_1. In response to the tax-induced shrinkage in the opportunity set,
the entrepreneur will choose a pattern of investment described by (M_2, S_2).
In this case, the entrepreneur adapts to the tax by increasing the supply of
risk taking and entrepreneurship. The result is an increase both in the
mean return and in the standard deviation, as shown by (M_4, S_4), once it is
recognized that government shares the profits and the losses of
entrepreneurial choices.

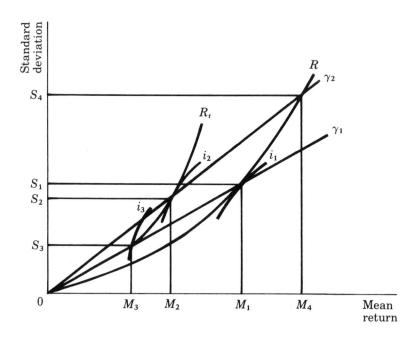

the net return after tax. Similar to the previous analysis of income taxation and the supply of labor, the introduction of a proportional income tax may increase, decrease, or leave unchanged the supply of risk taking and entrepreneurship. The tax reduces the expected return. But with full offsets for losses, government shares the losses as well as the profits, and it is quite possible for individual entrepreneurs to make choices in which the total expected return (the entrepreneur's plus the government's) and the total standard deviation are greater with the tax than without it.

This analysis of risk taking has much in common with the earlier analysis of labor supply, and it is subject to similar difficulties. In Figure 9.8, tax collections are equal to $M_4 - M_2$. The tax does not take resources away from the economy, but rather transfers them to alternative uses. If the tax revenue is spent to supply collective services, those services become a component of the return from the investment. The tax thus reduces the individual's private income from the investment, but the concomitant expenditure creates a form of collective return. The tax will almost surely create differential income effects among individuals, but, on average, income effects will sum to zero. Figure 9.9 illustrates the incorporation of public expenditure into the analysis. It is assumed that the collective expenditure is equally valuable at the margin with the private expenditure that is displaced by the taxation. Hence the collective expenditure becomes equivalent to a certain return. That the tax-cum-expenditure has no income effect on the average implies that the impact, within the framework of the analytical model, will be to unambiguously reduce the supply of risk taking and entrepreneurship.

Compared with a proportional income tax with full offsets for losses, a progressive tax with offsets for losses will place an additional tax on gains that exceeds the savings from offsets on losses, thus reducing the supply of risk taking and entrepreneurship from what it would be under proportional taxation. When losses cannot be used to offset gains, progressive taxation will further depress risk taking and entrepreneurship, compared with proportional income taxation with full offsets. Within the limits of the analytical models used here, the more progressive the rate of tax on gains, the lower the supply of entrepreneurship and risk taking that will exist in the economy.

FISCAL CHOICE AND PROGRESSIVE INCOME TAXATION

Much of the complexity associated with a system of income taxation arises because income is taxed at progressive rates. With a propor-

FIGURE 9.9 Entrepreneurial Choice with Tax-cum-Expenditure

The opportunity loci, $0R$ and $0R_t$, along with the associated indifference
curves, are replicated from Figure 9.8. The government's expenditure is
equal to its tax collections, and this expenditure appears as a certain
return, $0G$. Although any single person may face an uncertain return,
there is much less uncertainty about the aggregate of individual returns,
which gives public expenditure a more assured or certain status. Thus
people can essentially count on starting at G rather than at 0. Starting at
G, the individual faces the pretax opportunity locus, GR^*, which becomes
the posttax locus GR_t^*. Such a person will make the choice described by the
tangency of the indifference curve i_0 to GR_t^*. In this setting, the
combination of tax-cum-expenditure reduces the supply of risk taking and
entrepreneurship from S_2 to S_2^*.

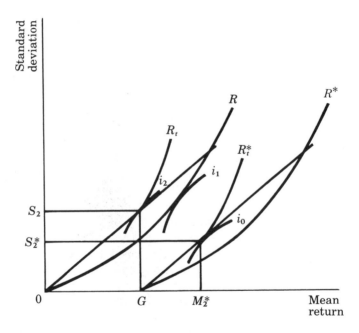

tional rate, there would be no problems of indexing for inflation because tax collections would rise in proportion to income instead of
rising faster than income, as they do under progressive taxation. Problems of averaging would likewise not arise under proportional income
taxation. Under a progressive income tax, people who have fluctuating
incomes pay a higher tax than people who have average but stable
incomes. A single person who has taxable income of $20,000 will incur
a tax liability of $3,752, according to the 1982 rate schedule shown
in Table 9.1 at the beginning of the chapter. But someone whose in-

come fluctuated with equal likelihood between $10,000 and $30,000 would pay an average tax of $4,202.50 on that average income of $20,000. Moreover, much of the effort to arrange transactions with an eye to their tax consequences results from the progression in marginal tax rates. Why, then, is income taxed under a complex system of progressive rates instead of a simple system of proportional rates?

Some people have suggested that progressive taxation is a form of collectively supplied charity that may be explained in the same way as private charity. Private charity is a product of utility interdependence, in which the donor's utility level depends on the level of consumption of the recipient. Donors derive utility from charitable contributions because they value the consumption of recipients. A donor will apportion his income between charity and his own consumption according to the ordinary principles of consumer choice. But if charity has elements of joint consumption combined with nonexclusion, for example, if person C benefits from A's transfer to B and if A is unable to prevent C's consumption, a market economy may supply a suboptimal amount of charity, according to the free-rider line of argument. Progressive taxation may likewise be viewed as a compact among the more wealthy members of society to tax themselves to subsidize the less wealthy, thereby supplying themselves with a collective good and increasing both their own utility and the utility of the less wealthy members of society.

This rationalization that progressive taxation reflects utility interdependence carries with it the implication that, among other things, the tax structure adopted by a society is invariant to the rules and procedures for making collective choices. Progressive taxation is chosen by those with relatively high incomes as an expression of utility interdependence, and the same tax structure would be chosen whether only those with high incomes could vote or whether everyone could vote. Both historical evidence about franchise extension and basic reasoning suggest that this invariance does not hold. But if the structure of taxation varies to some extent with changes in such things as voting rules, it would seem that a particular structure of taxation is chosen, at least to some extent, because it provides redistributive gains for a dominant coalition. When the income of the median voter is less than the mean income in society, for example, a majority of the voting populace has below-average incomes. Accordingly, progressive taxation might be a means by which a less wealthy majority coalition transfers income to its members from a more wealthy minority.

While this explanation of progressive taxation might possess some plausibility, it fails to explain why taxes are not even more progressive. That is, why isn't complete equality the outcome of the forma-

tion of coalitions by income? One possible explanation is that the
majority coalition is aware that it loses through the disincentive
effects that intensify with the progressivity of the tax. Such disincentive effects create a trade-off between the gains from greater equalization and the losses from the reduction in the total amount of
income available for redistribution. Progressive taxation thus becomes analogous to taking an increasing share of a shrinking pie. So
long as one's share of income increases more rapidly than the total
income shrinks, support of further progressivity is rational. Under
such circumstances, a majority coalition will choose a degree of progressivity that achieves less than complete equalization.

Another possible line of explanation is that the extent of progressivity may be limited by the inability of the less wealthy voters to
effectively outnumber the more wealthy voters. Because political competition is costly, people who have a comparative advantage in per-
suading others and people who have the wealth to assist in this per-
suasion will have more influence than others over political outcomes.
Coalitions will not form wholly along income lines, but instead they
will contain a mix of more wealthy and less wealthy voters.

A third possible explanation of the limits to progressivity is that
those in the lower income ranges do not expect to remain there permanently. People are mobile within the distribution of income. By
supporting extreme degrees of progression now, some members of
the less wealthy group will harm their chances to enjoy greater income
in the future, and by acquiescing in some amount of progressivity
now, some members of the more wealthy group will protect themselves against a run of bad financial luck in the future. This line of
explanation suggests that progessive taxation can be seen as having
some features of income insurance. Yet this insurance analogy can
be carried too far. Insurance is purchased before an accident, not
afterward. If insurance purchases were made after the outcome
was known, those without accidents would not want insurance, and
those with accidents would want comprehensive coverage. There
would be no room for agreement between the two groups, and insurance would be impossible without such agreement. By making
choices before outcomes are known, agreement becomes possible because the identities of accident victims are unknown. Tax institutions,
on the other hand, are chosen, at least to a substantial degree, after
the outcomes are known. Those who have high incomes will be in the
position of those who have had no accidents; they will desire little
coverage. Those with low incomes, by contrast, will be in a position
analogous to those who have had accidents and will tend to opt for
more extensive insurance in the form of progressive taxation than
they would otherwise choose.

PRODUCTION, DISTRIBUTION, AND TAX POLICY

Whatever reason might be thought most apt as an explanation for the choice of one tax pattern over another, it is useful to examine the economic consequences of that choice. The central point of controversy over tax policy probably concerns the balance to be achieved between the productive and the distributive aspects of tax policy. The present American system of income taxation essentially taxes saving twice as heavily as it taxes consumption. Between two people who earn the same income, the one who saves more will pay a higher rate of tax. This difference in treatment arises from the ability of saving to generate earnings in the future through the yield on the capital that is created. While earnings that are consumed are taxed only when they are earned, earnings that are saved are taxed twice, when they are earned and again when the return on the capital that is created accrues in the future. While this second aspect of the taxation of saving does not actually take place until the yields are realized, it is the original act of saving that creates the liability.

Some simple arithmetic can illustrate this proposition. If income is taxed at 50 percent, $200 of earnings will leave $100 remaining for consumption. If this $100 of posttax income is saved rather than spent, the total anticipated tax burden of earning $200 and saving the posttax $100 is actually $150, as long as the anticipated rate of return is equal to the rate of discount. Suppose the anticipated rate of return on saving is 10 percent. The $100 of saving will produce anticipated annual yields of $10, and these yields will carry with them anticipated tax burdens of $5. The present value of those future tax liabilities is $50, and the total tax burden associated with saving rather than consuming $100 when earnings are taxed at 50 percent is $150.[24] Although the share of income that is consumed is taxed at 50 percent, the share that is saved is actually taxed at 75 percent. More generally, for any particular anticipated rate of return and rate of discount, there is a present value of tax on the act of saving, which is the product of the marginal tax rate applicable at that level of income and the amount of saving. The American system of income taxation seems generally to discriminate against saving and, hence, capital formation. To avoid this double taxation, either saving or the yield from saving must be exempt from the income tax.

It might be argued that the double taxation of saving is desirable

[24] Alternatively, should the anticipated rate of return be 20 percent, the anticipated annual yields of $20 will carry with them anticipated liabilities of $10. With a 20 percent rate of discount, the present value of the tax liability will still be $50.

as a means for equalizing the distribution of income. When looked at for relatively short periods of time, tax policy seems primarily to concern the distribution of tax burdens and disposable income. In this short-run context, the fundamental issue concerning whether to exempt capital appreciation from the income tax would seem to be a matter of income distribution. But when looked at for a longer period of time, questions relating to the production — and destruction — of wealth become more significant.

This contrast between short-run and long-run contexts can be illustrated quite simply.[25] Suppose $10,000 is invested, with an anticipated annual return of 20 percent. The annual yield is taxed at 50 percent, and the revenues are distributed to recipients of public expenditure for their consumption. The exposition can be simplified by assuming that the posttax yield is reinvested. The first year the investment yields $2,000, of which $1,000 is taxed and the remaining $1,000 reinvested. The second year there is $11,000 of capital, the gross yield on which is $2,200. The tax is $1,100, and the same amount is left to be reinvested. The third year there is $12,100 of capital, which yields $2,420 in gross income. Tax collections are now $1,210, and an equal amount is reinvested to produce a capital base of $13,310 to start the fourth year.

In each year the budgetary process appears to deal essentially with a redistribution of wealth from savers to consumers. In the first year, the primary budgetary question appears to be whether to impose a tax of $1,000 on the recipients of capital income to finance, in one way or another, the consumption activities of other people. In each year, the question about distribution seems to be the same, with the amount rising each year. The central aspect of the budgetary process seems to be the use of taxes on capital income to finance the consumption of the beneficiaries of government expenditure.

When this process is examined over a sequence of years, however, this zero-sum perspective vanishes. If the yield from saving were not taxed, $2,000 would have been invested at the end of the first year, again assuming that the entire yield on saving is reinvested. In turn, the resulting capital base of $12,000 would have generated a yield of $2,400 the following year. The capital base of $14,000 at the start of the third year would have yielded $2,880, which would have left capital of $17,280 at the end of that year. When seen in this perspective, tax policy is responsible for the destruction of capital, and the value of capital destroyed has exceeded the amount of taxes collected. Instead of the accumulation of $7,280 of capital over the three-year

[25] This illustration is adapted from Irving Fisher and Herbert W. Fisher, *Constructive Income Taxation* (New York: Harper Bros., 1942).

period, only $3,310 has accumulated. The $3,310 of government expenditure has been financed by the destruction of $3,970 of capital, and the size of the capital destruction relative to the size of the expenditure increases starkly with the passage of time. If forty years are allowed to pass, wealth will be $453,000 and tax collections will have been $442,000. Since the amount of wealth would have been $14,800,000 in the absence of tax, the tax collection of $453,000 has been responsible for the destruction of $14,347,000 of capital.

The capital destruction that results from the double taxation of saving and capital means that less wealth is generally available within a society. This is not to argue against the taxation of capital to finance consumption, but only to note that more is involved in such taxation than the placement of penalties on losers so that winners may be rewarded. There is also a destruction of wealth, and this destruction harms nonsavers as well as savers. Labor and capital are complementary in production. An increase in the quantity of capital will increase the wages received by labor.[26] Tax policies that reduce the amount of saving and capital formation will reduce wages as well.

The assessment of tax policies does, of course, depend on the period of time over which the assessment is to be made, as the preceding numerical illustration showed. If the redistributive policy is assessed one year at a time, the policy is zero sum. But the longer the period of time over which the policy is assessed, the more strongly the negative-sum aspects come into focus. There is an interesting question of knowledge that arises in the assessment of tax policy in this case. Capital destruction need not refer to an actual reduction in the size of the capital stock. It can also refer to a reduction in its size compared with what it would have been had tax policy been different. With absolute capital destruction, people will experience declining standards of living. In this case people's memories provide bases for assessing the negative-sum aspects of the policy. Under what might be called relative capital destruction, living standards rise, but at a slower pace. The assessment of such a policy is not a matter of comparing the present with a memory of the past; rather it is a comparison of the present with some imaginative construction of an alter-

---

[26] Suppose production and distribution in an economy can be described by the Cobb-Douglas production function

$$X = AK^{\alpha}L^{1-\alpha} \quad (1 > \alpha > 0)$$

where X denotes aggregate output, A is a constant, and K and L denote the quantities of capital and labor, respectively. In a competitive economy, factors of production receive their marginal products. Accordingly, labor will receive

$$MP_L = (1 - \alpha) A L^{-\alpha} K^{\alpha}.$$

An increase in the quantity of capital will increase the marginal product and, hence, the wages of labor.

native present, if policy had been different over the past.[27] Moreover, many of the questions raised here deal with the various efforts by government to promote greater equality in the distribution of income, a topic that is examined in Chapter 17.

SUGGESTIONS FOR FURTHER READING

A thorough description and survey of a variety of issues concerning income taxation, including a strong defense of the Haig-Simons approach to the definition of income, is presented in Richard Goode, *The Individual Income Tax,* revised edition (Washington, D.C.: Brookings Institution, 1976). Various aspects of defining a comprehensive tax base are explored by the essayists in the conference volume *Comprehensive Income Taxation,* edited by Joseph A. Pechman (Washington, D.C.: Brookings Institution, 1977). A comprehensive description of the various provisions of the personal income tax appears in *Your Federal Income Tax,* an annual publication of the Internal Revenue Service.

The seminal expression of utility interdependence is Harold M. Hochman and James D. Rodgers, "Pareto Optimal Redistribution," *American Economic Review* 59 (September 1969), pp. 542–557. The view of progressive income taxation as a form of income insurance is developed in James M. Buchanan, *Public Finance in Democratic Process* (Chapel Hill: University of North Carolina Press, 1967), pp. 225–240. For empirical documentation of the use of fringe benefits as a form of compensation, see Wilbur G. Lewellen, *Executive Compensation in Large Industrial Corporations* (New York: Columbia University Press, 1968).

For a sample of the voluminous literature on the effect of income taxation on the supply of labor, see Richard Goode, "The Income Tax and the Supply of Labor," *Journal of Political Economy* 57 (October 1949), pp. 428–437; Richard A. Musgrave, *The Theory of Public Finance* (New York: McGraw-Hill, 1959), pp. 232–246; Marvin Kosters, "Effects of an Income Tax on Family Labor Supply," in *The Taxation of Income from Capital,* edited by Arnold C. Harberger and Martin J. Bailey (Washington, D.C.: Brookings Institution, 1969), pp. 301–321; and C. Duncan MacRae and Anthony M. J. Yezer, "The Personal Income Tax and Family Labor Supply," *Southern Economic Journal* 43 (July 1976), pp. 783–792.

For a sample of explorations into the effect of income taxation on risk taking, see Evsey D. Domar and Richard A. Musgrave, "Proportional Income Taxation and Risk Taking," *Quarterly Journal of Economics* 58 (May 1944), pp. 388–422; James E. Tobin, "Liquidity Preference as Be-

---

[27] For one interesting, and controversial, effort to make such an imaginative construction of an alternative present, see Martin S. Feldstein, "Social Security, Induced Retirement, and Aggregate Capital Accumulation," *Journal of Political Economy* 82 (October 1974), pp. 905–926.

havior Toward Risk," *Review of Economic Studies* 25 (February 1958), pp. 65–86; Martin S. Feldstein, "The Effects of Taxation on Risk Taking," *Journal of Political Economy* 77 (October 1969), pp. 755–764; and J. E. Stiglitz, "The Effect of Income, Wealth, and Capital Gains Taxation on Risk Taking," *Quarterly Journal of Economics* 83 (May 1969), pp. 263–283. Anthony B. Atkinson and Joseph E. Stiglitz explore from an advanced level the effects of income taxation on the supply of labor and of risk taking, in *Lectures on Public Economics* (New York: McGraw-Hill, 1980), especially pp. 23–61 and 97–127.

There have been several efforts to assess the overall progressivity of the entire system of taxation. Joseph A. Pechman and Benjamin A. Okner, in *Who Bears the Tax Burden?* (Washington, D.C.: Brookings Institution, 1974), argue that the overall tax system is roughly proportional to income. In contrast, Edgar K. Browning and William R. Johnson, in *The Distribution of the Tax Burden* (Washington, D.C.: American Enterprise Institute, 1979), argue, on the basis of somewhat different assumptions about tax incidence, that the overall tax burden is highly progressive. An increase in the progressivity of the tax system can, of course, be offset by a reverse change in the distributive impact of public expenditure. This realization has led several people to examine the combined effect of taxes and expenditures on the distribution of income. The book by Morgan Reynolds and Eugene Smolensky, cited in note 18 to this chapter, not only illustrates this type of approach but also contains bibliographical references to most other works with a similar intent.

Edgar K. Browning, "The Marginal Cost of Public Funds," *Journal of Political Economy* 84 (April 1976), pp. 283–298, argues that the personal income tax generates an excess burden of about 9 to 16 percent of the revenue collected. This excess burden results because the income tax drives a wedge between the social yield from a unit of labor and the private return. The article by Jerry Hausman, cited in note 15 of this chapter, argues that the excess burden is more on the order of 29 percent for husbands and 58 percent for wives. The excess burden of the income tax is related to public expenditure in Thomas S. McCaleb, "Excess Burden, Benefit Taxation, and Efficiency in Public Expenditure," *American Economic Review* 70 (June 1980), pp. 501–506.

10

Taxation of Corporation Income

The taxation of corporation income is an important source of revenue for both the federal government and state governments in the United States. The federal government raises about 30 percent as much revenue through its taxation of corporation income as it raises through its taxation of personal income. It raises about half as much revenue in this manner as it raises through its taxation of payrolls under the Social Security program, although Social Security revenues are officially classified not as tax revenues but as insurance trust revenues. State governments raise about 20 percent as much revenue from their taxation of corporation income as they raise from their predominant source of revenue, sales and excise taxation, and they raise about 40 percent as much revenue from taxing corporation income as they raise from taxing personal income. Since the taxation of corporation income by states raises no major issues beyond those raised by the federal tax, we will focus here on the federal tax.

INCOME, PROFIT, AND THE TAX BASE

The base of the corporation income tax essentially corresponds to profits in common financial statements; the tax base is the value of a corporation's sales less the expenses it incurs in doing business. The rate of tax applied against this base rises in stages to 46 percent on net income over $100,000. The intermediate stages are applied on increments of $25,000, and the intermediate rates of tax are 17, 20, 30, and 40 percent. A corporation with net income of $200,000 would pay a total tax of $72,750. It would pay $4,250 on its first $25,000 of income, $5,000 on its second $25,000, $7,500 on its third $25,000, $10,000 on its fourth $25,000, and $46,000 on the remaining $100,000 of net income. In form, the corporation income tax is progressive; higher marginal rates of tax are applied to larger incomes, which means the average rate of tax rises with income. In substance, however, the tax is essentially proportional at a 46 percent rate; more than 90 percent of total corporation income is taxed at the 46 percent rate. This is so even though only about one corporation in five has net income over $100,000. Although the majority of corporations are relatively small, the bulk of corporation income is earned by relatively large corporations.

Although income and profit are used interchangeably in common references to the taxation of corporations, there is an important difference between the two. Income is essentially equal to revenue less *contracted* expense. If a corporation issues $1 million worth of bonds and agrees to pay $150,000 per year in interest to the bondholders, that payment is a contracted expense. Table 10.1 describes a corporation that has revenues of $1 million, pays $150,000 in interest to bondholders, and incurs other expenses of doing business of $650,000. This corporation's income is $200,000. This amount is commonly described as profit, or before-tax profit, and it is the amount against which the corporation income tax is applied. The federal tax liability on $200,000 of corporation income is $72,750. After this tax is paid, $127,250 remains for stockholders.

Corporations also have noncontracted expenses of doing business, namely, payments to stockholders to attract and maintain their investment. Stockholders are residual claimants; they receive what is left after all contracted expenses have been paid. Although the payment to stockholders is not a contracted expense for a corporation, it is nonetheless a necessary one. If corporations are to attract and maintain capital, stockholders must anticipate receiving a return

TABLE 10.1   Income Versus Profit for a Corporation

Revenue	$1,000,000
Less cost of goods sold	650,000
Less interest to bondholders	150,000
Income	200,000
Less corporate income tax (federal)	72,750
Profit (as commonly denoted)	127,250
Less implicit interest to stockholders	150,000
Profit (loss)	(22,750)

from their investment that is sufficiently attractive to dissuade them from investing instead in bonds or in other contracted obligations. If the corporation has a capital stock of $1 million and if the rate of interest that is required to elicit and maintain this investment is 15 percent, $150,000 is really an implicit interest cost to the corporation.

Profit is a residual that remains after all expenses, contracted and noncontracted, have been paid. The corporation illustrated in Table 10.1 has actually lost $22,750. If stockholders anticipate that this pattern of return will continue in the future, they will be likely to shift out of the corporation into other investments.

DEPRECIATION AND CORPORATE TAXATION

A corporation's tax liability is, conceptually, a simple matter of subtracting its expenses from its revenues to determine its income and then taxing that income according to the appropriate rate schedule. The determination of income is quite complex in practice, however. There are many sources of complexity, but probably the most important is the one that arises in accounting for the expense of purchasing and using capital goods.

Methods of Depreciation

Suppose a corporation has sales of $100,000 per year and annual expenses for labor and materials of $50,000. If there were no other transactions involved, its net income would be $50,000 per year. But suppose the corporation uses capital goods that periodically must be replaced if the corporation is to maintain its ability to produce. Say the corporation manufactures furniture, and to do this it must purchase various pieces of equipment for sawing, sanding, and drilling, among other operations. Such equipment lasts, say, for five years and then must be replaced. Further, suppose the timing of these purchases is such that $50,000 is spent each fifth year, with nothing being spent in the other four years. What is the corporation's net income in this case? It could be regarded as zero in the year the capital equipment is purchased, and $50,000 in each of the other four years. Alternatively, the $50,000 outlay for the equipment could be treated as equivalent to a $10,000 outlay in each of the five years the equipment is used, in which case net income would be $40,000 in each of the five years. Other methods of apportioning the expense of the capital equipment over its lifetime would, of course, yield different measures of income for the various years.

Taxes are based on the consequences of transactions within a one-year period, and when expenses are incurred for items that last beyond one year, a question arises as to the method of determining the corporation's expenses for any particular year. This is the problem of *depreciation*. Saws that last five years and then must be replaced can be said to be used up over a five-year period. The replacement of the saws is a cost of production, because production will not continue unless the saws are replaced when they lose their serviceability. For tax purposes it is necessary to generate income figures for each year, which in turn requires that the expense of purchasing the saws be apportioned in some manner among their five years of life. There are three methods approved by the Internal Revenue Service (IRS) to assign depreciation to the various years of an asset's life. The simplest approach to depreciation is the straight-line method, in which depreciation is charged evenly over the life of an asset. For the $50,000 equipment with a five-year life, $10,000 is charged as expense for each year. Consequently, net income, against which the corporate tax would be levied, would be $40,000 in each of the five years.

The other two methods for charging depreciation that are allowed by the IRS are referred to as *double-declining balance* and *sum-of-the-years' digits*. Both methods concentrate depreciation in the earlier years of an asset's life, as Table 10.2 illustrates. The method of double-declining balance is a simple modification of the straight-line method. For any particular year, the undepreciated remainder is depreciated at double the amount it would have been depreciated under the straight-line method, under the assumption that the remaining balance is to be depreciated over the full life of the asset rather than over its remaining life. For the first year, $1,000 would have been depreciated under the straight-line method, so $2,000 is depreciated under double-declining balance. This gives a remaining balance of

TABLE 10.2 Annual Depreciation Charges under Three Methods

Year	Straight-Line	Double-Declining Balance	Sum-of-the-Years' Digits
1	$1,000	$2,000	$1,667
2	1,000	1,200	1,333
3	1,000	720	1,000
4	1,000	540	667
5	1,000	540	333

$3,000. Under straight-line depreciation, $3,000 for five years would have been depreciated at $600 per year, so double this amount, $1,200, is depreciated in the second year of double-declining balance. At the end of the second year, the remaining balance is $1,800. If this amount were depreciated for five years by the straight-line method, depreciation would be $360, so the double-declining balance method yields $720 depreciation for the third year.

If this method of computing depreciation were continued, in succeeding years less would be depreciated than would have been depreciated under the straight-line method; indeed, the sum of depreciation charges will never equal $5,000.[1] Consequently, double-declining balance converts to straight-line depreciation at the point where the amount that would be depreciated under the straight-line method exceeds that which would be depreciated under double-declining balance. For the fourth year, the remaining balance is $1,080. Application of the straight-line method would yield depreciation of $540 for each of the remaining two years, and these depreciation charges both would exceed what would have resulted under a continued application of double-declining balance. Moreover, the switch to straight-line depreciation at this point makes total depreciation charges equal to the initial price of the asset.

In the sum-of-the-years' digits method of determining depreciation, the amount of depreciation charged during the median year of an asset's life (assuming the lifetime is an odd number of years) is equal to the amount that would be charged each year under the straight-line method. For the earlier years, depreciation is greater with this method than with the straight-line method, and for the later years depreciation is less. The amount of depreciation charged each year is a fraction of the total amount to be depreciated over the asset's lifetime. The denominator of the fraction is the sum of the digits of the two years of the asset's life. For the case illustrated in Table 10.2, therefore, the denominator is 15. The numerator for any particular year is the number of years of life remaining at the start of that year. For the first year there are five years of life remaining, so 5/15 of $5,000 is charged as depreciation. For the succeeding

---

[1] This can be seen by considering the application of the continuation of this method to the fourth and fifth years. The remaining balance is $1,080, which if depreciated by straight-line over five years yields $216 per year, so double-declining balance yields $432. If this were done, the remaining balance to start the fifth year would be $648. For five years of asset life, straight-line depreciation would be $129.60, so double-declining balance would depreciate $259.20 the fifth year. The sum of depreciation charges over five years would thus be $4,611.20, which is less than the initial price of the asset. Indeed, the sum of charges will never reach $5,000, because the amount of depreciation is always less than the remaining balance, which itself is always positive.

years, the shares of $5,000 charged as depreciation are 4/15, 3/15, 2/15, and 1/15. A further relation between sum-of-the-years' digits and the straight-line method is that the sum of the charges for two years at equal distances from the median is equal to the amount that would have been charged for those two years under the straight-line method. In Table 10.2, the sum of depreciation in years 1 and 5 is $2,000, as it is also for years 2 and 4.

Besides these three allowable methods of charging depreciation, a fourth, currently nonallowable method for treating the purchase of capital assets is simply to count capital outlays as expenses in the year they are incurred. This so-called *expensing* of capital outlays has received increasing attention recently, principally because it is seen as a way of stimulating saving and capital formation by reducing the real rate at which corporate income is taxed. Although all methods of depreciation deduct the same amount from a corporation's gross income over the life of the asset, some methods of depreciation have a higher present value than others. This implies a lower real rate of tax because $100 of depreciation taken today is more valuable than $100 taken in one year. As long as the rate of interest is positive, the resulting tax reduction in the current year can earn a return that would not be available to the corporation if the depreciation occurred a year later. Consider the depreciation schedules illustrated in Table 10.2. The present value of the depreciation allowance under immediate expensing is, of course, $5,000, but it is less under the other methods for determining depreciation. Suppose the rate of discount is 10 percent. For the straight-line method, the present value of the depreciation allowance is $3,791, which is calculated by solving

$$PV = \frac{\$1,000}{1.1^1} + \frac{\$1,000}{1.1^2} + \frac{\$1,000}{1.1^3} + \frac{\$1,000}{1.1^4} + \frac{\$1,000}{1.1^5}.$$

By a similar procedure, which calls for inserting the proper amounts of depreciation charged to each year, the present value of the depreciation allowance is $4,055 under double-declining balance and $4,031 under sum-of-the-years' digits.

It is possible to make too much of differences in the present value of depreciation allowances under different methods of depreciation. For a corporation of stable size, with assets of various ages, it may make little difference which approach to depreciation is used. If the furniture company has equal amounts of equipment in each of the five age categories and replaces its five-year-old equipment with new equipment each year, the sum of depreciation charges will be the same under all three allowable methods as well as under expensing. Corporations in this situation might be called evenly rotating or steady-state corporations. The method for charging depreciation will make a difference to an expanding corporation, which of course characterizes all newly created corporations. When the value of capital assets increases each year, expenses will be higher and reported income lower the more rapidly those assets are depreciated.

Inflation and Depreciation

Perhaps more important than the choice among methods of charging depreciation is the convention of the IRS that the total amount of depreciation cannot exceed the original price of the asset. In a regime of rising prices, this limitation of depreciation will understate the corporation's real expenses and, hence, overstate its real income. Suppose a corporation depreciates a $50,000 asset over a five-year period, after which replacement is necessary if the corporation is to continue production. With stable prices, the depreciation allowance entails a reduction in the corporation's net income of an amount sufficient to replace the asset. Hence, net income represents a sustainable flow of consumption because the capital stock can in principle be maintained indefinitely.

Suppose prices have generally doubled over the five-year period. It will now take $100,000 to replace the asset, but only $50,000 will have been deducted from income to allow for replacement. The remainder of the expense of replacement must be financed from saving that otherwise could go into the provision of other, new capital goods. Consider the illustration of the straight-line method in Table 10.2, but suppose it is anticipated that prices will generally increase by 10 percent per year. As already noted, the present value of the straight-line depreciation is $3,791 when the rate of discount is 10 percent, and this present value is defined in terms of purchasing power in the initial year. But with inflation, the annual deductions of $1,000 are in depreciated dollars. The $1,000 of depreciation for the third year, for instance, is equivalent in initial purchasing power to only $751, assuming for ease of computation that the rise in prices takes place once per year rather than continuously throughout the year.[2] Stated alternatively, the anticipation of inflation raises the rate at which future dollars are discounted. If the rate of discount is 10 percent in the absence of inflation and if inflation is anticipated to be 10 percent annually, the rate of discount in the face of inflation is likely to be 20 percent. Accordingly, the present value of depre-

---

[2] That is, $751 = $1,000/1.1^3$, where 1.1^3 is the depreciation factor after three years of the 10 percent annual reduction (with annual rather than continuous compounding) in the value of the dollar.

ciation allowance under the straight-line method will be only $2,991, which can be calculated by solving

$$PV = \frac{\$1,000}{1.2^1} + \frac{\$1,000}{1.2^2} + \frac{\$1,000}{1.2^3} + \frac{\$1,000}{1.2^4} + \frac{\$1,000}{1.2^5}.$$

With the value of the depreciation in constant dollars being only $2,991 rather than $3,791, it can be said that $800 is the real present value of the capital consumption on which the corporation is taxed in the presence of inflation. To avoid this tax on capital consumption, it is necessary for the sum of the annual depreciation charges to exceed $5,000, for only in that way could the present value of those charges total $3,791 in constant dollars. To avoid a tax on capital consumption it is necessary that the nominal amount of depreciation allowed in each future year be sufficient to equal $1,000 in initial purchasing power. Accordingly, the sum of depreciation charges in current dollars must be $6,716, as can be found by solving

$$A = (\$1,000)1.1^1 + (\$1,000)1.1^2 + (\$1,000)1.1^3$$
$$+ (\$1,000)1.1^4 + (\$1,000)1.1^5.$$

CORPORATE TAX INCIDENCE IN THE SHORT RUN

Much interest has centered on the taxation of corporation income because of the possibility that such taxation might adversely affect saving, capital formation, and real income. Various controversies over depreciation, for instance, revolve around the extent to which such adverse effects might exist, as well as around the consequences of different approaches to remedy. Another point of substantial controversy about corporate taxation is the identification of who loses disposable income as a result of the corporation income tax. The question of incidence is, How is the nearly $80 billion that is collected from corporation taxation distributed among taxpayers? This question of incidence has evoked a substantial volume of conceptual and empirical analysis, in large part because different answers to the question of incidence imply different answers about the essential nature of the American economy. That is, if the American economy is considered to be organized essentially through a network of competitive markets, a different answer to the question of incidence is implied than if the economy is more aptly characterized as operating in some other manner.

If a tax is imposed on the net income of corporations, the short-run effect will be to reduce the net income of corporations by the amount of the tax, if corporations can be described as conforming to the central principles of the theory of competitive markets. According to this theory, firms seek to maximize profits by seeking to select a rate of output that equates marginal revenue and marginal cost. The taxation of corporation income affects neither the marginal revenue nor the marginal cost functions of corporations, so the tax will leave undisturbed the profit-maximizing strategy of the competitive corporation. By definition, the short run is a period of time during which the supply of equity capital is fixed; corporations may well vary the intensity with which they use the different items of capital stock they possess, but there is not enough time for expansions or contractions in this capital stock to take place. In the short run, stockholders — the suppliers of equity capital — will neither increase nor decrease the amount of capital they supply to corporations. With equity capital being in fixed supply, a tax on corporation income will reduce by the amount of the tax the net earnings by the suppliers of equity capital. The short-run incidence of the taxation of corporation income will lie wholly on stockholders.

The only way the corporation income tax can be shifted away from stockholders is for corporations to reduce their output and to increase their prices. But within the context of competitive firms seeking to maximize profits, any such reactions to the tax will lower profits even further from what they would have been in the absence of that reaction. In other words, if in the short run an increase in the tax on corporation income does not reduce the returns to owners of equity capital by the same amount as the tax, then corporations are not to be treated as maximizing profits, an implication that conflicts with much of the theory of markets that informs neoclassical economics. In this regard, there have been several suggestions put forward to the effect that the profit-maximizing formulation of contemporary corporations is inaccurate. It is sometimes suggested that the actual conduct of corporations results from the choices of corporate management, and owners have little ability to control the conduct of managers. If this is so — whether it is and the extent to which it might be is a subject of continuing controversy — the managers of corporations might use their positions to transfer wealth from owners to themselves. One way management might do this is by expanding the corporation's output beyond the rate required for profit maximization. It has been noted that managerial salaries rise directly with corporate sales. This relationship has in turn nurtured the argument that corporations might expand output beyond the profit-maximizing rate. If this happens, the income received by corporate managers increases, and the return received by stockholders declines.

A common formulation of this model of corporate conduct is that corporations seek to maximize sales subject to a constraint that profits must not fall below some minimally acceptable level. So long as profits remain above this minimal amount, management need not fear that the stockholders will seek a change in management. As evidence for this proposition that management seeks to maximize sales subject to a profit constraint, it has sometimes been noted that managerial salaries correlate more strongly with such measures of firm size as its sales than they correlate with measures of profitability.

While such evidence is consistent with this view of the corporation, it is also consistent with the profit-maximizing view. In a competitive market, all firms will tend to earn the same rate of return, so there will be no correlation between rates of profit and managerial salaries. At the same time, the productivity of management, gauged in terms of its ability to make correct choices and avoid incorrect ones, rises directly with the size of the firm. A manager who is able to improve a firm's performance by one percent is more valuable to a larger firm than to a smaller one. Therefore, even if the assumptions of competitive markets and profit-maximizing firms are accurate, managerial returns will be more strongly correlated with measures of corporate size than with measures of profitability.

If corporations are characterized as attempting to do something other than maximizing profits, perhaps seeking to maximize sales subject to a minimum profit constraint, an increase in the tax on corporation income will not be borne fully by stockholders. As Figure 10.1 illustrates, the tax will lead to some reduction in corporation output and increase in price. The tax reduces the corporation's profits to below the minimum level acceptable to stockholders. To maintain its position, management reduces output so as to increase profits. That this reduction in output increases profits is assured by the assumption that the firm has been operated so as to sacrifice profits for sales until the minimum profit constraint is reached. After the tax is imposed, output will be reduced and price increased until net income to stockholders again reaches its minimum acceptable level.

As noted above, the possibility that corporations are operated to a substantial degree in a way that transfers wealth from owners to managers is a controversial one and, moreover, one that cannot be resolved by examinations of the relations between profits, sales, and managerial returns. Resolution is possible, however, at least in principle, through an examination of the short-run response of corporations to changes in the rate of tax on corporation income. If corporations attempt to maximize their profits, a change in the rate of tax will have no short-run effect on their price and output choices. But if corporations do not attempt to maximize profits, perhaps because they attempt instead to maximize sales subject to a minimum profit constraint, a change in the rate of tax will bring about changes in

FIGURE 10.1 Corporate Tax Incidence and Alternative
Theories of the Firm

A profit-maximizing firm produces under conditions in which marginal
revenue equals marginal cost, which results in the rate of output X_0.
Suppose instead that the corporation seeks to maximize sales, subject to
the constraint that profit must not fall below some minimum level, say an
amount equal to $(P_1 - C_1)X_1$. The imposition of a tax of t percent will
reduce profit below this minimum acceptable level. To raise profit to an
acceptable level, the firm must reduce its output and increase its price, as
illustrated by X_2 and P_2. Letting the subscript 2 denote the posttax
situation, the posttax choice of the corporation's management will be that
for which

$$(1 - t) [(P_2 - C_2)X_2] = (P_1 - C_1)X_1;$$

that is, where the minimum acceptable level of profit is the same before
and after tax.

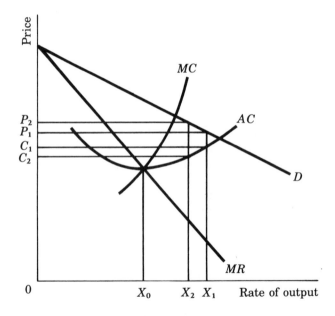

their price and output choices. In particular, an increase in tax will
reduce output and increase price, while a decrease in tax will increase
output and reduce price.[3] In both instances, a change in the rate of

[3] Figure 10.1 could have described a competitive firm, but nothing essential
would have changed. Since a competitive firm faces a horizontal demand curve,
output would change but price would not as the corporation responded to the
change in tax.

tax will bring about a change in the same direction in the before-tax income of corporations. In contrast, if corporations attempt to maximize profits, there will be no relation between changes in the rate of tax and before-tax income.

A finding that the corporation income tax is shifted from stockholders to consumers in the short run would have devastating implications for much of economic analysis because it would contradict the theory of the firm upon which the neoclassical analysis of the functioning of product and factor markets is based. For this reason, it is understandable that there has been strong interest in studies designed to estimate the short-run incidence of the corporation income tax. This interest was intensified since Marion Krzyzaniak and Richard Musgrave presented their findings that the corporation income tax is indeed shifted away from the owners of equity capital in the short run.[4] Krzyzaniak and Musgrave estimated a model of the gross rate of return on capital in manufacturing for the periods 1935–1942 and 1948–1959. The essential idea underlying their analysis is that the gross rate of return of corporate capital should not be affected by changes in the rate of tax on corporate income, if the tax is paid by the owners of corporate equity capital. If some or all of the tax is shifted forward to consumers, however, as is implied by various competitors to the neoclassical theory of firms and markets, the gross rate of return on corporate capital should rise in response to an increase in the rate of tax, thereby maintaining the same, minimally acceptable rate of return for corporate owners.

Krzyzaniak and Musgrave developed a model for testing the hypothesis of forward shifting of the corporate income tax, then estimated it and found that forward shifting did take place. In their model, they related the gross rate of return on corporate capital to (1) the corporation income tax as a percentage of the corporate capital stock, (2) the ratio of inventory to sales in manufacturing, which was lagged one year, (3) the change in the consumption-to-GNP ratio, which also was lagged one year, and (4) the current year's ratio of noncorporate tax accruals less government transfers to GNP. The acceptability of such an estimating equation depends, of course, on its acceptability as a model of the earnings of corporations. The extent of such acceptability may well be questioned, but if the model is regarded as reasonable, the coefficient on the first independent variable shows the impact of a change in corporate income tax on the gross rate of return on corporate capital. Krzyzaniak and Musgrave found this coefficient to be significant and equal to 1.34, which means that

[4] Marion Krzyzaniak and Richard A. Musgrave, *The Shifting of the Corporation Income Tax* (Baltimore: Johns Hopkins University Press, 1963).

for each 1 percent increase in the tax on corporation income, pretax corporation income increased by 1.34 percent. Interpreted literally, this finding is not free from difficulty, because it implies that increases in the taxation of corporate income actually increase the net income received by stockholders. If it is interpreted simply as a finding that increases in the taxation of corporate income do not reduce the net income received by owners, this finding supports some alternative to the neoclassical theory of the operation of the American economy.

As noted above, the acceptability of the Krzyzaniak-Musgrave formulation requires a prior acceptance that the model of corporate profits they used to construct their estimating equation is a reasonable model of corporate profits. If this assumption is rejected, their finding would lose its significance. But even if their model is accepted as at least approximately reasonable, a number of questions might still be raised about the significance of their findings. A criticism frequently levied against their formulation is that it does not allow adequately either for cyclical changes in economic conditions or for the peculiar circumstances created by the war years. Over the period examined by Krzyzaniak and Musgrave, there was a strong tendency for the simultaneous existence of low rates of return and low rates of tax on the one hand, and of high rates of return and high rates of tax on the other. Among other things, for instance, the depression of the 1930s was simultaneously a period of low taxes and low profits, while the prosperity of the 1950s was a period of simultaneous high taxes and high profits. To the extent that such a pattern resulted from cyclical and wartime conditions, the increased rate of return would be attributed incorrectly to the increase in the rate of tax.

In this regard, John Cragg, Arnold Harberger, and Peter Mieszkowski showed that the Krzyzaniak-Musgrave conclusion is highly sensitive to the way in which the estimating model is specified and that seemingly innocuous changes in specification can produce sharply different conclusions.[5] Using the Krzyzaniak-Musgrave procedures and data but introducing the employment rate and a dummy variable for the war years, Cragg, Harberger, and Mieszkowski re-estimated the Krzyzaniak-Musgrave model. When the employment rate was added to the original list of independent variables, the value of the tax coefficient fell by one-quarter, to 1.024. When the wartime variable was added to the list of independent variables, which took the form of introducing a dummy variable for the years 1941–1942 and 1950–1952, the value of the tax coefficient fell to 0.6002. More-

[5] John G. Cragg, Arnold C. Harberger, and Peter Mieszkowski, "Empirical Evidence on the Incidence of the Corporation Income Tax," *Journal of Political Economy* 75 (December 1967), pp. 811–821.

over, this coefficient, which might be thought to indicate that for each 1 percent increase in the tax on corporation income, posttax corporation income increased by 0.6 percent, was statistically not significantly different from zero. Thus, by making what seem to be two reasonable changes in the specification of the Krzyzaniak-Musgrave model, Cragg, Harberger, and Mieszkowski were able to reject the hypothesis of short-run shifting of the corporation income tax. The essential rationale of their analysis was not to present alternative estimates of short-run incidence but to show that the Krzyzaniak-Musgrave results are highly sensitive to seemingly minor and yet not unreasonable changes in the specifications that were used to estimate the impact of the corporate tax on the gross rate of return to corporate capital.

A major limitation in both analyses is that no alternative theory of the firm is specified from which their results can be derived. In response to this limitation, Robert Gordon examined the short-run shifting of the corporate tax through the development of a model in which firms set their prices as a markup of some percentage above their average costs.[6] An interesting feature of Gordon's model is that it can be reconciled with both the profit-maximizing and the sales-maximizing views of the firm, thereby giving it a position of a priori neutrality toward the competing theories of the firm.

Gordon also estimated a model of the gross rate of return on corporate capital, in which this rate of return was related to (1) gross sales as a percentage of real corporate capital, (2) maximum sales as a percentage of real corporate capital, (3) the rate of change in the price level, (4) the rate of change in real output, and (5) the rate of tax on corporation income. This model was estimated for both gross earnings as a percentage of sales and gross earnings as a percentage of capital. In both cases, the coefficient of the tax variable was not significantly different from zero. Changes in the rate of tax were found to have no effect on the gross earnings of corporations, which implies that the short-run effect of changes in tax rates is to bring about an equivalent and offsetting change in the posttax earnings of corporations.

Gordon's finding of no shift in the short run is consistent with the neoclassical theory of the firm. At the same time, Gordon found that gross sales as a percentage of corporate capital, which can be regarded as an indicator of the productivity of corporate capital, was highly significant. This indicated that much of the increase in the

[6] Robert J. Gordon, "The Incidence of the Corporation Income Tax in Manufacturing, 1925–62," *American Economic Review* 57 (September 1967), pp. 731–758.

rate of return on corporate capital during the periods he examined, 1925–1941 and 1946–1962, was the result of the increased productivity of corporate assets, which simply happened to concur with the rise in tax rates over that same period.

Other scholars have also explored the short-run incidence of the corporation income tax (some of these works are cited in the suggested readings at the end of this chapter). While there is much variation in the details of their results, reflecting, among other things, differences in models used and periods examined, for the most part they seem to portray the American economy as essentially competitive. This suggests that it is reasonable to view firms as seeking to maximize their net worth and that the nominal separation of ownership and control in large corporations is of little real significance. Yet the controversy surrounding the modern corporation and the service that alternative models of the contemporary corporation can provide to the various participants in the controversy suggest that the incidence of the corporation income tax will continue to be a subject of examination. Alternative answers to the question of incidence are pertinent to such issues, among others, as the place of corporations in contemporary society, whether federal chartering of large corporations should replace state chartering, and whether chartering provisions should be modified to reduce the degree of managerial discretion in the operation of corporations.

CORPORATE TAX INCIDENCE IN THE LONG RUN

In the short run, the imposition of a tax on corporation income (or an increase in the rate of an already existing tax) reduces the net return to stockholders. Yet corporate capital is only one type of investment; people may also invest in noncorporate enterprises, housing, and bonds, to mention a few possibilities. Indeed, a long-run equilibrium pattern of investment is one in which the rate of return investors anticipate receiving tends to be equal for the various types of investment — corporate capital, bonds, capital in unincorporated enterprises, farms, housing, and the like. Full equality in rates of return may not come about if different investments differ in their riskiness. If people prefer certainty to risk for the same expected return, as we discussed in Chapter 9, a riskier line of investment will have to offer a higher return in equilibrium than a safer investment, with the difference in return being sufficient to equalize the marginal investor's evaluation of the two investments. The imposition of a tax on the income generated by the supply of corporate capital, then, will induce people to reduce their investment in corporate capital as they expand their investment in areas not subject to corporate tax. The corporation income tax creates disequilibrium in the various capital markets in the short run, and the process by which market equilibrium is regained will entail some shifting of the corporate tax in the long run.

There are, of course, many particular forms of investment, so a complete rendition of the shifting of a tax on corporation income to achieve equilibrium would be relatively complex. Yet the essential point of the analysis can be captured by a simple model in which there are only two types of investment, for our purposes the supply of equity capital either to corporations or to unincorporated enterprises. Long-run equilibrium requires that the net return on corporate capital equal the net return on noncorporate capital. The imposition of a tax on the return on corporate capital creates disequilibrium in the capital market, and the process by which equilibrium is reattained will entail a shifting of the tax away from the owners of corporate capital. Figure 10.2 illustrates the process. Suppose the net rate of return is 10 percent in each sector before a tax is imposed on corporation income. The relative sizes of the corporate and noncorporate sectors will depend on the productivity of investment in those sectors, and changes in the productivity of investment in one sector or the other will change the allocation of the capital stock, but not the equality of net rates of return.

If a 50 percent tax is imposed on corporation income, the net return on corporate capital falls to 5 percent. In the short run, this reduction in income is borne by stockholders. But people will not continue to supply equity capital to corporations at 5 percent when they can earn 10 percent by supplying capital to noncorporate enterprises. Capital will shift away from corporations to unincorporated investments until the net rates of return are equal once again. The reduction in the supply of corporate capital might raise the gross rate of return from such investment to, say, 16 percent, leaving a net rate of return of 8 percent. Concomitantly, the increase in the supply of capital to unincorporated investments will reduce the (untaxed) rate of return to 8 percent. Owners of both types of capital then receive 8 percent on their investment, whereas they both received 10 percent before the imposition of the tax. Although the short-run effect of the corporate income tax is to reduce the net income received by corporate stockholders by the amount of the tax, *the long-run effect is to depress the net rate of return received by all investors.* In other words, part of the burden of the tax is shifted away from

FIGURE 10.2 Effect of Corporate Tax on Allocation of Capital

Assume that the total stock of capital is unaffected by the taxation of corporation income and that the size of this stock is equal to N_1C_1. The rate of return to suppliers of capital initially is r^*; $0C_1$ of their capital is invested in corporate enterprises and the remaining $0N_1$ is invested in noncorporate enterprises. The imposition of a 50 percent tax on the income earned by corporate capital reduces by half the rate of return on corporate capital in the short run. With capital being mobile in the long run (which can be a relatively short period of time in terms of the calendar), capital will shift from the corporate to the noncorporate sector. Equilibrium will be attained when the net rates of return are the same for the two types of investment, as indicated by r_n, at which time the size of the corporate sector will have shrunk to $0C_2$ while the size of the noncorporate sector will have expanded to $0N_2$. With this shrinkage in the size of the corporate sector, the gross rate of return rises to R_g, which is twice the net rate of return, r_n.

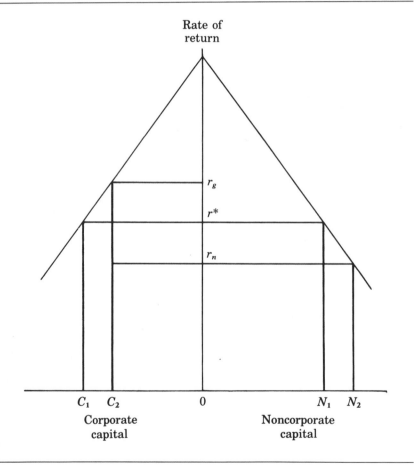

the suppliers of corporate capital to the suppliers of other forms of capital.[7]

A simple arithmetical model is useful in exploring the nature of this model of the long-run incidence of the corporation income tax.[8] Let X and Y denote two products, the outputs of the corporate and noncorporate sectors of the economy, respectively, and let K and L denote two factors of production, capital and labor, respectively. Assume that the demands for X and Y are unitarily elastic, which leads to the simplifying feature that price changes are offset by changes in quantity demanded so as to leave unchanged the total amount spent on the product. Likewise assume for computational simplicity that the elasticity of substitution in production between K and L is unitary in each industry. This assumption means that an increase in the price of capital relative to the price of labor will bring about a reduction in the use of capital relative to labor such that the shares of output received by each factor remain unchanged. Consistent with this assumption of a unitary elasticity of substitution, suppose that industry production can be described by the Cobb-Douglas production functions,

$$X = L_x^{\frac{1}{2}} K_x^{\frac{1}{2}} \text{ and } Y = L_y^{\frac{1}{2}} K_y^{\frac{1}{2}}.$$

Assume that the total income in the economy is $1,200, $600 in each sector. The exponents of $1/2$ on the production functions mean that each factor of production earns one-half of the income generated by that industry. Consequently, labor and capital each earn $300 in each industry. Further suppose that units of labor and capital are defined so as to make their price per unit equal to $1, implying that initially there are 300 units of each factor in each industry

Now suppose a 50 percent rate of tax is levied on income earned by capital employed in X, the corporate sector of this economy. In this case, long-run equilibrium requires that twice as much capital be employed in Y as in X, which in turn requires that 100 units of

[7] For documentation of a tendency toward equalization of net rates of return between corporate and noncorporate capital, despite considerable difference in tax treatment and pretax rates of return, see Laurtis R. Christensen, "Entrepreneurial Income: How Does It Measure Up?" *American Economic Review* 61 (September 1971), pp. 575–585. In 1969, for instance, when the corporate capital stock was $767.7 billion and the noncorporate capital stock was $532.6 billion, pretax rates of return were 18.8 percent and 14.1 percent in the corporate and noncorporate sectors, respectively, while posttax rates of return were 9.5 and 9.4 percent, respectively.

[8] The classic analysis of the long-run incidence of the corporation income tax is Arnold C. Harberger, "The Incidence of the Corporation Income Tax," *Journal of Political Economy* 70 (June 1962), pp. 215–240. The arithmetical model illustrated here is taken from the elementary case he describes on pages 217–219.

capital shift from X to Y in response to the tax. Because of the assumption of unitarily elastic demand functions, total spending on the output of each industry remains unchanged at $600. The assumption that the elasticity of substitution is unity, such as characterizes the Cobb-Douglas production function, means that the shares of income received by each factor of production are unchanged by any substitution between capital and labor that may result because of changes in their prices. Hence, capital and labor still receive $300 in each of the two sectors, but there are now only 200 units of capital employed in the corporate sector, while there are 400 units employed in the noncorporate sector. This means that the price of capital in the corporate sector is $1.50, while it is $0.75 in the noncorporate sector. Owners of capital in the corporate sector receive only $0.75 per unit, however, because the remaining $0.75 is collected by the government. Although the $150 of tax is nominally collected from the 200 units of capital employed in the corporate sector, in reality the tax is paid by all owners of capital through the reduction in the net price per unit of capital to $0.75.

As a result of the tax, corporate output falls and noncorporate output increases. If the products produced in these two sectors are different, the price of corporate output will rise while the price of noncorporate output will fall. This shift in relative price between the two sectors will not affect consumers as a class, of course, but it does mean that consumers with relatively strong demands for corporate output will lose while consumers with relatively strong demands for noncorporate output will gain. These price effects are, however, offsetting for the aggregrate of consumers, and so they are secondary to the question of incidence. That is, the rise in the price of corporate output does not mean that the tax is shifted forward to consumers, because the tax simultaneously lowers the price of noncorporate output. Moreover, in the event that corporate and noncorporate enterprises produce the same products, which is partially the case, the corporate tax will have no effect on the relative price of corporate and noncorporate output.

Although the capital market reaches a new long-run equilibrium in response to the taxation of corporation income, capital will come to be allocated inefficiently in the economy. The owners of corporate capital receive the same net rate of return as the owners of noncorporate capital. But this very equality in the presence of the tax on corporate income implies that the social or aggregate rate of return on capital invested in the corporate sector is higher than it is on capital invested in the noncorporate sector. This difference in rates of return means that a simple shift of capital from noncorporate to corporate enterprises will increase the value of all the output produced within the economy. This is so because the social rate of return is the gross or pretax rate of return, while the private return received by investors is the posttax rate of return. Suppose in the presence of a tax rate of 50 percent, the gross rate of return is 16 percent in the corporate sector and 8 percent in the noncorporate sector, which yields a posttax rate of return of 8 percent in each sector. Capital invested in the noncorporate sector yields an annual return of 8 percent, but capital invested in the corporate sector yields an annual return of 16 percent: 8 percent to investors and 8 percent to taxpayers (or to the government). Starting from this position, the shift of a unit of capital from the noncorporate to the corporate sector will increase by 8 percent the value of output produced in the economy. With the corporate tax, the total capital stock is less productive than it could be, and the lowered rate of return represents an excess burden of the corporate income tax, a burden that is rendered necessary by the imposition of a special tax on the income generated by corporate enterprise.[9]

In addition to reducing the supply of equity capital in the corporate sector relative to its supply in the noncorporate sector, the corporation income tax decreases the supply of equity relative to debt. Interest payments on debt are a deductible expense for a corporation, whereas the interest payments on equity that are necessary to elicit a supply of equity capital are not deductible in determining tax liability. Of two corporations with equal amounts of capital, the one that has all capital in equity will be taxed twice as heavily as the one that has its capital split evenly between debt and equity, assuming that the return on debt equals the expected return on equity. Changes in relative supplies of debt and equity will, of course, change the relative returns, but it is still the case that the differential tax treatment of equity capital relative to debt capital creates some incentive for the substitution of debt for equity as a source of capital.

More complex models of the taxation of corporation income could also be explored. One principal modification is to allow the tax to reduce the supply of saving and, hence, the stock of capital in society. In the numerical illustration we just described, the tax reduced the net price of all types of capital to $0.75. This model was

---

[9] One major form of substitution between types of capital in response to the taxation of corporation income is between the investment of capital in corporations and in housing. David J. Ott and Attiat F. Ott, "The Effect of Nonneutral Taxation on the Use of Capital by Sector," *Journal of Political Economy* 81 (August 1973), pp. 972–981, estimate that for 1969 the tax bias against corporate capital induced a shift of capital from the corporate sector to the housing sector of about $220 billion, on a capital base estimated at $1.74 trillion.

constructed under the assumption that the total supply of capital was unchanged and the only effect of the tax was to reallocate the supply of capital between the corporate and noncorporate sectors. But the fall in the net return to capital will reduce the supply of saving.

The extent to which this happens depends on the interest or net-return elasticity of saving. Michael Boskin has estimated that this elasticity is about 0.4.[10] This means that a 10 percent reduction in the net return will reduce the amount of saving by 4 percent. In terms of our numerical illustration, the 25 percent reduction in the net price of capital would bring about a 10 percent reduction in the size of the capital stock, lowering it from 600 units to 540 units. Real income would be reduced by the decline in capital stock, and the suppliers of labor as well as the suppliers of capital would suffer a decline in real income. Through such a reduction in saving and capital formation, part of the corporate income tax can be borne by the suppliers of labor services through a reduction in wages.[11]

INTEGRATION OF PERSONAL AND CORPORATION TAXES

Corporations cannot, of course, pay tax; only people can pay tax. The taxation of corporation income is really an indirect method of taxing the recipients of capital income. Moreover, the corporate income tax involves a double burden of taxation because the income is taxed once as it is earned by the corporation and it is taxed again when the remainder is distributed as dividends. Some might defend this practice on the distributive grounds that more equality is better then less. On average, the income of people who have capital income is higher than those who do not, so the taxation of corporation income might seem to be a means of placing more of the tax burden on those with relatively high incomes.

It is not unheard of for people in middle and lower income categories to be owners of capital, however, and many people in the upper income ranges own little or no capital. Although the relative

[10] Michael J. Boskin, "Taxation, Saving, and the Rate of Interest," *Journal of Political Economy* 86 (April 1978), part 2, pp. S3–S27.

[11] This is so unless the tax revenues are used by the government to support the provision of capital goods that are complementary to the activities of business enterprises. It appears to be the case, however, that government use of tax revenues is relatively weighted toward consumption, in comparison with how those revenues would be spent by the suppliers of capital.

significance of capital ownership rises with income, the correlation is certainly not perfect. If income is regarded as a better indicator of an ability to pay tax than any other indicator, the taxation of capital income will be inferior to a tax on income. It is the recognition of such difficulties that has inspired an interest in the possibilities for integrating the taxes on corporation and personal income.

Suppose corporations were to pay out all of their income as dividends. In this case, a simple elimination of the corporate income tax would eliminate the double taxation of corporate income, and the goals of tax integration would be achieved. Tax integration would be accomplished through tax elimination. If corporations retain some of their earnings, however, the capital value of shares of corporate ownership should rise. If so, and if capital appreciation is regarded as income as it is under the Haig-Simons approach, a simple elimination of the corporate income tax will not achieve the goals of tax integration unless unrealized capital gains are taxed.

If unrealized capital gains remain untaxed, the goals of tax integration can be largely accomplished, within the context of the Haig-Simons approach, by retaining the corporation income tax and by treating the payment of dividends as equivalent to withholding under the personal income tax. That is, corporations would still pay tax on their income, both on dividends and on retained earnings, but the recipients of dividend payments would receive a credit against their personal tax liability for their share of the corporate tax that is attributable to their dividends.

To illustrate this dividend-credit method of integration for very small numbers, suppose a corporation has income of $200 and is taxed at 50 percent. It pays half its net income as dividends and it has a single stockholder. The corporate tax is $100 and dividends paid and earnings retained are each $50. In this case 50 percent of the corporation's tax liability is attributable to dividends. This amount, $50, becomes taxable income to the stockholder, and at the same time the stockholder qua taxpayer is able to receive a credit for this amount because it is treated as a withholding tax, as tax is withheld from payments of salaries and wages. Dividend integration would seem to be relatively simple to accomplish and would do much to eliminate the double taxation of income on capital supplied to the corporation. (Elimination of the corporate tax would, of course, be simpler still to accomplish and would, within the Fisherian approach to the definition of income, eliminate entirely the double taxation of income from capital, setting aside complexities resulting from such omissions in the base of the personal income tax as the exclusion of the rental income of owner-occupied houses.)

So long as there are rate brackets in the personal income tax that exceed the highest rate of tax on corporation income, it is possible for an integration of the personal and corporate taxes to increase the rate of tax for some people. This can be seen most clearly under what is called the partnership method of integration and by assuming that all income is retained. Under the partnership method of integration, the corporation is treated as a partnership for tax purposes, in that the corporation's income is apportioned among the individual owners, as is the case within a partnership.

Although this approach to integration might be exceedingly difficult to implement, it is interesting to note that it conforms to the economic theory of the corporation, which treats the corporation essentially as a lower-cost substitute for what otherwise would be a set of contractual relations among various partners. Limited liability is clearly an important attribute of corporations, but it does not capture the essence of corporations because there is no reason in principle why limited liability could not operate in the relations between a partnership and its clients. In its essential features, then, a corporation is as much a network of contractual relations as is a partnership. Within the partnership method of integration, all corporate income is apportioned among the individual owners and taxed at the individually applicable rates. The treatment of dividends paid proceeds just as it does under the dividend-credit method of integration. But in addition, retained earnings are apportioned among owners.

Such an approach to integration reduces the use of retained earnings as long as the higher marginal-rate brackets within the personal tax exceed the highest marginal rate within the corporate tax. Consider a taxpayer in the 70 percent bracket in the personal income tax who owns shares in a corporation in which all earnings, prior to tax integration, are retained. Under the partnership method of integration, retained earnings are attributed to stockholders in proportion to their shares in the total amount of corporate equity. Under the corporate tax, such earnings in excess of $100,000 are taxed at 46 percent. But with tax integration, such earnings are taxed at 70 percent. Under the corporate income tax, dividends paid are taxed twice, once as corporate income and once as dividend income to the recipient. Retained earnings, however, are taxed only once, as corporate income. To the extent that such retained earnings increase the value of the corporation, they may eventually be taxed as capital appreciation, but nonetheless the tax is postponed as long as the shares of equity are not sold. With tax integration, retained earnings no longer entail this postponement of tax, so the advantage to stockholders of retained earnings will decline relative to the advantages of dividends, thereby leading to a greater use of dividends.

CORPORATE ENTERPRISE AND THE TAX STATE

Business enterprises generate a concentration of information that facilitates numerous aspects of tax administration, thereby making such enterprises central to the process of tax collection. Business enterprises, in fact, seem to have been essential for the development of the relatively large shares of taxation that characterize contemporary societies. Tax collection is surely less costly in a society characterized by relatively large enterprises than it would be in a nation of shopkeepers. The modern corporation seems to play a pivotal role in the financing of what Joseph Schumpeter referred to as the Tax State.[12]

Although taxes other than the tax on corporation income are apportioned according to such individual characteristics as income, wages, or spending, the various tax forms can easily be viewed as elements of a system of business taxation. Without the centralization of information about transactions that is made possible by business enterprises, the enactment and enforcement of a variety of personal taxes that are nominally levied on income and consumption would be much more difficult. Business enterprises represent a technological improvement in the process of tax extraction, and in their absence the ability of the state to tax incomes, wages, and spending would be weakened considerably. Personal income tax is assessed against individuals, for example, but collection of the tax takes place principally through businesses, both as businesses transmit portions of employee earnings directly to the government and as they serve as centralized sources of information about taxable transactions. The same is true for the collection of the Social Security tax. Liability for Social Security payments rests with individuals, but the entire process of collection and enforcement takes place through business enterprises rather than through individual citizens, who are vastly more numerous. Similarly, the taxation of consumer expenditure is also collected and enforced primarily by business enterprises, for in this case tax collections are determined by reported taxable sales of businesses.

While the bases of these various taxes are nominally related to such personal characteristics as income or expenditure, it is business enterprises and not individuals who are the nominally designated taxpayers. Although tax liabilities are stated with reference to the characteristics of individuals, business enterprises are indispensable

---

[12] Joseph A. Schumpeter, "The Crisis of the Tax State," *International Economic Papers,* No. 4 (London: Macmillan, 1954), pp. 5–38.

parties to modern forms of tax extraction. The more concentrated
the pattern of enterprise in a society, and hence the availability of
information, the less costly it is for government to extract taxes.
Indeed, of the major sources of tax revenue in the United States,
only the taxation of the value of personal residences is not administered through the offices of business enterprises.

The treatment of charitable contributions is instructive about the
symbiotic relationship between corporate organizations and the tax
state. If one person makes a charitable contribution directly to another person, the donor cannot claim a deduction under the personal
income tax for that contribution. The donor is in principle actually
liable for a transfer tax on the gift, although in practice a basic
exemption is allowed. But if the same contribution is made through
the offices of an organization approved by the Internal Revenue
Service, a deduction can be claimed by the donor and no liability
arises under the transfer tax. The tax system supports the organization of charitable contributions through corporatelike organizations.
Although it may be disputable whether corporatelike organizations
are more effective in providing charitable activities than are individuals, it seems clear that the encouragement of such organizations
facilitates tax extraction, compared with a regime where people could
choose on equal terms between acting charitably on their own or
through an organization.

Although the corporation serves directly as a source of tax revenue
only under the corporation income tax, even here the capital that is
supplied to corporations is not taxed; rather capital generally is taxed.
Yet it would be more costly to attempt to actually impose a tax on
all capital than to tax only corporate capital. But the imposition of
a tax on corporation income, which again is easily administered because of the centralization of information in the corporation, makes
for a relatively simple way of extending the reach of the tax state to
all owners of capital.

The tax state surely thrives on the corporation, and integration
of the personal and corporate taxes, while not proposing any disin-
tegration of the corporation and the centralization it represents, does
seem to represent a step backward in terms of the interests of the
tax state. Integration would restrict the reach of the tax state in
spite of the common pressures it faces to extend its reach. In this
respect, frequent arguments against integration claim that government revenues would decline on the order of $10 to $20 billion. This
decline in revenue represents, of course, the impact of the double
taxation of income from saving, so a reduction in revenue stemming
from the elimination of double taxation is hardly surprising. Integration may, however, run contrary to the *raison d'être* of the tax state,

which of course is not an argument against integration but rather is a recognition that the making of tax policy, like the making of expenditure policy, is potentially capable of positive examination.

SUGGESTIONS FOR FURTHER READING

The initial articulation of the proposition that the large, modern corporation is characterized by a separation of ownership and control, which allows managers to pursue their interests even though those interests may be contrary to the interests of stockholders, is Adolf A. Berle and Gardiner C. Means, *The Modern Corporation and Private Property* (New York: Macmillan, 1933). For a suggestion that the corporation might be more accurately viewed as seeking to maximize sales subject to a minimum profit constraint, see William J. Baumol, *Business Behavior, Value and Growth* (New York: Macmillan, 1959).

Although the nominal separation of ownership and control is undeniable, this separation may have little real import. For examinations of why this might be so, see Henry C. Manne, "Mergers and the Market for Corporate Control," *Journal of Political Economy* 73 (April 1965), pp. 110–120; Gordon Tullock, "A New Theory of Corporations," in *Roads to Freedom,* edited by Erich Streissler (London: Routledge and Kegan Paul, 1969), pp. 287–307; Brian Hindley, "Separation of Ownership and Control in the Modern Corporation," *Journal of Law and Economics* 13 (April 1970), pp. 185–221; and Michael C. Jensen and William H. Meckling, "Theory of the Firm: Managerial Behavior, Agency Costs, and Ownership Structure," *Journal of Financial Economics* 3 (October 1976), pp. 305–360.

The work examined in the text on the shifting of the corporation income tax considered shifting in terms of a relation between the rate of tax and the posttax rate of return on corporate capital. A constant posttax rate of return, however, will not imply shifting if technical change is increasing the marginal productivity of capital goods during the period under examination because in the absence of the tax the posttax rate of return on corporate capital will be rising. Some authors have accordingly examined corporate tax shifting in terms of a model of factor shares, instead of a model of rate of return. Within such an approach, Challis Hall, Jr., "Direct Sifting of the Corporation Income Tax in Manufacturing, 1919–59," *American Economic Review* 53, Proceedings (May 1963), pp. 258–271, is able to find support for the neoclassical theory of the firm. Similar support is given in Morris A. Adelman, "The Corporate Income Tax in the Long Run," *Journal of Political Economy* 65 (April 1957), pp. 151–157.

Besides the studies of rates of return cited in the text, William H. Oakland, "Corporate Earnings and Tax Shifting in U.S. Manufacturing," *Review of Economics and Statistics* 54 (August 1972), pp. 235–244, finds for the assumption of no shifting, while Richard Dusansky, "The Short

Run Shifting of the Corporate Income Tax," *Oxford Economic Papers* 24 (November 1972), pp. 351–371, finds in favor of an assumption of full shifting.

For a simple exposition of Arnold Harberger's approach to the analysis of corporate tax incidence, see Charles E. McLure, Jr., and Wayne R. Thirsk, "A Simplified Exposition of the Harberger Model," *National Tax Journal* 28 (March 1975), pp. 1–27. For an extension of Harberger's central framework to allow for an impact of the corporate tax on the rate of saving and capital formation, see J. Gregory Ballentine, "The Incidence of a Corporation Income Tax in a Growing Economy," *Journal of Political Economy* 86 (October 1978), pp. 863–875. Ballentine shows, among other things, that the extent to which the corporate tax reduces the net return to capital, rather than reducing the net return to labor, depends on the interest or net-return elasticity of saving, with an increasing share of the burden being shifted to suppliers of labor services as the supply of saving becomes more sensitive to changes in its net return.

A considerable amount of literature has arisen concerning the integration of the personal and corporate income taxes. For a symposium of articles devoted mainly to the subject, see *National Tax Journal* 28 (September 1975). Strong support for integration, along with a discussion of numerous pertinent issues, is presented in Charles E. McLure, Jr., "Integration of the Personal and Corporate Income Taxes: The Missing Element in Recent Tax Reform Proposals," *Harvard Law Review* 88 (January 1975), pp. 532–582. McLure accepts the Haig-Simons approach to the definition of income, as do most writers on integration, implying that simple abolition of the corporate tax would provide a loophole through retained earnings. Charles E. McLure, Jr., *Must Corporate Income Be Taxed Twice?* (Washington, D.C.: Brookings Institution, 1979), provides a careful survey of numerous issues that would arise in any actual effort to integrate the two taxes.

11

Taxation of Consumption

Market transactions are two-sided: One person's receipt of income is simultaneously another person's expenditure. Tax liability may be assessed against either side of the market. There is in principle an equivalence between a tax on the sources of income and a tax on the uses of income. In Chapters 9 and 10 we explored the former approach to taxation, and in this chapter we turn to the latter approach.

EXCISE TAXATION: INCIDENCE AND EXCESS BURDEN

Excise taxation is the taxation of particular transactions on the product side of the market. The federal government, for example, taxes distilled spirits at $10.50 per gallon, beer at $9 per barrel, cigarettes at $4 per thousand, and tires at 10 cents per pound. This form of excise taxation is referred to as *specific*, indicating that the tax is a specific amount per unit. Excise taxation may also be *ad valorem*, meaning that the tax is a percentage of the price at which the transaction occurs. The federal government levies a 6 percent tax on the price of telephone service, a 5 percent tax on the price of air travel, and a 10 percent tax on the price of firearms.

Although the government collects excise taxes from businesses, the taxes are paid by consumers. The brewers of beer actually transfer to the federal government $9 per barrel, but economists generally conclude that consumers rather than brewers truly pay the tax. Figure 11.1 illustrates how this conclusion is reached. Brewing is a competitive industry, and brewers must compete with other producers for such inputs as labor and capital goods. If inputs are unspecialized

FIGURE 11.1   Specific Excise Tax Paid Fully by Consumers

The market demand for the product of a competitive industry is described
by D. Inputs are unspecialized to the industry and are available in
comparatively unlimited supply (S) at the price P_1. The equilibrium rate of
output in the absence of tax is thus X_1. Suppose the government imposes a
tax per unit of output (a specific excise tax) of $P_2 - P_1$. The demand curve
D shows the gross price of a transaction, and the curve D_n shows the net
price after the tax has been deducted. For any rate of output, D_n lies below
D by the distance $P_2 - P_1$. After tax, inputs employed in the industry will
still receive P_1 per unit of output, and consequently the price of the product
must rise to P_2, which in turn implies a lower rate of industry output, X_2.

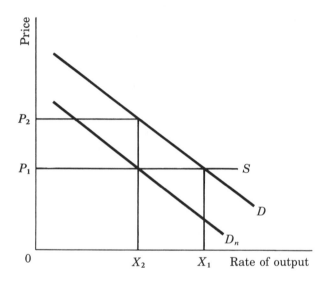

to the brewing industry, brewers will be able to attract inputs only
as long as they pay them what they could earn in other employments.
If a tax is imposed on the beer that is produced, there will be no decline in the price received by the suppliers of the inputs because any
such decline would cause the inputs to shift into other employments.
If the tax cannot reduce the price the brewers pay to suppliers of
inputs, its only effect will be to raise the price of beer to consumers.
With this rise in price, people will buy less beer, and fewer inputs
will be involved in the production of beer. The size of the industry
will be smaller because of the tax, but inputs employed in the production of beer will be earning the same amount after the tax as
they did before the tax because they will have shifted to alternative,
untaxed lines of employment. Consumers pay the tax and also re-

duce their rate of consumption in response to a tax-induced rise in price.

It need not be the case however, that an excise tax increases the price of a product by the amount of the tax. Indeed, there are circumstances in which an excise tax might produce no change in price but rather a decline in the price received by the suppliers of inputs to production. This is much less likely to occur under excise taxation than under a general sales tax, which we examine later. But we can demonstrate the possibility that an excise tax will be paid fully by the suppliers of resources to the taxed activity (see Figure 11.2). Suppose inputs are fully specialized to the taxed industry; that is, the taxed activity represents the only possible employment of those inputs. The price paid to the suppliers of the inputs has no effect on the amount supplied, and the payments to those suppliers

---

FIGURE 11.2 Specific Excise Tax Paid Fully by Factor Owners

Before tax, industry output is X_1 and the price of the product is P_1. The supply curve, S, is vertical, to indicate that inputs are fully specialized to that industry. Assume that a tax of $P_1 - P_2$ per unit of output is imposed. The demand curve D shows the gross price paid per unit of output, while the demand curve D_n shows the net amount after the tax has been subtracted. In this case, the price received per unit of output by suppliers of inputs falls by the full amount of the tax, to P_2, while the price paid by consumers remains unchanged, at P_1.

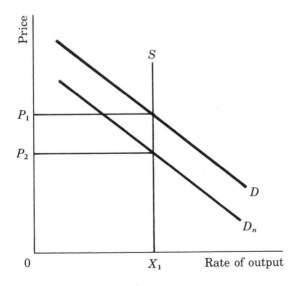

is called a *rent*, to indicate a surplus payment that is not necessary to cause the input to be supplied. In this situation, which for our purpose implies that brewers can only brew, that breweries can be used only for brewing, and so on, the tax will be fully absorbed by the suppliers of inputs. Industry output and the price paid by consumers will remain unchanged.

The case of wholly specialized inputs is remote under excise taxation; the case of unspecialized inputs more accurately describes the outcome of excise taxation. An intermediate position, most characteristic of short-run situations, is one in which some, but not all, inputs are specialized. As we saw when we considered the corporation income tax in Chapter 10, the supply of equity capital is fixed in the short run because the short run is defined to be of insufficient duration for changes in the size of plant and equipment to take place. Those inputs represented by plant and equipment are specialized to the industry in the short run, therefore, although generally they are not specialized in the long run.

When inputs are partially specialized, the supply curve to the industry slopes upward, which shows that some inputs will continue to be supplied to the industry even though the price suppliers receive for them may decline. When inputs are partially specialized, an excise tax will lead to some increase in the gross price of the product and some decline in the net price received by suppliers of inputs. This situation is described in Figure 11.3. The rise in gross price is referred to as *forward shifting*, to indicate that a portion of the tax is paid by consumers, and the decrease in net price is called *backward shifting*, to indicate that some of the tax is paid by suppliers of inputs to production. The relative degrees of forward and backward shifting will depend on the relative elasticities of demand and supply. As the elasticity of the supply function increases (that is, as productive inputs are less specialized), less tax is shifted backward to resource suppliers, for a given demand function. The less elastic the demand, the greater the share of the tax that will be shifted forward to consumers, for a given supply function.

EXCESS BURDEN

Questions of incidence concern the identity of those who transfer control over resources to the government in the form of taxes. Besides questions of incidence, excise taxation raises questions of excess burden, with *excess* indicating that the loss a tax imposes on consumers and suppliers exceeds the gain in revenue to the government. Figure 11.4 illustrates, for unspecialized inputs, how an excise tax can

FIGURE 11.3 Specific Excise Tax Shared Between Consumers and Factor Owners

The demand and supply functions pertaining to a competitive industry are described by D and S, respectively. Before tax, X_1 is the rate of output and P_1 is the price of the product. Suppose a specific excise tax is imposed, with the size of the tax being equal to the vertical distance ab, which in turn is equal to $P_2 - P_2^*$. The curve D_n shows the net price to producers after the tax is deducted from the gross price, which is described by D. The tax results in gross price rising to P_2 and the rate of output declining to X_2. Consumers pay P_2 for the product, while factor owners receive P_2^* per unit of product. The tax has been split between consumers and suppliers of inputs; the tax has increased the price paid by consumers by $P_2 - P_1$ per unit, and it has lowered the price received by input suppliers by $P_1 - P_2^*$ per unit.

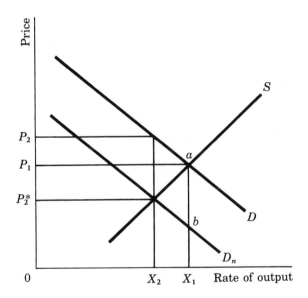

impose an excess burden. In the absence of tax, the price consumers must pay for a product (which is the value they place on an additional unit of that product) equals the marginal cost of that product (which is the value people place on an alternative product that must be sacrificed to make available the resources required to produce the product in question). The imposition of an excise tax raises the price above marginal cost, and when inputs are unspecialized this divergence is equal to the amount of the tax. In posttax equilibrium, the value people place on the product exceeds marginal cost by the amount of

FIGURE 11.4 Excess Burden of an Excise Tax with Unspecialized Inputs

In the absence of tax, the demand for the output of a competitive industry is described by D, and the supply curve for the industry is S. The rate of output is X_1 and the price of the industry output is P_1. The imposition of a specific excise tax of t dollars per unit of output raises the price by the amount of the tax, to P_2, as shown by the supply-cum-tax curve, S_t. In the presence of the tax, the rate of output is X_2. The value people place on one additional unit of output is P_2, which in general is given by the price-intercept on the demand function. To get one more unit of the product, however, requires the diversion of resources from other activities. The value of the production that is sacrificed is the marginal cost of the service, and for a one-unit expansion from X_2 this marginal cost is P_1. Hence, a one-unit increase in output from X_2 will entail an excess of gain over cost of ab. By extension of this line of reasoning, the excess burden of an excise tax that reduces output from X_1 to X_2 is illustrated by abc.

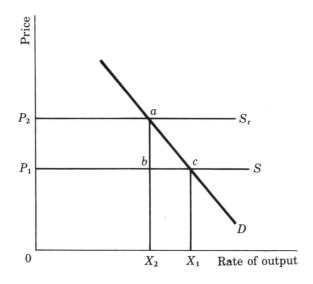

the tax. This inequality indicates that a shift in the composition of output away from untaxed products to taxed products results in the production of goods that are valued less highly than the output that would have been produced without the tax.

In Chapter 9 we saw that an excess burden resulted when a progressive income tax induced some people to work in occupations for lower monetary incomes rather than in occupations offering higher monetary incomes. In Chapter 10 we saw that excess burden resulted when the tax led people to shift some capital from corporate to noncorporate enterprises. Excess burden also results when an excise tax leads people to shift their purchases away from taxed products to other products. If people value all products equally at the margin in the absence of tax, the tax-induced shift in the pattern of consumption will show that people subsequently place a higher value on the taxed product than on the other products. The tax causes people to reallocate their budgets in favor of the untaxed products that are valued less highly at the margin than the taxed products, and the reduction in utility that results is the excess burden of the tax. The revenue that taxpayers transfer to government is the burden of the tax, described by the rectangular area P_1P_2ab in Figure 11.4. The additional loss in utility that taxpayers suffer is the *excess* burden of the tax, described by the area abc in Figure 11.4.

Excess burden in principle can be empirically measured. This can be seen most easily if the demand curve is assumed to be linear over the range of prices and quantities under consideration, although the principle can be extended to any form of demand function. For a linear demand function, the excess burden described by abc in Figure 11.4 is

$$E = \tfrac{1}{2}(\Delta P \Delta X).$$

The change in price, ΔP, is the amount of the tax, and the change in quantity, ΔX, shows the response of consumers to the higher prices brought about by the tax. The rate of the decline of consumption as price rises depends on the elasticity of demand, which is

$$\eta = \left(\frac{\Delta X}{\Delta P}\right)\left(\frac{P}{X}\right).$$

This formula for elasticity can be rewritten

$$\frac{X}{P}\eta = \frac{\Delta X}{\Delta P},$$

which, solving for ΔX, gives

$$\Delta X = \Delta P \frac{X}{P}\eta.$$

If this value for ΔX is substituted in the equation for E, above, the result is

$$E = \tfrac{1}{2}(\Delta P^2 \frac{X}{P}\eta).$$

Note in this equation that the excess burden rises with the square of the tax and that for any given tax the larger the elasticity of demand, the higher the excess burden.

Suppose that in the absence of tax 150 million barrels of beer would be sold annually at $50 per barrel. If a tax of $9 per barrel is imposed and if the elasticity of demand for beer is unity, the excess burden created by the excise tax is

$$E = \tfrac{1}{2} \, [9^2 \, (150{,}000{,}000/50) \, 1] = \$121{,}500{,}000.[1]$$

If the elasticity of demand is only, say, 0.7, the excess burden would be 70 percent of that shown above. If the state taxation of beer is also taken into account, the excess burden would increase. Under the conditions hypothesized here, the posttax price of beer is $59 per barrel and the amount sold is 123,000,000 barrels. The total amount people spend on beer is $7.257 billion, $1.107 billion of which is collected in tax. The excess burden is thus 1.7 percent of the total amount spent on beer, and it is 11 percent of the total amount of tax revenue collected. The principle underlying this calculation can be applied to all specific taxes.

EXCISE TAXATION AND PRODUCT CHARACTERISTICS

A product is actually a bundle of attributes. Milk varies in its butter-fat content and in the containers in which it is packaged. Eggs vary in size and in the color of their shells. Books come in cloth and paper covers and vary in the weight of the pages and in the boldness of the type. Any excise tax penalizes some of the attributes of a product relative to others. In consequence, the competition among producers for the patronage of customers will bring about a change in the characteristics of products, and those characteristics favored by the tax will be accentuated. The imposition of an excise tax, then, tends to change the nature of the product sold, with different forms of tax eliciting different alterations in the attributes of the product. This is obvious for a specific excise tax, but the same point holds as well for an *ad valorem* excise tax.

Cigarettes are taxed by the federal government at $4 per thousand, which is 8 cents per pack of 20. State taxes on cigarettes range from 2 cents per pack to over 20 cents, with a typical range of 10 to 15 cents. The total excise tax on cigarettes ranges from about 10 cents to 30 cents per pack, with a tax of 20 cents, or 1 cent per cigarette, being an approximate average. It is easy to see how this method of taxing cigarettes can influence the characteristics of the cigarettes that sup-

---

[1] It may not be immediately apparent that the excess burden is properly dimensioned. The dimension of price is $/X, and the dimension of the expression for excess burden is thus $(\$/X) \, (\$/X) \, (X/\$/X)$, which of course yields $ as its dimension.

pliers produce. Suppose that in the absence of a tax on cigarettes, cigarettes are 80 millimeters long and come 20 to a pack; a pack of cigarettes therefore contains 1,600 millimeters of tobacco shaped into cigarettes. Suppose a pack sells for 80 cents. The imposition of an excise tax on cigarettes of $10 per thousand, or 20 cents per pack, increases the price per pack to $1, assuming the model described in Figure 11.1 is applicable. (Alternatively, should there be specialized inputs involved in the production of cigarettes, the price of cigarettes will rise by less than 20 cents per pack because some of the tax will be paid by the input suppliers rather than by consumers.)

In the absence of tax, 1,600 millimeters of cigarettes sell for 80 cents, or 5 cents per 100 millimeters. If the only effect of the excise tax is to increase the price per pack to $1, the price of cigarettes rises to 6.25 cents per 100 millimeters. Cigarette manufacturers, however, can modify the nature of the cigarettes they produce. If they manufacture longer cigarettes, competition among producers will tend to bring about a decrease in price per 100 millimeters of cigarette in response to the tax.

Suppose cigarettes are lengthened to 100 millimeters, yielding 2,000 millimeters of cigarette per pack. If the cost of producing cigarettes is 5 cents per 100 millimeters, a pack of 100-millimeter cigarettes will sell for $1 in the absence of tax, or $1.20 in the presence of tax. By lengthening cigarettes from 80 to 100 millimeters, manufacturers lower the price per 100 millimeters of cigarette from 6.25 to 6 cents. In the absence of any change in the attributes of the product, the tax would increase the price per 100 millimeters of cigarette by 25 percent, from 5 cents to 6.25 cents. But in light of the increased length of cigarettes, the rise in price is only 20 percent, and this increase in price would be less still if the length of cigarettes were stretched further.

Distilled spirits are taxed by the federal government at $10.50 per gallon.[2] States also tax distilled spirits, typically through a tax that is nominally collected from wholesalers in the state but in some cases is collected through the monopoly pricing practices of state-owned liquor stores. The influence of the tax on market outcomes is the same regardless of the method by which it is collected. Whiskeys can, of course, differ from one another in many dimensions, but for our purposes, suppose they differ only in the length of aging, and an increase in age can be thought of as representing a variety of attributes that would constitute a higher-quality whiskey. Suppose in the absence of tax that whiskey aged six years sells for $25 per gallon and that whis-

[2] This is actually a gallon defined as containing 100 proof (50 percent) alcohol. The tax per gallon of 86-proof whiskey would accordingly be $9.03 (86 percent of $10.50).

key aged ten years sells for $50 per gallon, with this increase in price corresponding roughly to a 20 percent rate of interest. In the absence of tax, the price of ten-year whiskey is twice that of six-year whiskey, and in light of consumer preferences there will be an equilibrium distribution of production between the two types of whiskey.

Now suppose whiskey is taxed at $15 per gallon. Using the incidence model described in Figure 11.1, the price of six-year whiskey rises to $40 per gallon and the price of ten-year whiskey rises to $65. The tax on whiskey has made whiskey more expensive compared to other items of consumption, but it has also disturbed the price relationship between the two types of whiskey. Six-year whiskey has become more expensive relative to ten-year whiskey, or, conversely, ten-year whiskey has become cheaper relative to six-year whiskey. With cigarettes, the tax is imposed on the number of cigarettes and not on the amount of tobacco they contain, so one response to the tax is to expand the untaxed attribute, the amount of tobacco. With whiskey, the tax is imposed on the volume of alcohol, but not on the quality. In this case quality is an untaxed attribute, and one market response to the tax is an increase in the average quality of whiskey.

As a further illustration of the point, suppose light bulbs are of two types: a bulb that lasts for an average of one month and a bulb that lasts for twelve months. Suppose in the absence of tax that a package of two one-month bulbs sells for $1 and that a package of two twelve-month bulbs sells for $10. This pattern of prices means that people tend to regard as equivalent the payment of $1 per month and the payment of $10 once a year for bulbs. In present value terms, $10 paid now would equal $1 paid each month for 12 months. If a tax of $1 per package of bulbs is imposed, however, the price of one-month bulbs would rise to $2 and the price of twelve-month bulbs would rise to $11. The more durable bulbs would become relatively cheaper because the tax is imposed on the bulb, not on its durability. Durability is a tax-free attribute in this instance, so durability will be accentuated in response to the tax.

Numerous other examples could be given about the influence of taxation on the attributes of products. In the nineteenth century some cities taxed property according to its front footage. It is hardly surprising that lots became narrower and longer in response to the tax. It is likewise understandable why efforts in an earlier century to tax houses according to the number of windows led to an increased use of candles as a source of interior light. In some cases, it may well be the intent of tax policy to modify the attributes of products, as we explore in the next section. In many cases, however, such changes in attributes are likely to be simply unintended by-products of particular forms of taxation. Regardless of intention, the changes in product characteristics that result in response to an excise tax inject an additional element into the analysis of the economic effects of excise taxation.

CORRECTIVE TAXATION

An excise tax typically reduces the output of the taxed product, raises its price, and modifies its attributes. The modification of attributes may be an unintended consequence of the tax, and the change in price and output may impose an excess burden on consumers of the taxed product. But such a negative assessment of excise taxation is not inherent in the imposition of excise taxes. In some cases the *raison d'être* of an excise tax may be its ability to regulate the flow of resources into particular lines of economic activity. If so, we must examine excise taxes for their ability to regulate economic activity as well as for their ability to raise revenue, impose excess burdens, and modify product characteristics. It is possible that an excise tax on a product would raise little revenue because its high rate reduced the amount of the product demanded, which was the main purpose of the tax. The tax may alter the attributes of a product, with such alteration rather than increased revenue being the main purpose of the tax. There are several reasons why excise taxation is looked upon as a means of regulating economic activity, and they generally point to the use of taxes to correct defects in the outcome of market processes.

Externality as Justification

As we saw in Chapter 2, market transactions may be plagued by various externalities. It is easy to give a number of illustrations, although simply to give such illustrations does not render them valid. In the absence of tax, the market for distilled spirits, for instance, would attain an equilibrium such as that characterized in Figure 11.1, in which the price people pay for distilled spirits equals the marginal cost. But what constitutes the marginal cost of distilled spirits? The manufacturer's assessment of cost certainly includes such resources as labor, materials and equipment, and the waiting (interest forgone) that is necessary to produce the output.

What if the consumption of distilled spirits entails the use of other resources, the cost of which the manufacturer need not consider? Some consumers of distilled spirits may attempt to drive home, and injure or kill other people in the process. Such injury or damage could be regarded as a cost associated with the consumption of dis-

tilled spirits, but this cost is not reflected in the marginal cost of
the product. The imposition of a tax on the consumption of distilled
spirits might be thought to be a means of taking this external cost
into account, as Figure 11.5 describes. The rate of tax must be set
equal to the aspects of the marginal cost of the product that are
otherwise ignored in the market. If this can be done, the higher price

FIGURE 11.5 Welfare Gain from a Corrective Excise Tax

The supply curve for a competitive industry, the horizontal summation of
the marginal-cost curves of the firms in the industry, is described by S.
The marginal-cost functions from which this supply function is constructed
reflect the valuations of the alternative use of resources that firms must
acquire in order to produce. If there are other resources used in production
that the firms need not acquire, and if the evaluation of the alternative use
of those resources is added to the supply function S, the resulting supply
function is S_t. The competitive rate of output is X_1 and the price of the
product is P_1. At this rate of output, however, the value of the output
forgone by producing the product exceeds the value people place on that
product by the vertical distance ab. The imposition of a tax of ab per unit
will, in this case, make full marginal cost equal to the valuation placed on
the output. Accordingly, output will decline to X_0 and price will rise to P_0.
Part of the tax is paid by consumers as a higher gross price and part is
paid by suppliers through their receipt of lower net prices. Instead of an
excess burden, however, there is a welfare gain, as indicated by abc.

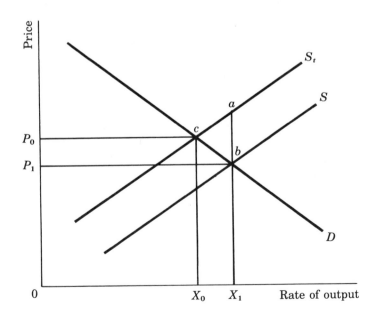

and lower output will reflect what would have occurred had the purchase of "damage rights" been a necessary element in the production of distilled spirits. There are two ways in which a system of damage rights might work. Manufacturers might purchase the agreement of people to participate in a lottery of sorts in which some participants will be killed and others injured each year. Or individual users might buy the agreement of those they might injure or kill. The central idea of a corrective excise tax is that it forces buyers and sellers to account for the cost of resources they use but, within the prevailing legal system, need not purchase.

We could easily develop an extensive list of occurrences of external costs to show how a properly chosen tax that reflects the costs not taken into account through the prevailing system of ownership can aid in the process of shifting resources from less valued to more valued uses. Most such cases can be described in terms of Figure 11.5. Most arguments for the use of excise taxation to correct market outcomes occur in the area of pollution. It can be argued that the use of throwaway bottles for beer and soft drinks, for instance, increases the amount of litter along highways and in parks, but the damage done by this litter, in terms of aesthetic valuation of the landscape, is not a component of the marginal cost of the beverages bottled in such containers. An excise tax on throwaway bottles might accordingly be thought of as a means of forcing producers and consumers to take this neglected component of marginal cost into account.

When pulp and paper firms discharge waste into rivers, they may inflict external costs on downstream users, either by increasing the expense that downstream users must incur before they can use the water or by rendering impossible such downstream activities as fishing and swimming. Once again, the imposition of an excise tax that reflects the marginal cost of the resources that the producer uses in the process of production, but which the producer need not purchase, might provide a welfare gain by making the price of those products reflect their full marginal cost rather than only a portion of that cost.

The ability of an excise tax to modify the characteristics of a product can also be thought of as a beneficial property of the tax. Power lawn mowers can be produced with a variety of attributes: width, weight, horsepower of their engines, noisiness, and rate of gasoline consumption. The marginal cost of power lawn mowers certainly includes the value of the labor and materials that the manufacturer must assemble to produce the mower, but suppose it does not include the value of the otherwise quiet environment that is disrupted by the mower. It might be argued that a tax on the decibel rating of power lawn mowers would be a means of forcing producers to take into account the damage done by such noise pollution, at the same time providing them with an incentive to modify the mechanical characteristics of their mowers. The result might be heavier mowers that consume more gas but make less noise. If people pay for the gas they use to run their mowers but do not pay for the noise pollution they create, it is possible that the attributes of mowers provided through the market will be lighter and noisier than they would be if noise pollution had to be taken into account. If so, a tax on one particular attribute, the decibel rating of the mower, might correct the composition of attributes that constitute the product, rather than correcting an overall rate of output.[3]

Problems of Knowledge and Incentive

To argue that if producers are able to ignore some costs of their production, a *properly* chosen tax will lead to the same choices regarding production that would result if those costs were taken into account is, of course, a truism. It does not follow, however, that the actual imposition of excise taxation for what seem to be corrective purposes performs in the manner implied by the model in Figure 11.5. For one thing, an issue of knowledge arises about the valuation to place on the neglected external costs. The corrective tax on distilled spirits in our previous example is set equal to the value of the output sacrificed by the resources that are used as a result of the consumption of distilled spirits but that need not be acquired by manufacturers. In the absence of a market for the purchase of agreements concerning the use of such resources, as might be embodied in the outcome of a damage lottery, there is no market test of the correctness of differing claims about valuation. A distiller's claim that his use of corn is more valuable than alternative uses is tested by the willingness of people to buy the product. This kind of market test provides an answer or an external check on claims about the value of resources in alternative employments. In the absence of such a test, people could reasonably judge different claims of value to be correct, which makes selection of a particular claim about value — that is, a particular rate of tax — a matter of political strength rather than of willingness to pay.

If various estimates of external cost are distributed normally about the "true" cost, and if legislation reflects an unbiased choice, the

---

[3] Charles J. Goetz and Italo Magnani, "Automobile Taxation Based on Mechanical Characteristics: Evidence from the Italian Case," *Public Finance* 24, no. 3 (1969), pp. 480–494, show that setting tax liability according to mechanical characteristics can induce considerable change in the character of the product.

"proper" rate of tax will result. But as Part II explained, such an outcome is atypical. Moreover, a tax is not the only way of taking those costs into account. Personal suits for damages are another possibility. Suppose it is possible to impute with reasonable accuracy a cost figure for the damage done in accidents caused by drunk drivers. (The development of such an imputation would be more or less of the same order of difficulty or complexity as the imputation of a marginal external cost of alcohol consumption.) If this damage figure is assessed against drunk drivers and paid to the victims, the marginal cost of consuming alcohol will rise and, furthermore, those who are damaged will at least receive some compensation.

The imposition of a corrective tax, in contrast, increases the government's revenues, but it does not compensate for the damages suffered by resource owners whose resources were used without their permission. For this to happen with corrective taxation, a separate act of appropriation by the legislature is required. With damage suits, compensation occurs directly, and damage suits will bring about more changes in the attributes of alcoholic consumption than will corrective taxation. When damages are paid through an excise tax on the purchases of distilled spirits, there will be some reduction in the total rate of consumption, but the composition of consumption will be essentially unchanged.

Some types of consumption may entail more external costs than others, just as some attributes of a power lawn mower may involve more external costs than others. The consumption of distilled spirits at home surely involves lower external costs than consumption elsewhere because the latter generally entails a subsequent drive in a car that the former does not. Moreover, some people are more likely than others to become drunken menaces. Corrective excise taxation cannot effectively distinguish among such attributes as the location of consumption or the drinking proclivities of consumers.[4] In contrast, the use of damage suits would result in some modification in the attributes of consumption by reducing attributes more likely to result in damage to others. This comparison of corrective taxes and personal liability is not meant to imply the superiority of personal liability as a way of taking external costs into account but only to suggest that corrective taxation often can be roughly duplicated by some corresponding change in legal liability.

---

[4] The location of consumption might be addressed by imposing a tax only on the sales of alcohol in bars and perhaps in restaurants. There would still be the matter of parties at the homes of others and also incentives for bars to bootleg because such a tax would create a divergence between the price wholesalers would charge to bars and the price they would charge to retailers for sale to private citizens.

Besides a problem of knowledge, a problem of incentive arises in the imposition of corrective excise taxes. Earlier we avoided this problem of incentive, as we did the problem of knowledge, by assuming that the political process somehow selects the mean estimate of external cost from among a set of normally distributed estimates. Even if the mean estimate is assumed to be that which would result under a market test, if such a test were possible, what is the basis for assuming that this estimate will be selected? Suppose an unbiased average estimate of the marginal external cost of distilled spirits is $5 per gallon. Why is this rate of tax a more likely outcome than taxes of $2 or $8 per gallon? If the unbiased average estimate of the rate of tax on disposable bottles were 3 cents, why is this a more likely outcome than a rate of 5 cents or 1 cent?

Corrective excise taxation is usually viewed as a means of procuring some general interest that is not satisfied through market transactions. Such taxation may modify the price relationships among products within the category subject to the tax. Such modifications may simply be unavoidable by-products of the corrective taxation, but they may also be one reason for the selection of one rate of tax over another. A 5-cent tax on disposable bottles might be chosen over a 3-cent tax because the higher tax does more to enhance the wealth of a producer who purchased an interest in the legislation. An $8 tax might be chosen over a $5 tax because the producers of relatively high-quality whiskey wanted to reduce competition from low-quality whiskeys and were able to purchase the necessary legislation. (Alternatively, a $2 tax might be chosen, indicating the political influence of the producers of low-quality whiskey.) Indeed, there are a variety of instances in which excise taxation conferred advantages to particular producers. Perhaps the most famous example in recent American history was the imposition of excise taxes on the sale of oleomargarine. By raising the price of margarine relative to butter, such a tax increases the demand for butter and enhances the wealth of butter producers.

GENERAL SALES TAXATION

Unlike an excise tax, which is applied to a specific item with different rates applicable to different items, a general sales tax is applied at a common rate to a broad range of transactions. In principle, a sales tax may be levied against any of several links in the chain of transactions from the initial manufacture of items to their ultimate sale to consumers. In the United States, sales taxes are imposed at the retail level by state governments and sometimes by local governments, with most rates clustering in the range of 4 to 6 percent.

Prices are quoted exclusive of tax, with the tax being added to the value of taxable sales.

An appliance store that sells televisions for $500 in a state where the sales tax rate is 5 percent will be liable for $25 of tax on that transaction. If that store reports sales of $50,000 in a month, it will turn over $2,500 to the state government. The firm, not the customer, bears the burden of compliance. (A sales tax could operate instead by deducting the tax from the price. With a tax rate of 4.76 percent, a television that sells for $525 would entail a tax liability of $25, leaving $500 for the retailer.) Adding the tax to the quoted prices is consistent with the legal fiction that the tax is paid by the buyer according to the amount of the purchase, and not by the firm according to the amount of sales. Economically, the distinction is inconsequential, except that the add-on method may lead people to be more fully aware of the taxes they pay and, in turn, this may lead to better-informed collective choices.

The dominant effect of an excise tax is generally thought to be an increase in the price paid by consumers rather than a decrease in the price received by suppliers of factors of production. Simple extension of this line of reasoning might lead to the conclusion that a sales tax is likewise paid through an increase in the price consumers pay for products. This is certainly the appearance created by the add-on method of taxation. What, after all, is a 5 percent sales tax but a set of 5 percent excise taxes on all products?

Regressivity of Sales Taxation

The assumption that sales taxation increases the price paid by consumers rather than lowering the price received by suppliers leads to the argument that a sales tax is a regressive form of taxation. With sales taxation being the primary source of revenue of state governments, this charge of regressivity has captured much attention because regressivity is commonly thought to be an undesirable characteristic of taxation, especially for major sources of revenue. It should be noted that, strictly speaking, sales taxes are proportional systems of taxation in which the rate of tax is constant regardless of the tax base. A tax of 5 percent on sales is a proportional tax.

The charge of regressivity arises when the tax base is changed from consumption to income. Table 11.1 illustrates the type of evidence on which this charge of regressivity is based. Suppose the share of income that is consumed falls as income rises, implying conversely that the share of income that is saved rises as income rises. People with incomes of $10,000 are found on average to spend 99.2 percent of their income on consumption, while people with incomes of $20,000

TABLE 11.1 Regressivity of Sales Taxation over One Year's Income

Person	Income	Consumption	Tax	Tax/Income
A	$10,000	$ 9,917	$496	4.96%
B	20,000	15,583	779	3.89

are found on average to consume only 77.9 percent of their income. Suppose the tax is 5 percent on consumption expenditures. Although each person's tax is 5 percent of consumption, the person with the lower income will have a larger share of income taken as tax. Such evidence leads to the conclusion that sales taxation is regressive.

The argument that sales taxation is regressive when related to the income base rests on two assumptions: (1) that the share of income consumed falls as income rises, and (2) that the tax leads to an increase in the price paid by consumers for products rather than to a decrease in price received by suppliers of inputs to production. Each assumption is open to question. Whether the share of income that is consumed falls as income rises or whether it is invariant to changes in income seems to depend largely on the length of time over which observations about income are made. For annual observations, the ratio of people's consumption expenditures to their income declines as income rises, as shown in Table 11.1. But when income is observed over several years, people's consumption as a share of their income seems to be approximately constant.

Milton Friedman has explained this difference in the short-run and long-run relationships between consumption and income as arising because consumption plans are based not so much on the income earned in a particular year as on an anticipated or permanent income over a horizon that extends into the future.[5] Income in any year has two components: a permanent component that reflects an expectation about the future and a transitory component that reflects the deviation from expected income for that year. Of those people who have below-average current incomes, more of them will have permanent incomes that exceed their current incomes than will have permanent incomes that fall short of their current incomes. Likewise, of all those people with above-average current incomes, more of them will have permanent incomes that are below their current income than will have permanent incomes above their current income.

[5] This perspective is developed in Milton Friedman, *A Theory of the Consumption Function* (Princeton: Princeton University Press, 1957).

A reconsideration of sales taxation in terms of permanent income gives a different perspective on regressivity, as Table 11.2 illustrates. (The data in Table 11.2 underlie the data presented in Table 11.1. Table 11.1 represents an averaging of the data in Table 11.2, with Person A being an average of persons A_1, A_2, and A_3 and similarly for Person B and B_1, B_2, and B_3.) In Table 11.2 it is assumed that consumption is 85 percent of permanent income. Each of the six people pays a sales tax that is 5 percent of consumption and 4.25 percent of permanent income. The sales tax is proportional with respect to permanent income as well as with respect to consumption.

The finding of regressivity, such as described in Table 11.1, results from a bias injected by aggregation. Persons A_3 and B_1 have identical permanent incomes and consumption and occupy an intermediate position in permanent income between A_1 and A_2 and B_2 and B_3. But when aggregation takes place by current income, A_3 is merged with A_1 and A_2, and B_1 is merged with B_2 and B_3. The result is the data portrayed in Table 11.1, where the various entries represent averages for the two groups. When liability under the sales tax is related to current income, it seems clearly regressive. But when tax liability is related to permanent income, it seems to be distributed in proportion to income, reflecting the approximate constancy that seems to characterize the relationship between consumption and permanent income.

Sales Taxation Versus Excise Taxation

Even when the sales tax is related to current income, its regressivity depends on the assumption that the tax increases the price paid by consumers. This assumption about incidence is an extension of the argument about an excise tax on a single product to an excise tax

TABLE 11.2 Sales Tax Regressivity and Permanent Income

Person	Current Income	Normal Income	Consumption	Tax
A_1	$10,000	$10,000	$ 8,500	$425.00
A_2	10,000	10,000	8,500	425.00
A_3	10,000	15,000	12,750	637.50
B_1	20,000	15,000	12,750	637.50
B_2	20,000	20,000	17,000	850.00
B_3	20,000	20,000	17,000	850.00

on all products. An excise tax of 5 percent on television sets will
raise the price of televisions by approximately 5 percent. This is
because suppliers of inputs engaged in the production of televisions
will not accept a lower price, which would be required if the price
of the product did not rise by the amount of the tax because they
would be able to receive a higher price by shifting to the production
of other, untaxed products.

But it does not follow that a 5 percent excise tax on all products,
which we have seen is what a general sales tax of 5 percent represents, will lead to a 5 percent rise in the price of products. The
assumption of a general sales tax means there are no untaxed products, so suppliers will have no untaxed alternative employments available. Consequently, the incidence of a general sales tax will correspond to the result of an excise tax in a situation in which suppliers
are fully specialized to the industry whose output is taxable. If suppliers cannot avoid the tax by shifting to alternative, untaxed employments, a general sales tax must lower the price they receive by
the amount of the tax. A truly general sales tax levied at a proportional rate is equivalent to a proportional income tax of that same
rate. The only difference is that the sales tax is nominally assessed
against the amount of sales and the income tax is assessed directly
against the earnings of factors of production.

As the taxation of retail sales is actually practiced, not all items
of consumption are included in the tax base. Services are almost
universally exempt, as are expenditures on housing. Food purchased
for home consumption, medicine, clothing, and utilities are commonly
exempt, although there is considerable variation among states in the
particular exemptions allowed. When exemptions are introduced, untaxed employments for factors of production arise, and it becomes
possible for suppliers to escape part of the tax. If suppliers' prices
do not fall by the full amount of the tax, the prices of products
purchased by consumers will rise to some extent. The shift of productive factors away from taxed activities into untaxed activities
will shift the composition of output in favor of untaxed activities.
In turn, the pattern of product prices will change: The price of taxed
activities will rise as their output is decreased and the price of untaxed activities will fall as their output is increased.

If the tax does not affect productivity within the economy, the
stock of money, or the demand for money, the tax will not affect the
average level of product prices. The structure of prices will be affected, with some products rising in price and other falling, but an
index of the average level of prices will be unchanged. To the extent
that this occurs and to the extent that patterns of consumption are
invariant among consumers, it cannot be said that consumers bear

any burden from the tax. The tax leads to a rise in the price of activities subject to tax, but it also leads to a fall in the price of activities exempt from the tax.

It is also true that not all of the stock of production is purchased by consumers; part is purchased by government with the proceeds of the tax. But government's purchase takes place because people in their capacity as suppliers of productive services receive lower net prices for their services. The government in effect claims a share of the income of factors of production. The analysis of a retail sales tax closely resembles that of the corporation income tax, at least in that the corporate tax is borne by suppliers of capital despite subsidiary and offsetting changes in the prices of corporate and noncorporate output. Even though some items are exempt from tax, suppliers of factors of production in the tax-exempt industries suffer a reduction in their net price because they face competition from factors of production that leave the taxed industries. A general tax on retail sales, even with significant exemptions from its base, seems to operate largely as a reduction in the price received by suppliers and, hence, to be equivalent to a proportional tax on income.[6]

VALUE-ADDED TAXATION

Sales taxes impose tax liability at a particular point in the process of production and distribution, whether that point is at the retail level or at another level in the process. Other methods of taxing consumption impose a tax at multiple stages in the process. With such multiple-stage forms of taxation, a tax is levied each time a product changes hands. A *turnover tax* is one in which the gross value of the merchandise sold is taxed at each transaction. If a manufacturer sells merchandise to a wholesaler for $100, who sells it to a retailer for $150, who in turn sells it to a consumer for $200, the tax base will be $450. Such a method clearly creates an incentive to reduce the number of stages through vertical integration.

Tax liability can be reduced by a consolidation of various stages in one firm. An integration or merger of the manufacturer and the

---

[6] Edgar K. Browning, "The Burden of Taxation," *Journal of Political Economy* 86 (August 1978), pp. 649–671, notes that the sales tax may actually be progressive in relation to income when transfer payments are taken into account. If consumption were financed wholly by factor income, the sales tax would be borne in proportion to income. But in the lower part of the income scale, transfer payments are an important source for financing consumption. If a sales tax is borne in proportion to factor income and if factor income is a smaller percentage of consumption in lower-income categories, the tax becomes progressive in relation to income.

wholesaler in the previous example will reduce the tax base by $100 because after integration, the manufacturer-wholesaler would sell to the retailer for $150 rather than a total of $250 for the two transactions before integration. The transactions of manufacturers and wholesalers who merge their operations are subject to less of a tax burden, and they are therefore at a competitive advantage. This incentive for vertical integration has been the main argument against a multiple-stage form of sales tax and in favor of a single-stage tax.

Tax liability can also be based on the net value rather than the gross value of transactions. The assessment of tax only against the value added at each stage in the process of production and distribution is referred to as the *value-added tax*, although it is really a method of assigning tax liability rather than a particular form of tax. In the previous example, the sale by the manufacturer to the wholesaler would have a tax base of $100, assuming that no tax is levied against the assembly of raw materials. When the wholesaler sells the product to the retailer, the tax base will be only $50, the difference between the selling price at that stage ($150) and the price the wholesaler paid for it ($100). When the retailer sells the product to the consumer for $200, the value added is $50. The total tax base is thus $200, which is the same as the base of the retail sales tax in this illustration, although that is not always the case. Unlike the use of turnover taxation, value-added taxation does not create any inducement to vertical integration. A merger of the manufacturer and wholesaler would merely make the value added $150 when the product passed from the manufacturer-wholesaler to the retailer, the same as the two separate values added of $100 and $50 before such a merger.

The precise base of a value-added tax varies depending on the types of deductions that are allowed at each stage in the process of production and distribution. The tax base could be made as broad as gross national product, which would result if the only deduction allowed is for the expense of intermediate goods used in preparing the product for sale. There would be no deduction for the expense of capital goods. The base of the tax, in terms of uses of income or objects of expenditure, would be expenditures on capital and consumer goods. Stated in terms of income categories, the base would include the depreciation of capital goods in addition to components of income such as wages and salaries, interest, rents, and profits. While the imposition of a value-added method of taxation against a base of gross national product is conceivable, it is not an option that receives much attention nor is it one that has been used in any countries that tax value added. Feasible options for value-added taxation involve some deduction for expenditures on capital goods; the two main options differ in their approach to the deduction of these expenditures.

The income type of value-added tax allows a deduction for the depreciation of capital assets from the base of the tax. A deduction is allowed to each seller for the expense of intermediate goods purchased from other firms and for the depreciation expense of capital goods attributable to production. This allowance for depreciation makes the base of this form of value-added taxation the net national product (gross national product less capital consumption, or depreciation). The taxation of value added at a constant rate is therefore equivalent to a proportional tax on income at that rate.

In the second option, the purchase price of capital goods can be deductible along with the price of intermediate goods. This method of taxation is simpler administratively because it avoids the need for depreciation schedules for capital goods. Perhaps partly for this reason it is the more popular form of value-added taxation. The base of this form of value-added taxation is consumption expenditures and is equivalent to a retail sales tax on consumer goods. In an evenly rotating or steady-state economy, investment is limited to the replacement of depreciated capital, and the income and consumption types of value-added tax are identical. In an expanding economy, where net capital accumulation is occurring, net capital accumulation would be taxed under the income type but not under the consumption type of value-added tax. Hence, the consumption type would be more favorable to saving and capital formation than would the income type.

In recent years there has been much interest in the possible replacement of the corporation income tax with a value-added tax. If such a replacement takes place and if the value-added tax is of the consumption type, the most common form of value-added tax, one major effect will be a change in personal incentives in the direction of saving rather than consumption. In two otherwise equivalent societies, with one taxing corporation income and the other imposing a value-added consumption tax, the latter society should have a higher rate of saving and capital formation and, hence, over time should experience a higher standard of living. Indeed, much of the recent interest in value-added taxation reflects an assumption that the American tax system encourages consumption rather than saving, thereby eroding future standards of living. A value-added tax, particularly of the consumption type, is seen as a means of restoring a parity between saving and consumption.[7]

---

[7] Some support for value-added taxation arises because it is seen as a means of improving the competitive position of American exporters. Within prevailing

SUGGESTIONS FOR FURTHER READING

The ability of excise taxation to induce changes in the attributes of products is explored in Yoram Barzel, "An Alternative Approach to the Analysis of Taxation," *Journal of Political Economy* 84 (December 1976), pp. 1177–1197. One of the important effects of taxation is to encourage a misstatement of taxable transactions. Taxes on distilled spirits, for instance, are administered by assessing wholesalers for the volume of distilled spirits they sell. The higher the tax, the greater the gain from an underreporting of such sales. Rodney T. Smith, "The Legal and Illegal Markets for Taxed Goods: Pure Theory and an Application to State Government Taxation of Distilled Spirits," *Journal of Law and Economics* 19 (August 1976), pp. 393–429, finds that wholesalers respond in this manner to higher taxes.

The theory of corrective taxation is complicated by such considerations as changes in the mix of inputs in response to the tax and institutional adjustments to offset some of the harmful effects that would otherwise result. On some of these points, see Charles R. Plott, "Externalities and Corrective Taxes," *Economica* 33 (February 1966), pp. 84–87; Otto A. Davis and Andrew Whinston, "Externalities, Welfare, and the Theory of Games," *Journal of Political Economy* 70 (June 1962), pp. 241–262; William J. Baumol, "On Taxation and the Control of Externalities," *American Economic Review* 62 (June 1972), pp. 307–322; and Hirofumi Shibata, "Pareto-Optimality, Trade, and the Pigovian Tax," *Economica* 39 (May 1972), pp. 190–202. James M. Griffin, "An Econometric Evaluation of Sulfur Taxes," *Journal of Political Economy* 82 (August 1974), pp. 669–688, explores the probable effects of a tax on sulfur designed to reduce emissions of sulfur dioxide resulting from the use of coal in the generation of electricity. John F. Morrall III, "Reducing Airport Noise," in *Benefit-Cost Analyses of Social Regulation*, edited by James C. Miller III and Bruce Yandle (Washington, D.C.: American Enterprise Institute, 1979), pp. 147–160, explores a proposal for imposing a tax on the noise produced by aircraft as a means of reducing noise near airports.

There has been much discussion about the possible regressivity of the taxation of retail sales. David G. Davies, "Progressiveness of a Sales Tax in Relation to Various Income Bases," *American Economic Review* 50 (December 1960), pp. 987–995, shows that the sales tax in Ohio in 1956, the source of his data, was regressive in terms of current income but was progressive in terms of permanent income. Jeffrey M. Schaefer, "Sales Tax Regressivity Under Alternative Tax Bases and Income Concepts," *National Tax Journal* 22 (December 1969), pp. 510–527, uses New Jer-

---

trade conventions, nations can give tax exemptions for excise-type taxes for exported goods, and at the same time they are able to impose such taxes on imported goods. No such exemption is allowable for payments under the corporate income tax, however. That is, to give a rebate on excise taxes attributable to exported goods is considered proper, but to give an equivalent subsidy to exports when a different tax system is used is considered dumping.

sey data for 1960–1961, and reaches conclusions quite similar to Davies's. If the sales tax is regressive in relation to income, sales tax revenues should increase less rapidly over time than income. The evidence on this question, however, seems generally to find that revenues and income increase at approximately the same rate, indicating probable proportionality when the sales tax is related to an income base. This literature includes, among others, David G. Davies, "The Sensitivity of Consumption Taxes to Fluctuations in Income," *National Tax Journal* 15 (September 1962), pp. 281–290; Robert Rafuse, "Cyclical Behavior of State-Local Finances," in *Essays in Fiscal Federalism*, edited by Richard A. Musgrave (Washington, D.C.: Brookings Institution, 1965), pp. 63–121; and Ann F. Friedlaender, Gerald J. Swanson, and John F. Due, "Estimating Sales Tax Revenue Changes in Response to Changes in Personal Income and Sales Tax Rates," *National Tax Journal* 26 (March 1973), pp. 103–110.

Peter Mieszkowski, "Tax Incidence Theory," *Journal of Economic Literature* 7 (December 1969), pp. 1103–1124, provides a comprehensive survey of incidence theory, including an analysis of the incidence of a general sales tax. Nicholas Kaldor, *An Expenditure Tax* (London: Allen & Unwin, 1955), argues in support of the principle that taxation should be based on expenditure rather than on income, on the grounds that it is preferable to tax people according to what they take from the stock of wealth than to tax them according to what they contribute. Value-added taxation is surveyed in Norman Ture, *The Value Added Tax: Facts and Fancies* (Washington, D.C.: Heritage Foundation, 1979); and in Clara K. Sullivan, *The Tax on Value Added* (New York: Columbia University Press, 1965). For an analysis of replacing the corporate income tax with a value-added tax, see Stephen P. Dresch, An-loh Lin, and David K. Stout, *Substituting a Value-Added Tax for the Corporate Income Tax* (Cambridge, Mass.: Ballinger, 1977).

12

Wealth as an Object of Taxation

The preceding three chapters examined different ways of assessing tax liability against the value of income or consumption in economic transactions undertaken during some interval of time. This chapter examines the imposition of tax liability against the value of stocks of assets as these exist at some point in time.

CAPITAL, INCOME, AND THE TAXATION OF WEALTH

For reasons we discussed in Chapter 9, it makes no difference, as long as income and capital are defined consistently, whether a tax is levied on an income flow or on the capital stock that generates that flow. The valuation of the stock is related to the valuation of the flow through the rate of interest. At base, income and wealth are simply different reflections of the same phenomenon: the ability to provide service that people value. Income and wealth are the same tax base, not independent bases for taxation. Although they are stated in different magnitudes, they are made commensurable through a rate of interest. An asset that is able to generate a net income of $50,000 per year will be valued at $500,000 if the rate of interest is 10 percent. Taxing the annual income at 20 percent is identical to taxing the capital value at 2 percent. Furthermore, starting from an existing income tax of 20 percent, imposing a 1 percent tax on capital value is equivalent to increasing the income tax to 30 percent. Income and wealth do not provide independent bases for taxation because each is merely an image of the other; there is a conceptual equivalence between taxing the value of an income flow and taxing the value of a capital stock.

Despite this conceptual equivalence of income and wealth and of taxes imposed on them, it is sometimes argued that the imposition of a tax on net worth would be a desirable addition to a system in which income tax is the primary source of revenue. Much of the interest in the taxation of net worth reflects a recognition that, even though income and wealth conceptually are images of each other, the actual tax on income diverges significantly from what it would be if it truly were to be equivalent to the taxation of capital.

If the taxation of wealth focused on areas that were incompletely covered under the income tax, it could be seen as a means of supplementing rather than duplicating the income tax. We discussed in Chapter 9 the treatment of the implicit rental income that the owners of housing receive. Consider now someone whose implicit net income is $10,000 per year. If the marginal rate of tax under the personal income tax is 40 percent, it could be said that that person's tax liability is $4,000 less than it would be if such implicit income were included in the tax base.[1] Suppose the discount rate is 10 percent, which implies that the net value of the house is $100,000. In this case, the imposition of a 4 percent tax on the net value of the house would remove this area of incompleteness within the personal income tax.[2]

The main argument in support of a tax on net worth to supplement a system of income taxation is that the personal income tax discriminates against human capital relative to physical capital. The basis of this argument is that the income tax applies to the net yield from physical capital, but it taxes the gross yield from human capital. The owners of physical capital are able to deduct depreciation and the expenses of maintaining productive capacity from the gross income generated by those capital goods. The net income that results is, moreover, defined in principle as a yield that can be sustained indefinitely.

There are some assets for which it is explicitly recognized that their yields cannot be sustained indefinitely. In many such cases the owners of those assets are able to deduct special depletion allowances.

[1] This statement is correct only as a first approximation. If implicit rental income were actually taxed, people would reduce their investment in such sources of income. There would be a lesser stock of owner-occupied housing, which in turn would yield a smaller annual flow of housing services.

[2] The taxation of the value of real estate by local governments in the United States is based on the gross value of real estate, not on its net value. The spirit of a tax on net worth to supplement areas of incompleteness in the income tax would require the tax to be assessed against net value because it is the net income that is omitted from the base of the income tax.

These allowances are common in various extractive industries, where the value of the land that contains mineral deposits declines as the minerals are extracted. Hence, the owners of such capital assets as deposits of oil, gas, sulfur, uranium, clay, and gravel can take an extra deduction from their gross income that is not available to the owners of other capital assets. This added deduction is rationalized on the ground that the net yield from such assets cannot be maintained indefinitely.

People in their ability to earn income can be thought of as constituting human capital. Although people own the human capital embodied in their persons, they are unable to deduct expenses for depreciation and for maintaining their ability to yield income in the future. There is, of course, a personal exemption of $1,000. In some crude sense this exemption might be thought of as an effort to allow a deduction for the maintenance of productive capacity. The exemption makes no allowance for differences in maintenance expenses among different types of human capital, however, although maintenance expenses differ among objects of physical capital. A Boeing 747 airplane clearly requires more expense to maintain its productive capacity than a Datsun 210 automobile. It is surely no different for different forms of human capital. Moreover, the yield from human capital is not indefinitely sustainable but rather is like an oil pool or uranium mine, except that the owners cannot deduct depletion allowances.

In the absence of suitable depletion allowances for the wasting asset that human capital represents, and without suitable deductions for depreciation and maintenance of productive capacity, the personal income tax would seem to discriminate against the owners of human capital compared to the owners of physical capital. The initial impact of such tax discrimination is to lower the net return on investing in human capital relative to investing in physical capital. Such a differential in net return is inconsistent with market equilibrium, of course, so the ultimate impact of such a tax would be to induce a shift in the pattern of capital formation. Investment in physical capital would increase and investment in human capital would decrease until the net returns to the two forms of capital were equal. In consequence, the gross return to human capital would exceed the gross return to physical capital, and this differential in gross returns would indicate an excess burden from the discrimination against human capital within the personal income tax.[3]

---

[3] This excess burden is of the same sort as that created by the corporation income tax, where the gross yield on corporate capital exceeds the gross yield on noncorporate capital.

A special tax on physical capital, which would result from the imposition of a tax on net worth, would be potentially capable of offsetting the discrimination against human capital in the personal income tax. Whether a particular proposal for the taxation of net worth would truly offset that discrimination is an open, empirical question. What would not seem open to question, within the context of the taxation of personal income, is the proposition that the personal income tax discriminates against human capital. Whether a particular proposal for taxation of net worth may more than offset the income tax discrimination against human capital or may be insufficient to offset that discrimination, it can still be said that some such effort at taxation of net worth offers the potential for offsetting that discrimination. Moreover, without such an offsetting effort the discrimination will continue.

The development of a tax on net worth would entail the creation of a new form of taxation for the American revenue system. Perhaps much the same effect could be accomplished, and in a less costly manner, by incorporating into the personal income tax a credit or exemption for the income from human capital. If it were thought, for example, that equality of treatment between the two forms of income required that the tax liability from the ownership of human capital be reduced by 20 percent, people could exclude 20 percent of their income from human capital in arriving at their taxable income. The idea of such a differential treatment of income from human and physical capital is often described as an earned-income credit, although the income generated by physical capital is as much "earned" as is the income generated by human capital. The income from physical capital is made possible through the application of effort to produce the specific capital goods and the postponement of consumption that saving represents and that is necessary to produce the capital goods. Regardless of nomenclature, some such method of reducing the tax associated with the income from human capital can be seen as an alternative to the imposition of an additional tax on the income from physical capital.

The discrimination against the earning of income from human capital under the personal income tax is clear, as Table 12.1 illustrates. Consider two people, each of whom invests $100,000. Person A invests in physical capital and Person B invests in his own person (human capital). Suppose the annual gross income in each case is $20,000 and that the expenses of maintaining that capital are $10,000. Net income in both cases is $10,000. The tax base of the personal income tax differentiates between the two types of investment; net income is the tax base for physical capital, but gross income is essentially the tax base for human capital. If income is taxed at 25

TABLE 12.1   Tax Treatment of Physical and Human Capital

	Person A Physical Capital	Person B Human Capital
Initial investment	$100,000	$100,000
Annual gross income	20,000	20,000
Less expenses of capital maintenance	10,000	10,000
Net income	10,000	10,000
Tax base under income tax	10,000	20,000
Less tax (at 25 percent)	2,500	5,000
Posttax net income	7,500	5,000
Posttax rate of return	7.5%	5%

percent, the income from physical capital carries a tax liability of $2,500, while the income from human capital carries a tax liability of $5,000 (25 percent of the $20,000 gross income). Consequently, net income after tax is $7,500 on the investment in physical capital and $5,000 on the investment in human capital. The posttax rate of return of 7.5 percent on the investment in physical capital is 50 percent higher than the posttax rate of return of 5 percent on the investment in human capital. This difference in posttax rates of return seems to indicate discrimination against income received from human capital. Such a difference in net rates of return, however, would actually alter the composition of investment in favor of physical capital so as to attain an equality in the net rates of return.

There is more than the personal income tax involved in the possible discrimination for or against physical capital vis-à-vis human capital. As we saw in Chapter 10, the corporation income tax is a tax on the income from physical capital and, moreover, one that takes place for the most part at a rate of 46 percent. In Table 12.1, A's net income would carry a tax liability of $4,600 under the corporate tax and the remaining $5,400 would then be taxed under the personal income tax. When this personal tax of $1,350 is added to the corporate tax of $4,600, the total tax of $5,950 leaves a posttax net income of only $4,050, which is less than the net income generated by the same investment in human capital. The taxation of real estate, to be discussed later in this chapter, is also a tax on the income from physical capital. These and other taxes on physical capital certainly reduce, and may well reverse, the discrimination between human and physical capital.

Furthermore, such public expenditure policies as subsidized education seem generally to discriminate in favor of the accumulation of human capital. Suppose the human capital that requires an investment of $100,000 in the absence of subsidization can be acquired for only $50,000, because the remaining $50,000 comes from tax revenues filtered through subsidized education. Even though B's posttax net income is still $5,000, his posttax rate of return has risen from 5 percent to 10 percent. In this instance, it is physical capital and not human capital that is discriminated against. In general, whether one form of capital is favored relative to another is clearly a complex matter. The personal income tax by itself seems to discriminate against human capital, although the double taxation of saving operates in the opposite direction. But it does not follow that a tax on net worth is required to restore equal treatment in taxation and thereby achieve greater efficiency in the allocation of capital between human and physical forms. On the one hand, the corporate income tax discriminates against physical capital and, on the other hand, the provision of subsidized public education discrimnates in favor of human capital.[4]

TAXATION OF REAL PROPERTY

The assessment of tax liability directly against capital value occurs in two forms in the United States. One is the assessment of liability when wealth is transferred from one person to another, either by gift or by bequest. The revenue raised by such taxation of wealth transfers is about 15 percent of the total revenues raised from the taxation of capital value. The predominant form of wealth taxation in the United States is the taxation of the value of property, which provides about 80 percent of the tax revenue of local governments. Property can be classified in two broad forms: real property and

---

[4] Perhaps one important difference between a tax on net worth and the use of an exemption for so-called earned income is that the net worth tax will probably expand the size of government budget, whereas the earned income exemption would probably contract it. If to some extent government is not subject to the control of the citizenry, as the models of majoritarian democracy described in Part II suggest, the expansion in tax bases available to government that would result from the development of a net worth tax would lead to an overall increase in the burden of taxation. In contrast, the creation of an earned-income exemption, by restricting the base available for taxation, would lead to a reduction in the size of government. For an argument that government acts to a significant extent to exploit the tax bases available to it so as to enhance its revenues at the expense of the general interest of the citizenry, see Geoffrey Brennan and James M. Buchanan, *The Power to Tax: Analytical Foundations of Fiscal Constitution* (Cambridge: Cambridge University Press, 1980).

personal property. Nearly 90 percent of the revenues from property taxation are collected from real property. As for personal property, a distinction is generally made between intangible assets and tangible assets.

Intangible assets are claims against the income from assets, represented by corporate stocks, bonds, mortgages, notes receivable, and the like. In a system of net worth taxation, intangible assets would constitute an important part of the tax base. Property taxation in the United States is not a personal tax levied according to the characteristics of the owner of the property, but rather it is an impersonal levy based on the characteristics of the property. This impersonal nature suggests that intangibles should be excluded from the tax base because to include them is to tax property twice. A corporation, for example, would be taxed on the real estate it owns, and this wealth would be taxed again as the value of its stock is taxed through a tax on intangible property. Although the taxation of intangible assets represents double taxation because the tangible assets represented by the intangibles are also taxed, the taxation of intangibles has received little practical use, principally because they can be hidden so easily from tax assessors. Whether this will continue to be the case in light of the continuing expansion of the ability of computer technology to store and process information remains to be seen.

As a source of revenue, the taxation of tangible property is only moderately more successful than the taxation of intangible property. Automobiles are the only element of individual tangible personal property that is taxed with any degree of success. The taxation of tangible property is somewhat more successful when it is levied on property such as inventories and equipment.

Property taxation, then, is predominantly the taxation of real property, and in the taxation of real property it is common to distinguish between the taxation of land and the taxation of the improvements placed on land. The bulk of the tax is currently levied on the improvements (buildings), with the tax base roughly evenly split between residential and nonresidential (commercial and industrial) real estate. The revenue produced by the property tax is, as with any tax, the product of a tax rate and a tax base. The definition of the tax base is particularly difficult in the taxation of real property for several reasons. Real estate typically changes hands only intermittently. For most real estate, current valuations, as reflected through market transactions, are nonexistent. The taxation of income or expenditure is based on the market valuations of various transactions that occur continually, but transactions in real property occur only intermittently.

The tax base for a piece of real estate could be taken as its value at an act of sale, with that value continuing to serve as the base of the tax until the property is sold again. When prices are generally rising, such a method of taxation will favor property that turns over infrequently relative to property that turns over often. If the participation of people in the common life of a community increases with the time of residence in a community, it might be argued that the favoritism engendered by such an approach to property taxation provides a rough measure of compensation for services rendered by longer-term residents. Nonetheless, such favoritism has generally been thought to be unwarranted. To avoid such favoritism when most property is sold intermittently requires that estimates be developed for the current values of most pieces of real estate. The appraisal of the value of property is thus a central feature of the administration of a system of property taxation.

Several techniques are used to assign an appraised value to a parcel of real estate. One method is to examine the sales price of properties that have recently been sold and that are judged to be approximately similar to the property being appraised and to use this information as a foundation on which to construct a judgment about the value of that property. Another method is simply to revise upward the appraised value of property by some average increase in real estate values. A third method, which is especially applicable to commercial and industrial property and to rental housing, is to determine the annual income derived from the property, from which it is a simple matter to capitalize that income flow to derive a capital value. In this manner, an apartment building that generates an annual net income of $40,000 would be appraised at $400,000 if the rate of discount is judged to be 10 percent and if that net income is judged to be sustainable indefinitely.

After property has been assigned an appraised value, an assessed value is established. While an appraised value is in principle an approximation to the market value of that property, an assessed value is set explicitly at some fraction of appraised value. The tax rate is then selected as some percentage of assessed value, and the product of the tax rate and the assessed value determines the tax liability for that piece of real estate. As a matter of arithmetic, it is irrelevant whether property is assessed at 100 percent of appraised value or at 25 percent because tax liability is a product of base and rate, so a tax rate of 1 percent when property is assessed at 100 percent of appraised value is equivalent to a tax rate of 4 percent when property is assessed at 25 percent of appraised value. Yet considerable variation exists in the relationship between assessed and appraised values. Oliver Oldman and Henry Aaron found that the average ratio of assessed value to sales price in Boston for 1962 ranged from 34.1 percent on single-family residences to 79 percent on commercial property.[5] Besides this variation among classes of property, there was also substantial variation among properties of the same class within the metropolitan Boston area. The ratio of assessed value to sales price for single-family residences ranged from 28.1 percent to 54.1 percent, and for commercial property the ratio ranged from 59 percent to 110.9 percent.

We should note that the variation in ratios of assessed value to sales price will overstate to some extent the degree of underlying variability in assessment practices. Suppose that there is no variation in assessment practices (that is, all properties that could reasonably be anticipated to sell for the same price carry the same assessed value) and, moreover, that the ratio of assessed value to anticipated selling price is the same for all properties. Despite this uniformity of assessment practices, an examination of ratios of assessed values to sales price is still likely to show variability. Not all properties that have the same anticipated selling price will actually sell for the same price. There will be some random variation of actual selling prices about the anticipated selling price for any set of properties. Even if assessment-sales ratios are uniform with respect to anticipated sales prices, variation in actual sales prices about the anticipated price will introduce dispersion into assessment-sales ratios. Some of the variation in assessment-sales ratios is surely attributable to random variation in market prices rather than to variation in assessment practices.[6]

Variation in assessment practices, even if overstated by common measures, still exists, and numerous suggestions have been advanced for dealing with the variability in ratios of assessed value to sales price. For the most part, these suggestions retain the essential framework of the tax, in that units of government would still assign assessed values to particular parcels of real estate. Typical suggestions for assessment reform involve greater professionalization of the assessment corps and expanded use of electronic data processing in developing comparisons among parcels of property. There has also been a growing use of 100 percent assessment, in which local governments are supposed to assess real estate at its appraised value.

Alternatively, the use of third parties to render judgments about the price at which other people would transact can be abandoned as a

[5] Oliver Oldman and Henry Aaron, "Assessment-Sales-Ratios Under the Boston Property Tax," *National Tax Journal* 18 (March 1965), pp. 36–49.

[6] This point is developed in Warner W. Doering, "The Use of Statistical Techniques in Equity Determination," *Proceedings of the National Tax Association, 1964* (Columbus, Ohio: National Tax Association, 1965), pp. 390–400.

means of reducing variability in assessment-sales ratios. At base, such third-party judgments seem to be an inescapable source of variability because even the most thorough comparison of transactions will never capture fully the effect of preference and circumstance on the value someone places on a parcel of real estate. A self-assessing form of property taxation has been put forward as a possible way of avoiding third-party difficulties.[7] With individual property owners able to declare their own valuations, some sanction would of course be required to prevent underassessment as a means of reducing tax liability. A common suggestion is that the owner be required to sell the property to any bidder at some percentage of the assessed value, say 150 percent. Some penalty could be levied for the privilege of changing one's declared assessment after receiving and rejecting an offer to buy at the required percentage of the self-assessed value.

Because an assessed value can be established only after an appraised value has been assigned, you might think that the use of assessed value is superfluous or that the additional step of computing an appraised value is an unnecessary expense. Local governments often have some incentive to lower their reported property value to increase their share of state aid. The distribution of state aid to local governments often varies inversely with a locality's share of the total assessed property value in the state. Thus, by lowering its assessed value, a locality can increase its share of state aid. The creation of boards of equalization by states, which set lower bounds to the ratios of assessed to appraised value, and the imposition of 100 percent assessment represent efforts by states to constrain such competition by localities.

As we noted, it is irrelevant whether property is assessed at 25 percent of its anticipated value and taxed at 4 percent or whether it is assessed at 100 percent and taxed at 1 percent. The tax liability is the same in either case. In terms of the actual operation of local budgetary processes, however, a difference may result. Responsibility for setting assessed value is separate from responsibility for setting the tax rates to be applied to those values. A tax assessor establishes assessed values, but a legislative council sets tax rates. Tax liability is thus the product of the actions of two separate offices.

---

[7] For a brief proposal for self-assessment in property taxation, see Arnold C. Harberger, "Issues of Tax Reform for Latin America," in *Fiscal Policy for Economic Growth in Latin America* (Baltimore: Johns Hopkins University Press, 1965), pp. 119–120. For a careful exploration of self-assessment, see Daniel M. Holland and William A. Vaughn, "An Evaluation of Self-Assessment Under a Property Tax," in *The Property Tax and Its Administration,* edited by Arthur D. Lynn, Jr. (Madison: University of Wisconsin Press, 1969), pp. 79–118.

The administrative theory behind this separation is that the appraisal of property value is a technical, nonpolitical matter of fact finding, but the selection of a rate of tax involves political questions. Yet tax assessors are commonly elected, and even if they weren't, they would have to be appointed through some political process. Elected assessors, and perhaps appointed assessors as well, might be generally motivated to support lower rather than higher assessed values as a means of cultivating support; indeed, it is essentially the only means they have for cultivating support. The city council must set the rate of tax and, other things equal, it would probably prefer to raise revenues by having the base rather than the rate of tax rise. Assessors and legislators thus seem to have somewhat different interests within the local budgetary process.

One effect of state-imposed requirements for uniform assessment, as represented by requirements for 100 percent assessment, may be to increase real rates of tax. Table 12.2 presents evidence that supports the proposition that an increase in the ratio of assessed to appraised value will not entail an offsetting reduction in the rate of tax. Rather, the nominal rate of tax seems to fall by less than the increase in the tax base, bringing about a rise in the real rate of tax. Localities with assessment ratios between 15 and 19.9 percent had nominal tax rates of 9.33 percent and real tax rates of 1.63 percent. Localities with assessment ratios between 50 and 59.9 percent had nominal rates of tax of only 5.23 percent, but their real rates of tax were 2.88 percent, nearly double those of the localities with the lower assessment ratio, despite their nominal tax rate being half as high. Programs to increase assessment ratios are commonly advocated as

TABLE 12.2   Assessment Ratios and Property Tax Rates, 1967

Assessed Value/ Appraised Value	Tax Rate		Real/ Nominal
	Nominal	Real	
15–19.9	9.33	1.63	17.5
20–24.9	8.85	1.99	22.5
25–29.9	7.86	2.16	27.5
30–34.9	6.23	2.02	32.4
35–39.9	5.37	2.01	37.4
40–49.9	5.24	2.36	45.0
50–59.9	5.23	2.88	55.1

Source: U.S. Department of Commerce, Bureau of the Census, *Taxable Property Values — 1967 Census of Governments* (Washington, D.C.: U.S. Government Printing Office, 1968), p. 15.

a means of reducing variability in assessment practices, thereby promoting equality in treatment among people with property of similar value. Such programs might also serve as a means of increasing tax collections.

WHO PAYS THE PROPERTY TAX?

The property tax, like the sales tax, has encountered much criticism on the ground that tax liability seems to be regressive when the tax is related to income. Because the property tax is the major form of tax revenue for local governments, the controversy surrounding the possible regressivity of the tax is understandable. The argument of regressivity has essentially the same structure as the argument about the regressivity of the sales tax. First, there is an assumption about the incidence of the tax; namely, that the tax is paid through a rise in the price of housing. Second, it is argued that the share of income people spend on housing falls as income rises, meaning that the share of income claimed by the property tax declines as income rises. Table 12.3 gives a simple illustration of this second argument. Person A, with an annual income of $20,000, spends 25 percent of that income on housing, while Person B, with $40,000 income, spends 20 percent on housing. The property tax is proportional to its base, which in Table 12.3 is assumed to be 20 percent of housing expenditure. Hence, Person A pays 5 percent of his income in tax, while Person B pays only 4 percent.

The Relation Between Housing and Income

As in the case of the sales tax, both assumptions on which the charge of regressivity rests are open to question. The observation that the percentage of income spent on housing falls as income rises depends critically on the definition of income. The relation between housing expenditure and income raises the same issue about the definition of income that arose in the examination of the relation between con-

TABLE 12.3 Income and Payments of Property Tax

Person	Income	Housing Expenditure	Property Tax	Tax/Income
A	$20,000	$5,000	$1,000	.05
B	40,000	8,000	1,600	.04

sumption and income in Chapter 11. If annual income is used as the measure, housing expenditure as a share of income declines as income rises.

But choices about housing are not changed annually to reflect changing economic circumstances. Rather, such choices are typically made in view of a horizon of several years — that is, they seem to reflect some notion of permanent income. Housing expenditures, however, seem to be approximately a constant percentage of normal income. If property taxes are consequently a constant percentage of permanent income, the property tax is roughly equivalent to a proportional tax on income, granting the assumption that the tax operates by increasing the price paid for housing services. In other words, if it is assumed that the property tax increases the price of housing services, the tax is seen to be regressive or proportional when related to an income base, depending on whether the question of regressivity is addressed by annual or permanent income, respectively. To the extent that permanent income is regarded as a better reflection of people's economic positions, the tax would seem to be paid roughly in proportion to income, assuming it is paid through a rise in the price of housing.

Property Taxation in a Single Locality

How reasonable is it to assume that the tax operates by raising the price of housing services? Consider the imposition of an annual tax of 2 percent on the value of all real estate, a tax rate that would be equivalent to an annual tax on rental value of 20 percent, assuming a 10 percent rate of discount. Initially assume that this tax is imposed by only one locality in the nation. The property tax in this instance operates essentially like a selective excise tax on a single product, as Figure 12.1 illustrates. In the short run, real estate is a specialized input into the provision of housing services, so the owner of the taxed real estate would bear the tax. Capital will not be invested in real estate in this particular locality, however, unless investors anticipate receiving a net rate of return equal to what they can anticipate receiving in other investments. As the supply of housing declines over time, the price of housing will rise. If real estate is an unspecialized input in the long run, the price of housing in the locality that imposes the tax will rise by the amount of the tax.

A Nationally Uniform Property Tax

Although the property tax is levied by individual units of local government, its use is general throughout the nation. To capture this

---

FIGURE 12.1 Incidence of a Narrowly Based Property Tax

Suppose initially that the supply of capital to real estate in a particular
locality is wholly specialized, as indicated by S_1. The demand for housing is
described by D, and the net demand function, D_n, is derived by subtracting
property tax payments from the gross price of housing. The immediate
effect of the tax is to reduce the price received by suppliers of housing
services to P_1^n. With the passing of time, disinvestment can occur in
housing, and as this happens the supply function becomes flatter, as shown
by the successive rotations to S_2 and S_3. Also with the passing of time,
suppliers of housing services experience a smaller reduction in the price
they receive, while consumers of housing experience a larger increase in
the price they pay. When the quantity of housing has declined to X_3, for
instance, consumers pay P_3 for housing, while suppliers of housing services
receive P_3^n.

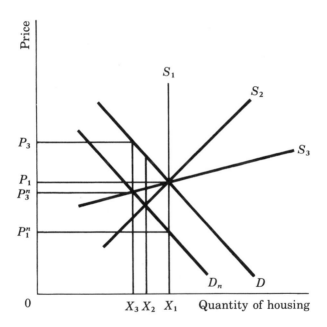

---

generality of the tax, assume there is a nationwide property tax of
2 percent. In the short run, this tax will be borne by the owners of
real estate, just as in the case where a single locality imposes a specific tax. If the supply of real estate is fixed in the short run and
the tax does not affect the demand for real estate, the tax will reduce
the return to owners of real estate. Disinvestment in the supply of
real estate will be accompanied by expanded investment in other
forms of capital. Because capital in the form of real estate is a sig-

nificant element in the total supply of capital, this process of re-allocation in the stock of capital will decrease the price received by the owners of nonrealty forms of capital. The tax on real estate creates disequilibrium in the capital market, and the restoration of equilibrium requires that the net rate of return on realty equals the net rate of return on nonrealty. This in turn requires a reduction in the supply of real property and an increase in the supply of nonrealty.

By this shift in the employment of capital, part of the tax that was originally paid by owners of real property becomes transmitted to owners of nonrealty capital. The long-run incidence of a national tax on real property is thus quite similar to the long-run incidence of the corporation income tax. The long-run decrease in the supply of real estate will bring about an increase in the price of housing services, but the long-run increase in the supply of other forms of capital will bring about a decrease in the prices of the services produced by that capital. On average, the price of consumption goods will be unchanged; the tax will be paid through a reduction in the net price received by suppliers of capital, as in the case of the corporate income tax.

Variable Rates of Tax Among Localities

The correct model for examining the incidence of the property tax is clearly not one in which a tax is levied by only one community. The property tax is imposed by units of local government, but it is used generally throughout the nation as a means of financing local government. This generality does not render the model of a national tax on property value the correct one for examining the incidence of the tax, however, because that model neglects the variation in the tax rates that exists among communities. Although 2 percent may be an average rate of tax, some communities have lower rates of tax and others impose higher rates. For our purposes we can assume that half of the communities tax property value at 1 percent and that the other half tax property value at 3 percent. But how would the analysis of tax incidence differ in this model from the analysis in the earlier model of a uniform tax of 2 percent?

The question is equivalent to asking how a model in which some localities tax income from real estate at 10 percent while others tax it at 30 percent differs from one in which all tax is levied at 20 percent. The question can be explored by assuming initially that there is a uniform tax of 2 percent and that subsequently some communities reduce their rate to 1 percent while others increase the rate to 3 percent. To avoid such complicating considerations as changes in local expenditure that changes in tax rates would imply, we can assume that localities leave their spending unchanged. This assumption implies that the communities that tax at 3 percent transfer 1 percent to those localities that tax at only 1 percent.

In Chapter 9 we saw that the progressive income tax can, for analytical purposes, be conceptualized as consisting of two parts: a proportional income tax and specific taxes and subsidies that vary among people. Similarly, the property tax can be conceptualized as consisting of two parts: a nationally uniform tax and specific taxes and subsidies that vary among localities. The effect of the nationally uniform tax is, in the short run, a reduction in the net price received by the owners of real estate, but in the long run its effect is a reduction in the net price received by owners of capital generally.

The variation in tax rates among localities adds a new element to the analysis. Assume a long-run equilibrium with a nationally uniform property tax and inject a set of taxes and subsidies. With reference to Figure 12.1, the effect of the tax is to drive D_n still further below D in those localities, while in the localities that receive the subsidy, D_n moves toward D. In the short run there is no change in either the supply of housing or the demand for housing in either locality. For localities whose tax rises to 3 percent, the initial effect of the tax will be to depress the net price that owners receive for their supply of housing services. For localities where the tax rate declines to 1 percent, the net price that the owners of housing services receive will rise by the amount of the tax reduction. The short-run effect of this system of taxes and subsidies, then, is to alter the pattern of net returns to the suppliers of housing services, leaving the price of housing to consumers unchanged.

Housing will become a more profitable investment in those localities where the tax is reduced. At the same time, it will become less profitable in those localities where the tax rate is increased. Suppose, as a first-order approximation, that the overall return to housing investment is not affected by the variation in rates of tax among localities. In this case, the tax will change the equilibrium distribution of housing investment among localities, but it will not affect the equilibrium distribution of capital between realty and nonrealty. Disinvestment will occur in those localities where the tax was increased, and this disinvestment will be offset by investment in realty in those localities where the tax rate was reduced.

Equilibrium requires that the net return to housing investment be the same in each type of locality as well as that the net return to housing be equal to the net return to other forms of capital. As the supply of housing expands in the low-tax communities, the net return falls. As the supply of housing contracts in the high-tax communities, the net return rises. In equilibrium, the net returns will be the same, but the quantities of housing will differ between the two types of localities. Suppliers of housing services will be earning the same net returns as they earned under the nationally uniform tax, but there will be a different distribution of housing between the two types of localities. Essentially, then, the long-run incidence of local taxes that vary in rates is the same as that of a nationally uniform tax, with the variation in rates affecting only the amount of realty in different localities.

The change in the relative amount of housing stock among types of localities will involve a movement of people as well as of housing. To see why this is so, suppose that people do not change their places of residence. The stock of housing will contract in the high-tax localities, and this contraction will increase the price of housing as the same number of people now compete for less housing. In the low-tax localities, the stock of housing expands, and with the same number of people competing for more housing, the price of housing will fall. But as housing becomes cheaper in some localities than in others, people will choose to locate where housing is cheaper. The demand for housing will fall in the high-tax localities, and it will rise in the low-tax localities. The variation in tax rate will have shifted the distribution of both the housing stock and the people in favor of the low-tax localities, but the incidence of the tax is essentially the same as under a nationally uniform tax — that is, on the suppliers of capital in much the same way as under the corporate income tax.

PROPERTY TAXATION IN A SYSTEM
OF LOCAL GOVERNMENT

Property tax rates do not vary among localities because some localities are being taxed especially heavily to provide subsidies for the other localities. Rather, tax rates differ mainly because localities differ in their choices of public expenditure. Communities with 3 percent and 1 percent rates of tax do not provide the same level of public expenditure. If they did, the low-tax community would clearly be more attractive compared with the high-tax community and with the case in which each community had a 2 percent rate of tax. Other things being equal, the low-tax community also supplies less public output than the high-tax community, and a consideration of the value people place on public output may modify substantially the preceding implication about the incidence of the property tax.

As before, assume the average rate of tax on property is 2 percent but that some localities tax property value at 3 percent and others tax it at 1 percent. For simplicity, it might be thought that one-half of the localities tax property at 2 percent, that one-quarter impose a tax rate of 1 percent, and that the other quarter taxes at 3 percent. The question of incidence concerns whether any significant difference arises among these localities because of the difference in tax rates.

For now, assume there are no initial differences in wealth among localities, but we will modify this assumption shortly. The assumption of equal wealth means that differences in tax rates relate directly to differences in public outputs, as measured by public expenditures. If public expenditures are of no value to residents, the difference in tax rates will induce mobility in real estate in the long run, thereby generating the conclusions about incidence that we reached earlier. Indeed, the assumption that the deviations in particular tax rates about the national average reflects a pattern of excise taxes and subsidies is, in effect, an assumption that public expenditures are of no value.

Recognizing that public expenditures have value can modify significantly the preceding analysis of incidence. Suppose patterns of public expenditure conform to the benefit principle in both the low-tax and the high-tax communities. In other words, the reason for the different rates of tax is that such a differential is necessary to give expression to differences in the demands for public output among the residents of the different localities. In this case, the low-tax communities will be composed mainly of relatively low demanders for public output, and the high-tax communities will be composed of relatively high demanders. If schooling is the primary form of public output, elderly people, single people, and childless people will generally have a lower demand for public output than will families with children. Other relevant factors including wealth being the same, communities consisting largely of the elderly and the childless will have a lower tax rate than communities consisting largely of people with children. But this difference in tax rates will be essentially the same as the difference in spending on beef between someone who likes steak for breakfast and dinner and someone who favors Japanese cuisine.

If the variation in tax rates among localities is a reflection of variation in desires for public output, the variation in tax rates will induce *no* changes in the market for housing. The differential in tax rates will be sustained over time, but without inducing any change in the location of capital because capital invested in real estate is earning the same net return in each locality. Although investors are paying a higher tax in the high-tax locality, they are also receiving a more highly valued pattern of public output, and the additional value placed on this output is equal to the added tax burden.

The property tax cannot be examined satisfactorily without analyzing its pivotal role in financing the services of local government, a subject that we discuss in more detail in Chapter 18. The property tax creates a tie-in sale between the purchase of public services and the purchase of housing. A person jointly consumes public services and housing, and the total price of this package is the sum of the property tax liability and the price of housing. As we will see in Chapter 18, the fiscal choices that emerge within a system of local government possess characteristics similar to the outcomes of market exchange. By permitting variation among localities in the provision of public services, a system of localities enables people to choose from bundles of public services in much the same way that the market enables people to choose among competing products. In a network of local governments, a property tax would thus perform approximately as a benefit tax in the sense of Wicksell's principle of taxation (Chapter 2).

The Charge of Regressivity

Despite the ability of a property tax to serve as a type of price for public output within local governments, the property tax has become the object of increased and vigorous attack from several directions. The charge of regressivity comes from one direction, although this charge may on closer inspection prove difficult to sustain. To the extent that the tax is really a price, questions of regressivity do not arise; it would make no more sense to speak of the regressivity of the property tax than to speak of the regressivity of the price of apples. It is, of course, the case that as income decreases, the price of an apple, or of any object, is a larger share of income, but this observation is merely a universal proposition about fractions with a constant numerator and a variable denominator. Questions of regressivity arise precisely as questions of pricing recede; if a tax is not a quasi-price, it serves no pricelike function, in which event it is reasonable to ask how its burden is distributed. Even if the property tax is not seen as a price for the services of local government, its incidence seems to be proportional, or possibly progressive, in relation to income.

Much of the recent criticism of the property tax as a means of financing local government is concerned not with its alleged regressivity, which is a relationship among taxpayers within a unit of government, but with its ability to allow wealthier communities to finance, say, education with less effort than poorer communities. Imagine two communities with equal numbers of residents, but one has twice the value of real estate as the other. The wealthier community will be able to provide a unit of any type of public output — a classroom, a fire truck, a tennis court — at a lower rate of tax, though not at a lower price, than the poorer community. If the object of expenditure costs $10,000 per year and if there are 1,000 members of the community, the price is $10 per person. But if that revenue is collected through a property tax, the collection of $10 per person will require a rate of tax on property that is twice as high in the poorer community than in the wealthier community.

At base, this observation is the truism that the cost of an object is a smaller share of income as income increases. If education were an ordinary object of consumption, financing education through the property tax would probably arouse little controversy. But education is also seen as a means of equipping people for the future, and the use of the local property tax to finance education favors children of relatively wealthy parents over children of relatively poorer parents. Increasingly, state governments have been taking over the financing of education, and as they do so, much of the direct relation between the wealth of individual communities and expenditure on education is removed.

Although wealth might confer an advantage, this is not necessarily the case. The advantage of wealth may in some cases be illusory, precisely because of market reactions to initial advantages. A community with an advantage in financing desired services, say because of higher wealth, is in a position analogous to the community with the 1 percent tax because it receives a subsidy from a community with a 3 percent tax. In that case, there was an initial short-run advantage to the owners of property in the low-tax community, but there was no advantage to subsequent owners in the long run because the initial advantage led to increases in the prices paid for housing in the initially advantaged community.

Consider a simple model in which initially there are two communities, each containing 100 houses valued at $40,000 each. A 2 percent tax is assessed against this tax base, giving each community a budget of $80,000. Suppose that subsequently one of the communities annexes adjacent territory containing ten businesses, each valued at $360,000. The tax base in this wealthier community nearly doubles, allowing it to finance the same budget at a tax rate of just over 1 percent. Alternatively, for the same 2 percent rate of tax it could finance twice the public output, or it could choose among a variety of intermediate positions in which public output was larger and the tax rate was smaller. This wealthier community is in essentially the same situation as the community that found its tax rate reduced from 2 percent to 1 percent because it received a subsidy financed by the increase in tax on another community; in this case, however, the annexed territory provides the subsidy.

To keep the example simple, suppose the increase in the tax base does not affect the desired rate of public output. As a result of the annexation, the tax assessed per house or business (assuming business property is taxed the same as residential property) falls from $800 toward $400. At a 10 percent rate of discount, this decline in tax liability will bring about a rise in the price of housing of nearly $4,000. The reduction in tax liability will have been *capitalized* into the value of real estate in that locality. As a condition of equilibrium, real estate will tend to earn the same net return among areas as well as the same net return as other forms of investment.

The ability of one locality to secure a tax reduction of $400 through its annexation of adjacent territory means that real estate in that locality earns a higher return than real estate in other localities. Houses that formerly sold for $40,000 will now sell for $44,000. This wealthier community will now have 100 houses valued at $44,000 each and 10 businesses valued at $360,000 each. It will be collecting $80,000 in revenues with a 1 percent tax rate. Simple arithmetic suggests that the residents of the wealthier community are better off than the residents of the poorer community because they are able to finance the same public output at a lower rate of tax.

Such an arithmetical comparison is not fully accurate, though. The owners of housing at the time of annexation are clearly better off because the annexation increased the value of their property by $4,000, but subsequent owners of property in that locality are not better off than owners of property in the poorer locality. These subsequent owners pay a tax rate of only 1 percent, or $440 per year, whereas they would have to pay a 2 percent tax, or $800 per year, in the poorer community. But this comparison is misleading because it neglects the $4,000 that subsequent residents had to pay to the initial residents to buy their houses to live in the wealthier community. Although annual taxes are $360 less in the wealthier community, an offsetting capital outlay of $4,000 was required to reside there, and this outlay is essentially equivalent and of opposite sign to the reduction in annual taxes. In effect, these subsequent residents financed their own annual tax reduction by making a lump-sum capital payment of $4,000.

This simple model is not intended to imply that differences in tax rates that can be attributed to differences in wealth among communities reflect nothing but the capitalization of those advantages and disadvantages and leave relatively recent residents in essentially the same position regardless of their community of residence. The advantages and disadvantages among communities will affect the demands for residency among those communities, which in turn will affect relative property values. If such capitalization of advantages and disadvantages occurs, simple arithmetical comparisons such as those we just used will give a misleading portrayal of gainers and losers. The very distinction between gainers and losers will depend on the identity of owners when the change in advantages and disadvantages occurred rather than on the current identity of owners, although there may of course be overlapping between the two sets of owners.

SITE-VALUE TAXATION

The taxation of the value of real property can in principle be separated into two taxes: a tax on the value of land and a tax on the value of the improvements placed on that land. It is sometimes suggested that this distinction between land and improvements should be sharpened and that increased emphasis should be placed on the taxation of land or site values.[8] Support for site-value taxation rests on two main premises. One is that land is in wholly inelastic supply and that taxation of land will not affect its supply. Moreover, such taxation will generate no excess burden.

The other premise is that site values are an unearned component of wealth. Changes in the value of land are thought to result not from the actions of the owners of land but from broad social tendencies regarding the size of the population and its location. A graphical portrait of the market for land would show a vertical supply curve intersected by a demand curve, with the intersection giving the price of land. The taxation of the value of land will have no effect on its supply, so there would be no loss of efficiency from the imposition of such a tax. Moreover, changes in the demand for land are not attributable to individual efforts. Such changes in demand, and in site values, are windfalls having nothing to do with individual effort or choice. Accordingly, there might seem to be little if any question of equity raised by the taxation of such unearned values.

The taxation of items in wholly inelastic supply for which changes in value are not attributable to the actions and choices of the owners would have much to recommend it as a form of taxation. How closely

[8] Site-value taxation is often associated with Henry George, who saw the taxation of site value as a practical means of replacing private ownership of land with common ownership. Several of his books explored this theme, the most famous of which is *Progress and Poverty* (1879; New York: Robert Schalkenbach Foundation, 1937).

a tax on site value would actually correspond to this common, paradigmatic representation of the tax is open to some question. Land
is not truly in zero elastic supply. After all, land has been produced
in a number of places in the world through the filling of bays, with
San Francisco and Tokyo providing two well-known illustrations. In
principle, the Rocky Mountains could be pared down and used to
fill the Gulf of Mexico.

Some may question the desirability of such actions to extend the
earth's land area, but it is undeniable that land can be produced if
the producer is willing to expend the required resources. Furthermore, the taxation of land values will induce some effort to substitute
capital for land. All that is required for this to happen is that land
and capital be substitutes in production, a relationship that holds
broadly. This is obviously true in agriculture, where fertilizer can be
substituted for land, but it is also true for much industry, where, for
instance, a factory can be built higher to economize on the use of
land. The decreased demand for land that thereby results will reduce
the value of land and, hence, the base of a site-value tax.[9]

Land cannot be measured only by such a quantitative measure as
acres, any more than the stock of housing can be measured simply
by counting the number of housing units. Housing units vary in
quality, and a higher-quality house can be treated as equivalent to
some multiple of a low-quality house. In other words, a house that
is valued at $80,000 can be treated as equivalent to two houses
valued at $40,000. In this manner, an increase in the quality of hous-
ing can be treated conceptually as equivalent to some increase in
quantity.

It is essentially the same with land. A marsh may be drained to
provide land for crops or houses, or a levee may be built along a river
to reduce the damage of flooding. The land in the surrounding flood
plain will be enhanced in quality, and this higher-quality land will
generate a larger supply of land services. The enhanced value of
service can be treated as equivalent to an expansion in the quantity
of land of the former, lower-quality type. Land is not truly in inelastic supply, which becomes clearer when it is recognized that the
quality of land can be modified through individual choice. Accordingly, a tax on site value will not be without excess burden, and
changes in the value of land will not be exclusively attributable to

[9] The ability of a tax on land to induce a substitution of capital for land is
discussed in Martin S. Feldstein, "The Surprising Incidence of a Tax on Pure
Rent: A New Answer to an Old Question," *Journal of Political Economy* 85
(April 1977), pp. 349–360.

general social forces. Individual efforts will also be able to change the value of land, mainly through changes in its quality but also through changes in actual quantity.

The taxation of site values does not seem to be as fiscally pure as it is sometimes suggested. This does not deny that the taxation of site values may generally entail less excess burden than other taxes, nor does it deny that much of the increase in land values reflects general social forces rather than individual effort. The arguments in favor of placing greater emphasis on the taxation of site values rather than improvements seems to have merit. Presently, the property tax is administered by making separate assessments for the value of land and improvements and then taxing the combined value at a uniform rate. Greater emphasis on the taxation of site values could be injected into the property tax by increasing the tax on land while reducing the tax on improvements.

TAXATION OF WEALTH TRANSFERS

For many years the United States imposed separate taxes on the value of estates that people left when they died and on the size of gifts people made during their lifetimes. Since 1976, the two taxes have been combined into one tax on wealth transfers. Most states also impose taxes on wealth transfers, either by taxing the value of the estates left by the decedents or by taxing the value of the inheritances received by the recipients. Although estate taxation and inheritance taxation are technical terms that are used to describe different approaches to imposing taxes on the transfer of wealth at death, *inheritance* is also a generic term that signifies such a transfer. All such transfers, along with the effort to tax them, will be described here by the generic term.

One of the main arguments for the taxation of inheritance is that such taxation is a means of providing a greater measure of equality of opportunity among people because a tax on the inheritance of material wealth will curtail one source of inequality. It might be questioned whether such taxation will effectively promote equality of opportunity or, indeed, whether it is possible to develop a meaningful conceptualization of equality of opportunity that truly differs from a notion of equality of outcomes. These issues were discussed in Chapter 3, and they are the most substantial issues that arise with respect to inheritance taxation. As a source of revenue, the taxation of inheritance is of minor significance, making up only about 1 percent of the revenues of the federal government. Nonetheless, inheritance taxation raises some interesting questions about incidence and its impact on saving, which we explore here.

People can be described in varying degrees as possessing demands to leave bequests to their heirs. Saving takes place during working years to provide for retirement, at which time dissaving occurs. Yet some people do not consume during their retirement years all the wealth they had accumulated; they leave some wealth for heirs. It might be thought that this results because people are uncertain about their time of death. In the face of such uncertainty, a prudent person might want to avoid running out of wealth while still alive. This situation can be avoided by reducing the rate of consumption to provide protection in the event of an unusually long life. As a result, some people will die without consuming all of their wealth, and the presence of such estates will reflect uncertainty about death rather than a demand for bequests. This argument certainly is plausible, but if it were correct it would be dominated by a strategy of buying annuities that guaranteed consumption during one's lifetime. Hence, it seems as though a demand for bequests is at least one of the factors that enter into choices to save.

The taxation of bequests operates through what can be conceptualized as a market for bequests, illustrated in Figure 12.2. The quantity of bequests is conceptualized most simply in dollars, which means that 100 units of bequest is an estate of $100. This conceptualization makes the price of a bequest unit constant at $1. In the absence of tax, a quantity of wealth will be bequeathed to descendants, B_0 in Figure 12.2. The estate tax operates as an excise tax on the market for bequests. A tax rate of 50 percent, for instance, reduces by half the net bequest from what it would be in the absence of tax. With a downward-sloping demand curve, testators will purchase fewer units of bequests, and heirs will thus receive less than they would have received in the absence of tax. But it does not follow that testators will save less in response to the imposition of the tax. The tax increases the gross price of a unit of bequest; with a 50 percent rate of tax, the price per $1 unit rises to $2. If the demand for bequests is inelastic, the rise in price will induce testators to spend more on bequests than before, even though they leave fewer bequests. Saving, however, is the amount spent on bequests, not the amount received by heirs. Hence, if the demand for bequests is inelastic, the imposition of a tax on bequests will increase the amount people save to leave bequests.

The effect of inheritance taxation on saving is thus an empirical matter, and at present there is no overwhelming consensus. The bulk of evidence at this time seems to support the proposition that the estate tax reduces saving. Michael Boskin has estimated that the

FIGURE 12.2 Effect of Inheritance Taxation on Saving

The demand curve, D, shows the number of bequest units a testator will bequeath at various prices. For simplicity, the dimension of a bequest unit is denoted as \$1, which makes the marginal cost of bequest units constant at \$1, as indicated by MC. In the absence of tax, the testator leaves an estate of B_0 units (or dollars) and pays a price of P_0 (\$1) per unit. Suppose a tax of 50 percent is imposed on the purchase of bequests. The net demand curve, D_n, subtracts the tax from the gross bequest. If bequests remain at B_0, the testator will bequeath the same amount of wealth as he or she bequeathed in the absence of tax but now the state will claim $(P_0 - P_0')B_0$ as tax, leaving $P_0' \cdot B_0$ as the net estate. In response to the tax, the testator will purchase fewer units of bequest, as indicated by the quantity B_1, where D_n intersects MC. The government now claims $(P_1 - P_0)B_1$ as tax, leaving $P_0 \cdot B_1$ as the net estate. The total amount of the testator's saving is the area under the demand curve. If $P_1 \cdot B_1$ is larger than $P_0 \cdot B_0$, which would happen if the demand for bequests were inelastic, total saving would rise even though net bequests would decline. With an elastic demand, though, total saving would decline, as would net bequests.

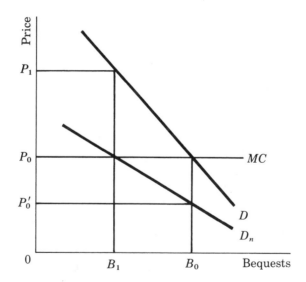

price elasticity of demand for charitable bequests is well in excess of unity and rises with the rate of tax.[10]

Charitable bequests are, of course, different from personal bequests, but it would be difficult to argue that the conditions of demand

[10] Michael J. Boskin, "Estate Taxation and Charitable Bequests," *Journal of Public Economics* 5, no. 1 (1976), pp. 27–56.

are radically different between the two types of bequests. There is, to be sure, some basis for arguing that people are probably less sensitive to changes in the price of personal bequests than they are to changes in the price of charitable bequests. This would reflect a personal preference in which the utility people derive from personal bequests is high compared to the utility they derive from charitable bequests, at least at lower levels of wealth. If this is so, the demand for personal bequests would be less elastic than the demand for charitable bequests. But as wealth rises, charitable bequests become relatively more important. In all, the argument based on price elasticity seems to support the proposition that the taxation of inheritance reduces the amount of saving.

In addition, the argument based on price elasticity is supported by one based on wealth elasticity. Besides raising the price of a unit of bequest, the taxation of bequests reduces the real wealth of the testator. Gary Becker has argued that the wealth elasticity of bequests exceeds unity.[11] If Becker is correct, the reduction in a testator's wealth through the taxing of bequests will reduce bequests by more than the increase in taxation. In other words, a decline of 10 percent in wealth due to the taxation of inheritance will reduce bequests by more than 10 percent. Overall, it seems quite plausible that taxing wealth transfers reduces the amount of saving.[12]

SUGGESTIONS FOR FURTHER READING

Alan A. Tait, *The Taxation of Personal Wealth* (Urbana: University of Illinois Press, 1967), explores wealth taxation as a means of offsetting omissions from the personal income tax. Net worth taxation, which is used in several countries but is not a major revenue source in any of them, is advocated in Lester C. Thurow, *The Impact of Taxes on the American Economy* (New York: Praeger, 1971).

The pioneering analysis of the property tax as a combination of a

[11] Gary S. Becker, "A Theory of Social Interactions," *Journal of Political Economy* 82 (December 1974), pp. 1063–1093.

[12] A further question arises concerning the subsequent use of the tax proceeds vis-à-vis the way the wealth would be used in the absence of the tax. Suppose the demand for bequests were unit elastic, so that saving by the testator will be unchanged by the tax. If the rate of tax is 50 percent, the heir will receive only one-half of what would have been received in the absence of tax, with the state collecting the remainder. If the heir and the state would use their shares of the wealth in essentially the same manner, there would be nothing more to explore. But the heir may maintain his share of the capital stock while the state consumes its share, or vice versa. In either case, there will be subsequent second-order effects on saving and capital formation because of different saving and consumption choices of the various recipients of the estate.

national tax on property and a set of particular taxes on property in particular locations is Peter Mieszkowski, "The Property Tax: An Excise Tax or a Profits Tax?" *Journal of Public Economics* 1 (April 1972), pp.73–96. Mieszkowski's work represents an extension of the analytical framework Arnold Harberger developed for the corporate income tax, which we discussed in Chapter 10; within this perspective of the property tax as essentially a tax on capital, the tax is seen to be progressive when its liability is related to income. The same analytical framework is pursued and the progressivity of the property tax affirmed in Henry J. Aaron, *Who Pays the Property Tax?* (Washington, D.C.: Brookings Institution, 1975).

Dick Netzer is one of the main antagonists to what has become the orthodox view that the property tax is a tax on capital. Although he recognizes some validity in the application of Harberger's model of the corporate income tax to the property tax, Netzer argues that the property tax, while roughly proportional to income, is regressive in its residential component because an important part of the tax operates through increasing the price of housing. A careful discussion of differing perspectives on the incidence of the tax is presented in Dick Netzer, "The Incidence of the Property Tax Revisited," *National Tax Journal* 26 (December 1973), pp. 515–535. Netzer's earlier work, *Economics of the Property Tax* (Washington, D.C.: Brookings Institution, 1966), is a useful survey of numerous aspects of the property tax that reflects more strongly than his subsequent article the formerly standard view that the property tax is paid by consumers of housing, with the business portion of the tax paid by consumers in the form of higher prices for products.

As noted in the text, the relation between income and expenditures on housing is itself open to question. Housing expenditures seem to be at least constant with respect to permanent income and may well rise with it. Even if the tax were assumed to result in higher prices for consumers, the tax would accordingly be proportional or even progressive in relation to permanent income. On the relation between income and housing expenditure, see Margaret G. Reid, *Housing and Income* (Chicago: University of Chicago Press, 1962); and Richard F. Muth, "The Demand for Non-Farm Housing," in *The Demand for Durable Goods*, edited by Arnold C. Harberger (Chicago: University of Chicago Press, 1960), pp. 29–96.

The capitalization into property values of a tax increase that was not accompanied by a change in expenditures occurred in California when the legislature mandated a change in assessment practices that roughly doubled property taxes. A $200 increase in taxes was found to reduce property values by about $2,800, indicating a discount rate of about 7 percent. For a discussion of this episode, see R. Stafford Smith, "Property Tax Capitalization in San Francisco," *National Tax Journal* 23 (June 1970), pp. 177–193.

For a statement of the general necessity to consider public expenditure as well as taxation in exploring possible capitalization into property values, see the seminal study by Wallace E. Oates, "Effects of Property

Taxes and Local Public Spending on Property Values," *Journal of Economy* 77 (December 1969), pp. 957–971. A considerable literature has subsequently developed concerning the capitalization of property taxes, a sample of which includes Matthew Edel and Elliott Sclar, "Taxes, Spending, and Property Values: Supply Adjustment in a Tiebout-Oates Model," *Journal of Political Economy* 82 (October 1974), pp. 941–754; Bruce W. Hamilton, "Capitalization of Intrajurisdictional Differences in Local Tax Prices," *American Economic Review* 66 (December 1976), pp. 743–753; Harvey S. Rosen and David J. Fullerton, "A Note on Local Tax Rates, Public Benefit Levels, and Property Values," *Journal of Political Economy* 85 (April 1977), pp. 433–440; and Jon C. Sonstelie and Paul R. Portney, "Gross Rents and Market Values: Testing the Implications of Tiebout's Hypothesis," *Journal of Urban Economics* 7 (January 1980), pp. 102–118. The work that inspired this whole literature is Charles M. Tiebout, "A Pure Theory of Local Expenditure," *Journal of Political Economy* 64 (October 1956), pp. 416–424.

For argument in support of taxing land values more heavily and reducing the taxation of improvements, see Dick Netzer, "Is There Too Much Reliance on the Local Property Tax?," in *Property Tax Reform*, edited by George E. Peterson (Washington, D.C.: The Urban Institute, 1973), pp. 13–23. Phillip Finkelstein, *Real Property Taxation in New York City* (New York: Praeger, 1975), is a case study that supports some shift of the tax burden in New York City from improvements to land.

Various aspects of inheritance are treated, from somewhat different perspectives, in John A. Brittain, *Inheritance and the Inequality of Wealth* (Washington, D.C.: Brookings Institution, 1978); and Richard E. Wagner, *Inheritance and the State* (Washington, D.C.: American Enterprise Institute, 1977).

13

Borrowing and Inflationary Finance

Instead of taxing people, governments can finance their activities by borrowing from them. This method of finance involves the replacement of present taxes with future taxes, with the future taxes being necessary to pay interest on the debt as well as perhaps eventually to amortize it. Much controversy has arisen over the similarities and differences between taxing and borrowing as methods of financing government, and our main interest in this chapter is to explore the various points of controversy.

Governments may also finance their activities through the creation of money, a method of inflationary finance that has become more prominent in recent years. Although we discuss inflationary finance in this chapter, most of the questions that arise in an examination of money creation and inflationary finance are treated in courses on macroeconomics and monetary theory and so are not considered here. Only to the extent that inflationary finance touches on important aspects of public economics will it be examined here.

WHY DO GOVERNMENTS BORROW?

Not too long ago, it was common for public borrowing to be discussed under the general rubric of "extraordinary finance," to indicate that it was a method of finance used in extraordinary times such as war and depression.[1] Fiscal history with regard to borrowing could be

---

[1] See, for instance, the discussion of public loans versus extraordinary taxes in Antonio de Viti de Marco, *First Principles of Public Finance,* translated from the Italian by Edith Pavlo Marget (London: Jonathan Cape, 1936), pp. 377–398.

written largely in terms of borrowing taking place during wars and depressions, with there being some effort to retire debt during normal times. Between 1795 and 1811, the debt of the federal government was reduced by nearly half, from $83.8 million to $45.2 million. The War of 1812 brought on a series of deficits, but between 1815 and 1836 eighteen surpluses in twenty-one years subsequently reduced the national debt from $127 million to $337,000. A major depression occurred from 1837 to 1843, and four years later the Mexican-American War broke out. The 1850s saw eight years of surplus and then came the Civil War. The national debt was $2.7 billion by the war's end, in 1865, but twenty-eight consecutive years of budget surplus reduced the national debt to $961 million by the end of 1893.

During this period, about 25 percent of all federal expenditure was devoted to amortization of the debt. Federal debt increased during the Spanish-American War to $1.4 billion and was then reduced, though slowly in comparison with earlier experience, to $1.2 billion in 1916. The financing of World War I increased the national debt to $25.5 billion by the end of 1918. Eleven consective years of surplus reduced the debt to $16.2 billion by 1930. Then came the Great Depression and World War II, leaving a national debt of $169.4 billion in 1946. The fourteen years between 1947 and 1960 saw seven years of surplus and seven years of deficit, with essentially no change in the national debt, although the Korean War was also fought during that period.

Only during the past two decades does the record on the use of public borrowing appear to differ significantly from its previous history. In the 1960s, the gross amount of national debt increased from $291 billion to $382 billion, and even this increase in debt was not totally unprecedented, as the Vietnam War was being fought during this period. In the 1970s, generally a period of peace and full employment, the national debt increased from $382 billion to $899 billion, and it has since come to exceed $1 trillion. This recent history suggests that government borrowing is no longer confined to such extraordinary events as wars and depressions, yet most work on borrowing continues to focus on its use in such extraordinary settings.

Borrowing involves an exchange of temporal command over resources. Public borrowing is no different from personal borrowing in this regard. The borrower receives command from the lender over resources now in exchange for giving up command over resources to the lender in the future as the loan is repaid. At base, borrowing does not affect the wealth of the borrower or the lender but only the timing of the use of wealth, although of course this change in timing is mutually advantageous. The borrower receives an asset, in the form of a car, cash, or some other item but also incurs the offsetting liability of a note owed to the lender. The lender reduces one asset, in the form of cash or a car in stock, and receives an offsetting asset in the borrower's note.

The essence of personal borrowing is a change in the timing of the use of wealth. Instead of borrowing to buy a car, a person could reduce current consumption until he had saved enough to buy it. Borrowing allows the borrower to increase consumption in the present while requiring that the borrower decrease consumption in the future to pay the lender. A person might borrow for many reasons. Present consumption might be valued more highly than future consumption. Future income might be thought very likely to be significantly higher than present income, and borrowing transfers some of that income to the present. Present income might have fallen unexpectedly but future prospects remain better, in which case borrowing allows the borrower to achieve some smoothing of the time pattern of consumption. Regardless of the reasons for a decision to borrow, what is mainly involved in such a choice is achieving some more highly desired pattern of consumption through time.

The same reasons that hold for personal borrowing also hold in general for public borrowing; indeed, this point underlies the notion of extraordinary finance. A war might increase public spending substantially above normal levels. The imposition of an extraordinary tax is one means of financing those added expenditures. If this were done, some people would borrow from others to pay their share of that extraordinary tax. If government finances the war by borrowing rather than by taxing its citizens, the public loan in effect replaces the network of private loans that would otherwise have arisen. If the public loan is less costly than the network of private loans as a means of arranging to change the timing of consumption that the war entails, public borrowing becomes an efficient means of financing such extraordinary situations. Borrowing is a way people can smooth out their patterns of consumption through time in situations when government is confronted with sudden, extraordinary variation in its revenues or expenditures. This is not to say that borrowing is only used as a vehicle of extraordinary finance. More recently, borrowing has become an ordinary means of finance as well.[2]

[2] For an examination of the change in borrowing from a means of extraordinary finance to its substantial use for purposes of ordinary finance, see James M. Buchanan and Richard E. Wagner, *Democracy in Deficit* (New York: Academic Press, 1977).

BORROWING VERSUS TAXING:
THE RICARDIAN PERSPECTIVE

What difference does it make, and to whom, whether public expenditures are financed by taxes or by loans? Given the amount of public expenditure to be financed, what, if anything, is the consequence of substituting debt finance for tax finance? With tax finance, the analysis is in principle straightforward. Suppose tax liability is assessed through a proportional tax on personal income. Individual taxpayers will pay for the public output in proportion to their respective incomes. Naturally, the use of different forms of taxation may generate different distributions of the cost of public output among the citizenry. Regardless of which form of taxation is used, the cost of the public expenditure will be borne by taxpayers at the time the expenditure is undertaken.

The central issue in debt finance is whether it is a means of shifting the time the burden is borne — in particular, whether it shifts the burden from present taxpayers to future taxpayers. Suppose the alternative means of financing the expenditure are through a proportional income tax or through the creation of public debt, with that debt subsequently to be amortized by proportional income taxation as well.[3] Starting from a position in which the expenditure is financed by a proportional income tax, what difference will result if the expenditure is financed by the creation of public debt?

At first glance, it might seem obvious that the resort to borrowing shifts the burden of the expenditure from present taxpayers to future taxpayers because taxes are delayed until the future when the debt is amortized. But this is not necessarily correct. Whether public output is financed by taxing or by borrowing, the resources that are devoted to the supply of public output are withdrawn from other uses at the time that output is produced. Consequently, the burden of the expenditure might seem to rest on taxpayers at the time the public expenditure is undertaken. If so, whether financing takes place

---

[3] Debt finance could be compared with a different form of taxation, a tax on corporation income or a progressive income tax, for example. Because the comparison between tax finance per se and debt finance is of interest, it is of central importance that the same form of taxation be used to finance the public expenditure and to amortize the debt. Given the existence of a particular form of taxation to finance the supply of public output, it is of interest whether there is any difference between an expenditure financed currently by taxation or currently by debt issue, with the debt subsequently to be amortized by the same tax that would have been used to finance the expenditure currently. The particular form of tax that is used in the analysis is less important than is the consistent use of that form of tax. The assumption of a proportional income tax is merely a simplifying device that does not alter the central thrust of the analysis.

through current taxation or through debt issue would be irrelevant because the burden of the expenditure is represented by the resources expended, and the utilization of resources necessarily occurs in the present.

This line of argument can be illustrated by war finance. To fight a war, the state must provide various types of military capital. The state could acquire command over the required resources by taxing its citizens at sufficiently high rates. Suppose instead that the state acquires command over those resources by selling bonds to some of its citizenry. Whether the military capital is financed by taxes or by loans, the resources required to produce the military capital are extracted from people at the time the military production takes place. The shift from taxes to loans as a means of financing the war would seem to be merely a matter of bookkeeping. Cost must be borne at the time resources are committed to one use rather than to another, so tax finance and debt finance would seem to be identical: With neither form of finance does it seem possible to shift the burden of public expenditure from the present to the future.

This equivalence of borrowing and taxing is commonly called the *Ricardian equivalence theorem*, after David Ricardo, the English economist who articulated the notion:

> Government might at once have required the twenty millions in the shape of taxes; in which case it would not have been necessary to raise annual taxes to the amount of a million. This, however, would not have changed the nature of the transaction. An individual, instead of being called upon to pay £100 per annum, might have been obliged to pay £2000 once for all. It might also have suited his convenience rather to borrow this £2000, and to pay £100 per annum for interest to the lender, than to spare the larger sum from his own funds.[4]

Ricardo's proposition about the equivalence of borrowing and taxing is one illustration of the conceptual equivalence of capital and income. With a 5 percent rate of interest, a perpetual liability for annual payments of £100 is equal to a current liability to make a single payment of £2000. Whether an extraordinary tax is levied currently or the government borrows the revenues and amortizes the debt in the future is inessential; in either case current taxpayers experience a reduction in wealth equal to their share in the extraordinary tax that was financed instead by borrowing. Granted, some taxpayers may prefer borrowing to the extraordinary tax because they have strong preferences for present consumption. In the event the

---

[4] David Ricardo, *Principles of Political Economy and Taxation* (1817; Homewood, Ill.: Richard D. Irwin, 1963), p. 139.

extraordinary tax was imposed, those taxpayers would have borrowed to finance their tax payments and in doing so would have assumed a liability for debt repayment that was equivalent in present value to their share in the extraordinary tax. Public borrowing replaces a network of individual borrowings and repayments, possibly saving on transaction costs in the process.

Debt finance simultaneously involves two distinct transactions. With one transaction, bondholders give up present purchasing power to government in exchange for a greater amount of purchasing power in the future (that is, repayment of principal plus payment of interest on that principal). With the other transaction, taxpayers avoid paying tax in the present by incurring an obligation to pay tax in the future. Debt finance allows taxpayers to defer paying for public output until taxes are assessed to amortize the debt. Debt finance does not, however, make taxpayers any wealthier because the present value of the future tax payments they incur by virtue of the borrowing is equal to the one-time reduction in consumption they would have incurred under tax finance.

In effect, public borrowing is a means by which people with relatively low preference for present consumption lend to those with relatively high preference for present consumption. All people will be taxpayers, but only some will be bondholders. Although bondholders will be taxpayers, their liability for taxes to amortize public debt will be substantially less than the value of the debt they hold. Bondholding taxpayers can be thought of as net bondholders, but for linguistic simplicity the central distinction in the following discussion is between taxpayers and bondholders, recognizing that the bondholders' perspective as taxpayers is overshadowed by their perspective as bondholders.

Public borrowing alters intertemporal patterns of personal consumption. The replacement of tax finance by debt finance can be looked on as an agreement between bondholders and taxpayers in which bondholders agree to contribute additional resources toward the supply of public output in exchange for the agreement of taxpayers to make compensating payments in the future. Debt finance thus allows taxpayers to defer paying their share of the cost of supplying public output by borrowing from bondholders in the present and repaying them in the future. Debt finance clearly entails a different intertemporal location of the cost of public output than tax finance, just as buying a car on credit entails a different intertemporal location of cost than buying one for cash. The essence of debt finance is that it accommodates individual differences in time preference by allowing people who do not want to reduce their present consumption to borrow from those who are willing to do so. Taxpayers cannot, however, escape the burden of that public output; they can only postpone the time when the actual reduction in consumption occurs.

This view that debt finance is not a method by which the cost of public output can be shifted from present taxpayers to future taxpayers should not be confused with the proposition that the imposition of taxes to amortize debt represents no burden to society because "we owe it to ourselves," as the adage goes. The treatment of debt interest within the national income accounts reflects acceptance of this adage because such payments are treated as transfer payments and not as income payments for services rendered. If a nation is thought of as a single person and if all debt is owed by members of the nation, in one sense it can be said that the members owe their nation's debt to themselves, which gives the imposition of taxes to pay the obligations that the debt entails the appearance of a transfer payment from one pocket to another.

This perspective can be applied equally to the payment associated with any transaction. A customer, for instance, pays a farmer $1 for a dozen eggs. If the accounts of the customer and the farmer are added together, as they are from the perspective of national income accounting, the exchange of the eggs and the dollar is seen merely as a transfer. All transactions can be looked on as transfer payments from such an ex post accounting point of view. The test of whether a particular transaction constitutes a transfer payment or a payment for services rendered resides in the absence or presence of agreement among the parties. A transfer payment represents a taking from one person and a giving to another, and so will not be agreeable to at least one of the parties. But mutual agreeableness describes the relationship between the farmer and the customer, and market transactions generally. Both the farmer and the customer are better off by virtue of the transaction, and the $1 represents a payment in exchange for services rendered, rather than a transfer payment.

Does the payment of taxes for interest and debt amortization represent only a transfer of wealth, or does it represent payment for services rendered? If the repayment of debt is said to constitute a transfer payment, the initial creation of the debt must have constituted a transfer payment as well. Or if the initial payment of debt constituted a mutually agreeable exchange, the subsequent payment for interest and amortization must constitute payment for services rendered. In the absence of public borrowing, the imposition of an extraordinary tax will lead those with relatively high preferences for present consumption to borrow from those with relatively high preferences for future consumption. When the borrowers subsequently pay principal and interest to the lenders, the payment of interest is treated as a payment for a service rendered — namely, for the borrower's being able to achieve a more desirable pattern of consumption over time — and such payments of interest are treated as income in the national income accounts.

Public borrowing essentially involves a replacement of a network of individual borrowings with a public borrowing. The debt transaction is agreeable to the lenders, who choose to become net bondholders rather than net taxpayers, and it is simultaneously agreeable to the borrowers, who choose to remain net taxpayers rather than undergo an immediate reduction in their consumption by becoming net bondholders. Interest payments on public debt, then, would seem to be as much a payment for services rendered as are interest payments on other forms of financial transactions.

CAN PUBLIC BORROWING BURDEN THE FUTURE?

It is possible to conceptualize public debt as the replacement of a network of individual debt transactions with a single transaction made by government. But how reasonable is this conceptualization? Is it the case that public debt entails no essential difference from tax finance? Or is this proposition about equivalence simply a possibility, with nonequivalence also a possibility? David Ricardo, who articulated the proposition about equivalence, thought that actual equivalence was unlikely:

> From what I have said, it must not be inferred that I consider the system of borrowing as the best calculated to defray the extraordinary expenses of the state. It is a system which tends to make us less thrifty — to blind us to our real situation. If the expenses of a war be 40 millions per annum, and the share which a man would have to contribute towards that annual expense were £100, he would endeavour, on being at once called upon for his portion, to save speedily the £100 from his income. By the system of loans, he is called upon to pay only the interest of his £100, or £5 per annum, and considers that he does enough by saving this £5 from his expenditure, and then deludes himself with the belief that he is as rich as before.[5]

If people systematically underestimate the future tax payments that public borrowing entails, they will perceive themselves as being wealthier than they really are. This possibility is referred to as *debt illusion*, and it is a controversial point. It is one thing to say that people will not be perfectly accurate in assessing the present conse-

[5] Ibid., p. 140.

quences of future tax obligations entailed by public borrowing. Making mistakes is not contrary to the principles of economic analysis. Economics, after all, takes people as they are, and making mistakes is a normal part of life. The argument grounded in debt illusion, however, does more than imply that people make mistakes. It implies that a systematic bias occurs in those mistakes. With debt illusion, it is not a matter of some people underestimating the present value of the reduction in wealth that public debt entails while other people overestimate the present value of that reduction. Rather, it is that most, if not all, people underestimate the present value of the wealth reduction, which in turn leads them to consume more than they would under tax finance.

Arguments based on illusion have generally been greeted with skepticism in economics, principally because no generally satisfactory argument has yet been developed within a theory of learning as to why such perceptual errors will be systematically biased rather than randomly distributed about the correct perception. Regardless of the controversial status of debt illusion, there are other, less controversial reasons why taxpayers might see debt finance as less costly than tax finance. If such a difference in perceptions of cost exists, debt issue can be a means of shifting the burden of public output from the present set of taxpayers to a future set.

If private borrowing in the face of extraordinary expenditure is used instead of public borrowing, the liability for debt amortization resides with the borrower. Should the borrower die before the obligation has been fulfilled, the remaining obligation becomes a claim on the borrower's estate. And should that borrower migrate to another country, the debt obligation remains, although in this case the remedy available to the lender in the event of default depends on the existence of treaties between the two nations regarding such matters.

When national debt is issued, however, no personal obligations are created. There is an obligation to collect taxes in the future to make the payments of interest and principal, but there is no personalized liability assigned to specific people. Migration can allow a person to escape liability for debt amortization as can death. This is not to say that a person will choose to die to escape paying taxes to cover debt amortization, but there can be systematic variation in the cost of debt finance relative to tax finance, depending on someone's life expectancy as a taxpayer. Moreover, a person's life expectancy as a taxpayer will generally be shorter than actual life expectancy, because the years of retirement often mean little or no payment of taxes.

Consider the choice between paying an extraordinary tax of $1,000 now or issuing a perpetual bond (a consol) that pays $100 per year, which is illustrated in Table 13.1. With an interest rate of 10 percent, these two methods of finance are equivalent: both have present values of $1,000. But with public finance, obligations under debt finance do not become part of a taxpayer's estate. For someone with a taxpaying life expectancy of ten years, the present value of financing government through public debt is only $614. For such a person, public borrowing reduces the cost of government by nearly 40 percent from what it would be under tax finance. For someone with a taxpaying life expectancy of twenty years, the present value under loan finance is $851, which still represents a 15 percent reduction in the cost of public output compared with that cost under tax finance. For someone relatively young, say with forty years of taxpaying life expectancy, the present value of loan finance is $978, or practically the same as it would be under tax finance.

With higher rates of discount, the divergence between loan finance and tax finance would become larger. The ability of public debt to shift some burden from present members of society to future members need not arise from illusion, for this ability can also arise because of systematic differences in constraints confronted by people of different ages.

The extent to which someone will treat loan finance as less costly than tax finance because the imminence of death (or retirement) reduces the present value of loan finance depends also on the extent that people treat those who survive them as extensions of themselves. Suppose each couple in society exactly reproduce themselves and treat their survivors as extensions of themselves. In such a model, the passing of generations into history is of no consequence, for the effect of the model is to treat people as if they live forever; debt finance is equivalent to tax finance, and so the choice between the two methods of finance would have no consequence for the relation between present and future generations. In this context, an increase

---

TABLE 13.1 Cost of Public Debt and Taxpaying Life Expectancy

Taxpaying Life Expectancy	Present Value of Debt [a]
10 years	$614
20 years	851
40 years	978

[a] Burden of repayment is assumed to be $100 per year indefinitely, with an interest rate of 10 percent.

in public borrowing will be accompanied by an increase in saving that would be sufficient to pay the remaining tax liability at the time of death. Borrowing replaces a present liability with a future liability. If people do not use this postponement of payment as a means of placing some of the cost of public spending on future taxpayers, they must increase their current saving by an amount sufficient to pay the future tax obligations that will remain after their death.

Whether, or the extent to which, public borrowing can shift wealth from people in the future to people in the present depends, then, on the strength of this bond between generations, which has been called the *intergenerational bequest motive*. As we saw in Chapter 12, a bequest motive seems to be an element in personal saving decisions, but such a motive can be present without leading people to treat their heirs as extensions of themselves. Whether an increase in public debt will bring about an increase in saving is an empirical question. The answer will provide information about the strength of the bequest motive.

On this point, Randall Holcombe, John Jackson, and Asghar Zardkoohi have examined the relationship between debt creation and saving, and they estimate that about 20 percent of the increase in debt is compensated for by an increase in savings.[6] They developed this estimate by constructing a model of saving between 1929 and 1976 in which per capita real saving was estimated to be a function, among several other variables, of public debt creation during the year. They estimated the coefficient on the debt variable to be 0.20 and found it statistically to be significantly greater than zero and less than one. This coefficient indicates that a $100 increase in government debt will, other things remaining the same, increase saving by $20. Their finding suggests that present taxpayers act to some extent to increase their saving in response to the creation of public debt, but it also suggests that to an even larger degree they push the burden of the debt onto future taxpayers.

With debt finance, people increase their consumption compared with what it would be under tax finance. They do not increase their saving sufficiently to offset the future tax liability the debt entails, according to the evidence compiled by Holcombe, Jackson, and Zard-

[6] Randall G. Holcombe, John D. Jackson, and Asghar Zardkoohi, "The National Debt Controversy," *Kyklos* 34, no. 2 (1981), pp. 186–202. A related argument, along with supporting evidence, is presented in Randall G. Holcombe and Asghar Zardkoohi, "Public Investment in a Democracy," *Southern Economic Journal* 47 (July 1980), pp. 210–217. A reinforcing line of argument, also with supporting evidence, is developed in W. Mark Crain and Robert B. Ekelund, Jr., "Deficits and Democracy," *Southern Economic Journal* 44 (April 1978), pp. 813–828.

koohi. If this evidence is accurate, borrowing is not equivalent to taxation because borrowing brings about an increase in the consumption of present taxpayers. This larger consumption concomitantly reduces the consumption opportunities available to future taxpayers because it lowers the future capital stock from what it would otherwise have been. To recognize this difference between tax finance and loan finance is not necessarily to render any specific normative judgment. If future generations will generally be wealthier than the present generation, debt finance seems to be one means of allowing the present generation to capture some of that increased future wealth. Moreover, the present generation may bequeath a larger stock of public capital to future generations, and the increase in public debt may be a way of passing onward some amount of offsetting liability.[7]

BORROWING BY STATE AND
LOCAL GOVERNMENTS

Debt finance can shift some of the burden of public expenditures onto future taxpayers as long as present taxpayers do not increase their saving sufficiently to amortize the debt. Present taxpayers would rationally do this as long as they do not view heirs as extensions of themselves. Present taxpayers might also prefer debt to tax finance if they expected to emigrate. With respect to the national government, emigration is of little significance. But state and local governments can also choose between debt and tax finance, and people can emigrate among such units of government within a nation. Conceptually, an increase in the likelihood of emigration is equivalent to a reduction in taxpaying life expectancy.

For state and local governments, it might seem at first glance that debt finance might operate even more strongly than at the national level to place the burden of public expenditures on future taxpayers. With tax finance, residents of the locality must reduce their disposable income to pay for public output. But with debt finance, disposable income is unaffected initially because the public output is financed by borrowing, with the bulk of the lending coming from people who reside in other parts of the nation. Should people leave the locality before the debt is amortized, it might seem as though they have been able to escape paying for public output because the obligation for debt amortization resides with the locality

---

[7] On the contrary, however, the present generation may bequeath a smaller capital stock as a result of environmental degradation or war.

and not with individual residents. A resident who moves prior to amortization cannot be held liable for a share of the cost of amortization.

Debt finance might not operate so easily to increase the net wealth of taxpayers in a particular locality, however. Suppose local governments can finance their activities either by borrowing or by imposing a property tax and that all local residents own property within the locality. An issue of debt by the locality is used to reduce the property tax, with this debt to be amortized over ten years. For residents who anticipate residing in the locality more than ten years, public output is equally costly under debt finance and tax finance. Borrowing reduces taxes initially, but amortization raises taxes in subsequent years, and the present value of those higher taxes is equal to the amount of the initial tax reduction. For those residents, the situation is precisely the one described by the Ricardian equivalence theorem.

It might seem that residents who anticipate leaving before ten years have passed can escape liability for the debt and escape it more fully the sooner they move, which implies that the shift from tax finance to loan finance increases their wealth. But how are they able to escape this liability for debt amortization? They own property in the locality, and the debt is to be amortized by the imposition of higher future taxes on property. The future taxes that debt finance requires create, in effect, a lien against property in the locality, and this quasi-lien is essentially equivalent to an increase in the mortgage against the property. Unlike the necessity to pay off the mortgage, the owner will not have to pay this future tax at the time of migration when the house is sold. Should people have knowledge of the quasi-lien that debt finance entails, houses in that locality will sell for less because of the future tax assessment implied by the debt.

Future tax payments will tend to be capitalized into the value of property in the locality issuing the debt. No one locality will be able to affect the market rate of return to investment in housing. Suppose initially that equivalent houses sell for $50,000 in different localities, and one locality has substituted debt for taxes so that the present value of the additional future taxes is $2,000. In a competitive market for housing, property in this locality will tend to sell for $48,000 because only at this price will the rate of return on housing be equal to that in other localities. Although the subsequent owner ends up making the nominal payment of tax, the actual payment has been made by the initial property owner who received less for the property because the debt liability made the property less attractive to potential buyers. The ownership of property and the use of the property tax to finance local government converts local borrowing into a quasi-personal obligation of property owners.[8]

TAXATION THROUGH INFLATION

Government may also be financed through the creation of money. (Private individuals may also, of course, finance their activities through the creation of money, and this is called counterfeiting.) The effect of money creation is to reduce the value of the stock of previously existing money. Whether money is created by private individuals or by government, its value declines as each unit of money is able to command fewer goods than it could before the money expansion. That is, it requires more units of money to acquire command over goods than it required before the money expansion. This general rise in prices, or, alternatively, this decline in the value of money, is what is meant by *inflation.*

In numerous historical episodes governments have directly resorted to creating money to finance their activities. The operation of such inflationary finance may be illustrated quite simply. Suppose a government prints money equal to the existing stock of money. The existing stock of money will subsequently be worth only one-half of its former value, and the creation of money by government constitutes a tax on the holders of money essentially equivalent to the imposition of a 50 percent tax on existing money stocks. The burden of the tax is distributed among citizens in proportion to their holding of money. In the case of a forthright tax on money stocks, assuming such a tax could be enforced, people will lose one-half of their money balances to the government. But when government creates new money, each person's nominal money balance remains unchanged, and the tax reduces the real value of those balances by half. In either case

[8] Recognition that local residents may be renters rather than property owners does nothing to change the effective transformation of the property tax into a quasi-personal obligation of property owners, assuming the property tax to be paid by suppliers of capital. Should the property tax be paid by consumers of housing, a quite different situation can arise, particularly in instances where renters are a majority in the locality. In this case, debt finance offers renters an opportunity to avoid paying for public output. By replacing taxes with borrowing, renters can avoid the future taxes to amortize the debt by emigrating before the debt is amortized. Renters would have an incentive to favor borrowing over taxing, and in communities where renters are dominant a rising amount of debt might be anticipated. But if the property tax is paid by suppliers of capital, the choice between borrowing and taxing will be inessential for renters, and no conflict of interest between renters and property owners will arise, at least with regard to the different methods of financing public output.

a tax has been imposed on the money balances people possess. Inflation, or money creation, is therefore one means of taxation, the burden of which is distributed roughly in proportion to the ownership of money balances.

Within the prevailing American monetary system, the government does not directly create money. Instead, money is created as the Federal Reserve system increases its ownership of national debt. Money creation thus involves the use of national debt, and this process of monetary expansion is referred to as *debt monetization*. This means that the government is immediately responsible for borrowing, but not for money creation or inflation.

Borrowing and inflation, however, are confounded within our present monetary system because both occur through transactions in national debt. The government borrows by incurring obligations to make future payments, and money creation takes place when the Federal Reserve system buys government debt. Such purchases of debt increase the quantity of reserves in the banking system, and these reserves supply a base for the expansion of bank lending and deposit creation. In principle, whether the Federal Reserve system increases or decreases its ownership of national debt, or the rate at which it does so, bears no necessary relationship to whether the federal budget is in surplus or deficit or to the amount of that surplus or deficit. In principle, the Federal Reserve system can increase its ownership of national debt even though the federal budget is in surplus and the federal government is retiring its debt. It may also reduce its ownership of national debt even though the federal budget is in deficit, with the national debt thereby expanding.

Immediate responsibility for money creation and inflation rests with the Federal Reserve system, not with the federal government. Moreover, within a fractional reserve system of banking, most of the tax revenues represented by the decline in the real money balances of existing holders of money will accrue to the banking system and not to the government. Nonetheless, there is reason to think that some positive association exists between government budget policies and subsequent money creation, particularly if the Ricardian equivalence theorem does not hold completely. Although the Federal Reserve system is nominally independent of the government, there is reason to think that a general congruence of interests will arise, especially if the same party controls both the executive and legislative branches of the government.

Assume, for example, that government runs a balanced budget. The ability of individuals to borrow is limited by the willingness of people to lend. People who save have chosen to relinquish their control over resources now in exchange for repayment of principal and interest at some later time. Repayment is made by borrowers or investors, and this repayment is made possible by the yield on the investment. The rate of interest indicates the rate of return to savers from lending, but it is also the price of borrowing. Consequently, the higher the rate of interest, the greater the amount of saving but the less the desired amount of borrowing. Figure 13.1 illustrates this point and shows the impact of government borrowing in the absence of debt monetization. If the government runs a budget deficit, the demand for loanable funds will increase by the amount of the deficit. The resulting excess demand for loans will lead to a rise in the rate of interest, owing to the competition among borrowers for funds. As

---

FIGURE 13.1   Budget Deficits and the Market for Loanable Funds

The demand for loans on the part of investors is described by D_1, and the supply of loans by savers is described by S. The equilibrium quantity of loans (and saving) will be L_0 and the rate of interest will be R_0. The demand curve D_2 adds the government's deficit to the private demand for loanable funds. The rate of interest will rise to R_1 and the quantity of loans (and saving) will rise to L_1. Of this quantity, $L_1 - L_1'$ is taken by government, leaving l_1' for private investors. The budget deficit has crowded out $L_0 - L_1'$ of private investment.

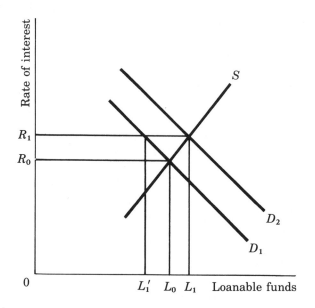

the rate of interest rises, some potential borrowers will curtail their desire to borrow. This process of reduction in the amount of loans must continue until the excess demand for loans disappears.

Suppose in the absence of the budget deficit that the rate of interest would be 8 percent and the amount of saving and borrowing would be $100 billion. Now introduce a budget deficit of $40 billion. The $140 billion of desired borrowing exceeds the $100 billion of desired saving. This excess demand for loans will drive the rate of interest above 8 percent, which reduces the amount that borrowers wish to borrow. They might wish to borrow $100 billion at an 8 percent rate of interest, but only $85 billion at 9 percent.

The rise in the rate of interest also increases the desire of people to save to, say, $105 billion at a 9 percent rate of interest. The rate of interest will continue to rise until the excess demand for loans disappears. Should this require the rate of interest to rise to 10 percent, the amount of saving is $110 billion. Government will borrow $40 billion of this total, and private citizens will borrow the remaining $70 billion. The $40 billion budget deficit will have crowded out $30 billion of private investment, for private borrowing will have been reduced from $100 billion to $70 billion.

There is likely to be political gain from some resistance to this crowding out. The government will have chosen the budget deficit because the governing party thinks that deficits strengthen its political support more than a reduction in expenditure or an increase in taxes would. Suppose the gain in political support varies directly with the degree of diffusion of the costs of the deficits over the population. A cost of $10 billion spread over 100 million people would generally provoke less opposition than the same cost spread over only one million people. When budget deficits are financed by genuine borrowing, the costs of deficit finance are concentrated on the investors who are crowded out.

In contrast, money creation diffuses the cost more generally among the population, as Figure 13.2 illustrates. With debt monetization, the supply of loanable funds is no longer limited to what people save. Money creation shifts outward the supply of loanable funds, creating an excess supply. This excess supply puts downward pressure on the rate of interest, and this decline in the rate of interest will reduce the amount of private saving. Consistent with Figure 13.2, suppose the rate of interest that ultimately results is 9 percent and that people save $105 billion at this rate. When the money creation of $10 billion is added, the total amount of loanable funds supplied is $115 billion. With $40 billion being used to finance the government's budget deficit, $75 billion remains available for private investors. As

FIGURE 13.2 Debt Monetization and the Market for
Loanable Funds

The curves D_1 and D_2 and the supply curve S_1 have the same meaning as
in Figure 13.1, as do the rates of interest R_1 and R_0 and the amounts of
loanable funds (and saving) L_1', L_0, and L_1. Figure 13.2 adds debt
monetization to Figure 13.1, represented by an outward shift in the supply
of loanable funds to S_2, where the horizontal distance between S_1 and S_2
represents the amount of money created. The rate of interest falls from R_1
in the absence of debt monetization to R_2, which is still higher than it
would be in the absence of the budget deficit, R_0. The total amount of
loanable funds supplied is L_2, of which L_2^* comes from saving and the
remainder comes from money creation. The government borrows $L_2 - L_2'$,
leaving L_2' for private investors. In this case, the amount of crowding out is
$L_0 - L_2'$, which is less by $L_2' - L_1'$ than what it would be without debt
monetization.

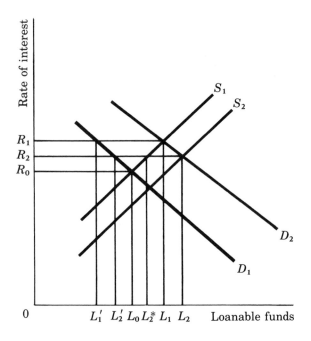

a result of the debt monetization, the amount of crowding out is
reduced from \$30 billion to \$25 billion. Debt monetization reduces
the extent of crowding out because the inflation in the stock of money
is used to provide the resources necessary to finance the additional
private investment. The money creation reduces the real value of

the existing stock of money, and this erosion of value provides the means for reducing the extent of crowding out.[9]

By diffusing the cost of deficit finance, a budget deficit accompanied by some debt monetization would seem likely to evoke less opposition than a deficit unaccompanied by monetization. Should the interests of the governing party be reflected in the actions of the Federal Reserve system, budget deficits seem likely to result in money creation as debt monetization is used to offset some of the crowding out that would otherwise occur. Because the Federal Reserve system is nominally independent of the government, debt monetization is unlikely to proceed in the same manner as it would if monetary expansion were directly under governmental control. The interests of the banking system, however, also seem generally to be facilitated by debt monetization, and as the Federal Reserve system reflects banking interests, some debt monetization can also be anticipated in response to budget deficits.

IS ECONOMIC INSTABILITY POLITICALLY INSPIRED?

Discussions of postwar economic policy have largely reflected the implicit political assumption that the process of policy formation will put the tools of economic policy to the best possible use, limited only by such things as irreducible ignorance, unavoidable errors, or unforeseeable events. In recent years much interest has emerged in the possibility that in pursuing its political interests an incumbent government might use economic policy in ways that promote economic disorder. This disorder might arise inadvertently as a by-product of other policies or it might arise directly as a policy objective. In either case, recognition that public policy emerges from a political process, facets of which were explored in Part II, has only recently begun to be incorporated into the analysis of economic policy.

One of the interesting lines of recent thought concerning efforts to integrate the economic interests of incumbent governments into the formation of economic policy has been a recognition that government may sometimes act to create economic instability rather than acting to alleviate it. In large measure, most literature on economic

[9] The increase in prices owing to the monetary expansion will also lead to an upward shift in the nominal rate of interest. Figure 13.2 does not account for this inflation premium, but the analysis could easily be modified to do so. The result would be a more complicated narrative, but with no change in the essential point of the analysis.

policy has tacitly assumed either that an incumbent government will act selflessly to promote economic stability or that its own political survival will require it to promote such stability. But if the interests of the government actually are enhanced by policies that create instability, the promotion of stability is unlikely to be pursued single-mindedly.

Policies are instruments available to a party in its efforts to maintain its incumbency. Numerous observers have suggested that a systematic relationship exists between general economic conditions and political success. Such economic indicators as rates of inflation and unemployment seem to vary inversely with the electoral prospects of the incumbent government, while an indicator such as the growth of real income seems to vary positively. If this is so, incumbent governments might try to use economic policy to enhance their electoral prospects.

In several related studies, Bruno Frey and Friedrich Schneider have examined the relation between these economic indicators and the popularity of incumbent governments.[10] They found that incumbent governments become less popular as rates of inflation and unemployment increase, but they become more popular as the rate of growth in real consumption increases. They also found that incumbent governments use their budgetary powers to change programs of public expenditure to enhance their electoral prospects. While the findings in other studies differ among themselves in many ways, they give a fairly consistent portrayal of the ability of economic conditions to influence the political success of incumbent governments and of the effort of incumbent governments to use economic policy to influence their electoral prospects. These studies generally support the notion that there is some inconsistency between the promotion of economic stability and the attainment of electoral success.

A simple formulation of how an incumbent government might be able to enhance its electoral prospects through the creation of economic instability is described in Figure 13.3. We assume that inflation and unemployment are evaluated negatively by voters, who are less likely to support the incumbent government as the rates of inflation and unemployment increase. The ability of the incumbent

[10] Their general framework is presented in Bruno S. Frey and Friedrich Schneider, "On the Modelling of Politico-Economic Interdependence," *European Journal of Political Research* 3 (December 1975), pp. 339–360. Also see Frey and Schneider, "An Empirical Study of Politico-Economic Interaction in the United States," *Review of Economics and Statistics* 60 (May 1978), pp. 174–183, and "A Politico-Economic Model of the United Kingdom," *Economic Journal* 88 (June 1978), pp. 243–253.

FIGURE 13.3   Economic Conditions, Policy, and Electoral Support

Assume the state of an economy can be described by its rates of inflation and unemployment. The preferences of voters are described by the indifference curves that rise toward the origin. These indifference curves represent the probability that the incumbent government will be reelected. For instance, i_1u_1 might represent, say, 56:44 odds that the incumbent government will be reelected, whereas the indifference curve i_2u_2 represents 52:48 odds, with the incumbent's odds of success declining as the economic indicators move toward the upper right.

It is also assumed that the economy faces a short-run trade-off as described by the pp curves, although the long-run Phillips curve is vertical at P. If the economy is initially in long-run equilibrium at a, an incumbent government can increase its electoral prospects by pursuing an inflationary policy that moves the economy to b. The reduction in unemployment will be temporary, as described by the movement to c, where all that remains is inflation. Should a deflationary policy then be pursued, the economy would initially move to d, where the incumbent government's popularity would be low, but as the economy adjusted to the lower prices, a would be attained once again.

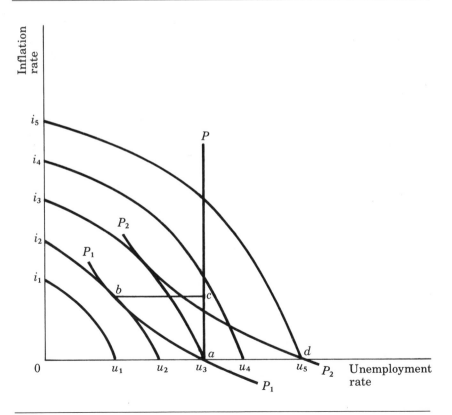

government to influence economic conditions is described by a Phillips-curve relationship between inflation and unemployment. Figure 13.3 assumes that no long-run trade-off occurs between the two variables but that a short-run trade-off is exploitable by the incumbent government.

Within this framework it is easy to describe how politically induced instability could increase the electoral prospects of the incumbent government. If the incumbent party is able to pursue an inflationary policy that reduces unemployment in the short run, electoral support will increase, as represented by the movement from *a* to *b*. Inflation will be able to stimulate employment only in the short run while anticipations about future prices are incorrect. These incorrect anticipations reflect an inability of producers to distinguish with full clarity between a general rise in prices and a relative rise in the particular prices for their output. As these anticipations become correct, inflation will lose its ability to stimulate employment. Consequently, the natural rate of unemployment, described by the long-run Phillips curve, will again be attained.

A temporary reduction in unemployment will be purchased by a permanent inflation of prices, as represented by the movement from *b* to *c*. If the incumbent government then maintains a stable policy until the next election, it will face lower odds of success than it faced in the previous election, as can be seen by a comparison of *a* and *c* (or by a comparison of *b* and the corresponding point of tangency on the short-run Phillips curve through *c*). However, the incumbent government could pursue a deflationary policy after the election, moving the economy to the position of low popularity described by *d*. As people come to anticipate correctly the lower level of inflation in the economy, the short-run Phillips curve will shift downward until the natural rate of unemployment is attained again, this time at the inflationless position described by *a*.

An electoral cycle is the result. An inflationary policy, described by the movement from *a* to *b*, is instituted before the election to gain support. The long-run erosion of the government's support caused by the permanent inflation described by *c* is eliminated by incurring still greater disfavor by pursuing a deflationary policy, described by the movement to *d*, after the election but well in advance of the next election. When the next election draws near, the incumbent government is ready to repeat the cycle.

Within this common analytical framework, voters are seen as weighting recent experiences more heavily than more distant experiences. A policy that provides for a constant rate of unemployment and inflation over the entire electoral period will be less successful in achieving political support than a policy that contracts an economy soon after an election and expands it before the next election. In principle, this analytical framework yields a stable business cycle that has a period equal to the length of the election period.

Such stability is not, of course, part of economic experience. Economies cannot be controlled as simply as some of the models suggest. Moreover, to assume that such an electoral cycle can be repeated indefinitely is to assume that voters are myopic and remain so in the long run. Voters who are assumed to prefer stability to instability nonetheless support the government that creates instability. They do this because their evaluation of that government weights recent experiences more heavily than distant experiences, which in turn implies that voters never recognize that they are being manipulated according to the timing of elections. These questions of myopia notwithstanding, what is especially noteworthy about the emerging interest in integrating the electoral interests of incumbent governments and the conduct of economic policy is that it represents a recognition that the conduct of economic policy will reflect the interests of the governing party, even though those interests may run contrary to some notion of general interest.

Once self-interest is introduced as a consideration in the formation of economic policy, a focus on rates of inflation and unemployment requires some displacement. Suppose there is some inverse statistical relation between, say, the rate of unemployment and a measure of support for an incumbent party. This evidence might show a 55 percent chance of electoral success when the unemployment rate is 5 percent and only a 45 percent chance of success when the unemployment rate is 10 percent, given the rate of inflation. A reduction in the rate of unemployment increases the total amount of working time within the population. This increase is not distributed uniformly among the population but rather is concentrated among particular people.

An inverse relation between the unemployment rate and the degree of support for the incumbent party may exist because a rise in unemployment indicates a reduction in real income for some people, and these people will be less likely to support the incumbent party. The success of the policy would thus result not because of the general or aggregate increase in working time but because this increase is concentrated in particular people, who will be more likely to support the incumbent party. The success of the policy thus seems better understood in its impact on individuals and their real incomes rather than in its impact on some aggregate measure of unemployment.

The last word on the relation between the electoral interests of incumbent governments and the conduct of economic policy, includ-

ing questions of whether that interest may in some instances promote instability over stability, is certainly not in sight. The entire
interest in the topic reflects the growing interest in trying to understand the actual conduct of economic policy as reflecting the operation of self-interest within a particular institutional order rather than
looking at policy outcomes as the choices of some benevolent, self-
effacing public officials who try their best but who sometimes fall
innocent victims to ignorance, error, or unforeseen events.

SUGGESTIONS FOR FURTHER READING

Robert J. Barro, "Are Government Bonds Net Wealth?" *Journal of
Political Economy* 82 (December 1974), pp. 1095–1017, develops a
model of overlapping generations that treats households as if they existed forever and shows that an increase in public borrowing will elicit
an offsetting increase in private saving, so that taxpayers at the time
the debt is created will not act as if their wealth has been increased.
Starting from this equivalence of borrowing and taxing, Robert J. Barro,
"On the Determination of the Public Debt," *Journal of Political Economy* 87 (October 1979), pp. 940–971, explains the creation of public
debt as an effort to minimize the present value of the excess burden
associated with raising revenue when there are intermittent occurrences
of extraordinary expenditures. For further discussion of these points, see
Robert J. Barro, "Public Debt and Taxes," in *Federal Tax Reform: Myths
and Realities,* edited by Michael J. Boskin (San Francisco: Institute
for Contemporary Studies, 1978), pp. 189–209.

James M. Buchanan, *Public Principles of Public Debt* (Homewood,
Ill.: Richard D. Irwin, 1958), provides the modern classic statement of
the ability of loan finance to shift the burden of public output to taxpayers in the future. Buchanan's book sparked an intense controversy soon
after its publication. *Public Debt and Future Generations,* edited by
James M. Ferguson (Chapel Hill: University of North Carolina Press,
1964), reprints many of the articles that arose in this controversy. George
C. Daly, "The Burden of the Debt and Future Generations in Local
Finance," *Southern Economic Journal* 36 (July 1969), pp. 44–51, discusses the capitalization into property values of borrowing by local governments.

The ability of inflation to serve as a form of taxation is explored in
Milton Friedman, "Government Revenue from Inflation," *Journal of
Political Economy* 79 (August 1971), pp. 846–856. Like other forms of
taxation, inflation also entails an excess burden. For examinations of this
excess burden, see Martin J. Bailey, "The Welfare Cost of Inflationary
Finance," *Journal of Political Economy* 64 (April 1956), pp. 93–110;
and Alvin L. Marty, "Growth and the Welfare Cost of Inflationary
Finance," *Journal of Political Economy* 75 (February 1967), pp. 71–76.
For an analysis of crowding out, see Keith M. Carlson and Roger W.

Spencer, "Crowding Out and Its Critics," *Federal Reserve Bank of St. Louis, Review* 57 (December 1975), pp. 2–17.

Edward R. Tufte, *Political Control of the Economy* (Princeton: Princeton University Press, 1978), finds evidence for the pro-cyclical use of economic policy as a means of enhancing electoral prospects in nineteen of the twenty-seven democracies he surveyed. A sample of efforts to explore conceptual foundations of what is sometimes referred to as the political business cycle are William D. Nordhaus, "The Political Business Cycle," *Review of Economic Studies* 42 (April 1975), pp. 169–190; C. Duncan MacRae, "A Political Model of the Business Cycle," *Journal of Political Economy* 85 (April 1977), pp. 239–263; Bruno S. Frey, "Politico-Economic Models and Cycles," *Journal of Public Economics* 9 (April 1978), pp. 203–220; and Richard E. Wagner, "Boom and Bust: The Political Economy of Economic Disorder," *Journal of Libertarian Studies* 4 (Winter 1980), pp. 1–37. *Models of Political Economy,* edited by Paul Whiteley (London: Sage, 1980), contains a number of essays on the relation between economic conditions and the formation of economic policy by incumbent governments.

IV

ECONOMIC CALCULATION AND THE CONDUCT OF PUBLIC PROGRAMS

14

Budget Concepts and Budgetary Processes

The various models we explored in Part II described budget outcomes essentially as being chosen by a median voter or a controlling coalition. Actual budgetary processes are considerably more complex than those simple models seem to imply. An analysis of budgetary choice must, of course, necessarily be based on simplified abstractions or models of actual budgetary processes. To the extent that such models are able to explain satisfactorily the central characteristics of budgetary choices, they would seem to be useful ways of conceptualizing budgetary outcomes.

This chapter provides basic background about the prevailing process through which the budget of the federal government emerges. Chapter 15 examines the effort to develop analytical techniques to assist in promoting efficiency in public budgeting, and the following three chapters explore three major areas of budgetary interest: spending for national defense, the various programs of the welfare state, and the relations among the units of government that arise in a federalist system.

ECONOMIC CALCULATION
AND BUDGET FORMATS

A budget is not a unique, self-defining entity. It is a form for presenting information, and it contains much room for choice about the types of information to present as well as about the format in which to present it. Prior to fiscal year 1969, the federal government's budget was actually presented as three different budgets: an administrative budget, a consolidated cash budget, and a national income accounts budget.

The administrative budget formed the basis for appropriations legislation. It excluded expenditures and receipts in trust funds such as those for Social Security and highways because those expenditures were not subject to annual legislative choice. The consolidated cash budget incorporated those trust fund activities, as it represented a comprehensive statement on a cash basis of all government payments and receipts. The national income accounts budget differed from the consolidated cash budget in that taxes and expenditures were computed on an accrual basis rather than on a cash basis. Taxes were entered into the national income accounts budget when the liability for the tax was incurred, not when the payment was received. Similarly, expenditures were recorded when the goods were received by the government rather than when the payment was made. Additionally, certain types of what would be considered purely financial transactions, as when a bureau bought a used typewriter, were excluded from the national income accounts budget, just as the price paid for the typewriter would be excluded from the definition of national income (although the income of the vendor who sells the typewriter would be included in national income).

With the submission of the 1969 budget, these three budgets were replaced by a unified budget. The information that was formerly presented in three formats is now presented in one. Proposals for other budget formats have also been advanced from time to time. We made note of the tax expenditure budget in Chapter 9. There have also been proposals for capital budgets, performance budgets, credit budgets, and off-budget budgets. Since a budget is a method for presenting information, the proper format depends on the type of information that is desired by users, and several types of budgets may be required if several different types of information are pertinent to users.

The primary purpose of the unified budget is to serve as an instrument for measuring the impact of the national government on such aggregate economic variables as national income and total employment. This budget concept provides information about the impact of government's fiscal activities on those macroeconomic variables, although the ability to use government budgets systematically to control macroeconomic variables is presently a controversial question in macroeconomic theory that is not addressed in this book.

Another possible objective toward which budgets could be directed is efficiency in the allocation of public resources. The unified budget does not present information in a manner that is useful for such tasks of public management. A budget designed to assist as a management tool for promoting efficiency in public spending would need to provide information relating to various programs that government undertakes.

There are numerous ways government activities can be put into program categories. Among other things, programs can be defined quite broadly or relatively narrowly. "Life, liberty, and the pursuit of happiness" could be defined as a program, in which event the entire budget might be said to constitute a single program. In this case there would be no possibility for comparison among programs, so this budgetary information would be of little value for the evaluation of public programs. Programs could be defined less broadly in general categories such as education, health, and community development. The programs could be defined in narrower terms still, as when education might be divided into, say, programs for general and for vocational education. Moreover, general education might be further narrowed by identifying programs for remedial education, for the education of gifted children, and so on.

Since macroeconomic theory and policy are outside the scope of this book, the focus here is on the possible use of budgeting as a means of calculating the value or efficiency of government's alternative uses of resources. More generally, if government's economic activities are thought to have significance from several different perspectives, several types of budgets will be necessary, each one emphasizing certain types of information and not covering other types.

THE BUDGET PROCESS OF
THE FEDERAL GOVERNMENT

The creation of the federal government's budget takes place in two stages: the development of a proposal by the president, followed by the enactment of a budget by the Congress. It normally takes about eighteen months to prepare and enact the federal budget, with about nine months required for executive preparation and about nine months for legislative authorization and appropriation. Budgets are developed for fiscal years, with the year of the budget actually ending on September 30. The budget for fiscal 1982, for instance, began on October 1, 1981, and ended on September 30, 1982.

This budget was submitted by the president to Congress in January 1981, but its preparation began in early 1980 when the different bureaus within the various cabinet departments, as well as the various independent agencies, formulated their initial budgetary plans for fiscal 1982.[1] During the spring of 1980, the budget offices in the various cabinet departments and administrative agencies worked with their subordinate bureaus in formulating preliminary budget estimates. These estimates were then submitted to the Office of Management and Budget for a preliminary review in light of guidelines announced by the president. During the summer of 1980, the departments and independent agencies revised their budget requests according to those guidelines. The revised estimates were then submitted to the Office of Management and Budget, which reviewed departmental requests in detail, held hearings on those requests, and then compiled the overall budget document for submission to the president. The president reviewed the budget, making changes where desired, and submitted it to Congress in January 1981.

The second phase of the budget cycle begins when Congress receives the budget. In 1974, the Congressional Budget and Impoundment Control Act instituted what appeared to be a major change in congressional budgetary procedures. The announced intention, if not the actual impact, of the 1974 act was to allow Congress better control over spending.

Before the Congressional Budget Act, there was no formal effort by Congress to decide about total budgetary magnitudes. The House of Representatives initiated budgetary action by submitting the budget to the House Appropriations Committee, which was organized into subcommittees along such functional lines as military services, public works, agriculture, and education and labor. Each subcommittee examined those portions of the budget that were relevant to it and eventually made a report to the full appropriations committee, which in turn reported its budget bill to the House of Representatives.

After approval by the House, the Senate acted on the budget, following a procedure similar to that in the House, with subcommittees of the Senate Appropriations Committee examining the House appropriations bills and with the Senate Appropriations Committee reporting to the Senate. Any difference that resulted between the appropriations bills approved by the House and by the Senate were reconciled in a conference committee, and the resulting bill was then sent to the president for veto or approval.

Much criticism developed over this budget process because there

---

[1] The following describes what happens under normal or typical circumstances. The budget for fiscal 1982 was not treated in this typical fashion. The budget was prepared by and presented to Congress by President Jimmy Carter, but President Ronald Reagan took office a few days later and proceeded to revise the budget immediately. The dates in the text illustrate the general schedule that is followed in most years; they do not describe the history of the budget for fiscal 1982, or for any other particular year.

was never any consideration of total budgetary magnitudes. Each appropriations subcommittee recommended the budget its members desired, and the resulting budget reported out of the appropriations committee was generally the sum of the recommendations of the subcommittees, as the various subcomittees generally operated under a norm of reciprocity. Nowhere was there any effort to impose overall constraints on the size of the budget.

The Congressional Budget Act of 1974 changed that procedure by creating budget committees in the House and the Senate and assigning to those committees the task of submitting resolutions that set targets for overall expenditures and revenue and also for spending on the major functional categories. This act required the budget committees to submit their budget resolutions by April 15 (with the fiscal year to begin October 1) and for congressional agreement on a joint budget resolution to be reached by May 15. Appropriations legislation would then take place within the confines of that joint budget resolution. The Budget Act required that by September 15 Congress would enact a second, and in this case binding, budget resolution. Congress would thus have to act to reconcile any discrepancy between the first and the second budget resolutions by raising budget targets for the second resolution, by curtailing the recommendations of the appropriations committees, and so on. Within this framework of budget committees and budget resolutions, the rest of the congressional budget process remained generally unchanged: The functional organization of appropriations subcommittees was maintained, and the House retained initial responsibility over appropriations.

Whether the Budget Act of 1974 has made any substantial difference in budgetary outcome is an open question. The required schedule has not always been kept: The second budget resolution was two months late for fiscal 1981 and was ignored entirely for fiscal 1982. Moreover, the resolutions are based on projections of revenues and expenditures. Appropriations legislation can conform to the budget resolution even though actual appropriations may deviate substantially from that resolution.

Supplemental appropriations can be, and often are, used as a means of avoiding the constraints the second budget resolution seems to impose. With supplemental appropriations, agencies are able to increase their spending beyond that authorized by the second budget resolution, if during the fiscal year the Congress enacts, upon recommendation of the appropriations committees, requests for additional appropriations for agencies that otherwise would run out of money. In some cases supplemental appropriations can arise because the projections about spending were underestimated, possibly as a result of errors in economic forecasts. If the actual rate of unemployment turns out to be higher than what was projected, for instance, spending will likewise turn out to be higher than was initially projected. Supplemental appropriations can also arise out of an interest to avoid having explicitly to raise the spending limits in the second budget resolution. The spending level in the second resolution can be kept unrealistically low, with the discrepancy resolved through supplemental appropriations. It may, of course, be difficult, or even impossible, to judge whether supplemental appropriations in a particular case arise out of genuinely unforeseen circumstances or as a matter of political tactics.

INCREMENTALISM, RATIONALISM, AND BUDGETARY CHOICE

The Congressional Budget Act of 1974 was widely advocated as a means of injecting greater rationality into the budgetary process. The act, it was thought, would require Congress to consider simultaneously the costs and benefits of various proposals for expenditure. Within the guidelines set by the first budget resolution, a proposal by an appropriations subcommittee to increase spending would require that committee to consider simultaneously some offsetting reduction in some other program under its jurisdiction. In this manner, the actions of the appropriations committees would reflect a rough balancing of the benefits thought to result from different ways of spending money allotted by the budget committees. The effort of the budget committees to propose targets for revenues and expenditures would likewise reflect a rough balancing of the benefits and the costs of public spending, for these would be reflected in the extent to which Congress was willing to tax the citizenry.

The Congressional Budget Act so far does not seem to have brought about that increased rationality. But the difficulties of the Congressional Budget Act are not unparalleled. In the mid-1960s, an effort was made to institute *program budgeting* throughout the federal government. The idea behind program budgeting was that the development of budgetary information in terms of various governmental programs would make for more rational and efficient budgeting than is possible when budgets are presented simply in line-item fashion by each agency. Program budgeting survived, in its formal usage, for only a few years. More recently, there has been some interest in *zero-based budgeting*. For the most part, budgetary choice usually involves changes in the base of the previous year, with that base itself not subject to examination. The principle of zero-based budgeting, in contrast, is that each agency's budget would start each year from zero, and so the legislature would decide on the total amount of appropriation *de novo* rather than simply deciding on increments to an existing base. Zero-based budgeting also seems to have had little impact on budgetary outcomes.

Incrementalism and Budgetary Outcomes

These experiences with the Congressional Budget Act, program budgeting, and zero-based budgeting, along with other experiences that could be adduced, might seem to point to a conflict between the rationality required for economic calculation and the incremental, nonrational nature of budgetary choice. At first glance, there seem to be reasons why this might be so. The process by which budgetary choices are made seems clearly to be an incremental one in which the appropriation for the coming year is generally some relatively small change (normally upward) from the present budget. This incremental perspective on budgeting suggests that an agency's budget for the coming year will tend to be some percentage markup from its budget for this year. Table 14.1, which shows the percentage increase in annual budgetary appropriations for thirty-seven bureaus over a twelve-year period, illustrates the incremental nature of the budgetary process. In nearly 35 percent of the 444 cases examined,

TABLE 14.1 [a]   Distribution of Annual Percentage Increases in Appropriations

Rate of Increase	Number of Cases
0–5%	149
6–10	84
11–20	93
21–30	51
31–40	21
41–50	15
51–100	24
100+	7

[a] Figures recalculated from those supplied by Richard Fenno. The table shows the number of cases of thirty-seven domestic bureaus over a twelve-year period that fall into various percentages of increase over the past year (444 cases in all).

Source: Aaron Wildavsky, *The Politics of the Budgetary Process,* 3rd ed., p. 14. Copyright © 1979 by Aaron Wildavsky. Reprinted by permission of the publisher, Little, Brown and Company.

the appropriations increased between zero and 5 percent over the
preceding year's appropriation. This annual increment ranged between 6 and 10 percent in 20 percent of the cases, and between 11
and 20 percent in another 20 percent of the cases. Thus the empirical
record seems to suggest that an agency's budget for the current year
tends to be some percentage markup from its budget during the past
year. The current year's budget is in turn used as a base to which
a markup is added to determine next year's budget.

The incremental nature of the budgetary process was demonstrated
strikingly in empirical work by Otto Davis, M. A. H. Dempster, and
Aaron Wildavsky.[2] Davis, Dempster, and Wildavsky formulated two
simple decision rules that seemed to explain most budgetary choices
quite well. X_t denotes the appropriations requested for some bureau
by the president, and Y_t denotes the appropriations approved for
that bureau by the Congress. The budgetary process follows a two-
step pattern. The president, with full knowledge of the bureau's
budget for the current year, initially proposes a budget for the coming year. Then the Congress, with full knowledge of the president's
proposed budget for the coming year, enacts an appropriation for
that year.

The incrementalist perspective on budgetary processes suggests a
simple set of bureau and congressional decision rules, and those rules
seemed to perform relatively well in explaining the empirical regulari-
ties. For the set of sample bureaus, Davis, Dempster, and Wildavsky
estimated the relation $X_{it} = \beta Y_{it-1} + \epsilon_{it}$, where X_{it} is the president's
request for bureau i during year t, Y_{it-1} is the budget of bureau i
during year $t-1$, and ϵ_{it} is a randomly distributed disturbance term
with mean zero. That is, the president's request for any bureau is
equal to the appropriation made by Congress for the preceding year
multiplied by some constant factor, β. If $\beta = 1.1$, for instance, the
rule states that the president will request 10 percent more for the
bureau this year than the Congress appropriated for it last year.
Similarly, Davis, Dempster, and Wildavsky estimated the relation
$Y_{it} = \alpha X_{it} + \eta_{it}$, where Y_{it} is the amount appropriated by Congress for
bureau i during year t, X_{it} is the president's proposal, and η_{it} is a randomly distributed disturbance term with mean zero. In this formula-
tion, the congressional appropriation for a bureau is some percentage
of the presidential request for that same year. If $\alpha = 0.95$, for instance,

[2] Otto A. Davis, M. A. H. Dempster, and Aaron Wildavsky, "On the Process
of Budgeting: An Empirical Study of Congressional Appropriation," *Public
Choice* 1 (Fall 1966), pp. 63–132; and Otto A. Davis, M. A. H. Dempster, and
Aaron Wildavsky, "A Theory of the Budgetary Process," *American Political
Science Review* 60 (September 1966), pp. 529–547.

the congressional appropriation will equal 95 percent of the president's request.

To test their empirical formulation, Davis, Dempster, and Wildavsky used time series data for fifty-eight nondefense agencies of the national government over the period 1947–1963. The budgetary data seemed to be explained fairly well by these simple linear decision rules. If the budgetary process is inherently incremental, perhaps because the sheer volume of information involved makes anything else unmanageable, it would be no mystery why such nonincremental processes as zero-based budgeting, program budgeting, and the Congressional Budget Act of 1974 seem to have had little impact. These alternative approaches to budgeting attempt to inject some rational comparison of options into what is inherently an incremental, nonrational process of choice.

Rationalism and Budgetary Outcomes

Is there any real conflict between an incremental view of the budgetary process and a rationalist view, in which budget choices would be explained not simply by some mechanical decision rule but by reference to such notions as preferences of median voters or controlling coalitions? While the mechanical, incremental formulation of the budgetary process seems to predict budgetary choices reasonably well, especially over the short run, the incremental formulation contains some obvious weaknesses that become especially glaring as the time interval lengthens beyond a few years. Davis, Dempster, and Wildavsky found that the values of α and β varied both among bureaus and for any single bureau over time. The estimate of β for the Bureau of Indian Affairs from 1948 to 1954 was 0.832, for example, but it increased to 1.037 for the period 1956–1963. Similarly, the estimate of α was 1.321 from 1947 to 1953, but it fell to 1.081 during the period 1954–1963.

As Davis, Dempster, and Wildavsky noted, various shifts seemed to have occurred in the underlying functions during the mid-1950s. Moreover, the value of β for the Bureau of Mines from 1948 to 1954 was 0.915, a significantly higher figure than the 0.832 estimated for the Bureau of Indian Affairs. Likewise, the estimated value of α for the Bureau of Mines from 1947 to 1955 was 1.116, significantly less than the value of 1.321 estimated for the Bureau of Indian Affairs. While the estimated values of α and β for the Bureau of Mines also shifted after the mid-1950s, the amount of shift was quite small in comparison with the shift that occurred for the Bureau of Indian Affairs. The incremental theory of budgetary choice is unable to explain either why the coefficient of any single bureau varies over time or why the coefficient varies among bureaus at a single point in time.

Oliver Williamson has shown that such variation can be explained within an essentially rationalist perspective on the budgetary process.[3] Accordingly, an incremental theory of the budgetary process is but a short-run approximation to outcomes that at base reflect the considerations examined by a rational theory of budgeting. The reasons why α and β are higher for some bureaus than for others (that is, why budgets increase faster for some bureaus than for others) can be explained by introducing some concept of demand for the services supplied by the various bureaus: α and β are higher for bureaus that face relatively strong demand for their services than for bureaus that do not. Similarly, some concept of demand can explain why the values of α and β change over time: α and β increase more rapidly for those bureaus that are experiencing more rapidly increasing demand for their services. The ability of the incremental formulation of the budgetary process to give close fits over a short period of time indicates only that the demand for most services changes at a relatively slow rate. But as the time interval lengthens, these changes can become substantial, in which case a shift in parameters must be incorporated into the incremental formulation of the budgetary process.

The incremental approach to budgetary processes can be reconciled relatively easily with a rational approach. Consider the formulation of the decision rule that describes the president's markup of an agency's appropriation for the past year, $X_{it} = \beta Y_{it-1} + \epsilon_{it}$. As we noted above, the parameter β is a constant markup term, although its value may shift both over time and among bureaus. If average cost equals marginal cost over the relevant range of output, a simple rule of markup pricing can be equivalent to profit maximization. A simple model of markup pricing is one in which $P_i = b_i(AC_i)$, where P_i is the price of commodity i, AC_i is the average cost of i, and b_i is the appropriate coefficient of markup, a coefficient that differs among commodities according to the elasticity of demand for the various commodities. The more elastic the demand, the lower the markup coefficient. For profit-maximizing firms, then, a commodity with a more elastic demand would carry a lower markup than would a commodity with a less elastic demand.

A political model of markup pricing can be developed by extending the standard model of markup pricing, as Williamson showed. Poli-

[3] Oliver E. Williamson, "A Rational Theory of the Federal Budgetary Process," *Public Choice* 2 (Spring 1977), pp. 71–89. For a related effort showing that budgetary policies reflect citizen demands, see John E. Jackson, "Politics and the Budgetary Process," *Social Science Research* 1 (April 1972), pp. 35–60.

ticians support various public expenditures because they yield political value. If the president's budgetary problem is construed as one of maximizing the political value produced by a budget, subject to a total budget constraint, a relationship arises relating the president's proposal for the coming year to the legislative appropriation for the current year; that relationship is essentially the same as that described by Davis, Dempster, and Wildavsky. In this case, however, the shift in parameter over time depends on conditions of demand — that is, on the ability of different bureaus to provide political value to the president.

A similar formulation can be given to the relationship expressing the legislature's appropriations as a percentage of the president's recommendation. The incremental approach to the budget process seems to be accurate in the short run, perhaps descriptively more accurate than the rationalist models described in Part II. The incremental perspective does not seem to be an alternative to a rational theory of budgetary choice but rather a special case of a rational theory: The various parameters shift over time because demand does not grow uniformly over time for all bureaus, and the shifts in budgetary parameters are a response of politicians to the change in the demand for different programs of public expenditure.

PLANNING-PROGRAMMING-BUDGETING SYSTEM

The commonly drawn conflict between budgeting as a nonrational, incremental process and budgeting as a rational activity seems inappropriate. Incrementalism describes budgeting in terms of such apparently nonrational concepts as habitual percentage markups in budgets. Zero-based budgeting, in contrast, proposes to reconsider explicitly the existing base by conceptually starting all budgets at zero for each year. On the surface, zero-based budgeting seems to be the epitome of rationality. Each year all programs would be looked at afresh and thereby brought under the scrutiny of some calculation of benefits and costs. Incrementalism, on the other hand, sees any such calculations as limited, at the most, to the annual additions to the budget. Most of those additions, it appears, are perhaps more a product of habit than of thought. Despite the interest that has sometimes been expressed in zero-based budgeting, it has had little impact on budgetary processes, and it seems unlikely that it will ever have much impact. Incrementalism seems clearly to describe more accurately the process of budgeting.

Zero-based budgeting would, in principle, require annual review of the full range of budgetary options. Conceptually, roughly $700 billion of accounts would be set to zero, the various uses of funds examined, and choices made about the amounts to allocate to different uses. This might be rational if the evaluation of budgetary options were costless, or even if demand and cost conditions changed substantially and unpredictably from year to year. But it is quite costly to examine budgetary options, and demand and cost conditions for the most part change relatively slowly. It is hardly rational to engage in a costly process of reconsidering that which has changed very little. Zero-based budgeting (if it is truly zero-based budgeting in substance and not just in form) in fact conflicts with rationality because it neglects the costliness of budgeting. Incremental budgeting, on the other hand, is fully consistent with rationality, in a context of costly budgeting and demand and cost conditions that change relatively slowly.

Program budgeting and the planning-programming-budgeting system (PPBS) are alternative formats that have been advocated as means of generating more useful information than can be produced by the line-item format of the present system of budgeting. Program budgeting and PPBS are essentially consistent with the incremental nature of budgetary processes, but they would expand the ways in which budgetary information is presented. As we have seen, the present format in which federal budget information is presented is useful mainly as a means of assessing the aggregate impact of government spending on the economy. That format is also useful as a means of controlling expenditures. A budget is presented by each agency, with line-item allocations for various expenditure categories. This budget format makes it possible to ensure through auditing that the expenditures were directed to the line-item categories called for.

In contrast, performance budgeting and PPBS entail the presentation of information in a format that is useful for assessing options about the allocation of resources. Program budgeting seeks to present budgetary information in terms of resources directed to particular programs. It is thought that such a presentation of information provides a more accurate idea of government activities, which in turn should result in more informed budgetary choices. Whereas budgeting traditionally focuses on inputs, program budgeting seeks to present budgetary information in terms of outputs, or at least to group spending on various inputs in terms of the outputs to which those inputs are applied in production. The presentation of budgetary information in a manner that relates to outputs is clearly useful in principle.

Performing program budgeting is often no trivial task. A hospital's input budget can be described by such categories as rent, labor, medicines, supplies, and equipment. There are many ways a program budget for the hospital might be constructed. Programs could be defined in terms of emergency care, preventive medicine, and treatment, or in terms of specific illnesses and surgical procedures. Other possible classifications of a hospital's activities into programs could be imagined.

When economic activity is organized through property and contract, no question arises about how to specify the output because the contract represents a meeting of the minds as to the rights and duties of each person. The owner of a hospital that is organized through property and contract will have available a number of ways of organizing accounts and records to provide information. The owner will choose a particular format because it is thought to be most effective in advancing the owner's objectives, whatever those might be. An owner who wants to retire by age fifty to a sybaritic life might well want a different presentation of information than one who wants to be written about in future histories as a pioneer in treatment and surgical procedure.

Owners may well use different budget formats because their objectives require different forms for the presentation of information. The absence of a unique format for the presentation of budgetary information is resolved privately through the ability of entrepreneurs to choose formats best suited to their purposes. Through a regime of property and contract, consensus generally reigns within individual firms.[4] It is not the same with governmental agencies because there may be no consensus as to the objectives to be achieved by a hospital or by any other agency. Without such consensus, there can be no unique set of programs into which the government's budget can be separated. Different political interests will prefer different classifications of programs.

Program budgeting and PPBS represent efforts to provide information on the allocative consequences of different government programs, which, in principle, might seem to be only beneficial. This would be beneficial in a system of consensual decision making concerning the use of resources, but it might not be in some nonconsensual system characterized by the absence of property and contract. Such information need not be unambiguously beneficial if there is no consensus as to the proper form for the presentation of information. Consequently, program budgeting may make explicit much of

---

[4] On the prevalence of consensus within firms as an outcome of a regime of property and contract, see Harry De Angelo, "Competition and Unanimity," *American Economic Review* 71 (March 1981), pp. 18–27.

the conflict over the use of resources that is inherent within a system of majoritarian democracy. Within the present system of budgeting, such conflict may be less explicit.

PERFORMANCE CONTRACTING

Program budgeting and PPBS have been supported as additional budgetary formats because they represent an effort to focus on outputs, not just on inputs. Performance contracting reflects a similar focus on outputs but without getting involved with the development of new budget formats. Performance contracting operates within a line-item focus on inputs of the prevailing budgetary system, but it suggests that different ways of contracting for services will affect the amount that government spends for the various items. Issues of contracting are perhaps of special interest in military spending, aspects of which are examined in Chapter 16. Such issues are also of general budgetary interest, and we will briefly consider them here.

Competitive Bidding and Forms of Contract

Suppose a government has decided it wants to equip its high officials with specially designed briefcases. These briefcases are not generally available for sale, so the government must contract with a producer for their production and purchase. One way it might do so is through offering a *fixed-fee contract*, say $10 million for 100,000 briefcases that conform to the government's specifications. Alternatively, it might offer a *cost-plus-fixed-fee contract*, which might allow the contractor a fixed profit based on some percentage of the initial estimate of cost and then cover the actual costs of producing the briefcases. If the profit rate were 20 percent and the initial estimate of cost were $10 million, the government would offer to pay the contractor $2 million plus the contractor's actual expenses in producing the briefcases. If those expenses turned out to be only $7 million, the contractor would receive $9 million, and if they turned out to be $12 million, the government would pay $14 million to the contractor.

Contracts, particularly military contracts, are often negotiated between the government and a contractor, but competitive bidding is frequently used as well. With competitive bidding, the contract typically goes to the lowest bidder unless exceptional circumstances support some other choice, such as a record of unreliability of the low bidder or an interest in giving some bids to minority contractors. Contractors will typically vary in their efficiency. One contractor may be able to produce the specified briefcases for $8 million while another requires $9 million.

For the most part, contractors will have more knowledge than the government about their comparative efficiency. Indeed, if this were not the case, there would be no reason for bidding, for the government would be able to select the most efficient contractor without having to go through the expense of bidding. With fixed-fee contracting, the high-cost contractor will have no incentive to bid below $9 million for the contract, assuming that there were adequate safeguards against cheating on specifications, because it would not be able to cover its costs with such a bid. The low-cost contractor will have an incentive to raise its bid so long as it thinks it will remain the low-cost contractor. Although the low-cost contractor might raise its bid above $8 million, it will still offer some bid below $9 million. From an ex ante perspective, the more efficient contractor will be chosen within a system of fixed-fee contracting. To the extent the bid is higher than $8 million, the contractor can anticipate receiving rents on the contract; that is, the contractor will receive more from the contract than is necessary to get the service supplied. At the same time, however, market competition will generally operate to keep such rents relatively low, assuming no one person has a peculiar monopoly on the talent or materials required for making the product. If the contractor guesses wrong and actually requires $10 million to make the briefcases, a loss will be taken, and perhaps the other contractor would actually have been more efficient. There is, of course, no way of knowing this in advance. What can be said, however, is that from an ex ante perspective this method of bidding tends to give contracts to relatively efficient producers.

Cost-plus-fixed-fee contracting does not operate so strongly to give business to the more efficient contractor. Suppose the contract calls for the government to pay for the cost of the briefcases plus 20 percent of the initial bid. Under a fixed-fee contract, one contractor would bid $8 million and another $9 million. But the incentives are somewhat different under cost-plus-fixed-fee contracting. On the one hand, the more efficient firm can possibly gain by overstating its initial estimate of cost. If it estimates its cost to be $8.5 million instead of $8 million, it will increase its profit from $1.6 million to $1.7 million if it gets the bid regardless of its actual cost. On the other hand, the less efficient firm can possibly gain by understating its initial estimate of cost. If it estimates its cost to be $8 million instead of $9 million, it reduces its profit from $1.8 million to $1.6 million, but it also increases its likelihood of being the lower bidder. Should the contractor actually spend $10 million in making the briefcases, the $2 million overrun will be paid for by the government.

The contractor will receive a $1.6 million profit regardless of the actual cost of the briefcases. Cost-plus-fixed-fee contracting thus reduces the likelihood that a system of competitive bidding will lead to the selection of the contractor who from an ex ante perspective seems to be the most efficient producer. Moreover, the cost-plus part of the contract gives an incentive for being slack in the use of resources, as well as an incentive to the contractor to transfer wealth from taxpayers by such indirect means as paying higher than required expenses to subcontractors and other business activities in which the contractor retains some interest.

One prominent type of contract is a combination of fixed-fee and cost-plus-fixed-fee. This contract is like a cost-plus-fixed-fee contract, except that cost overruns are shared between the government and the contractor according to some stipulated rate. If that rate is 50 percent, the contractor who bids $8 million for the briefcases and then spends $10 million in producing them will receive $9 million from the government — the $8 million as initial bid plus 50 percent of the $2 million overrun. The contractor will also receive the fixed fee, which will be $1.6 million if it is 20 percent of the initial bid. This type of contract softens some of the peculiar incentives of cost-plus-fixed-fee contracting, but it does not eliminate them.

Performance Contracting in Education

Even fixed-fee contracting may fail to promote efficiency as fully as outright residual claimancy would. It all depends on the terms of the contract in the first place, and governments may have reasons for setting terms that would be unlikely to arise under a regime of property and contract, even though the contract is of a fixed-fee type. The Gary, Indiana, school district, for example, contracted with the Behavioral Research Laboratories to provide education for its students. The idea was to use performance contracting as a means of strengthening the incentive faced by the producer from what it was thought to be under the prevailing form of public education.[5]

Behavioral Research Laboratories was to receive $800 per year for each pupil who after three years surpassed nationwide grade norms on standardized achievement tests on mathematics and reading. It should come as no surprise that mathematics and reading became more heavily emphasized in the curriculum because the contract placed a value only on mathematics and reading scores. More-

[5] This case is discussed in George E. Peterson, "The Distributional Impact of Performance Contracting in Schools," in *Redistribution Through Public Choice,* edited by Harold M. Hochman and George E. Peterson (New York: Columbia University Press, 1974), pp. 115–135.

over, this type of contract created an incentive for the firm to spend differently on educating different children. Some children of high ability can be expected to exceed grade norms regardless of the amount of attention they receive in school. From the perspective of the firm under its contract with the Gary School District, any expenditure on those children would have been wasted, so the firm could reasonably be expected to slight such children. There also are children of low ability who perhaps could not be expected to surpass the nationwide average no matter how much attention they received. These children too could be expected to be slighted under the terms of the performance contract. Most of the effort would reasonably be directed at children of average ability who probably could not be expected to surpass the grade norms without assistance but who would be likely to do so with assistance.

Table 14.2 presents some evidence that confirms the analysis of this particular contract. Relative to the degree of nationwide improvement in mathematics and reading, students at the Banneker School generally did better in mathematics than in reading; their improvement exceeded the national average in mathematics in four of the five categories, whereas in reading it fell below the national average in all five categories. Of special interest, however, is the differential performance in relation to the standings of students at the start of the year. In mathematics, Banneker fared strongest

TABLE 14.2   Test Gains Nationwide and at Banneker School

	Relation to Grade Norm at Start of Year				
	−40% or more	−40% to −20%	−20% to 0%	% to +20%	+20% or more
Mathematics					
National (N)	0.68	0.73	0.92	1.10	1.15
Banneker (B)	0.80	1.15	1.20	1.14	1.04
B − N	0.12	0.42	0.28	0.04	−0.11
Reading					
National (N)	0.75	0.77	0.95	1.06	1.17
Banneker (B)	0.68	0.76	0.82	0.85	0.74
B − N	−0.07	−0.01	−0.13	−0.21	−0.43

Source: George E. Peterson, "The Distributional Impact of Performance Contracting in Schools," in *Redistribution Through Public Choice,* edited by Harold M. Hochman and George E. Peterson (New York: Columbia University Press, 1974), pp. 130–131. Reprinted by permission of Columbia University Press.

relative to the national average among those whose starting points were between 40 percent below the national norm and the national norm. And in reading, those who generally fared best were those who were in the same range below the national norm, although the pattern is not so strikingly apparent in this case. For both exams, students who started the year 20 percent or more above the national norm experienced sharp relative declines in their progress.

Different types of performance contracts would, of course, elicit different responses from the contractor. If the contractor had been paid according to the aggregate increase in the number of points scored by pupils, a more uniform system of instruction and pattern of test scores would surely have resulted. A different pattern of instruction would have resulted if the payments under the terms of the contract had been based on other criteria such as the number of U.S. presidents that students could name or the average lengths of time for which pupils could do a flex-arm hang. A still different pattern of instruction and outcomes could be expected if it were not the school district that contracted with a contractor but individual parents who contracted with individual contractors of their choosing.

CAPITAL BUDGETING

Capital budgeting is a method of presenting budgetary information that also seeks to provide it in a manner that is more useful for economic calculation than the present method of budgeting. Unlike PPBS and program budgeting, capital budgeting does not seek to present the entire sum of budgetary information in a different format. It seeks only to distinguish between those expenditures that represent the current using up of resources and those that actually represent a type of current saving through the acquisition of capital goods that will be used up only in the future. It can be argued that the present method of budgeting overstates the expenses of government because the government's purchase of capital assets is treated as an expense in the year they are purchased. If such purchases of assets are treated as capital acquisitions and depreciated over a period of time, each year's operating budget would contain only charges for depreciation. The purchase of the assets would be placed in the capital budget, with the balance in this budget drawn down as the assets are depreciated. An office building that the government has constructed for $100 million, for instance, would be placed into a capital budget. If it is depreciated on a straight-line basis over twenty years, in each subsequent year the operating budget will record a $5 million expenditure for depreciation on the building.

Capital budgeting is advocated on the ground that it entails a more accurate presentation of information about the actual annual expenses of government. The expenses of corporations are treated in this manner because capital expenditures are depreciated over a period of years. Hence, the use of capital budgeting by government would seem to produce a closer comparability between government and businesses. Capital budgeting, like program budgeting and PPBS, is a means of providing information, and like program budgeting and PPBS, the value of different formats for presenting information depends on the objectives of those who are responsible for taking action. An owner of an enterprise may or may not choose to engage in capital budgeting, with this choice depending on the owner's objectives and the relation between the information and the objectives. The depreciation of assets is a congressional requirement for purposes of taxation and is not necessarily and universally undertaken for its informational value. In the absence of such a tax requirement, an owner may choose to treat capital assets as an expense immediately rather than to depreciate them, depending on which budgetary format is thought to provide the more valuable information.

Budgeting may well vary depending on the institutional or political system. A hotel provides a variety of collective goods within an institutional framework of property and contract, as we noted in Chapter 7. A hotel might well choose to use budgetary formats that differ from those of a national government, not because of the fundamental nature of the transactions that are made but because of differences in the degree of consensus concerning the utilization of resources that typify the institutional orders.

What would determine the rate of depreciation within a system of capital budgeting? Corporate rates of depreciation are currently determined by the government, and in the absence of such tax requirements the rate of depreciation (including 100 percent depreciation the first year) would be determined according to how the owner values the information provided under different methods of depreciation. But government faces no external authority that can impose on it particular rates of depreciation, nor is it typically subject to the institutional order of property and contract that tends to generate consensus concerning resource utilization.

Governments might set depreciation rates relatively low so as to make current expenditures seem lower than otherwise. They might also place current expenditures in the capital budget to make the current budget seem smaller than it would otherwise be. Indeed, this practice was one of the devices that led to New York City's so-called fiscal crisis in the mid-1970s: To reduce the size of its operating budget, in 1966 New York City shifted its expenditures for manpower training from its expense budget to its capital budget.[6] Although capital budgeting is a format for the presentation of information, the value of alternative formats depends ultimately on the institutional framework within which choices concerning resource utilization are made.

CREDIT PROGRAMS AND OFF-BUDGET TRANSACTIONS

The government's budget is becoming less significant as an indicator of the extent of government's economic activities. The most rapidly growing way in which government participates in decisions concerning the utilization of resources is in making and guaranteeing loans. Such credit transactions have been rising about five times as rapidly as measured federal spending in recent years. In fiscal 1980 and 1981 the Federal Housing Administration and the Veterans Administration issued more than $60 billion in new loan guarantees. The Farmers Home Administration and the Rural Electrification Administration issued more than $24 billion in new credit to rural areas in fiscal 1980 and 1981.[7]

Foreign countries that buy military equipment from the United States receive loans that do not appear in the budget. New York City and the Chrysler Corporation are subsidized by the government through a program of loan guarantees, but neither the amount of the loan nor even the amount of the subsidy the guarantee represents appears in the budget. Credit to such favored industries as shipbuilding, automobile manufacturing, aircraft manufacturing, and steel production was about $4 billion in fiscal 1980 and 1981. For 1981, such credit activities were about one-fourth of budgeted federal spending.

Although such loans and loan guarantees amounted to about $140 in fiscal 1981, only about $5 billion actually entered the budget because federal outlays are registered only if the borrower defaults. Credit programs are a massive way in which government can influence the utilization of resources and yet do so in a way that

[6] Damodar Gujarati, *Pensions and New York City's Fiscal Crisis* (Washington, D.C.: American Enterprise Institute, 1978).

[7] For a survey of credit programs and budgeting, see Congressional Budget Office, *Federal Credit Activities: An Analysis of the President's Credit Budget for 1981* (Washington, D.C.: U.S. Government Printing Office, 1980).

hardly appears at all in budgetary magnitudes. The loans and loan guarantees reduce the price of credit to recipients. In consequence, resources are transferred to the recipients of loans and guarantees away from other potential borrowers.

In the absence of subsidized credit, there tends to be an allocation of credit among potential claimants such that the anticipated marginal productivity of credit in one use equals that in other uses. This equalization of anticipated returns is a consequence of a competitive market for credit. But if certain types of credit transactions are subsidized by government, the composition of credit will shift in the direction of those favored transactions. Such a program of subsidies operates similarly to the corporation income tax in creating an excess burden, but rather than taxing some forms of capital investment, it subsidizes some forms of investment. Regardless, the allocation of resources shifts in response to the subsidy so as to equalize anticipated net rates of return. Although the subsidized activities will offer the same anticipated net rate of return as the other activities, the gross or social return will be lower on resources employed in the subsidized activities. The loan guarantees and subsidies will impose an excess burden on the economy, but such activities are excluded from the budget, except to the extent of actual defaults.

In a growing number of cases credit transactions are moved off the budget entirely. If the Farmers Home Administration guarantees a loan, the reduced interest rate is not treated as a government subsidy, even though that is the effect of the program. In the event of default by the borrower, however, the Farmers Home Administration will have to pay the lender, and the amount of this payment will be reflected in the agency's budget the year the payment takes place. But if the Farmers Home Administration sells its loans to the Federal Financing Bank, even the potential budgetary impact of its loan guarantee vanishes. The credit transaction has been moved off the budget entirely. Should default occur after the loan has been sold to the Federal Financing Bank, the lender will be paid not by an expenditure from the Farmers Home Administration, but from the issuance of public debt by the U.S. Treasury.

For fiscal 1981, the net loan outlays by the Federal Financing Bank were roughly equivalent to the recorded federal budget deficit. Much concern has been registered over the past several years about the growth of government spending, but government participation in decisions concerning the utilization of resources increasingly takes place in ways that are not reflected in budgetary magnitudes, although they do affect the allocation of resources in society through their impact on credit markets.

THE ELUSIVE SEARCH FOR
BUDGETARY CONTROL

The concern with budgetary control has been a persistent theme in American fiscal history, although the intensity of this concern has perhaps risen in step with the expansion in the size of government. The Congressional Budget Act of 1974 was only the most recent manifestation of this concern, and various proposals for balanced budgets, regulatory budgets, and tax and spending limits are further reflections of it. If some of these proposals actually are instituted, historical extrapolation would yield the inference that the problem would persist nonetheless, although perhaps in somewhat modified form.

With respect to a requirement of a balanced budget, for instance, just what budget is to be balanced? In terms of the government's actual revenues and expenditures, many past instances of budget deficits have been described as representing a balanced budget. This is done simply by defining the pertinent budget not as the actual budget, but as the budget that someone projects will occur at some higher level of employment. At this higher level of employment, expenditures would presumably be lower and revenues higher than at the actual level of employment. Such a high-employment budget is a hypothetical construct that can never be tested, but it perhaps lends a greater appearance of control than might otherwise be ascribed to the process of budgeting.

Even in terms of actual budgetary totals, a requirement of a balanced budget seems likely to encourage a greater use of credit programs and off-budget transactions to escape the constraint the balanced budget requirement would otherwise impose. If so, the concern with budgetary control would persist, but it would cover new issues in response to the change in the nature of government activity that in turn was induced by the preceding effort at promoting control.

Almost all of the concerns about budgetary control arise because government operates outside the institutional framework of property and contract. The analysis of majoritarian and consensual democracy developed in Part II is pertinent to a consideration of government budgeting. Budgetary processes and outcomes are reflections of politically manifested interests operating within a particular institutional order. People who are high bidders in the market for legislation may acquire subsidies through expenditure programs in the ordinary budget. But they might also acquire subsidies through regulation and credit programs instead. In all such cases, it is the ability of government to operate by taking and giving rather than by buying and selling — that is, its ability to operate outside the framework of property and contract — that both generates a demand on the part of citizens for such legislation and induces a supply on the part of politicians for that type of legislation. So long as the basic mode of operation of government remains that of taking and giving rather than of buying and selling, changes in budget concepts or budgetary processes seem likely to have a comparatively limited ability to offset the negative-sum destruction of wealth that is one attribute of a system of majoritarian democracy.

SUGGESTIONS FOR FURTHER READING

An incrementalist approach to budgetary processes is put forward in Charles E. Lindbloom, "The Science of Muddling Through," *Public Administration Review* 19 (Spring 1959), pp. 79–88; Aaron Wildavsky, *The Politics of the Budgetary Process,* 3rd ed. (Boston: Little, Brown, 1979), and *Budgeting: A Comparative Theory of Budgetary Processes* (Boston: Little, Brown, 1975). An incrementalist perspective on budgeting is contrasted with a rationalist or analytical perspective in Allen Schick, "Systems Politics and Systems Budgeting," *Public Administration Review* 29 (March/April 1969), pp. 137–151.

Public Budgeting: Program Planning and Evaluation, 3rd ed., edited by Fremont J. Lyden and Ernest G. Miller (Chicago: Rand McNally, 1978), contains a collection of essays on the political and economic aspects of budgeting, program budgeting, zero-based budgeting, and program evaluation. Allen Schick, "A Death in the Bureaucracy: The Demise of Federal PPB," *Public Administration Review* 33 (March/April 1973), pp. 146–156, describes how PPBS operated to heighten conflict over resource utilization, thereby leading to its demise because prevailing budgetary institutions generally act to reduce or control overt conflict. Peter C. Sarant, *Zero-Base Budgeting in the Public Sector* (Reading, Mass.: Addison-Wesley, 1978), describes a procedure for implementing zero-based budgeting.

Performance contracting is discussed in John J. McCall, "The Simple Economics of Incentive Contracting," *American Economic Review* 60 (December 1970), pp. 837–846. Charles L. Schultze, *The Politics and Economics of Public Spending* (Washington, D.C.: Brookings Institution, 1968), discusses various aspects of bringing economic analysis to bear on budgetary choices.

15

Analytical Techniques to Promote Economic Calculation

As we saw in Chapter 14, the development of program budgeting and PPBS are particular reflections of a general and continuing interest in the promotion of efficiency in public expenditure. Many of the specific techniques and methods that have been developed to assist in this promotion can be subsumed under the rubric of *benefit-cost analysis*, which, as it is used in public economics, represents an effort to impart concrete substance to a universal principle of human conduct: People seek to attain their goals effectively rather than ineffectively.[1] Benefit-cost analysis is used in public economics to develop information about the probable consequences of various public programs and policies. The use people make of such information will, of course, depend on their incentives to utilize that information.

ECONOMIC CALCULATION, BENEFIT-COST, AND SOCIAL PROFITABILITY

When it is treated as an analytical method or procedure, benefit-cost analysis represents an effort to apply the concepts and categories of

---

[1] For a clear statement of the universality of this principle, see William H. Meckling, "Values and the Choice of the Model of the Individual in the Social Sciences," *Schweizerische Zeitschrift für Volkswirtschaft und Statistik* 112 (December 1976), pp. 545–560.

economics to the assessment of potential programs of public expenditure. The origins of benefit-cost analysis can be traced to the 1920s, but it came into widespread use after World War II, when water resource investments under the aegis of the Army Corps of Engineers and the Bureau of Reclamation provided the material for analysis. In the early 1960s, military applications became prominent, although they were typically referred to as *systems analysis*. Subsequently, such areas as health, education, transportation, recreation, and regulation, among others, came to provide material for benefit-cost analysis.

Benefit-cost analysis is used to develop estimates of the benefits and costs that are anticipated from various government programs. If the analysis is conducted properly, it tells whether a public program will shift resources into more valuable or less valuable employments compared with the existing pattern of resource utilization. There is substantial outward similarity between benefit-cost analysis as applied to programs of public expenditure and investment analysis as practiced by business firms.

From the perspective of a business, a properly executed investment analysis would reflect, from an ex ante perspective, an effort to maximize the present value of the firm. Anticipations may be treated harshly by reality, of course, so choices that were anticipated to be efficient or profitable may turn out not to be so. After careful analysis, a brewer may conclude that the development of a new beer should increase the value of the brewery. From an ex ante perspective, the brewer would anticipate that the benefits from developing the new beer will exceed the costs.

The use of benefit-cost analysis to assist in making budgetary choices by government falls within the same essential perspective of profitability, but with profitability understood from a social rather than an individual perspective. In the presence of complete ownership rights, profit maximization is synonymous with economic efficiency, as discussed in Chapter 2. But if ownership is incomplete and nontransferable, various externalities can arise through market transactions. In such instances, the price of a product may not reflect fully the value of the resources used in its production. When electricity is generated by coal, for example, the utility company may pay for all the resources necessary to generate the electricity except those that are used in the form of damage done by the soot and sulfur dioxide that are emitted. If the cost of trading with respect to the use of the air is sufficiently high, the utility company may be able to avoid paying for all the resources it uses in its generating electricity. The utility may maximize profits, as described by an equality of its own marginal revenue and marginal cost. But this maximization of profits does not imply that resources are being employed in their most highly valued uses.

In the presence of externalities, choices by firms concerning the use of resources will not necessarily promote the use of resources in their most valuable employments. The social marginal cost of the generation of electricity includes the damage done by the emission of soot and sulfur dioxide, whereas the private marginal cost includes only the various resources the firm must hire to produce its output. The value people place on the marginal unit of electricity is less than the social marginal cost, which in turn implies that a change in the pattern of resource usage to one in which less electricity is produced will increase the value yielded from the same stock of resources.

So long as the output of the utility is excessive, as judged by a consideration of what would happen if the utility had to purchase the right to emit soot and sulfur dioxide, the benefit from a reduction in output will exceed the cost. An efficient curtailment of the utility's output will have taken place when the marginal benefit from that curtailment equals the marginal cost. Stated alternatively, an efficient program of curtailment will generate the same outcome as would result if the utility made an effort to maximize its profits while counting as a cost of production the purchase of the right to emit soot and sulfur dioxide. Benefit-cost analysis operates within a framework of "social profitability," in that it seeks to assess public programs and policies from the perspective of the pattern of resource utilization that would have taken place under some alternative, but perhaps nonimplementable pattern of ownership rights.

THE CENTRAL STRUCTURE OF
BENEFIT-COST ANALYSIS

Benefit-cost analysis applies economic analysis to develop information about the salient economic differences among options for public policy or expenditure. To this end, it is an attempt to provide empirical solutions to economic models. A benefit-cost analysis might be conducted of options for reducing the level of emissions of carbon monoxide and hydrocarbons from automobiles. Those options might be limited to various degrees of stringency as to what constitutes an acceptable level of emissions. The policy options might further allow for differences in acceptable emissions among automobiles, trucks, and motorcycles and for regional variation in emission standards. In other words, benefit-cost analysis is an effort to assess the anticipated consequences of policy options, but the selection of those options is not part of the analysis.

The articulation of possible policy options is a preanalytical activity; therefore, the value of any benefit-cost analysis depends on the value of the options presented for analysis. Policy options typically are expressed in terms of the objectives to be attained by public policy; these might be of narrow interest such as increasing the wealth of campaign contributors, or they might be of broader interest. Regardless, it is possible to conceptualize this preanalytical stage as consisting of a statement of the goals or objectives to be attained through a program of public expenditure and a statement of different possible ways of attaining that objective.

Objectives can be stated with varying degrees of generality, with more specific objectives producing a sharper focus on possible programs for analysis. An objective to increase the quality of life by 10 percent is so general as to be unobjectionable, and its generality probably impedes the development of policy options because there are almost a limitless number of policy options that could be developed. Alternative objectives such as increasing air quality by 10 percent or reducing crime by 10 percent seem to relate to the general objective, but they narrow the range of options so as to offer the possibility of analytical manageability.

Even these narrower objectives are sufficiently broad to contain much ambiguity, however. Crime is not a homogeneous category. A simple counting of the total number of crimes and then seeking to reduce that number by 10 percent would treat murder as equivalent to petty larceny. Instead of seeking a 10 percent reduction in crime, a 10 percent reduction in the loss from crime could be sought. But to state the objective this way requires some selection of weights or values for the losses suffered in different crimes. Burglaries may be assessed by the value of what is stolen, but crimes such as murder, rape, and assault are not so readily measured. Nonetheless, some effort at placing a value on different crimes will be part of any assessment of programs for reducing the loss from crime.

The specific programs that might be proposed to reduce the loss from crime will be articulated through essentially the same process that is used to state objectives, and the two processes take place more or less simultaneously rather than sequentially. A listing of possible programs might include increases in the size of the investigative force of the police department, increases in the number of units patrolling the streets, options for different time distributions of such patrols, inducing people to install better locks on their doors and windows, subsidizing personal purchases of guard dogs, paying bounties to vigilantes who apprehend criminals, increasing punishments for criminals, and changing the laws that define crime.

Benefit-cost analysis takes place with respect to concrete options for public policy, and it involves an effort to estimate empirically an economic model of the anticipated consequences of various policy options. The desirable consequences of a program are placed on the benefit side of the ledger and the undesirable consequences are placed on the cost side. The benefits from a program of crime reduction would mainly involve anticipated reductions in the losses from crime. The main feature of cost generally entails the value of the output that is sacrificed because the program alters the pattern of output in society. The benefits and costs typically extend over a number of years, and some difficult issues arise in trying to assess programs that differ in the timing of benefits and costs.

After benefits and costs have been assessed and the problems of their timing overcome, how is a selection made from among the numerous options that have been examined? The efficient choice among options is the option that maximizes the difference between the anticipated benefits and anticipated costs. This is identical to maximizing the difference between marginal benefits and marginal costs, but it is quite different from selecting a project because its benefit-cost ratio exceeds unity.

Figure 15.1 illustrates the total benefits and total costs for different sizes of a project, say patrol forces. It is easy to see that the project at size B, which entails the largest difference between benefits and costs (that is, the largest net benefit), is the efficient choice. An increase in the scale of the program from A to B entails added costs of $75 (perhaps in thousands of dollars), but it would involve added benefits of $100. By contrast, expansions in the size of the program beyond B increase benefits less than costs. In expanding from B to C, for instance, costs increase by $75 while benefits increase by only $50. Scale B, at which the net benefit is maximized (that is, where marginal benefit equals marginal cost), is the most efficient scale of the project. The ratio of benefits to costs, though frequently bandied about in popular discourse, is of little significance. All projects smaller than D have benefit-cost ratios in excess of unity and yet those larger than B represent inefficiently large scales of activity. Benefit-cost ratios also exceed unity for projects smaller than B, and yet those projects represent inefficiently small scales of activity. A benefit-cost ratio in excess of unity is therefore no indicator of desirability, although a benefit-cost ratio of less than unity is certainly an indicator of undesirability.

FIGURE 15.1 Benefits, Costs, and the Choice Among
Program Options

The total benefits and the total costs that are anticipated to result from
various sizes of a project are illustrated by *TB* and *TC*, respectively. The
project at size *A* has benefits of $150 and costs of $50; at size *B* the
benefits are $250 and costs are $125, and the project at size *C* has benefits
of $300 and costs of $200. *B* is the size with the largest difference between
benefits and costs, $125; it is the size of the project for which marginal
benefits equal marginal costs. For a size such as *A*, marginal benefits
exceed marginal cost, while the reverse relationship holds for *C*. (Marginal
benefit and marginal cost for a particular scale of project are measured by
the slope of lines drawn tangent to *TB* and *TC*, respectively.) Note that all
projects smaller than *D* have a benefit-cost ratio in excess of unity, which
shows the lack of significance of such a ratio.

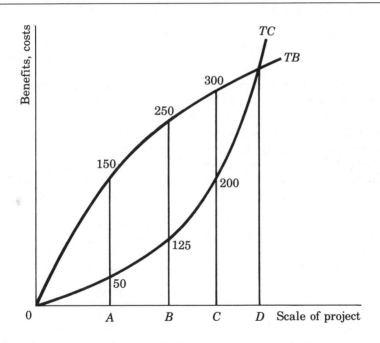

TIME AND THE DISCOUNT RATE

Programs of public expenditure typically have patterns of benefits
and costs that extend over a number of years, and any analysis of
benefits and costs must be consistent with the observation that a
dollar of benefit or cost that occurs at some date in the future is
not equal to a dollar of benefit or cost now. The receipt of $1 now is

more valuable than the receipt of \$1 in one year because the dollar received now can be invested and earn interest. If the rate of interest is 10 percent, the receipt of \$1 now is equivalent to the receipt of \$1.10 in one year. Accordingly, a project that yields a benefit of \$1.10 in one year is equivalent to a project that yields a benefit of \$1 now. Stated alternatively, a program that yields a benefit of \$1 in one year is equivalent to a program that yields a benefit of 91 cents currently, because 91 cents invested at 10 percent compounded annually will yield \$1 in one year. In this case, the 91 cents is the *present value* of the \$1 benefit (or cost) that arises one year from now.

When interest is compounded annually, the present value of the future receipt or payment of any amount A_i in year i can be determined from the formula

$$PV = \sum_{i=1}^{n} [A_i/(1+r)^i],$$

where r is the rate of interest (rate of discount of future values) and i is the number of years. Table 15.1 shows the present value of \$1 for a variety of rates of interest and periods of time. With an interest rate of 5 percent, \$1 in one year is equivalent to \$0.95 now, while it is equivalent to only 61 cents ten years in the future. When the rate of interest is 20 percent, \$1 in one year is equivalent to only 83 cents now, and \$1 in ten years is equivalent to only 16 cents now.

TABLE 15.1 Present Value of \$1 for Selected Discount Rates and Time Periods

	Discount Rate			
Year	5%	10%	15%	20%
1	\$0.952	\$0.909	\$0.870	\$0.833
2	0.907	0.826	0.756	0.694
3	0.864	0.751	0.658	0.579
4	0.823	0.683	0.572	0.482
5	0.784	0.621	0.497	0.402
10	0.614	0.386	0.247	0.162
15	0.481	0.239	0.123	0.065
20	0.377	0.149	0.061	0.026
30	0.231	0.057	0.015	0.004
40	0.142	0.022	0.004	0.001
50	0.087	0.009	0.001	—

As you can see from a quick inspection of Table 15.1, the rate at which future benefits and costs are discounted can significantly affect the present value of those benefits and costs and, hence, the evaluation of the programs those benefits and costs represent.

In many cases the costs of public programs are borne mainly in the present, as when a dam is built to control flooding from a river, while the benefits occur mainly in the future, as when damage is avoided because a flood was averted. The lower the rate at which future benefits and costs are discounted in such cases, the larger the net benefits of any particular project size will appear and the larger the project size that maximizes the net benefit will be.

Table 15.2 illustrates this point. Suppose the dam to control flooding takes one year to construct and requires an initial outlay of $10 million. For the subsequent fifty years of expected life of the dam, the annual benefits from the estimated reduction in damage owing to flooding are anticipated to be $1 million. If those benefits are discounted at 5 percent, their present value will be $18.3 million, leaving a net benefit of $8.3 million. But if the future benefits are discounted at 15 percent, their present value will be only $6.7 million, which leaves a negative net benefit of $3.3 million. With a discount rate of 10 percent, the present value of the future benefits is $9.9 million, indicating a zero net benefit. The choice of a discount rate above or below 10 percent is essentially a choice of whether the project will show positive or negative net benefits. Moreover, the lower the rate of discount, the larger the net benefits will be. With a 1 percent rate of discount, for instance, the present value of the benefits will be $39.2 million, giving a net benefit of $29.2 million.

TABLE 15.2 Benefit-Cost Calculations with Different Interest Rates[a]

Interest Rate	Present Value (in millions)		Net Present Value
	Benefit	Cost	
1%	$39.2	$10	$29.2
5%	18.3	10	8.3
10%	9.9	10	−0.1
15%	6.7	10	−3.3

[a] Cost of $10 million is borne initially, and the annual benefits are $1 million per year for fifty years.

Two Categories of Discount Rate

In light of the pivotal importance that the choice of a rate of discount can have, it is understandable that much interest has arisen over the principles that might guide the choice of that rate. There are, of course, numerous rates of discount that might be chosen; a perusal of the financial pages of any major newspaper will show numerous rates of interest that could be used. The possible rates of discount can be put into two categories for our purposes. One category refers to a rate of interest confronted by citizens acting privately. Although there are many such rates of interest, including the rates of return on various corporate equities and the rates corporations must pay to borrow, we can conceptualize an abstract notion of a private interest rate.

The other category is the rate of interest confronted by citizens acting collectively through government. Although there are numerous particular rates of interest at which units of government borrow, it is possible to conceptualize an abstract notion of a collective or public interest rate, and some such collective interest rate is generally taken to be the other main option for a discount rate. The choice between these two categories is important because the collective interest rate is generally several percentage points below the private interest rate.

Within the framework of social profitability, the choice of a rate of discount reduces primarily to a matter of which rate conforms more closely with the essential spirit of the profitability criterion. If government takes $100 from private citizens to invest in a program, with the return on this investment to accrue in one year, what is the return in one year that should be anticipated if the investment is to be consistent with the profitability criterion? In other words, what is given up when this resource transfer takes place? What is the opportunity cost of public investment?

Effect of the Corporation Income Tax
on the Discount Rate

In the absence of taxes on capital and on the income from capital, a rate of interest equates the rate of time preference — that is, the rate at which people are willing to sacrifice present for future consumption — and the rate of return on investment. A 10 percent rate of interest, for instance, means that savers are willing to save as long as they receive a 10 percent return on their abstinence from current consumption and, simultaneously, that investors receive a 10 percent return on the use to which they put the savings. The rate of interest represents both the productivity of investment and the rate at which people discount future consumption relative to present consumption.

The corporate income tax creates a divergence between the two rates. Suppose all economic activity in the private sector is organized through corporations and that the corporation tax is 50 percent (to simplify the arithmetic from the actual current rate of 46 percent). Even if investors evaluated government and business firms as equally safe investments, corporations would have to promise a rate of return double that promised by government. If government is able to attract capital by promising a 10 percent rate of return, business firms will have to promise 20 percent before tax in order to return 10 percent to investors. The opportunity cost of the investment is 20 percent, which is the output that would be sacrificed if the investment is not undertaken. But the rate of time preference indicates that people would be willing to make the investment for a return of only 10 percent. The corporate tax creates a divergence between the rate of time preference and the opportunity cost of investment.

So long as the corporate tax exists, however, 20 percent, not 10 percent, indicates the opportunity cost of public investment and, hence, the appropriate rate of discount. An investment of $100 in corporate activity returns $20 per year, with $10 accruing to investors and $10 accruing to people generally in their capacity as taxpayers-cum-citizens. Suppose $100 is transferred from corporate to government use, where the rate of return is 10 percent. The investment of $100 yields a return of $10 to taxpayers-cum-citizens, and that is all. Taxpayers-cum-citizens are equally well off in either case, but investors are worse off as a result of the transfer of resources. The criterion of social profitability would in this case call for resources to be shifted from activities in which the return is 10 percent into activities in which they earn 20 percent.[2]

Differences in Degree of Risk

Public and private interest rates also diverge because of differences in risk confronted by the suppliers of capital. A supplier of capital

[2] It has often been argued that societies tend to invest too little because they discount the future too heavily. Some who advance this argument do so on the grounds that the time horizons of the particular members of society are largely limited by their life expectancies, while the time horizon of a society is not so limited. Low rates of discount on public investment have been advocated as a means of offsetting this short-sightedness. But even if this argument is granted, and there is no consensus on its veracity, it does not argue for a policy favoring public investment over private investment. Rather, it argues for a general policy of subsidizing investment. That is, it argues that rates of time preference are too high generally, the rectification of which requires some means of lowering real interest rates, as through some general subsidization of investment.

to a corporation can be less assured of being paid than a supplier of capital to government. So long as people prefer a more assured to a less assured return of the same value, the private interest rate will exceed the public interest rate by the amount of the necessary risk premium.

In the absence of a corporation income tax, people might supply capital to corporations for a promised return of 10 percent, but they might supply capital to government for a promised return of 8 percent, with the 2-point differential reflecting the value people place on the greater certainty of return from supplying capital to government. In the absence of a corporation income tax, it could be asked whether the discount rate consistent with the criterion of social profitability should be 8 or 10 percent. In the presence of a 50 percent tax on corporation income, which would increase the pretax return on corporate capital to 20 percent, it can be asked whether the appropriate discount rate should be 20 percent or 16 percent, where the 16 percent option represents the effect of imposing a 50 percent tax on corporation income in the absence of the risk premium paid on corporate investment. In either case, the issue is essentially whether the risk premium paid on corporate investment is an element of the opportunity cost of public investment. If it is, the discount rate should be 20 percent in the presence of a 50 percent corporation tax and 10 percent in its absence. If it is not, the discount rate should be 16 percent in the presence of the tax and 8 percent in its absence.

From the point of view of society as a whole, private and public investment seem to be of essentially equal risk. Although government investment is essentially riskless to individual suppliers of capital, government investment is not riskless to everyone in society. Investment programs often fail to yield the returns that were anticipated, and expenses may prove higher than expected, which likewise reduces the return. The reason government investment is essentially riskless for investors is that the risk is shifted onto taxpayers.

An investment in a flood control project may be undertaken because it is thought to be socially profitable. But such things as cost overruns and changes in the pattern of land development may render the project socially unprofitable. A business enterprise that provided this project, setting aside for purposes of discussion the problems of ill-defined ownership that might make such an effort impossible in the first place, might well go bankrupt and not pay the investors the initially promised returns. But if the project is provided by government, taxes are simply increased to cover any losses. Thus the risk of government investments is borne by taxpayers.

The risk premium paid on private capital results simply because the risk on the supply of capital to government is shifted from the suppliers of capital to taxpayers generally. Privately, the locus of risk resides with the suppliers of capital; publicly, it resides with taxpayers. Accordingly, the opportunity cost of public investment seems more properly captured by a market rate of interest that includes a risk premium; since underlying riskiness is essentially the same for either class of investment, it seems that the rate of return offered privately reflects more accurately what is sacrificed by transferring resources from private to public use.

ASSESSMENT OF BENEFIT AND COST

Benefit-cost analysis represents on the one hand a rejection of the criterion of profitability as used by firms, for otherwise there would be no reason for government not to act like private firms in selling its services at a profit. On the other hand, it represents an effort to follow the profitability criterion as it would operate under an alternative system of ownership that does not actually exist. Benefit-cost analysis is to a large extent an exercise in conjectural history, in that it attempts to assess what would take place under a system of ownership rights in which problems associated with the incompleteness of ownership are absent.

In undertaking an assessment of the benefits and costs anticipated from the possible programs of public expenditure, a distinction is commonly made between direct and indirect benefits and costs. This distinction is a matter of judgment, reflecting some notion of immediacy or proximity. With respect to the construction of a subway line, for instance, the value to users of the time they save in traveling would be considered a direct benefit, while the value of the time saved by people who continue to use automobiles, because of lessened traffic congestion, would be viewed as an indirect benefit.

It is also common to distinguish between tangible and intangible benefits and costs, although this distinction is also ultimately a matter of judgment. If the subway reduces traffic noise on nearby highways, the value that people living close to the highways place on the quieter surroundings is an intangible benefit. A distinction is also made between real and pecuniary effects, and pecuniary effects are excluded because to include them would be to engage in double counting: The increased business done by merchants located near the subway terminals may have been offset by a decreased business done by merchants located elsewhere, possibly along the highway. If such an increase in business is to be treated as a benefit of the subway, the decrease in business suffered by merchants elsewhere must be counted as a cost. Such changes in the income positions of various people can also be ignored because when they are aggregated they sum to zero.

Some general issues concerning the assessment of benefits and costs may be illustrated by considering a hypothetical government that has decided to replace its dilapidated prison facility with a new one and that must decide which of several types of facility to construct.[3] One type might be a purely incarcerating facility in which no provision is made for rehabilitation. A second type might be one in which the prisoners are trained for one of a narrow range of vocational skills. A third might be one in which prisoners are trained for one occupation among a broad range. The assessment of benefits and costs entails the application of economic analysis in an effort to describe the benefits and costs that might be anticipated from the different types of facilities. After describing the assessment of benefits and costs in this hypothetical illustration, we will examine three actual applications of benefit-cost analysis.

Benefits

Before any measurement can be undertaken, a benefit-cost analysis must describe the various types of benefits and costs that are anticipated to result from the program. One benefit of investment in prisoner rehabilitation might be a reduction in future prison expenses that would result from a lowered rate of recidivism. Other benefits might be a reduction in losses suffered by the victims of crime because of a lowered crime rate and an increase in tax payments and reduction in welfare costs that result from increased earnings of released prisoners. The reduction in recidivism might lower the equilibrium prison population, which in turn might make possible a saving in future prison costs.

As we mentioned before, any effort to estimate benefits and costs entails an effort to solve empirically an economic model that reflects the system that is influenced by the program under examination. Consider the benefit from the reduction in the rate of recidivism. The first step in assessing the probable magnitude of this benefit might entail the construction of a model of the prison population. At any time, a prison contains a mixture of prisoners described by their criminal record. Some are first offenders, others are recidivists. Each year some prisoners are released and others are incarcerated. Some

---

[3] For treatments of various issues relating to the application of benefit-cost analysis to prisons, see Thomas F. Tabasz, *Toward an Economics of Prisons* (Lexington, Mass.: D.C. Heath, 1975); and John Holahan, "Measuring Benefits from Prison Reform," in *Public Expenditure and Policy Analysis*, 2nd ed., edited by Robert H. Haveman and Julius Margolis (Chicago: Rand McNally, 1977), pp. 301–328.

who are incarcerated are first offenders, while the remainder are recidivists. Among those who are released, some will not be imprisoned again, while others will return.

Information about the probable pattern of the prison population can be used to develop a model of the steady-state equilibrium of the prison population. Suppose the equilibrium prison population is 2,000 inmates and that each prisoner serves a five-year term. Accordingly, each year 400 prisoners are released and 400 are incarcerated in their place. If recidivism takes place only once and at a rate of 50 percent, 200 of the 400 prisoners who are released each year will be incarcerated again. Moreover, if all of the recidivists are returned to prison in the year following their release, 200 of the 400 entering prisoners will be recidivists. Under these conditions, the prison will contain 1,000 inmates who are first offenders and 1,000 who are recidivists.

When such a model of the determinants of the size and composition of the prison population has been constructed, it is possible to assess the benefits from different types of prison programs. Suppose, for instance, one program for investment in prisoner rehabilitation is anticipated to reduce the rate of recidivism to 25 percent.[4] In consequence, only 100 rather than 200 of the 400 prisoners who are released will be incarcerated again. If 200 first offenders are still incarcerated each year, the equilibrium prison population will fall from 2,000 to 1,335 inmates. Once this new equilibrium is attained, 267 prisoners will be incarcerated each year, and as that inmate class is released, only 67 will be incarcerated again. In this model, the reduction in the rate of recidivism from 50 to 25 percent eventually brings about a 33 percent reduction in the equilibrium size of the prison population.

From this anticipated reduction in the size of the prison population, we can develop an assessment of benefit. One form of benefit would be a reduction in the expenses of operating the prison. Suppose the benefits are to be assessed over a ten-year horizon, assuming a 10 percent rate of discount. In the model just described, it is a simple task to estimate the size of the prison population for each of the next ten years. (It would be equally simple to develop estimates for longer periods into the future.) While the prison population will still be 2,000 during the first year of the program, it will decline by 100 inmates per year during the second through sixth years of the program.

[4] The development of this estimate would itself require the construction of an economic model of the supply of labor, because it would be necessary to estimate the impact of an increase in a released prisoner's expected earnings in a legitimate occupation relative to his or her expected earnings in criminal activity. For a treatment of criminal activity within the framework of a theory of occupational choice, see Gary S. Becker, "Crime and Punishment: An Economic Approach," *Journal of Political Economy* 76 (April 1968), pp. 169–217.

This reduction results because each year's class of 400 is replaced by a class of only 300. In turn, during the seventh through tenth years of the program, the prison population will decline by 25 inmates each year, thus producing an inmate population of 1,400 during the tenth year. During these years, an exiting class of 300 is replaced by an entering class of 275, consisting of 200 first offenders and 75 recidivists (25 percent of the 300 released the previous year).

Once this model has been developed, it is a relatively simple matter of accounting to develop an estimate of the benefit from this reduction in the size of the prison population. Suppose the direct expense of operating the prison is $10,000 per inmate per year. The first reduction in the number of inmates will occur in the second year of the new program. With the inmate population reduced by 100 that year, the reduction in required outlays will be $1 million. In the third through sixth years, required outlays can be anticipated to decline each year by $1 million from the previous year. In the seventh through tenth years, the prison population will be declining by only 25 inmates per year, which means that the cost of operation will decline by an additional $250,000 each year. The present value of this decline in the direct expense of operating the prison is $19,695,850, computed from the formula

$$PV = \frac{\$1,000,000}{(1.1)^2} + \frac{\$2,000,000}{(1.1)^3} + \ldots + \frac{\$5,000,000}{(1.1)^6} +$$
$$\frac{\$5,250,000}{(1.1)^7} + \ldots + \frac{\$6,000,000}{(1.1)^{10}}.$$

The $6,000,000 entry for the tenth year indicates that in the absence of the program, direct spending on prisons would have been $6,000,-000 higher that year than it would be with the program.[5]

The reduction in recidivism, moreover, will ultimately expand the labor force by 665 members, with the timing of this expansion corresponding to the reduction in the size of the prison population. By becoming gainfully employed, these former prisoners will contribute to the tax base, which in turn can be thought of either as allowing for tax reductions generally or as allowing for an expanded provision of public services without a concomitant increase in taxes. (Alternatively, the tax payments could be substracted from the cost of the program, to indicate that prisoners partially finance their own rehabilitation.) The reduction in recidivism also can be translated into

[5] The present value of the benefit anticipated to accrue in the tenth year is $2,316,000. As Table 15.1 shows, the present value of $1 in ten years is 38.6 cents, assuming a 10 percent rate of discount. Hence, the present value of $6 million is $2.316 million.

a reduction in the number of crimes committed. By placing some value on different types of crimes and estimating the reduction in crime that results from the lower rate of recidivism, a value for the reduction in the loss from crime can be estimated and attributed to the program.

Furthermore, the reduction in the size of the prison population reduces the anticipated future expense of building and maintaining prison facilities. Alternatively, suppose the current growth rate of the prison population is 100 inmates per year. If the prison's capacity is 2,200, its capacity will be reached in two years in the absence of the rehabilitation program, at which time additional facilities will be required. With the rehabilitation program, the 2,200 limit will not be reached until the seventh year. In this instance, the rehabilitation program permits postponement of the need for additional capacity for five years; the benefit of this postponement can be measured by the difference between the expense of construction now and the present value of that expense in five years. If the expense of the additional capacity is estimated at $1 million, the present value of having to make that outlay in five years is $621,000 assuming a 10 percent rate of discount, which implies a benefit of $379,000 from the five-year delay in construction.

Although these various problems of valuation are often difficult to implement empirically, they are nonetheless relatively amenable to monetary assessment. Not all elements of benefit are so assessable in monetary terms. In one prison facility inmates may live under less brutal conditions than in another. But what value should be placed on the alleviation of brutal living conditions? Such a question might be answered conceptually by determining how much people would be willing to pay for upgrading the living conditions in a prison, even if that upgrading produced no reduction in recidivism. It is possible that people may place a negative value on such an upgrading. Regardless of whether upgrading is valued negatively or positively, intangible benefits and costs pose difficult problems of assessment, and these difficulties support the point that benefit-cost analysis is more properly regarded as a method for developing and presenting information about expenditure options than as a rule to apply in making choices among options.

Costs

The assessment of cost is commonly thought to be a simpler task than the assessment of benefit. Unlike many elements of benefit, cost is usually assigned a clear monetary dimension. It is simple to say that the price of a ticket to a movie is $5 and to call this amount the cost of going to the movie. Yet the benefit from going to the movie does not readily allow such a monetary measure. If cost is considered a benefit forgone, as explained in Chapter 8, then one part of the cost of going to a movie is the benefit forgone by not doing something else. The cost of attending the movie is the alternative benefit that could have been acquired with the $5 price of the ticket and the three hours of time that attendance at the theater required.

Cost is generally thought to be more objective and hence more readily measurable than benefit because it is commonly confounded with price. Actually, at the margin of choice, price is simultaneously a measure of cost and of benefit.[6] Cost and benefit are not separate, distinct features of a situation subject to choice; rather, they are mirror images of each other.

In enumerating the various types of cost associated with some proposed project, it is customary to distinguish those that are attributable directly to constructing and maintaining the project and those that accrue indirectly as a consequence of the project's existence and operation. An investment in prisoner rehabilitation will require some initial capital outlay for the equipment necessary to provide the desired training. If the prisoners are to be trained as automobile mechanics, the training program will require a capital investment in such items as garage facilities, tools and equipment, and a supply of automobiles. Besides these capital outlays, operating expenses will be incurred for training personnel and for material and equipment used to train them. Suppose the program entails an initial capital outlay of $2 million and annual expenditures of $1 million for each of the following ten years. With a 10 percent rate of discount and assuming that the capital equipment will have no salvage value at the conclusion of the ten years, the present value of the ten-year program is $8,144,565, computed from the formula

$$PV = \$2,000,000 + \frac{\$1,000,000}{(1.1)^1} + \frac{\$1,000,000}{(1.1)^2} + \cdots + \frac{\$1,000,000}{(1.1)^{10}}.$$

Forms of indirect cost associated with prison rehabilitation do not seem as evident as they might for some other programs. One form of indirect cost might stem from an increase in traffic congestion around the prison, especially if part of the training program contains a garage offering repair service to the public at subsidized prices. Given information about traffic patterns, one could estimate the loss of time associated with the increased congestion. In turn, this estimate could

[6] This is explained in James M. Buchanan, *Cost and Choice* (Chicago: Markham, 1969).

be multiplied by some value of time to develop an estimate of the cost of congestion.

DISTRIBUTIONAL WEIGHTS

As it is commonly used, benefit-cost analysis aggregates benefits and costs without regard to the identity of the recipients of benefits or the bearers of cost. This neutrality is not required by any law of nature, and it is sometimes suggested that it might beneficially be replaced by an effort to weight benefits and costs according to such criteria as the income of the beneficiaries. If this were done, two programs each with anticipated benefits assessed at $100 would be evaluated differently if the beneficiaries of the two programs differed in income. The benefit to people whose income was twice the average might be evaluated at only $50, while the benefit to people whose income was half the average might be evaluated at $200. In proposals for distributional weighting, the weights w would generally be determined by a formula such as

$$w = (y_k/\bar{y})^{-\lambda},$$

where $\bar{y}$ is average income and y_k is the income of the kth class of beneficiaries. The parameter λ can take on any value, although $\lambda = 1$, $\lambda = 2$, $\lambda = 3$ are commonly used in discussions of distributional weighting.

The operation of distributional weights can be illustrated quite simply with reference to the formula. Consider two possible additions to a flood control project, each of which is anticipated to cost $3 million in present value terms. One addition would primarily protect the property of relatively wealthy people with valuable property. The present value of the benefits of this addition, conceived of as a reduction in the anticipated loss due to flooding, is estimated to be $4 million.

The other addition would protect against flooding where the property belongs to people with relatively low incomes. Because the property is less valuable, the benefits from flood control are lower. Suppose these benefits are estimated at $2 million, essentially because property in the poorer area is only half as valuable as property in the wealthier area. Further suppose that income of people in the poorer area is one-half the average income and that income of people in the wealthier area is twice the average income. (As we noted above, a project cannot be evaluated on the basis of the benefit-cost ratio, but a comparison of ratios is nonetheless a simple way of illustrating the central point here.) Without distributional weights, the project to protect the wealthier area from flooding is more efficient than the project to protect the poorer area.

Now suppose a set of distributional weights is used to assess the two projects. If $\lambda = 1$, benefits in the poorer area will be given a weight of $w = 2$, and benefits in the wealthier area will be given a weight of $w = 0.5$. The weighted benefit from the flood control project in the poorer area will be $4 million, and the weighted benefit in the wealthier area will be $2 million. In this case, the use of distributional weights exactly reverses the assessment of the two projects. For higher values of λ, the benefits received by residents of the poorer area will be increased still further, and the benefits received by the residents of the wealthier area will be reduced further. For $\lambda = 2$, benefits in the poorer area are given a weight of $w = 4$, while benefits in the wealthier area are given a weight of $w = 0.25$. For $\lambda = 3$, benefits are weighted at $w = 8$ in the poorer area and at $w = 0.125$ in the wealthier area.

Distributional weights make the assessment of projects more favorable as those projects confer a larger share of their benefits on people with below-average incomes. The application of distributional weights makes explicit the use of public expenditures as a means of changing the distribution of real consumption opportunities. To a large extent, the use of distributional weights makes explicit only what is done anyway through a variety of public programs to equalize consumption opportunities. A food stamp program that provides subsidized food for people with low incomes could be treated not as a subsidy but as a socially profitable program within the framework of benefit-cost analysis, simply by applying an appropriately chosen set of distributional weights to the benefits.

Perhaps the main concern with distributional weights is that they can allow a substantial degree of resource wastage. With $\lambda = 3$ and an average income of the beneficiary group of one-half the national average, a program that wasted up to seven-eighths of its output would appear warranted through the use of distributional weights. This point is illustrated in Figure 15.2. The opportunity locus reflects various distributions of income, under the assumption of full efficiency in resource utilization.

A program that imposes more cost on relatively wealthy taxpayers than it awards in benefits to relatively poor recipients is warranted by the distributional weighting scheme. Both areas might consist of chicken farmers whose farms are subject to damage from flooding. The use of a distributional weight of $w = 3$ when the poor farmers have half the average income and the wealthy farmers have twice the average would evaluate as more favorable a program that saved only 100 chickens owned by poor farmers than a program that for

FIGURE 15.2 Distributional Weights and Economic Efficiency

The opportunity locus describes alternative distributions of income between two sets of people, H denoting those with relatively high incomes and L denoting those with relatively low incomes. Initially, H-type people have incomes of H_1 and L-type people have incomes of L_1, described by A. Suppose the government institutes a program that has costs in excess of benefits but is justified through a system of distributional weights. The costs are equal to $H_1 - H_2$ and the benefits are equal to $L_2 - L_1$. The resulting outcome is described by B. Although this outcome is justified by the use of distributional weights, any movement to some other position within the area CBD—that is, toward the opportunity locus—can increase the wealth of both sets of people.

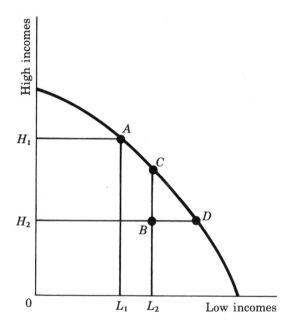

the same expense saved up to 800 chickens owned by the wealthier farmers. If the chickens of the wealthier farmers were saved instead, society would have available up to 700 more chickens for the same outlay as that entailed by the flood control project. It would be possible to transfer to the poorer farmers more than 100 chickens, which would leave them even wealthier than they would have been with the flood control project and at the same time leave the rest of society wealthier as well. Whether this potential might be realized is, however, another matter.

THREE EXERCISES IN BENEFIT-COST ANALYSIS

Numerous efforts have been made to apply benefit-cost analysis to various options for public expenditure, three of which are described here.

Project Crossroads[7]

Between September 1968 and August 1970, the District of Columbia instituted a program of counseling, job placement and training, and remedial education for youthful first offenders. The ages of the participants were between eighteen and twenty-five, and they were arrested for such crimes as burglary, robbery, larceny, and auto theft, with a few also arrested for prostitution and forgery. The activities of Project Crossroads took place during the three-month period between arrest and trial. The court would dismiss charges on the recommendation of the project's director. During the two-year life of the project, 460 people participated.

Three main categories of benefit were thought to arise from Project Crossroads. One category was an anticipated reduction in the various costs of operating the court system. Since the project's participants would not stand trial, the claim on court resources would obviously be reduced. If the project reduced the future commission of crimes by the participants, future court costs would be reduced as well. The second category of expected benefit was a reduction in the rate of recidivism among participants. Participants were trained for gainful employment, and it was thought that the increase in anticipated earnings in legitimate occupations relative to the anticipated earnings through crime would reduce the crimes, and hence the cost of crimes, committed by participants. The third category of anticipated benefit was the increased productivity of program participants.

The basic data about the project were developed by studying the first 200 participants for one year after they left the project. To form a basis of comparison, a control group of 107 people was selected from among youthful first offenders arrested for the same types of crimes as committed by the participants in Project Crossroads. These people were all arrested in the twelve-month period prior to September 1968. As far as possible, the members of the control group and the participants in Project Crossroads differed only in their participation in the project. During the one-year period following each participant's release from the project, 26 percent of the participants in

---

[7] The discussion of Project Crossroads is taken from Holahan, "Measuring Benefits from Prison Reform."

Project Crossroads were arrested for further crimes, and 36.4 percent of the control group were arrested.

The benefit generated by the project was estimated by comparing the experience of the 460 participants with their experience had the project not existed, in which event the participants would have gone to trial and would have had a 10.4 percent higher rate of recidivism. Table 15.3 presents the basic data in a benefit-cost analysis of Project Crossroads. The reduction in the cost of crime owing to the reduced rate of recidivism was the primary category of benefit. With a 5 percent rate of discount, the present value of this benefit was estimated at nearly $250,000, or about $500 per participant (about $5,000 per recidivist prevented). With a 15 percent rate of discount, the present value of the benefit was estimated at slightly over $210,000.

Such marked changes in interest rate make relatively small changes in the present value of benefit in this case because the project was considered for only one year in the future. If a longer period of time had been considered, the benefit would have been larger, assuming the difference in rates of recidivism persisted, and the present value of the benefits associated with different rates of discount would have diverged more sharply. Table 15.3 presents a lower-bound estimate of the benefit from reduced recidivism. If the 10.4 percent differential holds for one year and is erased thereafter, the benefit from reduced recidivism is as shown in the first row. If the differential

TABLE 15.3   Benefits and Costs of Project Crossroads

	Discount Rate		
	5%	10%	15%
Category of benefit			
Reduced Recidivism	$249,507	$228,215	$210,029
Diversion from court system	109,995	104,995	100,430
Earnings of participants	190,282	170,729	156,074
Total benefit	549,784	503,939	466,533
Total cost	233,256	233,256	233,256
Benefits: Costs	2.4	2.2	2.0

Source: John Holahan, "Measuring Benefits from Prison Reform," in *Public Expenditure and Policy Analysis,* 2nd ed., edited by Robert H. Haveman and Julius Margolis (Chicago: Rand McNally, 1977), p. 326. Originally published as Urban Institute Working Paper 963-14, March 20, 1973. Reprinted by permission of the Urban Institute Press.

persisted in subsequent years, the present value of the benefit from the reduced rate of recidivism would be even higher.

The benefits from the diversion of the resources of the court system and from the increased productivity of participants in the project are estimated in similar fashion by comparing the experience of the participants with that of the members of the control group. The reduction in court costs and the increase in earnings constitute these forms of benefit, both of which are also assumed to cease after one year. The cost of the project is invariant to the rate of discount and is slightly over $500 per participant. The rate of discount has no effect on the present value of cost because all costs are assumed to be borne immediately, as they are limited to the three-month period following the initial arrest. All of the benefit from the project, on the other hand, occurs after this three-month period.

The Mid-State Project[8]

The Mid-State project was proposed by the U.S. Bureau of Reclamation to divert water from the Platte River in Nebraska for use in irrigation as a means of curtailing the use of wells as a source of water. The central elements of the bureau's assessment of benefits and costs are shown in Table 15.4, as they were appraised in 1967.

The bureau's assessment projected annual benefits of $5,661,500. Most of those benefits were estimated to result from the conversion of 44,000 acres of land from dry farming to irrigation. The direct benefits of the increased production were estimated at $59.86 per acre per year, yielding an estimated annual benefit of $2,471,000. It was further estimated that 96,000 acres that were irrigated by wells would be relieved of pumping expenses after the project was instituted. The reduction in pumping expense was estimated at $12.17 per acre per year, the total estimated value of this benefit being $1,096,000 per year. The switch from wells to water diverted from the Platte River would keep the water table from declining further, the bureau argued. When the groundwater stabilization occurred, pumping expenses would be reduced throughout the area affected by the project. The bureau estimated that 163,000 acres would be so affected and that the annual value of this reduction in expense was $5.05 per acre, yielding an annual benefit of $772,000.

These three categories of estimated benefit totaled $4,339,000, which is approximately three-quarters of the total estimated benefit of $5,661,500. The other categories of benefit were relatively small.

---

[8] The following discussion is derived from Steve H. Hanke and Richard A. Walker, "Benefit-Cost Analysis Reconsidered: An Evaluation of the Mid-State Project," *Water Resources Research* 10 (October 1974), pp. 898–908.

TABLE 15.4   Bureau of Reclamation's Benefit-Cost Analysis

Description	Value
Benefits	
Direct, 44,000 acres at $59.86	$2,471,000[a]
Indirect, 44,000 acres at $12.11	204,000[b]
Reduced pumping expenses, 96,000 acres at $12.17	1,096,000[a]
Groundwater stabilization, 163,000 acres at $5.05	772,000[a]
Recreation	175,500
Fish and wildlife	425,000
Flood control	518,000
Total annual benefits	$5,661,500
Costs	
Annual capital cost	
($112,334,000 for 100 years at 3.125%)	$3,680,000
Annual operation, maintenance, and replacement	863,000
Total annual costs	4,543,000
Benefit: Cost	1.24

[a] Irrigation benefits are discounted by 0.938 to take account of a five-year development lag before full benefits are realized.

[b] The actual figure was over $500,000, but the bureau presented a net figure by subtracting the land lost to such things as rights-of-way and reservoirs rather than showing these losses separately.

Source: Steve H. Hanke and Richard A. Walker, "Benefit-Cost Analysis Reconsidered: An Evaluation of the Mid-State Project," *Water Resources Research* 10 (October 1974), p. 900. Copyrighted by the American Geophysical Union. Reprinted by permission.

The indirect benefits of converting 44,000 acres from dry farming to irrigation were estimated at $12.11 per acre, or $204,000. Recreation benefits were estimated at $175,000, while the value of such activities as fishing and hunting were estimated to be $425,000. Finally, the value of flood control protection was estimated at $518,000.

The annual cost of the project, which contains two elements, was estimated to be $4,543,000. The estimated capital cost of the project, $112,334,000, was capitalized over a one-hundred-year period at a 3.125 percent interest rate to determine an annual equivalent. That is, the estimated capital cost of $112,334,000 is equivalent in present value terms to one hundred annual payments of $3,680,000, when the rate of discount is 3.125 percent. In addition to this annual equivalent of the initial capital expense, it was estimated that the annual expenses for operation and maintenance would be $863,000. Hence, the total annual expense of the project was estimated to be $4,543,000. According to the bureau's analysis, the Mid-State project had a benefit-cost ratio of 1.24, indicating, in the bureau's judgment, that the project was worthwhile. (Although it was noted above that a ratio of total benefits to total costs is not an adequate indicator of social profitability, the main interest here is not in constructing some "better" estimate, but only in illustrating a particular benefit-cost analysis. Therefore, the focus on the benefit-cost ratios that follow provides valid points for illustration, even if those ratios reflect an underlying conceptual inadequacy.)

Hanke and Walker suggest a number of ways in which the bureau's analysis of the benefits and costs of the Mid-State project could be reassessed, with the bases for these alternative assessments being well grounded in analytical principle. The main component of cost is the conversion of the initial capital study outlay to an annual equivalent by spreading that outlay over 100 years and using a discount rate of 3.125 percent. Hanke and Walker suggest that an alternative life of fifty years has reasonable grounds for support, and that different rates of discount are possible. The 3.125 percent rate that was used by the Bureau of Reclamation was the coupon rate prevailing at the time on long-term government bonds. Even then, the actual rate on long-term bonds was 4.85 percent, and, moreover, the rate of discount called for by the Water Resources Planning Act of 1965 was 5.375 percent. With a discount rate of 5.375 percent and a fifty-year life, the annual cost of the project was estimated to be $6,487,000, which gave a benefit-cost ratio of 0.87, accepting the bureau's initial figures for benefits. Guidelines issued by the Office of Management and Budget as to the opportunity cost of public funds set the proper discount rate at 10 percent. Use of this discount rate would increase the annual cost to $12,193,000, giving a benefit-cost ratio of 0.46.

Some of the Bureau of Reclamation's projections of benefits were also questioned by Hanke and Walker. The bureau projected annual fish and wildlife benefits to be $425,000, but Hanke and Walker advanced a plausible basis for thinking that the project would dry up much of the habitat for wildlife and, consequently, much of the opportunity for fishing. Rather than providing the positive benefit of an enhanced opportunity for fishing and hunting, the project might actually destroy much of the existing opportunity. Accordingly, Hanke and Walker estimated that the fish and wildlife benefits would actually be negative, −$347,000.

The direct benefits of converting 44,000 acres from dry farming to irrigation was nearly half of the total benefit from the project. Yet Hanke and Walker showed that a substantial share of this benefit represented a double counting because it included such things as the increased farm income attributable to price support programs, but it did not include the negative benefit to taxpayers of providing the larger subsidies to farmers. Through the elimination of such pecuniary transfers, the projected benefit from converting the 44,000 acres from dry farming to irrigation became $1,136,400, less than half its initial projection. Moreover, Hanke and Walker also argued that a plausible figure for flood control benefits was $341,000 rather than the $518,000 used by the bureau.

The impact of the various emendations offered by Hanke and Walker is both startling and instructive. The annual benefits were projected by Hanke and Walker to be only $2,879,000. Even if the bureau's use of a 3.125 percent discount rate and a one hundred-year life is accepted, the benefit-cost ratio is only 0.63. Use of a 5.375 percent discount rate and a fifty-year life yields a benefit-cost ratio of 0.44.When a 10 percent rate of discount is used, the benefit-cost ratio declines to 0.23.

The lesson to be gleaned from this reconsideration of the Mid-State project is not that the Bureau of Reclamation made an erroneous analysis of benefits and costs that Hanke and Walker corrected. If this were the lesson, benefit-cost analysis would be properly regarded as a rule for decision making, and the primary problem of public administration would be to employ people who could conduct benefit-cost analyses correctly. The proper lesson seems to be that benefit-cost analysis cannot be looked on as a strictly objective method for making choices among policy options. The same facts can lead people to construct quite different interpretations. Each entry in a table of benefits and costs represents an empirical estimation of an economic model of the policy or program under consideration. Even totally disinterested analysts can differ in their views about proper approaches to modeling the phenomenon in question as well as in their views about how to form empirical estimates. Moreover, benefit-cost analysis is by no means typically generated by disinterested analysts; as Hanke and Walker conclude, "The selection of appropriate water projects is a political process, no matter how deeply hidden the political choices are beneath the complex analytics of benefit-cost analysis." [9]

The Trans-Alaska Pipeline [10]

The importance of political considerations in the choice among projects is aptly illustrated by Charles Cicchetti and Myrick Freeman's

[9] Ibid., p. 907.
[10] The following discussion comes from Charles J. Cicchetti and A. Myrick Freeman III, "The Trans-Alaska Pipeline: An Economic Analysis of Alternatives," in Pollution, Resources, and the Environment, edited by Alain C. Enthoven and A. Myrick Freeman III (New York: Norton, 1973), pp. 271–284.

study of the trans-Alaska pipeline. (The low prices cited for oil reflect that fact that the study was prepared in 1972). Two alternative routes for shipping oil from northern Alaska were considered. The trans-Alaska route would entail the construction of a pipeline to Valdez, Alaska, from which point the oil would be shipped by sea to the western United States. The route would be 789 miles long, and the pipeline would cross two mountain ranges, one of which is seismically quite active. The other route would run along the Mackenzie River valley to Edmonton, Canada, where the pipeline would connect with existing pipelines to the midwestern United States. This pipeline would be between 1,600 and 1,800 miles long, and there seems to be little doubt that in minimizing environmental damage the Mackenzie Valley route would be superior. The primary question for benefit-cost analysis is whether the other considerations weigh sufficiently heavily in favor of the trans-Alaska pipeline to offset its environmental inferiority.

At the time of the study, the cost of the oil that would be displaced by the Alaskan oil was $2.49 per barrel in Los Angeles, which would receive the oil from the trans-Alaskan pipeline, and $2.74 per barrel in Chicago, the recipient of oil from the Mackenzie Valley pipeline. The question at issue is which pipeline option offers the greater net benefit, given that a decision has already been made to exploit the northern Alaskan oil. If oil costs the same to transport to either Los Angeles or Chicago, and if environmental consequences are the same for both routes, the Mackenzie Valley pipeline would have the higher net benefits because the oil shipped to Chicago would displace more costly oil than the oil shipped to Los Angeles.

Each barrel of oil shipped to Chicago would represent a social saving of 25 cents ($2.74 − $2.49) over the alternative of shipping it to Los Angeles. If the oil is more costly to ship to Chicago, however, the social saving from shipping it there is reduced. If the cost of shipping it to Chicago exceeds by more than 25 cents per barrel the cost of shipping it to Los Angeles, there will be a social loss in shipping the oil to Chicago, unless the possible environmental costs of shipment to Los Angeles are regarded as sufficiently large to offset the otherwise higher cost of the Mackenzie Valley pipeline.

As for the costs of the two routes, Cicchetti and Freeman used the cost data supplied by the oil companies for the Mackenzie Valley pipeline to Chicago and for the combination of trans-Alaska pipeline and tanker to Los Angeles. These data were discounted at 10 percent over a twenty-five-year life. To reflect some of the uncertainty that necessarily exists in such estimates, low, medium, and high estimates of cost were developed. Although the Mackenzie Valley route was more costly under all three estimates, the added costliness was always less than the added costliness of midwestern oil over western oil.

The high estimate of transit cost was $1.23 per barrel for the Mackenzie Valley pipeline and $1.10 for the trans-Alaska pipeline. The higher cost of 13 cents per barrel for shipment to Chicago means a social saving of 12 cents per barrel for shipping to Chicago via the Mackenzie Valley route, considering that Chicago oil is 25 cents per barrel more costly than Los Angeles oil. Actually, this is a lower-bound estimate because the intangible environmental benefits always favor the Mackenzie Valley route. The medium estimates of savings were $1.09 per barrel for the Mackenzie Valley pipeline and $1.01 per barrel for the trans-Alaska pipeline. If shipment to Chicago is only 8 cents per barrel more expensive than shipment to Los Angeles, there is a 17-cents-per-barrel advantage plus whatever value might be attached to the environmental superiority of the Mackenzie Valley route. The low cost estimates were 94 cents per barrel for the Mackenzie Valley pipeline and 91 cents per barrel for the trans-Alaska pipeline. If it costs only 3 cents more per barrel to ship to Chicago, the Mackenzie Valley route yields a social saving of 22 cents per barrel, in addition to its environmental advantages.

The greater social benefit from shipment to Chicago seems to be matched by greater profits to the oil companies, as the data in Table 15.5 show. The selling prices of oil at the time were $3.17 per barrel in Los Angeles and $3.81 per barrel in Chicago. Wellhead prices (selling price minus transportation costs) were $2.16 per barrel for oil shipped to Los Angeles and $2.72 for oil shipped to Chicago.

TABLE 15.5   Oil Company Net Revenue per Barrel for Two Routes

	Trans-Alaska Pipeline	Mackenzie Valley
Market price	$3.17	3.81
Less transportation cost	1.01	1.09
Wellhead price	2.16	2.72
Less 20% tax on wellhead price	.43	.54
Less production cost	.25	.25
Net revenue	$1.48	$1.93

Source: Adapted from Charles J. Cicchetti and A. Myrick Freeman III, "The Trans-Alaska Pipeline: An Economic Analysis of Alternatives," in *Pollution, Resources, and the Environment,* edited by Alain C. Enthoven and A. Myrick Freeman III (New York: Norton, 1973), pp. 277–280.

The state of Alaska imposed an excise tax of 20 percent of the well-head price, or 43 cents per barrel of oil shipped to Los Angeles and 54 cents per barrel of oil shipped to Chicago. When this tax and the actual production cost of 25 cents per barrel are subtracted from the wellhead price, oil company revenue appears to be $1.48 per barrel on oil shipped to Los Angeles and $1.93 per barrel on oil shipped to Chicago. The benefit-cost analysis that supported the Mackenzie Valley pipeline seems also to support the interests of the oil companies in their profits.

Yet the oil companies strongly supported the trans-Alaska pipeline. An analysis of why this might have been rational at the time shows some of the ways in which different public policies interact. The U.S. government had at that time a Mandatory Oil Import Quota Program, which was ended in 1973. Under this program a company that exported oil was entitled also to import an equivalent amount of oil. Oil could be shipped from Valdez to Japan, and for each barrel exported the exporter could import a barrel of oil at the east coast where its price was higher. At the time, the market price of oil in Japan was only $2 per barrel. With transportation cost estimated at 80 cents per barrel, the wellhead price on oil exported to Japan was $1.20, so the excise tax would have been 24 cents. With a production cost of 25 cents per barrel, the resulting revenue derived from the sale of oil in Japan would be only 81 cents per barrel, in contrast to $1.48 per barrel derived from oil shipped to Los Angeles and $1.93 per barrel from oil shipped to Chicago.

However, the export of oil to Japan also entitled the shipper to import an equal amount of oil at the east coast. The difference between the price of oil on the east coast and the price for which the shipper could obtain that oil was estimated to be $1.75 per barrel. Consequently, the combination of shipping Alaskan oil to Japan and importing other oil to the east coast under the import quota program would seem likely to produce a net revenue of $2.56 per barrel. This is a considerably higher yield for the oil companies than they would realize by direct shipment to the Midwest. The total stock of resources devoted to the shipment of oil would, of course, be much higher, which illustrates the social waste promoted by the import quota program.

THE PROBLEM OF FIDUCIARY RESPONSIBILITY

It should be clear by now that the use of benefit-cost analysis to promote economic efficiency is a difficult task. The assessment of benefit and cost is subject to much uncertainty: Estimates must be based on necessarily incomplete data; arbitrary choices of models and estimates are often required; various types of noncommensurable elements are usually present; and there is no uniquely correct rate of discount. Even if these limitations are ignored, however, and a benefit-cost analysis unambiguously reveals one project as more efficient than the others to those who examine the analysis, the use of benefit-cost analysis cannot avoid some issues of fiduciary responsibility concerning the construction and presentation of the options about which a choice is to be made.

Suppose a benefit-cost analysis reveals that one size or type of prison is the most efficient choice. This analysis implies that given the necessity to choose among different options, one of those at hand is the most efficient choice. But why is analysis and choice restricted to the options under consideration in the first place? Among other things, a prison is but one part of an overall judicial system, and a quite different option, say instituting some type of judicial reform, may be preferable to building a new prison. Rather than a choice among types and sizes of prisons, the choice could be construed as one among such options as a new prison, an increase in the number of judges, or a change in procedures to allow speedier trials. The benefit-cost frame of reference is also appropriate for this choice, but the options are more difficult to define, and noncommensurable elements become more pronounced.

Benefit-cost analysis is a technique that can be helpful in developing and presenting information relating to the choice among options. It is not a rule for making choices, but it may lead to a more informed choice among the options that have been advanced for analysis. *The actual making a choice, as well as the development of the options from which a choice will be made in the first place, is essentially a product of the incentives contained within political institutions*, with different institutions imparting different incentives, as we explored in Part II.

As we noted earlier, benefit-cost analysis, understood as a principle of conduct, is applicable to all choices. A distinction can be made, however, between the ex ante judgment (that is, one made in anticipation of a result) that leads to a particular choice and the ex post evaluation of the actual consequences of that choice. A brewery may expand its capacity because it anticipates that the extra revenues generated by the added capacity will exceed the extra costs. A government agency may dam a river or prohibit the sale of a product because it judges that the benefits from doing so will exceed the costs. These judgments of benefits and costs are ex ante; that is, they reflect an anticipation about what will result from the decision to be made. The actual result may be quite different. Ex ante, all investment projects are viewed by their initiators as having benefits in excess of costs. Ex post, however, some investments will turn out to have been failures. Ex ante, the Ford Motor Company's creation of the Edsel surely seemed to be a profitable choice; ex post, it turned out to be a disaster.

Recognition that the lack of omniscience implies a possible divergence between an ex ante assessment of prospective outcomes and an ex post determination of actual outcomes raises a question of fiduciary responsibility in decision making. Suppose someone thinks that a new product will make a profitable addition to a company's line because a benefit-cost analysis reveals anticipated benefits in excess of anticipated costs. This judgment is based on beliefs about the future, which cover such things as the future expenses of production and the future demands for the product. There is no way of knowing with certainty what the actual future states of these circumstances will be, so a decision must be based only on informed judgments about the future.

How knowledgeable are those judgments likely to be? Suppose the new product is, for whatever reason, a pet project of the person in charge of making the recommendation. Questions of capability aside, that person's reading of the evidence about the future may turn out naturally to be roseate. What would prevent such a reading of the evidence? For a person or for a business, the presence of a residual-claimant status creates an incentive to temper one's hopes, wishes, or prejudices because inefficient decisions will redound to the harm of the decision maker. While mistakes cannot be avoided, the system of profit and loss creates a relatively disinterested, ex post check on the veracity of ex ante judgments of benefit and cost.

It is somewhat different in government. The absence of price and profit information weakens the cognitive basis of a benefit-cost analysis and lessens the incentive of decision makers to pursue efficient over inefficient courses of action. This possible clash between the requisites for economic efficiency and the system of incentives that operates within government was examined in Part II. While economic efficiency may result in some instances, it does not seem to be an inherent tendency within government. Business and government are similar in that the central perspective of benefit-cost analysis is equally appropriate in both settings, but they differ because of systematic differences in the information that is produced regarding the success of different choices.

Price and profit provide information on which to base an analysis of benefits and costs in business, but this information is not available in government. Moreover, the record of actual experiences can be useful in helping to make a more informed judgment in other, related instances that might arise. Additionally, the presence of an unambiguous measure of ex post success — profit — serves to harness the natural tendency toward overoptimism that otherwise would almost certainly be present when someone else's money is being spent. The necessity of putting one's money on the line and of being responsible for the ultimate outcome surely has a sobering effect on the assessment of the prospects for such projects, an effect that is weakened when tax money is used in a setting where no judgment about profitability has to be faced.

If a firm builds a campground because it thinks it will be profitable, it has in effect made a judgment that it thinks the benefits to consumers will exceed the costs of the campground — that is, the value to consumers of other uses of the resources embodied in the campground. If the firm is correct in this judgment, it will make a profit. In government, however, there is no direct scope for profitability to operate, so there cannot be any unambiguous judgment rendered after the fact about the value or profitability of a previous decision to commit resources to a particular use. The general usefulness of such techniques as benefit-cost analysis depend on the institutional environment within which the demand for benefit-cost analysis emerges.

In a setting in which public officials are seeking to have their agencies prosper and grow, benefit-cost analysis may well be an instrument for assisting in the selection of policies and programs that promote that growth. In this regard, it is perhaps curious that the application of benefit-cost analysis in government is conducted in terms of economic variables, as if the agency is aiming to maximize some indicator of social profitability or value. Votes or some other measure of political support might be a more appropriate framework around which to organize an assessment of the benefits and costs of possible programs, at least with respect to providing information truly of interest to those responsible for making decisions.

Why not evaluate the Mid-State project by the additions to and subtractions from the Bureau of Reclamation's base of political support? Why does benefit-cost analysis proceed within the language and categories of profit maximization when the institutional setting within which government operates is one in which the "profits" resulting from the operation of government are nonappropriable? Perhaps the relatively poor standing of the Mid-State project in terms of an efficiency notion of social profitability would be seen differently if the benefit-cost analysis were conducted in terms of the benefits and costs borne by those with interests in the activities of the Bureau of Reclamation. The study of the trans-Alaska pipeline suggests this may be a possibility. Perhaps projects that are shown to be inefficient by a benefit-cost analysis conducted from the perspective of social profitability would be efficient when conducted from the perspective of the interests that dominate the legislation pertaining to those programs and projects.[11]

SUGGESTIONS FOR FURTHER READING

The literature on benefit-cost analysis is voluminous. E. J. Mishan, *Cost-Benefit Analysis* (New York: Praeger, 1976), is a comprehensive text. For more practice-oriented treatments, see Peter G. Sassone and William A. Schaffer, *Cost-Benefit Analysis: A Handbook* (New York: Academic Press, 1978); and Lee G. Anderson and Russell F. Settle, *Benefit-Cost Analysis: A Practical Guide* (Lexington, Mass.: D. C. Heath, 1977). A. R. Prest and Ralph Turvey, "Cost-Benefit Analysis: A Survey," in *Surveys of Economic Theory*, vol. 3, *Resource Allocation* (New York: St. Martin's Press, 1966), pp. 155–207, present a thorough survey of the literature before 1966. Roland N. McKean, *Efficiency in Government Through Systems Analysis* (New York: Wiley, 1958), is an important treatise that presents the state of the subject at the time it was written and that is still a valuable treatment of many subjects.

Raymond F. Mikesell, *The Rate of Discount for Evaluating Public Projects* (Washington, D.C.: American Enterprise Institute, 1977), surveys the considerable literature and controversy that have arisen over the rate of discount in benefit-cost analysis. For further discussions of corporation taxation and risk premiums, see William J. Baumol, "On the Social Rate of Discount," *American Economic Review* 58 (September 1968), pp. 788–802. On the transfer of risk to taxpayers from the suppliers of capital to government, see Mark V. Pauly, "Risk and the Social Rate of Discount," *American Economic Review* 60 (March 1970), pp. 195–198.

---

[11] It is also possible to find cases in which projects that seem to be justified by a benefit-cost analysis are not undertaken. Vernon W. Ruttan, "Bureaucratic Productivity: The Case of Agricultural Research," *Public Choice* 35, No. 5 (1980), pp. 529–547, adduces much evidence to show that the rate of return on agricultural research is in the range of 30 to 60 percent. This is much higher than rates of return in many other activities, which suggests that a transfer of resources from other areas into agricultural research would have positive net benefits. But if most of the gain from agricultural research is passed on to consumers, and if consumers are generally ineffective in having their interests represented, the opportunities for social profitability that such a shift seems to offer may not be marshaled effectively through prevailing political institutions. Just as it is possible for majoritarian democracy to overexpand some activities and underprovide others, as we discussed in Part II, so it is possible for a benefit-cost analysis of various programs to show insufficient investment from the perspective of social profitability in some areas and excessive investment in other areas.

Martin S. Feldstein, "Distributional Preferences in Public Expenditure Analysis," in *Redistribution Through Public Choice,* edited by Harold M. Hochman and George E. Peterson (New York: Columbia University Press, 1974), pp. 136–161, advocates the use of distributional weights as supplying additional information about various programs of public expenditure, with those who ultimately make such choices choosing whichever of the various forms of information they prefer, including the unweighted form. For a careful examination of the possible inefficiency consequences of distributional weighting, see Arnold C. Harberger, "On the Use of Distributional Weights in Social Cost-Benefit Analysis," *Journal of Political Economy* 86 (April 1978), part 2, pp. S87–S120. See also Harberger's essay, "Three Basic Postulates for Applied Welfare Economics: An Interpretative Essay," *Journal of Economic Literature* 9 (September 1971), pp. 785–797, in which he argues in favor of distributional neutrality over distributional weighting in benefit-cost analysis.

Many public projects deal with changes in risks of injury, illness, and death, and a considerable literature has arisen over the treatment of reductions of such risks in benefit-cost analysis. A thorough survey of the literature on the risk of death is presented in Martin J. Bailey, *Reducing the Risks to Life* (Washington, D.C.: American Enterprise Institute, 1980). Allan Williams, "Cost-Benefit Analysis: Bastard Science? and/or Insidious Poison in the Body Politik?" *Journal of Public Economics* 1 (August 1972), pp. 199–226, explains that benefit-cost analysis is best understood as a means of developing and presenting information and not as a rule for decision making.

16

The Protective State

National defense was the largest category of expenditure in the federal budget until 1974, when expenditures on income security, which are discussed in Chapter 17, began to occupy first place. Military spending still accounts for more than half of the total amount the federal government spends on the purchase of goods and services, and national defense is by far the most significant item of expenditure in the federal budget in terms of the allocation of resources.

The maintenance of order, both external and internal, is generally thought to be the most essential function of government. The maintenance of external order through protection against disruption from abroad is the task of military spending and is the province of the federal government. The maintenance of internal order through protection against disorder from within the country is covered by police spending and is undertaken in various ways at all levels of government. This chapter focuses on the category of military spending, mainly because it is about ten times as large as that of police spending. Although military spending is by far the largest resource-using category of public expenditure, it is one that often is less amenable to economic analysis than many smaller categories. In part this chapter explores the contribution economics can make to an understanding of military spending, and in part it explains the limitations of an economic analysis of military spending. Regardless of those limitations, the central importance of military spending in the federal budget would seem to make military spending worthy of consideration.

ARMS, POLICE, AND CONUNDRUMS
IN PUBLIC GOODS THEORY

National defense is typically advanced as an archetypical or paradigmatic example in the theory of public goods. A military force that protects one person from foreign aggression is generally thought to simultaneously protect all other members of the nation. Examples can be adduced, of course, in which the protection of one person does not imply the protection of all. People who live close to military installations or to other likely targets of aggression may in some cases receive less protection than people who live in more remote areas. Moreover, there have been numerous cases in which an aggressor occupied only part of a country. In those cases, those who live in the unoccupied parts appear to have received more protection than those who live in the occupied parts. Although such examples can be developed to illustrate the presence of some rivalry in consumption, national defense is widely thought to conform more closely than most government activities to the common definition of a public good — that is, a good for which one person's consumption is not in rivalry with someone else's consumption.

National defense may be nonrivalrous in consumption, but it may not correspond fully to the theory of public goods. As we described that theory in Figure 2.4, an efficient rate of output results when the sum of the marginal evaluations of the individual members of society equals the marginal cost of providing a good, in this case national defense.

Cost has two dimensions in the theory of public goods: the number of people in the jurisdiction and the total amount produced. Given the amount produced, nonrivalry in consumption means that the marginal cost of adding one more person to the jurisdiction is zero. Given the population of the jurisdiction, there is a positive cost of producing more of the good. The marginal-cost function as described in Figure 2.4 represents the rate at which civilian goods must be sacrificed to produce military goods. This marginal cost is equated to the vertical summation of the individual marginal valuations or demand functions to develop a description of the efficient provision of a public good within the framework of the benefit principle.

How appropriate is it to speak of a trade-off between civilian goods and military goods? Suppose spending on military goods is zero. Without protective expenditures, people will not be safe from violence, either by other members of the nation or by foreigners. It is arguable that the consumption of civilian goods will be zero as well, or, alternatively, will correspond to some subsistence level. So long as one nation has resources, human or physical, that are coveted by people in other nations and valued at more than the anticipated cost of conquest, efforts at conquest are likely to occur. The abolition of the expenditures of the protective state would reduce the cost of conquest to foreign nations. The expenditures of the protective state are essential, at least over some range of activity, for social life and the accumulation of wealth. Within that range, there seems to be no rivalry between military goods and civilian goods because it is impossible to consume civilian goods beyond a subsistence level without the concomitant provision of military goods.

Over some range of output, the production of military goods is complementary to rather than rivalrous with the production of civilian goods. Figure 16.1 illustrates a range of output over which the consumption of civilian goods increases simultaneously with the production of military goods. The provision of military goods, along with the other activities of the protective state, increases the security that the members of the nation have against aggression. With increased security, saving and wealth formation increase. People can rationally make plans that extend longer into the future, and the rate at which possible future returns are discounted becomes lower. The less the fear of foreign invasion or expropriation through internal violence, the greater the present value of activities that promise future returns. An increase in saving and capital formation causes an increase in the sustainable rate of consumption. Hence, there will be a range in which increased security will increase the sustainable rate of production of civilian goods because of the stronger incentive to engage in capital formation.

At some point, increased production of military goods will no longer increase civilian output, and military and civilian goods will become rivalrous. When this happens, it is possible to speak of the marginal cost of military output as the value of the sacrificed civilian output that is required by the increase in military output. Military goods are not valued as items of consumption, however, but only for their anticipated ability to increase the sustainable value of civilian output. Therefore, the optimal provision of military goods will be that which maximizes the value of civilian goods, point A in Figure 16.1. Provision of M_1 of military goods will require resources that might otherwise have gone into the provision of civilian goods, had there been no threat from internal or external aggressors. In the absence of such aggressors, the alternative transformation function CAM might be said to hold, in which case $C - C_1$ would represent the amount of civilian goods sacrificed to produce M_1 of military goods. In the absence of internal and external aggressors, however, the consumption of civilian goods would take place at C and there

FIGURE 16.1 Military Expenditures and the Theory of
Public Goods

The transformation function $0AM$ shows the amounts of military goods and
civilian goods available to a society that faces internal and external
sources of aggression. An increase in the provision of military goods until
M_1 is reached will, via an increased security of property, increase the
production of civilian goods, as shown by the $0A$ segment of the
transformation function. The production of M_1 military goods entails no
sacrifice of civilian goods, but rather makes possible the production of C_1
civilian goods. There is, nonetheless, a question of how to organize the
provision of the military goods, which presumably involve some
transformation of civilian goods into military goods. It is, however,
incorrect to conceptualize some transformation function like CAM, in which
case $C - C_1$ is viewed as the cost in terms of sacrificed civilian goods that
is necessary to produce the M_1 military goods.

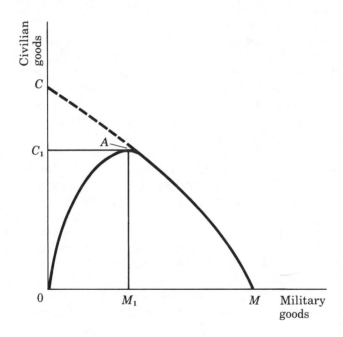

would be no military production. The resources implicit in the $C - C_1$
of civilian goods that are transformed into the production of M_1 of
military goods make possible the production and consumption of C_1
of civilian goods.

A question obviously arises as to how to undertake the resource
extractions necessary to produce the military goods, but the standard

construction of the benefit principle does not fit the activities of the protective state. According to the benefit principle, military spending should be increased until the concomitant increase in civilian goods made possible by the increase in military goods equals the decrease in civilian goods necessitated by the transfer of resources into the production of military goods. At that point of equality, point A in Figure 16.1, the distribution of the increase in civilian goods made possible by increase in military goods can also be equated with the distribution of the reduction in civilian goods made necessary by the transfer of resources into the production of military goods. This pattern of distribution is comparable to the equality of marginal valuations and marginal tax-prices in the benefit principle of public economics.

Although the activities of the protective state can be conceptualized in the manner described by Figure 16.1, that construction begs many questions about knowledge. At base, it assumes that all people are of the same mind about the dangers of potential aggression and about the proper way to protect against such threats. If people are not of the same mind, they will place different values on the extent of activities of the protective state. Much controversy over military and foreign policy reflects such differences in presumptions about knowledge. Some people may think that the attainment of a position such as point A in Figure 16.1 requires the ability to project decisive military power simultaneously in Western Europe, the Persian Gulf, and eastern Asia. Others may think that such a substantial military force entails a sacrifice of civilian output rather than serving as an indirect means of producing such output. Those people might view a position such as point A as attainable by a nuclear deterrent in conjunction with an ability to project decisive military power only in North America. In a median voter model, the amount of military spending that would be chosen would correspond to the median value of M_1 (or location of A) in the population. With other models of collective choice, different outcomes may result that would reflect the preferences of the members of the dominant coalition.

RATIONAL BASES FOR WAR

The protective activities of the state are grounded in the assumption that aggression, from both internal and external sources, would be rife in the absence of those activities. Aggression from within is called crime, and aggression from without is often called war; both types of aggression can be thought of as reflecting a benefit-cost estimate on the part of the aggressor. War or crime has a cost to the aggressor that includes the physical and human resources used in the act of aggression as well as the losses that might be suffered if the aggression fails. These losses include confiscation of wealth, possible enslavement, and death. War also offers potential benefits: the capital that might be captured or the destruction of a potential aggressor before its potential is realized, as in the case of Israel's bombing of what it suspected was Iraq's nuclear weapons plant.

Aggression offers gains and it imposes costs, and an increase in gains relative to costs will elicit an increase in aggression. Other things equal, an increase in a nation's wealth is an increase in the benefit of aggression to other nations that might covet that wealth. On the other hand, an increase in a nation's military capabilities increases the cost of aggression to other nations. Should there be a nation that possesses no resources valued by another nation and whose inhabitants are generally lazy, ill, or feeble-minded, it is unlikely to be coveted by other nations. But if deposits of oil or other valued minerals are discovered within its boundaries, the capital in that nation is likely to be coveted by others. In turn, if that nation has no military capacity and no alliances, it is more likely to be attacked than if it had military capacity, either directly or through alliances. Other things equal, then, an increase in a nation's coveted capital — the part of a nation's capital stock that is valued by potential aggressors — will increase the likelihood that other nations will choose to fight over that capital. An increase in defense capability, however, can offset that likelihood.

In the absence of an interdependency among nations such as that created by an alliance, the assessment of benefits and costs involves only two nations: the potential aggressor and the nation being coveted. The aggressor's wealth may be $400 and the victim's $200. If the aggressor anticipates the war will cost $100 and that the victim will be so devastated in the process that its wealth will be reduced to $50, the aggressor will anticipate gaining only $50 for its $100 investment and will refrain from aggression. On the other hand, if the aggressor anticipates that conquest will result in a destruction of only $50 of the victim's wealth, it will be able to anticipate increasing its wealth by $150 in exchange for giving up $100. The victim may assess the likelihood and the cost of defeat to be so high as to render resistance not worthwhile, as may have been the case for Czechoslovakia against the Germans in 1938 and against the Russians in 1948 and 1968. Alternatively, the aggressor might judge the costs of aggression to exceed the benefits, as perhaps characterizes the Soviet Union's choice to treat Yugoslavia's resistance differently from the way it treated Czechoslovakia's. The Yugoslavs were better armed, the terrain was more rugged, and the Yugoslavs had a demonstrated history of resistance to aggression. For a number of reasons, Soviet action against Yugoslavia could have been more costly than its action against Czechoslovakia.

When more than one nation covets the potential victim, the benefit-cost estimation of a single potential aggressor may be altered. Aggression might invite entry by the other, possibly stronger potential aggressors. This scenario is the basis for the theory of balance of power as a means for preserving peace. When the anticipated cost of this possibility is taken into account, the cost of aggression may be seen to exceed the benefits. Such strategic factors do not deny that aggression can be understood from a benefit-cost perspective, but they do imply that the benefit-cost calculation must be applied strategically or interdependently rather than independently in a nation-by-nation comparison. Despite the complexities that might arise in an interdependent relationship, aggression is as rational an activity as other human activities. This creates some range of complementarity between the provision of protective activities and the pursuit of ordinary economic activities such as production and consumption.

THE MILITARY BUDGET

In thinking about military spending, we must distinguish between budget authorizations and budget outlays. Budget authorizations refer to permissions given by Congress to spend, although the actual spending might not take place until some future year. Budget outlays refer to the expenditures actually made during a year, much of which might have been authorized in previous years. It has been estimated that on average only about 12 percent of the money authorized for a new weapons system is spent in the first year. The Trident nuclear submarines for example, were authorized in 1969 as a replacement for the Polaris, with delivery scheduled to start in 1983. The actual outlays, however, occurred as the submarines were constructed.

The outgoing Carter administration projected budget authorizations for military spending of $196.4 billion, $224 billion, and $253.1 billion for fiscal years 1982, 1983, and 1984, respectively. The incoming Reagan administration initially proposed $213.8 billion, $244.1 billion, and $279.8 billion for those three years, increases over the Carter projections of 8 percent, 9 percent, and more than 10 percent, respectively. The proposed budget outlays showed similar increases.

Within a line-item framework of budgeting, defense spending can be divided into three main categories: about 55 percent for current expenditures such as salaries, retirement payments, operating expenses, and maintenance; 35 percent for procurement; and 10 percent for research and development, testing, and evaluation.

The military buildup that the Reagan administration has pursued has engendered much controversy, fueled perhaps by the intent of the administration to curtail the size of various programs of income transfer. (Income transfer, which is covered in Chapter 17, basically involves the government's transferring income from some people to others.) Overall, the Reagan administration proposes to shift the structure of federal activity away from programs of income transfer and toward military activity. The 1983 budget, which was introduced into Congress in January 1982 and was the first original budget submitted by President Reagan, called for military outlays of $215.9 billion, 6.3 percent of estimated gross national product (GNP). In contrast, military outlays for fiscal 1982 were projected at $182.8 billion, 5.9 percent of estimated GNP. Military spending in 1983 would be larger in real terms than that in 1982 by 10.5 percent. Authorizations requested for fiscal 1983 were $258 billion, a 13.3 percent increase in real terms over fiscal 1982. Moreover, by 1987 military spending is projected by the Reagan administration to have risen to 7.4 percent of GNP.

Much of the controversy over military spending arises no doubt because of the Reagan administration's sharp reversal of the direction taken by the Carter administration, a direction that continued a trend throughout the 1960s and 1970s of reducing the relative importance of military spending in the federal budget. Although military spending was in the range of 9 to 10 percent of GNP during the Eisenhower and Kennedy administrations, it had declined more or less steadily afterward, until it was about 5 percent of GNP by the end of the 1970s. The Reagan administration proposals would boost the relative share of military spending in GNP roughly halfway back to its share during the Eisenhower and Kennedy administrations.

The Reagan administration advances several reasons for this shift in federal budgetary emphasis, most of which reduce to an unfavorable comparison between the United States and the Soviet Union. Table 16.1 presents some of those comparisons. The Soviet Union has been increasing military spending in real terms by about 4 to 5 percent per year for the past two decades; American military spending has been declining in real terms during those years. Consequently, the Soviet Union now spends 35 to 50 percent more on military activities than the United States does. Essentially the same point can be made by comparing the efforts of the NATO and the Warsaw Pact countries.

What was once a clear American dominance in weaponry has been

TABLE 16.1 Military Spending in Constant 1977 Dollars
(in billions)

Nation or Alliance	Year		
	1969	1974	1978
United States	$132.3	$104.8	$100.9
NATO	186.6	167.8	169.1
Soviet Union	107.9	128.5	143.0
Warsaw Pact	125.5	150.1	165.1

Source: Statistical Abstract of the United States: 1980 (Washington, D.C.: U.S. Government Printing Office, 1980), p. 369.

replaced by a rough parity and, some would say, a Soviet dominance in some areas. The Soviet Union, for example, has about 1,400 intercontinental ballistic missiles (ICBMs), whereas the United States has 1,054. The Soviet Union has 950 submarine-launched ballistic missiles (SLBMs), along with 62 submarines to launch them; in contrast, the United States has 656 SLBMs and only 41 submarines for launching them. The Reagan administration often asserts that the Soviet Union is close to amassing the ability to quickly overrun Western Europe. Such assertions are based on the estimation that the Warsaw Pact nations possess larger numbers of personnel, tanks, and other military apparatus than do the NATO countries, and a variety of other specific indicators have been marshaled to support the argument that the United States occupies an inferior military position to that of the Soviet Union.

The election of President Reagan in 1980 seems to reflect to some extent a general acceptance of the contention that the United States has slipped behind the Soviet Union. The argument of the "window of vulnerability" in the mid-1980s, which presumes that the Soviet Union will by then be capable of destroying the U.S. ICBMs in their silos, have perhaps been the most noted of the various specific arguments. This argument, which is used to support deployment of the MX missile, has proven quite controversial, however. The degree of accuracy that would be required for Soviet missiles to destroy American ICBMs seems to exceed the accuracy that has been achieved by repeated test firings along an east-west flight path. Moreover, any missile attack would come over the North Pole, a route over which there have never been any test firings.

The notion of a window of vulnerability is based on the assumption that the United States would absorb a first strike before retaliating, with retaliation coming from SLBMs if the ICBMs were in fact destroyed. Soviet ICBMs would take up to thirty minutes to reach the United States and would have been detected within a few minutes of their launching. A policy of firing the Minuteman ICBMs at that time (or soon thereafter to allow time for confirmation to avoid a mistaken launching of a first strike) is another way of closing such a window of vulnerability. This is not to advocate the launching of ICBMs at the warning of an impending Soviet strike, but only to note that there is an interdependence between choices about nuclear strategy and military budgets: What is seen as a position of vulnerability under one strategy, and which may thereby call for budgetary expansion, may not be a position of vulnerability under an alternative strategy and, therefore, may not call for budgetary expansion.

MILITARY SPENDING AS THE PRICE
OF A FOREIGN POLICY

Some questions about defense spending relate to the actual amount of military spending required to bring about an outcome such as that described by point A in Figure 16.1 Even if it is assumed, for simplicity, that people are of the same mind concerning the threat of foreign aggression, defense budgeting is intimately connected with issues of military strategy. Different strategic perspectives imply different budgetary choices. Although military strategy lies outside the purview of public economics, some consideration must be given to the relation between military strategy and defense budgeting.

A particular military budget is the price of a particular foreign policy.[1] A particular foreign policy and its associated military budget describe a particular hypothesis about what is required to attain a position such as point A in Figure 16.1. Recall the Reagan administration's requested budget authorization of $258 billion for fiscal 1983. This $258 billion is the price tag of a foreign policy that has two primary components: the prevention of nuclear attack by the Soviet Union and the projection of American influence throughout most of the world. Of the $258 billion requested for 1983, roughly $54 billion is for strategic nuclear forces and the remaining $204 billion is for general-purpose forces designed to project American influence in

[1] The relation between options for military spending and options for foreign policy is described in Earl C. Ravenal, *Reagan's 1983 Defense Budget: An Analysis and an Alternative* (Washington, D.C.: Cato Institute, 1982).

various parts of the world. Of the latter amount, approximately $129 billion is earmarked for projecting American influence in Europe, $39 billion in Asia, and $36 billion to the other areas of the world.[2]

Although there is room for economizing on individual weapons and the like, as we discuss below, most military spending is affected relatively little by any such economizing. The level of military spending is a reflection of a particular choice about foreign policy, just as a person's entertainment budget reflects his or her individual policy on entertainment. An army division costs about $3.75 billion per year, and choices among options for tanks, personnel carriers, rifles, and the like affect this basic price tag very little. Similarly, an aircraft carrier task force costs about $11 billion per year, and choices among nuclear powered and smaller, oil-fired carriers make comparatively little difference to the price tag. For the most part, the military budget offers relatively little scope for a choice about size, once a foreign policy has been chosen. There is, of course, some choice about types of weapons, but the effect of such choices on the size of the budget is clearly of a second order. The choice of foreign policy primarily determines the level of military spending.

If the defense of Western Europe is to be an element of American foreign policy, there may be some scope for reducing the amount spent below $129 billion, or even for increasing it above that amount, but the deviations will cover a relatively small range. If an army division costs about $3.75 billion per year, and if the defense of Western Europe requires twelve divisions, this component of American foreign policy will cost about $45 billion per year. (Similar statements can be made about the expenses of providing air and naval protection.) By using less advanced weapons and equipment, the price of a division might be reduced to, say, $3.25 billion per year. This would reduce the expense of defending Western Europe by $6 billion, or about 5 percent — assuming that military effectiveness was not impaired, for otherwise some offsetting increase in other types of expenditure would be required. The price tag of a foreign policy that entails the defense of Western Europe is largely determined by the capacities and interests of the Soviet Union and the requirements of technology. And it is the same for a choice of such other foreign policy objectives as defending eastern Asia or maintaining access to the Persian Gulf. The defense budget is inseparable from, and largely determined by, the foreign policy commitments a nation makes. In examining alternative defense budgets, the basic point of departure must be the costs and gains of different foreign policy choices.

[2] Ibid.

A BENEFIT-COST PERSPECTIVE ON FOREIGN AND MILITARY POLICY

If the United States chooses through its foreign policy to defend Western Europe, this policy will carry a military price tag of approximately $129 billion. If it chooses to defend South Korea and Japan, the price tag will be about $39 billion. These amounts might be changed, though by only a few percent, through such things as increased efficiency in the procurement of weapons. Is a particular foreign policy a worthwhile purchase for a nation? Is it worthwhile for the United States to spend $129 billion in defense of Western Europe? Is it a worthwhile investment to purchase protection for eastern Asia, the Persian Gulf, and so on?

Economics cannot provide answers to such questions, as we saw in Chapter 15, but it can help organize thinking about such questions. At base, a foreign policy choice to defend Western Europe reflects an assumption that the increased value of civilian consumption made possible by doing so exceeds the amount of civilian consumption forgone for military production. If $129 billion is the price tag of defending Western Europe, it is reasonable to ask whether the benefits of that expenditure are sufficient to make the investment worthwhile. Economics cannot judge whether a particular investment is worthwhile, but it can provide a framework for examining more carefully and systematically the various elements involved in a proposed investment.

Trading Value of a Nation

To ask about the benefit side of any U.S. foreign policy choice is to ask about the value of specific nation or region to the United States.[3] One source of benefit is the gain from trade that might be forgone in the event of a military conquest. The United States imports about $45 billion annually from Western European nations and about $35 billion from Japan and South Korea. If that trade ceases because of foreign conquest made possible by the absence of American military protection, a loss to residents of the United States would result. This loss is represented by Figure 16.2, another application of the notion of excess burden, which we explored in Chapter 11. The loss to the United States of, say, eastern Asia or Western Europe as a trading partner is equal to the value of those countries as sources of imports, less the value of the substitutes that would arise in the absence of

[3] See the development of this theme in Charles Wolf, Jr., "Some Aspects of the 'Value' of Less-Developed Countries to the United States," *World Politics* 15 (July 1963), pp. 623–634.

FIGURE 16.2 Loss from One Nation's Disappearance as a
Trading Partner

In the presence of trade with a particular nation (or set of nations), the
United States buys X_1 units of some service X at price P_1 per unit. If that
nation disappears as a trading partner, say through military conquest,
supply is reduced from S_1 to S_2. Consequently, there is a lower rate of
output for the United States, X_2, and a higher price, P_2. For the United
States, the loss can be represented as the loss of consumers' surplus, which
in this case is the area P_1P_2ab.

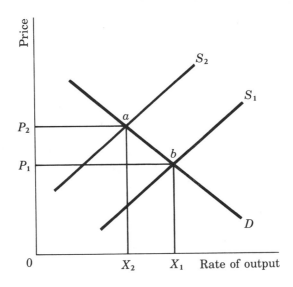

these sources. The value to residents of the United States of Japan
as a source of automobiles is the value of Japanese automobiles to
American residents, less the value of the automobiles American residents would have to choose if Japan were no longer a source because
of Soviet conquest resulting from the lack of U.S. military protection.

It is conceptually possible for the demand for a product supplied
by a particular nation to be so inelastic in the United States that
the excess burden suffered by a disappearance of that product will
actually exceed the amount that was being spent on the product. The
loss suffered by the disappearance of the source for a rare but vital
mineral might, for example, exceed the amount initially being spent
on it. But, in general, the excess burden associated with the loss of a
particular source of supply will be less than the initial expenditure
on the product. If the only value of Western Europe and eastern

Asia to the United States is as a source of gain from trade, $45 billion and $35 billion, respectively, might plausibly be taken as upper-bound estimates of the value to the United States of providing those areas with military protection. When judged only from this perspective, the approximately $39 billion spent on the defense of eastern Asia would appear to be a more favorable investment than the $129 billion spent on the defense of Western Europe.

If American protection ensures the continuation of a nation as a source of imports and if the elimination of that source results from the absence of such protection, the measure of welfare loss attributable to a nation's disappearance as a trading partner is an accurate measure of the gain from American military protection. Otherwise, it is not. If the probability that Japan and South Korea will be lost as sources of imports in the absence of American military protection is only 0.9 (rather than 1.0), and if the probability that they will be lost despite an American military presence is 0.2 (and not zero), the expected gain from American military sepnding is only 70 percent of the $35 billion welfare loss that would be suffered by the disappearance of Japan and South Korea as trading partners.

Military Value of a Nation

There is more to the value of a particular nation or region than its value as a trading partner in the international division of labor. A nation or region might have value as a more efficient place of defense than other places, including the continental United States. The value of Western Europe as a trading partner is surely less than the expense of defending it, and the same may be true for eastern Asia. But the defense of Western Europe may offer a more efficient place to defend the United States than a defense limited to the U.S. boundaries. In Chapter 15, we noted that each entry in a benefit-cost analysis represents an effort to solve empirically an economic model pertaining to the situation described by that entry. This holds for the benefits and costs of various options for foreign policy and defense spending.

Whether the defense of Western Europe or eastern Asia offers a lower cost option than the direct defense of the American perimeter depends on the most appropriate model of the conduct of the Soviet Union, among other things. Perhaps in some model of worldwide Soviet imperialism, the fall of Western Europe would be a stepping-stone in the Soviet Union's conquest of the United States. In such a model, the defense of Western Europe is a means of defending the United States without directly destroying American territory. There is certainly a value in having destruction wrought in someone else's land. In an alternative model that sees the Soviet Union as essentially cautious but surrounded by increasingly strong and hostile nations, it is not so clear that the defense of Western Europe is only a choice of a less costly location for the defense of the United States. Economics cannot provide an answer to such questions, but it can help put the central questions in starkest relief. The United States is choosing to spend $129 billion on the defense of Western Europe, $39 billion on the defense of eastern Asia, and so on, and it is surely reasonable to attempt to articulate the returns that such investments might offer.

Benefit-cost analysis suggests that with respect to trade benefits the defense of eastern Asia is more worthwhile than the defense of Western Europe. Intangible benefits might also arise in extending American military protection, and these benefits are as legitimate as those from trade and reductions in the cost of defending the United States. There is little doubt that the benefits are higher for Western Europe than for eastern Asia. The United States' heritage largely lies with Western Europe, though this is becoming less so as the source of American citizens shifts away from Western Europe. Whether the benefits are worth the costs is an open question.

Stated differently, for the defense of Western Europe to be a worthwhile investment or component of American foreign policy, the combination of intangible benefits and the superior location of Europe over the United States as a place for warfare with the Soviet Union must be worth an expenditure on the order of $84 billion annually. Economic analysis cannot answer whether this is the case, although it can indicate that the value of Western Europe as a trading partner is likely to be substantially less than the expense the United States would bear in supporting the defense of Western Europe. This statement cannot be made as strongly for eastern Asia. Perhaps it could not be made at all for the Persian Gulf.

A defense budget is essentially a price paid to purchase a foreign policy. In a nonimperialist nation, the primary purpose of a foreign policy is to maximize the anticipated value of the opportunities open to the members of that nation, as described in Figure 16.1. Whether a particular foreign policy can accomplish this is a difficult and open question.

LOWER-LEVEL TACTICAL CHOICES
AND WEAPONS PROCUREMENT

Current military expenditures are governed substantially by the assumption that the protection of Western Europe against Soviet aggression is central to the maintenance of American interests. An opposing assumption would have great budgetary ramifications. Even if the former assumption is maintained, lower-level strategic choices also influence military spending, although these influences are less significant than those already discussed.

Present American military strategy is heavily geared to positional warfare in Europe, which leads to a specific selection of weapons and troop requirements. The main assumption of positional warfare is that two armies will meet in pitched battle, and in such a setting victory is likely to go to the side that is able to bring the most deadly firepower to bear on the battlefield. This is sometimes called warfare by attrition, a style that emphasizes high body counts. This tactic of warfare is consistent with a personnel policy in which the annual rate of turnover is on the order of 100 percent. Units are not kept together for very long; rather, individuals are continually coming and going because the only function of an individual is to fire the weapon that represents firepower. The continual substitution of individuals within fighting units is of no consequence in this approach to military tactics because the units themselves represent nothing but the means by which firepower is delivered.

An alternative approach that has gained support in recent years is what might be called a mobile or maneuver-based warfare. This approach is based not on massed, pitched battles, but on quickness and mobility, as in armored penetrations through enemy lines. The German invasion of France in World War II, where France had the superior firepower but where the Germans simply outmaneuvered them, is an excellent example of such an approach to warfare, as is the American landing at Inchon during the Korean War (although the rest of the Korean War was based on firepower and attrition). The purpose of tactics based on mobility and maneuver is to disrupt the ability of the enemy to communicate among themselves. When this can be done, an enemy turns into a mob. Regardless of the firepower it may have had as an organized army, an armed mob is a much less threatening adversary.

Warfare based on maneuver requires other choices concerning weapons and personnel, and these choices are reflected in budgetary choices. Maneuver warfare requires troops that work well together in a way that is possible only when units have trained together for a substantial period of time. Such an approach requires an emphasis in weapons on speed and mobility rather than on firepower in a massed battle. The M-1 tank, for example, offers enormous firepower on a battlefield, but it may be of less value for a strategy of mobility: It can attain a speed of 45 m.p.h., but its high rate of breakdowns and the requirement that it travel with an assemblage of supporting vehicles might be liabilities in a tactics based on maneuver.[4] Whether to prepare for a war of attrition in Europe or to prepare for a war of maneuver is a low-order question of tactics, the answer to which carries budgetary implications, although those implications are clearly less substantial than the budgetary implications of a choice about the value of defending Western Europe in the first place.

Weapons Procurement and Common Versus Particular Interest

The procurement of weapons for the military, while constituting only about 35 percent of the military budget, has long been the most controversial aspect of military budgeting. Supporters of military spending often seem to suggest that a posture of frugality in military spending is to ask the military to fight with technologically obsolete weapons, and such a suggestion is often advanced in support of increased spending to replace older weapons systems with more advanced, and more expensive, systems. Critics of military spending argue that the result of buying the latest weapons is often to buy the most expensive weapons rather than those best suited for the tasks they must serve. They argue furthermore that the main beneficiaries of many decisions about weapons procurement are the military contractors who build the weapons systems and the senior military officers who subsequently are employed by military contractors, who in turn are seeking to elicit additional contracts from the military.

That there is a symbiotic relationship between military contractors, senior military officers, and the military appropriations committees in Congress is difficult to deny. Contracts for major weapons systems are exceedingly expensive, and the production of those systems resides with a handful of large corporations for whom a major share of business is with the military, although they subcontract much of the work to small firms. Rockwell International, General Dynamics, McDonnell Douglas, Lockheed, Chrysler, FMC, Martin Marietta, and Boeing are familiar names that supply weapons systems to the military. Moreover, more than 2,000 former military officers of senior rank are employed in various capacities by such companies. No doubt many military officers make recommendations about procurement decisions and hope to find employment with such private firms in the future. Legislators with seats on the military

---

[4] The M-1 tank averages only 77 miles between breakdowns, whereas the M-60 averages 493 miles. For an interesting examination of what might be called grade inflation in reports on the testing of weapons and equipment, see Dina Rasor, "Fighting with Failures," *Reason* 18 (April 1982), pp. 19–28.

committees in Congress have a personal interest in arranging contracts for businesses in their districts. To the extent that congressional committees are dominated by legislators who reflect the interests of high demanders, which, as we saw in Chapter 5, is a trait of majoritarian democracy, there is a positive correlation between the awarding of military contracts and positions on armed services committees.

The same principles of legislation and bureaucracy that we discussed in Part II with reference to various civilian activities are applicable to military activities as well. Military spending is supposed to provide a general or universal benefit of security from external aggression, but it can also provide a specific or selective benefit through transferring income to those who are engaged in the provision of military services.

Legislators with authority over military appropriations may be motivated by some general concern of providing security throughout the nation, but to some extent they may face a trade-off between providing universal benefits and providing particular benefits to people who have an interest in military legislation as military contractors or as constituents employed by military contractors. If so, there may be a tendency toward expansion in military spending beyond what is consistent with maximizing the anticipated value of civilian goods. This possibility is illustrated by Figure 16.3. If there were no room for particular interests to use military spending as a means of transferring wealth, a foreign policy and a size of military budget would be chosen that maximize the anticipated value of civilian output. But if military production can be used as a vehicle for transferring income to particular interests, a larger military budget can result, as shown by the excess of M_2 over M_1.

Many procurement choices are difficult to explain based on an exclusive service to the general interest in protection from aggression as against an interest in using procurement as a particular means of transferring income. Given the link between budgeting and strategy, what may appear to be budgetary choices that reflect the use of procurement as a means of transferring income might be interpreted alternatively using a different assumption about strategy. Under the very best circumstances, it may be exceedingly difficult to determine whether a particular pattern of spending represents a transfer of income to those with interests in military production, as represented by the movement from M_1 to M_2 in Figure 16.3, or whether it represents an optimum expenditure at M_2 in light of a strategy that can maximize the anticipated value of civilian consumption, as described by the opportunity set $0A'M$.

FIGURE 16.3 Military Spending and Income Transfers

The rate of military output that is most preferred by citizens generally is
M_1, assuming that all people have the same perceived relation between
military spending and the anticipated value of civilian consumption. The
thesis that the military-industrial complex and related legislative interests
are able to use military production to some extent as a means of
transferring income results in an alternative distribution of production
such as that characterized by M_2. The added military output is the vehicle
by which income is transferred and, with less civilian consumption
possible, citizens attain a lower level of satisfaction, as shown by the move
from indifference curve i_1 to i_2. (The indifference curves are horizontal lines
to show that military output has no direct value to citizens.)

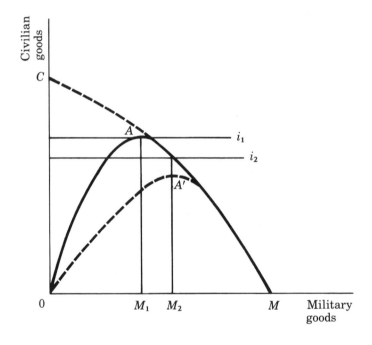

Simplicity, Complexity, and the Cost of Weapons

The primary way of increasing the cost of weapons systems is to
purchase technologically advanced systems, and some controversy
has arisen over whether the most modern, advanced, and complex
systems are necessarily the best buys. On the drawing board, more
advanced technology seems to provide an advantage over less advanced technology. In the absence of a budget constraint, it seems
better to produce highly advanced planes than to produce the same

number of less advanced planes. Indeed, this was the rationalization given for the production of the F-14 and F-15 fighter planes. It was estimated that in one-on-one battles between the advanced F-15s and such comparatively simple aircraft as F-5s, A-10s, or MIG-21s, the F-15 would win 74 battles out of 75. Even though an F-15 might cost $15 to $25 million, and an F-5 $4 million, the F-15 would be a bargain with its 74:1 kill ratio.[5] In simulated fights where four of the advanced planes confronted four of the simpler planes, however, the advanced planes achieved a kill ratio of only about 2.5:1.

The F-14s and F-15s are so expensive, along with their overwhelming advantage in one-on-one combat, because of technical sophistication such as all-weather capability and radar-guided missiles. When the radar on an F-15 spots an enemy plane, the pilot can guide the missile onto its target. To do this, however, the pilot must stay locked on the enemy plane while the missile travels its course. If there is only one enemy plane in the sky, this presents no problem, and, apparently, the enemy plane will be downed 74 times out of 75.

But one-on-one air combat is rare. In the presence of other planes, the sophistication built into the F-14s and F-15s loses some of its value. The radar used to locate other planes can also signal one's position to the enemy. Many victories in air combat come through surprise, and the large size of the F-14s and F-15s reduces the scope for surprise. Also, the flight pattern of a plane that locks onto the enemy plane to guide the missile to its target becomes more predictable, making it easier prey for other enemy planes.[6] Simpler equipment also is often more reliable than more complex equipment. The F-5 averages more than 3,000 hours between engine breakdowns, whereas the F-15s and F-16s average less than 400 hours. Once a breakdown has occurred, the F-5 requires less than 50 hours on average for repair, whereas the F-15s and F-16s require more than 300 hours.

[5] The cost estimates of weapons and equipment often have a substantial range. The estimate used here is an average expense, derived by dividing the total estimated expense of developing and producing the item by the number of items to be produced. A different figure for expense, and generally a lower figure, is the marginal cost of building one more item. For instance, the cost of an F-15 fighter is estimated at $25 million when the total production and development costs are divided by the number of planes to be produced, but it is estimated to cost $15 million when cost is taken only as the direct expense of building one more plane.

[6] Another and related case of jeopardy to "friendly" personnel is the TOW (tube-launched, optically tracked, wire-guided) antitank missile. The person who fires this weapon must keep the sight of the TOW on the target vehicle to guide the missile to its target. While the TOW achieves practically perfect scores in tests, the firer in those tests is not being fired upon. The missile travels at 200 meters per second and creates a recognizable backblast on being fired. If the target is 1,000 meters away, the operator must keep the weapon sighted on the target for five seconds. It may be difficult to visualize this happening very often in combat.

Other examples could be described in which the advantages of sophisticated weapons seem to be small under actual combat conditions, even though sophistication nearly always wins in one-on-one tests. Such one-on-one tests assume the absence of a budget constraint and the presence of conditions that may rarely, if ever, be found in combat. It may be better to build ten F-15s than to build ten F-5s at the same price. But if the real option is on the order of fifty F-5s or ten F-15s, the advantage in protection from aggression may go to simplicity over sophistication. An F-5 is able to average 2.5 sorties per day, but an F-15 can average only one. Thus the choice may not be between fifty F-5s and ten F-15s, but rather between 125 sorties with F-5s or 10 sorties with F-15s.

It is common in critical or reformatory discussions of military spending to look for savings on items such as ships, planes, and tanks. Some people question whether a $3.5-billion nuclear-powered aircraft carrier provides sufficient additional benefit over an oil-fired carrier to justify the additional $1 billion expense. As we have seen, the choice between these two types of carrier will do little to affect the price tag of a carrier task force because a particular choice about foreign policy places a lower bound on military spending. This is illustrated in Figure 16.4. Nonetheless, given a particular choice about foreign policy, it is certainly reasonable to wish to have that policy achieved in the least costly manner.

It has been suggested by the Department of Defense in its budget request, as well as by friendly critics, that several billions a year have been or could be saved by instituting various reforms in such activities as making procurement choices.[7] Sixty percent of all procurement contracts are negotiated between the Department of Defense and a sole supplier, 32 percent with competitive suppliers, and only 8 percent are formally advertised and put to bid. It is estimated that an expanded use of competitive bidding could reduce defense spending by about $2.7 billion annually.[8] It has similarly been estimated that the use of five-year budgets in place of annual budgets would save $700 million annually, while a more vigorous effort to control technological frills could save about $2.3 billion per year. In total, the Pentagon has estimated that actual spending for fiscal 1983 would have been $7.4 billion higher than actually proposed, had it not been for various cost-cutting efforts.

Such efforts are, of course, always to be supported, for the excess of an outlay such as a in Figure 16.4 above an alternative outlay

---

[7] Robert Foelber, *Cutting the High Cost of Weapons* (Washington, D.C.: Heritage Foundation, 1982).

[8] Ibid., p. 16.

FIGURE 16.4 Relation Between Foreign Policy, Military
Spending, and Waste

Different foreign policies can be characterized by the extent of American
involvement in other parts of the world. The curve $0C$ represents a cost
function that relates different foreign policy choices to different military
budgets. A cost function is a boundary that separates what is possible from
what is not. It is impossible to produce any particular foreign policy for a
price below $0C$. It is, of course, possible to produce a particular foreign
policy in a more-than-minimally costly manner. For instance, the degree of
American intervention represented by foreign policy F_1 can be produced in
the least costly manner by a military budget of size M_1. It can also be
produced by the higher military budgets M_2 and M_3, which represent waste
resulting from production of a particular output with something other than
a least-cost combination of inputs. (The same relationship holds between
budget sizes M_2 and M_3 as alternative ways of producing the more
interventionist foreign policy, F_2.)

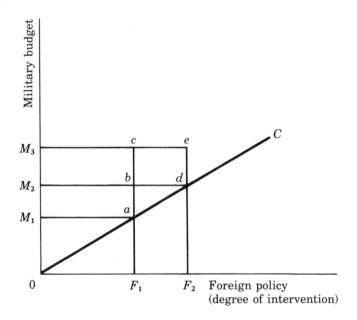

such as b represents waste. But it should also be remembered that
the \$7.4 billion saving will purchase only about two army divisions.
This saving represents only about 20 percent of the cost of the foreign policy choice to defend eastern Asia and only about 5 percent
of the cost of the choice to defend Western Europe.

CONSCRIPTION AND VOLUNTARISM
IN THE PROCUREMENT OF PEOPLE

Prior to 1973, the personnel needs of the military were met ultimately through conscription. Many people who served in the military before 1973 were volunteers rather than conscriptees, but conscription was available to fill any gap between the number of people who volunteered and the number of people the military wanted. Moreover, some people volunteered in anticipation of being drafted, either because they could assure themselves of the timing of their military service or because they could have more choice in their assignments. Under conscription, in periods other than those of full mobilization, the number of people drafted is only a small percentage of the number of people eligible for the draft. Presently, the number of military replacements is about 200,000 annually, but there are about 2 million people in each age category. Even if women are excluded, only about one person in five would see military service.

Conscription is used when the military finds that it cannot attract as many people as it wants at the wage it offers. Business firms that find themselves in this position have to increase their wage offers. In the absence of conscription, so would the military. But under conscription, the military can draft people to obtain the desired number of personnel. The difference between the wage rate actually paid by the military under conscription and the wage rate that would have to be paid to achieve the desired level of strength represents, among other things, an implicit tax-in-kind that conscription imposes on conscriptees under the draft. This is illustrated by Figure 16.5. Under conscription, those who are drafted pay an implicit tax through a reduction in the wage rate they receive. Under voluntary service, this implicit tax does not exist because people are paid sufficiently to induce them to volunteer. This larger wage payment becomes an explicit tax on taxpayers.

The issue of conscription versus voluntarism involves more than the locus of the tax burden between conscriptees and taxpayers. Conscription also distorts military choices. Under conscription, the price of labor to the military is less than the opportunity cost of that labor. The military has incentives to make excessive use of labor because of its relative cheapness, illustrated by a company marching across a parade field looking for cigarette butts or standing in line at a mess hall that seats only one-quarter their number. There are also more substantial ways in which the excessive use of labor might come about. The military might refrain from using capital equipment that would economize on labor. The higher the price of labor, the stronger the incentive to substitute capital for labor in the produc-

FIGURE 16.5 Conscription as a Tax

The supply function, S, relates the number of people who will voluntarily join the military to the wage rate the military offers. If a force of L_v is wanted, the rate of pay will have to be W_v. Alternatively, the military could impose a wage of W_c, at which price it will get only L_c volunteers, and it can fill the gap by drafting the remainder. The triangular area abc represents the total implicit tax imposed on draftees who would not volunteer at W_c, and bc indicates the size of that tax borne by the L_vth person. The area W_cW_vca represents a rent that accrues to military personnel under voluntary service and to taxpayers under conscription.

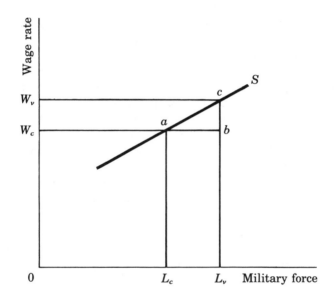

tion of military goods; at a sufficiently high price for labor, the military might even look to robots. Voluntary service can be seen as a means of having the opportunity cost of labor more accurately reflected in military choices, which in turn induces more rational decision making within the military.

The advertising efforts the armed services make to attract volunteers highlight the potential vocational benefits from gaining experience in working with sophisticated equipment. But the gap between the high skill required to operate much modern equipment and the lack of such skills throughout the military, especially the army, has received increasing attention and concern. Much of what is required in the military, particularly in the army and the marines, has relatively little direct value as training for civilian employment. If the production of military output is seen as essentially comparable to all other economic activities, it would be desirable to staff military positions with people whose opportunity cost in other occupations is lowest. Such an approach to efficient staffing would not have an electrical engineer toting a rifle and sleeping in a tent. The procurement of personnel through voluntary services accomplishes this efficient pattern of staffing.

The composition of the military has changed under voluntary service to reflect the mix of talents and capacities it requires. The military has increased its proportion of minority groups and high school dropouts, for whom the opportunity cost of military service is relatively low. The proportion of people in the military who were eventually destined for universities and professional schools has declined because for these people the opportunity cost of military service is relatively high. On the grounds of economic efficiency, voluntary service seems to have achieved a distribution of personnel that more fully reflects the employment of people according to their comparative advantages. The common pay scale for all services despite the generally higher technological requirements in the air force and navy have understandably created problems in staffing some positions.

In principle, such deficiencies can be corrected by allowing greater variation in payments to reflect differences in the scarcity of different types of talent. Under voluntary service, a mix of skills can be attracted only through the use of a differentiated pattern of compensation. Someone whose best alternative employment is working on a street-repair crew has a lower opportunity cost than someone whose best alternative employment is servicing computers, and compensation will have to reflect those differentials under voluntary service, although it need not under conscription.

Is the procurement of people to be assessed purely from a perspective of economic efficiency? If military service were simply one of many consumption goods, this question should probably be answered affirmatively; or at least the normative assumptions of a liberal society, as reflected in the benefit principle, would require an affirmative answer. From the standpoint of economic efficiency, if defense is seen as a publicly provided item of consumption, the mix of personnel that results under voluntary service would reflect a more efficient assignment of people to tasks than the mix that would result under conscription. But if military service is seen not as a collectively provided consumption good, but rather as a foundation for continued social existence, it might not be so clear that voluntary service is superior to conscription. The benefit principle seems less applicable to the protective activities of government than to its productive activities, even granted the normative assumptions of a liberal society. Moreover, under voluntary service, substantial segments of the population — namely, those with high opportunity costs of military service — may cease to have military experience. It is an open question whether a society will deal more effectively with that set of policies most vital to its continued existence if exposure to military life becomes concentrated among people in the lower classes, who do not inhabit the dominant positions in American life, or if military experience comes more fully to inform the central body of the polity. It is an equally open question whether there is any relation at all between the diffusion of military experience throughout the population and the effectiveness with which a society is able to deal with threats posed by possible aggression. Such questions are, of course, well outside the purview of economics, but, then, this is characteristic of many of the central issues about military spending.

SUGGESTIONS FOR FURTHER READING

Arguments that national defense is not properly understood as a consumer good as defined by the theory of public goods are set forth in Earl A. Thompson, "Taxation and National Defense," *Journal of Political Economy* 82 (August 1974), pp. 755–782; and Jacob Meerman, "Are Public Goods Public Goods?" *Public Choice* 35, no. 1 (1980), pp. 45–57. Thompson, along with Gordon Tullock, *The Social Dilemma: The Economics of War and Revolution* (Blacksburg, Va.: University Publications, 1974), sets forth clearly and thoroughly a rationalist approach to war as reflecting a consideration of costs and gains.

Over the past two decades, there has been a substantial infusion of economic thinking into approaches to military budgeting. An influential early work is Charles J. Hitch and Roland N. McKean, *The Economics of Defense in the Nuclear Age* (Cambridge: Harvard University Press, 1960). The years during which Robert McNamara was secretary of defense, the early 1960s, were regarded as the halcyon years for economic thinking in military matters, and Edward S. Quade, ed., *Analysis for Military Decisions* (Chicago: Rand McNally, 1966), presents a series of essays on the application of economic reasoning to military matters. The propitiousness of economic thinking in military matters is questioned sharply in Jeffrey G. Barlow, ed., *Reforming the Military* (Washington, D.C.: Heritage Foundation, 1981). A roughly similar perspective is developed in James Fallows, *National Defense* (New York: Random House, 1981).

Various aspects of military conscription versus voluntary service are explored in James C. Miller II, ed., *Why the Draft?* (Baltimore: Penguin, 1968); Sol Tax, ed., *The Draft: Facts and Alternatives* (Chicago: University of Chicago Press, 1967); Walter Y. Oi, "The Economic Cost of the Draft," *American Economic Review,* Proceedings, 57 (May 1967), pp. 39–62; and Edward F. Renshaw, "The Economics of Conscription," *Southern Economic Journal* 27 (October 1960), pp. 111–117.

As noted in the text, questions of military strategy fall outside the purview of public economics and of economics generally. Oskar Morgenstern, *The Question of National Defense* (New York: Random House, 1959), is long outdated in terms of the particular options described, but it is nonetheless interesting as it reflects the thinking of one of the seminal writers in the effort to incorporate questions of strategy into economics via the theory of games. Kenneth E. Boulding, *Conflict and Defense* (New York: Harper & Row, 1962); and Thomas C. Schelling, *The Strategy of Conflict* (Cambridge, Mass.: Harvard University Press, 1960), likewise extend economics to questions of strategy and conflict. Andrew Schotter and Gerhard Schwoediauer, "Economics and Game Theory: A Survey," *Journal of Economic Literature* 18 (June 1980), pp. 479–525, is a thorough survey of game theory in economics, although it does not consider international applications. G. Warren Nutter, *Kissinger's Grand Design* (Washington, D.C.: American Enterprise Institute, 1975), explores the relation between foreign and military policy and strategy from the perspective of an economist who participated in such matters as an assistant defense secretary during the Nixon administration. James F. Dunnigan, *How to Make War* (New York: Morrow, 1982), is a thorough examination and description of weapons and strategies, both nuclear and conventional.

The War Economy of the United States, edited by Seymour Melman (New York: St. Martin's Press, 1971), is a set of essays dealing with, among other things, the pork barrel aspects of military spending and the relation of that spending to economic well-being. Melman has been one of the primary scholars who has studied the impact of military spending on economic well-being. Two of his main works are *Pentagon Capitalism: The Political Economy of War* (New York: McGraw-Hill, 1970), and *The Permanent War Economy: American Capitalism in Decline* (New York: Simon and Schuster, 1974).

17

The Welfare State

Since 1974 the various programs of income transfer that constitute the welfare state have been the largest category of expenditure in the federal budget. These welfare programs can be divided into social insurance and public assistance. Social insurance programs include Old Age and Survivors Insurance, which is the basic Social Security program, Medicare, and unemployment insurance. The main programs of public assistance are Medicaid, Aid to Families with Dependent Children (AFDC), food stamps, Supplemental Security Income, Head Start, and free school lunches and breakfasts. While federal spending on these social welfare programs was about 5 percent of gross national product (GNP) in 1960, that share had risen to about 12 percent in 1980. For all levels of government combined, social welfare expenditures increased from about 10 percent of GNP in 1960 to about 20 percent in 1980.

Social insurance programs are designed to provide general or universal support, whereas public assistance programs are designed to provide support only for the poorer members of society. Accordingly, eligibility for Social Security, Medicare, and unemployment insurance is practically universal. Eligibility for the various public assistance programs is in principle limited to disadvantaged groups. Medicaid is designed to support the medical expenses of those who are relatively poor, and the Food Stamp Program is designed to subsidize their food purchases. Aid to Families with Dependent Children is designed to provide support for children whose families are so poor as to be unable to support them in what is regarded as a reasonable manner. Supplemental Security Income awards cash payments to various categories of the aged, the blind, and the disabled. Head Start is a program of subsidized preschool education for the disadvantaged, and the program of free school lunches and breakfasts is likewise restricted to various categories of the poor.

Although the distinction between insurance programs designed to provide security and public assistance programs designed to alleviate poverty might be clear conceptually, the insurance and assistance aspects are often confounded in practice. The payments people can expect to receive under such social insurance programs as Social Security bear only a weak relationship to the amounts they are required to pay. This is because social insurance is used simultaneously as a type of public assistance program in that payments of benefits are skewed in favor of people with relatively low incomes.

GOVERNMENT AND THE EQUALIZATION OF INCOME

The programs of the welfare state, including the social insurance programs but particularly the public assistance programs, are generally seen as governmental efforts to reduce inequality in the distribution of income. As Table 17.1 shows, the distribution of income that results from market transactions seems to be characterized both by a significant degree of inequality and by an apparent persistence of this inequality throughout the postwar period. The 20 percent of families with the lowest incomes have earned about 5 percent of total income throughout that period, and the second-lowest quintile of families has earned about 12 percent of total income throughout that period. The remaining three quintiles show a similar pattern of persistence in their shares of income over the postwar period, with the highest 20 percent of families consistently receiving a little over 40 percent of the total income.

There are many possible ways to describe the degree of inequality

TABLE 17.1   Percentage Income Shares for Families

Year	Lowest	2nd	3rd	4th	Highest	Top 5%
			Quintile			
1952	4.9	12.2	17.8	24.0	41.3	15.9
1965	5.2	12.2	17.8	23.9	40.9	15.5
1970	5.4	12.2	17.6	23.8	40.9	15.6
1975	5.4	11.8	17.6	24.1	41.1	15.5
1979	5.3	11.6	17.5	24.1	41.6	15.7

Source: Statistical Abstract of the United States, 1981 (Washington, D.C.: U.S. Government Printing Office, 1981), p. 438.

in the distribution of income. The data in Table 17.1 are one such way, and similar tables could be constructed but with the population grouped differently. Data like those in Table 17.1 can be plotted as in Figure 17.1. The resulting plot is called a *Lorenz curve*. If income were distributed equally, the Lorenz curve would be a diagonal line, *A*. The area between the diagonal line and the actual Lorenz curve, then, is an indicator of the degree of inequality. A *Gini coefficient* is calculated by dividing the area between the diagonal and the Lorenz curve by the total area beneath the diagonal; it ranges from zero for full equality to 1 for complete inequality, in which case one person receives all the income. (For the various observations shown in Table 17.1, the Gini coefficient lies in the vicinity of 0.40.)

How unequal must the distribution of income be before a problem of inequality can be said to exist? Or at what degree of equality can it be said that there is no problem of inequality? It is commonly

FIGURE 17.1 Lorenz Curve and Gini Coefficient to Describe Income Inequality

The diagonal line describes a distribution of income in which all recipients have the same income. The bowed line roughly describes the distribution of income shown in Table 17.1. This line is referred to as a Lorenz curve. If the area between the Lorenz curve and the diagonal is divided by the total area beneath the diagonal, the result, $A/(A + B)$, is called the Gini coefficient.

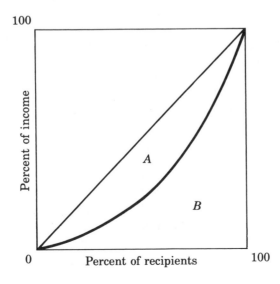

thought that any program that promotes equality in the distribution of income is beneficial, or at least that greater equality is a point in favor of a program. Similarly, programs that render the distribution of income more unequal are generally regarded as undesirable, or at least greater inequality is regarded as a negative feature of a program. Within what limit is this sentiment to apply? If it is to apply without limit, the implication is that any Gini coefficient greater than zero shows undesirable inequality. If perfect equality is not the requirement, then there must be a Gini coefficient that is regarded as too small — that is, for too little inequality to exist.[1]

Measured Inequality and Real Equality

In a market economy, the distribution of income is to an important extent the result of the personal choices of the participants in the economic process. Indeed, a pattern of inequality in the distribution of income tends to arise to provide an underlying equality in the net advantages of different occupations. Such inequality is a necessary condition for equilibrium in the markets for labor and capital. If employments differ in their nonmonetary returns and in the monetary expenses of entering and pursuing them, they must differ as well in their monetary returns in order for equilibrium to be attained in the labor market. As we saw in Chapter 9, occupations that require long and extensive training before one can earn a livelihood must yield higher money returns than unskilled occupations just to compensate for the greater cost of preparation. Occupations with greater variability in employment must pay more than occupations with steady employment; the larger payment is a type of insurance payment for the higher chance of becoming unemployed.

In a variety of ways, an inequality in measured income in a market economy offsets opposing inequalities in other relevant characteristics of different occupations. Once such natural economic forces as differences in the expenses of preparing for and practicing certain occupations are taken into account, the area between the diagonal line

---

[1] It is generally thought that the promotion of equality in the distribution of income will reduce the total amount of output. This will happen if those who bear the tax burdens reduce their labor supply, as well as if those who receive the subsidies reduce their labor supply. Even within an analytical framework that sees the optimal Gini coefficient as zero in the absence of any such disincentive effects, the optimal Gini coefficient can turn out to be quite substantial if output falls relatively rapidly as equalization takes place. See, for instance, Martin S. Feldstein, "On the Optimal Progressivity of the Income Tax," *Journal of Public Economics* 2, no. 4 (1973), pp. 357–376; and James A. Mirrlees, "An Exploration in the Theory of Optimum Income Taxation," *Review of Economic Studies* 38 (April 1971), pp. 175–208.

and a Lorenz curve takes on less significance as an indicator of the degree of inequality. In some cases the attribution of a particular measure of inequality raises questions about the appropriate time horizon to apply apply in making such an attribution. These questions are essentially the same as those that arise in choosing between permanent and current income in studies of tax incidence, which we discussed in Chapters 11 and 12.

Consider the relationship between age and income. It is well known that a charting of people's incomes over their lifetime produces a profile in which income rises during the earlier years of a working life, peaks during the middle years, and declines thereafter. This general profile holds for high school graduates and for college graduates, although the peak is more pronounced for college graduates. There are two reasons why the profile is humped rather than flat. In the early years of working, people become increasingly proficient as they gain experience. In the later years, their endurance lessens and their health declines.

Imagine a set of people who have identical income profiles over their lifetimes but who are different ages. If the incomes of such people are merged to produce a distribution of income for a particular year, inequality will appear despite the perfectly equal distribution of lifetime income. Consider a set of people who are identical in their preferences and abilities and who must choose between two occupations. Table 17.2 shows the essential data. For ease of computation, it is assumed that a person's working life lasts only five years and that the rate of interest is zero. Occupation A yields an income of $15,000 per year for five years. Occupation B requires a two-year period of training, and this training entails no personal expense. With a zero rate of interest, equilibrium in the labor market requires the annual income in occupation B to be $25,000. When looked at from the perspective of earnings in any one year, practitioners of occupation B are earning 67 percent more per year than practitioners of occupation A. If there are equal numbers of both

TABLE 17.2   Relation Between Income and Age

| Occupation | Age (or Years from First Potential Employment) | | | | |
	1	2	3	4	5
A	$15,000	$15,000	$15,000	$15,000	$15,000
B	0	0	25,000	25,000	25,000

practitioners, the lowest 50 percent of earners will receive only 37.5 percent of the income, while the highest 50 percent will receive 62.5 percent. It is a mistake, however, to interpret this disparity as evidence of inequality because the people who choose between the two occupations and their associated earnings profiles view them as equivalent.[2]

Morton Paglin has conjectured that a proper analysis of the relation between income and age would reduce the Gini coefficient of inequality for 1972 by about one-third and would also show more decline in that coefficient over the postwar period than is indicated by such data as those shown in Table 17.1.[3] The actual Gini coefficient declined only slightly over the postwar period Paglin examined, from 0.378 in 1947 to 0.359 in 1972. But during this same period, the percentage of families headed by people under twenty-five years of age or over sixty-five increased from 14 percent in 1947 to 22 percent in 1972. By itself, this 50 percent increase in the relative importance of younger and older households would have increased the Gini coefficient, even though the underlying distribution of lifetime income remained unchanged. That the Gini coefficient did not increase in the presence of this change in age composition implies that it would have declined had the age composition of the population remained unchanged. Paglin estimates that the amount of age-related inequality that is nonetheless consistent with lifetime equality was 0.075 in 1947 and 0.120 in 1972. If these coefficients are subtracted from the actual coefficients, the resulting measures are 0.303 in 1947 and 0.239 in 1972.

These alternative measures are estimates of the extent of inequality that would have resulted if the incomes that were recorded for people had been the average of their incomes over their lifetimes, instead of their actual incomes in a particular year. If such an alternative measure were used to portray the extent of inequality, there would have been about a 20 percent decline in inequality over the postwar period. The estimated Gini coefficients advanced by Paglin are efforts to describe observations that are inherently unobservable; namely, lifetime incomes for a set of living people. Any such effort

[2] Recognition that actual interest rates are positive serves only to increase even more the amount of inequality that is necessary for competitive equilibrium. With a 20 percent rate of interest, for instance, the present value of the income profile offered by occupation A is $44,859. To achieve an equivalent present value, occupation B must offer an annual income of $30,666.

[3] Morton Paglin, "The Measurement and Trend of Inequality: A Basic Revision," *American Economic Review* 65 (September 1975), pp. 598–609.

TABLE 17.3   Families Below Poverty Level in 1976

Form of Income	Number of Families	Percent of All Families
Earnings	21,436,000	27.0
Earnings plus cash transfers	10,716,000	13.5
Earnings plus cash and in-kind transfers	6,441,000	8.1

Source: Statistical Abstract of the United States, 1980 (Washington, D.C.: U.S. Government Printing Office, 1980), p. 463.

must necessarily be fraught with pitfalls and ambiguities.[4] Nonetheless, the central point raised by Paglin about the interpretation of measures of income inequality is certainly valid, at least as long as the age-income profile is humped and the age composition of the population changes over time.

Inequality and Benefits from Public Spending

Data on the distribution of income such as those presented in Table 17.1 count as income only what people earn on their own. But people also receive benefits from public programs. Some of these benefits accrue in cash, as with Social Security, unemployment insurance, Supplemental Security Income, and Aid to Families with Dependent Children. Other benefits accrue in kind, through subsidies of specific forms of consumption. These include payments for food stamps, child nutrition, housing assistance, Medicare, and Medicaid. Table 17.3 gives one indication of how substantial these various benefits are. If only earnings are considered, 27 percent of family units fell below the poverty line in 1976. If cash transfers are counted as income as well, the number of family units below the poverty line was only 13.5 percent. If the various in-kind benefits are also counted as income, the number of family units below the poverty line fell still further, to 8.1 percent.

It should be noted that a dollar of in-kind subsidy will not generally be valued by the recipient as equivalent to a dollar of cash payment. People may pay 75 cents for lunches in the absence of a

[4] See, for instance, the comments on Paglin's article by Eric R. Nelson; William R. Johnson; Sheldon Danziger, Robert Haveman, and Eugene Smolensky; Joseph J. Minarik; and C. John Kurien; along with Paglin's reply, in *American Economic Review* 67 (June 1977), pp. 497–531.

subsidy. For people who buy lunches each day, the provision of lunches free of charge is equivalent to an increase in their weekly income of $3.75. But for someone who might have bought lunch only four days per week, or who might have bought a smaller lunch for 60 cents each day, the provision of free lunches costing 75 cents per day is not equivalent to an increase in weekly income of $3.75. The free lunches in this case are equivalent to an increase in money income of some amount between $3 and $3.75. The recipient of the free lunches now has approximately $3 available to spend on other things and also has more food available than before.

This extra food has some value to the recipient, although the value is probably less than 15 cents per lunch. By buying the 60-cent lunches rather than the 75-cent lunches, the recipient has demonstrated a preference for 15 cents in cash over the additional food. Therefore, when the additional food is provided through the free lunch program, its value to the recipient is something less than 15 cents. Although the in-kind benefits of various programs of public assistance may not be identical to the receipt of cash of the same amount, such programs nonetheless expand the recipient's consumption opportunities. The amount spent in making those in-kind subsidies available is at least a first-order approximation of the income equivalence of the in-kind benefits provided by various public assistance programs.

When the benefits provided by various public programs are treated as forms of income, the portrayal of the degree of inequality and its trend changes quite substantially from that indicated in Table 17.1, as Table 17.4 shows. The distribution of income appears to be substantially more equal when the value of public assistance programs is included in the definition of income. The share of income received by the lowest quintile in 1972, for instance, is more than

TABLE 17.4 Percentage Income Shares for Families (Adjusted)

	Quintile				
Year	Lowest	2nd	3rd	4th	Highest
1952	7.8	14.8	18.8	23.3	35.3
1962	9.0	15.1	19.1	22.9	34.0
1972	12.6	16.1	18.4	20.9	31.9

Source: Edgar K. Browning, "The Trend Toward Equality in the Distribution of Net Income," *Southern Economic Journal* 43 (July 1976), p. 919. Reprinted by permission of the *Southern Economic Journal* and the author.

twice what it is if only earnings are counted as income. Table 17.4 also shows that there has been substantial equalization in the distribution of income over the postwar period. Indeed, the income received through various public assistance programs appears to be roughly equal to the money income of people officially judged to be below the poverty income level.[5] In 1973, the 23 million people who were officially judged to be poor had money income of $20.8 billion, while they would have required $30.5 billion to reach the poverty line. These people also received in-kind transfers estimated to be worth $18.8 billion, however, which increased their total income to $39.6 billion, 30 percent above the official poverty income level. Poverty appears to have been essentially eliminated in the United States, if the transfer programs of the welfare state are counted as income.

INCOME MAINTENANCE

The programs of social insurance and public assistance are commonly referred to as income maintenance programs, to indicate that they are designed to maintain a person's income or ability to consume despite that person's lack of ability to earn income. The amount paid to a recipient under most income maintenance programs varies inversely with the recipient's other income. For Social Security recipients between ages sixty-five and seventy-two, any earnings beyond $6,000 are offset 50 cents on the dollar by a reduction in benefits. For recipients of AFDC payments, each dollar of income earned reduces payments by 67 cents. For food stamp recipients, each dollar earned reduces the subsidy received by about 30 cents. Under the Supplemental Security Income program, each dollar earned reduces payments by 50 cents. The idea behind the negative relation between income earned and benefits received is that the programs are designed to maintain some minimal standard of living for those who could not on their own provide such a standard, and as income increases, less subsidy is needed to provide that standard.

The programs of the welfare state are typically looked upon as subsidies, for they enable people to consume more than their incomes would allow them to consume. But income maintenance programs are, in another sense, a type of tax. Although recipients are subsidized, the amount of subsidy declines as income rises. From the perspective of the recipient, the earning of income entails a tax in the form of a reduction in the receipt of various payments from social insurance

---

[5] Edgar K. Browning, "The Trend Toward Equality in the Distribution of Net Income," *Southern Economic Journal* 43 (July 1976), pp. 912–923.

and public assistance. Someone might be earning, say, $3,000 and receive $3,000 of additional income through such programs as food stamps, Medicaid, and AFDC. If that person's earnings subsequently increase to, say, $6,000, the amount received through various income maintenance programs would decline, say to $1,000. In this case, the earning of an additional $3,000 results in a $2,000 reduction in payments under income maintenance programs. This reduction in subsidy as income rises is equivalent to a tax that increases as income rises. In this illustration, the rate of tax is 67 percent.

The income maintenance programs of the welfare state amount more or less to what has been called a *negative income tax*. Negative income taxation would use the tax system to assist more directly people with low incomes and to do so with a minimum of administrative involvement in their lives. Rather than a number of different programs administered by different agencies, there could be a single, general program of support. Particular programs of income maintenance typically pay a maximum amount to people with no income, reduce the amount paid as income rises, and eventually reach a level of income, called a break-even level, at which payments are no longer made. A negative income tax would have this same central structure, but it would be a single, universal program. A negative income tax, like numerous programs of public assistance, contains two main features: a guaranteed floor of consumption (or a maximum payment) and a tax on income, which actually takes the form of a reduction in the actual payment from the maximum amount.

Suppose the guarantee is set at $3,000, with a 50 percent rate of tax. A person with zero income would receive a payment of $3,000. Increases in income would be offset by reductions at a rate of 50 percent in the amount of payment. A person with income of $2,000 would lose $1,000 of subsidy, leaving a total income of $4,000. The subsidy would vanish when income reached $6,000, the break-even level, for the 50 percent tax on that income would equal the amount of the guarantee. Beyond $6,000 of income, the normal tax schedule would take effect: people would pay positive taxes on their earnings over $6,000.

A negative income tax is clearly subject to trade-offs among the guaranteed level of income, the rate of tax, and the break-even level of income. Given the rate of tax, the higher the income guarantee, the higher the rate of income before the subsidy stops. A 50 percent tax rate with a guarantee of $5,000 will provide subsidies to all people with incomes below $10,000. Lower rates of tax might seem generally superior to higher rates of tax because higher rates may more strongly discourage the supply of labor. But the lower the rate of tax, the wider the spread between the base guarantee and the income at which the subsidy stops. With a base guarantee of $5,000 and a tax rate of 25 percent, all people with incomes of less than $20,000 would receive some subsidy.

To maintain a low tax rate while restricting the subsidy to relatively low incomes requires a low guarantee. To restrict the subsidy to people with incomes less than $8,000 allows a guarantee of $4,000 if the tax rate is set at 50 percent, but it allows a guarantee of only $2,000 if the tax rate is set at 25 percent. To allow a higher guarantee while still restricting the subsidy to relatively low incomes requires a comparatively high rate of tax. If the subsidy is to be restricted to people with incomes below $8,000, a $4,000 guarantee will require a tax rate of 50 percent, and a $6,000 guarantee will require a tax rate of 75 percent. In general, the relation between the tax rate, T, the amount of the guarantee, G, and the break-even income at which the subsidy stops, B, is $T = G/B$.

THE INCENTIVE EFFECTS OF INCOME MAINTENANCE

Welfare recipients face marginal rates of "tax" that are generally higher than those faced by wage earners with annual incomes below about $10,000. Indeed, marginal tax rates in the range of 80 percent are not unheard of. In such a case, a welfare recipient who takes a job that pays $5,000 will net only $1,000 because welfare payments will have been reduced by $4,000. The tax decreases the opportunity cost of leisure. At the same time, the guarantee increases the recipient's income. As long as leisure is a normal good, both the substitution and the income effect of a negative income tax would generally work in the direction of increasing leisure — that is, of reducing the amount of labor that recipients supply.

The effect of a negative income tax on the amount of leisure demanded and, hence, the amount of labor supplied can be examined with reference to Figure 17.2. For the income range between the base guarantee and the break-even level, the negative income tax represents an outward shift in a person's opportunity set for earning income and for taking leisure. With income and leisure both being normal goods, people whose income was less than the break-even level will respond to the negative income tax by taking more leisure. This is illustrated by the indifference curves i_1 and i_1' in Figure 17.2. For people whose initial income-leisure choice produces an income substantially in excess of the break-even level, the negative income tax will have no impact on the supply of labor. This outcome is indicated by indifference curve i_3. For people near the break-even

FIGURE 17.2   Negative Taxation and the Supply of Labor

The effect of a negative income tax on the demand for leisure and the
supply of labor can be explored using the same analytical apparatus by
which we examined the impact of income taxation on the supply of labor in
Chapter 9. In the absence of a negative income tax, a person faces the
budget constraint il, with the slope being the negative of the wage rate.
The kinked budget constraint, ibg, shows the effect of introducing a
negative income tax with a base guarantee g and a break-even income b.
For people initially to the right of b on il, the negative tax will expand
their opportunity set, and they will choose more leisure. This case is
illustrated by the shift from indifference curve i_1 (with leisure l_1) to
indifference curve i_1' (with leisure l_1'). For people with income near b, the
effect of the negative income tax will depend on their preferences for
income and leisure. Indifference curves i_2 and i_2' describe someone who
initially was earning slightly more than the break-even income by taking
only l_2 of leisure but who increases leisure by more than enough to
compensate for the reduced income, as shown by the choice of l_2' of leisure.
The person described by the indifference curve i_3 is unaffected by the
negative income tax.

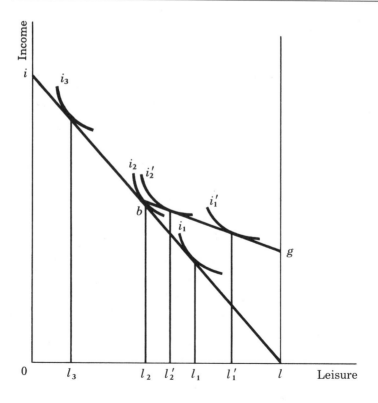

level of income, the negative income tax will induce them either to reduce the amount of labor they supply or to leave it unchanged.

The indifference curves i_2 and i_2' illustrate a case in which the amount of labor supplied is reduced, as shown by the increase in leisure from l_2 to l_2'. Although this person incurs a reduction in income, the increase in leisure is judged to be more valuable than what could have been purchased with the extra income that could have been earned. As long as leisure is a normal good, a negative income tax will never induce an increase in the amount of labor that recipients supply.

The negative income tax reduces the amount of labor recipients supply both because the substitution effect of the tax component lowers the price of leisure (by reducing the net return to an hour of labor) and because the income effect of the guaranteed income encourages the consumption of leisure, if leisure is viewed as a normal good. The negative income tax further entails an increase in the taxes imposed on the remainder of the citizenry who pay for the program. These taxes raise the same issues about their impact on the supply of labor as income taxes raise in general. As we discussed in Chapter 9, the imposition of taxes to finance income subsidies probably also reduces the amount of labor that people supply.

The actual extent of the negative impact of a negative income tax on the supply of labor is an empirical question that is difficult to answer because of the absence of a general negative income tax. There have been a few efforts to introduce experimental negative income taxes for short periods of time. One experiment was conducted in Gary, Indiana, between 1971 and 1974. Drawing on a study of 380 participants in that experiment, Gary Burtless and Jerry Hausman concluded that the negative income tax had a significant though perhaps small impact on the supply of labor.[6] This experiment contained marginal tax rates of 40 and 60 percent. A worker with a pretax wage of $3.50 per hour was found to work, on average, 40 hours per week in the absence of the negative income tax. A negative income tax that guaranteed $3,500 per year and had a marginal tax rate of 60 percent was found to decrease hours worked, on average, to 37 per week. This 8 percent reduction in hours worked was accompanied by a slight increase in weekly income, from $115.54 without the tax to $119.07 with the tax. This outcome corresponds to the conceptual characterization given by i_1 and i_1' in Figure 17.2.

[6] Gary Burtless and Jerry A. Hausman, "The Effect of Taxation on Labor Supply: Evaluating the Gary Negative Income Tax Experiment," *Journal of Political Economy* 86 (December 1978), pp. 1103–1130.

THE GUARANTEE STATE AND
WELFARE DEPENDENCY

Income maintenance programs are seen primarily as ways of over-coming poverty. In some cases income is transferred in cash, as with Supplemental Security Income and AFDC, while in other cases it is transferred in kind, as with food stamps, Medicaid, and school lunches. Regardless of whether the transfer is in cash or in kind, the intent of the various programs is to expand the ability to consume of people whose incomes would otherwise keep them beneath a level of consumption deemed reasonable or adequate. Poverty is defined in terms of a level of income, and, as noted in Tables 17.3 and 17.4, the development of various income maintenance programs during the postwar era can be said generally to have eliminated poverty, aside from a few isolated pockets.

Instead of being defined with reference to a standard of consumption, poverty could be defined with reference to an ability to support oneself independently of the benevolence of others. If poverty is seen as a state of independence, poverty can hardly be said to have been eliminated by the various programs of the welfare state; in fact, it may have been intensified by those programs. As noted above, the share of income received by families in the bottom quintile has remained approximately constant throughout the postwar period, although the share of total income received by this quintile appears to increase significantly if the benefits of various transfer programs are included as income. This observation is consistent with the assumption that the welfare state has reduced poverty.

During this same postwar period, the percentage of families in the lowest quintile of the income distribution that are headed by someone who is employed has declined from around 60 percent to about 40 percent. The percentage of families in the lowest quintile that receive no income from earnings has increased from about 20 percent to nearly 40 percent. Essentially the same pattern emerges for the second quintile, but with lower magnitudes. For the upper three quintiles, however, there has been essentially no change in the pattern of employment: 90 percent of families in those quintiles are headed by someone who is employed, and less than 1 percent receive no income from earnings. Such observations as these might seem to suggest that there has been some reduction in the ability of people to support themselves independently of the benevolence of others.

Minimum Wage Legislation, Unemployment,
and Welfare Guarantees

To the extent that the guarantee programs of the welfare state bring about some reduction in participation in the labor force by heads of families, some status of welfare dependency might be promoted in the long run. Minimum wage legislation provides a good illustration of this possibility. The effect of minimum wage legislation on wages and employment depends on whether the legislation is universal or selective in coverage. In the initial years after the imposition of minimum wage legislation, coverage was selective, but now it is almost universal. In 1938, only 43 percent of nonsupervisory employment was covered by the minimum wage, and, moreover, those occupations that were covered tended generally to have relatively high wages. In 1981, coverage under the minimum wage had been extended to 84 percent of the labor force. The minimum wage has generally ranged between 40 and 50 percent of the average wage in manufacturing. The effect of a selective minimum wage is illustrated in Figure 17.3.

FIGURE 17.3 Effect of a Selective Minimum Wage

The demand and supply functions for labor in covered and uncovered occupations are indicated by D_c and S_c and D_u and S_u, respectively. Initially the wage rate and the amount of employment are W_c and L_c, respectively, in the covered occupations and W_u and L_u in the uncovered occupations. Suppose a minimum wage of W_{min} is imposed in the covered industries. The amount of employment in those industries will decline to L_c'. This reduction in employment in the covered industries will bring about an increase in the supply of labor to the uncovered industries. If it is assumed, for geometrical simplicity, that the increased supply of labor in the uncovered industries is equal to the reduction in employment in the covered industries, the new supply function S_u' will shift rightward by the amount of reduced employment in the covered industries. The wage rate will fall to W_u' and the amount of employment will increase to L_u'.

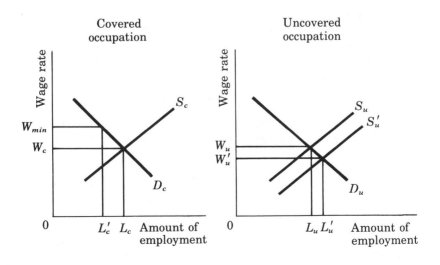

The low-wage labor force can be separated into those who work in employments covered by the legislation and those who work in employments excluded from coverage. The imposition of a minimum wage reduces the quantity of labor demanded in the employments covered. The resulting reduction in employment implies an equivalent increase in the supply of labor to employments not covered, which reduces the wage in those employments. In this situation, the minimum wage has no effect on the amount of employment. Its main effect is to increase the wage received by those low-wage workers who remain employed in the covered employments, while lowering the wage received by low-wage workers in the noncovered employments (including those workers who were displaced from the covered employments).

If coverage under the minimum wage is universal, as it nearly is now, there will not exist any uncovered industries to which people displaced by the minimum wage can supply their labor. As Figure 17.4 describes for this situation, the minimum wage reduces the amount of labor demanded and the amount of employment, although those who remain employed receive higher wages than before. Those who become unemployed have no uncovered markets for their labor; for them, zero income seems to be the consequence of becoming unemployed through a universal minimum wage. The analysis of a universal minimum wage is straightforward, and it implies that minimum wage legislation harms a substantial segment of the low-wage labor force. Not all members of the low-wage labor force are harmed, of course, because some find employment at a higher wage than they formerly received. But those for whom the option is unemployment at the minimum wage or employment at a (lower) market-clearing wage certainly seem to be harmed.

Minimum wage legislation often receives stronger support in legislative districts as the percentage of low-wage workers in those districts increases. Keith Leffler presents evidence that this support reflects not ignorance about the employment effects of minimum wages but a rational interest in securing greater transfers through various programs of income maintenance.[7] The model described in Figure 17.4 implies that the alternative to working at the market wage is not working and having no income. But this does not seem to be the relevant option, once the various programs of public assistance and income maintenance are taken into account. The option of employment at the market wage is not unemployment at a zero wage and income, but unemployment combined with a payment from the welfare state in compensation.

[7] Keith B. Leffler, "Minimum Wages, Welfare, and Wealth Transfers to the Poor," *Journal of Law and Economics* 21 (October 1978), pp. 345–358.

FIGURE 17.4 Effect of a Universal Minimum Wage

For the low-wage occupations shown here, the amount of employment will
be L_0 and the wage rate will be W_0 in the absence of a minimum wage.
Suppose a minimum wage is set at W_{min} and that there are no uncovered
industries available for employment. The amount of labor demanded,
shown by D, and hence the amount of employment, will decline to L_m. At
this higher wage, the amount of labor people would be willing to supply, S,
is L_m'. The amount of unemployment at the minimum wage is actually
$L_m' - L_m$, with only $L_0 - L_m$ representing the amount of formerly
employed labor that is now unemployed, and with $L_m' - L_0$ representing
the labor that formerly was withheld from the labor force but is now
attracted into the labor force by the higher wage.

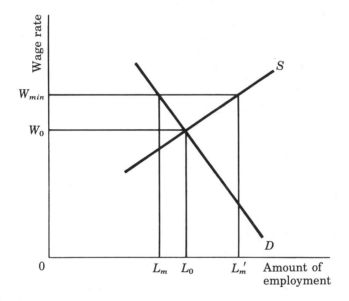

Payments under the AFDC program are a case in point. Since
the unemployed parent amendment to Title IV of the Social Security
Act in 1961, the AFDC program has increased its payments in the
event of parental unemployment. Not all states have chosen to use
this amendment; although AFDC is financed by the federal government, administration is by states, and eligibility rules differ among
states. Leffler examined welfare payments in California, which adopted
the unemployed parent amendment. For the period he examined,
1952 to 1974, Leffler found a significantly positive relation between
an increase in the minimum wage (and the associated unemployment) and an increase in welfare payments, both for general relief

and for AFDC. Over the period Leffler examined, welfare payments generally were about 80 percent of what income would have been had the recipient worked instead at the minimum wage. Furthermore, the various expenses of working are commonly estimated to run in the vicinity of 15 percent of income.

When the level of welfare payments is combined with the cost of earning income (estimated to be about 15 percent of income), it appears that the unemployment that results from minimum wage legislation may actually have little effect on the income of those who become unemployed. Some people may even reach a preferred position, in that the small reduction in income may be regarded as worthwhile in light of the increased leisure that also results. Someone who works 40 hours per week at a minimum wage of $3.35 per hour earns $134 per week. If various welfare benefits pay 80 percent of that amount, $107.20 per week, the unemployed person actually loses only $26.80 per week, not accounting for any possible costs of employment. Becoming employed would in this case offer a net gain of only $26.80 for a work week of 40 hours, or 67 cents per hour. As long as leisure is valued at more than 67 cents per hour, the unemployed person who becomes a recipient of welfare attains a position preferable to having a slightly higher income and having to work.

Welfare Dependency

Although welfare programs may offset the loss of real income that results from the unemployment caused by minimum wage legislation, they may also create a type of welfare dependency that comes about because human capital is not accumulated in a state of unemployment. Most low-wage jobs are initial and not terminal employments. They are entry points into the world of work. As people accumulate the skills and traits that are required for successful employment, they typically move on to higher-paying jobs. Mopping storeroom floors at half the minimum wage may have been the first step to becoming a machinist at three times that minimum before mandatory minimum wages and union barriers to entry foreclosed such initial steps.

If entry-level jobs are foreclosed, however, an opportunity for the creation of skills and traits is also foreclosed. Without the opportunities for personal development afforded by mopping floors, the chance to become a machinist is foreclosed. With the experience afforded by initial employment at a low wage, human capital may accumulate initially at a rate of, say, 10 percent. In the absence of such experience, human capital will accumulate at a lower rate, or perhaps not at all. This point is illustrated by Figure 17.5. At the time of potential entry into the labor force, two people may be equivalent in all relevant respects. The person who subsequently finds employment accumulates skills and cultivates personal traits conducive to occupational success such as being punctual and being courteous to others. The person who does not find employment but nonetheless is able to receive the same initial income through welfare is not able to accumulate those skills and traits. For this person, human capital accumulates more slowly, if at all, and so the ability to earn income

---

FIGURE 17.5 Age-Income Relationship With and Without Welfare

Someone who works initially, say at the minimum wage W_{min}, will accumulate more valuable skills and traits through experience, and this accumulation is reflected in the rising portion of the income profile AB. (The declining portion comes about when such natural features of aging as more illness and less endurance come to dominate the accumulation of skills.) If the alternative to finding employment is receiving the same initial amount through welfare, the person will not be able to accumulate the work experience that is reflected in the income profile AB. The lack of accumulated work experience is equivalent to a reduction in the rate of interest in the accumulation of human capital. The lessened rate of accumulation results in a lower, flatter age-income profile, as represented by AC. For any given age, the distance between the two curves, de for example, shows the subsequent disadvantage owing to the initial reduction in the ability to accumulate human capital.

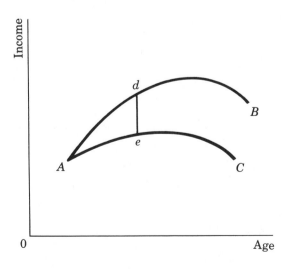

in future years grows more slowly than it otherwise would. Welfare may be the largest permanent source of income for such a person. If so, a status of welfare dependency will have been created.

Minimum wage legislation is but one example of legislation that to some extent seems to prevent people from employing their talents in ways that will lead to their fuller development. In conjunction with child labor legislation, it is surely an important factor in preventing the accumulation of human capital among those who, through aptitude or ability, are likely to end their formal education upon graduation from high school, if not before. For college students, the effects of minimum wage and child labor legislation are largely irrelevant because they do not apply, except in those cases where a student's only hope for a college education requires some substantial support from a job while in school. But for those whose formal education ends before college, the foreclosure of options to gain initial experience in the world of work can be an important factor in reducing the rate of subsequent accumulation of human capital.

In assessing a variety of ways in which the opportunities to gain initial experience are foreclosed, Walter Williams offered the following conjecture: "I would guess that if we abolished the minimum wage law, reduced licensing restrictions, changed labor legislation and reorganized the delivery of education, in twenty to thirty years hence there would be no 'Negro problem' as there is no Japanese, Chinese, Jewish or other earlier-immigrant problem. Those people were able to start off poor and progress because they did not face the market restrictions that today's minorities face." [8] The extent to which the programs of the welfare state create, as a by-product of their provision of a base of support, a longer-term welfare dependency is a topic that awaits future research, although the apparent persistence of the economic difficulties of blacks and Hispanics in light of the temporary nature of the difficulties encountered by other minorities such as the Japanese, Chinese, Jews, and Poles has been argued cogently by George Gilder and Thomas Sowell, among others, to be attributable to an important degree to the growth of the welfare state. [9] Although much research will doubtless be done on these issues, it already seems clear that the various guarantees of the welfare state may constitute a two-edged sword: They provide support

[8] Walter E. Williams, "Government Sanctioned Restraints that Reduce Economic Opportunities for Minorities," *Policy Review*, no. 2 (Fall 1977), pp. 7–30.
[9] The economic history of ethnic groups in the United States is examined in Thomas Sowell, *Ethnic America* (New York: Basic Books, 1981). George Gilder, *Wealth and Poverty* (New York: Basic Books, 1981), argues that poverty is escaped through work and the support of family and that welfare programs tend to create welfare dependency through their various disincentives.

for people and they weaken the ability of people to provide their own support (and often various restrictions on labor markets foreclose options by which people could support themselves).

TWO FORMS OF SOCIAL SECURITY

Social Security began in 1935 as a small program designed essentially to provide a base of protection for people after their retirement. It was initially conceived as an insurance program and was modeled after private retirement programs that were in operation at the time. The program was not as thoroughly contractual as the private programs, but principles of contract were central: People's contributions would be invested to earn a return, and upon their retirement people would receive the principal plus interest.

Such a funded form of social security would accumulate reserves in an actuarially sound manner, just as an insurance company accumulates reserves to fund its commitments. The Social Security system was never fully funded, but the extent of funding was substantial. Under funding, the Social Security system would hold people's savings plus accumulated interest until they retired, when it would make payments according to the amount people had contributed. Moreover, the projected benefits initially were small because the program was seen only as providing a basic floor of protection. It was assumed that people generally would undertake various plans of personal saving to provide most of their retirement income.

The substantial degree of funding that initially characterized Social Security was eliminated in 1939 when a tax-and-transfer system of social security was established. The change from one type of Social Security system to another took place quietly through a change in the formula for paying benefits. The link between taxes paid and retirement benefits received was not severed entirely, but it was loosened considerably. People began receiving payments because of the mere fact of their retirement, and not because of their previous contributions. Tax payments no longer became part of a capital fund that was invested to earn interest. Instead, tax revenues were appropriated as expenditures to pay people who were retired or were otherwise eligible to receive payments. No longer could the contributions made during the years of work be said to constitute the basis on which benefits were received during retirement. Those benefits were now received by an act of appropriation from the legislature, with the amount of such appropriation reflecting the willingness of the legislature to impose taxes on those who currently were working.

On the tax side of the account, in 1982 people paid a Social Security tax of 13.4 percent on all earnings up to $32,400. Nominally, this amount is split evenly between employee and employer, but the tax is really equivalent to a proportional tax on wage and salary income of 13.4 percent. The expansion of the program since its inception can be seen by considering its alphabetic evolution. It presently is known as OASDHI, for Old Age, Survivors, Disability, and Health Insurance. In 1935 it was simply OAI for Old Age Insurance. In 1939 it became OASI, when benefits for survivors were incorporated into the program. With the addition of payments for disability in 1954, the program became OASDI. When health care was added through Medicare in 1965, Social Security reached its present format, OASDHI.

A chasm separates the rhetoric about Social Security from the reality. The rhetoric speaks of "social insurance," with people making "contributions" to the program during their working years. It does not speak of workers as paying taxes and of recipients as receiving transfer or welfare payments from the government. It can perhaps be argued that the insurance rhetoric has been important in gaining public acceptance for the system, but such argument does not increase the accuracy of the rhetoric. Moreover, if Social Security is viewed as insurance, it would also have to be recognized as bankrupt. Based on benefit promises presently in force, Social Security appears to have an actuarial deficit of about $5 trillion, which indicates the extent of the bankruptcy of a private insurance program that had made benefit promises to people but had not accumulated the capital fund necessary to fulfill those promises.

The change in the operation of the Social Security program since 1939 has been dramatic. In 1940 the accumulated trust fund was estimated to be equal to thirty-three years of expenditure. This accumulation of a fund is precisely what would happen in the initial years of any funded insurance program. Since 1940, however, reserves have been paid out to recipients and the fund has been dissipated. By 1950 the trust fund was equal only to thirteen years of expenditure, and by 1960 it had declined to two years of expenditure. In recent years the trust fund has hovered around three months of expenditure.

Rather than being treated as an insurance program, Social Security can be treated as a tax-and-transfer program among generations. Those who currently are working are taxed. Those taxes do not provide a fund to finance future retirement, but are transferred to people who currently are retired. When people who are presently of working age subsequently retire, they in turn will be supported by the imposition of taxes on people who are in the labor force at that time. In this way, a continual process of taxing people who are in the labor force and transferring the proceeds to people who are retired (or who are surviving spouses, disabled, or ill) is set in motion.

If this tax-and-transfer process is looked on as a type of implicit contract among generations, people can be seen as receiving a rate of return on their taxes equal to the rate of growth in the tax base. Suppose there is no growth in population and that real income, the tax base, and tax collections all grow at 2 percent per year. In this case, people will receive during their retirement years a 2 percent rate of return on the tax payments they made during their working years. If population grows over time, the rate of return will be higher because population growth also increases the tax base. If population grows at 1 percent per year and real income per person grows at 2 percent, the rate of return on Social Security taxes will be 3 percent — the sum of the two rates of growth, which is made up of the rate of growth in the economy, the tax base, and tax collections.

Until the 1970s, 3 percent had conformed fairly well to the real rate of growth in the American economy, and it seemed to indicate the long-run rate of return people might be able to anticipate receiving under a tax-and-transfer form of Social Security. Whether they could do better under a funded system is problematical. What is not problematical is that the people who have retired under Social Security to date would have generally done worse under a funded system. The main reason is that those people spent only a partial working life under the program and that the tax base was expanding rapidly as more people were incorporated into the system. Those people have made less than full lifetime tax payments and have received benefit payments based on a tax base that was temporarily expanding more rapidly than was possible permanently. It is no wonder that Social Security enjoys the strong support it does among people of retirement age and those close to it.

What is not so clear is the support Social Security might command in the future as a mature system. Assuming the 1970s turn out to have been a momentary dip in a long-term trend of 3 percent annual growth in the economy, a tax-and-transfer system of social security will be beneficial to people only if 3 percent exceeds the rate of return they could receive through some funded system of social security. Setting the 1970s aside, the pretax rate of return on capital investment has run in the vicinity of 10 percent. It thus might seem as though some funded system of social security, including a personal investment program, could yield a return about triple that which could be yielded in the long run under a tax-and-transfer system.

As we noted in Part III, however, the yield on investment is taxed in a number of ways. Corporate income is taxed at nearly 50 percent.

Saving is taxed twice under the personal income tax, and realty is taxed under the property tax. In all, the tax burden on the income from capital may range in the vicinity of 70 or 80 percent. Thus, the posttax return to a funded system of social security — the net return that could also be attained through a program of personal investment — seems to run in the vicinity of 2 to 3 percent as well. Such an investment may well yield 10 percent in real terms before tax, but if the yield from that investment is taxed at 70 percent, the posttax return to the investor will be only 3 percent. In a steady-state comparison when the return to saving is taxed heavily, tax-and-transfer and funded systems of social security might seem to offer roughly similar rates of return.

WEALTH, WELFARE, AND SOCIAL SECURITY

Although funded and tax-and-transfer systems of social security seem to offer roughly similar net rates of return when judged from a steady-state perspective and based on prevailing rates of tax on capital income, much interest has arisen recently in the possibility that a tax-and-transfer system of social security might lower the rate of saving and capital formation from what it would be under a funded system. If this happens, real income will decline as well. This possible consequence of a tax-and-transfer system of social security was advanced initially by Martin Feldstein in an article that understandably has proven controversial.[10]

The conceptual basis for Feldstein's argument rests on a life cycle model of saving, in which people save during their years of work to provide for their retirement. The saving that takes place forms a capital fund that is invested through the creation of capital goods. If a system of personal responsibility for retirement is replaced by a funded system of social security, no essential difference results. Instead of saving, people pay social security taxes. These taxes, however, still constitute a supply of saving that is used to finance investment. The participants in a funded system of social security essentially are an investment club. People contribute to the club what they would otherwise have saved on their own, and this saving provides funds for investment, just as would happen under a regime of individual investment. The funded system of social security provides people with wealth that can be converted into income to pro-

---

[10] Martin Feldstein, "Social Security, Induced Retirement, and Aggregate Capital Accumulation," *Journal of Political Economy* 82 (October 1974), pp 905–926.

vide support during their retirement. Whether retirement is financed through personal responsibility or through a funded system of social insurance, the impact on saving and capital accumulation is the same, assuming that the government's operation of the funded system reflects what would have taken place through a regime of personal responsibility; that is, assuming that government earns a competitive rate of return on its social insurance fund.[11]

Like a funded system of social security, a tax-and-transfer system also provides a source of wealth, at least as viewed from the perspective of individual retirees. People will be able to support themselves during their retirement by the social security payments they will receive. These payments are essentially equivalent to the payments based on accumulated capital and interest they would have received under a funded system of social security. Unlike funding, however, social security taxes are not saved to provide for the accumulation of capital. Instead, the taxes are transferred from current workers to retirees to support their consumption.

An asymmetry occurs between a funded system and a tax-and-transfer system. They are identical in that the payments they offer during the years of retirement are a substitute form of wealth for the personal saving and capital accumulation that would otherwise be necessary. But they differ in the use they make of the taxes collected. In the funded system the tax revenues represent a supply of saving that is invested in capital goods to provide future income. But in the tax-and-transfer system, the revenues represent a source of consumption for people who are currently retired. In terms of the market for loanable funds described in Chapter 13, a tax-and-transfer system entails a leftward shift in the supply of saving, compared with a funded system of social security. With a lower rate of saving, the equilibrium capital stock will be lower as well.

As for the possible magnitude involved, Feldstein estimates that Social Security has been responsible for about a 40 percent reduction in the rate of saving. Although a 40 percent reduction in the amount of saving in any one year will have a small impact on the size of the capital stock, the long-run impact of a sustained reduction in saving will be an equivalent reduction in the capital stock. A

[11] If the federal government actually operated a funded system of social security, it would likely dominate the supply side of the capital market. For instance, total personal saving in 1980 was roughly $100 billion, while Social Security revenues, which would have been saved under a funded system, were about $115 billion. Hence, a funded system of social security would seem likely to provide more than half the total supply of saving in the United States, assuming there were no other significant changes in response to the funded system. The potential opportunity for the socialization of investment would perhaps bring up a variety of new questions.

lower capital stock implies in turn a reduction in the sustainable or permanent level of consumption. Just what a 40 percent reduction in capital stock implies for a reduction in permanent income or consumption depends on the relation between capital and income. Feldstein assumed that this relation could be described by the Cobb-Douglas production function that we described in Chapter 10.

By estimating particular values for the pertinent parameters for 1975, and by then postulating a 40 percent increase in the amount of capital, Feldstein developed a conjecture about what total national output would have been under a funded system of social security. Feldstein estimated that GNP would have been $285 billion higher in 1975, which translates to about $1,300 per person or about $3,500 per family unit. Put differently, this aggregate figure was about 30 percent of total consumer spending at the time and more than twice the total amount of personal income tax payments or total spending on national defense. Furthermore, the use of a funded system, Feldstein estimated, would have produced a real rate of interest that was 30 percent lower as a result of the larger capital stock. Feldstein also estimated that the larger capital stock would have raised the wages of labor, which is complementary in production with capital, by 15 percent.

There are, of course, numerous other ways by which the impact of social security on saving can be estimated. Much controversy has arisen over the particular empirical magnitudes, and no consensus has yet been reached about them. Alicia Munnell, for instance, finds that Social Security has had little overall impact on saving to date, but she predicts that such an effect is likely to exert itself in the future.[12] Social Security has two opposing effects on saving. It induces people to save less because it is a substitute for personal saving. But to the extent Social Security encourages people to retire earlier, it induces them to save more because they will have to support themselves during a longer period of retirement.

Munnell estimated for 1969, as evaluated in 1958 dollars, that the wealth effect of Social Security reduced saving by $11.4 billion. The retirement effect was estimated to have increased saving by $8.5 billion. This net reduction of $2.9 billion can be gauged against total personal saving of $35.2 billion in 1969, as evaluated in 1958 dollars. However, Munnell notes, the retirement effect seems likely to have run its course, as there is little scope remaining for further reduction in participation in the labor force by the elderly. (Whereas 50 percent of all males over sixty-five worked before Social Security, 20

[12] Alicia H. Munnell, "The Impact of Social Security on Personal Savings," *National Tax Journal* 27 (December 1974), pp. 553–567.

percent do so now.) The benefits have been increasing rapidly, however, and this wealth effect, which by Munnell's estimate reduced saving by over 30 percent, seems likely to continue to grow.

There is probably more consensus about the conceptual point that a tax-and-transfer system of social security will bring about some reduction in saving than there is about the probable extent of that reduction. But even this conceptual point is not free from some points of contention. The conceptual issues that arise are closely related to those concerning the incidence of debt finance that were discussed in Chapter 13, issues that can be explored from the perspective of both retirees and their children.

Although the life cycle model views people largely as saving to provide for their own retirement, it is possible that retirees will be supported by contributions from their children. Indeed, investment in children may perhaps be seen as one possible option as a source of investment for retirement support. If the government then institutes a program of transfers to retired parents, the children of those parents will be able to offset those transfers to some extent by reducing their own support of their parents. Indeed, if all retirement support for parents initially comes from their children rather than from their own assets, the injection of a program of governmental transfers to retired parents will be fully offset by an equivalent reduction in the support given by children. But as long as children provide only partial support for retired parents, the governmental transfer to parents cannot be fully offset by a reduction in transfers from children.

The effect of the tax-and-transfer form of social security on saving also depends on the response of parents as savers. If social security reduces the saving that parents undertake to support themselves, parents will bequeath a smaller capital stock to their survivors than they would have bequeathed under either a regime of personal saving for retirement or a funded system of social security. But if people view their heirs as perfect extensions of themselves, the reduction in saving that results from the tax-and-transfer system of social security interferes with parental preferences for bequeathing wealth to their survivors.

This interference can be negated if parents increase their saving to offset the reduction in saving that would otherwise take place through the tax-and-transfer system. If this happens, social security will have no impact on saving, regardless of how it is financed. Not everyone has heirs, of course, and of those who do, there are probably differences in the strengths of bequest motives. When bequest motives are imperfect — when parents do not treat their children fully as extensions of themselves — a tax-and-transfer system of social security will bring about some reduction in personal saving. How much of a reduction is an empirical matter, about which a consensus is presently lacking. The question is obviously of great importance and will doubtless continue to be a topic of continued study for some time to come.

OPTIONS FOR SOCIAL SECURITY

The past decade or so has seen episodic expressions of concern about the solvency of Social Security. From time to time Social Security has been pronounced in critical condition, with death at hand unless a transfusion of revenues is forthcoming. This financial aspect of the program has received much more attention than the possible impacts on saving of the Social Security program. As noted earlier, statements are commonly made about the actuarial bankruptcy of Social Security, with the extent of bankruptcy placed at about $5 trillion.

But a tax-and-transfer system cannot become actuarially bankrupt because actuarial principles are inapplicable. It can, however, encounter an inconsistency between the benefits promised and the taxes imposed. The schedule of benefits promised has tended to generate a more rapid growth in Social Security payments than the announced schedule of tax rates has generated revenues. In such a situation, the Social Security system would be unable to make payments unless payments were reduced or revenues increased.

The past decade or two has seen great increases in the generosity of Social Security payments. The replacement ratio — Social Security payments as a percentage of earnings the year before retirement — rose from 30 percent in 1965 to 50 percent a decade later, for a single retiree earning the median wage income. In 1977, Congress enacted massive increases in Social Security taxes, with the maximum tax being increased by 43 percent in 1981 and by 52 percent in 1986 from their previously scheduled rates. These tax increases were argued at the time to be sufficient to solve the financial problem of Social Security until sometime in the twenty-first century. Concerns about the impending crisis in Social Security emerged again before the decade had even ended, however.

The crises that periodically have occurred in Social Security have always been treated as financial. When projections show expenditures in excess of revenues available, the response has always been to increase taxes. As recently as 1947, the maximum tax that could be collected from one person was $60. Thirty-five years later, the maximum tax was $4,340. An imbalance between revenues and expenses can, of course, also be rectified by reducing expenses. The reduction of benefits, however, has rarely been undertaken. In 1981, the benefit for students aged nineteen or over was phased out, payment of the lump-sum death benefit was restricted to cases in which a spouse was living with the decedent, and the minimum benefit was eliminated. Increasing consideration has been given to raising the retirement age, from sixty-five to sixty-eight, and to reducing the benefit from early retirement.

To reduce benefits is, of course, to reduce the wealth of retirees from what they could otherwise have anticipated based on the legislation enacted by Congress. But how is making a change in the benefits promised to retirees any different from changing the tax commitments that were made to workers? An increase in taxes reduces the wealth of workers from what they could otherwise have anticipated based on the legislation enacted by Congress. If taxes are increased, taxpayers must necessarily suffer a reduction in their anticipated standard of living, just as retirees must suffer a reduction in their standard of living if their benefits are reduced. Economically, the situation is totally symmetric: There are always two ways of closing a gap between revenue and expenditure.

Politically, there may well be an important difference between reducing benefits and increasing taxes. For those retired, or close to retirement, changes in Social Security benefits are a substantial and often dominant element in their future income. For those working and supporting the retired, an increase in Social Security taxes involves a smaller percentage of their present and future income. Their earnings from work are larger than the impact of changes in Social Security taxes. The losses to workers will at least equal the gains to retirees, but those losses will be less noticed than will the gains.[13]

One adult in seven is in the sixty-five-or-over age category. Moreover, people in this category vote more frequently than others, often perhaps because the opportunity cost of their time is lower. The percentage of the total eligible electorate that voted in the 1980 election was just over 50 percent; nearly two-thirds of those over age sixty-five voted. It is perhaps no accident that average hourly earnings in such industries as steel and automobiles rose about 150 percent during the 1970s and that average Social Security benefits rose by 240 percent in the same time. The asymmetrical political treatment of discrepancies between the tax and payment sides of Social Security seem explicable. Inconsistent legislation concerning benefits and taxes may be an understandable feature of a tax-and-transfer

[13] Losses will equal gains if Social Security entails nothing but a set of taxes and transfers. But if it reduces saving and future wealth as well, the gain to retirees will be less than the loss suffered by workers.

system of social security, when it is considered as an element of majoritarian democracy. In contrast, a funded system of social security seems to belong instead to a regime of consensual democracy. The ultimate crisis of Social Security, in other words, may properly be seen as political rather than financial. That is, the pattern of evolution of Social Security since 1940 might be but a natural development of the redistributive potential of the tax-and-transfer system that was given a strong boost in 1939.

If the course of Social Security is seen not as an unfortunate set of exogenous circumstances always skewing otherwise reasonable projections but rather as a predictible and understandable working out of a tax-and-transfer system within a framework of majoritarian democracy, options for reform can be seen in a different light. Efforts to close projected gaps between revenues and expenditures might command less interest because those gaps are a natural attribute of a system of majoritarian democracy. Interest in reform would turn more to changes in the incentives to engage in taxing and transferring.

A return to a funded system has been advocated as a means of overcoming the harmful consequences for saving and capital formation. Funding can be a vehicle for establishing a quid pro quo relationship between the taxes people pay and the benefits they anticipate receiving upon retirement. Any effort to establish a funded system will encounter difficulties in making the transition. The existing actuarial deficit means that the amount of funds on hand is less than the benefit commitments already made. Even if Social Security henceforth is operated actuarially as a funded system, it would be necessary somehow to deal with the present actuarial deficit.

There are two polar possibilities, along with a variety of intermediate options. The actuarial deficit could be closed by reducing benefit payments, in which case the bulk of the deficit would be borne by retirees and people close to retirement. The deficit could also be closed by increasing taxes. One simple way of doing this would be to treat the actuarial deficit as a national debt and to make that debt explicit by issuing bonds to raise the necessary funds. As an intermediate measure, budget surpluses could be run, with the cumulative amount of surplus eventually coming to exceed the amount of the present deficit.

If funding is viewed as an option, a regime of personal responsibility might also be considered. When the original Social Security legislation was being developed, the Senate passed the Clark Amendment, which would have allowed people to opt out of Social Security if they were able to produce evidence of comparable coverage elsewhere.[14] It might be argued that there is some collective interest in assuring that people are able to have a minimal level of income during their retirement. But this argument does not imply that Social Security must be provided collectively or that it must be mandatory. Private provision is equally able to assure support during retirement. The Clark amendment would have required merely that people be able to demonstrate some ability to provide for their retirement. If social security is to be operated as a tax-and-transfer system, however, people cannot be allowed to replace Social Security with personal provision. In a mature tax-and-transfer system, the return any one generation receives is the rate of growth in the tax base, and to allow opting out by those who are presently working would erode the very basis of the intergeneration compact that a tax-and-transfer system represents.

Much of the opposition to allowing personal choice in the provision for retirement arises because the welfare and the insurance components of the program are presently confounded. Social Security has some characteristics of insurance, but it also has attributes of public assistance. Benefit payments are skewed to provide relatively larger payments to people with relatively smaller past earnings. If the public assistance and the insurance aspects of Social Security were separated, a more knowledgeable assessment of policy options possibly would result. It would then be possible for social insurance policy to focus on the ways people might provide for their retirement, with public assistance policy focusing on impoverishment regardless of age.

SUGGESTIONS FOR FURTHER READING

Colin D. Campbell, ed., *Income Redistribution* (Washington, D.C.: American Enterprise Institute, 1977), presents a series of papers on various aspects of income redistribution, including the extent to which there might be a genuine desire for equality; the fairness of market processes of income determination; the trade-off between production and redistribution; the effectiveness of actual efforts at redistribution; and possible conflicts between redistribution and liberty. On the almost complete elimination of poverty in the United States, when poverty is defined in terms of some minimal amount of consumption, see Edgar K. Browning, *Redistribution and the Welfare System* (Washington, D.C.: American Enterprise Institute, 1975); Martin Anderson, "Welfare Reform," in

[14] This amendment, named after Senator Bennett C. Clark of Missouri, died in the conference committee in which the House and Senate resolve the differences between their bills.

The United States in the 1980s, edited by Peter Duignan and Alvin Rabushka (Stanford, Calif.: Hoover Institution Press, 1980), pp. 139–179; and Morton Paglin, "Poverty in the United States: A Reevaluation," *Policy Review* 8 (Spring 1979), pp. 7–24. Milton Friedman, "Choice, Chance, and the Personal Distribution of Income," *Journal of Political Economy* 61 (August 1953), pp. 277–290, describes how a substantial portion of the observed inequality of income is a reflection of people's preferences as these influence the occupational choices they make.

The literature on minimum wage legislation is extensive. Finis Welch, *Minimum Wages: Issues and Evidence* (Washington, D.C.: American Enterprise Institute, 1978), is a concise survey, complete with references to this literature. The various difficulties of finding a satisfying approach to the reform of welfare programs are explored in Henry J. Aaron, *Why Is Welfare So Hard to Reform?* (Washington, D.C.: Brookings Institution, 1973); and Martin Anderson, *Welfare: The Political Economy of Welfare Reform in the United States* (Stanford, Calif.: Hoover Institution Press, 1978). Although the basic concepts of negative income taxation are simple, the implementation of any particular plan will require choices concerning such issues as (1) the definition of income, (2) the definition of the family unit, (3) rules for membership in the family unit, (4) selection of the allowance schedule for units of various sizes, (5) relation of negative income taxation to prevailing public assistance programs, and (6) treatment of fluctuating income. For an exploration of these issues, see James Tobin, Joseph A. Pechman, and Peter Mieszkowski, "Is a Negative Income Tax Practical?" *Yale Law Journal* 77 (November 1967), pp. 1–27. The disincentive effects of unemployment insurance are described in Martin Feldstein, "The Economics of the New Unemployment," *The Public Interest,* no. 33 (Fall 1973), pp. 3–42.

Contrasting conceptions of Social Security are examined in Colin D. Campbell, "Social Insurance in the United States: A Program in Search of an Explanation," *Journal of Law and Economics* 12 (October 1969), pp. 249–265. *The Crisis in Social Security,* edited by Michael J. Boskin (San Francisco: Institute for Contemporary Studies, 1977), contains a number of essays concerning the financial difficulties and the antisaving bias of the present system of Social Security. The political popularity of Social Security, despite its imposition of losses on a majority of the citizenry, is examined in William C. Mitchell, *The Popularity of Social Security: A Paradox in Public Choice* (Washington, D.C.: American Enterprise Institute, 1977).

The ultimately political nature of the Social Security crisis as an understandable outcome of a system of majoritarian democracy is explored in Carolyn L. Weaver, *The Crisis in Social Security: Economic and Political Dimensions* (Durham, N.C.: Duke University Press, 1982); and Peter Ferrara, *Social Security: The Inherent Contradiction* (San Francisco: Cato Institute, 1980). Weaver emphasizes the historical development of Social Security as a natural process set in motion by the replacement of an essentially contractual system, created in 1935, by the tax-and-transfer system created in 1939. Ferrara emphasizes that although

Social Security produced a transitory period of extraordinarily high rates of return, the mature system offers a lower rate of return than people could gain on their own. He also discusses a way of replacing the present system with a regime of personal provision. Both Weaver and Ferrara see the present difficulties with Social Security as an inevitable product of its noncontractual nature.

18

Public Economics in a Compound Republic

In previous chapters we have not paid particular attention to the unique features that arise when government is organized as a federal or compound republic in which exists a multiplicitly of governments whose jurisdictions often overlap. In law and political science, federalism describes a constitutional order in which people are simultaneously members of two autonomous units of government. Federalism is embodied in the American Constitution, with the federal government and the state governments possessing autonomous spheres of jurisdiction.

As it is commonly used in public economics, however, federalism refers not so much to nominal constitutional arrangements as to the existence of a multiplicity of overlapping governments, each possessing some autonomy in legislating and budgeting.[1] Although nations such as Belguim and the United Kingdom would not be described as federalist by constitutional criteria, lower levels of government in those nations do possess much autonomy. For most questions that arise in public economics related to federalism, what matters most is the presence of a system of government characterized by a multiplicity of overlapping governments possessing substantial autonomy.

Within this notion of federalism as a compound republic, we can pursue two lines of examination. One concerns the relations among units of government at different levels when a hierarchy of governments exist. Under such a hierarchy a person is governed simultaneously by a city, a state, and the federal government. The other

[1] This approach is taken in such primary contributions to federalism in public economics as Wallace E. Oates, *Fiscal Federalism* (New York: Harcourt Brace Jovanovich, 1972); and Albert Breton and Anthony Scott, *The Economic Constitution of Federal States* (Toronto: University of Toronto Press, 1978).

line of inquiry arises from the possibility that people have some choice about which of several units of government will govern them. A person who works in New York City can choose to be governed by New York, Connecticut, or New Jersey. If the person chooses to reside in New York State, he or she faces a further choice about residing in and being governed by New York City, Scarsdale, New Rochelle, White Plains, or wherever. The first several sections of this chapter examine issues that arise when people are governed simultaneously by two or more levels of government; the last few sections address issues that arise when people can choose which among several units of government they will be governed by.

FEDERALISM AND FISCAL EFFICIENCY

Choices regarding the supply of education, or of any other service provided by government, might be made by the federal government for the entire nation. The implementation of those choices could take place through local schools, much as local offices administer many of the activities of the Social Security Administration. But autonomy over policy choices would rest with the federal government. Alternatively, choices about education, or about any other service, might be made by a number of smaller, autonomous units of government. Much of the literature on fiscal federalism is concerned with the differences that are likely to arise among assignments of autonomy over activities. With respect to the United States government as it presently functions, autonomy over an activity might reside with the federal government or it could reside with the fifty state governments.

At a more general level, the number of autonomous jurisdictions can also be treated as variable. Indeed, autonomy might be regarded as the province of 80 million units of government, with each family considered self-governing with regard to, say, education. Moreover, autonomy can in principle be divided among units of government at different levels. Individual families might be autonomous with respect to education of children and the federal government autonomous with respect to the education of veterans. The sphere of autonomy is not self-defining, and divided autonomy often characterizes federal systems of government. Nonetheless, it is often convenient for discussion to proceed as if autonomy over a function is indivisible and is assigned exclusively to one level of government or another.

Accommodation of Preferences

With respect to the locus of autonomy for a particular service, economists have focused on such questions as the degree to which

TABLE 18.1 Preference Accommodation in Federal and
Unitary States

	Options	
Territory	X	Y
A	20,000	30,000
B	35,000	15,000
Total	55,000	45,000

different levels of government are able to satisfy differing preferences among people and the costliness of services at different levels of government. As autonomy comes to reside with smaller units of government, the overall system of government becomes better able to accommodate variation in the preferences of individual citizens. This point is illustrated, in abstract terms, by Table 18.1.

Suppose an area contains 100,000 residents, 55,000 of whom prefer option X and 45,000 of whom prefer option Y. Under a unitary system of government, X will be chosen under majority rule, and 45,000 people will find their preferences unfulfilled or contradicted. But if that territory can be divided into two smaller regions, A and B, the degree to which preferences are unfulfilled may be reduced. If residents of A prefer Y to X by 30,000 to 20,000 while residents of B prefer X to Y by 35,000 to 15,000, Y will be the choice in A and X will be the choice in B. As a result, only 35,000 people, and not 45,000, will have their preferences unfulfilled. The more fully people come to apportion themselves between the two territories according to the similarity between their preferences and those of their neighbors, the less people will find their preferences unfulfilled.

In the limiting case, no one's preference will be unfulfilled. This will happen if A comes to contain 45,000 people, all of whom prefer Y, and B comes to contain 55,000 people, all of whom prefer X. At the very worst, the devolution of autonomy will have no effect in reducing the degree to which people's preferences go unfulfilled. This will happen if a majority in each government after devolution still prefers option X.[2]

Suppose two options provide for elementary and secondary education. One may be labeled a progressive education, characterized, among other things, by teaching reading through a look-and-say

[2] This point is developed in J. Roland Pennock, "Federal and Unitary Government — Disharmony and Frustration," *Behavioral Science* 4 (April 1959), pp. 147–157.

method, in which the materials assigned are chosen predominantly from contemporary authors who write in a vernacular style. The other might be called a saber-toothed (or Neanderthal) education, characterized by such things as teaching reading through phonics, with the materials that are read coming largely from classical sources, including the Bible.

If 55,000 people prefer the progressive curriculum and 45,000 people prefer the saber-toothed curriculum, the progressive curriculum will be chosen under majority rule in a unitary state. But in a federal state, different curricula may be chosen in different states. If so, there will be a fuller accommodation of variation in personal preferences in a federal state. Moreover, the various jurisdictions will be better able to discern the value of different potential curricula when they are able to experiment with their curricula.

Suppose the children in one jurisdiction seem to develop in a civil and energetic manner, while in another they appear to develop in a rude and lazy manner. If the main difference between the jurisdictions appears to be their approach to education, the jurisdictions may have valuable information on which to base decisions, depending also on the value judgment they make about which type of personality is preferable. A federal system of government means a greater range of experimentation in addition to allowing for a greater accommodation of variation in personal preferences.

People differ in their preferences for various types of activities and services, those provided publicly as well as privately. The organization of economic activity within a market economy allows fulfillment of those many preferences for services offered privately. In broadly similar fashion, the various jurisdictions within a federal system of government can accommodate differences in preferences for service provided publicly.[3] Figure 18.1 illustrates the gain in the enhanced ability to fulfill disparate preferences that results from a devolution in autonomy over the provision of a particular service. The point described by this figure — that a devolution of autonomy enhances the ability of government to reflect differences in personal preferences — is essentially the same as the one developed above, but the illustration here is in continuous rather than discrete form.

Economies of Scale

Although the devolution of autonomy offers gains from a fuller accommodation of personal preferences, such devolution may also en-

[3] For an interesting description of such variations in preference for public services, see Thomas R. Dye, "City-Suburban Social Distance and Public Policy," *Social Forces* 44 (September 1965), pp. 100–106.

FIGURE 18.1 Welfare Loss From Single Government

Two governments, *A* and *B*, contain equal numbers of people, and all the people in each government have identical preferences. This situation is described by the demand curves D_A and D_B. If *A* and *B* are autonomous and if the tax-price faced by each resident is P^*, people in *A* will choose Q_A and people in *B* will choose Q_B. If *A* and *B* are replaced by a single government, preferences could not be satisfied so fully, as long as a common tax-price is to be charged to all residents. Suppose the output under a single government is Q^*, the midpoint between Q_A and Q_B, with all people still paying P^* per unit. At Q^*, the value people in *A* place on the service is less than the price they must pay, by *cb*, and over the entire range, Q_A to Q^*, the sum of those welfare loses is *abc*. In similar fashion residents of *B* are suffering a welfare loss of *cde*, but in this case the loss arises because output is less than what they would desire. (Essentially the same point could be made by assuming Q_A or Q_B was the output, in which case the entire welfare loss would rest on people who preferred the alternative output.)

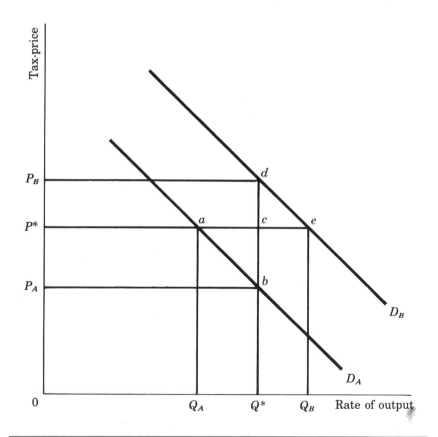

counter offsetting costs. Suppose public output is produced according to some U-shaped average cost function, as illustrated by Figure 18.2. If so, it is possible for jurisdictions to be too small to exploit fully the economies of scale in production. Police protection might cost $10 per person when it is provided for 30,000 people and $7 per person when it is provided for 60,000 people. If so, it will be more costly to provide police protection for two jurisdictions of 30,000 each than to provide it for a single jurisdiction of 60,000. In this instance, a trade-off might arise between the higher costliness of smaller jurisdictions and their superior ability to accommodate variations in personal preferences. In the presence of such a trade-off, the smaller jurisdictions might be warranted only if the value

---

FIGURE 18.2 Economies of Scale and Jurisdictional Size

Suppose the average cost of public output varies with the size of the jurisdiction that provides that output in the manner described by AC. A jurisdiction of size X_1 has the lowest cost of public output, C_1. For a smaller jurisdiction such as that represented by X_2, public output is more expensive, as shown by C_2. The same is true for a larger jurisdiction such as that represented by X_3, where the average cost of output is C_3. If X_2 is one-half the size of X_1, a merger of two such jurisdictions would appear to reduce the unit cost of public output from C_2 to C_1.

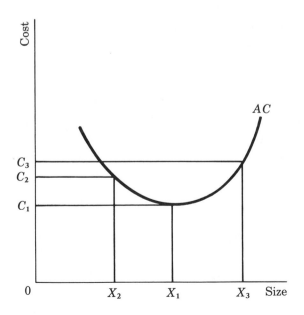

people place on the greater accommodation of preferences is more than $3 per person, which would be the cost of maintaining those smaller jurisdictions.

These considerations of economies of scale, while perhaps having intuitive appeal, are less than fully satisfactory. Even though it may be cheaper to organize police services to serve 60,000 people than to serve 30,000, this does not mean that cities must contain 60,000 people to take advantage of the economies of scale. Other options for exploiting those economies of scale are available. One city could contract with the other for police services. In this way, one city containing 30,000 residents would produce at a rate of output that would serve 60,000 residents, thereby exploiting the economies of scale. The other city would produce no police services but would buy those services from the producing city. Alternatively, the two cities could agree to some cooperative arrangement for the joint production of police services, or both cities could purchase police services from a third jurisdiction.

Regardless of particular options, there is no reason why the unit that organizes production must be identical with the unit that has the demand. In principle, it is entirely possible for demands for police services to be made by communities of 5,000 and yet for production to take place on a scale that would serve 60,000. This simply means that each producer would serve twelve customers.

The cost of organizing economic activity, and not the cost of production as such, is of central importance. It is these organizational costs that place the primary limit on the devolution of autonomy. If all police activity is provided by jurisdictions of 5,000, or even 30,000, for instance, traffic control may take place smoothly and neighborhood disturbances quieted peacefully. But the apprehension of car thieves or kidnappers is likely to be almost impossible for such jurisdictions. To cover the wider geographical range required for investigation and apprehension in these instances, police in one jurisdiction must be able to receive the assistance of police in other jurisdictions. To establish such a network of assistance may entail such high costs of contracting, communicating, and the like that dealing with wide-ranging criminal activities within a highly decentralized system will be ineffective. The devolution of autonomy will thus have proceeded too far. The less fully the devolution of autonomy takes place, the less burden will be placed on coordination among units of government.

The economic analysis of federalism, then, sees the primary benefit of the devolution of autonomy as its ability to accommodate variations in personal preferences and values as well as to offer sources of experimentation, which, in turn, promotes learning through a quasi-laboratory situation. This accommodation is limited by the costliness of coordinating actions among autonomous units of government. Such organizational costs mean that governments will be larger than they would otherwise be if the accommodation of differing preferences and values was the only organizing force. Indeed, in the absence of such organizational costs, there would be no case for governments of any size because preferences will always be accommodated most fully within a regime of personal autonomy. (In like manner and as we saw in Chapter 10, in the absence of organizational costs there also would be no business firms.)

Once it is recognized that functions can typically be subdivided, the separation of functions among levels of government would seem to be more effectively approached in somewhat different fashion. Such questions as the proper level for providing police service would diminish in importance. Questions concerning the types of police services to be undertaken by local, state, and federal agencies would become relatively more important. The Federal Bureau of Investigation, for instance, provides much information to local police departments, and the FBI may well be the efficient-sized unit for organizing the collection and provision of information that it makes available, even though it may not be the efficient-sized unit to possess autonomy over decisions concerning such matters as traffic control.

MISCOORDINATION IN A FEDERAL SYSTEM

The ability to accommodate differing demands through autonomous jurisdictions constitutes the benefit side of a federal system of government. Budgetary choices within any unit of government will be based on a comparison of the benefits and costs of its own activities to its own residents. To the extent that preferences are homogeneous within a jurisdiction, a model of choice by a median voter will be equivalent to one of unanimous consent. Budgetary choices will tend to be consensual or optimal when viewed from the perspective of a single jurisdiction. The inability to achieve some forms of coordination among those jurisdictions constitutes the cost side of a federal system of government. Such failures of coordination can render the output choices of any jurisdiction as either excessive or insufficient, as judged by the standard of the benefit principle. Which category of outcome emerges depends on the type of miscoordination that results.

Cost Spillovers

If one jurisdiction is able to transfer some of the cost of its activities to people who reside in other jurisdictions, the price its own residents pay for public output will fall. This reduction in price will bring about an increase in the rate of output, as Figure 18.3 illustrates. The members of that jurisdiction will choose a rate of output that equates marginal cost and marginal value. In a median voter model, this equality will refer to the person whose preferences are median within the jurisdiction; and in a consensual model, this equality will characterize all residents. But if some of the cost of the public output can be transferred to people in other jurisdictions, the marginal cost borne by the jurisdiction's residents will fall, and this will lead them to choose an even larger rate of output. At this larger rate of output, the full marginal cost of the community's output will exceed the

---

FIGURE 18.3 Cost Spillovers and Budgetary Size

D_A describes the demand curve for X on the part of the members of a community. MC describes the marginal cost of X, and MC_A describes the marginal cost borne by the members of the community, with the divergence between MC and MC_A resulting because of tax exporting or cost spillover. In the presence of such tax exporting, X_A is the chosen rate of output. At this rate of output, the value of the X_Ath unit of output is less than the full marginal cost by ba. The total welfare loss attributable to the expansion in output from X to X_A through tax exporting is abc.

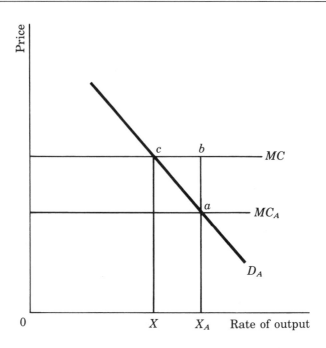

marginal benefit, and an inefficient pattern of resource utilization will result.

As for possible empirical magnitudes, Charles McLure has estimated that about 25 percent of state and local taxes are exported across state boundaries.[4] This happens mainly through the deductibility of state and local taxes from the federal income tax. Deductibility lowers the price to state and local residents of public services that are financed by taxation. If a locality increases property taxes by $100, a local resident in the 40 percent tax bracket will be able to reduce federal taxes by $40. To such a person, the price of the local output is thus only $60.

In some cases, however, what might appear to be tax exporting might not turn out to be so when public expenditures are taken into account. A city that is an attractive place for tourists might place a tax on hotel rooms. If this tax raises the price of hotel rooms, it might be thought to be exported to tourists. But if the city also offers various services to tourists, the ultimate effect of the tax may be on the order of a charge for services rendered rather than an export of taxes.

Benefit Spillovers

Although the spillover of the cost of the output choices of subnational jurisdictions apparently can be substantial, most attention on the fiscal aspects of federalism has focused on the spillover of the benefits from public expenditures. The effect of expenditure spillover is simply the reverse of tax spillover, and it is illustrated in Figure 18.4. The independent budgetary choice of the jurisdiction under examination will result in a budget that is inefficiently small because the value placed on additional output by residents of other jurisdictions is not taken into account. Should that value received by outsiders be somehow taken into account, output will expand until the sum of the marginal valuations placed on that jurisdiction's output by the residents of all jurisdictions equals the marginal cost. Unless the interests of residents of other jurisdictions are taken into account, something that is precluded momentarily by the assumption of autonomous jurisdictions, the budgetary choices of a set of autonomous jurisdictions will generate inefficiency in the utilization of resources.

Spillovers raise issues pertaining both to efficiency and to equity. With efficiency, the output of activities subject to benefit spillovers

[4] Charles E. McLure, Jr., "The Interstate Exporting of State and Local Taxes: Estimates for 1962," *National Tax Journal* 20 (March 1967), pp. 49–77.

FIGURE 18.4 Benefit Spillovers and Budgetary Choice

The demand curve of the median voter in jurisdiction A is D_A. Facing a marginal tax price of P_0, the median voter chooses X_A as the rate of output. Some residents of jurisdiction B also benefit from A's output, and the demand function $D_A + D_B$ represents the addition of this demand to A's own demand. At the rate of output X_A, the sum of the marginal valuations placed on A's output exceeds the marginal cost of that output by ab. This excess of value over cost indicates the extent of resource misallocation. Only at the output rate X_{A+B} will the sum of the marginal valuations equal the marginal cost.

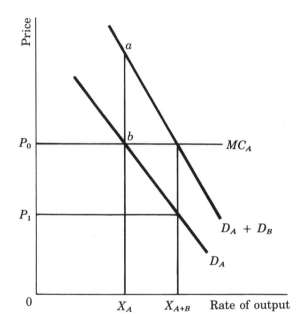

will be too small, according to the benefit principle. For those activities, the value yielded by additional output will exceed the cost. An increase in the production of those services subject to benefit spillover will increase the value yielded by the existing stock of resources in society. With equity, transfers of income take place as a result of spillovers. Jurisdictions that are the recipients of benefit spillovers gain income, and those that are on the supplying end lose income. As we will see, the relationship between central cities and outlying suburbs is often advanced as an example of such a transfer of income.

REMEDIES FOR MISCOORDINATION

If spillovers of either benefit or cost create miscoordination or in-efficiency among a set of autonomous governments, the amalgamation or merger of those governments will obviously eliminate the scope for spillovers. It will, however, also destroy the federal system of government. It cannot therefore be presented as a remedy within a federalist system because it represents instead the replacement of a federalist system with a unitary system of government. In a federalist system, the main categories of remedy are grants-in-aid, usually from a higher to a lower level of government, and contracts among units of government.

Intergovernmental Grants

Conditional grants-in-aid from a higher to a lower level of government can be a means of offsetting the miscoordination that might otherwise result in a federal system of government. Suppose a community is contemplating an improvement in its system of traffic control. The overall effect of this improvement will be a more rapid movement of traffic through town. Different degrees of improvement might be chosen. Among other things, the number of streets included within the new system can be varied. Options also exist for the equipment purchased, with the more expensive types being able to adapt the timing of signals to the flow of traffic almost continuously.

The equipment and the coverage that the community chooses will depend on both the preferences of the members of the community and the cost they must incur for the equipment. If the members bear the full cost, they will make an optimizing choice, essentially the kind illustrated in Figure 18.4. Suppose that half the traffic in the community and, hence, half the total demand for the new equipment, comes from nonresidents who for a number of reasons must travel through the community. As Figure 18.4 illustrated, too little output will be provided in the presence of such spillovers, as judged from the perspective of the benefit principle. But if a higher level of government, possibly the federal government, offers a grant-in-aid, with the grant covering half the cost of the new equipment, the price will be reduced to the members of the community, and accordingly, they will choose a larger rate of output. With reference to Figure 18.4, if the grant reduces the price paid by the members of the community from P_0 to P_1, the efficient rate of output, $X_{A + B}$, will be supplied.

The grant in the example is open-ended in that the size of the grant is residually determined as the product of the lower jurisdiction's choice of output and the announced rate of matching. The matching feature of the grant reduces the price of public output to members of particular jurisdictions. A grant that simply transfers a lump sum will not accomplish this change in price but will only increase the income of residents in the jurisdiction.

Contracting Among Governments

Although matching grants have the ability to offset the inefficiency that might otherwise result, they are not the only means of doing so. The presence of spillovers also creates an incentive for the jurisdictions to reach some agreement that will offset the effects of the spillover. In terms of the model described in Figure 18.4, the residents in each jurisdiction can gain by reaching some agreement to establish $X_{A + B}$ as the rate of output. Figure 18.5 provides further illustration of this point. Starting from the output that is chosen under independent action, X_A, the jurisdiction whose members benefit from the new traffic equipment (or, more generally, who benefit from the spillover) will be willing to pay something for additional output beyond X_A. This amount is described by its own demand function for that output, D_B. The jurisdiction that provides the traffic equipment will likewise be willing to expand output if it receives sufficient compensation. The terms on which it would be willing to expand output are essentially described by the extent to which the cost of the added output exceeds its own evaluation of that output. As long as the actual rate of output is less than the efficient rate, gains from trade will exist between the two jurisdictions. The jurisdiction receiving the spillover will be willing to make some payment to the producing jurisdiction in exchange for the latter's agreement to expand production.[5]

Ordinary assumptions about inefficiency under spillover fail to account for the full range of processes for exploiting the gains from trade. Inefficiency implies the existence of unexploited gains from trade, and the development of an agreement among the jurisdictions affected by such spillovers can alleviate the inefficiency. In principle, the development of an agreement among the affected jurisdictions

---

[5] Spillovers may perhaps create issues of equity, even though no questions of efficiency arise. Suppose in Figure 18.5, D_B is positive at rates of output less than X_A, but it becomes zero at X_A. In this case, residents of B still receive a gain from the spill-in provided by A's production, but the marginal valuation placed upon A's output by residents of B is zero. The efficient rate of output in this situation will be X_A.

FIGURE 18.5 Spillovers and Gain from Intergovernmental
Agreement

The demand curves D_A and D_B describe the demands of the median voters
in A and B for some service, X, supplied by jurisdiction A. If the
jurisdictions act independently, A will provide X_A, as this is the optimizing
choice for the median voter in A. At this rate of output, the median voter
in B values a marginal expansion in A's output at P_B. On the one hand,
this amount indicates the extent of allocative inefficiency under
independent action. On the other hand, it also indicates the extent of the
incentive the two jurisdictions have to reach some agreement to increase
A's supply of X. For jurisdiction B, its median voter would be willing to
pay any amount up to the amount shown by D_B for an expansion in A's
output beyond X_A. The minimum amount A must receive to be willing to
do so is the vertical distance between MC and D_A. Until the rate of output
X_{A+B} is attained, the maximum amount that B will be willing to pay for an
expansion in output, given by D_B, will exceed the minimum amount that A
must receive, as given by $MC - D_A$.

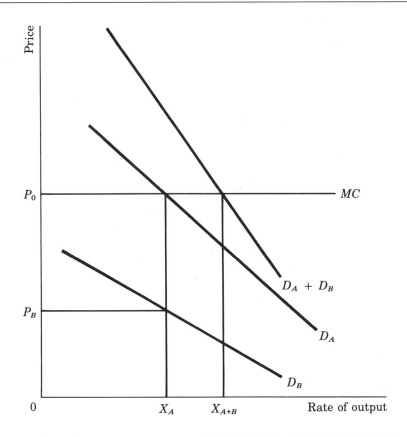

and the use of grants-in-aid by a higher level government can operate identically to offset inefficiencies that might otherwise arise. This statement about principle is identical to the conceptual equivalence of imposing a corrective excise tax on a manufacturer who dumps waste into a river and establishing transferable ownership rights to the water in the river.

An equivalence in principle does not, of course, imply an equivalence in practice. Processes of intergovernmental negotiation may founder on the costliness of securing agreement when large numbers of jurisdictions are involved, just as processes for the transfer of ownership rights may founder on the high costs of policing and enforcing such a system. Grants-in-aid from a higher level of government may be a means of overcoming the high cost of reaching an agreement among a large number of autonomous governments, but they may also serve as an instrument for transferring income to winning coalitions by lowering the prices those coalitions pay for public output. If this happens, grants-in-aid, as they actually work rather than as they conceptually might work, can become instruments for the creation of inefficiency just as actual excise taxes may perform quite differently from the way the rationalization for corrective excise taxation sees them as performing.

SOME INSTITUTIONAL FEATURES OF GRANTS-IN-AID

Federal grants-in-aid to state and local governments were nearly $90 billion in fiscal 1980. Over three-quarters of that amount went for categorical grants, which are awarded for specific programs. The remaining amount was spent on revenue sharing, which is awarded for general support, and block grants, which are awarded for broad purposes such as health care, crime control, and community development. Of the categorical grants, about one-third were project grants, in which a specific amount of money is awarded for a specific project. The remainder of categorical grants were formula grants, which often have the characteristics of open-ended matching grants. The 1980 budget contained $1.375 billion in formula grants for urban mass transportation. Those grants were awarded by a formula in which the federal government paid 80 percent of construction expenses for urban mass transit and 50 percent of the expenses of operation.

Grants in a System of Majoritarian Democracy

Formula grants conform more closely than project grants to our model of the way matching grants can be used to correct resource misallocations that might otherwise result through spillovers. The construction of such a model does not imply, however, that actual matching grants necessarily promote efficiency. The presence of a federal matching grant of 50 percent for the operating expenses of local mass transit does not imply that the rate of spillover is 50 percent. This might be the rate of spillover, but there are other circumstances under which such a rate of matching might be attached to a federal grant, especially within a system of majoritarian democracy.

Matching grants may be used by winning coalitions as vehicles for the transfer of income, with the transfer taking place through the choice of a rate of matching that exceeds the rate of spillover. Suppose a nation contains three states, with each state having the same population and income and with each state paying one-third of federal taxes. Further suppose that the major cities in two of the states are relatively old, predating the automobile and thus having high population density and much difficulty in handling automobile traffic. In contrast, the major city in the third state postdates the automobile, has a low population density, and handles automobile traffic smoothly. If mass transit is a local function, the older cities will choose to invest in mass transit to the point where the marginal benefit its members (or its median voter) anticipate receiving from that investment equals the marginal cost.

Under state provision, suppose the two states that contain the older cities form a coalition to support a program of federal grants for mass transit. As long as these states can keep the grants to themselves, they will receive transfers of income from the residents of the third state.[6] Even though spillovers may be absent, a program of federal grants may be created nonetheless. The effect of such a matching grant is shown in Figure 18.6. In the absence of a matching grant, A and B bear the full costs of their choices. When the grant is

[6] There are a number of ways they might be able to restrict the grant program to themselves. Eligibility for grants could be written in terms of criteria such as average age of housing stock, average speed of automobile traffic at 5 P.M. on weekdays, and so on, so as to preclude the major city in the third state from participating in the program. Alternatively, the rate of matching could be selected so that the third state would have no incentive to participate. With full federal funding, the third state would have an incentive to participate to the point where the marginal benefit to its residents equals the marginal cost, with this marginal cost being one-third of the actual marginal cost. If the share the state must pay is raised above zero, the incentive to participate is reduced. The third state would withdraw its participation first, and a rate of matching could be chosen such that, even in the absence of other rules concerning eligibility for the program, only two of the three states would choose to participate, namely the two states with the relatively strong demands for mass transit.

FIGURE 18.6 Use of Matching Grants to Transfer Income

The demand for mass transit on the part of the median voters in states A and B is described by D_A and D_B. The marginal cost of mass transit in each state is P_0. If mass transit is chosen by individual states, A and B will each choose X_0 as its rate of provision. But suppose they can get mass transit provided through a matching grant. Doing so will bring in contributions from residents of state C, who have no demand for mass transit. The effect of the grant is to reduce the price to residents in A and B to MC_G. Consequently, residents in A and B will choose larger programs of mass transit, as described by X_1.

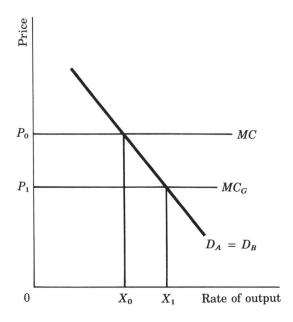

financed by taxes imposed equally on residents in all three states, with benefits being divided evenly between states A and B, the marginal cost to residents of A and B is reduced by one-third. As a result, states A and B will choose a greater investment in mass transit than they would have chosen otherwise. If the pregrant individual budgetary choices of the states reflected fiscal efficiency, the grant will have created inefficiency in the use of resources as a by-product of the transfer of income from residents of C to residents of A and B. Even though spillovers may be absent, a controlling coalition may profit from a program of grants-in-aid from the federal government to state and local governments.

Besides transferring income from the residents of some jurisdictions to the residents of other jurisdictions, federal grants can also transfer income among the residents within a jurisdiction. Differences in the systems under which states and the federal government raise their revenues can create an incentive for some people to support a transfer of financial responsibility from the states to the federal government. The federal government raises most of its revenues through a progressive income tax. State governments raise their revenues through taxes that are roughly proportional to income. A federal grant replaces proportional state taxes with the progressive federal tax. As long as income is distributed so that the median income is less than the average income, the replacement of a proportional income tax with a progressive tax will benefit people with below-average incomes. A program of federal grants is a way of bringing about such a substitution of taxes and, hence, of transferring income among the residents of a jurisdiction.[7]

Nullification and the Constitutional Contract

The federal government can use the tax revenues it collects to award grants-in-aid. The grant is a type of contract, and as a condition of receipt the federal government may impose whatever conditions it chooses. States are in principle free to accept or reject a grant under the terms offered. Through the use of grants, the federal government is able to nationalize what would otherwise be state activities. Traffic control, for instance, is constitutionally a state function. However, the federal government has been able to gain control of such features as speed limits and roadside advertising by making the receipt of highway grants conditional on the states' adhering to such things as 55-m.p.h. speed limits and the prohibition of roadside billboards. There has been a growing interest in using federal grants to gain the adherence of the states to a set of penalties for drunken driving.

The relationship between the federal government and the state governments contains a significant asymmetry. States individually are in a large-number analog to the prisoners' dilemma we described in Chapter 2. Each state is given the option either of accepting a grant on the terms offered by the federal government or of rejecting it. States need not impose 55-m.p.h. speed limits; they need only impose such requirements if they wish to receive federal highway grants. If a state rejects a federal grant, however, its residents will continue to pay federal taxes to finance the grant program.

[7] This possibility is explored in Kenneth V. Greene, "Some Institutional Considerations in Federal-State Fiscal Relations," *Public Choice* 9 (Fall 1970), pp. 1–18.

The residents of a state that rejects a grant program suffer a transfer of income to the residents of those states that accept the grant. When states act individually, each will be strongly motivated to participate in grant programs even though the various states might choose to reject such participation and retain the tax revenues instead, if they could act collectively.

A grant-in-aid effectively changes the division of responsibility within the federal system. Grants involve a revision of the Constitution but without formal amendment.[8] The direct nationalization of authority for setting highway speed limits, because it violates the constitutional assignment of responsibility, should be possible only through the process of constitutional amendment, in which case the consent of three-quarters of the state legislatures would ultimately be required before the setting of speed limits. But through the use of grants-in-aid, this constitutional revision takes place and without recourse to the formal process of constitutional amendment.

The formal procedures for amendment ensure that changes in the division of responsibility between the federal and state governments take place consensually. Informal amendment through such nonconsensual processes as grants-in-aid can be prevented only through some extension of the central principle of formal amendment to effective amendment via grants-in-aid. The basic principle of consensual democracy as reflected in the process of constitutional amendment is that if one-quarter plus one of the state legislatures judge a proposed amendment to be undesirable, there is insufficient consensus in support of that amendment. To close the informal loophole on nonconsensual amendments offered by grants-in-aid, it would be necessary to allow one-quarter plus one of the state legislatures to veto a grant program. Such a requirement of state consent would allow states to escape the prisoners' dilemma they are caught in when they must choose individually to accept or reject a grant. Grants might thus be transformed from an instrument of majoritarian democracy into one of consensual democracy.

REVENUE SHARING AND GENERAL-PURPOSE GRANTS

Nearly one-quarter of federal grants support the general activities of state and local governments. Revenue sharing can be described

[8] This constitutional theme is developed in William A. Niskanen, "The Prospect for Liberal Democracy," in *Fiscal Responsibility in Constitutional Democracy,* edited by James M. Buchanan and Richard E. Wagner (Leiden: Martinus Nijhoff, 1978), pp. 157–174.

as an unconditional grant; in contrast to conditional or categorical grants, revenue sharing is not designated to be spent on particular activities but rather is available to support a range of activities. Nonetheless, revenue sharing has strings or conditions attached, although the strings are much more subtle than those associated with matching grants.[9] Other things equal, revenue sharing awards more money to units of government with higher tax rates and also to those that collect larger shares of their revenues through an income tax. Accordingly, revenue sharing creates some incentive for use of income taxation and for replacement of fees and charges with taxes, both of which increase the amount of revenue a unit of government receives. In spite of the various incentives that revenue sharing contains, it is less dependent on responses by recipient governments than are categorical grants, even if it is not awarded entirely unconditionally.

Block Grants

Block grants are commonly thought to represent a compromise between categorical grants and unconditional grants such as revenue sharing. They are awarded for a broader range of activities than are categorical grants, and they seem to offer less flexibility than unconditional grants. Block grants for community development, for instance, cannot be used to pay for elementary education, although there are many things they can be used for. So long as the amount of a block grant is less than what the recipient government would spend on the activity in question in the absence of the grant, a block grant is actually indistinguishable from revenue sharing.

Suppose a state spends $1 billion each on education and health and that one-quarter of any increase in disposable income is also spent on public services, with that increased spending distributed evenly between education and health. If the state receives an unconditional grant of $200,000, net public spending will rise by $50,000, with an additional $25,000 spent on each function. The state's accounting system may show that it spends the entire $200,000 grant divided evenly between education and health. The grant will actually lead to only a $50,000 increase in spending. State taxes will also be reduced by $150,000, or, equivalently in a situation of growth through time, state taxes will rise by $150,000 less than they would have risen. The unconditional grant is equivalent to an increase in the

[9] On the various conditions associated with revenue sharing, see Robert D. Reischauer, "General Revenue Sharing — the Program's Incentives," in *Financing the New Federalism,* edited by Wallace E. Oates (Baltimore: Johns Hopkins University Press, 1975), pp. 40–87.

income of state residents, and the resulting impact on spending is the same as an increase in the residents' personal income.

Now suppose that the $200,000 is given as a block grant for education. The grant does not change the desire of state residents to devote one-quarter of increases in disposable income to the provision of state services and three-quarters to the provision of personal services. Nor does it alter the desire of state residents to distribute public spending equally between education and health. Consequently, the $200,000 grant will lead to a $50,000 increase in state spending and a $150,000 increase in personal spending, the latter coming about through a $150,000 reduction in state taxes. Moreover, this increase in state spending will be divided equally between education and health.

The state's accounting records, however, will show that it spent the entire $200,000 on education. The state's own spending on education will be $175,000 less than it otherwise would have been, its spending on health will be $25,000 greater, and its taxes will be $150,000 less. This outcome will tend to come about as long as the block grant is less than what the state would spend on the activity in the absence of the grant.[10] Thus there seem to be only two types of grant programs at base: categorical or conditional grants and unconditional grants, exemplified by revenue sharing and block grants.

Revenue Sharing

Conditional grants are often rationalized on the ground that they are necessary to correct the resource misallocations that would otherwise result from benefit spillovers among units of government. But unconditional grants have nothing to do with spillovers, for they entail income but not substitution effects. Unconditional grants such as revenue sharing are commonly rationalized on the ground that a federal system of government tends to contain some systematic imbalance between the national government and state and local governments. The federal government receives the dominant share of its revenue from a progressive tax on income, in which 10 percent growth in national income generates about a 17 percent increase in tax

[10] The possible scope for nonmatching grants to alter the spending patterns of recipient governments is examined in Paul N. Courant, Edward M. Gramlich, and Daniel L. Rubinfeld, "The Stimulative Effects of Intergovernmental Grants; Or Why Money Sticks Where It Hits"; and Wallace E. Oates, "Lump-Sum Intergovernmental Grants Have Price Effects," both in *Fiscal Federalism and Grants-in-Aid,* edited by Peter Mieszkowski and William H. Oakland (Washington, D.C.: Urban Institute, 1979), pp. 5–21 and 23–30, respectively.

revenue. In contrast, state and local governments receive their revenues through various taxes that grow roughly in proportion to income. Revenue sharing, then, might be seen as a means of providing state and local governments with some of the added revenues that accrue to the federal government because of its progressive tax structure.

If revenues grow more rapidly than demands at the federal level and less rapidly than demands at the state and local levels, however, why not rectify the imbalance through a combination of reduction in federal taxes and increase in state and local taxes? Why isn't fiscal imbalance at most simply a transitory phenomenon that can be eliminated through reductions in federal taxes and increases in state and local taxes? The common characterization of fiscal imbalance seems to require some assumption that people perceive the fiscal environment in terms of the prevailing rate structure rather than of the particular rate of tax they pay. If that is so, a tax increase that occurs naturally through income growth within the context of a progressive rate structure will be seen as less burdensome than a tax increase that occurs through a deliberate increase in the tax rate within the context of a proportional tax structure.

Pieces of evidence support the proposition that people tend to confound a tax structure and a rate of tax. In a study of the extent to which people are aware of their tax payments, Van Wagstaff found that people with below-median incomes systematically overestimated the taxes they paid, while people with above-median incomes systematically underestimated their tax payments.[11] Wagstaff's evidence implies that as a person's income increases, the estimated additional tax payments would be less than the actual additional tax payments. A person with increasing income would underestimate the impact of the "natural" tax increase that was produced by progressivity in the rate structure; to some degree the rate structure rather than the rate of tax would be seen as the fiscal environment. Relatedly, Wallace Oates found evidence to suggest that spending increases more rapidly in states with relatively elastic revenue systems than in states with relatively inelastic systems.[12]

A large body of causal observation also seems to support the existence of such a systematic misperception of the elements that con-

[11] J. Van Wagstaff, "Income Tax Consciousness Under Withholding," *Southern Economic Journal* 32 (July 1965), pp. 73–80.

[12] Wallace E. Oates, " 'Automatic' Increases in Tax Revenues — the Effect on the Size of the Public Budget," in Wallace E. Oates, *Financing the New Federalism,* pp. 139–160.

stitute a change in the fiscal environment. Whenever a legislative assembly considers possible changes in tax rates, much discussion takes place and much publicity is given to the deliberations. Yet no similar attention is paid to the continual, automatic increases in tax rates that are produced by progressivity in the revenue structure. Although people seem to be well aware of any proposal to enact a special surcharge on taxes, they seem relatively unaware that such a surcharge is enacted automatically each year under a progressive tax system. The so-called budget reductions associated with the start of the Reagan administration, for instance, were not budget reductions at all but simply proposed reductions in the rate at which expenditures were to increase. Should such a faulty perception exist, federal fiscal imbalance may arise from differences among levels of government in the elasticities of their revenue systems.

Such a possible source of fiscal imbalance may be intensified if the federal government occupies a relatively monopolistic position vis-à-vis state and local governments. If all levels of government conform essentially to the Wicksellian-like characteristics of consensual democracy, questions of fiscal imbalance could not arise. However, if state and local governments conform to those characteristics, but the national government contains some of the monopolistic elements of majoritarian democracy, fiscal imbalance may result. Indeed, this proposition is implicitly recognized in statements in the literature on federalism to the effect that redistribution must be undertaken by the federal government because state and local governments are too competitive with one another to permit much redistributive activity. When the national government is able to act as a fiscal monopolist, national expenditures will expand relative to state and local expenditures.

Figure 18.7 illustrates the effect of the development of fiscal monopoly at the federal level on the mix of governmental output within a federal system. The various zero subscripts in Figure 18.7 describe the pertinent facts under the assumption that both the federal and the state and local governments conform to the competitive features of the benefit principle. The subscripts 1 describe the change that results if the federal government is able to act as a fiscal monopolist. As we saw in Part II, there are two main elements in the theory of fiscal monopoly: the ability of government to capture consumers' surplus through various types of price discrimination and the ability of government to produce in a more costly manner than it could under competition, with the higher cost being a means of transferring income to favored groups. Figure 18.7 is constructed through a combination of both possibilities, with the result being an increase in federal output and the federal budget. This higher budget reduces

FIGURE 18.7 Fiscal Imbalance in a Federal System

Part a describes the budgetary choice of the federal government, and part b that choice for state and local governments. Within a system of consensual democracy corresponding to the benefit principle, the marginal cost of federal output is P_0^F, the demand is D_0^F, and the resulting rate of output is X_0^F. Similarly, the marginal cost of local output is P_0^L, the demand is D_0^L, and the resulting rate of output is X_0^L.

Suppose instead that the federal government is a fiscal monopolist. Two polar models of fiscal monopoly are combined here: There is some increase in the cost of providing public output and there is some increase in output. Part a is constructed on the assumption that both models have some applicability. Marginal cost increases to P_1^F and "demand" is shifted outward to D_1^F. As a result, public output expands to X_1^F, and at this higher output the federal budget is larger than it would be under a system of consensual democracy. With a larger federal budget, people have less income to spend on state and local output and on personal consumption. The demand for state and local output shifts inward to D_1^L, so state and local output falls to X_1^L.

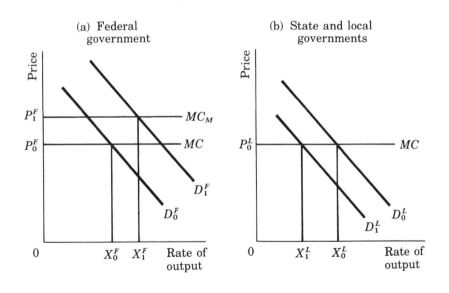

(a) Federal government

(b) State and local governments

disposable income, which in turn reduces the demand for state and local services.[13]

[13] State and local output and federal output might be substitutes or complements, and such relationships would complicate the analysis somewhat. If the relationship is complementary, the increase in federal output will increase the demand for state and local output from what it would otherwise be. If the two outputs are substitutes, the increase in federal output will reduce still further the demand for state and local output.

One implication of the line of analysis suggested by Figure 18.7 is that even though people may think that federal taxes and not state and local taxes are too high in relation to benefits received, their response, nonetheless, may be to seek reductions in state and local taxes. To achieve a reduction in federal taxes will require the formation of a coalition containing supporters from many different state and local governments, whereas a tax reduction within any single state or local government requires the development of support only within that jurisdiction. The residents of a majority of individual jurisdictions may prefer federal tax reduction to state and local tax reduction, but if it is more costly to organize a national coalition in support of federal tax reduction than to organize state and local coalitions, they may pursue a reduction in state and local taxes instead.

Revenue sharing can be rationalized as a means of offsetting the monopoly position of the federal government, but such imbalance can be corrected instead through a reduction in federal tax rates. For this reason, it seems problematical to maintain that revenue sharing is a means for rectifying a fiscal imbalance that is attributable to the monopoly position of the federal government because federal tax reduction is also capable of serving that purpose. Perhaps revenue sharing is a means by which state and local governments are able to capture part of the monopoly revenues accumulated by the federal government. Revenue sharing may represent some sharing of the fiscal monopoly of the federal government with state and local governments.

Why might such sharing take place? It can be rational from the perspective of politicians at both levels as long as the support of politicians at one level of government provides complementary inputs to the success of politicians at the other level. This does seem to be the case in the American federal system. Federal politicians can award grants to favored state and local politicians in exchange for support, which is useful to federal politicians because they must be elected from local districts. The relationship between federal and state and local politicians seems to be one of complementarity rather than of independence, let alone of substitution. In such a relationship, it may well be rational for the higher level monopoly government to share some of its profits with the lower level competitive government.[14]

---

[14] The complementarity of interests between federal and state and local politicians, and the rationality of grants in light of this complementarity, is explored, though with somewhat different emphasis, in Roger L. Faith, "Local Fiscal Crises and Intergovernmental Grants: A Suggested Hypothesis," *Public Choice* 34, nos. 3–4 (1979), pp. 317–351.

A POLYCENTRIC SYSTEM
OF URBAN GOVERNMENT

The organization of government in metropolitan areas exemplifies the conflicting perspectives toward a federal form of government. Lower levels of government seem generally to conform more closely to the conditions for consensual democracy than does the federal government, especially if the federal government is so large, as in the United States, that the cost of moving elsewhere is comparatively high.

If people can choose to live among several localities within the metropolitan area in which they work, individual units of government will have little scope to implement monopolistic practices that transfer wealth from some people to others through the buying and selling of legislation. The ability of units of local government to place tax burdens on people in excess of the valuations those people place on public services will be limited to the cost of moving elsewhere. If the cost of migration is zero, local governments will have no ability to impose budgetary outcomes that do not conform to the benefit principle. As migration becomes costly, local governments will be able to implement budgetary policies that impose welfare losses on people, but still only to the extent of the cost of migration. The cost of migration is relatively low among local governments within a metropolitan area, certainly lower than it is among national governments. With such a low cost of migration, local governments will tend to be organized according to the outcomes of the benefit principle and the theory of consensual democracy.

It is often suggested that the organization of government within metropolitan areas, in which a central city and numerous suburbs must compete for residents and business (or for a tax base generally), encounters difficulty because spillovers arise that cannot be handled within the fragmented system of government that characterizes such metropolitan areas. Many suburban residents work in the central city, and they use city services such as roads and police but pay the major portion of their local taxes to the suburbs in which they live. This is frequently used to suggest that some means be found for requiring suburban residents to contribute more fully to the support of central cities. Such support could take place in several ways. Special taxes could be levied on suburban residents who work in the central city, perhaps through a tax on income earned within the city, as is done by New York City, among others. Some type of consolidation of the central city and the outlying suburbs could be instituted, as has occurred in such places as Nashville and Jacksonville, among others.

Regardless of how suburban residents might be required to pay for city services, it is clearly possible that resources will be allocated inefficiently if suburban residents do not pay for their use of city services. As we have seen, in such a situation the private cost of city residency will be higher than the social cost, which will cause too few people to live in the city and will make city budgets inefficiently small. Likewise, the private cost of suburban residency will be lower than the social cost, which means that there will be too many suburban residents, with suburban budgets being inefficiently large. If suburban residents were somehow charged for their use of city services, the price of city residency relative to suburban residency would fall, and the relative amounts of city and suburban residency would equalize.

In their travels to the city to work, to shop, and to play, suburban residents use public facilities supplied by the central city, such as police and road services, among others. Suppose the central business district during a working day has a population made up of 50 percent city residents and 50 percent suburban residents. If the daily expenditure on police in the city is $20,000, it is possible to say that the central city spends $10,000 in giving police services to suburban residents. Similar computations could be undertaken for other services provided by the city such as road maintenance, parks, and the like.[15]

Suppose that the central city spends $20,000 daily in providing services that are used by suburban residents and, moreover, that suburban residents pay no direct taxes for city services. This absence of tax payment might come about because city revenues are derived wholly from a tax on real estate and because suburban residents own no real estate in the central city. In this situation, the issues of equity and efficiency arise. It might be argued that suburban residents exploit city residents because they receive services that are paid for exclusively by city residents. Suburban residents do not share in the cost of the services that are undertaken for the benefit of both city and suburban residents. It is, of course, certainly possible for suburban residents to benefit from the total city services while placing no marginal value on an expansion of those services. If so, no question of inefficiency arises, although a question of equity might.

A question of inefficiency will arise only to the extent that suburban residents place a marginal value on an expansion of city output. In this situation, gains from trade will exist, as Figure 18.5 described.

[15] This would be a statement about average cost, not marginal cost. In other words, in the absence of those suburban residents, police expenditures might not decline to $10,000, because of overhead expenses and the like.

In the presence of unexploited gains from trade, it is difficult to argue that one type of resident is gaining advantages at the expense of the other. Rather, both are being disadvantaged relative to what would happen if the gains from trade could somehow be exploited.

Do suburban residents in fact fail to contribute to the provision of the services they use? There are many ways in which suburban residents might contribute to the support of such services. Even if they make no direct contribution to city services, they may contribute indirectly. By working, shopping, or playing in the central city, the suburbanites increase the value of city businesses, which increases the city's tax base.

Suppose a city constructs an arena and sponsors a number of events each year. Part of the expense of the arena is covered by admissions, and the remainder is covered through the property tax on city businesses and residents. Half of those who use the arena live outside the city. If the city appropriates $1 million per year to cover the arena's expenses not covered by admissions, can it be said that suburban residents are receiving a transfer of income of $500,000 from city residents, or that an inefficiently small allocation of resources is being made to the arena? If both questions are answered positively, it would be simple to stop both the inequity and the inefficiency by limiting admission to city residents, perhaps by giving them passes similar to library cards. There would no longer be any opportunity for suburban residents to use the arena, so there could be no claim of a transfer of income from city residents to suburbanites.

If the city could restrict attendance at arena events to its own residents, but if it chooses not to do so, this would seem to imply that city residents think they would be better off by allowing suburbanites to use the arena. Perhaps by eating in city restaurants while attending events at the arena or shopping in city stores, suburban residents contribute to the income of city businesses. The arena, in other words, may be viewed as an investment undertaken to increase the wealth of city residents whose businesses are complementary to the arena, such as restaurants, stores, and hotels. If this is so, an observation that the central city is not covering the costs of serving suburban residents would seem to be little more than an observation that the city has made an unwise or unprofitable investment in the arena. For any business that is losing money, it can be said that the business is paying more to provide the service to customers than those customers are paying in return. It is understandable nonetheless why central cities would be interested in expanding their tax base, although we can ask whether such an expansion is a means of transferring income or a means of overcoming allocative inefficiencies.

INTERGOVERNMENTAL VARIATION
IN FISCAL CAPACITY

Great variation in per capita income exists among state and local governments. In 1979, per capita income in the United States was $8,773. Four states plus the District of Columbia had per capita incomes over $10,000: Alaska at $11,219, the District of Columbia at $10,570, Nevada at $10,521, Connecticut at $10,129, and California at $10,047. At the other end of the spectrum, three states had per capita incomes under $7,000: Mississippi at $6,178, Arkansas at $6,933, and Alabama at $6,962. (The variation among local governments is larger than among states.) The higher a jurisdiction's per capita income, the greater the public output it can supply at any given tax rate. For a 10 percent rate of tax, Nevada will be able to spend $1,052 per person on public services. To spend the same amount on public services, residents of Mississippi would have to tax themselves at more than 17 percent. Alternatively stated, for the same rate of tax, residents in Mississippi would be able to spend only 59 percent as much on public services as residents of Nevada would be able to spend. The differences are even larger for lower levels of government.

Such variations in the relationship between per capita income and the supply of public services have often been used to support efforts to equalize that relationship across jurisdictions. With respect to education, the ability of wealthier jurisdictions to provide education on more favorable terms has been a main argument in the general substitution of state financing for local financing of education. More generally, grant programs often contain terms that award larger grants to jurisdictions with lower per capita income. In some cases jurisdictions with below-average income receive larger grants than jurisdictions with above-average income, other relevant circumstances being the same. In other cases, jurisdictions with lower per capita income are faced with lower rates of required matching than are jurisdictions with higher per capita income. General revenue sharing similarly provides larger revenues for jurisdictions with lower per capita income.

Such efforts at fiscal redistribution are generally supported on the same grounds that redistribution among people is supported — that is, as a means of equalizing opportunities for consumption.[16] Advocacy

---

[16] Equalization with respect to education has been advocated not just as a means of promoting greater equality in consumption opportunities, but as a means of providing greater equality in the opportunities of people to prepare themselves to choose their future courses in life. Other things equal, pupils in wealthier school districts will have more opportunities opened to them than

of fiscal redistribution among political units does, however, raise some questions generally as to the effectiveness of such policies, accepting for purposes of discussion the interest in promoting equalization that such advocacy reflects.

Suppose the per capita income of state B exceeds that of state A, and that each state contains 1 million residents. Take a hypothetical revenue transfer of $10 million from B to A. Political units can neither enjoy benefits nor bear costs; only people can do so. Therefore, it is illusory to speak of income as being transferred among political units; income can be transferred only among the people who reside in those units. The transfer from one state to the other will take place through some form of public expenditure, and different programs of expenditure will entail different patterns of benefit.

Regardless of the pattern, however, the transfer will benefit particular citizens. If the usual variation exists in the distribution of personal incomes, there will be overlap in the incomes of the residents of the two states. Although the per capita income of B exceeds that of A, many residents of A will have personal incomes greater than the average income in B, and many residents of B will have personal incomes less than the average income in A.

Table 18.2 illustrates some of the issues created by policies of fiscal redistribution. Assume that two states, A and B, each have five residents. Initial personal income is shown in column 1. Per capita income is $6,400 in A and $8,000 in B. The coefficient of variation, a measure of inequality, is 41.1 percent among personal incomes and 11.1 percent among state per capital incomes.[17] There is clearly less inequality among state incomes than among personal incomes. Per capita income can be equalized between the two states by transferring $4,000 from B to A. The equalization achieved through this transfer between states can be compared with the equalization that could be achieved through a $4,000 transfer between persons. Columns 2 and 3 illustrate a transfer between governments; columns 4 and 5 illustrate a transfer among persons. There are many ways that such transfers might be made, and Table 18.2 considers two possibilities. Columns 2 and 4 present the maximum possible equalization of personal incomes that is compatible with the assumptions of the illus-

---

will pupils in poorer school districts, and the future histories of pupils will reflect those differential opportunities, in addition to reflecting possible differences in talents and interests. The equalization of spending on education is advocated as a means of reducing the influence of jurisdictional wealth on the future of pupils, rather than of equalizing consumption opportunities per se.

[17] The coefficient of variation is the ratio of the standard deviation of a distribution to the mean value of that distribution.

TABLE 18.2   Impact of Alternative Forms of Income Redistribution

Person	Personal Income (1)	$4,000 Redistribution Among Governments		$4,000 Redistribution Among Persons	
		Maximum Equalization (2)	Standard Case (3)	Maximum Equalization (4)	Standard Case (5)
A_1	$ 3,000	$ 5,500	$ 3,800	$ 5,000	$ 3,800
A_2	4,000	5,500	4,800	5,000	4,800
A_3	6,000	6,000	6,800	8,000	6,800
A_4	8,000	8,000	8,800	8,000	7,348
A_5	11,000	11,000	11,800	9,667	10,100
B_1	4,000	4,000	3,600	5,000	4,800
B_2	6,000	6,000	5,400	6,000	6,800
B_3	8,000	8,000	7,200	8,000	7,348
B_4	10,000	9,000	9,000	9,667	9,184
B_5	12,000	9,000	10,800	9,667	11,020

tration: High incomes are pared down from the top and low incomes are built up from the bottom. Columns 3 and 5 present what might be regarded as a standard case: Those who provide the subsidy are taxed in proportion to their incomes, and the recipients of the subsidy share equally in the subsidy, perhaps as implied by some simplistic notion of one person–one vote.

The transfer of $4,000 between the two states reduces the coefficient of variation in state per capita incomes to zero. At the same time, the coefficient of variation in personal incomes is also reduced. Under the hypothesis of maximum equalization described in column 2, the coefficient of variation is reduced to 28.2 percent. In the standard case illustrated in column 3, in which residents of B are each taxed at 10 percent and each resident of A receives a subsidy of $800, the coefficient of variation in personal incomes falls to 37.7 percent.

Suppose it is assumed that the $4,000 is transferred among persons. The result will be to increase the inequality in state per capita incomes and to decrease the inequality in personal incomes, when these measures of inequality are compared against the outcome of a $4,000 transfer between the two states. The maximum equalization, shown in column 4, results when the entire $4,000 is extracted from the three wealthiest persons, leaving each of them with net incomes of $9,667, and given to the three poorest individuals, raising each of their net incomes to $5,000. The coefficient of variation among state per capita incomes rises from zero to 6.5 percent, while the coefficient of variation among personal incomes falls from 28.2 percent to 26.7 percent.

In the standard case shown in column 5, it is assumed that the $4,000 is raised by levying a proportional tax of about 8.2 percent on the five persons with above-average incomes. It is simultaneously assumed that each person with a below-average income receives a transfer of $800. In this case the coefficient of variation in state per capita incomes rises from zero to 8.8 percent, while the coefficient of variation in personal incomes falls from 37.7 percent to 31.2 percent. When contrasted with a program of transfers among states, the transfer of income among persons has increased the inequality in the distribution of state per capita income, but at the same time it has reduced the inequality in the distribution of personal income.

Although specific numerical illustrations can be misleading, the principles illustrated here are generally applicable. Because income transfers can take place ultimately only among persons, any transfer from a political unit with an above-average per capita income to one with a below-average per capita income will generate a substantial volume of transfers from poorer people residing in the wealthier unit to wealthier people residing in the poorer unit. Intergovernmental income redistribution, then, would seem to be an inefficient means of narrowing the variations in personal income. Any amount of equalization of personal income that results from some program of intergovernmental redistribution can be achieved at a lower budgetary outlay if the transfers take place among persons. Or, for the same budgetary outlay, greater income equality can be achieved through a program of interpersonal income redistribution. To the extent that taxes generate excess burdens, any program of intergovernmental equalization would seem to be dominated by some program of interpersonal equalization, if it is assumed that equalization is truly the objective of the equalizing aspects of the grant, rather than arising as a by-product of the market for legislation, and if the normative case for such equalization is accepted.

SUGGESTIONS FOR FURTHER READING

The ability of a polycentric urban area to accommodate differences in preferences for public output has been the subject of a vast literature. The seminal work in the economics literature is Charles M. Tiebout, "A Pure Theory of Local Expenditures," *Journal of Political Economy* 64 (October 1956), pp. 416–24. This central theme is developed further in Vincent Ostrom, Charles M. Tiebout, and Robert Warren, "The Organization of Government in a Metropolitan Area," *American Political Science Review* 55 (December 1961), pp. 831–842. The relation between local governments in a polycentric urban area and profit-seeking firms in a competitive industry is explored in Jon C. Sonstelie and Paul R. Portney, "Profit Maximizing Communities and the Theory of Local Public Expenditure," *Journal of Urban Economics* 5 (April 1978), pp. 263–277.

More generally on the organization of governments in metropolitan areas, see Robert L. Bish, *The Public Economy of Metropolitan Areas* (Chicago: Markham, 1971); and Robert L. Bish and Vincent Ostrom, *Understanding Urban Government: Metropolitan Reform Reconsidered* (Washington, D.C.: American Enterprise Institute, 1973). James A. Maxwell and J. Richard Aronson, *Financing State and Local Governments,* 3rd ed. (Washington, D.C.: Brookings Institution, 1977), is a standard reference work on all aspects of state and local finance.

Whether there is a sense in which the residents of suburban areas can be said to exploit the residents of central cities is an interesting and important empirical and conceptual question. A positive answer is provided for Detroit for 1965 in William B. Neenan, "Suburban–Central City Exploitation Thesis: One City's Tale," *National Tax Journal* 23 (June 1970), pp. 117–139. Neenan's work in this article is described in more detail in his book *Political Economy of Urban Areas* (Chicago: Markham, 1972), pp. 53–139. In an examination of the relation between Washington, D.C., and the outlying suburban areas in Maryland and Virginia, Kenneth V. Greene, William B. Neenan, and Claudia D. Scott, *Fiscal Interactions in a Metropolitan Area* (Lexington, Mass.: Heath, 1974), reach the perhaps agnostic conclusion that identifying the exploiter and the exploited depends on the assumptions made about the incidence of the benefits from various expenditures made by the central city, with the central city being exploited under one set of assumptions and the suburbs being exploited under another set. David F. Bradford and Wallace E. Oates, "Suburban Exploitation of Central Cities and Governmental Structure," in *Redistribution Through Public Choice,* edited by Harold M. Hochman and George E. Peterson (New York: Columbia University Press, 1974), pp. 43–90, argue that in northeastern New Jersey in 1960 such a pattern of city-suburb exploitation did not seem to exist, and they emphasize that considerable variation seemed to exist in the relations among the various suburban communities. Evidence presented in John C. Weicher, "The Effect of Metropolitan Fragmentation on Central City Budgets," in *Models of Urban Structure,* edited by David C. Sweet (Lexington, Mass.: D.C. Heath, 1972), pp. 177–203, portrays suburban residents as being exploited by city residents. John E. Filer and Lawrence W. Kenny, "Voter Reaction to City-County Consolidation Referenda," *Journal of Law and Economics* 23 (April 1980), pp. 179–190, explores the extent to which proposed consolidations are means for achieving efficiency or for transferring income from some jurisdictions to others.

Vincent Ostrom, *The Political Theory of a Compound Republic* (Blacksburg, Va.: Center for Study of Public Choice, Virginia Polytechnic Institute, 1971), is a valuable study of the political theory contained in the

Federalist Papers. Gottfried Dietze, *The Federalist: A Classic on Federalism and Free Government* (Baltimore: Johns Hopkins University Press, 1960), presents a thorough analysis not only of the eighty-five essays that constitute the *Federalist Papers,* but of the intellectual and historical background that informed them. Bernard Dafflon, *Federal Finance in Theory and Practice: With Special Reference to Switzerland* (Bern: Verlag Paul Haupt, 1977), is an integrated political-economic treatment that recognizes that the political and constitutional features of a federalism cannot be separated from the economic features and that emphasizes a focus on procedures of policy formation rather than on specific policy measures. Bhajan S. Grewal, Geoffrey Brennan, and Russell L. Mathews, eds., *The Economics of Federalism* (Canberra: Australian National University Press, 1980), is a collection of previously published essays on such aspects of federalism as the division of responsibility among units of government, spillovers among jurisdictions, income inequality among units of government, and grants-in-aid. Werner W. Pommerehne, "Quantitative Aspects of Federalism: A Study of Six Counties," in *The Political Economy of Fiscal Federalism,* edited by Wallace E. Oates (Lexington, Mass.: D.C. Heath, 1977), pp. 275–355, contains rich detail for Canada, France, Switzerland, the United Kingdom, the United States, and West Germany.

Index